EIGHTH EDITION
GLOBAL EDITION

PROBLEM SOLVING AND
PROGRAM DESIGN

in C

EIGHTH EDITION
GLOBAL EDITION

PROBLEM SOLVING AND PROGRAM DESIGN

in C

Jeri R. Hanly, University of Wyoming

Elliot B. Koffman, Temple University

Global Edition Contributions by
Mohit P. Tahiliani, National Institute of Technology, Surathkal

PEARSON

Boston   Columbus   Indianapolis   New York   San Francisco   Hoboken
Amsterdam   Cape Town   Dubai   London   Madrid   Milan   Munich   Paris   Montreal   Toronto   Delhi
Mexico City   Sao Paulo   Sydney   Hong Kong   Seoul   Singapore   Taipei   Tokyo

Vice President and Editorial Director, ECS: Marcia Horton
Executive Editor: Tracy Johnson
Product Marketing Manager: Bram van Kempen
Field Marketing Manager: Demetrius Hall
Marketing Assistant: Jon Bryant
Project Management Team Lead: Scott Disanno
Program Manager: Carole Snyder
Senior Project Manager: Camille Trentacoste
Assistant Acquisitions Editor, Global Edition: Aditee Agarwal

Associate Project Editor, Global Edition: Sinjita Basu
Media Production Manager, Global Edition: Vikram Kumar
Senior Manufacturing Controller, Production, Global Edition: Trudy Kimber
Operations Supervisor: Vincent Scelta
Operations Specialist: Maura Zaldivar-Garcia
Full-Service Project Management: Cenveo® Publisher Services
Cover Design: Lumina Datamatics
Cover Photo Source: Shutterstock
Cover Printer: RR Donnelley Moore Langen

Pearson Education Limited
Edinburgh Gate
Harlow
Essex CM20 2JE
England

and Associated Companies throughout the world

Visit us on the World Wide Web at:
www.pearsonglobaleditions.com

© Pearson Education Limited 2016

The rights of Jeri R. Hanly and Elliot B. Koffman to be identified as the authors of this work have been asserted by them in accordance with the Copyright, Designs and Patents Act 1988.

Authorized adaptation from the United States edition, entitled Problem Solving and Program Design in C, 8th Edition, 978-0-134-01489-0, by Jeri R. Hanly and Elliot B. Koffman, published by Pearson Education © 2016.

ISBN 10: 1-292-09881-3
ISBN 13: 978-1-292-09881-4

British Library Cataloguing-in-Publication Data

A catalogue record for this book is available from the British Library.

10 9 8 7 6 5 4 3 2 1
19 18 17 16 15

Typeset in New Caledonia 10/12 by Cenveo® Publisher Services.

Printed and bound by RR Donnelley Westford in the United States of America.

This book is dedicated to

Jeri Hanly's family:
Brian, Kevin, Laura, Grace, and Caleb
Trinity, Alex, Eva, Eli, and Jonah
Eric, Jennifier, Mical, Micah, Josiah, and Rachel

Elliot Koffman's family:
Caryn and Deborah
Richard, Jacquie, and Dustin
Robin, Jeffrey, Jonathan, and Eliana

PREFACE

Problem Solving and Program Design in C teaches a disciplined approach to problem solving, applying widely accepted software engineering methods to design program solutions as cohesive, readable, reusable modules. We present as an implementation vehicle for these modules a subset of ANSI C—a standardized, industrial-strength programming language known for its power and portability. This text can be used for a first course in programming methods: It assumes no prior knowledge of computers or programming. The text's broad selection of case studies and exercises allows an instructor to design an introductory programming course in C for computer science majors or for students from a wide range of other disciplines.

New to This Edition

Several changes to this edition are listed below. The majority of these changes are in response to the recommendations of our reviewers.

- Chapter 0 information on professional opportunities in computing has been extensively updated.
- Hardware examples in Chapter 1 have been brought up-to-date to reflect current technology.
- Discussion of programming languages in Chapter 1 has been revised to list the most popular languages in use today.
- Chapters on arrays, strings, files, and dynamic data structures have been renamed and reworked to place greater emphasis on the use of pointers.
- Chapter 6 coverage of levels of testing has been updated.
- All chapters contain new programming project problems, and beginning with Chapter 5, some projects are marked as especially appropriate for team programming.
- Three chapters contain new "C in Focus" articles—"Team Programming" (Chapter 5), "Defensive Programming" (Chapter 8), and "Evolving Standards" (Chapter 10).
- Format of many tables, including those that trace execution of code, has been altered to improve readability.
- Exercises on bitwise operations have been added to Appendix C.

Using C to Teach Program Development

Two of our goals—teaching program design and teaching C—may be seen by some as contradictory. C is widely perceived as a language to be tackled only after one has learned the fundamentals of programming in some other, friendlier language. The perception that C is excessively difficult is traceable to the history of the language. Designed as a vehicle for programming the UNIX operating system, C found its original clientele among programmers who understood the complexities of the operating system and the underlying machine and who considered it natural to exploit this knowledge in their programs. Therefore, it is not surprising that many textbooks whose primary goal is to teach C expose the student to program examples requiring an understanding of machine concepts that are not in the syllabus of a standard introductory programming course.

In this text, we are able to teach both a rational approach to program development and an introduction to ANSI C because we have chosen the first goal as our primary one. One might fear that this choice would lead to a watered-down treatment of ANSI C. On the contrary, we find that the blended presentation of programming concepts and of the implementation of these concepts in C captures a focused picture of the power of ANSI C as a high-level programming language, a picture that is often blurred in texts whose foremost objective is the coverage of all of ANSI C. Even following this approach of giving program design precedence over discussion of C language features, we have arrived at coverage of the essential constructs of C that is quite comprehensive.

Pointers and the Organization of the Book

The order in which C language topics are presented is dictated by our view of the needs of the beginning programmer rather than by the structure of the C programming language. The reader may be surprised to discover that there are multiple chapter titles that include the word "Pointers." This follows from our treatment of C as a high-level language, and our recognition that the critical role of pointers in C is often a challenging concept for students to grasp.

Whereas other high-level languages have separate language constructs for output parameters and arrays, C openly folds these concepts into its notion of a pointer, drastically increasing the complexity of learning the language. We simplify the learning process by discussing pointers from these separate perspectives where such topics normally arise when teaching other programming languages, thus allowing a student to absorb the intricacies of pointer usage a little at a time. Our approach makes possible the presentation of fundamental concepts using traditional high-level language terminology—output parameter, array, array subscript, string—and makes it easier for students without prior assembly language background to master the many aspects of pointer usage. This approach is also helpful for students studying C as a second programming language, since it facilitates their understanding of the many aspects of pointer use as simply C's means of implementing constructs they have already met.

Therefore, this text has not one but five chapters that discuss pointer concepts. Chapter 6 (Pointers and Modular Programming) begins with a discussion of pointers, indirect reference, and the use of pointers to files. It then discusses the use of pointers as simple output and input/output parameters, Chapter 7 deals with arrays, Chapter 8 presents strings and arrays of pointers. Chapter 11 discusses file pointers again. Chapter 13 describes dynamic memory allocation after reviewing pointer uses previously covered.

Software Engineering Concepts

The book presents many aspects of software engineering. Some are explicitly discussed and others are taught only by example. The connection between good problem-solving skills and effective software development is established early in Chapter 1 with a section that discusses the art and science of problem solving. The five-phase software development method presented in Chapter 1 is used to solve the first case study and is applied uniformly to case studies throughout the text. Major program style issues are highlighted in special displays, and the coding style used in examples is based on guidelines followed in segments of the C software industry. There are sections in several chapters that discuss algorithm tracing, program debugging, and testing.

Chapter 3 introduces procedural abstraction through selected C library functions, parameterless void functions, and functions that take input parameters and return a value. Chapters 4 and 5 include additional function examples including the use of a function as a parameter, and Chapter 6 completes the study of functions that have simple parameters. The chapter discusses the use of pointers to represent output and input/output parameters.

Case studies and sample programs in Chapters 6, 7, and 10 introduce by example the concepts of data abstraction and encapsulation of a data type and operators. Chapter 12 presents C's facilities for formalizing procedural and data abstraction in personal libraries defined by separate header and implementation files. Chapter 14 (on the textbook website) introduces essential concepts of multiprocessing, such as parent and child processes, interprocess communication, mutual exclusion locking, and deadlock avoidance. Chapter 15 (on the textbook website) describes how object-oriented design is implemented by C++.

The use of visible function interfaces is emphasized throughout the text. We do not mention the possibility of using a global variable until Chapter 12, and then we carefully describe both the dangers and the value of global variable usage.

Optional Graphics Sections

Many computer science faculty find that the use of graphics is an excellent motivator in the study of introductory programming and as a vehicle to help students understand how to use libraries and to call functions. This text offers three optional sections with graphics examples:

Section 3.6:   Introduction to Computer Graphics
Section 5.11:   Loops in Graphics Programs
Section 7.10:   Graphics Programs with Arrays

To reduce the overhead required to introduce graphics, we use WinBGIm (Windows BGI with mouse), which is a package based on the Turbo Pascal BGI

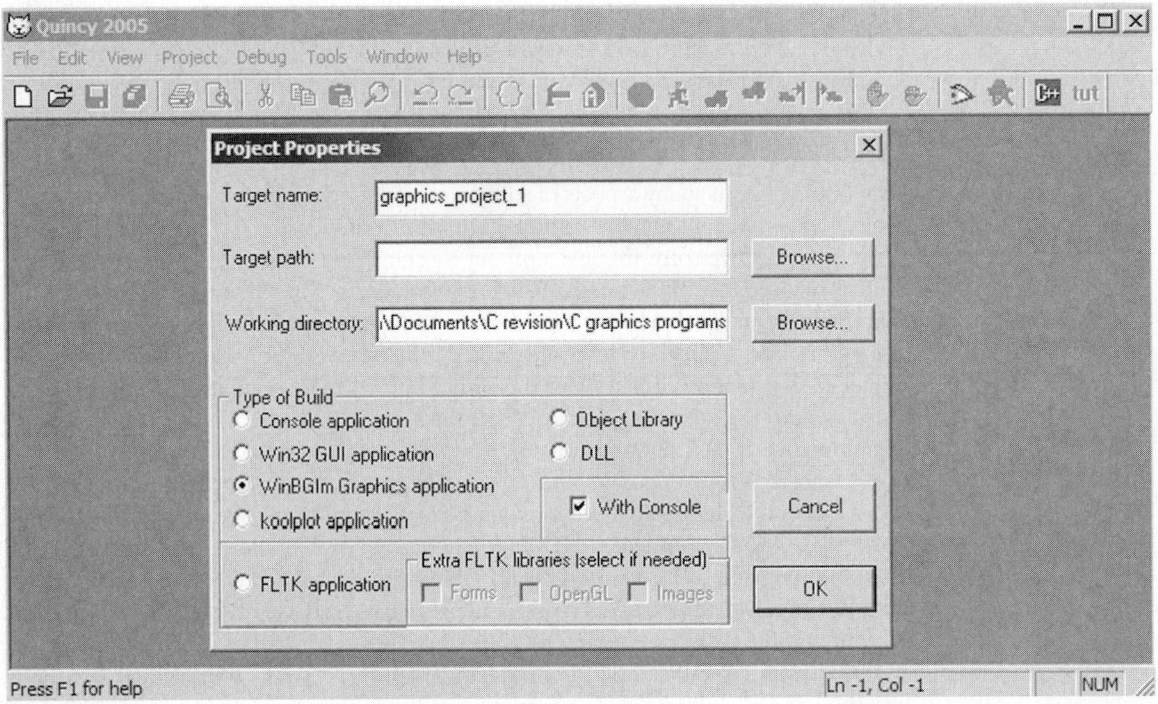

FIGURE 1

(Borland Graphics Interface) library. WinBGIm was created to run on top of the Win32 library by Michael Main and his students at the University of Colorado. Several development platforms appropriate for CS 1 courses have incorporated WinBGIm. Quincy (developed by Al Stevens) is an open-source student-oriented C++ IDE that includes WinBGIm as well as more advanced libraries (http://www .codecutter.net/tools/quincy). Figure 1 shows the Quincy new project window (File → New → Project) with WinBGIm Graphics application selected.

A command-line platform based on the open-source GNU g++ compiler and the emacs program editor is distributed by the University of Colorado (http://www .codecutter.net/tools/winbgim). WinBGIm is also available for Bloodshed Software's Dev-C++ and Microsoft's Visual Studio C++.

Pedagogical Features

We employ the following pedagogical features to enhance the usefulness of this book as a learning tool:

End-of-Section Exercises　　Most sections end with a number of Self-Check Exercises. These include exercises that require analysis of program fragments as well as short programming exercises.

Examples and Case Studies The book contains a wide variety of programming examples. Whenever possible, examples contain complete programs or functions rather than incomplete program fragments. Each chapter contains one or more substantial case studies that are solved following the software development method. Numerous case studies give the student glimpses of important applications of computing, including database searching, business applications such as billing and sales analysis, word processing, and environmental applications such as radiation level monitoring and water conservation.

Syntax Display Boxes The syntax displays describe the syntax and semantics of new C features and provide examples.

Program Style Displays The program style displays discuss major issues of good programming style.

Error Discussions and Chapter Review Each chapter concludes with a section that discusses common programming errors. The Chapter Review includes a table of new C constructs.

End-of-Chapter Exercises Quick-Check Exercises with answers follow each Chapter Review. There are also review exercises available in each chapter.

End-of-Chapter Projects Each chapter ends with Programming Projects giving students an opportunity to practice what they learned in the chapter.

Appendices

Reference tables of ANSI C constructs appear on the inside covers of the book. Because this text covers only a subset of ANSI C, the appendices play a vital role in increasing the value of the book as a reference. Throughout the book, array referencing is done with subscript notation; Appendix A is the only coverage of pointer arithmetic. Appendix B is an alphabetized table of ANSI C standard libraries. The table in Appendix C shows the precedence and associativity of all ANSI C operators; the operators not previously defined are explained in this appendix. Exercises for practicing some of the bitwise operators are included. Appendix D presents character set tables, and Appendix E lists all ANSI C reserved words.

Supplements

The following supplemental materials are available to all readers of this book at www.pearsonglobaleditions.com/Hanly:

- Source code
- Known errata
- Answers to odd-numbered Self-Check exercises.

The following instructor supplement is available only to qualified instructors at the Pearson Instructor Resource Center. Visit www.pearsonglobaleditions.com/Hanly or contact your local Pearson sales representative to gain access to the IRC.

- Solutions Manual

Acknowledgments

Many people participated in the development of this textbook. The reviewers for this edition, who suggested most of the changes, include Michael Geiger, UMASS Lowell, Lowell, MA; Qi Hao, University of Alabama, Tuscaloosa, AL; Haibing Lu, Santa Clara University, Santa Clara, CA; Susan Mengel, Texas Tech University, Lubbock, TX; Shensheng Tang, Missouri Western State University, St. Joseph, MO; Kevin Mess, College of Southern Nevada, Las Vegas, NV; Samir Iabbassen, Long Island University, Brooklyn, NY; and Ray Lauff, Temple University, Philadelphia, PA. We would also like to acknowledge Michael Main for his assistance with the graphics examples and his students at the University of Colorado who adapted WinBGI to create WinBGIm (Grant Macklem, Gregory Schmelter, Alan Schmidt, and Ivan Stashak).

We also want to thank Charlotte Young of South Plains College for her help in creating Chapter 0, and Jeff Warsaw of WaveRules, LLC, who contributed substantially to Chapter 14. Joan C. Horvath of the Jet Propulsion Laboratory, California Institute of Technology, contributed several programming exercises, and Nelson Max of the University of California, Davis suggested numerous improvements to the text. Jeri acknowledges the assistance of her former colleagues at Loyola University Maryland—James R. Glenn, Dawn J. Lawrie, and Roberta E. Sabin—who contributed several programming projects. We are also grateful for the assistance over the years of several Temple University, University of Wyoming, and Howard University former students who helped to verify the programming examples and who provided answer keys for the host of exercises, including Mark Thoney, Lynne Doherty, Andrew Wrobel, Steve Babiak, Donna Chrupcala, Masoud Kermani, Thayne Routh, and Paul Onakoya.

It has been a pleasure to work with the Pearson team in this endeavor. Tracy Johnson (Executive Editor), Carole Snyder (Program Manager), and Camille Trentacoste (Senior Project Manager) provided ideas and guidance throughout the various phases of manuscript revision.

J.R.H.
E.B.K.

Pearson wishes to thank and acknowledge the following reviewers for their work on the Global Edition:

Vikas Deep Dhiman, *Amity University*

Ll Xin Cindy, *The Hong Kong University of Science and Technology*

Piyali Sengupta, *Freelance Writer*

CONTENTS

PROBLEM SOLVING AND PROGRAM DESIGN

in C

Computer Science as a Career Path

CHAPTER OBJECTIVES

- To learn why computer science may be the right field for you
- To become familiar with different computer disciplines and related college majors
- To find out about career opportunities

Introduction

In order to choose a course of study and eventually a desirable career path, we may ask many important questions. Why would we choose this field? Will we be good at it? Will there be jobs for us when we finish our education? Will we enjoy our work? This chapter sheds some light on these types of questions for anyone contemplating a degree in computer science or a related field.

Section 1   Why Computer Science May Be the Right Field for You

Reasons to Major in Computer Science

Millennials Those born from 1982 on are said to be confident, social and team-oriented, proud of achievement, prone to use analytic skills to make decisions, and determined to seek security, stability, and balance for themselves

Almost everything we do is influenced by computing. Today's generation of college students, dubbed the **Millennials**, are not surprised by this statement. They have grown up with computers, the Internet, instant communication, social networking, and electronic entertainment. They embrace new technology and expect it to do fantastic things.

However, previous generations are not as comfortable with technology and try to solve problems without always thinking of technology first. Many people in the workforce resist the changes that technology requires. They often turn to the youngest employees to take over technology issues and to make choices that will have important consequences.

This difference among generations creates a great environment for bright and dedicated students to choose to major in computer science or a related field. The computer industry is one of the fastest-growing segments of our economy and promises to continue to see growth well into the future. In order to be competitive, businesses must continue to hire well-trained professionals not only to produce high-quality products for the present, but also to plan creative scientific and engineering advances for the future.

A person who is part of the computer industry can choose from a wide variety of fields where many interesting and challenging problems will need to be solved. In addition to all the business and communication jobs that may first come to mind, people with degrees in computer science are working on problems from all spectrums of life. A quick review of technical articles highlights such areas as developing electronic balloting for state and national elections, using signals from wireless devices to update vehicle and pedestrian travel times in order to make the best decisions for traffic signals or management of construction zones, and using a supercomputer-powered "virtual earthquake" to study benefits of an early warning system using 3-D models of actual geographic locations and damage scenarios.

Some problems being worked on right now by computer professionals in the medical world include understanding how the human brain works by modeling brain activation patterns with emphasis on helping people impacted by autism or disorders like paranoid schizophrenia; customizing a wide array of helpful devices for the physically impaired, from programmable robotic prostheses to digital "sight"; gathering information from implanted pacemakers in order to make timely decisions in times of crisis; developing a computer system capable of recognizing human emotional states by analyzing a human face in real time; and developing human–computer interfaces that allow a computer to be operated solely by human gestures in order to manipulate virtual objects.

The fields of security and law enforcement present many challenges to the computer professional, and include the following: The U.S. government is performing observational studies on normal behavior in online worlds in hopes of developing techniques for uncovering online activities of terrorist groups. Advancements in voice biometrics technology allow speech to be analyzed by computer software to determine identity, truthfulness, and emotional states. Electronic protection against malicious software is of great concern to national economies and security interests.

Some of our world's most challenging problems will be worked on by teams of professionals from many disciplines. Obviously, these teams will include computer professionals who are creative and possess the knowledge of how to best use technology. In the near future, we will see much innovation in the areas of the human genome project, environmental monitoring, AIDS vaccine research, clean fuels, tracking weather changes by using robots in potentially dangerous areas, and using supercomputers to simulate the earth's architecture and functions in order to predict natural disasters. A way to make a positive difference in the world would be to study computing, either as your primary focus or as a means of advancing technology in another field.

Traits of a Computer Scientist

An individual's personality and character traits typically influence the field he or she chooses to study and eventually in which he or she will work. The demands of certain fields are met by individuals with certain capabilities. It makes sense that people who are successful computer science students will have many common traits. Read the following description and decide if it sounds like you.

Foremost, you must love the challenge of solving problems. Computer science is more about finding solutions to problems than it is about using the current computer hardware or programming language. Solving problems requires being creative and "thinking outside the box." You must be willing to try things that are different from the "accepted" solution.

You enjoy working with technology and enjoy being a lifelong learner. You enjoy puzzles and work tenaciously to find solutions. You probably don't even notice that the hours have flown by as you are narrowing in on the answer. You enjoy building things, both in the actual world and in a "virtual world." You can see how to customize a particular object to make it work in a specific environment. You like to tackle large projects and see them to completion. You like to build things that are useful to people and that will have a positive impact on their lives.

To be successful in the workplace, you must also be a good communicator. You should be able to explain your plans and solutions well to both technical and non-technical people. You must be able to write clearly and concisely in the technical environment. Since most projects involve multiple people, it is important to work well in a group. If you plan to become a manager or run your own company, it is very important to be able to work with different personalities.

Frederick P. Brooks, famous for leading the team that developed the operating system for the IBM System/360, wrote a book in the 1970s titled *The Mythical Man Month—Essays on Software Engineering*. Even though much has changed in the computing world since he wrote the book, his essays still hold a lot of relevance today. He listed the "Joys of the Craft" as the following: First is the sheer joy of making things of your own design. Second is the pleasure of making things that are useful to and respected by other people. Third is the joy of fashioning complex puzzle-like entities into a system that works correctly. Fourth is the joy of always learning because of the nonrepetitive nature of the work. Finally, there is the joy of working with a very tractable medium. The programmer can create in his or her imagination and readily produce a product that can be tested and easily changed and reworked. Wouldn't the sculptor or civil engineer enjoy such easy tractability!

The IBM System/360 was a mainframe computer system family announced by IBM in 1964. It was the first family of computers making a clear distinction between architecture and implementation, allowing IBM to release a suite of compatible designs at different price points. The design is considered by many to be one of the most successful computers in history, influencing computer design for years to come (see Figure 0.1).

FIGURE 0.1

IBM introduced the system/360 family of business mainframe computers in 1964. (©2012 akg-images/Paul Almasy/ Newscom. Unauthorized use not permitted.)

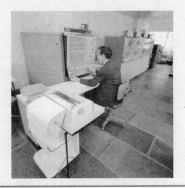

Section 2   The College Experience: Computer Disciplines and Majors to Choose From

Most professionals in the computing industry have at least an undergraduate degree in mathematics, computer science, or a related field. Many have advanced degrees, especially those involved primarily in research or education.

Computing is a broad discipline that intersects many other fields such as mathematics, science, engineering, and business. Because of such a wide range of choices, it is impossible for anyone to be an expert in all of them. A career involving computing requires the individual to focus his or her efforts while obtaining a college degree.

There are many different degrees that involve computing offered at institutions of higher learning. These degrees can even be from different departments within the same institution. Although computing degrees can share some of the same courses, they can also be quite different from each other. Choosing among them can be confusing.

To ease this confusion, it is wise for students to consult with academic advisors in the computer science department, the computer or electrical engineering department, and the business school to explore the options available in their specific institution. Next we summarize some of the degree programs that your institution may offer.

Computer Science

Computer science as a discipline encompasses a wide range of topics from theoretical and algorithmic foundations to cutting-edge developments. The work computer scientists are trained to do can be arranged into three categories:

- Designing and implementing useful software
- Devising new ways to use computers
- Developing effective ways to solve computing problems

A computer science degree consists of courses that include computing theory, programming, and mathematics. These courses ultimately develop the logic and reasoning skills integral to becoming a computer scientist. The math sequence includes calculus I and II (and in many cases, calculus III) as well as discrete mathematics. Some students also study linear algebra and probability and statistics. A computer science degree offers a comprehensive foundation that permits graduates to understand and adapt to new technologies and new ideas. Computer science departments are often found at universities as part of the science, engineering, or mathematics divisions.

Computer scientists take on challenging programming jobs, supervise other programmers, and advise other programmers on the best approaches to be taken. Computer science researchers are working with scientists from other fields to perform such tasks as using databases to create and organize new knowledge, making robots that will be practical and intelligent aides, and using computers to help decipher the secrets of human DNA. Their theoretical background allows them to determine the best performance possible for new technologies and their study of algorithms helps them to develop creative approaches to new (and old) problems.

Computer Engineering

For students who are more interested in understanding and designing the actual computing devices, many opportunities are available in computer engineering, which is concerned with the design and construction of computers and computer-based systems. A computer engineering degree involves the study of hardware, software, communications, and the interaction among them, and is a customized blend of an electrical engineering degree with a computer science degree.

The computer engineering curriculum includes courses on the theories, principles, and practices of traditional electrical engineering as well as mathematics through the standard calculus sequence and beyond. This knowledge is then applied in courses dealing with designing computers and computer-based devices. In addition, programming courses are required so that the computer engineer can develop software for digital devices and their interfaces.

Currently, an important area for computer engineers involves embedded systems. This involves the development of devices that have software and hardware embedded in them such as cell phones, digital music players, alarm systems, medical diagnostic devices, laser surgical tools, and so on. The devices a computer engineer might work with are limitless as he or she applies his or her knowledge of how to integrate hardware and software systems.

Information Systems

The information systems (IS) field focuses on integrating technology into businesses and other enterprises to manage their information in an efficient and secure manner. In this area, technology is viewed as an instrument for generating, processing, and distributing information. Therefore, the focus in this field is on business and organizational principles.

Most IS programs are located in the business school of a university or college, and IS degrees combine business and computing coursework, and the math that is required has a business application focus. These degrees may be found under such programs as Computer Information Systems (CIS) or Management Information Systems (MIS). Degree program names are not always consistent, but they all have their focus on business principles and applications of technology with less emphasis on the theory of computer science or the digital design of computer engineering.

IS specialists must understand both technical and organizational factors, and must be able to help an organization determine how to use information and technology to provide a competitive edge. These professionals serve as a bridge between the technical community and the management community within an organization. They are called on to determine the best way to use technology, organize information, and communicate effectively.

Information Technology

An Information Technology (IT) program prepares students to meet the computer technology needs of business, government, healthcare, schools, and other organizations. IT has its emphasis on the technology itself, more than on the information handled, the theory behind it, or how to design hardware or software. IT professionals work with computer systems to ensure they work properly, are secure, are upgraded and maintained, and are replaced as appropriate.

Because computers have become integral parts of the work environment for all employees at all levels of the organization, many enterprises must maintain departments of IT workers. Organizations of every kind are dependent on information technology on a daily basis and the need for qualified workers is great.

Degree programs in IT are commonly found in business or information management departments, or as an alternate degree in a computer science department. IT programs in business departments focus on using applications to meet the requirements of networking, systems integration, and resource planning. The emphasis is less on programming and more on using programs already written to the best advantage. IT programs in computer science departments often have more emphasis on programming for computer users, with a focus on writing software for interactive web pages, multimedia, and cloud computing.

IT specialists select appropriate hardware and software products for an organization and then integrate these products within the existing infrastructure. They install and customize and maintain the software as needed. Other examples of responsibilities include network administration and security, design and implementation of web pages, development of multimedia resources, oversight of e-mail systems, and installation of communication components. User support and training are often important responsibilities for the IT professional as well.

Software Engineering

Software engineering (SE) is the discipline of developing and maintaining large software systems. These systems must behave reliably and efficiently, be affordable, and satisfy all requirements defined for them. SE seeks to integrate the theory of computer science and mathematics with the practical engineering principles developed for physical objects.

An SE degree program is closely related to the computer science degree program, and they are usually offered within the same department. In fact, most computer science curricula require one or more software engineering courses. An SE degree can be considered a specialized degree within the confines of the field of computer science.

SE students learn more about software reliability and maintenance of large systems and focus more on techniques for developing and maintaining software that is engineered to be correct from its inception. Most programs require SE students to participate in group projects for the development of software that will be used in earnest by others. Students assess customer needs, develop usable software, test the product thoroughly, and analyze its usefulness.

Professionals who hold a software engineering degree expect to be involved with the creation and maintenance of large software systems that may be used by many different organizations. Their focus will be on the design principles that make the system viable for many people and through many years.

Although an SE degree has a recognized description, the term *software engineer* is merely a job label in the workplace. There is no standard definition for this term when used in a job description, and its meaning can vary widely among employers. An employer may think of a programmer or an IT specialist as a software engineer.

FIGURE 0.2

Illustrations of the overlapping fields within mixed disciplinary majors

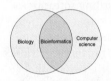

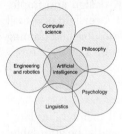

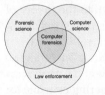

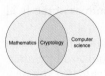

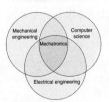

Mixed Disciplinary Majors

Technology is opening doors for fields of study that combine different sciences or engineering fields with computing as illustrated by Figure 0.2. Institutes of higher learning have responded by offering courses or programs for multidisciplinary majors. Some examples follow.

- **Bioinformatics** is the use of computer science to maintain, analyze, and store biological data as well as to assist in solving biological problems—usually on the molecular level. Such biological problems include protein folding, protein function prediction, and phylogeny (the history, origin, and evolution of a set of organisms). The core principle of bioinformatics involves using computing resources to help solve problems on scales of magnitude too great for human observation.

- **Artificial Intelligence** (AI) is the implementation and study of systems that can exhibit autonomous intelligence or behaviors. AI research draws from many fields including computer science, psychology, philosophy, linguistics, neuroscience, logic, and economics. Applications include robotics, control systems, scheduling, logistics, speech recognition, handwriting recognition, understanding natural language, proving mathematical theorems, data mining, and facial recognition.

- **Computer Forensics** is a branch of forensic science pertaining to legal evidence that may be found in computers and digital storage devices. The collection of this evidence must adhere to standards of evidence admissible in a court of law. Computer forensics involves the fields of law, law enforcement, and business.

- **Cryptology** (or cryptography) is the practice and study of hiding information and involves mathematics, computer science, and engineering. Electronic data security for commerce, personal uses, and military uses continue to be of vast importance.

- **Mechatronics** is the combination of mechanical engineering, electronic engineering, and software engineering in order to design advanced hybrid systems. Examples of mechatronics include production systems, planetary exploration rovers, automotive subsystems such as anti-lock braking systems, and autofocus cameras.

Even when the definitions are given for the different computing disciplines mentioned in this chapter, it is easy to see that there is great overlap among all of them.

In fact, many professionals who have earned a computer science degree may be working in jobs that are closer to an information systems description or vice versa. The student is encouraged to choose a computing field that seems closest to his or her personal goals.

Section 3 Career Opportunities

The Bureau of Labor Statistics is the principal fact-finding agency for the U.S. Federal Government in the field of labor economics and statistics. This agency publishes *The Occupational Outlook Handbook*, which is a nationally recognized source of career information, designed to provide valuable assistance to individuals making decisions about their future work lives. The *Handbook* is revised every two years. Table 0.1 gives an overview of some of the major computer occupations tracked by the U.S. Bureau of Labor Statistics.

The Demand in the United States and in the World

According to the *BLS Occupational Outlook Handbook,* software developer, database administrator, and network/computer systems administrator are three of the occupations projected to grow at the fastest rates over the 2010–2020 decade. Strong employment growth combined with a limited supply of qualified workers will result in excellent employment prospects. Those with practical experience and at least a bachelor's degree in one of the computing fields described in Section 2 should have the best opportunities. Employers will continue to seek computer professionals with strong programming, systems analysis, interpersonal, and business skills.

The growing need for computer professionals is increased by the ongoing retirement of a generation of baby boomers, and all of this is occurring as the U.S. government projects continued rapid growth in many computer science and IT occupations.

Today's students need not worry about the impact that outsourcing computer jobs to other countries will have on their ability to find a job. The fact is that many companies have been disappointed in the results when outsourcing entire projects. Some of the more mundane aspects of coding can be outsourced, but the more creative work is best kept in house. For example, during the design and development of a new system, interaction with specialists from other disciplines and communication with other team members and potential system users are of utmost importance. These activities are negatively impacted by communication difficulties across cultures and long distances. Many companies are rethinking outsourcing and doing more system development at home.

The number of graduates from the computing fields will not meet the demand in the marketplace in the foreseeable future. Projections and statistics show that there will be plenty of jobs to be offered to the qualified computer professional and the salaries will be higher than the average full-time worker earns in the United States.

TABLE 0.1   Computer, Computer Engineering, and Information Technology Occupations

Occupation	Job Summary	Entry-Level Education
Computer and Information Research Scientists	Computer and information research scientists invent and design new technology and find new uses for existing technology. They study and solve complex problems in computing for business, science, medicine, and other uses.	Doctoral or professional degree
Computer Programmers	Computer programmers write code to create software programs. They turn the program designs created by software developers and engineers into instructions that a computer can follow.	Bachelor's degree
Computer Support Specialists	Computer support specialists provide help and advice to people and organizations using computer software or equipment. Some, called technical support specialists, support information technology (IT) employees within their organization. Others, called help-desk technicians, assist non-IT users who are having computer problems.	Some college, no degree
Computer Systems Analysts	Computer systems analysts study an organization's current computer systems and procedures and make recommendations to management to help the organization operate more efficiently and effectively. They bring business and information technology (IT) together by understanding the needs and limitations of both.	Bachelor's degree
Database Administrators	Database administrators use software to store and organize data, such as financial information and customer shipping records. They make sure that data are available to users and are secure from unauthorized access.	Bachelor's degree
Information Security Analysts, Web Developers, and Computer Network Architects	Information security analysts, web developers, and computer network architects all use information technology (IT) to advance their organization's goals. Security analysts ensure a firm's information stays safe from cyber attacks. Web developers create websites to help firms have a public face. Computer network architects create the internal networks all workers within organizations use.	Bachelor's degree
Network and Computer Systems Administrators	Network and computer systems administrators are responsible for the day-to-day operation of an organization's computer networks. They organize, install, and support an organization's computer systems, including local area networks (LANs), wide area networks (WANs), network segments, intranets, and other data communication systems.	Bachelor's degree

Software Developers	Software developers are the creative minds behind computer programs. Some develop the applications that allow people to do specific tasks on a computer or other device. Others develop the underlying systems that run the devices or control networks.	Bachelor's degree
Computer Hardware Engineers	Computer equipment such as chips, circuit boards, or routers. By solving complex problems in computer hardware, these engineers create rapid advances in computer technology.	Bachelor's degree

Excerpted with permission from U.S. Bureau of Labor Statistics, Office of Occupational Statistics and Employment Projections, March 29, 2012

The Demand for Underrepresented Groups

The demand for women and minorities to fill computer-related jobs is higher than ever. The computer-related fields have traditionally seen small numbers of women and minorities in the workplace. Colleges and universities want to attract these groups to computer science and IS departments and often offer good scholarships and opportunities.

According to a study by the National Center for Women and Information Technology, the most successful IT teams were also the most diverse. The study showed that diversity of thought leads to innovation, and that companies should be aware of the significance of diversity. Prospective students should not be turned away by the stereotypical view of a "computer geek" who sits in front of a computer all day, but should realize all the opportunities to be found in such a diverse and fast-growing field. Computer professionals will be creating the applications that allow computers to solve real-world problems.

New Careers Constantly on the Horizon

It is clear that there will be a healthy need for computer professionals in the career paths that are known about today. For the student just starting to plan a career, there will surely be opportunities that have not even been imagined yet. The possibilities are amazing and the rewards are many.

One such window into the future can be seen in the work of Bruce Donald, a professor of Computer Science and of Biochemistry at Duke University. Through his research, Professor Donald has developed microscopic robots that can be controlled individually or as a group. These robots (see Figure 0.3) are measured in microns (millionths of a meter) and are almost 100 times smaller than previous robotic designs of their kind. Each robot can respond differently to the same single

FIGURE 0.3

Scanning-electron micrograph of a microrobot consisting of an untethered scratch-drive actuator (USDA) that provides forward motion, and a curved steering-arm actuator (i) that moves robot in straight line or turns. (© 2013 *The International Journal of Robotics Research*)

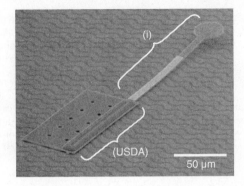

"global control signal" as voltages charge and discharge on their working parts. A budding computer scientist should see many fantastic applications for these devices!

The student who chooses to major in computer science or a related field can look forward to challenging and interesting classes. The job market will be wide open upon graduation, with the assurance that such degrees will be highly marketable. A new employee or researcher will have opportunities to be at the forefront of innovative technology in a constantly changing world. The prospects are limited only by the imagination.

Overview of Computers and Programming

CHAPTER OBJECTIVES

- To learn about the different categories of computers
- To understand the role of each component in a computer
- To understand the purpose of an operating system
- To learn the differences between machine language, assembly language, and higher-level languages
- To understand what processes are required to run a C program
- To learn how to solve a programming problem in a careful, disciplined way
- To understand and appreciate ethical issues related to the use of computers and programming

In developed countries, life in the twenty-first century is conducted in a veritable sea of computers. From the coffeepot that turns itself on to brew your morning coffee to the microwave that cooks your breakfast to the automobile that you drive to work to the automated teller machine you stop by for cash, virtually every aspect of your life depends on **computers**. These machines which receive, store, process, and output information can deal with data of all kinds: numbers, text, images, graphics, and sound, to name a few.

computer a machine that can receive, store, transform, and output data of all kinds

The computer program's role in this technology is essential; without a list of instructions to follow, the computer is virtually useless. Programming languages allow us to write those programs and thus to communicate with computers.

You are about to begin the study of computer science using one of the most versatile programming languages available today: the C language. This chapter introduces you to the computer and its components and to the major categories of programming languages. It discusses how C programs are processed by a computer. It also describes a systematic approach to solving programming problems called the *software development method* and shows you how to apply it.

1.1 Electronic Computers Then and Now

In our everyday life, we come in contact with computers frequently, some of us using computers for creating presentations and other documents, tabulating data in spreadsheets, or even having studied programming in high school. But it wasn't always this way. Not so long ago, most people considered computers to be mysterious devices whose secrets were known only by a few computer wizards.

The first electronic computer was built in the late 1930s by Dr. John Atanasoff and Clifford Berry at Iowa State University. Atanasoff designed his computer to assist graduate students in nuclear physics with their mathematical computations.

The first large-scale, general-purpose electronic digital computer, called the ENIAC, was completed in 1946 at the University of Pennsylvania with funding from the U.S. Army. Weighing 30 tons and occupying a 30-by-50-foot space, the ENIAC was used to compute ballistics tables, predict the weather, and make atomic energy calculations.

These early computers used vacuum tubes as their basic electronic component. Technological advances in the design and manufacture of electronic components led to new generations of computers that were considerably smaller, faster, and less expensive than previous ones.

FIGURE 1.1

The Intel® Core™ i7 processor chip contains the full circuitry of a central processing unit in an integrated circuit whose small size and low power requirements make it suitable for use in mobile internet devices. (Intel Corporation Pressroom Photo Archives)

computer chip (processor chip) a silicon chip containing the circuitry for a computer processor

Using today's technology, the entire circuitry of a computer processor can be packaged in a single electronic component called a **computer** or **processor chip** (Fig. 1.1), which is less than one-fourth the size of a standard postage stamp. Their affordability and small size enable computer chips to be installed in watches, cellphones, GPS systems, cameras, home appliances, automobiles, and, of course, computers.

Today, a common sight in offices and homes is a personal computer, which can cost less than $500 and sit on a desk (Fig. 1.2a) and yet has as much computational power as one that 40 years ago cost more than $100,000 and filled a 9-by-12-foot room. Even smaller computers can fit inside a briefcase or purse (Fig. 1.2b, c) or your hand (Fig. 1.2d).

Modern computers are categorized according to their size and performance. *Personal computers*, shown in Fig. 1.2, are used by a single person at a time. Large real-time transaction processing systems, such as ATMs and other banking networks, and corporate reservations systems for motels, airlines, and rental cars use *mainframes*, very powerful and reliable computers. The largest capacity and fastest computers are called *supercomputers* and are used by research laboratories and in computationally intensive applications such as weather forecasting.

FIGURE 1.2

(a) Desktop Computer, iMac. (© Hugh Threlfall/Alamy). (b) Hewlett Packard Laptop. (© Hewlett-Packard Company). (c) iPad. (© D. Hurst/Alamy). (d) Android phone, LG Thrill 4G. (© Handout/MCT/Newscom).

a

b

c

d

hardware   the actual computer equipment

software   the set of programs associated with a computer

program   a list of instructions that enables a computer to perform a specific task

binary number   a number whose digits are 0 and 1

The elements of a computer system fall into two major categories: hardware and software. **Hardware** is the equipment used to perform the necessary computations and includes the central processing unit (CPU), monitor, keyboard, mouse, printer, and speakers. **Software** consists of the **programs** that enable us to solve problems with a computer by providing it with lists of instructions to perform.

Programming a computer has undergone significant changes over the years. Initially, the task was very difficult, requiring programmers to write their program instructions as long **binary numbers** (sequences of 0s and 1s). High-level programming languages such as C make programming much easier.

EXERCISES FOR SECTION 1.1

Self-Check

1.   Is a computer program a piece of hardware or is it software?
2.   For what applications are mainframes used?

1.2   Computer Hardware

Despite significant variations in cost, size, and capabilities, modern computers resemble one another in many basic ways. Essentially, most consist of the following components:

- Main memory
- Secondary memory, which includes storage devices such as hard disks, CDs, DVDs, and flash drives
- Central processing unit
- Input devices, such as keyboards, mice, touchpads, touch screens, scanners, joysticks, and microphones
- Output devices, such as screens, printers, and speakers

Figure 1.3 shows how these components interact in a computer, with the arrows pointing in the direction of information flow. The program must first be transferred from *secondary storage* to *main memory* before it can be executed. Normally, the person using a program (the *program user*) must supply some data to be processed. These data are entered through an *input device* and are stored in the computer's *main memory*, where they can be accessed and manipulated by the *central processing unit*. The results of this manipulation are then stored back in *main memory*. Finally, the information in main memory can be displayed through an *output device*. In the remainder of this section, we describe these components in more detail.

Memory

Memory is an essential component in any computer. Let's look at what it consists of and how the computer works with it.

FIGURE 1.3

Components of a Computer

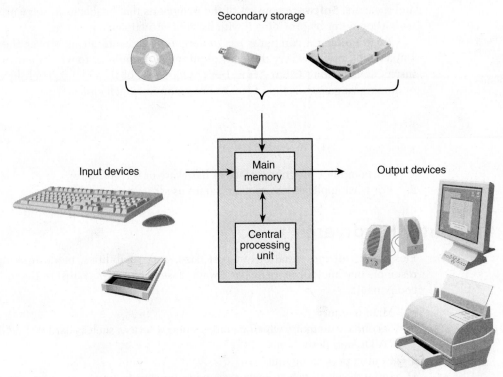

Anatomy of Memory   Imagine the memory of a computer as an ordered sequence of storage locations called **memory cells** (Fig. 1.4). To store and access information, the computer must have some way of identifying the individual memory cells. Therefore, each memory cell has a unique **address** that indicates its relative position in memory. Figure 1.4 shows a computer memory consisting of 1000 memory cells with addresses 0 through 999. Most computers, however, have millions of individual memory cells, each with its own address.

The data stored in a memory cell are called the **contents** of the cell. Every memory cell always has some contents, although we may have no idea what they are. In Fig. 1.4, the contents of memory cell 3 are the number −26 and the contents of memory cell 4 are the letter H.

Although not shown in Fig. 1.4, a memory cell can also contain a program instruction. The ability to store programs as well as data is called the **stored program concept**: A program's instructions must be stored in main memory before they can be executed. We can change the computer's operation by storing a different program in memory.

memory cell   an individual storage location in memory

address of a memory cell   the relative position of a memory cell in the computer's main memory

contents of a memory cell   the information stored in a memory cell, either a program instruction or data

stored program concept   a computer's ability to store program instructions in main memory for execution

Memory

Address	Contents
0	-27.2
1	354
2	0.005
3	-26
4	H
⋮	⋮
998	X
999	75.62

FIGURE 1.4

1000 Memory Cells in Main Memory

|00101100|
←Byte→   Bit

FIGURE 1.5

Relationship Between a Byte and a Bit

Bytes and Bits A memory cell is actually a grouping of smaller units called bytes. A **byte** is the amount of storage required to store a single character, such as the letter H in memory cell 4 of Fig. 1.4. The number of bytes a memory cell can contain varies from computer to computer. A byte is composed of even smaller units of storage called bits (Fig. 1.5). The term **bit**, derived from the words **b**inary dig**it**, is the smallest element a computer can deal with. Binary refers to a number system based on two numbers, 0 and 1, so a bit is either a 0 or a 1. Generally, there are 8 bits to a byte.

Storage and Retrieval of Information in Memory Each value in memory is represented by a particular pattern of 0s and 1s. A computer can either store a value or retrieve a value. To **store** a value, the computer sets each bit of a selected memory cell to either 0 or 1, destroying the previous contents of the cell in the process. To **retrieve** a value from a memory cell, the computer copies the pattern of 0s and 1s stored in that cell to another storage area for processing; the copy operation does not destroy the contents of the cell whose value is retrieved. This process is the same regardless of the kind of information—character, number, or program instruction—to be stored or retrieved.

Main Memory Main memory stores programs, data, and results. Most computers have two types of main memory: **random access memory (RAM)**, which offers

byte the amount of storage required to store a single character

bit a binary digit; a 0 or a 1

data storage setting the individual bits of a memory cell to 0 or 1, destroying its previous contents

data retrieval copying the contents of a particular memory cell to another storage area

random access memory (RAM) the part of main memory that temporarily stores programs, data, and results

read-only memory (ROM) the part of main memory that permanently stores programs or data

volatile memory memory whose contents disappear when the computer is switched off

temporary storage of programs and data, and read-only memory (ROM), which stores programs or data permanently. RAM temporarily stores programs while they are being executed (carried out) by the computer. It also temporarily stores such data as numbers, names, and even pictures while a program is manipulating them. RAM is usually volatile memory, which means that everything in RAM will be lost when the computer is switched off.

ROM, on the other hand, stores information permanently within the computer. The computer can retrieve (or read), but cannot store (or write) information in ROM, hence its name, read-only. Because ROM is not volatile, the data stored there do not disappear when the computer is switched off. Start-up instructions and other critical instructions are burned into ROM chips at the factory. When we refer to main memory in this text, we mean RAM because that is the part of main memory that is normally accessible to the programmer.

Secondary Storage Devices   Computer systems provide storage in addition to main memory for two reasons. First, computers need storage that is permanent or semipermanent so that information can be retained during a power loss or when the computer is turned off. Second, systems typically store more information than will fit in memory.

secondary storage units such as disks or flash drives that retain data even when the power to the drive is off

disk thin platter of metal or plastic on which data are represented by magnetized spots arranged in tracks

optical drive device that uses a laser to access or store data on a CD or DVD or Blu-ray Disk

Figure 1.6 shows some of the most frequently encountered **secondary storage** devices and storage media. Most personal computers use two types of disk drives as their secondary storage devices—hard drives and optical drives. Hard **disks** are attached to their disk drives and are coated with a magnetic material. Each data bit is a magnetized spot on the disk, and the spots are arranged in concentric circles called tracks. The disk drive read/write head accesses data by moving across the spinning disk to the correct track and then sensing the spots as they move by. The hard disks in personal computers usually hold several hundred gigabytes (GB) of data, but clusters of hard drives that store data for an entire network may provide as much as several terabytes (TB) of storage (see Table 1.1).

Many of today's personal computers are equipped with **optical drives** for storing and retrieving data on compact disks (CDs) or digital versatile disks (DVDs) that can be removed from the drive. A CD is a silvery plastic platter on which a laser records data as a sequence of tiny pits in a spiral track on one side of the disk. One CD can hold 680 MB of data. A DVD uses smaller pits packed in a tighter spiral. Some Blu-ray disks (high-density optical disks read with a blue-violet laser) can hold multiple layers of data—for a total capacity of 200 GB, sufficient storage for many hours of studio-quality video and multi-channel audio.

FIGURE 1.6

Secondary Storage Media

DVD   Flash   Hard
             drive   disk

TABLE 1.1   Terms Used to Quantify Storage Capacities

Term	Abbreviation	Equivalent to	Comparison to Power of 10
Byte	B	8 bits	
Kilobyte	KB	1,024 (2^{10}) bytes	> 10^3
Megabyte	MB	1,048,576 (2^{20}) bytes	> 10^6
Gigabyte	GB	1,073,741,824 (2^{30}) bytes	> 10^9
Terabyte	TB	1,099,511,627,776 (2^{40}) bytes	> 10^{12}
Petabyte	PB	1,125,899,906,842,624 (2^{50}) bytes	> 10^{15}

flash drive   device that plugs into USB port and stores data bits as trapped electrons

Flash drives such as the one pictured in Fig. 1.6 use flash memory packaged in small plastic cases about three inches long that can be plugged into any of a computer's USB (Universal Serial Bus) ports. Unlike hard drives and optical drives that must spin their disks for access to data, flash drives have no moving parts and all data transfer is by electronic signal only. In flash memory, bits are represented as electrons trapped in microscopic chambers of silicon dioxide. Typical USB flash drives store several GB of data, but drives holding up to one terabyte (1 TB) are also available.

file   named collection of data stored on a disk

Information stored on a disk is organized into separate collections called **files**. One file may contain a C program. Another file may contain the data to be processed by that program (a *data file*). A third file could contain the results generated by a program (an *output file*). The names of all files stored on a disk are listed in the disk's **directory**. This directory may be broken into one or more levels of subdirectories or folders, where each **subdirectory** stores the names of files that relate to the same general topic. For example, you might have separate subdirectories of files that contain homework assignments and programs for each course you are taking this semester. The details of how files are named and grouped in directories vary with each computer system. Follow the naming conventions that apply to your system.

directory   a list of the names of files stored on a disk

subdirectory   a list of the names of files that relate to a particular topic

Central Processing Unit

central processing unit (CPU) coordinates all computer operations and performs arithmetic and logical operations on data

The **central processing unit (CPU)** or **processor** has two roles: coordinating all computer operations and performing arithmetic and logical operations on data. The processor follows the instructions contained in a computer program to determine which operations should be carried out and in what order. It then transmits coordinating control signals to the other computer components. For example, if the instruction requires scanning a data item, the CPU sends the necessary control signals to the input device.

fetching an instruction   retrieving an instruction from main memory

To process a program stored in main memory, the CPU retrieves each instruction in sequence (called **fetching an instruction**), interprets the instruction to determine what should be done and then retrieves any data needed to carry out that instruction. Next, the CPU performs the actual manipulation, or processing, of the data it retrieved. The CPU stores the results in main memory.

The CPU can perform such arithmetic operations as addition, subtraction, multiplication, and division. The CPU can also compare the contents of two memory cells (for example, Which contains the larger value? Are the values equal?) and make decisions based on the results of that comparison.

The circuitry of a modern CPU is housed in a single integrated circuit or chip, millions of miniature circuits manufactured in a sliver of silicon. A processor's current instruction and data values are stored temporarily inside the CPU in special high-speed memory locations called **registers**.

register high-speed memory location inside the CPU

multiprocessor a computer with more than one CPU

Some **multiprocessor** computers have multiple CPU chips or a multi-core processor (a single chip containing multiple CPUs). These computers are capable of faster speeds because they can process different sets of instructions at the same time.

Input/Output Devices

We use *input/output (I/O) devices* to communicate with the computer. Specifically, they allow us to enter data for a computation and to observe the results of that computation.

cursor a moving place marker that appears on the screen

function keys special keyboard keys used to select a particular operation; operation selected depends on program being used

mouse, touchpad input devices that move a cursor on the computer screen to select an operation

icon a picture representing a computer operation

hard copy a printed version of information

You will be using a *keyboard* as an input device and a *monitor* (display screen) as an output device. When you press a letter or digit key on a keyboard, that character is sent to main memory and is also displayed on the screen at the position of the **cursor**, a moving place marker (often a blinking line or rectangle). A computer keyboard has keys for letters, numbers, and punctuation marks plus some extra keys for performing special functions. The twelve **function keys** along the top row of the keyboard are labeled F1 through F12. The activity performed when you press a function key depends on the program currently being executed; that is, pressing F1 in one program will usually not produce the same results as pressing F1 in another program. Other special keys enable you to delete characters, move the cursor, and "enter" a line of data you typed at the keyboard.

Other common input devices provide pointing capability to allow you to select an operation. Moving a **mouse** around on your desktop or dragging your finger across a **touchpad** moves the *cursor* (normally an arrow, vertical line, or a small rectangle) displayed on the screen. You select an operation by moving the cursor to a word or **icon** (picture) that represents the computer operation you wish to perform and then clicking a button to activate the operation selected.

A screen provides a temporary display of information. If you want **hard copy** (a printed version) of some information, you must send that information to an output device called a *printer* .

Computer Networks

local area network (LAN) computers, printers, scanners, and storage devices connected by cables for intercommunication

The explosion we are experiencing in worldwide information access is primarily due to the fact that computers are now linked together in networks so they can communicate with one another. In a **local area network (LAN)**, computers and other

FIGURE 1.7

Local Area
Network

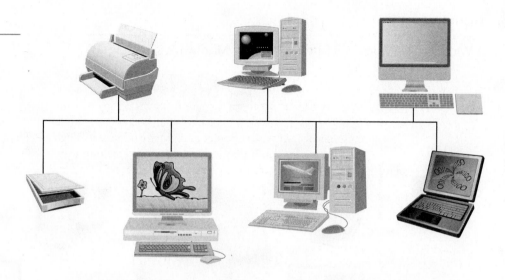

file server   the computer in a network that controls access to a secondary storage device such as a hard disk

wide area network (WAN)   a network such as the Internet that connects computers and LANs over a large geographic area

World Wide Web (WWW)   a part of the Internet whose graphical user interfaces make associated network resources easily navigable

graphical user interface (GUI)   pictures and menus displayed to allow user to select commands and data

modem   device that converts binary data into analog signals that can be transmitted between computers over telephone lines

devices in a building are connected by cables or a wireless network, allowing them to share information and resources such as printers, scanners, and secondary storage devices (Fig. 1.7). A computer that controls access to a secondary storage device such as a large hard disk is called a **file server**.

Local area networks can be connected to other LANs using the same technology as telephone networks. Communications over intermediate distances use phone lines, fiber-optics cables or wireless technology, and long-range communications use either phone lines or microwave signals that may be relayed by satellite (Fig. 1.8).

A network that links many individual computers and local area networks over a large geographic area is called a **wide area network (WAN)**. The most well-known WAN is the Internet, a network of university, corporate, government, and public-access networks. The Internet is a descendant of the computer network designed by the U.S. Defense Department's 1969 ARPAnet project. The goal of the project was to create a computer network that could continue to operate even if partially destroyed. The most widely used aspect of the Internet is the **World Wide Web (WWW)**, the universe of Internet-accessible resources that are navigable through the use of a **graphical user interface (GUI)**.

If you have a computer with a modem, you can connect to the information superhighway through a telephone line, television or fiber-optic cable, or through wireless or satellite communications. A **modem** (**mo**dulator/**dem**odulator) converts binary computer data into audio tones that can be transmitted to another computer over a normal telephone circuit. At the computer on the receiving end, another modem converts the audio tones back to binary data.

Early modems for telephone lines transmitted at only 300 baud (300 bits per second). Today's modems can transmit over 150 megabits per second, if attached to a line that handles such speeds.

FIGURE 1.8

A Wide Area Network with Satellite Relays of Microwave Signals

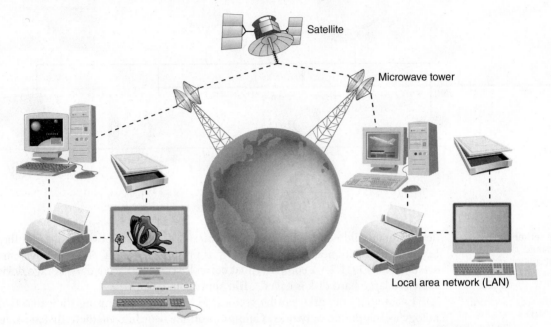

Satellite

Microwave tower

Local area network (LAN)

cable Internet access two-way high-speed transmission of Internet data through two of the hundreds of channels available over the coaxial cable that carries cable television signals

Cable Internet access brings Internet data to your computer at speeds of several billion bits per second using the same coaxial cable that carries cable TV. Wireless and satellite communications provide data speeds comparable to cable.

 EXERCISES FOR SECTION 1.2

Self-Check

1. If a computer executes instructions to sum the contents of memory cells 2 and 999 in Fig. 1.4 and store the result in cell 0, what would then be the contents of cells 0, 2, and 999?
2. One bit can have two values, 0 or 1. A combination of 2 bits can have four values: 00, 01, 10, and 11. List all of the values you can form with a combination of 3 bits. Do the same for 4 bits.
3. List the following in order of smallest to largest: byte, bit, WAN, main memory, memory cell, LAN, secondary storage.

1.3   Computer Software

In the previous section, we surveyed the components of a computer system, components referred to collectively as hardware. We also studied the fundamental operations that allow a computer to accomplish tasks: repeated fetching and execution of instructions. In this section, we focus on these all-important lists of instructions called computer programs or computer software. We will consider first the software that makes the hardware friendly to the user. We will then look at the various levels of computer languages in which software is written and at the process of creating and running a new program.

Operating System

operating system (OS) software that controls interaction of user and computer hardware and that manages allocation of computer resources

The collection of computer programs that control the interaction of the user and the computer hardware is called the **operating system (OS)**. The operating system of a computer is often compared to the conductor of an orchestra, for it is the software that is responsible for directing all computer operations and managing all computer resources. Usually, part of the operating system is stored permanently in a read-only memory (ROM) chip so that it is available as soon as the computer is turned on. A computer can look at the values in read-only memory, but cannot write new values to the chip. The ROM-based portion of the OS contains the instructions necessary for loading into memory the rest of the operating system code, which typically resides on a disk. Loading the operating system into memory is called **booting the computer**.

booting a computer loading the operating system from disk into memory

Here is a list of some of the operating system's many responsibilities:

1. Communicating with the computer user: receiving commands and carrying them out or rejecting them with an error message.
2. Managing allocation of memory, of processor time, and of other resources for various tasks.
3. Collecting input from the keyboard, touchpad, mouse, and other input devices, and providing this data to the currently running program.
4. Conveying program output to the screen, printer, or other output device.
5. Accessing data from secondary storage.
6. Writing data to secondary storage.

In addition to these responsibilities, the operating system of a computer with multiple users must verify each individual's right to use the computer and must ensure that each user can access only data for which he or she has proper authorization. When multiple programs are running on a computer concurrently, the OS makes sure that each one accesses only the memory and other resources specifically allocated to it.

An operating system that uses a command-line interface displays a brief message, called a *prompt*, that indicates its readiness to receive input, and the user then types a command at the keyboard. Figure 1.9 shows an entry of a UNIX command (`ls temp/misc`) requesting a list of the names of all the files (`Gridvar.c,`

FIGURE 1.9   Entering a UNIX Command for Directory Display

```
1.  mycomputer:~> ls temp/misc

2.  Gridvar.c      Gridvar.exe      Gridok.txt

3.

4.  mycomputer:~>
```

Gridvar.exe , Gridok.txt) in subdirectory misc of directory temp. In this case, the prompt is mycomputer:~> (In this figure, and in all subsequent figures showing program runs, input typed by the user is shown in color to distinguish it from computer-generated text.)

Most modern operating systems have a graphical user interface that provides the user with a system of icons and menus. To issue commands, the user moves the mouse or touchpad cursor to point to the appropriate icon or menu selection and clicks a button once or twice. Figure 1.10 shows the window that

FIGURE 1.10

Accessing
Secondary Storage
Devices Through
Windows

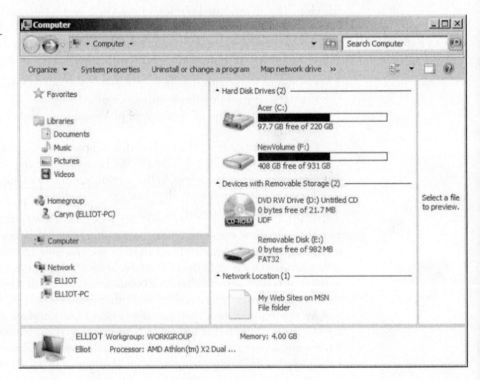

pops up in Microsoft Windows 7 when you left-click on the Start icon and then left-click on Computer. You can view the directories of the hard drive (C:), backup drive (F:), optical drive (D:), or flash drive (E:) by double-clicking the appropriate icon.

Application Software

application software used for a specific task such as word processing, accounting, database management, playing a game, or checking the weather forecast

Application programs are developed to assist a computer user in accomplishing specific tasks. For example, a word-processing application such as Microsoft Word or OpenOffice.org Writer helps to create a document, a spreadsheet application such as Microsoft Office Excel helps to automate tedious numerical calculations and to generate charts that depict data, and a database management application such as Microsoft Office Access or Oracle assists in data storage and quick keyword-based access to large collections of records.

install make an application available on a computer by copying it to the computer's hard drive

Computer users typically purchase application software by downloading files from the Internet and **install** the software by following on-screen directions that copy the programs to the hard disk. When buying software, you must always check that the program you are purchasing is compatible with both the operating system and the computer hardware you plan to use. We have already discussed some of the differences among operating systems; now we will investigate the different languages understood by different processors.

Computer Languages

Developing new software requires writing lists of instructions for a computer to execute. However, software developers rarely write in the language directly understood by a processor, since this **machine language** is a collection of binary numbers. Another drawback of machine language is that it is not standardized: There is a different machine language for every type of CPU. This same drawback also applies to the somewhat more readable **assembly language**, a language in which computer operations are represented by mnemonic codes rather than binary numbers and variables can be given names rather than binary memory addresses. Table 1.2 shows a tiny machine language program fragment that adds two numbers and the equivalent fragment in assembly language. Notice that each assembly language instruction corresponds to exactly one machine instruction: The assembly language memory cells labeled A and B are space for variables; they are not instructions. The symbol ? indicates that we do not know the contents of the memory cells with addresses 00000101 and 00000110.

machine language binary number codes understood by a specific CPU

assembly language mnemonic codes that correspond to machine language instructions

high-level language machine-independent programming language that combines algebraic expressions and English symbols

To write programs that are independent of the processor on which they will be executed, software designers use **high-level languages** that combine algebraic expressions and symbols taken from English. For example, the machine/assembly

TABLE 1.2 A Machine Language Program Fragment and Its Assembly Language Equivalent

Memory Addresses	Machine Language Instructions	Assembly Language Instructions
00000000	00000000	CLA
00000001	00010101	ADD A
00000010	00010110	ADD B
00000011	00110101	STA A
00000100	01110111	HLT
00000101	?	A ?
00000110	?	B ?

language program fragment shown in Table 1.2 would be a single statement in a high-level language:

$$a = a + b;$$

This statement means "add the values of variables a and b, and store the result in variable a (replacing a's previous value)."

There are many high-level languages available. Table 1.3 lists some of the most widely used ones along with some information about their origins and the application areas that first popularized them. Although programmers find it far easier to express problem solutions in high-level languages, there remains the problem that computers do NOT understand these languages. Thus, before a high-level language program can be executed, it must first be translated into the target processor's machine language. The program that does this translation is called a **compiler**. Figure 1.11 illustrates the role of the compiler in the process of developing and testing a high-level language program. Both the input to and the output from the compiler (when it is successful) are programs. The input to the compiler is a **source file** containing the text of a high-level language program. The software developer creates this file by using a word processor or editor. The format of the source file is text, which means that it is a collection of character codes. For example, you might type a program into a file called `myprog.c`. The compiler will scan this source file, checking the program to see if it follows the high-level language's **syntax** (grammar) rules. If the program is syntactically correct, the compiler saves in an **object file** the machine language instructions that carry out the program's purpose. For program `myprog.c`, the object file created might be named `myprog.obj`. Notice that this file's format is binary. This means that you should not send it to a printer, display it on your screen, or try to work with it in a word processor

compiler software that translates a high-level language program into machine language

source file file containing a program written in a high-level language; the input for a compiler

syntax grammar rules of a programming language

object file file of machine language instructions that is the output of a compiler

TABLE 1.3 High-Level Languages

Language	Origin / Application Area
C	Systems programming language originally used in the development of the UNIX operating system; now used in a wide range of applications
C++	Adds object-oriented features to C; used in a wide range of applications including game development
Objective C	Adds to C object capabilities and messaging; used by Apple for systems programming and iPhone application software
Perl	Used in creation of interactive web pages, graphics, and network programming
Python	General-purpose high-level language that emphasizes readability of code
Java	General-purpose language used in wide range of applications including Web programming and Android application software
JavaScript	Used in web browsers both for client-side interaction with user and in web server programs
PHP	Designed for web development; code is interpreted by a program running on a web server to generate a dynamic web page
C#	Adds object-oriented and component-oriented features to C; developed by Microsoft for its .NET initiative

because it will appear to be meaningless garbage to a word processor, printer, or screen. If the source program contains syntax errors, the compiler lists these errors but does not create an object file. The developer must return to the word processor, correct the errors, and recompile the program.

Although an object file contains machine instructions, not all of the instructions are complete. High-level languages provide the software developer with many named chunks of code for operations that the developer will likely need. Almost all high-level language programs use at least one of these chunks of code called *functions* that reside in other object files available to the system. The **linker** program combines these prefabricated functions with the object file, creating a complete machine language program that is ready to run. For your sample program, the linker might name the executable file it creates `myprog.exe`.

linker software that combines object files and resolves cross-references to create an executable machine language program

As long as `myprog.exe` is just stored on your disk, it does nothing. To run it, the loader must copy all its instructions into memory and direct the CPU to begin execution with the first instruction. As the program executes, it takes input data from one or more sources and sends results to output and/or secondary storage devices.

integrated development environment (IDE) software package combining a word processor, compiler, linker, loader, and tools for finding errors

Some computer systems require the user to ask the OS to carry out separately each step illustrated in Fig. 1.11. However, most high-level language compilers are sold as part of an **integrated development environment (IDE)**, a package that combines a simple word processor with a compiler, linker, and loader. Such environments give the developer menus from which to select the next step, and if the developer tries a step

FIGURE 1.11

Entering, Translating, and Running a High-Level Language Program

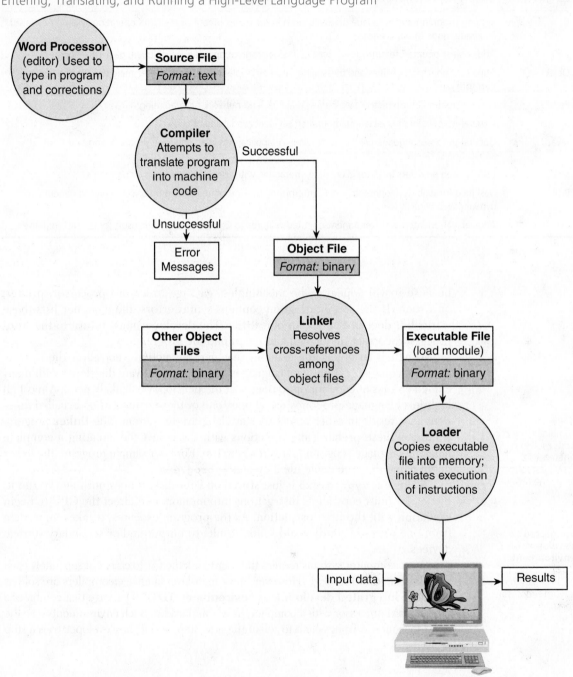

that is out of sequence, the environment simply fills in the missing steps automatically. An IDE will frequently use the term *build* to mean "compile and link."

The user of an integrated development environment should be aware that the environment may not automatically save to disk the source, object, and executable files. Rather, it may simply leave these versions of the program in memory. Such an approach saves the expenditure of time and disk space needed to make copies and keeps the code readily available in memory for application of the next step in the translation/execution process. However, the developer can risk losing the only copy of the source file in the event of a power outage or serious program error. To prevent such a loss when using an IDE, be sure to explicitly save the source file to disk after every modification before attempting to run the program.

Executing a Program

To execute a machine language program, the processor must examine each program instruction in memory and send out the command signals required to carry out the instruction. Although the instructions normally are executed in sequence, as we will discuss later, it is possible to have the CPU skip over some instructions or execute some instructions more than once.

During execution, data can be entered into memory and manipulated in some specified way. Special program instructions are used for entering or scanning a program's data (called **input data**) into memory. After the input data have been processed, instructions for displaying or printing values in memory can be executed to display the program results. The lines displayed by a program are called the **program output**.

input data   the data values that are scanned by a program

program output   the lines displayed by a program

Let's use the situation described in Fig. 1.12—executing a water bill program stored in memory—as an example. The first step of the program scans into memory data that describe the amount of water used. In step 2, the program manipulates the data and stores the results of the computations in memory. In the final step, the computational results are displayed as a water bill.

EXERCISES FOR SECTION 1.3

Self-Check

1. What do you think these five high-level language statements mean?

   ```
   x = a + b + c;    x = y / z;    d = c - b + a;
   z = z + 1;    kelvin = celsius + 273.15;
   ```

2. List two reasons why it would be preferable to write a program in C rather than in machine language.

FIGURE 1.12

Flow of Information During Program Execution

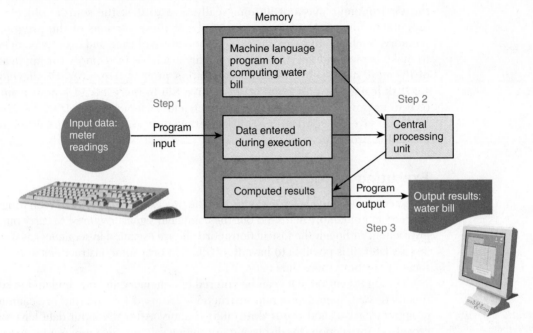

3. Would a syntax error be found in a source program or an object program? What system program would find a syntax error if one existed?
4. Explain the differences among the source program, the object program, and an executable program. Which do you create, and which does the compiler create? Which does the linker create?

1.4 The Software Development Method

Programming is a problem-solving activity. If you are a good problem solver, you have the potential to become a good programmer. Therefore, one goal of this book is to help you improve your problem-solving ability. Problem-solving methods are covered in many subject areas. Business students learn to solve problems with a *systems approach* while engineering and science students use the *engineering and scientific method*. Programmers use the *software development method*.

Software Development Method

1. Specify the problem requirements.
2. Analyze the problem.

3. Design the algorithm to solve the problem.
4. Implement the algorithm.
5. Test and verify the completed program.
6. Maintain and update the program.

PROBLEM

Specifying the problem requirements forces you to state the problem clearly and unambiguously and to gain a clear understanding of what is required for its solution. Your objective is to eliminate unimportant aspects and zero in on the root problem. This goal may not be as easy to achieve as it sounds. You may find you need more information from the person who posed the problem.

ANALYSIS

Analyzing the problem involves identifying the problem (a) *inputs*, that is, the data you have to work with; (b) *outputs*, that is, the desired results; and (c) any additional requirements or constraints on the solution. At this stage, you should also determine the required format in which the results should be displayed (for example, as a table with specific column headings) and develop a list of problem variables and their relationships. These relationships may be expressed as formulas.

If steps 1 and 2 are not done properly, you will solve the wrong problem. Read the problem statement carefully, first, to obtain a clear idea of the problem and second, to determine the inputs and outputs. You may find it helpful to underline phrases in the problem statement that identify the inputs and outputs, as in the problem statement below.

Compute and display the total cost of apples given the number of <u>pounds of apples</u> purchased and the <u>cost per pound of apples</u>.

Next, summarize the information contained in the underlined phrases:

Problem Inputs

```
quantity of apples purchased (in pounds)
cost per pound of apples (in dollars per pound)
```

Problem Output

```
total cost of apples (in dollars)
```

Once you know the problem inputs and outputs, develop a list of formulas that specify relationships between them. The general formula

$$Total\ cost = Unit\ cost \times Number\ of\ units$$

computes the total cost of any item purchased. Substituting the variables for our particular problem yields the formula

$$Total\ cost\ of\ apples = Cost\ per\ pound \times Pounds\ of\ apples$$

abstraction the process of modeling a problem by extracting the essential variables and their relationships

In some situations, you may need to make certain assumptions or simplifications to derive these relationships. This process of modeling a problem by extracting the essential variables and their relationships is called **abstraction**.

DESIGN

Designing the algorithm to solve the problem requires you to develop a list of steps called an **algorithm** to solve the problem and then to verify that the algorithm solves the problem as intended. Writing the algorithm is often the most difficult part of the problem-solving process. Don't attempt to solve every detail of the problem at the beginning; instead, discipline yourself to use top-down design. In **top-down design** (also called *divide and conquer*), you first list the major steps, or subproblems, that need to be solved. Then you solve the original problem by solving each of its subproblems. Most computer algorithms consist of at least the following subproblems.

algorithm a list of steps for solving a problem

top-down design breaking a problem into its major subproblems and then solving the subproblems

ALGORITHM FOR A PROGRAMMING PROBLEM

1. Get the data.
2. Perform the computations.
3. Display the results.

stepwise refinement development of a detailed list of steps to solve a particular step in the original algorithm

Once you know the subproblems, you can attack each one individually. For example, the perform-the-computations step may need to be broken down into a more detailed list of steps through a process called **stepwise refinement**.

You may be familiar with top-down design if you use an outline when writing a term paper. Your first step is to create an outline of the major topics, which you then refine by filling in subtopics for each major topic. Once the outline is complete, you begin writing the text for each subtopic.

desk checking the step-by-step simulation of the computer execution of an algorithm

Desk checking is an important part of algorithm design that is often overlooked. To **desk check** an algorithm, you must carefully perform each algorithm step (or its refinements) just as a computer would and verify that the algorithm works as intended. You'll save time and effort if you locate algorithm errors early in the problem-solving process.

IMPLEMENTATION

Implementing the algorithm (step 4 in the software development method) involves writing it as a program. You must convert each algorithm step into one or more statements in a programming language.

TESTING

Testing and verifying the program requires testing the completed program to verify that it works as desired. Don't rely on just one test case. Run the program several times using different sets of data to make sure that it works correctly for every situation provided for in the algorithm.

MAINTENANCE

Maintaining and updating the program involves modifying a program to remove previously undetected errors and to keep it up-to-date as government regulations or company policies change. Many organizations maintain a program for five years or more, often after the programmers who originally coded it have left or moved on to other positions.

A disciplined approach is essential if you want to create programs that are easy to read, understand, and maintain. You must follow accepted program style guidelines (which will be stressed in this book) and avoid tricks and programming shortcuts.

Caution: Failure Is Part of the Process

Although having a step-by-step approach to problem solving is helpful, we must avoid jumping to the conclusion that if we follow these steps, we are *guaranteed* a correct solution the first time, every time. The fact that verification is so important implies an essential truth of problem solving: The first (also the second, the third, or the twentieth) attempt at a solution *may be wrong.* Probably the most important distinction between outstanding problem solvers and less proficient ones is that outstanding problem solvers are not discouraged by initial failures. Rather, they see the faulty and near-correct early solutions as a means of gaining a better understanding of the problem. One of the most inventive problem solvers of all time, Thomas Edison, is noted for his positive interpretation of the thousands of failed experiments that contributed to his incredible record of inventions. His friends report that he always saw those failures in terms of the helpful data they yielded about what did *not* work.

EXERCISES FOR SECTION 1.4

Self-Check

1. List the steps of the software development method.
2. In which phase is the algorithm developed? In which phase do you identify the problem inputs and outputs?

1.5 Applying the Software Development Method

Throughout this book, we use the first five steps of the software development method to solve programming problems. These example problems, presented as Case Studies, begin with a *problem statement*. As part of the problem *analysis*, we identify the data requirements for the problem, indicating the problem inputs and the desired outputs. Next, we *design* and refine the initial algorithm. Finally, we *implement* the algorithm as a C program. We also provide a sample run of the program and discuss how to *test* the program.

We walk you through a sample case study next. This example includes a running commentary on the process, which you can use as a model in solving other problems.

CASE STUDY   Converting Miles to Kilometers

PROBLEM

Your summer surveying job requires you to study some maps that give distances in kilometers and some that use miles. You and your coworkers prefer to deal in metric measurements. Write a program that performs the necessary conversion.

ANALYSIS

The first step in solving this problem is to determine what you are asked to do. You must convert from one system of measurement to another, but are you supposed to convert from kilometers to miles, or vice versa? The problem states that you prefer to deal in metric measurements, so you must convert distance measurements in miles to kilometers. Therefore, the problem input is **distance in miles** and the problem output is **distance in kilometers**. To write the program, you need to know the relationship between miles and kilometers. Consulting a metric table shows that one mile equals 1.609 kilometers.

The data requirements and relevant formulas are listed below. `miles` identifies the memory cell that will contain the problem input and `kms` identifies the memory cell that will contain the program result, or the problem output.

DATA REQUIREMENTS

Problem Input
```
miles    /* the distance in miles*/
```

Problem Output
```
kms    /* the distance in kilometers */
```

Relevant Formula

1 mile = 1.609 kilometers

DESIGN

Next, formulate the algorithm that solves the problem. Begin by listing the three major steps, or subproblems, of the algorithm.

ALGORITHM

1. Get the distance in miles.
2. Convert the distance to kilometers.
3. Display the distance in kilometers.

Now decide whether any steps of the algorithm need further refinement or whether they are perfectly clear as stated. Step 1 (getting the data) and step 3 (displaying a value) are basic steps and require no further refinement. Step 2 is fairly straightforward, but some detail might help:

Step 2 Refinement

2.1 The distance in kilometers is 1.609 times the distance in miles.

We list the complete algorithm with refinements below to show you how it all fits together. The algorithm resembles an outline for a term paper. The refinement of step 2 is numbered as step 2.1 and is indented under step 2.

ALGORITHM WITH REFINEMENTS

1. Get the distance in miles.
2. Convert the distance to kilometers.
   2.1 The distance in kilometers is 1.609 times the distance in miles.
3. Display the distance in kilometers.

Let's desk check the algorithm before going further. If step 1 gets a distance of 10.0 miles, step 2.1 would convert it to 1.609 × 10.00 or 16.09 kilometers. This correct result would be displayed by step 3.

IMPLEMENTATION

To implement the solution, you must write the algorithm as a C program. To do this, you must first tell the C compiler about the problem data requirements—that

FIGURE 1.13   Miles-to-Kilometers Conversion Program

```
1.  /*
2.   * Converts distance in miles to kilometers.
3.   */
4.  #include <stdio.h>              /* printf, scanf definitions */
5.  #define KMS_PER_MILE 1.609      /* conversion constant       */
6.
7.  int
8.  main(void)
9.  {
10.        double miles,  /* input - distance in miles.        */
11.               kms;    /* output - distance in kilometers */
12.
13.        /* Get the distance in miles. */
14.        printf("Enter the distance in miles> ");
15.        scanf("%lf", &miles);
16.
17.        /* Convert the distance to kilometers. */
18.        kms = KMS_PER_MILE * miles;
19.
20.        /* Display the distance in kilometers. */
21.        printf("That equals %f kilometers.\n", kms);
22.
23.        return (0);
24.  }
```

Sample Run
```
Enter the distance in miles> 10.00
That equals 16.090000 kilometers.
```

is, what memory cell names you are using and what kind of data will be stored in each memory cell. Next, convert each algorithm step into one or more C statements. If an algorithm step has been refined, you must convert the refinements, not the original step, into C statements.

Figure 1.13 shows the C program along with a sample execution or run. For easy identification, the program statements corresponding to algorithm steps are in color as is the input data typed in by the program user. Don't worry about understanding the details of this program yet. We explain the program in the next chapter.

TESTING

How do you know the sample run is correct? You should always examine program results carefully to make sure that they make sense. In this run, a distance of 10.0 miles is converted to 16.09 kilometers, as it should be. To verify that the program works properly, enter a few more test values of miles. You don't need to try more than a few test cases to verify that a simple program like this is correct.

 EXERCISES FOR SECTION 1.5

Self-Check

1. Change the algorithm for the metric conversion program to convert distance in kilometers to miles.
2. List the data requirements, formulas, and algorithm for a program that converts a volume from quarts to liters.

1.6 Professional Ethics for Computer Programmers

We end this introductory chapter with a discussion of professional ethics for computer programmers. Like other professionals, computer programmers and software system designers (called software engineers) need to follow certain standards of professional conduct.

Privacy and Misuse of Data

As part of their jobs, programmers may have access to large data banks or databases containing sensitive information on financial transactions, personnel, or private health data, information that is classified as "secret" or "top secret." Programmers should always behave in a socially responsible manner and not retrieve information that they are not entitled to see. They should not use information to which they are given access for their own personal gain, or do anything that would be considered illegal, unethical, or harmful to others. Just as doctors and lawyers must keep patient information confidential, programmers must respect an individual's rights to privacy.

computer theft (computer fraud) Illegally obtaining money by falsifying information in a computer database

A programmer who changes information in a database containing financial records for his or her own personal gain—for example, changes the amount of money in a bank account—is guilty of **computer theft** or **computer fraud**. This is a felony that can lead to fines and imprisonment.

Computer Hacking

You may have heard about "computer hackers" who break into secure data banks by using their own computer to call the computer that controls access to the data bank. Classified or confidential information retrieved in this way has been sold to intelligence agencies of other countries. Other hackers have tried to break into computers to retrieve information for their own amusement or as a prank, to gain media attention, or just to demonstrate that they can do it. Regardless of the intent, this activity is illegal, and the government will prosecute anyone who does it. Your university probably addresses this kind of activity in your student handbook. The punishment is likely similar to penalties for other criminal activity, because that is exactly what hacking is—a crime.

virus Code attached to another program that spreads through a computer's disk memory, disrupting the computer or erasing information

Another illegal activity sometimes practiced by hackers is attaching harmful code, called a **virus**, to another program so that the virus code copies itself throughout a computer's disk memory. A virus can cause sporadic activities to disrupt the operation of the host computer—for example, unusual messages may appear on the screen at certain times—or cause the host computer to erase portions of its own disk memory, destroying valuable information and programs. Viruses are spread from one computer to another in various ways—for example, if you copy a file that originated on another computer that has a virus, or if you open an e-mail message that is sent from an infected computer. A computer **worm** is a virus that can replicate itself on other network computers, causing these computers to send multiple messages over the network to disrupt its operation or shut it down. Certainly, data theft and virus propagation should not be considered harmless pranks; they are illegal and carry serious penalties.

worm A virus that can disrupt a network by replicating itself on other network computers

Plagiarism and Software Piracy

Using someone else's programs without permission is also unprofessional behavior. Although it is certainly permissible to use modules from libraries that have been developed for reuse by their own company's programmers, you cannot use another programmer's personal programs or programs from another company without getting permission beforehand. Doing so could lead to a lawsuit, with you or your company having to pay damages.

Modifying another student's code and submitting it as your own is a fraudulent practice—specifically, plagiarism—and is no different than copying paragraphs of information from a book or journal article and calling it your own. Most universities have severe penalties for plagiarism that may include failing the course and/or being dismissed from the university. Be aware that even if you modify the code slightly or substitute your own comments or different variable names, you are still guilty of plagiarism if you are using another person's ideas and code. To avoid any question of plagiarism, find out beforehand your instructor's rules about working with others on a project. If group efforts are not allowed, make sure that you work independently and submit only your own code.

software piracy
Violating copyright agreements by illegally copying software for use in another computer

Many commercial software packages are protected by copyright laws against **software piracy**—the practice of illegally copying software for use on another computer. If you violate this law, your company or university can be fined heavily for allowing this activity to occur. Besides the fact that software piracy is against the law, using software copied from another computer increases the possibility that your computer will receive a virus. For all these reasons, you should read the copyright restrictions on each software package and adhere to them.

Misuse of a Computer Resource

Computer system access privileges or user account codes are private property. These privileges are usually granted for a specific purpose—for example, for work to be done in a particular course or for work to be done during the time you are a student at your university. The privilege should be protected; it should not be loaned to or shared with anyone else and should not be used for any purpose for which it was not intended. When you leave the institution, this privilege is normally terminated and any accounts associated with the privilege will be closed.

Computers, computer programs, data, and access (account) codes are like any other property. If they belong to someone else and you are not explicitly given permission to use them, then do not use them. If you are granted a use privilege for a specific purpose, do not abuse the privilege or it will be taken away.

Legal issues aside, it is important that we apply the same principles of right and wrong to computerized property and access rights as to all other property rights and privileges. If you are not sure about the propriety of something you want to do, ask first. As students and professionals in computing, we set an example for others. If we set a bad example, others are sure to follow.

 EXERCISES FOR SECTION 1.6

Self-Check

1. Some computer users will not open an e-mail message unless they know the person who sent it. Why might someone adopt this policy?
2. Find out the penalty for plagiarism at your school.
3. Why is it a good policy to be selective about opening e-mail attachments?
4. Define the terms *virus* and *worm*.

Chapter Review

1. The basic components of a computer are main memory and secondary storage, the CPU, and input and output devices.
2. All data manipulated by a computer are represented digitally, as base 2 numbers composed of strings of the digits 0 and 1.

3. Main memory is organized into individual storage locations called memory cells.
   - Each memory cell has a unique address.
   - A memory cell is a collection of bytes; a byte is a collection of 8 bits.
   - A memory cell is never empty, but its initial contents may be meaningless to your program.
   - The current contents of a memory cell are destroyed whenever new information is stored in that cell.
   - Programs *must* be loaded into the memory of the computer before they can be executed.
   - Data cannot be manipulated by the computer until they are first stored in memory.

4. Information in secondary storage is organized into files: program files and data files. Secondary storage provides a low-cost means of storing large quantities of information in semipermanent form.

5. A CPU runs a computer program by repeatedly fetching and executing simple machine-code instructions.

6. Connecting computers in networks allows sharing of resources—local resources on LANs and worldwide resources on a WAN such as the Internet.

7. Programming languages range from machine language (meaningful to a computer) to high-level language (meaningful to a programmer).

8. Several system programs are used to prepare a high-level language program for execution. An editor enters a high-level language program into a file. A compiler translates a high-level language program (the source program) into machine language (the object program). The linker links this object program to other object files, creating an executable file, and the loader loads the executable file into memory. All of these programs are combined in an integrated development environment (IDE).

9. Through the operating system, you can issue commands to the computer and manage files.

10. Follow the first five steps of the software development method to solve programming problems: (1) specify the problem, (2) analyze the problem, (3) design the algorithm, (4) implement the algorithm, and (5) test and verify the completed program. Write programs in a consistent style that is easy to read, understand, and maintain.

11. Follow ethical standards of conduct in everything you do pertaining to computers. This means do not copy software that is copyright protected, do not hack into someone else's computer, do not send files that may be infected to others, and do not submit someone else's work as your own or lend your work to another student.

Quick-Check Exercises

1. A _____ translates a high-level language program into _____.
2. A(n) _____ provides access to system programs for program entry and compilation, database maintenance, web browsing, and so on.
3. Specify the correct order for these operations: execution, translation, linking, loading.
4. A high-level language program is saved on disk as a(n) _____ file.
5. The _____ finds syntax errors in the _____.
6. Before linking, a machine language program is saved on disk as a(n) _____ file.
7. After linking, a machine language program is saved on disk as a(n) _____ file.
8. Computer programs are _____ components of a computer system while a disk drive is _____.
9. A(n) _____ is a package that combines a simple word processor with a compiler, linker, and loader.
10. _____ have no moving parts, and all data transfers occur via electronic signal only, unlike in the case of hard drives, which must spin their disks for access to data.
11. On a magnetic disk, data are represented as _____ arranged in concentric tracks.
12. On a CD, DVD, or Blu-ray disk, data are represented as laser-written pits arranged in a(n) _____.
13. A(n) _____stores the names of files that are related to the same general topic.
14. A _____ converts binary computer data into audio tones that can be transmitted between computers over telephone lines.

Answers to Quick-Check Exercises

1. compiler, machine language
2. operating system
3. translation, linking, loading, execution
4. source
5. compiler, source file
6. object
7. executable
8. software, hardware
9. integrated development environment (IDE)
10. Flash drives
11. magnetized spots
12. spiral
13. subdirectory
14. modem

Review Questions

1. List at least three kinds of information stored in a computer.
2. List two functions of the CPU.
3. List two input devices, two output devices, and two secondary storage devices.
4. Describe three categories of programming languages.
5. What is a syntax error?
6. What processes are needed to transform a C program to a machine language program that is ready for execution?
7. Explain the relationship between memory cells, bytes, and bits.
8. Name three high-level languages and describe their application areas.
9. What are the differences between RAM and ROM?
10. What is the World Wide Web?
11. What is computer theft?
12. What is software piracy?
13. How many bytes equal 1 TB?

Overview of C

CHAPTER OBJECTIVES

- To become familiar with the general form of a C program and the basic elements in a program

- To appreciate the importance of writing comments in a program

- To understand the use of data types and the differences between the data types `int`, `double`, and `char`

- To know how to declare variables

- To understand how to write assignment statements to change the values of variables

- To learn how C evaluates arithmetic expressions and how to write them in C

- To learn how to read data values into a program and to display results

- To understand how to write format strings for data entry and display

- To learn how to use redirection to enable the use of files for input/output

- To understand the differences between syntax errors, run-time errors, and logic errors, and how to avoid them and to correct them

T his chapter introduces C—a high-level programming language developed in 1972 by Dennis Ritchie at AT&T Bell Laboratories. Because C was designed as a language in which to write the UNIX® operating system, it was originally used primarily for systems programming. Over the years, however, the power and flexibility of C, together with the availability of high-quality C compilers for computers of all sizes, have made it a popular language in industry for a wide variety of applications.

This chapter describes the elements of a C program and the types of data that can be processed by C. It also describes C statements for performing computations, for entering data, and for displaying results.

2.1   C Language Elements

One advantage of C is that it lets you write programs that resemble everyday English. Even though you do not yet know how to write your own programs, you can probably read and understand the program in Fig. 1.14. Figure 2.1 repeats this figure with the basic features of C highlighted. We identify them briefly below, and explain them in detail in Sections 2.2 to 2.4. The line numbers shown in all code figures are not part of the C programming.

Preprocessor Directives

preprocessor directive
a C program line
beginning with # that
provides an instruction
to the preprocessor

preprocessor a
system program that
modifies a C program
prior to its compilation

library a collection
of useful functions and
symbols that may be
accessed by a program

The C program in Fig. 2.1 has two parts: preprocessor directives and the main function. The **preprocessor directives** are commands that give instructions to the C **preprocessor**, whose job it is to modify the text of a C program *before* it is compiled. A preprocessor directive begins with a number symbol (#) as its first nonblank character. The two most common directives appear in Fig. 2.1: #include and #define.

The C language explicitly defines only a small number of operations: Many actions that are necessary in a computer program are not defined directly by C. Instead, every C implementation contains collections of useful functions and symbols called **libraries**. The ANSI (American National Standards Institute) standard for C requires that certain *standard libraries* be provided in every ANSI C implementation. A C system may expand the number of operations available by supplying additional libraries; an individual programmer can also create libraries of functions. Each library has a standard header file whose name ends with the symbols .h.

FIGURE 2.1   C Language Elements in Miles-to-Kilometers Conversion Program

```
/*
 * Converts distances from miles to kilometers.
 */
                              standard header file          comment
preprocessor
directive          #include <stdio.h>              /* printf, scanf definitions */
                   #define KMS_PER_MILE 1.609       /* conversion constant       */

constant
                   int  ←                reserved word
                   main(void)
                   {
                       double miles, /* distance in miles
variable                 kms;      /* equivalent distance in kilometers */

                                                          comment
                       /* Get the distance in miles. */ ←
standard               printf("Enter the distance in miles> ");
identifier             scanf("%lf", &miles);

                       /* Convert the distance to kilometers. */
                       kms = KMS_PER_MILE * miles;
                                                 special symbol
                       /* Display the distance in kilometers. */
                       printf("That equals %f kilometers.\n", kms);
                                                     punctuation
reserved
word                   return (0); ←
                   } ←        special symbol
```

The `#include` directive gives a program access to a library. This directive causes the preprocessor to insert definitions from a standard header file into a program before compilation. The directive

```
#include <stdio.h>              /* printf, scanf definitions */
```

notifies the preprocessor that some names used in the program (such as `scanf` and `printf`) are found in the standard header file `<stdio.h>`.

The other preprocessor directive in Fig. 2.1

```
#define KMS_PER_MILE 1.609     /* conversion constant */
```

constant macro a name that is replaced by a particular constant value before the program is sent to the compiler

associates the **constant macro** KMS_PER_MILE with the meaning 1.609. This directive instructs the preprocessor to replace each occurrence of KMS_PER_ MILE in the text of the C program by 1.609 before compilation begins. As a result, the line

```
kms = KMS_PER_MILE * miles;
```

would read

```
kms = 1.609 * miles;
```

by the time it was sent to the C compiler. Only data values that never change (or change very rarely) should be given names using a #define, because an executing C program cannot change the value of a name defined as a constant macro. Using the constant macro KMS_PER_MILE in the text of a program for the value 1.609 makes it easier to understand and maintain the program.

comment text beginning with /* and ending with */ that provides supplementary information but is ignored by the preprocessor and compiler

The text on the right of each preprocessor directive, starting with /* and ending with */, is a **comment**. Comments provide supplementary information making it easier for us to understand the program, but comments are ignored by the C preprocessor and compiler.

Syntax Displays for Preprocessor Directives

For each new C construct introduced in this book, we provide a syntax display that describes and explains the construct's syntax and shows examples of its use. The following syntax displays describe the two preprocessor directives. The italicized elements in each construct are discussed in the interpretation section.

#include Directive for Defining Identifiers from Standard Libraries

SYNTAX: #include <*standard header file*>

EXAMPLES: #include <stdio.h>
              #include <math.h>

INTERPRETATION: #include directives tell the preprocessor where to find the meanings of standard identifiers used in the program. These meanings are collected in files called *standard header files*. The header file stdio.h contains information about standard input and output functions such as scanf and printf. Descriptions of common mathematical functions are found in the header file math.h. We will investigate header files associated with other standard libraries in later chapters.

#define Directive for Creating Constant Macros

SYNTAX: #define *NAME value*

EXAMPLES: #define MILES_PER_KM 0.62137
               #define PI 3.141593
               #define MAX_LENGTH 100

INTERPRETATION: The C preprocessor is notified that it is to replace each use of the identifier *NAME* by *value*. C program statements cannot change the value associated with *NAME*.

Function main

The two-line heading

```
int
main(void)
```

marks the beginning of the main function where program execution begins. Every
C program has a main function. The remaining lines of the program form the *body*
of the function, which is enclosed in braces {, }.

declarations the part
of a program that tells
the compiler the names
of memory cells in a
program

A function body has two parts: declarations and executable statements. The
declarations tell the compiler what memory cells are needed in the function (for
example, miles and kms in Fig. 2.1). To create this part of the function, the programmer uses the problem data requirements identified during problem analysis.

executable statements
program lines that are
converted to machine
language instructions
and executed by the
computer

The **executable statements** (derived from the algorithm) are translated into
machine language and later executed.

The main function contains *punctuation* and *special symbols* (*, =). Commas
separate items in a list, a semicolon appears at the end of several lines, and braces
({, }) mark the beginning and end of the body of function main.

---

main Function Definition

SYNTAX: int
               main(void)
               {
                       function body
               }

(continued)

```
EXAMPLE:    int
            main(void)
            {
               printf("Hello world\n");
               return (0);
            }
```

INTERPRETATION: Program execution begins with the main function. Braces enclose the main *function body*, which contains declarations and executable statements. The line `int` indicates that the main function returns an integer value (`0`) to the operating system when it finishes normal execution. The symbols (`void`) indicate that the main function receives no data from the operating system before it begins execution.

Reserved Words

reserved word a word that has special meaning in C

Each line of Fig. 2.1 contains a number of different words classified as **reserved words**, identifiers from standard libraries, and names for memory cells. All the reserved words appear in lowercase; they have special meaning in C and cannot be used for other purposes. A complete list of ANSI C reserved words is found in Appendix E. Table 2.1 describes the reserved words in Fig 2.1.

Standard Identifiers

standard identifier a word having special meaning but one that a programmer may redefine (but redefinition is not recommended!)

The other words in Fig. 2.1 are identifiers that come in two varieties: standard and user-defined. Like reserved words, **standard identifiers** have special meaning in C. In Fig. 2.1, the standard identifiers `printf` and `scanf` are names of operations defined in the standard input/output library. Unlike reserved words, standard identifiers can be redefined and used by the programmer for other purposes—however, we don't recommend this practice. If you redefine a standard identifier, C will no longer be able to use it for its original purpose.

TABLE 2.1 Reserved Words in Fig. 2.1

Reserved Word	Meaning
`int`	integer; indicates that the main function returns an integer value
`void`	indicates that the main function receives no data from the operating system
`double`	indicates that the memory cells store real numbers
`return`	returns control from the main function to the operating system

User-Defined Identifiers

We choose our own identifiers (called *user-defined identifiers*) to name memory cells that will hold data and program results and to name operations that we define (more on this in Chapter 3). The first user-defined identifier in Fig. 2.1, `KMS_PER_MILE`, is the name of a constant macro.

You have some freedom in selecting identifiers. The syntax rules and some valid identifiers follow. Table 2.2 shows some invalid identifiers.

1. An identifier must consist only of letters, digits, and underscores.
2. An identifier cannot begin with a digit.
3. A C reserved word cannot be used as an identifier.
4. An identifier defined in a C standard library should not be redefined.[*]

Valid Identifiers

`letter_1, letter_2, inches, cent, CENT_PER_INCH, Hello, variable`

Although the syntax rules for identifiers do not place a limit on length, some ANSI C compilers do not consider two names to be different unless there is a variation within the first 31 characters. The two identifiers

```
per_capita_meat_consumption_in_1980
per_capita_meat_consumption_in_1995
```

would be viewed as identical by a C compiler that considered only the first 31 characters to be significant.

Table 2.3 lists the category of each identifier appearing in the main function of Fig. 2.1.

TABLE 2.2 Invalid Identifiers

Invalid Identifier	Reason Invalid
1Letter	begins with a letter
double	reserved word
int	reserved word
TWO*FOUR	character * not allowed
joe's	character ' not allowed

---

[*]Rule 4 is actually advice from the authors rather than ANSI C syntax.

TABLE 2.3   Reserved Words and Identifiers in Fig. 2.1

Reserved Words	Standard Identifiers	User-Defined Identifiers
int, void, double, return	printf, scanf	KMS_PER_MILE, main, miles, kms

Uppercase and Lowercase Letters

The C programmer must take great care in the use of uppercase and lowercase letters because the C compiler considers such usage significant. The names Rate, rate, and RATE are viewed by the compiler as *different* identifiers. Adopting a consistent pattern in the way you use uppercase and lowercase letters is helpful to the readers of your programs. You will see that all reserved words in C and the names of all standard library functions use only lowercase letters. One style that has been widely adopted in industry uses all uppercase letters in the names of constant macros. We follow this convention in this text; for other identifiers, we use all lowercase letters.

Program Style   *Choosing Identifier Names*

We discuss program style throughout the text in displays like this one. A program that "looks good" is easier to read and understand than one that is sloppy. Most programs will be examined or studied by someone other than the original programmers. In industry, programmers spend considerably more time on program maintenance (that is, updating and modifying the program) than they do on its original design or coding. A program that is neatly stated and whose meaning is clear makes everyone's job simpler.

Pick a meaningful name for a user-defined identifier, so its use is easy to understand. For example, the identifier salary would be a good name for a memory cell used to store a person's salary, whereas the identifier s or bagel would be a bad choice. If an identifier consists of two or more words, placing the underscore character (_) between words will improve the readability of the name (dollars_per_hour rather than dollarsperhour).

Choose identifiers long enough to convey your meaning, but avoid excessively long names because you are more likely to make a typing error in a longer name. For example, use the shorter identifier lbs_per_sq_in instead of the longer identifier pounds_per_square_inch.

If you mistype a name so that the identifier looks like the name of another memory cell, often the compiler cannot help you detect your error. For this reason and to avoid confusion, do not choose names that are similar to each other. Especially avoid selecting two names that are different only in their use of uppercase and lowercase letters, such as LARGE and large. Also try not to use two names that differ only in the presence or absence of an underscore (xcoord and x_coord).

 EXERCISES FOR SECTION 2.1

Self-Check

1. Which of the following identifiers are (a) C reserved words, (b) standard identifiers, (c) conventionally used as constant macro names, (d) other valid identifiers, and (e) invalid identifiers?

```
void      MAX_ENTRIES    double    time      G       Sue's
return    printf         xyz123    part#2    "char"  #insert
this_is_a_long_one
```

2. Why should E (2.7182818) be defined as a constant macro?
3. What part of a C implementation changes the text of a C program just before it is compiled? Name two directives that give instructions about these changes.
4. Why shouldn't you use a standard identifier as the name of a memory cell in a program? Can you use a reserved word instead?

2.2 Variable Declarations and Data Types

Variable Declarations

variable a name associated with a memory cell whose value can change

variable declarations statements that communicate to the compiler the names of variables in the program and the kind of information stored in each variable

The memory cells used for storing a program's input data and its computational results are called **variables** because the values stored in variables can change (and usually do) as the program executes. The **variable declarations** in a C program communicate to the C compiler the names of all variables used in a program. They also tell the compiler what kind of information will be stored in each variable and how that information will be represented in memory. The variable declarations

```
double miles; /* input - distance in miles.       */
double kms;   /* output - distance in kilometers   */
```

give the names of two variables (miles, kms) used to store real numbers. Note that C ignores the comments on the right of each line describing the usage of each variable.

A variable declaration begins with an identifier (for example, double) that tells the C compiler the type of data (such as a real number) stored in a particular variable. You can declare variables for any data type. C requires you to declare every variable used in a program.

Syntax Display for Declarations

SYNTAX: `int` *variable_list;*
            `double` *variable_list;*
            `char` *variable_list;*

EXAMPLES: ```
            int count,
                large;
            double x, y, z;
            char first_initial;
            char ans;
            ```

INTERPRETATION: A memory cell is allocated for each name in the *variable_list*. The type of data (`double`, `int`, `char`) to be stored in each variable is specified at the beginning of the statement. One statement may extend over multiple lines. A single data type can appear in more than one variable declaration, so the following two declaration sections are equally acceptable ways of declaring the variables `rate`, `time`, and `age`.

```
double rate, time;          double   rate;
int age;                    int      age;
                            double   time;
```

Data Types

data type   a set of values and operations that can be performed on those values

A **data type** is a set of values and a set of operations on those values. Knowledge of the data type of an item (a variable or value) enables the C compiler to correctly specify operations on that item. A standard data type in C is a data type that is predefined, such as `char`, `double`, and `int`. We use the standard data types `double` and `int` as abstractions for the real numbers and integers (in the mathematical sense).

Objects of a data type can be variables or constants. A positive numeric constant (or number) in a C program can be written with or without a + sign. A numeric constant cannot contain a comma.

Numeric constants in C are considered nonnegative numbers. Although you can use a number like −10500 in a program, C views the minus sign as the negation operator (applied to the positive constant `10500`) rather than as a part of the constant.

Data Type int   In mathematics, integers are whole numbers. The `int` data type is used to represent integers in C. Because of the finite size of a memory cell, not all integers can be represented by type `int`. ANSI C specifies that the range of data type
```

int must include at least the values –32767 through 32767. You can store an integer in a type int variable, perform the common arithmetic operations (add, subtract, multiply, and divide), and compare two integers. Some values that you can store in a type int variable are

–10500   435   +15   –25   32767

Data Type double   A real number has an integral part and a fractional part that are separated by a decimal point. In C, the data type double is used to represent real numbers (for example, 3.14159, 0.0005, and 150.0). You can store a real number in a type double variable, perform the common arithmetic operations (add, subtract, multiply, and divide), and compare them.

We can use scientific notation to represent real numbers (usually for very large or very small values). In normal scientific notation, the real number 1.23×10^5 is equivalent to 123000.0 where the exponent 5 means "move the decimal point five places to the right." In C scientific notation, we write this number as 1.23e5 or 1.23E5. Read the letter e or E as "times 10 to the power": 1.23e5 means 1.23 times 10 to the power 5. If the exponent has a minus sign, the decimal point is moved to the left (for example, 0.34e-4 is equivalent to 0.000034). Table 2.4 lists some real numbers and indicates which ones can be stored in a type double variable. The last line shows we can write a type double constant in C scientific notation without a decimal point.

Data type double is an abstraction for the real numbers because it does not include them all. Some real numbers are too large or too small, and some real numbers cannot be represented precisely because of the finite size of a memory cell. However, we can certainly represent enough of the real numbers in C to carry out most of the computations we wish to perform with sufficient accuracy.

TABLE 2.4   Type double Constants (real numbers)

Valid double Constants	Invalid double Constants
3.14159	150 (no decimal point)
0.005	.12345e (missing exponent)
12345.0	15e-0.3 (0.3 is invalid exponent)
15.0e-04 (value is 0.0015)	
2.345e2 (value is 234.5)	12.5e.3 (.3 is invalid exponent)
1.15e-3 (value is 0.00115)	34,500.99 (comma is not allowed)
12e+5 (value is 1200000.0)	

FIGURE 2.2
_____

Internal Formats of
Type int and Type
double

type `int` format   type `double` format

| binary number |

| sign | exponent | mantissa |

Differences Between Numeric Types

You may wonder why having more than one numeric type is necessary. Can the data type `double` be used for all numbers? Yes, but on many computers, operations involving integers are faster than those involving numbers of type `double`. Less storage space is needed to store type `int` values. Also, operations with integers are always precise, whereas some loss of accuracy or _round-off error_ may occur when dealing with type `double` numbers.

These differences result from the way numbers are represented in the computer's memory. All data are represented in memory as _binary strings,_ strings of 0s and 1s. However, the binary string stored for the type `int` value 13 is not the same as the binary string stored for the type `double` number 13.0. The actual internal representation is computer dependent, and type `double` numbers usually require more bytes of computer memory than type `int`. Compare the sample `int` and `double` formats shown in Fig. 2.2.

Positive integers are represented by standard binary numbers. If you are familiar with the binary number system, you know that the integer 13 is represented as the binary number 01101.

The format of type `double` values (also called _floating-point format_) is analogous to scientific notation. The storage area occupied by the number is divided into three sections: the sign (0 for positive numbers, 1 for negative numbers), the _mantissa_, and the _exponent_. The mantissa is a binary fraction between 0.5 and 1.0. The exponent is an integer. The mantissa and exponent are chosen so that the following formula is correct.

$$real\ number = mantissa \times 2^{exponent}$$

If 64 bits are used for storage of a type `double` number, the sign would occupy 1 bit, the exponent 11 bits, and the mantissa 52 bits. Because of the finite size of a memory cell, not all real numbers in the range allowed can be represented precisely as type `double` values. We will discuss this concept later.

We have seen that type `double` values may include a fractional part, whereas type `int` values cannot. An additional advantage of the type `double` format is that a much larger range of numbers can be represented as compared to type `int`. Actual ranges vary from one implementation to another, but the ANSI standard for C specifies that the minimum range of positive values of type `int` is from 1 to 32,767 (approximately 3.3×10^4). The minimum range specified for positive values

TABLE 2.5 Integer Types in C

Type	Range in Typical Implementation
short	−32,767 .. 32,767
unsigned short	0 .. 65,535
int	−2,147,483,647 .. 2,147,483,647
unsigned	0 .. 4,294,967,295
long	−2,147,483,647 .. 2,147,483,647
unsigned long	0 .. 4,294,967,295

of type double is from 10^{-37} to 10^{37}. To understand how small 10^{-37} is, consider the fact that the mass of one electron is approximately 10^{-27} grams, and 10^{-37} is one ten-billionth of 10^{-27}. The enormity of 10^{37} may be clearer when you realize that if you multiply the diameter of the Milky Way galaxy in kilometers by a trillion, your numeric result is just one ten-thousandth of 10^{37}.

ANSI C provides several integer data types in addition to int. Table 2.5 lists these types along with their ranges in a typical C implementation (short <= int <= long). Notice that the largest number represented by an unsigned integer type is about twice the magnitude of the largest value in the corresponding signed type. This results from using the sign bit as part of the number's magnitude.

Similarly, ANSI C defines three floating-point types that differ in their memory requirements: float, double, and long double. Values of type float must have at least six decimal digits of precision; both type double and long double values must have at least ten decimal digits. Table 2.6 lists the range of positive numbers representable by each of these types in a typical C implementation.

Data Type char

Data type char represents an individual character value—a letter, a digit, or a special symbol. Each type char value is enclosed in apostrophes (single quotes) as shown here.

'A'   'z'   '2'   '9'   '*'   ':'   '"'   ' '

TABLE 2.6 Floating-Point Types in C

Type	Approximate Range*	Significant Digits*
float	10^{-37} .. 10^{38}	6
double	10^{-307} .. 10^{308}	15
long double	10^{-4931} .. 10^{4932}	19

*In a typical C implementation

In the line above Table 2.6, the character value `'"'` represents the character "; the character value `' '` represents the blank character, which is typed by pressing the apostrophe key, the space bar, and the apostrophe key.

Although a type `char` value in a program requires apostrophes, a type `char` data value should not have them. Thus, for example, when entering the letter z as a character data item to be read by a program, press the z key instead of the sequence `'z'`.

The ASCII Code

ASCII code   a particular code that specifies the integer representing each `char` value

You should know that a character is represented in memory as an integer. The value stored is determined by the code used by your C compiler. The **ASCII code** (American Standard Code for Information Interchange) is the most common. Table 2.7 shows the ASCII (pronounced "askey") code values for several characters. Appendix D shows the complete ASCII code.

The digit characters `'0'` through `'9'` have code values of 48 through 57 (decimal). The order relationship that follows holds for the digit characters (i.e., `'0'` < `'1'`, `'1'` < `'2'`, and so on).

`'0'` < `'1'` < `'2'` < `'3'` < `'4'` < `'5'` < `'6'` < `'7'` < `'8'` < `'9'`

In ASCII, uppercase letters have the decimal code values 65 through 90. The order relationship that follows holds for uppercase letters.

`'A'` < `'B'` < `'C'` < ... < `'X'` < `'Y'` < `'Z'`

Lowercase letters have the consecutive decimal code values 97 through 122, and the following order relationship holds:

`'a'` < `'b'` < `'c'` < ... < `'x'` < `'y'` < `'z'`

TABLE 2.7   ASCII Codes for Characters

Character	ASCII Code
`' '`	32
`'*'`	42
`'A'`	65
`'B'`	66
`'Z'`	90
`'a'`	97
`'b'`	98
`'z'`	122
`'0'`	48
`'9'`	57

In ASCII, the *printable characters* have codes from 32 (code for a blank or space) to 126 (code for the symbol ~). The other codes represent nonprintable *control characters*. Sending a control character to an output device causes the device to perform a special operation such as returning the cursor to column one, advancing the cursor to the next line, or ringing a bell.

EXERCISES FOR SECTION 2.2

Self-Check

1. a.   Write the following numbers in normal decimal notation:

    `103e-4     1.2345e+6     123.45e+3`

    b.   Write the following numbers in C scientific notation:

    `1300     123.45     0.00426`

2. Indicate which of the following are valid type `int`, `double`, or `char` constants in C and which are not. Identify the data type of each valid constant.

    `'PQR'     15E-2     35     'h'     -37.491     .912     4,719     'true'     "T"`
    `& 4.5e3     '$'`

3. What would be the best variable type for the area of a circle in square inches? Which type for the number of cars passing through an intersection in an hour? The first letter of your last name?

Programming

1. Write the `#define` preprocessor directive and declarations for a program that has a constant macro for `PI` (3.14159) and variables `radius`, `area`, and `circumf` declared as `double`, variable `num_circ` as an `int`, and variable `circ_name` as a `char`.

2.3 Executable Statements

The executable statements follow the declarations in a function. They are the C statements used to write or code the algorithm and its refinements. The C compiler translates the executable statements into machine language; the computer executes the machine language version of these statements when we run the program.

Programs in Memory

Before examining the executable statements in the miles-to-kilometers conversion program (Fig. 2.1), let's see what computer memory looks like before and

FIGURE 2.3
Memory (a) Before
and (b) After
Execution of a
Program

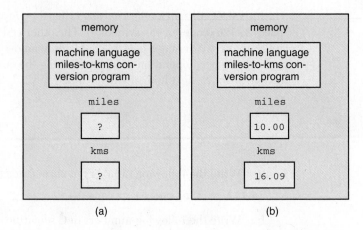

after that program executes. Figure 2.3a shows the program loaded into memory and the program memory area before the program executes. The question marks in memory cells `miles` and `kms` indicate that the values of these cells are undefined before program execution begins. During program execution, the data value `10.00` is copied from the input device into the variable `miles`. After the program executes, the variables are defined as shown in Fig. 2.3b. We will see why next.

Assignment Statements

assignment statement
an instruction that
stores a value or a
computational result
in a variable

An **assignment statement** stores a value or a computational result in a variable, and is used to perform most arithmetic operations in a program. The assignment statement

```
kms = KMS_PER_MILE * miles;
```

assigns a value to the variable `kms`. The value assigned is the result of the multiplication (`*` means multiply) of the constant macro `KMS_PER_MILE` (1.609) by the variable `miles`. The memory cell for `miles` must contain valid information (in this case, a real number) before the assignment statement is executed. Figure 2.4 shows the contents of memory before and after the assignment statement executes; only the value of `kms` is changed.

In C the symbol = is the assignment operator. Read it as "becomes," "gets," or "takes the value of" rather than "equals" because it is *not* equivalent to the equal sign of mathematics. In mathematics, this symbol states a relationship between two values, but in C it represents an action to be carried out by the computer.

FIGURE 2.4

Effect of kms =
KMS_PER_MILE *
miles;

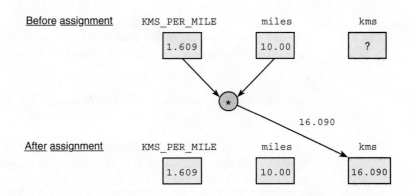

Before assignment

After assignment

Assignment Statement

FORM: *variable* = *expression*;

EXAMPLE: x = y + z + 2.0;

INTERPRETATION: The *variable* before the assignment operator is assigned the value of the *expression* after it. The previous value of *variable* is destroyed. The *expression* can be a variable, a constant, or a combination of these connected by appropriate operators (for example, +, -, /, and *).

EXAMPLE 2.1   In C you can write assignment statements of the form

    sum = sum + item;

where the variable sum appears on both sides of the assignment operator. This is obviously not an algebraic equation, but it illustrates a common programming practice. This statement instructs the computer to add the current value of sum to the value of item; the result is then stored back into sum. The previous value of sum is destroyed in the process, as illustrated in Fig. 2.5. The value of item, however, is unchanged.

FIGURE 2.5

Effect of sum =
sum + item;

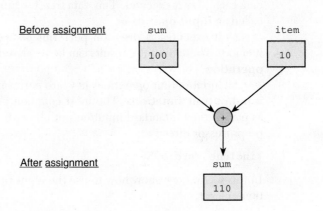

Before assignment

After assignment

EXAMPLE 2.2   You can also write assignment statements that assign the value of a single variable or constant to a variable. If x and new_x are type `double` variables, the statement

```
new_x = x;
```

copies the value of variable x into variable new_x. The statement

```
new_x = -x;
```

instructs the computer to get the value of x, negate that value, and store the result in new_x. For example, if x is 3.5, new_x is -3.5. Neither of the assignment statements above changes the value of x.

Section 2.5 continues the discussion of type `int` and `double` expressions and operators.

Assignment to a `char` Variable

The `char` variable next_letter is assigned the character value 'A' by the assignment statement

```
next_letter = 'A';
```

A single character variable or value may appear on the right-hand side of a character assignment statement.

Input/Output Operations and Functions

Data can be stored in memory in two different ways: either by assignment to a variable or by copying the data from an input device into a variable using a function like `scanf`. You copy data into a variable if you want a program to manipulate different data each time it executes. This data transfer from the outside world into memory is called an **input operation**.

input operation an instruction that copies data from an input device into memory

As it executes, a program performs computations and stores the results in memory. These program results can be displayed to the program user by an **output operation**.

output operation an instruction that displays information stored in memory

All input/output operations in C are performed by special program units called **input/output functions**. The most common input/output functions are supplied as part of the C standard input/output library to which we gain access through the preprocessor directive

input/output function a C function that performs an input or output operation

```
#include <stdio.h>
```

In this section, we show how to use the input function `scanf` and the output function `printf`.

function call calling
or activating a function

In C a **function call** is used to call or activate a function. Calling a function is analogous to asking a friend to perform an urgent task. You tell your friend what to do (but not how to do it) and wait for your friend to report back that the task is finished. After hearing from your friend, you can go on and do something else.

The printf Function

To see the results of a program execution, we must have a way to specify what variable values should be displayed. In Fig. 2.1, the statement

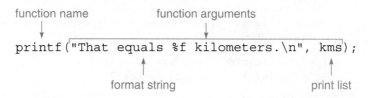

function argument
enclosed in parentheses
following the function
name; provides
information needed by
the function

format string in a call
to printf, a string
of characters enclosed
in quotes ("), which
specifies the form of the
output line

print list in a call to
printf, the variables
or expressions whose
values are displayed

placeholder a symbol
beginning with % in
a format string that
indicates where to
display the output value

calls function printf (pronounced "print-eff") to display a line of program output. A function call consists of two parts: the function name and the **function arguments**, enclosed in parentheses. The arguments for printf consist of a **format string** (in quotes) and a **print list** (the variable kms). The function call above displays the line

That equals 16.090000 kilometers.

which is the result of displaying the format string "That equals %f kilometers.\n" after substituting the value of kms for its placeholder (%f) in the format string. A **placeholder** always begins with the symbol %. Here the placeholder %f marks the display position for a type double variable.

Table 2.8 shows placeholders for type char, double, and int variables. Each placeholder is an abbreviation for the type of data it represents. C uses %f (or %lf) and not %d with type double because programmers often refer to real numbers as *floating-point numbers.*

The placeholders used with scanf are the same as those used with printf except for variables of type double. Type double variables use a %f placeholder in a printf format string and a %lf placeholder in a scanf format string.

**newline escape
sequence** the
character sequence
\n, which is used in
a format string to
terminate an output
line

The format string shown above also contains the **newline escape sequence** \n. Like all C escape sequences, \n begins with the backslash character. Including this sequence at the end of the format string terminates the current output line.

Multiple Placeholders Format strings can have multiple placeholders. If the print list of a printf call has several variables, the format string should contain the same number of placeholders. C matches variables with placeholders in left-to-right order.

TABLE 2.8 Placeholders in Format Strings

Placeholder	Variable Type	Function Use
%c	char	printf/scanf
%d	int	printf/scanf
%f	double	printf
%lf	double	scanf

EXAMPLE 2.3

If `letter_1`, `letter_2`, and `letter_3` are type `char` variables and `age` is type `int`, the `printf` call

```
printf("Hi %c%c%c - your age is %d\n",
      letter_1, letter_2, letter_3, age);
```

displays a line such as

```
Hi EBK - your age is 35
```

The placeholders `%c%c%c` indicate the display position of the letters (E, B, and K) stored in the three type `char` variables, and the placeholder `%d` indicates the position of the value of `age` (35).

Syntax Display for printf Function Call

SYNTAX: printf(*format string, print list*);
            printf(*format string*);

EXAMPLES: printf("I am %d years old, and my gpa is %f\n",
                   age, gpa);
            printf("Enter the object mass in grams> ");

INTERPRETATION: The `printf` function displays the value of its *format string* after substituting in left-to-right order the values of the expressions in the *print list* for their placeholders in the *format string* and after replacing escape sequences such as \n by their meanings.

---

cursor a moving place marker that indicates the next position on the screen where information will be displayed

More About \n   The **cursor** is a moving place marker that indicates the next position on the screen where information will be displayed. When executing a `printf` function call, the cursor is advanced to the start of the next line on the screen if the \n escape sequence is encountered in the format string.

We often end a `printf` format string with a \n (newline escape sequence) so that the call to `printf` produces a completed line of output. If no characters are printed on the next line before another newline character is printed, a blank line will appear in the output. For example, the calls

```
printf("Here is the first line\n");
printf("\nand this is the second.\n");
```

produce two lines of text with a blank line in between:

```
Here is the first line

and this is the second.
```

The blank line appears because the newline character terminates the first format string and begins the second. Notice that because the format strings of these calls to `printf` contain no placeholders, no print list of variables is needed.

If a `printf` format string contains a \n in the middle of the string

```
printf("This sentence appears \non two lines.\n");
```

the characters after the \n appear on a new output line:

```
This sentence appears
on two lines.
```

In the next section, we will see examples where the newline escape sequence is omitted.

Displaying Prompts   When input data are needed in an interactive program, you should use the `printf` function to display a **prompting message**, or **prompt**, that tells the program user what data to enter. The `printf` statement below

prompt (prompting
message)   a message
displayed to indicate
what data to enter and
in what form

```
printf("Enter the distance in miles> ");
scanf("%lf", &miles);
```

displays a prompt for square meters (a numeric value). The `printf` statement displays the format string and advances the cursor to the screen position following this string. The program user can then type in the data value requested, which is processed by the `scanf` function as described next. The cursor is advanced to the next line when the user presses the <return> or <enter> key.

The scanf Function

The statement

```
scanf("%lf", &miles);
```

calls function `scanf` (pronounced "scan-eff") to copy data into the variable `miles`. Where does function `scanf` get the data it stores in the variable `miles`? It copies the data from the standard input device. In most cases, the standard input device is the keyboard; consequently, the computer will attempt to store in `miles` whatever data the program user types at the keyboard.

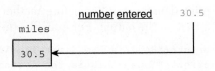

The format string "%lf" consists of a single placeholder that tells scanf what kind of data to copy into the variable miles. Because the placeholder is %lf, the input operation will proceed without error only if the program user types in a number. Figure 2.6 shows the effect of the scanf operation.

Notice that in a call to scanf, the name of each variable that is to be given a value is preceded by the ampersand character (&). The & is the C *address-of* operator. In the context of this input operation, the & operator tells the scanf function *where* to find each variable into which it is to store a new value. If the ampersand were omitted, scanf would know only a variable's current value, not its location in memory, so scanf would be unable to store a new value in the variable.

When scanf executes, the program pauses until the required data are entered and the <return> or <enter> key is pressed. If an incorrect data character is typed, the program user can press the backspace key (←) to edit the data. However, once <return> or <enter> is pressed, the data are processed exactly as typed in and it is too late to correct any data entry errors.

The function call

```
scanf("%c%c%c", &letter_1, &letter_2, &letter_3);
```

causes the scanf function to copy data into each of the three variables, and the format string includes one %c placeholder for each variable. Assuming these variables are declared as type char, one character will be stored in each variable. The next three characters that are entered at the keyboard are stored in these variables. Note that case is important for character data, so the letters B and b have different representations in memory. Again, the program user should press the <return> or <enter> key after typing in three characters. Figure 2.7 shows the effect of this statement when the letters Bob are entered.

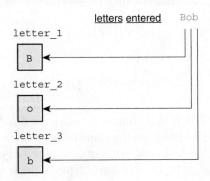

The number of input characters consumed by the `scanf` function depends on the current format placeholder, which should reflect the type of the variable in which the data will be stored. Only one input character is used for a `%c` (type `char` variable). For a `%lf` or `%d` (type `double` or `int` variable), the program first skips any spaces and then scans characters until it reaches a character that cannot be part of the number. Usually, the program user indicates the end of a number by pressing the space bar or by pressing the <return> or <enter> key.

If you would like `scanf` to skip spaces before scanning a character, put a blank in the format string before the `%c` placeholder. If you type more data characters on a line than are needed by the current call to `scanf`, the extra characters will be processed by the next call to `scanf`.

Some C compilers require you to use the format string `"\n%c"` to read the first character of a data line. The `\n` causes `scanf` to skip over any extra characters (including the newline character) not scanned from the previous data line.

Syntax Display for scanf Function Call

SYNTAX: `scanf(`*format string, input list*`);`

EXAMPLE: `scanf("%c%d", &first_initial, &age);`

INTERPRETATION: The `scanf` function copies into memory data typed at the keyboard by the program user during program execution. The *format string* is a quoted string of place-holders, one placeholder for each variable in the *input list*. Each `int`, `double`, or `char` variable in the *input list* is preceded by an ampersand (`&`). Commas are used to separate variable names. The order of the placeholders must correspond to the order of the variables in the *input list*.

You must enter data in the same order as the variables in the *input list*. You should insert one or more blank characters or carriage returns between numeric items. If you plan to insert blanks or carriage returns between character data, you must include a blank in the format string before the `%c` placeholder.

The return Statement

The last line in the main function (Fig. 2.1)

```
return (0);
```

transfers control from your program to the operating system. The value in paren-theses, `0`, is considered the result of function `main`'s execution, and it indicates that your program executed without error.

Syntax Display for return Statement

SYNTAX: return *expression*;

EXAMPLE: return (0);

INTERPRETATION: The **return** statement transfers control from a function back to the activator of the function. For function **main**, control is transferred back to the operating system. The value of *expression* is returned as the result of the function execution.

EXERCISES FOR SECTION 2.3

Self-Check

1. Show the output displayed by the following program lines when the data entered are 5 and 7:

```
printf("Enter two integers> ");
scanf("%d%d", &m, &n);
m = m + 5;
n = 3 * n;
printf("m = %d\nn = %d\n", m, n);
```

2. Show the contents of memory before and after the execution of the program lines shown in Exercise 1.

3. Show the output displayed by the following lines if the value of exp is 11:

```
printf("My name is ");
printf("Jane Doe.");
printf("\n");
printf("I live in ");
printf("Ann Arbor, MI\n");
printf("and I have %d years ", exp);
printf("of programming experience.\n");
```

4. How could you modify the code in Exercise 3 so that "My name is Jane Doe." and "I live in Ann Arbor, MI" would appear on the same line without running together (i.e., with a space between the period and the "I")?

Programming

1. Write a statement that asks the user to type three integers and another statement that stores the three user responses into first, second, and third.

2. a. Write a statement that displays the following line with the value of the type int variable n before the period.

   The value of n is _____.

b. Assuming that `side` and `area` are type `double` variables containing the length of one side in cm and the area of a square in square cm, write a statement that will display this information in this form:

```
The area of a square whose side length is _____ cm
is _____ square cm.
```

3. Write a program that asks the user to enter the radius of a circle and then computes and displays the circle's area. Use the formula

$$Area = PI \times Radius \times Radius$$

where *PI* is the constant macro `3.14159`.

2.4   General Form of a C Program

Now that we have discussed the individual statements that can appear in C programs, we review the rules for combining them into programs. We also discuss the use of punctuation, spacing, and comments in a program.

As shown in Fig. 2.8, each program begins with preprocessor directives that serve to provide information about functions from standard libraries and definitions of necessary program constants. Examples of such directives are `#include` and `#define`. Unlike the declarations and executable statements of the main function body, the preprocessor directives we have seen do not end in semicolons.

A simple C program defines the main function after the preprocessor directives. An open curly brace (`{`) signals the beginning of the main function body. Within this body, we first see the declarations of all the variables to be used by the main function. These variables are followed by the statements that are translated into machine language and are eventually executed. The statements we have looked at so far perform computations or input/output operations. The end of the main function body is marked by a closing curly brace (`}`).

C treats most line breaks like spaces so a C statement can extend over more than one line. You should not split a statement that extends over more than one line in the middle of an identifier, a reserved word, a constant, or a format string.

FIGURE 2.8

General Form of a
C Program

```
preprocessor directives
main function heading
{
    declarations
    executable statements
}
```

You can write more than one statement on a line. For example, the line

```
printf("Enter distance in miles> "); scanf("%lf", &miles);
```

contains a statement that displays a prompt and a statement that gets the data requested. We recommend that you place only one statement on a line because it improves readability and makes it easier to maintain a program.

Program Style   *Spaces in Programs*

The consistent and careful use of blank spaces can improve the style of a program. A blank space is required between consecutive words in a program line.

The compiler ignores extra blanks between words and symbols, but you may insert space to improve the readability and style of a program. You should always leave a blank space after a comma and before and after operators such as *, -, and =. You should indent the body of the main function and insert blank lines between sections of the program.

Although stylistic issues have no effect whatever on the meaning of the program as far as the computer is concerned, they can make it easier for people to read and understand the program. Take care, however, not to insert blank spaces where they do not belong. For example, there cannot be a space between the characters that surround a comment (/* and */). Also, you cannot write the identifier MAX_ITEMS as MAX ITEMS.

Comments in Programs

program documentation information (comments) that enhances the readability of a program

Programmers can make a program easier to understand by using comments to describe the purpose of the program, the use of identifiers, and the purpose of each program step. Comments are part of the **program documentation** because they help others read and understand the program. The compiler, however, ignores comments and they are not translated into machine language.

A comment can appear by itself on a program line, at the end of a line following a statement, or embedded in a statement. In the following variable declarations, the first comment is embedded in the declaration, while the second one follows the declaration.

```
double miles,  /* input - distance in miles      */
       kms;    /* output - distance in kilometers */
```

We document most variables in this way.

Program Style   *Using Comments*

Each program should begin with a header section that consists of a series of comments specifying

- the programmer's name
- the date of the current version
- a brief description of what the program does

Program Comment

SYNTAX: /* *comment text* */

EXAMPLES:
```
/* This is a one-line or partial-line comment */
/*
 * This is a multiple-line comment in which the stars
 * not immediately preceded or followed by slashes
 * have no special syntactic significance, but simply
 * help the comment to stand out as a block. This
 * style is often used to document the purpose of a
 * program.
 */
```

INTERPRETATION: A slash-star indicates the start of a comment; a star-slash indicates the end of a comment. Comments are listed with the program but are otherwise ignored by the C compiler. A comment may be put in a C program anywhere a blank space would be valid.

Note: ANSI C does not permit the placement of one comment inside another.

C++ Style Comment

SYNTAX: // *comment text*

EXAMPLES:
```
// This is a one-line comment
int sales;  // input - amount of sales
```

INTERPRETATION: A slash-slash indicates the start of a comment; the comment continues until the end of the line.

Note: C++ style comments were added to standard C in 1999. However, it is possible that the options set for a compiler may prevent it from recognizing them. For that reason, we do not use them in this book.

If you write the program for a class assignment, you should also list this class identification and your instructor's name.

```
/*
 * Programmer: William Bell    Date completed: May 9, 2015
 * Instructor: Janet Smith     Class: CIS61
 *
 * Calculates and displays the area and circumference of a
 * circle
 */
```

Before you implement each step in the initial algorithm, you should write a comment that summarizes the purpose of the algorithm step. This comment should describe what the step does rather than simply restate the step in English. For example, the comment

```
/* Convert the distance to kilometers. */
kms = KMS_PER_MILE * miles;
```

is more descriptive and hence preferable to

```
/* Multiply KMS_PER_MILE by miles and store result in kms. */
kms = KMS_PER_MILE * miles;
```

EXERCISES FOR SECTION 2.4

Self-Check

1. Change the following comments so they are syntactically correct.

   ```
   /* This is a comment? *\
   /* This one /* seems like a comment */ doesn't it */
   ```

2. Correct the syntax errors in the following program, and rewrite the program so that it follows our style conventions. What does each statement of your corrected program do? What output does it display?

   ```
   /*
    * Calculate and display the difference of two input values
    *)
   #include <stdio.h>
   int
   main(void) {int X, /* first input value */ x, /* second
      input value */
   sum; /* sum of inputs */
   scanf("%i%i"; X; x); X + x = sum;
   printf("%d + %d = %d\n"; X; x; sum); return (0);}
   ```

Programming

1. Write a program that stores the values 'x' and 76.1 in separate memory cells. Your program should get the values as data items and display them again for the user when done.

2.5 Arithmetic Expressions

To solve most programming problems, you will need to write arithmetic expressions that manipulate type int and double data. This section describes the operators used in arithmetic expressions, and rules for writing and evaluating the expressions.

TABLE 2.9 Arithmetic Operators

Arithmetic Operator	Meaning	Examples
`+`	addition	`5 + 2 is 7` `5.0 + 2.0 is 7.0`
`-`	subtraction	`5 - 2 is 3` `5.0 - 2.0 is 3.0`
`*`	multiplication	`5 * 2 is 10` `5.0 * 2.0 is 10.0`
`/`	division	`5.0 / 2.0 is 2.5` `5 / 2 is 2`
`%`	remainder	`5 % 2 is 1`

Table 2.9 shows all the arithmetic operators. Each operator manipulates two *operands,* which may be constants, variables, or other arithmetic expressions. The operators +, -, *, and / may be used with type int or double operands. As shown in the last column, the data type of the result is the same as the data type of its operands. An additional operator, the remainder operator (%), can be used with integer operands to find the remainder of longhand division. We will discuss the division and remainder operators in the next subsection.

Operators / and %

When applied to two positive integers, the division operator (/) computes the integral part of the result of dividing its first operand by its second. For example, the value of 7.0 / 2.0 is 3.5, but the value of 7 / 2 is the integral part of this result, or 3. Similarly, the value of 299.0 / 100.0 is 2.99, but the value of 299 / 100 is the integral part of this result, or 2. If the / operator is used with a negative and a positive integer, the result may vary from one C implementation to another. For this reason, you should avoid using division with negative integers. The / operation is undefined when the divisor (the second operand) is 0. Table 2.10 shows some examples of integer division.

TABLE 2.10 Results of Integer Division

`3 / 15 = 0`	`18 / 3 = 6`
`15 / 3 = 5`	`16 / -3 varies`
`16 / 3 = 5`	`0 / 4 = 0`
`17 / 3 = 5`	`4 / 0 is undefined`

The remainder operator (%) returns the *integer remainder* of the result of dividing its first operand by its second. For example, the value of 7 % 2 is 1 because the integer remainder is 1.

```
7 / 2                    299 / 100
  |                         |
  v                         v
  3                         2
2 |7                   100 |299
  6                        200
  1 <-- 7 % 2              99 <-- 299 % 100
```

You can use longhand division to determine the result of a / or % operation with integers. The calculation on the left shows the effect of dividing 7 by 2 by longhand division: we get a quotient of 3 (7 / 2) and a remainder of 1 (7 % 2). The calculation on the right shows that 299 % 100 is 99 because we get a remainder of 99 when we divide 299 by 100.

The magnitude of m % n must always be less than the divisor n, so if m is positive, the value of m % 100 must be between 0 and 99. The % operation is undefined when n is zero and varies from one implementation to another if n is negative. Table 2.11 shows some examples of the % operator.

The formula

$$m \ equals \ (m / n) * n + (m \% n)$$

defines the relationship between the operators / and % for an integer dividend of m and an integer divisor of n. We can see that this formula holds for the two problems discussed earlier by plugging in values for m, n, m / n, and m % n. In the first example that follows, m is 7 and n is 2; in the second, m is 299 and n is 100.

```
7      equals (7 / 2) * 2 + (7 % 2)
       equals    3    * 2 +    1
299    equals (299 / 100) * 100 + (299 % 100)
       equals      2       * 100 +      99
```

TABLE 2.11 Results of % Operation

3 % 5 = 3	5 % 3 = 2
4 % 5 = 4	5 % 4 = 1
5 % 5 = 0	15 % 5 = 0
6 % 5 = 1	15 % 6 = 3
7 % 5 = 2	15 % -7 varies
8 % 5 = 3	15 % 0 is undefined

EXAMPLE 2.4 If you have `p` pieces of candy and `c` children and want to distribute the candy equally, the expression

```
p / c
```

tells you how many pieces to give each child. For example, if `p` is 18 and `c` is 4, give each child 4 pieces. The expression

```
p % c
```

tells you how many pieces would be left over (18 % 4 is 2).

Data Type of an Expression

The data type of each variable must be specified in its declaration, but how does C determine the data type of an expression? The data type of an expression depends on the type(s) of its operands. Let's consider the types of expressions involving operands that are integers of type `int` or real numbers of type `double`°. For example, the expression

```
ace + bandage
```

is type `int` if both `ace` and `bandage` are type `int`; otherwise, it is type `double`. In general, an expression of the form

```
ace arithmetic_operator bandage
```

is of type `int` if *both* `ace` and `bandage` are of type `int`; otherwise, it is of type `double`.

An expression that has operands of both type `int` and `double` is a **mixed-type expression**. The data type of such a mixed-type expression will be `double`.

mixed-type expression an expression with operands of different types

Mixed-Type Assignment Statement

When an assignment statement is executed, the expression is first evaluated; then the result is assigned to the variable listed to the left of the assignment operator (=). Either a type `double` or a type `int` expression may be assigned to a type `double` variable, so if `m` and `n` are type `int` and `p`, `x`, and `y` are type `double`, the statements that follow assign the values shown in the boxes.

```
m = 3;
n = 2;
p = 2.0;
x = m / p;
y = m / n;
```

°C defines additional integer and real data types besides `int` and `double`, but these two types can represent most numbers used in programming applications.

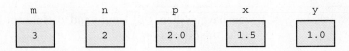

mixed-type assignment the expression being evaluated and the variable to which it is assigned have different data types

In a **mixed-type assignment** such as

```
y = m / n;
```

the expression has a different data type from the variable y getting its value. A common error is to assume that because y is type double, the expression will be evaluated as if m and n were also type double instead of type int. Remember, the expression is evaluated before the assignment is made, and the type of the variable being assigned has no effect whatsoever on the expression value. The expression m / n evaluates to the integer 1. This value is converted to type double (1.0) before it is stored in y.

Assignment of a type double expression to a type int variable causes the fractional part of the expression to be lost since it cannot be represented in a type int variable. The expression in the assignment statements

```
x = 9 * 0.5;
n = 9 * 0.5;
```

evaluates to the real number 4.5. If x is of type double, the number 4.5 is stored in x, as expected. If n is of type int, only the integral part of the expression value is stored in n, as shown.

```
      x              n
   ┌──────┐      ┌──────┐
   │ 4.5  │      │  4   │
   └──────┘      └──────┘
```

Type Conversion Through Casts

type cast converting an expression to a different type by writing the desired type in parentheses in front of the expression

C allows the programmer to convert the type of an expression by placing the desired type in parentheses before the expression, an operation called a **type cast**. In the previous section, we saw that the fractional part of a real value is lost when it is assigned to an int. Use a type cast to show that this happens.

```
n = (int)(9 * 0.5);
```

Two common uses of type casts are shown in Table 2.12—avoiding integer division when computing an average and rounding a type double value by adding 0.5 and converting the result to int.

Characters as Integers

Since characters are represented by integer codes, C permits conversion of type char to type int and vice versa. For example, you could use the following to find out the code your implementation uses for a question mark:

```
qmark_code = (int)'?';
printf("Code for ? = %d\n", qmark_code);
```

TABLE 2.12   Examples of the Use of Type Casts

Application	Example	Explanation

Avoiding integer division	`int num_students; /* number of students who took a test */`
	`int total_score;  /* total of all students' test scores */`
	`double average;`
	`average = (double)total_score / (double)num_students;`
		If the assignment statement were written
		
		`average = (double) (total_score / num_students);`
		
		integer division would cause the loss of the fractional part of the average.

Rounding a positive number	`double x;`
	`int rounded_x;`
	`/* code to give x a value omitted */`
	`rounded_x = (int)(x + 0.5);`
		Consider cases when x's fractional part is greater than or equal to 0.5, and cases when it is less. On the left we see how 35.51 is rounded to 36; on the right how 35.12 is rounded to 35.
		
		  35.51 35.12
		+0.50 +0.50
		───── ─────
		36.01 35.62

You can perform arithmetic operations on characters. For example, the expression `'A' + 1` adds 1 to the code for `'A'` and its value is the next character after `'A'` which is `'B'` in ASCII.

Expressions with Multiple Operators

In our programs so far, most expressions have involved a single arithmetic operator; however, expressions with multiple operators are common in C. Expressions can include both unary and binary operators. **Unary operators** take only one operand. In these expressions, we see the unary negation (–) and plus (+) operators.

unary operator   an operator with one operand

```
x = -y;
p = +x * y;
```

binary operator   an operator with two operands

Binary operators require two operands. When + and – are used to represent addition and subtraction, they are binary operators.

```
x = y + z;
z = y - x;
```

To understand and write expressions with multiple operators, we must know the C rules for evaluating expressions. For example, in the expression x + y / z, is + performed before / or is + performed after /? Is the expression x / y * z evaluated as (x / y) * z or as x / (y * z)? Verify for yourself that the order of evaluation does make a difference by substituting some simple values for x, y, and z. In both of these expressions, the / operator is evaluated first; the reasons are explained in the C rules for evaluation of arithmetic expressions that follow. These rules are based on familiar algebraic rules.

Rules for Evaluating Expressions

a. *Parentheses rule:* All expressions in parentheses must be evaluated separately. Nested parenthesized expressions must be evaluated from the inside out, with the innermost expression evaluated first.

b. *Operator precedence rule:* Operators in the same expression are evaluated in the following order:

    unary +, –   first
    *, /, %   next
    binary +, –   last

c. *Associativity rule:* Unary operators in the same subexpression and at the same precedence level (such as + and –) are evaluated right to left (*right associativity*). Binary operators in the same subexpression and at the same precedence level (such as + and –) are evaluated left to right (*left associativity*).

These rules will help you understand how C evaluates expressions. Use parentheses as needed to specify the order of evaluation. Often it is a good idea in complicated expressions to use extra parentheses to document clearly the order of operator evaluation. For example, the expression

```
x * y * z + a / b - c * d
```

can be written in a more readable form using parentheses:

```
(x * y * z ) + (a / b) - (c * d)
```

EXAMPLE 2.5   The formula for the area of a circle

$$a = \pi r^2$$

can be written in C as

```
area = PI * radius * radius;
```

where the meaning of the constant macro PI is 3.14159. Figure 2.9 shows the *evaluation tree* for this formula. In this tree, which you read from top to bottom, arrows connect each operand with its operator. The order of operator evaluation is shown by the number to the left of each operator; the letter to the right of the operator indicates which evaluation rule applies.

FIGURE 2.9

Evaluation Tree
for area = PI *
radius * radius;

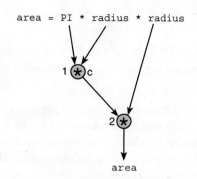

In Fig. 2.10, we see a step-by-step evaluation of the same expression for a
radius value of 2.0. You may want to use a similar notation when computing by
hand the value of an expression with multiple operators.

FIGURE 2.10

Step-by-Step
Expression
Evaluation

area	=	PI	*	radius	*	radius
		3.14159		2.0		2.0
		6.28318				
				12.56636		

EXAMPLE 2.6

The formula for the average velocity, v, of a particle traveling on a line between
points p_1 and p_2 in time t_1 to t_2 is

$$v = \frac{p_2 - p_1}{t_2 - t_1}$$

This formula can be written and evaluated in C as shown in Fig. 2.11.

FIGURE 2.11

Evaluation Tree
and Evaluation for
v = (p2 - p1) /
(t2 - t1);

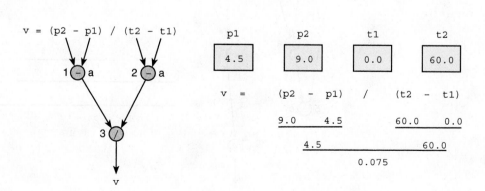

EXAMPLE 2.7   Consider the expression

```
z - (a + b / 2) + w * -y
```

containing type int variables only. The parenthesized expression

```
(a + b / 2)
```

is evaluated first (rule a) beginning with b / 2 (rule b). Once the value of b / 2 is determined, it can be added to a to obtain the value of (a + b / 2). Next, y is negated (rule b). The multiplication operation can now be performed (rule b) and the value for w * -y is determined. Then, the value of (a + b / 2) is subtracted from z (rule c). Finally, this result is added to w * -y. The evaluation tree and step-by-step evaluation for this expression are shown in Fig. 2.12.

Writing Mathematical Formulas in C

You may encounter two problems in writing a mathematical formula in C. First, multiplication often can be implied in a formula by writing the two items to be multiplied next to each other, for example, $a = bc$. In C, however, you must always use the * operator to indicate multiplication, as in

```
a = b * C;
```

The other difficulty arises in formulas with division. We normally write the numerator and the denominator on separate lines:

$$m = \frac{y - b}{x - a}$$

FIGURE 2.12

Evaluation Tree
and Evaluation for
z - (a + b / 2)
+ w * -y

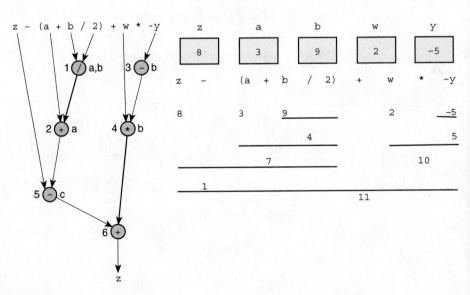

TABLE 2.13 Mathematical Formulas as C Expressions

Mathematical Formula	C Expression
1. $b^2 - 4ac$	`b * b - 4 * a * c`
2. $a + b - c$	`a + b - c`
3. $\dfrac{a + b}{c + d}$	`(a + b) / (c + d)`
4. $\dfrac{1}{1 + x^2}$	`1 / (1 + x * x)`
5. $a \times -(b + c)$	`a * -(b + c)`

In C, however, the numerator and denominator are placed on the same line. Consequently, parentheses are often needed to separate the numerator from the denominator and to indicate clearly the order of evaluation of the operators in the expression. The above formula would be written in C as

```
m = (y - b) / (x - a);
```

Table 2.13 shows several mathematical formulas rewritten in C.

The points illustrated in these examples can be summarized as follows:

- Always specify multiplication explicitly by using the operator `*` where needed (formulas 1 and 4).
- Use parentheses when required to control the order of operator evaluation (formulas 3 and 4).
- Two arithmetic operators can be written in succession if the second is a unary operator (formula 5).

Numerical Inaccuracies

representational error an error due to coding a real number as a finite number of binary digits

One of the problems in processing data of type `double` is that sometimes an error occurs in representing real numbers. Just as certain fractions cannot be represented exactly in the decimal number system (e.g., the fraction 1/3 is 0.333333 . . .), so some fractions cannot be represented exactly as binary numbers in the mantissa of the type `double` format. The **representational error** (sometimes called *round-off error*) will depend on the number of bits used in the mantissa: the more bits, the smaller the error.

cancellation error an error resulting from applying an arithmetic operation to operands of vastly different magnitudes; effect of smaller operand is lost

Errors may occur when manipulating very large and very small real numbers. When you add a large number and a small number, the larger number may "cancel out" the smaller number, resulting in a **cancellation error**. If x is much larger than y, then $x + y$ may have the same value as x (for example, 1000.0 + 0.0000001234 is equal to 1000.0 on some computers).

arithmetic underflow
an error in which a very small computational result is represented as zero

arithmetic overflow
an error that is an attempt to represent a computational result that is too large

If two very small numbers are multiplied, the result may be too small to be represented accurately, so it will be represented as zero. This phenomenon is called **arithmetic underflow**. Similarly, if two very large numbers are multiplied, the result may be too large to be represented. This phenomenon, called **arithmetic overflow**, is handled in different ways by different C compilers. (Arithmetic overflow can occur when processing very large integer values as well.)

CASE STUDY   Supermarket Coin Processor

This case study demonstrates the manipulation of type int data (using / and %) and type char data.

PROBLEM

You are drafting software for the machines placed at the front of supermarkets to convert change to personalized credit slips. In this draft, the user will manually enter the number of each kind of coin in the collection, but in the final version, these counts will be provided by code that interfaces with the counting devices in the machine.

ANALYSIS

To solve this problem, you need to get the customer's initials to use in personalizing the credit slip along with the count of each type of coin (dollars, quarters, dimes, nickels, and pennies). From the counts, you can determine the total value of the coins in cents. Once you have that figure, you can do an integer division using 100 as the divisor to get the dollar value; the remainder of this division will be the leftover change. In the data requirements, list the total value in cents (total_cents) as a program variable, because it is needed as part of the computation process but is not a required problem output.

DATA REQUIREMENTS

Problem Inputs

```
char first, middle, last  /* a customer's initials */
int dollars               /* number of dollars    */
int quarters              /* number of quarters   */
int dimes                 /* number of dimes      */
int nickels               /* number of nickels    */
int pennies               /* number of pennies    */
```

Problem Outputs

```
int total_dollars        /* total dollar value    */
int change               /* leftover change       */
```

Additional Program Variables

```
int total_cents          /* total value in cents  */
```

DESIGN

INITIAL ALGORITHM

1. Get and display the customer's initials.
2. Get the count of each kind of coin.
3. Compute the total value in cents.
4. Find the value in dollars and change.
5. Display the value in dollars and change.

Steps 3 and 4 may need refinement. Their refinements are:

Step 3 Refinement

3.1 Find the equivalent value of each kind of coin in pennies and add these values.

Step 4 Refinement

4.1 total_dollars is the integer quotient of total_cents and 100.
4.2 change is the integer remainder of total_cents and 100.

IMPLEMENTATION

The program is shown in Fig. 2.13. The statements

```
scanf("%c%c%c", &first, &middle, &last);
printf("\n%c%c%c, please enter your coin information.\n",
       first, middle, last);
```

copy three data characters into first, middle, and last and display those characters as part of the instructions to the customer.

The statement

```
total_cents = 100 * dollars + 25 * quarters + 10 * dimes +
              5 * nickels + pennies;
```

implements algorithm step 3.1. The statements

```
total_dollars = total_cents / 100;
change = total_cents % 100;
```

implement steps 4.1 and 4.2. The last call to printf displays the results.

FIGURE 2.13 Supermarket Coin Value Program

```
1.  /*
2.   * Determines the value of a collection of coins.
3.   */
4.  #include <stdio.h>
5.  int
6.  main(void)
7.  {
8.     char first, middle, last;  /* input - 3 initials            */
9.     int pennies, nickels;      /* input - count of each coin type */
10.    int dimes, quarters;       /* input - count of each coin type */
11.    int dollars;               /* input - count of each coin type */
12.    int change;                /* output - change amount          */
13.    int total_dollars;         /* output - dollar amount          */
14.    int total_cents;           /* total cents                     */
15.
16.        /* Get and display the customer's initials. */
17.        printf("Type in your 3 initials and press return> ");
18.        scanf("%c%c%c", &first, &middle, &last);
19.        printf("\n%c%c%c, please enter your coin information.\n",
20.               first, middle, last);
21.
22.        /* Get the count of each kind of coin. */
23.        printf("Number of $ coins > ");
24.        scanf("%d", &dollars);
25.        printf("Number of quarters> ");
26.        scanf("%d", &quarters);
27.        printf("Number of dimes   > ");
28.        scanf("%d", &dimes);
29.        printf("Number of nickels > ");
30.        scanf("%d", &nickels);
31.        printf("Number of pennies > ");
32.        scanf("%d", &pennies);
33.
34.        /* Compute the total value in cents. */
35.        total_cents = 100 * dollars + 25 * quarters + 10 * dimes +
36.                      5 * nickels + pennies;
37.
38.        /* Find the value in dollars and change. */
39.        total_dollars = total_cents / 100;
40.        change = total_cents % 100;
41.
42.        /* Display the credit slip with value in dollars and change. */
```

(continued)

```
43.      printf("\n\n%c%c%c Coin Credit\nDollars: %d\nChange: %d cents\n",
44.             first, middle, last, total_dollars, change);
45.
46.      return (0);
47. }
```

```
Type in your 3 initials and press return> JRH
JRH, please enter your coin information.
Number of $ coins > 2
Number of quarters> 14
Number of dimes   > 12
Number of nickels > 25
Number of pennies > 131

JRH Coin Credit
Dollars: 9
Change:  26 cents
```

TESTING

To test this program, try running it with a combination of coins that yield an exact dollar amount with no leftover change. For example, 1 dollar, 8 quarters, 0 dimes, 35 nickels, and 25 pennies should yield a value of 5 dollars and 0 cents. Then increase and decrease the quantity of pennies by 1 (26 and 24 pennies) to make sure that these cases are also handled properly.

EXERCISES FOR SECTION 2.5

Self-Check

1. a. Evaluate the following expressions with 7 and 22 as operands.

    22 / 7   7 / 22   22 % 7   7 % 22

    Repeat this exercise for the following pairs of integers:

    b. 15, 16
    c. 3, 23
    d. −3, 16

2. Do a step-by-step evaluation of the expressions that follow if the value of celsius is 38.1 and salary is 38450.00.

```
1.8 * Celsius + 32.0
(salary - 5000.00) * 0.20 + 1425.00
```

3. Given the constants and variable declarations

```
#define PI 3.14159
#define MAX_I 1000
. . .
double x, y;
int a, b, i;
```

indicate which of the following statements are valid, and find the value stored by each valid statement. Also indicate which are invalid and why. Assume that a is 3, b is 4, and y is -1.0.

a. i = a % b;
b. i = (989 - MAX_I) / a;
c. i = b % a;
d. x = PI * y;
e. i = a / -b;
f. x = a / b;
g. x = a % (a / b);
h. i = b / 0;
i. i = a % (990 - MAX_I);
j. i = (MAX_I - 990) / a;
k. x = a / y;
l. i = PI * a;
m. x = PI / y;
n. x = b / a;
o. i = (MAX_I - 990) % a;
p. i = a % 0;
q. i = a % (MAX_I - 990);
r. x = (double) a / b;

4. What values are assigned by the legal statements in Exercise 3, assuming a is 7, b is 3, and y is 2.0?

5. Assume that you have the following variable declarations:

```
int color, lime, straw, red, orange;
double white, green, blue, purple, crayon;
```

Evaluate each of the statements below using the following values: color is 2, crayon is -1.3, straw is 1, red is 3, purple is 0.3E+1.

a. white = color * 2.5 / purple;
b. green = color / purple;

```
c.   orange = color / red;
d.   blue = (color + straw) / (crayon + 0.3);
e.   lime = red / color + red % color;
f.   purple = straw / red * color;
```

6. Let a, b, c, and x be the names of four type `double` variables, and let i, j, and k be the names of three type `int` variables. Each of the following statements contains one or more violations of the rules for forming arithmetic expressions. Rewrite each statement so that it is consistent with these rules.

    a.   a = a *remainder* c;
    b.   x = 3a ÷ bc;
    c.   j = 4(i + k);

7. Evaluate the following, assuming that letters have consecutive character codes.

    a.   `(int)'D' - (int)'A'`
    b.   `(char)((int)'C' + 2)`
    c.   `(int)'6' - (int)'7'`

8. How does cancellation error differ from representational error?
9. If squaring 10^{-20} gives a result of zero, the type of error that has occurred is called _____.
10. Evaluate the following expressions if x is `10.5`, y is `7.2`, m is `5`, and n is `2`.

    a.   `x / (double)m`
    b.   `x / m`
    c.   `(double)(n * m)`
    d.   `(double)(n / m) + y`
    e.   `(double)(n / m)`

Programming

1. Write an assignment statement that might be used to implement the following equation in C.

$$q = \frac{kA(T_1 - T_2)}{L}$$

2. Write a program that stores the values `'A'`, `'B'`, `19`, and `-0.42E7` in separate memory cells that you have declared. Use an assignment statement to store the first value, but get the other three values as input data from the user.

2.6 Formatting Numbers in Program Output

C displays all numbers in its default notation unless you instruct it to do otherwise. This section explains how to specify the format or appearance of your output.

Formatting Values of Type int

Specifying the format of an integer value displayed by a C program is fairly easy. You simply add a number between the % and the d of the %d placeholder in the printf format string. This number specifies the **field width**—the number of columns to use for the display of the value. The statement

field width the number of columns used to display a value

```
printf("Results: %3d meters = %4d ft. %2d in.\n",
       meters, feet, inches);
```

indicates that 3 columns will be used to display the value of meters, 4 columns will be used for feet, and 2 columns will be used for inches (a number between 0 and 11). If meters is 21, feet is 68, and inches is 11, the program output will be

```
Results:   21 meters =   68 ft. 11 in.
```

In this line, notice that there is an extra space before the value of meters (21) and two extra spaces before the value of feet (68). The reason is that the placeholder for meters (%3d) allows space for 3 digits to be printed. Because the value of meters is between 10 and 99, its two digits are displayed *right-justified,* preceded by one blank space. Because the placeholder for feet (%4d) allows room for 4 digits, printing its two-digit value right-justified leaves two extra blank spaces. We can use the placeholder %2d to display any integer value between −9 and 99. The placeholder %4d works for values in the range −999 to 9999. For negative numbers, the minus sign is included in the count of digits displayed.

Table 2.14 shows how two integer values are displayed using different format string placeholders. The character ▮ represents a blank character. The last line shows that C expands the field width if it is too small for the integer value displayed.

Formatting Values of Type double

To describe the format specification for a type double value, we must indicate both the total *field width* needed and the number of *decimal places* desired. The total field width should be large enough to accommodate all digits before and after the decimal point. There will be at least one digit before the decimal point because a

TABLE 2.14 Displaying 234 and −234 Using Different Placeholders

Value	Format	Displayed Output	Value	Format	Displayed Output
234	%4d	▮234	−234	%4d	−234
234	%5d	▮▮234	−234	%5d	▮−234
234	%6d	▮▮▮234	−234	%6d	▮▮−234
234	%1d	234	−234	%2d	−234

TABLE 2.15   Displaying x Using Format String Placeholder %6.2f

Value of x	Displayed Output	Value of X	Displayed Output
-99.42	-99.42	-25.554	-25.55
.123	▉▉0.12	99.999	100.00
-9.536	▉-9.54	999.4	999.40

zero is printed as the whole-number part of fractions that are less than 1.0 and greater than -1.0. We should also include a display column for the decimal point and for the minus sign if the number can be negative. The form of the format string placeholder is %n.mf where n is a number representing the total field width, and m is the desired number of decimal places.

If x is a type double variable whose value will be between -99.99 and 999.99, we could use the placeholder %6.2f to display the value of x to an accuracy of two decimal places. Table 2.15 shows different values of x displayed using this format specification. The values displayed are rounded to two decimal places and are displayed right-justified in six columns. When you round to two decimal places, if the third digit of the value's fractional part is 5 or greater, the second digit is incremented by 1 (-9.536 becomes -9.54). Otherwise, the digits after the second digit in the fraction are simply dropped (-25.554 becomes -25.55).

Table 2.16 shows some values that were displayed using other placeholders. The last line shows it is legal to omit the total field width in the format string placeholder. If you use a placeholder such as %.mf to specify only the number of decimal places, the value will be printed with no leading blanks.

TABLE 2.16   Formatting Type double Values

Value	Format	Displayed Output	Value	Format	Displayed Output
3.14159	%5.2f	▉3.14	3.14159	%4.2f	3.14
3.14159	%3.2f	3.14	3.14159	%5.1f	▉▉3.1
3.14159	%5.3f	3.142	3.14159	%8.5f	▉3.14159
.1234	%4.2f	0.12	-.006	%4.2f	-0.01
-.006	%8.3f	▉▉-0.006	-.006	%8.5f	-0.00600
-.006	%.3f	-0.006	-3.14159	%.4f	-3.1416

Program Style   *Eliminating Leading Blanks*

As shown in Tables 2.14 through 2.16, a value whose whole-number part requires fewer display columns than are specified by the format field width is displayed with leading blanks. To eliminate extra leading blanks, omit the field width from the format string placeholder. The simple placeholder %d will cause an integer value to be displayed with no leading blanks. A placeholder of the form % . *m*f has the same effect for values of type `double`, and this placeholder still allows you to choose the number of decimal places you wish.

  EXERCISES FOR SECTION 2.6

Self-Check

1. Correct the statement

    ```
    printf("Salary is %2.10f\n", salary);
    ```

2. Show how the value -3.6175 would be printed using the formats %8.4f, %8.3f, %8.2f, %8.1f, %8.0f, %.2f.

3. Assuming x (type `double`) is 12.335 and i (type `int`) is 100, show the lines displayed by the following statements. For clarity, use the symbol ▌ to denote a blank space.

    ```
    printf("x is %6.2f  i is %4d\n", x, i);
    printf("i is %d\n", i);
    printf ("x is %.1f\n", x);
    ```

Programming

1. If the variables a, b, and c are 504, 302.558, and -12.31, respectively, write a statement that will display the following line. (For clarity, a ▌ denotes a blank space.)

    ```
    ▌▌504▌▌▌▌▌302.56▌▌▌▌-12.3
    ```

2.7   Interactive Mode, Batch Mode, and Data Files

interactive mode
a mode of program execution in which the user responds to prompts by entering (typing in) data

There are two basic modes of computer operation: batch mode and interactive mode. The programs that we have written so far run in interactive mode. In **interactive mode**, the program user interacts with the program and types in data while it is running. We include prompts so the program user knows when to enter each

batch mode   a mode
of program execution
in which the program
scans its data from a
previously prepared
data file

data item. In **batch mode**, the program scans its data from a data file prepared beforehand instead of interacting with its user.

Input Redirection

Figure 2.14 shows the miles-to-kilometers conversion program rewritten as a batch program. We assume here that the standard input device is associated with a batch data file instead of with the keyboard. In most systems, this association can be accomplished relatively easily through *input/output redirection* using operating system commands or by changing settings in your development environment. For example, in the UNIX® operating system, you can instruct your program to take its input from file `mydata.txt` instead of from the keyboard by placing the symbols `<mydata.txt` at the end of the command line that causes your compiled and linked program to execute. You should use a word processor to create the text file `mydata.txt` before attempting to run the program. If you normally used the command line

```
metric
```

to execute this program, your new command line would be

```
metric <mydata.txt
```

Program Style   *Echo Prints versus Prompts*

In Fig. 2.14, the statement

```
scanf("%lf", &miles);
```

gets a value for `miles` from the first (and only) line of the data file. Because the program input comes from a data file, there is no need to precede this statement with a prompting message. Instead, we follow the call to `scanf` with the statement

```
printf("The distance in miles is %.2f.\n", miles);
```

This statement *echo prints* or displays the value just stored in `miles` and provides a record of the data manipulated by the program. Without it, we would have no easy way of knowing what value `scanf` obtained for `miles`. Whenever you convert an interactive program to a batch program, make sure you replace each prompt with an echo print that follows the call to `scanf`.

Output Redirection

You can also redirect program output to a disk file instead of to the screen. Then you can send the output file to the printer (using an operating system command) to obtain a hard copy of the program output. In UNIX, use the symbols `>myoutput.txt` to redirect output from the screen to file `myoutput.txt`. You do not need to create file `myoutput.txt` before running the program, but if you do have an

FIGURE 2.14   Batch Version of Miles-to-Kilometers Conversion Program

```
1.   /* Converts distances from miles to kilometers.       */
2.
3.   #include <stdio.h> /* printf, scanf definitions       */
4.   #define KMS_PER_MILE 1.609 /* conversion constant      */
5.
6.   int
7.   main(void)
8.   {
9.        double miles,  /* distance in miles              */
10.             kms;      /* equivalent distance in kilometers */
11.
12.       /* Get and echo the distance in miles. */
13.       scanf("%lf", &miles);
14.       printf("The distance in miles is %.2f.\n", miles);
15.
16.       /* Convert the distance to kilometers. */
17.       kms = KMS_PER_MILE * miles;
18.
19.       /* Display the distance in kilometers. */
20.       printf("That equals %.2f kilometers.\n", kms);
21.
22.       return (0);
23.   }

The distance in miles is 112.00.
That equals 180.21 kilometers.
```

existing file with this name, its contents will be overwritten when your program runs. The command line

```
metric >myoutput.txt
```

executes the compiled and linked code for program `metric`, taking program input from the keyboard and writing program output to file `myoutput.txt`. However, interacting with the running program will be difficult because all program output, including any prompting messages, will be sent to the output file. It would be better to use the command line

```
metric <mydata.txt >myoutput.txt
```

which takes program input from data file `mydata.txt` and sends program output to output file `myoutput.txt`.

If you are creating and running your program through an integrated development environment, you will need to set your options so the IDE will know where to

FIGURE 2.15

An IDE (Quincy 2005) Allows Developer to Set Command-Line Options.

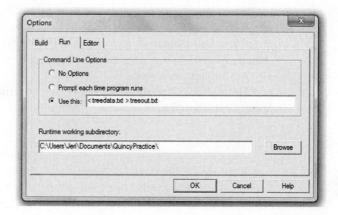

find your data file and store your output file. Alternatively, you can select an option to have the IDE prompt you each time you run the program. Figure 2.15 shows a screen that is collecting the developer's preferences.

 EXERCISES FOR SECTION 2.7

Self-Check

1. Explain the difference in placement of calls to `printf` used to display prompts and calls to `printf` used to echo data. Which calls are used in interactive programs, and which are used in batch programs?
2. How is input data provided to an interactive program? How is input data provided to a batch program?

Programming

1. Rewrite the program in Fig. 2.13 as a batch program. Assume that the data file will be made accessible through input redirection.

2.8 Common Programming Errors

As you begin to program, soon you will discover that a program rarely runs correctly the first time it executes. Murphy's Law, "If something can go wrong, it will," seems to have been written with the computer program in mind. In fact, errors are so common that they have their own special name—*bugs*—and the process of correcting them is called **debugging** a program. (According to computer folklore, computer pioneer Dr. Grace Murray Hopper diagnosed the first hardware error caused by a large insect found inside a computer component.) To alert you to potential problems, we will provide a section on common programming errors at the end of each chapter.

debugging removing errors from a program

When the compiler detects an error, the computer displays an *error message,* which indicates that you have made a mistake and what the likely cause of the error might be. Unfortunately, error messages are often difficult to interpret and are sometimes misleading. As you gain experience, you will become more proficient at locating and correcting errors.

Three kinds of errors—syntax errors, run-time errors, and logic errors—can occur, as discussed in the following sections.

Syntax Errors

syntax error
a violation of the
C grammar rules,
detected during
program translation
(compilation)

A **syntax error** occurs when your code violates one or more grammar rules of C and is detected by the compiler as it attempts to translate your program. If a statement has a syntax error, it cannot be translated and your program will not be executed.

Figure 2.16 shows a compiler listing of the miles-to-kilometers conversion program. A compiler listing is a listing created by the compiler during program translation that shows each line of the source program (preceded by a line number) and any syntax errors detected by the compiler. For this particular compiler, errors are indicated by lines that begin with five asterisks. The program contains the following syntax errors:

- Missing semicolon at the end of the variable declaration (in line 271)
- Undeclared variable `miles` (detected in lines 275 and 278)
- Last comment is not closed because of blank in `*/` close-comment sequence (in line 280)

The actual formats of the listing and the error messages produced by a compiler may differ from those in Fig. 2.16. Indeed, many C compilers do not produce a listing at all, but merely display error messages. In this listing, whenever an error is detected, the compiler displays a line starting with five asterisks followed by the error message. Notice that the line marked for an error is not always the line containing the programmer's mistake. (For example, the error occurring in line 271 is marked after line 274.)

The compiler attempts to correct errors wherever it can. Look at line 271 in the listing; it is missing a semicolon at the end. The compiler cannot be sure that this semicolon is missing until it processes the `printf` symbol on line 274. Because the `printf` is not a comma or a semicolon, the compiler then knows that the variable declaration statement begun on line 271 is not being continued to another line.

We see several cases in this listing where one mistake of the programmer leads to the generation of multiple error messages. For example, the missing declaration for variable `miles` causes an error message to be printed each time `miles` is used in the program. This message would also occur if we remembered to declare `miles` but mistyped it (perhaps as `milles`) in the declaration statement. The missing declaration for `miles` also causes the second error message on line 275. Because the address-of operator must have a variable as its operand, the fact that `miles` is not declared as a variable makes it an invalid operand.

FIGURE 2.16 Compiler Listing of a Program with Syntax Errors

```
221 /* Converts distances from miles to kilometers. */
222
223 #include <stdio.h>              /* printf, scanf definitions  */
266 #define KMS_PER_MILE 1.609  /* conversion constant        */
267
268 int
269 main(void)
270 {
271       double kms
272
273       /* Get the distance in miles. */
274       printf("Enter the distance in miles> ");
***** Semicolon added at the end of the previous source line
275       scanf("%lf", &miles);
***** Identifier "miles" is not declared within this scope
***** Invalid operand of address-of operator
276
277       /* Convert the distance to kilometers. */
278       kms = KMS_PER_MILE * miles;
***** Identifier "miles" is not declared within this scope
279
280       /* Display the distance in kilometers. * /
281       printf("That equals %f kilometers.\n", kms);
282
283       return (0);
284 }
***** Unexpected end-of-file encountered in a comment
***** "}" inserted before end-of-file
```

The mistyped close-comment character sequence also causes multiple messages. Because any text is valid inside a comment, the compiler is unaware that there is a problem until it comes to the end of the source file without having encountered a } to end the program! After complaining about this unexpected turn of events (see line following line 284), it does what it can to correct the situation by closing the comment at the end of the source file text and adding a } to end the program properly.

Mistyping a close-comment sequence can cause errors that are very difficult to find. If the comment that is not correctly closed is in the middle of a program, the compiler will simply continue to treat program lines as comment text until it comes to the */ that closes the *next* comment. When you begin getting error messages that make you think your compiler isn't seeing part of your program, recheck your comments carefully. In the worst case, treating these executable statements as comments may not cause a syntax error—then the program will simply run incorrectly. Mistyping the open-comment sequence /* will make the compiler attempt to process the comment as a C statement, causing a syntax error.

Your strategy for correcting syntax errors should take into account the fact that one error can lead to many error messages. It is often a good idea to concentrate on correcting the errors in the declaration part of a program first. Then recompile the program before you attempt to fix other errors. Many of the other error messages will disappear once the declarations are correct.

Syntax errors are often caused by the improper use of quotation marks with format strings. Make sure that you always use a quote (") to begin and end a string.

Run-Time Errors

run-time error
an attempt to perform an invalid operation, detected during program execution

Run-time errors may be detected and displayed by the computer during the execution of a program. A run-time error occurs when the program directs the computer to perform an illegal operation, such as dividing a number by zero. When a run-time error is discovered, the computer will stop executing your program and will display a diagnostic message that indicates the line where the error was detected.

The program in Fig. 2.17 compiles successfully, but should not run to completion if the first integer entered is greater than the second. In this case, integer division causes the value assigned to temp in line 271 to be zero. Using temp as a divisor in

FIGURE 2.17   A Program with a Run-Time Error

```
111 #include <stdio.h>
262
263 int
264 main(void)
265 {
266      int    first, second;
267      double temp, ans;
268
269      printf("Enter two integers> ");
270      scanf("%d%d", &first, &second);
271      temp = second / first;
272      ans = first / temp;
273      printf("The result is %.3f\n", ans);
274
275      return (0);
276 }


Enter two integers> 14 3
Arithmetic fault, divide by zero at line 272 of routine main
```

line 272 causes the divide by zero error shown. Some execution environments would not detect this error, but would run to completion with meaningless results.

Undetected Errors

Many execution errors may not prevent a C program from running to completion, but they may simply lead to incorrect results. Therefore, it is essential that you predict the results your program should produce and verify that the actual output is correct.

A very common source of incorrect results in C programs is the input of a mixture of character and numeric data. Errors can be avoided if the programmer always keeps in mind scanf's different treatment of the %c placeholder on the one hand and of the %d and %lf placeholders on the other. We noted that scanf first skips any blanks and carriage returns in the input when a numeric value is scanned. In contrast, scanf skips nothing when it scans a character unless the %c placeholder is preceded by a blank.

Figure 2.18 shows what appears to be a minor revision to the start of function main for the supermarket coin processor program from Fig. 2.13. We have added an integer variable year, and we ask for a value of year before getting the user's

FIGURE 2.18   Revised Start of main Function for Supermarket Coin Value Program

```
1.   int
2.   main(void)
3.   {
4.         char first, middle, last; /* input - 3 initials            */
5.         int pennies, nickels;    /* input - count of each coin type */
6.         int dimes, quarters;     /* input - count of each coin type */
7.         int dollars;             /* input - count of each coin type */
8.         int change;                /* output - change amount       */
9.         int total_dollars;         /* output - dollar amount        */
10.        int total_cents;           /* total cents                   */
11.        int year;                  /* input — year                  */
12.
13.        /* Get the current year.                                    */
14.        printf("Enter the current year and press return> ");
15.        scanf("%d", &year);
16.
17.        /* Get and display the customer's initials.                 */
18.        printf("Type in 3 initials and press return> ");
19.        scanf("%c%c%c", &first, &middle, &last);
20.        printf("\n%c%c%c, please enter your coin information for %d.\n",
21.                first, middle, last, year);
     ...
```

initials. If the user types in 2015 and then the letters BMC, we would expect the second call to printf to display the message

BMC, please enter your coin information for 2015.

Instead, it displays a blank line followed by

BM, please enter your coin information for 2015.

To understand why, let's examine the status of memory at the time of the call to printf.

The value of year is correct, but the three characters stored are not 'B', 'M', 'C', but '\n', 'B', and 'M'. The \n in first is the character that results from the user pressing the <enter> key after entering the number 2015. The scan of 2015 stopped at this character, so it was the first character processed by the statement

```
scanf("%c%c%c", &first, &middle, &last);
```

Because the letter C was not yet scanned, it will be scanned during the next scanf call. This will lead to further problems. The statement

```
scanf("%d", &dollars);
```

does not copy a value into dollars because the next character to scan is C, which is not a digit character. Consequently, dollars will retain whatever value it happens to have. The same is true for variables quarters, dimes, nickels, and pennies, and, therefore, the results displayed by the program will be meaningless.

One simple way to repair the program would be to insert a space before the first %c placeholder. Then scanf will skip spaces (including carriage returns) before scanning a character.

```
scanf(" %c%c%c", &first, &middle, &last);
```

Figure 2.19 shows another error that may or may not cause the program to abort with a run-time error message. The programmer has left out the & (address-of) operators on the variables in the call to scanf. Because scanf does not know where to find first and second, it is unable to store in them the values entered by the user. In this instance, if the program runs to completion, it will use whatever "garbage" values were originally in the memory locations named first and second.

Logic Errors

logic error an error caused by following an incorrect algorithm

Logic errors occur when a program follows a faulty algorithm. Because logic errors usually do not cause run-time errors and do not display error messages, they are very difficult to detect. The only sign of a logic error may be incorrect program output. You can detect logic errors by testing the program thoroughly,

FIGURE 2.19 A Program That Produces Incorrect Results Due to & Omission

```
1.    #include <stdio.h>
2.
3.    int
4.    main(void)
5.    {
6.        int    first, second, sum;
7.
8.        printf("Enter two integers> ");
9.        scanf("%d%d", first, second); /* ERROR!! should be &first, &second */
10.       sum = first + second;
11.       printf("%d + %d = %d\n", first, second, sum);
12.
13.       return (0);
14.   }
```

```
Enter two integers> 14    3
5971289 + 5971297 = 11942586
```

comparing its output to calculated results. You can prevent logic errors by carefully desk checking the algorithm and the program before you type it in.

Because debugging can be time-consuming, plan your program solutions carefully and desk check them to eliminate bugs early. If you are unsure of the syntax for a particular statement, look it up in the text or in the syntax guide printed on the inside back covers. Following this approach will save time and avoid trouble.

Chapter Review

1. Every C program has preprocessor directives and a main function. The main function contains variable declarations and executable statements.
2. Variable names must begin with a letter or an underscore (the latter is not recommended) and consist of letters, digits, and underscore symbols. A reserved word cannot be used as an identifier.
3. C's data types enable the compiler to determine how to store a particular value in memory and what operations can be performed on that value. Three standard data types are int, double, and char. The data type of each variable must be declared.
4. The executable statements are derived from the algorithm and are translated into machine language. Assignment statements are used to perform computations and store results in memory. Function calls are used to get data (function scanf) and to display values stored in memory (function printf).

NEW C CONSTRUCTS

Construct	Effect
#include directive	
`#include <stdio.h>`	Tells the preprocessor to give the program access to the header file for standard I/O library. This includes information about the `printf` and `scanf` functions.
#define directive for naming constant macros	
`#define PI 3.14159` `#define STAR '*'`	Tells the preprocessor to use `3.14159` as the definition of the name `PI` and `'*'` as the meaning of the identifier `STAR`.
main function heading	
`int` `main(void)`	Marks the start of the function where program execution begins.
variable declaration	
`double pct, wt;` `int high, mid, low;`	Allocates memory cells named `pct` and `wt` for storage of double-precision real numbers, cells named `high`, `mid`, and `low` for storage of integers.
assignment statement	
`distance = speed * time;`	Stores the product of `speed` and `time` as the value of the variable `distance`.
calls to input functions	
`scanf("%lf%d", &pct, &high);`	Copies input data from the keyboard into the type `double` variable `pct` and the type `int` variable `high`.
calls to output functions	
`printf("Percentage is %.3f\n", pct);`	Displays a line with the string `"Percentage is"` followed by the value of `pct` rounded to three decimal places.
return statement	
`return (0);`	Final statement of function `main`.

Quick-Check Exercises

1. What value is assigned to the type integer variable p by the statement

   ```
   p = 3200.0 / 4.0 - 10.0 + 120.0;
   ```

2. What value is assigned to p by the following statement, assuming p is 93.5?

   ```
   p = p / 0.5;
   ```

3. Show the exact form of the output line displayed when p is 9.

   ```
   printf("Four values of p are %2d*%3d*%4d*%d\n",
           p, p, p, p);
   ```

4. Show the exact form of the output line displayed when p is `12.7092`.

```
printf("Four values of p are %3.1f*%5.1f*%6.2f*%f\n",
       p, p, p, p);
```

5. What data types would you use to represent the following items: number of children at school, a letter grade on an exam, the average number of school days a child is absent each year?
6. In which step of the software development method are the problem inputs and outputs identified?
7. If function scanf is getting two numbers from the same line of input, what characters should be used to separate them?
8. How does the computer determine how many data values to get from the input device when a scanf operation is performed?
9. In an interactive program, how does the program user know how many data values to enter when the scanf function is called?
10. Does the compiler flag syntax or run-time errors?

Answers to Quick-Check Exercises

1. `910`
2. `187.0`
3. `Four values of p are   ∎9*∎∎9*∎∎∎9*9 (∎ = 1 blank)`
4. `Four values of p are 12.7*∎ 12.7*∎ 12.71*12.709200`
5. `int, char, double`
6. analysis
7. blanks
8. It depends on the number of placeholders in the format string.
9. from reading the prompt
10. syntax errors

Review Questions

1. What type of information should be specified in the block comment at the very beginning of the program?
2. Which variables below are syntactically incorrect?

```
MAX              peta
_mid             hash%
double           old avg
var@             #num
```

3. What is the output of the following program fragment?

```c
#include <stdio.h>
int main (void)
{
    int p, l;
            p = 0;
            l = 5;
    p = 4 * l;
            l++;
    printf("Value of p = %d\n", p);
            return (0);
}
```

4. Stylistically, which of the following identifiers would be good choices for names of constant macros?

```
gravity    G    MAX_SPEED    Sphere_Size
```

5. Write the data requirements, necessary formulas, and algorithm for Programming Project 9 in the next section.
6. The average pH of citrus fruits is 2.2, and this value has been stored in the variable `avg_citrus_pH`. Provide a statement to display this information in a readable way.
7. List three standard data types of C.
8. Convert the program statements below to take input data and echo it in batch mode.

```c
printf("Enter two characters> ");
scanf("%c%c", &c1, &c2);
printf("Enter three integers separated by spaces> ");
scanf("%d%d%d", &n, &m, &p);
```

9. Write an algorithm that finds the area of a rectangle, stores the result in the variable called area, and displays it.

Programming Projects

1. Write a program that calculates taxi fare at a rate of $1.50 per mile. Your program should interact with the user in this manner:

```
TAXI FARE CALCULATOR
Enter beginning odometer reading=> 78602.5
Enter ending odometer reading=> 78622.7
You traveled a distance of 20.2 miles. At $1.50 per mile,
your fare is $30.30.
```

2. Write a program to assist in the design of a hydroelectric dam. Prompt the user for the height of the dam and for the number of cubic meters of water that are projected to flow from the top to the bottom of the dam each second. Predict how many megawatts ($1MW = 10^6W$) of power will be produced if 90% of the work done on the water by gravity is converted to electrical energy. Note that the mass of one cubic meter of water is 1000 kg. Use 9.80 m/sec² as the gravitational constant g. Be sure to use meaningful names for both the gravitational constant and the 90% efficiency constant. For one run, use a height of 170 m and flow of 1.30×10^3 m³/s. The relevant formula (w = work, m = mass, g = gravity, and h = height) is: $w = mgh$.

3. Write a program that estimates the temperature in a freezer (in °C) given the elapsed time (hours) since a power failure. Assume this temperature (T) is given by

$$T = \frac{4t^2}{t + 2} - 20$$

where t is the time since the power failure. Your program should prompt the user to enter how long it has been since the start of the power failure in whole hours and minutes. Note that you will need to convert the elapsed time into hours. For example, if the user entered 2 30 (2 hours 30 minutes), you would need to convert this to 2.5 hours.

4. Write a program to convert a sum of money in US dollars to British pounds.

DATA REQUIREMENTS

Problem Input

```
float dollar /* currency in US dollars */
```

Problem Output

```
float pound  /* currency in British pounds */
```

Relevant Formula

1 USD = 0.65 GBP

5. Hospitals use programmable pumps to deliver medications and fluids to intravenous lines at a set number of milliliters per hour. Write a program to output information for the labels the hospital pharmacy places on bags of I.V. medications indicating the volume of medication to be infused and the rate at which the pump should be set. The program should prompt the user to enter the quantity of fluid in the bag and the number of minutes over which it should be infused. Output the VTBI (volume to be infused) in ml and the infusion rate in ml/hr.

Sample run:

```
Volume to be infused (ml) => 100
Minutes over which to infuse => 20

VTBI: 100 ml
Rate: 300 ml/hr
```

6. Write a program that predicts the score needed on a final exam to achieve a desired grade in a course. The program should interact with the user as follows:

```
Enter desired grade> B
Enter minimum average required> 79.5
Enter current average in course> 74.6
Enter how much the final counts
as a percentage of the course grade> 25

You need a score of 94.20 on the final to get a B.
```

In the example shown, the final counts 25% of the course grade.

7. Write a program that calculates how many BTUs of heat are delivered to a house given the number of gallons of oil burned and the efficiency of the house's oil furnace. Assume that a barrel of oil (42 gallons) has an energy equivalent of 5,800,000 BTU. (*Note:* This number is too large to represent as an int on some personal computers.) For one test use an efficiency of 65% and 100 gallons of oil.

8. Metro City Planners proposes that a community conserve its water supply by replacing all the community's toilets with low-flush models that use only 2 liters per flush. Assume that there is about 1 toilet for every 3 persons, that existing toilets use an average of 15 liters per flush, that a toilet is flushed on average 14 times per day, and that the cost to install each new toilet is $150. Write a program that would estimate the magnitude (liters/day) and cost of the water saved based on the community's population.

9. Write a program that takes the length and width of a rectangular yard and the length and width of a rectangular house situated in the yard. Your program should compute the time required to cut the grass at the rate of two square feet a second.

10. Write a program that outputs the equation of the perpendicular bisector of the line segment between two points. Your program should

- prompt for and input the coordinates of the two points [for example, try the points (2.0, –4.0) and (7.0, –2.0)];
- compute the slope of the line between those two points;
- compute the coordinates of the midpoint of the line segment between the two points by averaging the two x-coordinates and the two y-coordinates;
- compute the slope of the perpendicular bisector by taking the negative reciprocal of the slope of the line segment;

FIGURE 2.20

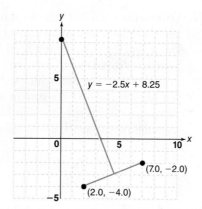

- compute the y-intercept of the perpendicular bisector (you now have the slope m of the bisector and a point (x_{mid}, y_{mid}) on the bisector, so the y-intercept is $y_{mid} - m\, x_{mid}$); and
- output with labels the original two points, and output in $y = mx + b$ format the equation of the perpendicular bisector. Figure 2.20 illustrates the sample line segment mentioned above and its perpendicular bisector.

Test your program to be sure it works on different pairs of points. However, there will be some pairs of points for which you can't make your program work (at least not at this stage). Think about what points will cause your program to fail, and write a paragraph describing which points fall in this category.

11. The Pythagorean theorem states that the sum of the squares of the sides of a right triangle is equal to the square of the hypotenuse. For example, if two sides of a right triangle have lengths of 3 and 4, then the hypotenuse must have a length of 5. Together the integers 3, 4, and 5 form a *Pythagorean triple*. There are an infinite number of such triples. Given two positive integers, m and n, where $m > n$, a Pythagorean triple can be generated by the following formulas:

$$side1 = m^2 - n^2$$
$$side2 = 2mn$$
$$hypotenuse = m^2 + n^2$$

The triple (*side1* = 3, *side2* = 4, and *hypotenuse* = 5) is generated by this formula when $m = 2$ and $n = 1$. Write a program that takes values for m and n as input and displays the values of the Pythagorean triple generated by the formulas above.

12. Write a program that calculates the acceleration (m/s²) of a jet fighter launched from an aircraft-carrier catapult, given the jet's takeoff speed in km/hr and the distance (meters) over which the catapult accelerates the jet from rest to takeoff. Assume constant acceleration. Also calculate the time (seconds) for the fighter to be accelerated to takeoff speed. When you prompt the user, be sure to indicate the units for each input. For one run, use a takeoff speed of 278 km/hr and a distance of 94 meters. Relevant formulas (v = velocity, a = acceleration, t = time, and s = distance)

$$v = at$$

$$s = \tfrac{1}{2}at^2$$

13. Write a program that predicts how many whole sections of a batch would need to be created given the number of students enrolled in the batch. Assume that each section accommodates 30 students. Prompt the user to enter the number of students enrolled. Echo print the number of students enrolled and then display both the number of sections that will be required and the number of students that will be left over.

Top-Down Design with Functions

CHAPTER OBJECTIVES

- To learn about functions and how to use them to write programs with separate modules

- To understand the capabilities of some standard functions in C

- To introduce structure charts as a system documentation tool

- To understand how control flows between function `main` and other functions

- To learn how to pass information to functions using input arguments

- To learn how to return a value from a function

Programmers who use the software-development method to solve problems seldom tackle each new program as a unique event. Information contained in the problem statement and amassed during the analysis and design phases helps the programmer plan and complete the finished program. Programmers also use segments of earlier program solutions as building blocks to construct new programs.

In the first part of this chapter, we demonstrate how you can tap existing information and code in the form of predefined functions to write programs. In addition to using existing information, programmers can use top-down design techniques to simplify the development of algorithms and the structure of the resulting programs. To apply top-down design, the programmer starts with the broadest statement of the problem solution and works down to more detailed subproblems. In the second part of this chapter, we demonstrate top-down design and emphasize the role of modular programming using functions.

3.1 Building Programs from Existing Information

Programmers seldom start off with a blank slate (or empty screen) when they develop a program. Often some—or all—of the solution can be developed from information that already exists or from the solution to another problem, as we demonstrate in this section.

Carefully following the software development method generates important system documentation before you even begin to code a program. This system documentation, consisting of a description of a problem's data requirements (developed during the Analysis phase) and its solution algorithm (developed during the Design phase), summarizes your intentions and thought processes.

You can use this documentation as a starting point in coding your program. For example, you can begin by editing the data requirements to conform to the C syntax for constant macro definitions and variable declarations, as shown in Fig. 3.1 for the miles-to-kilometers conversion program. This approach is especially helpful if the documentation was created with a word processor and is in a file that you can edit.

To develop the executable statements in the main function, first use the initial algorithm and its refinements as program comments. The comments describe each algorithm step and provide program documentation that guides your C code. Figure 3.1 shows how the program will look at this point. After the comments are in place in the main function, you can begin to write the C statements. Place the C code for an unrefined step directly under that step. For a step that is refined, either edit the refinement to change it from English to C or replace it with C code. We illustrate this entire process in the next case study.

FIGURE 3.1   Edited Data Requirements and Algorithm for Conversion Program

```
1.  /*
2.   * Converts distance in miles to kilometers.
3.   */
4.
5.  #include <stdio.h>              /* printf, scanf definitions */
6.  #define KMS_PER_MILE 1.609      /* conversion constant */
7.
8.  int
9.  main(void)
10. {
11.       double miles;   /* input - distance in miles.      */
12.       double kms;     /* output - distance in kilometers  */
13.
14.       /* Get the distance in miles.                     */
15.
16.       /* Convert the distance to kilometers.            */
17.          /* Distance in kilometers is
18.               1.609 * distance in miles.                 */
19.
20.       /* Display the distance in kilometers.            */
21.
22.       return (0);
23. }
```

CASE STUDY   Finding the Area and Circumference of a Circle

PROBLEM

Get the radius of a circle. Compute and display the circle's area and circumference.

ANALYSIS

Clearly, the problem input is the circle's radius. Two outputs are requested: the circle's area and circumference. These variables should be type double because the inputs and outputs may contain fractional parts. The geometric relationships of a circle's radius to its area and circumference are listed below, along with the data requirements.

DATA REQUIREMENTS

Problem Constant

```
PI      3.14159
```

Problem Input

```
radius      /* radius of a circle          */
```

Problem Outputs

```
area      /* area of a circle          */
circum    /* circumference of a circle */
```

Relevant Formulas

area of a circle $= \pi \times radius^2$
circumference of a circle $= 2\pi \times radius$

DESIGN

After identifying the problem inputs and outputs, list the steps necessary to solve the problem. Pay close attention to the order of the steps.

INITIAL ALGORITHM

1. Get the circle radius.
2. Calculate the area.
3. Calculate the circumference.
4. Display the area and the circumference.

ALGORITHM REFINEMENTS

Next refine any steps that do not have an obvious solution (steps 2 and 3).

Step 2 Refinement

2.1 Assign PI * radius * radius to area.

Step 3 Refinement

3.1 Assign 2 * PI * radius to circum.

IMPLEMENTATION

Figure 3.2 shows the C program so far. The main function lists the initial algorithm and its refinements as comments. To write the final program, convert the refinements (steps 2.1 and 3.1) to C and write C code for the unrefined steps (steps 1 and 4). Figure 3.3 shows the final program.

FIGURE 3.2   Outline of Program Circle

```
1.  /*
2.   * Calculates and displays the area and circumference of a circle
3.   */
4.
5.  #include <stdio.h> /* printf, scanf definitions */
6.  #define PI 3.14159
7.
8.  int
9.  main(void)
10. {
11.       double radius;    /* input - radius of a circle  */
12.       double area;      /* output - area of a circle   */
13.       double circum;    /* output - circumference      */
14.
15.       /* Get the circle radius */
16.
17.       /* Calculate the area */
18.          /* Assign PI * radius * radius to area. */
19.
20.       /* Calculate the circumference */
21.          /* Assign 2 * PI * radius to circum */
22.
23.       /* Display the area and circumference */
24.
25.       return (0);
26. }
```

FIGURE 3.3   Calculating the Area and the Circumference of a Circle

```
1.  /*
2.   * Calculates and displays the area and circumference of a circle
3.   */
4.
5.  #include <stdio.h> /* printf, scanf definitions */
6.  #define PI 3.14159
7.
8.  int
9.  main(void)
```

(continued)

FIGURE 3.3 (continued)

```
10.  {
11.          double radius; /* input - radius of a circle */
12.          double area;    /* output - area of a circle   */
13.          double circum; /* output - circumference       */
14.
15.          /* Get the circle radius */
16.          printf("Enter radius> ");
17.          scanf("%lf", &radius);
18.
19.          /* Calculate the area */
20.          area = PI * radius * radius;
21.
22.          /* Calculate the circumference */
23.          circum = 2 * PI * radius;
24.
25.          /* Display the area and circumference */
26.          printf("The area is %.4f\n", area);
27.          printf("The circumference is %.4f\n", circum);
28.
29.          return (0);
30.  }
```

```
Enter radius> 5.0
The area is 78.5397
The circumference is 31.4159
```

TESTING

The sample output in Fig. 3.3 provides a good test of the solution because it is relatively easy to compute by hand the area and the circumference for a radius value of 5.0. The radius squared is 25.0 and π is approximately 3, so the value of the area appears to be correct. The circumference should be 10 times π, which is also an easy number to compute by hand.

CASE STUDY   Computing the Weight of a Batch of Flat Washers

Another way in which programmers use existing information is by *extending the solution for one problem to solve another*. For example, you can easily solve this problem by building on the solution to the previous one.

PROBLEM

You work for a hardware company that manufactures flat washers. To estimate shipping costs, your company needs a program that computes the weight of a specified quantity of flat washers.

ANALYSIS

A flat washer resembles a small donut. To compute the weight of a single flat washer, you need to know its rim area, its thickness, and the density of the material used in its construction. The last two quantities are problem inputs. However, the rim area (see Fig. 3.4) must be computed from two measurements that are provided as inputs: the washer's outer diameter and its inner diameter (diameter of the hole).

In the following data requirements, we list the washer's inner and outer radius (half the diameter) as program variables. We also list the rim area and weight of one washer (`unit_weight`) as program variables.

DATA REQUIREMENTS

Problem Constant
```
PI      3.14159
```

Problem Inputs
```
double hole_diameter /* diameter of hole */
double edge_diameter /* diameter of outer edge */
double thickness     /* thickness of washer */
double density       /* density of material used */
double quantity      /* number of washers made */
```

FIGURE 3.4

Computing the Rim Area of a Flat Washer

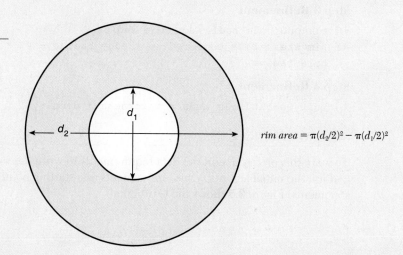

$$rim\ area = \pi(d_2/2)^2 - \pi(d_1/2)^2$$

Problem Outputs

```
double weight        /* weight of batch of washers */
```

Program Variables

```
double hole_radius   /* radius of hole */
double edge_radius   /* radius of outer edge */
double rim_area      /* area of rim */
double unit_weight   /* weight of 1 washer */
```

Relevant Formulas

area of a circle $= \pi \times radius^2$
radius of a circle = diameter / 2
rim area = area of outer circle – area of hole
unit weight = rim area × thickness × density

DESIGN

We list the algorithm next, followed by the refinement of steps 3 and 4.

INITIAL ALGORITHM

1. Get the washer's inner diameter, outer diameter, and thickness.
2. Get the material density and quantity of washers manufactured.
3. Compute the rim area.
4. Compute the weight of one flat washer.
5. Compute the weight of the batch of washers.
6. Display the weight of the batch of washers.

Step 3 Refinement

3.1 Compute `hole_radius` and `edge_radius`.
3.2 `rim_area` is `PI * edge_radius * edge_radius - PI * hole_radius * hole_radius`

Step 4 Refinement

4.1 `unit_weight` is `rim_area * thickness * density`

IMPLEMENTATION

To write this program, edit the data requirements to write the variable declarations and use the initial algorithm with refinements as a starting point for the executable statements. Figure 3.5 shows the C program.

FIGURE 3.5 Flat Washer Program

```
1.  /*
2.   * Computes the weight of a batch of flat washers.
3.   */
4.
5.  #include <stdio.h> /* printf, scanf definitions */
6.  #define PI 3.14159
7.
8.  int
9.  main(void)
10. {
11.        double hole_diameter; /* input - diameter of hole       */
12.        double edge_diameter; /* input - diameter of outer edge */
13.        double thickness;     /* input - thickness of washer    */
14.        double density;       /* input - density of material used */
15.        double quantity;      /* input - number of washers made  */
16.        double weight;        /* output - weight of washer batch */
17.        double hole_radius;   /* radius of hole                 */
18.        double edge_radius;   /* radius of outer edge           */
19.        double rim_area;      /* area of rim                    */
20.        double unit_weight;   /* weight of 1 washer             */
21.
22.        /* Get the inner diameter, outer diameter, and thickness.*/
23.        printf("Inner diameter in centimeters> ");
24.        scanf("%lf", &hole_diameter);
25.        printf("Outer diameter in centimeters> ");
26.        scanf("%lf", &edge_diameter);
27.        printf("Thickness in centimeters> ");
28.        scanf("%lf", &thickness);
29.
30.        /* Get the material density and quantity manufactured. */
31.        printf("Material density in grams per cubic centimeter> ");
32.        scanf("%lf", &density);
33.        printf("Quantity in batch> ");
34.        scanf("%lf", &quantity);
35.
36.        /* Compute the rim area. */
37.        hole_radius = hole_diameter / 2.0;
38.        edge_radius = edge_diameter / 2.0;
```

(continued)

FIGURE 3.5 (continued)

```
39.        rim_area = PI * edge_radius * edge_radius -
40.                   PI * hole_radius * hole_radius;
41.
42.        /* Compute the weight of a flat washer. */
43.        unit_weight = rim_area * thickness * density;
44.        /* Compute the weight of the batch of washers. */
45.        weight = unit_weight * quantity;
46.
47.        /* Display the weight of the batch of washers. */
48.        printf("\nThe expected weight of the batch is %.2f", weight);
49.        printf(" grams.\n");
50.
51.        return (0);
52. }
```

```
Inner diameter in centimeters> 1.2
Outer diameter in centimeters> 2.4
Thickness in centimeters> 0.1
Material density in grams per cubic centimeter> 7.87
Quantity in batch> 1000

The expected weight of the batch is 2670.23 grams.
```

TESTING

To test this program, run it with inner and outer diameters such as 2 centimeters and 4 centimeters that lead to easy calculations for rim area (3 * PI square centimeters). You can verify that the program is computing the correct unit weight by entering 1 for quantity, and then verify that the batch weight is correct by running it for larger quantities.

EXERCISES FOR SECTION 3.1

Self-Check

1. Describe the problem inputs and outputs and write the algorithm for a program that computes an employee's gross salary given the hours worked and the hourly rate.

2. Write a preliminary version of the program from your solution to Self-Check Exercise 1. Show the declaration part of the program and the program comments corresponding to the algorithm and its refinements.

3. In computing gross salary, what changes should you make to extend the payroll algorithm in Self-Check Exercise 1 to include overtime hours to be paid at 1.5 times an employee's normal hourly rate? Assume that overtime hours are entered separately.

Programming

1. Add refinements to the program outline that follows and write the final C program.

```
/*
 * Compute the sum and average of two numbers.
 */

#include <stdio.h> /* printf, scanf definitions */

int
main(void)
{
      double one, two, /* input - numbers to process   */
             sum,      /* output - sum of one and two   */
             average;  /* output - average of one and two */
      /* Get two numbers. */
      /* Compute sum of numbers. */
      /* Compute average of numbers. */
      /* Display sum and average. */

      return (0);
}
```

2. Write a complete C program for Self-Check Exercise 1.
3. Write a complete C program for the revised payroll algorithm developed in Self-Check Exercise 3.
4. Assume that flat washers are manufactured by stamping them out from a rectangular piece of material of uniform thickness. Extend the washer program to compute (a) the number of square centimeters of material needed to manufacture a specified quantity of flat washers and (b) the weight of the leftover material.

3.2 Library Functions

Predefined Functions and Code Reuse

A primary goal of software engineering is to write error-free code. *Code reuse*, reusing program fragments that have already been written and tested whenever possible, is one way to accomplish this goal. Stated more simply, "Why reinvent the wheel?"

C promotes reuse by providing many predefined functions that can be used to perform mathematical computations. C's standard math library defines a function named sqrt that performs the square root computation. The function call in the assignment statement

function call

$$y = sqrt(x);$$

function   argument
name

activates the code for function sqrt, passing the argument x to the function. You activate a function by writing a function call. After the function executes, the function result is substituted for the function call. If x is 16.0, the assignment statement above is evaluated as follows:

1. x is 16.0, so function sqrt computes the √16.0 or 4.0.
2. The function result, 4.0, is assigned to y.

A function can be thought of as a "black box" that receives one or more input values and automatically returns a single output value. Figure 3.6 illustrates this for the call to function sqrt. The value of x (16.0) is the function input, and the function result, or output, is √16.0 (result is 4.0).

If w is 9.0, the assignment statement

```
z = 5.7 + sqrt(w);
```

is evaluated as follows:

1. w is 9.0, so function sqrt computes the square root of 9.0, or 3.0.
2. The values 5.7 and 3.0 are added together.
3. The sum, 8.7, is stored in z.

EXAMPLE 3.1   The program in Fig. 3.7 displays the square root of two numbers provided as input data (first and second) and the square root of their sum. To do so, it must call the C function sqrt three times:

FIGURE 3.6

Function sqrt as a "Black Box"

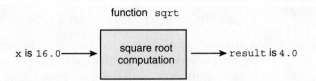

function sqrt

x is 16.0 ⟶ square root computation ⟶ result is 4.0

```
first_sqrt = sqrt(first);
second_sqrt = sqrt(second);
sum_sqrt = sqrt(first + second);
```

For the first two calls, the function arguments are variables (`first` and `second`). The third call shows that a function argument can also be an expression (`first + second`). For all three calls, the result returned by function `sqrt` is assigned to a variable. Because the definition of the standard `sqrt` function is found in the standard math library, the program begins with an additional `#include` directive.

If you look closely at the program in Fig. 3.7, you will see that each statement contains a call to a library function (`printf`, `scanf`, `sqrt`)—we have used C's predefined functions as building blocks to construct a new program.

Use of Color to Highlight New Constructs

In Fig. 3.7, program lines that illustrate new constructs are in color, so that you can find them easily. We will continue to use color for this purpose in figures that contain programs.

FIGURE 3.7 Square Root Program

```
1.  /*
2.   * Performs three square root computations
3.   */
4.
5.  #include <stdio.h> /* definitions of printf, scanf */
6.  #include <math.h>  /* definition of sqrt           */
7.
8.  int
9.  main(void)
10. {
11.       double first, second,    /* input - two data values     */
12.              first_sqrt,        /* output - square root of first */
13.              second_sqrt,       /* output - square root of second */
14.              sum_sqrt;          /* output - square root of sum   */
15.
16.       /* Get first number and display its square root. */
17.       printf("Enter the first number> ");
18.       scanf("%lf", &first);
19.       first_sqrt = sqrt(first);
20.       printf("The square root of the first number is %.2f\n", first_sqrt);
```

(continued)

FIGURE 3.7   (continued)

```
21.        /* Get second number and display its square root. */
22.        printf("Enter the second number> ");
23.        scanf("%lf", &second);
24.        second_sqrt = sqrt(second);
25.        printf("The square root of the second number is %.2f\n", second_sqrt);
26.
27.        /* Display the square root of the sum of the two numbers. */
28.        sum_sqrt = sqrt(first + second);
29.        printf("The square root of the sum of the two numbers is %.2f\n",
30.               sum_sqrt);
31.
32.        return (0);
33. }
```

```
Enter the first number> 9.0
The square root of the first number is 3.00
Enter the second number> 16.0
The square root of the second number is 4.00
The square root of the sum of the two numbers is 5.00
```

C Library Functions

Table 3.1 lists the names and descriptions of some of the most commonly used functions along with the name of the standard header file to #include in order to have access to each function. A complete list of standard library functions appears in Appendix B.

If one of the functions in Table 3.1 is called with a numeric argument that is not of the argument type listed, the argument value is converted to the required type before it is used. Conversions of type int to type double cause no problems, but a conversion of type double to type int leads to the loss of any fractional part, just as in a mixed-type assignment. For example, if we call the abs function with the type double value -3.47, the result returned is the type int value 3. For this reason, the library has a separate absolute value function (fabs) for type double arguments.

Most of the functions in Table 3.1 perform common mathematical computations. The arguments for log and log10 must be positive; the argument for sqrt cannot be negative. The arguments for sin, cos, and tan must be expressed in radians, not in degrees.

TABLE 3.1   Some Mathematical Library Functions

Function	Standard Header File	Purpose: Example	Argument(s)	Result
abs(x)	`<stdlib.h>`	Returns the absolute value of its integer argument: if x is −5, abs(x) is 5	int	int
ceil(x)	`<math.h>`	Returns the smallest integral value that is not less than x: if x is 45.23, ceil(x) is 46.0	double	double
cos(x)	`<math.h>`	Returns the cosine of angle x: if x is 0.0, cos(x) is 1.0	double (radians)	double
exp(x)	`<math.h>`	Returns e^x where e = 2.71828...: if x is 1.0, exp(x) is 2.71828	double	double
fabs(x)	`<math.h>`	Returns the absolute value of its type **double** argument: if x is −8.432, fabs(x) is 8.432	double	double
floor(x)	`<math.h>`	Returns the largest integral value that is not greater than x: if x is 45.23, floor(x) is 45.0	double	double
log(x)	`<math.h>`	Returns the natural logarithm of x for x > 0.0: if x is 2.71828, log(x) is 1.0	double	double
log10(x)	`<math.h>`	Returns the base-10 logarithm of x for x > 0.0: if x is 100.0, log10(x) is 2.0	double	double
pow(x, y)	`<math.h>`	Returns x^y. If x is negative, y must be integral: if x is 0.16 and y is 0.5, pow(x,y) is 0.4	double, double	double
sin(x)	`<math.h>`	Returns the sine of angle x: if x is 1.5708, sin(x) is 1.0	double (radians)	double
sqrt(x)	`<math.h>`	Returns the nonnegative square root of x ($\sqrt{x}$) for x ▢ 0.0: if x is 2.25, sqrt(x) is 1.5	double	double
tan(x)	`<math.h>`	Returns the tangent of angle x: if x is 0.0, tan(x) is 0.0	double (radians)	double

EXAMPLE 3.2   We can use the C functions pow (power) and sqrt to compute the roots of a quadratic equation in x of the form

$$ax^2 + bx + c = 0$$

The two roots are defined as

$$root_1 = \frac{-b + \sqrt{b^2 - 4ac}}{2a} \qquad root_2 = \frac{-b - \sqrt{b^2 - 4ac}}{2a}$$

when the *discriminant* ($b^2 - 4ac$) is greater than zero. If we assume that this is the case, we can use these assignment statements to assign values to `root_1` and `root_2`.

```
/* Compute two roots, root_1 and root_2, for disc > 0.0 */
disc = pow(b,2) - 4 * a * c;
root_1 = (-b + sqrt(disc)) / (2 * a);
root_2 = (-b - sqrt(disc)) / (2 * a);
```

In the first assignment statement above, the expression begins with `pow(b, 2)`, which calls function `pow` with `b` and `2` as arguments; the function result (`b²`) is substituted for the function call when the expression is evaluated.

EXAMPLE 3.3

If we know the lengths of two sides (b and c) of a triangle and the angle between them in degrees (α), we can compute the length of the third side (a) using the following formula (see Fig. 3.8).

$$a^2 = b^2 + c^2 - 2bc \cos \alpha$$

To use the math library cosine function (`cos`), we must express its argument angle in radians instead of degrees. To convert an angle from degrees to radians, we multiply the angle by $\pi/180$. If we assume `PI` represents the constant π, the C assignment statement that follows computes the unknown side length:

```
a = sqrt(pow(b,2) + pow(c,2)
      - 2 * b * c * cos(alpha * PI / 180.0));
```

FIGURE 3.8

Triangle with
Unknown Side *a*

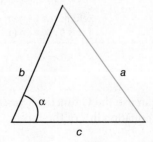

A Look at Where We Are Heading

C also allows us to write our own functions. Let's assume that we have already written functions `find_area` and `find_circum`:

- Function `find_area(r)` returns the area of a circle with radius `r`.
- Function `find_circum(r)` returns the circumference of a circle with radius `r`.

We can reuse these functions in two programs shown earlier in this chapter (see Figs. 3.3 and 3.5). The program in Fig. 3.3 computes the area and the circumference of a circle. The statements

```
area = find_area(radius);
circum = find_circum(radius);
```

can be used to find these values. The expression part for each of the assignment statements is a function call with argument `radius` (the circle radius). The result returned by each function execution is stored in an output variable for the program (`area` or `circum`).

For the flat washer program (Fig. 3.5), we can use the statement

```
rim_area = find_area(edge_radius) - find_area(hole_radius);
```

to compute the rim area for a washer. This statement is clearer than the one shown in the original program (lines 39 and 40).

 EXERCISES FOR SECTION 3.2

Self-Check

1. Rewrite the following mathematical expressions using C functions:

   a. $\sqrt{u + v} \times w^2$ c. $\sqrt{(x - y)^3}$

   b. $\log_e (x^y)$ d. $|xy - w/z|$

2. Evaluate the following:

   a. `log10(10000.0)`

   b. `ceil(16.2)`

   c. `floor(-7.5) * pow(3.0, 2.0)`

   d. `floor(21.8 + 0.8)`

   e. `sqrt(ceil(fabs(-7.4)))`

Programming

1. Write statements that compute and display the absolute difference of two type `double` variables, x and $y (|x - y|)$.

2. Write a complete C program that prompts the user for the coordinates of two 3-D points (x_1, y_1, z_1) and (x_2, y_2, z_2) and displays the distance between them computed using the following formula:

$$distance = \sqrt{(x_1 - x_2)^2 + (y_1 - y_2)^2 + (z_1 - z_2)^2}$$

3.3 Top-Down Design and Structure Charts

top-down design
a problem-solving method in which you first break a problem up into its major subproblems and then solve the subproblems to derive the solution to the original problem

structure chart a documentation tool that shows the relationships among the subproblems of a problem

Often the algorithm needed to solve a problem is more complex than those we have seen so far, and the programmer must break up the problem into subproblems to develop the program solution. In attempting to solve a subproblem at one level, we introduce new subproblems at lower levels. This process, called **top-down design**, proceeds from the original problem at the top level to the subproblems at each lower level. The splitting of a problem into its related subproblems is analogous to the process of refining an algorithm. The case study below introduces a documentation tool—the **structure chart**—that will help you to keep track of the relationships among subproblems.

CASE STUDY   Drawing Simple Diagrams

PROBLEM

You want to draw some simple diagrams on your printer or screen. Two examples are the house and female stick figure in Fig. 3.9.

ANALYSIS

The house is formed by displaying a triangle without its base on top of a rectangle. The stick figure consists of a circular shape, a triangle, and a triangle without its base. We can draw both figures with these four basic components:

- a circle
- a base line
- parallel lines
- intersecting lines

FIGURE 3.9

House and Stick Figure

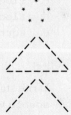

DESIGN

To create the stick figure, you can divide the problem into three subproblems.

INITIAL ALGORITHM

1. Draw a circle.
2. Draw a triangle.
3. Draw intersecting lines.

ALGORITHM REFINEMENTS

Because a triangle is not a basic component, you must refine step 2, generating the following subproblems:

Step 2 Refinement

2.1 Draw intersecting lines.
2.2 Draw a base.

You can use a structure chart to show the relationship between the original problem and its subproblems, as in Fig. 3.10, where the original problem (level 0) is in the darker color and its three subordinate subproblems are shown at level 1. The subproblem *Draw a triangle* is also in color because it has its own subproblems (shown at level 2).

The subproblems appear in both the algorithm and the structure chart. The algorithm, not the structure chart, shows the order in which you carry out each step to solve the problem. The structure chart simply illustrates the subordination of subproblems to each other and to the original problem.

FIGURE 3.10

Structure Chart for Drawing a Stick Figure

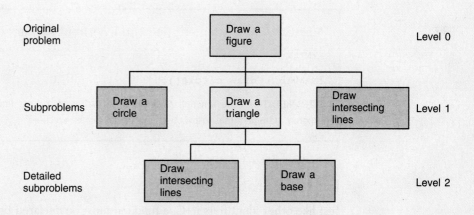

EXERCISES FOR SECTION 3.3

Self-Check

1. In which phase of the software-development method do you apply top-down design to break the problem into suitable subproblems?
2. Draw the structure chart for the problem of drawing the house shown in Fig. 3.9.

3.4 Functions Without Arguments

One way that programmers implement top-down design in their programs is by defining their own functions. Often, a programmer will write one function subprogram for each subproblem in the structure chart. In this section, we show how to use and define your own functions, focusing on simple functions that have no arguments and return no value.

As an example of top-down design with functions, you could use the main function in Fig. 3.11 to draw the stick figure of a person. In Fig. 3.11, the three algorithm steps are coded as calls to three function subprograms. For example, the statement

```
draw_circle();
```

calls a function (`draw_circle`) that implements the algorithm step *Draw a circle*.

We call function `draw_circle` just like we call function `printf`. The empty parentheses after the function name indicate that `draw_circle` requires no arguments.

Function Call Statement (Function Without Arguments)

SYNTAX: *fname*();

EXAMPLE: `draw_circle();`

INTERPRETATION: The function *fname* is called. After *fname* has finished execution, the program statement that follows the function call will be executed.

Function Prototypes

Just like other identifiers in C, a function must be declared before it can be referenced. One way to declare a function is to insert a function prototype before the

FIGURE 3.11 Function Prototypes and Main Function for Stick Figure

```
1.  /*
2.   * Draws a stick figure
3.   */
4.
5.  #include <stdio.h>              /* printf definition */
6.
7.  /* function prototypes */
8.
9.  void draw_circle(void);         /* Draws a circle              */
10.
11. void draw_intersect(void);      /* Draws intersecting lines    */
12.
13. void draw_base(void);           /* Draws a base line           */
14.
15. void draw_triangle(void);       /* Draws a triangle            */
16.
17. int
18. main(void)
19. {
20.         /* Draw a circle. */
21.         draw_circle();
22.
23.         /* Draw a triangle. */
24.         draw_triangle();
25.
26.         /* Draw intersecting lines. */
27.         draw_intersect();
28.
29.         return (0);
30. }
```

main function. A function prototype tells the C compiler the data type of the function, the function name, and information about the arguments that the function expects. The data type of a function is determined by the type of value returned by the function. The functions declared in Fig. 3.11 are **void functions** (that is, their type is void) because they do not return a value. In the function prototype

void function
a function that does
not return a value

```
void draw_circle(void);     /* Draws a circle     */
```

the second void indicates that draw_circle expects no arguments.

Function Prototype (Function Without Arguments)

FORM: *ftype fname*(`void`);

EXAMPLE: `void draw_circle(void);`

INTERPRETATION: The identifier *fname* is declared to be the name of a function. The identifier *ftype* specifies the data type of the function result.

Note: ftype is `void` if the function does not return a value. The argument list (`void`) indicates that the function has no arguments. The function prototype must appear before the first call to the function.

Function Definitions

Although the prototype specifies the number of arguments a function takes and the type of its result, it does not specify the function operation. To do this, you need to provide a definition for each function subprogram similar to the definition of the main function. Figure 3.12 shows the definition for function `draw_circle`.

The function heading is similar to the function prototype in Fig. 3.11 except that it is not ended by the symbol `;`. We have adopted a style that places the function type on a separate line. (Industrial C developers often use this style to make function definitions easy to find in long source files.) The function body, enclosed in braces, consists of three calls to function `printf` that cause the computer to display a circular shape. We omit the `return` statement because `draw_circle` does not return a result.

FIGURE 3.12   Function draw_circle

```
1.  /*
2.   * Draws a circle
3.   */
4.  void
5.  draw_circle(void)
6.  {
7.        printf("   *   \n");
8.        printf(" *     *\n");
9.        printf(" *   * \n");
10. }
```

The function call statement

```
draw_circle();
```

causes these `printf` statements to execute. Control returns to the main function after the circle shape is displayed.

Function Definition (Function Without Arguments)

SYNTAX: *ftype*
            fname(`void`)

            `{`
                local declarations
                executable statements
            `}`

EXAMPLE: ```
            /*
             * Displays a block-letter H
             */
            void
            print_h(void)
            {
                    printf("** **\n");
                    printf("** **\n");
                    printf("*****\n");
                    printf("** **\n");
                    printf("** **\n");
            }
            ```

INTERPRETATION: The function *fname* is defined. In the function heading, the identifier *ftype* specifies the data type of the function result. Notice that there are no semicolons after the lines of the function heading. The braces enclose the function body. Any identifiers that are declared in the optional *local declarations* are defined only during the execution of the function and can be referenced only within the function. The *executable statements* of the function body describe the data manipulation to be performed by the function.

*Note: ftype* is `void` if the function does not return a value. The argument list `(void)` indicates that the function has no arguments. You can omit the `void` and write the argument list as `()`.

---

Each function body may contain declarations for its own variables. These variables are considered *local* to the function; in other words, they can be referenced only within the function. There will be more on this topic later.

The structure chart in Fig. 3.10 shows that the subproblem *Draw a triangle* (level 1) depends on the solutions to its subordinate subproblems *Draw intersecting*
            ```

FIGURE 3.13 Function draw_triangle

```
1.  /*
2.   * Draws a triangle
3.   */
4.  void
5.  draw_triangle(void)
6.  {
7.        draw_intersect();
8.        draw_base();
9.  }
```

lines and *Draw a base* (both level 2). Figure 3.13 shows how you can use top-down design to code function `draw_triangle`. Instead of using `printf` statements to display a triangular pattern, the body of function `draw_triangle` calls functions `draw_intersect` and `draw_base` to draw a triangle.

Placement of Functions in a Program

Figure 3.14 shows the complete program with function subprograms. The subprogram prototypes precede the main function (after any `#include` or `#define` directives) and the subprogram definitions follow the main function. The relative order of the function definitions does not affect their order of execution; that is determined by the order of execution of the function call statements.

FIGURE 3.14 Program to Draw a Stick Figure

```
1.  /* Draws a stick figure */
2.
3.  #include <stdio.h>            /* printf definition */
4.
5.  /* Function prototypes */
6.  void draw_circle(void);           /* Draws a circle              */
7.
8.  void draw_intersect(void);        /* Draws intersecting lines    */
9.
10. void draw_base(void);             /* Draws a base line           */
11.
12. void draw_triangle(void);         /* Draws a triangle            */
13.
```

(continued)

FIGURE 3.14   (continued)

```c
14.  int
15.  main(void)
16.  {
17.
18.          /* Draw a circle.              */
19.          draw_circle();
20.
21.          /* Draw a triangle.            */
22.          draw_triangle();
23.
24.          /* Draw intersecting lines.    */
25.          draw_intersect();
26.
27.          return (0);
28.  }
29.
30.  /*
31.   * Draws a circle
32.   */
33.  void
34.  draw_circle(void)
35.  {
36.       printf("   *   \n");
37.       printf(" *     * \n");
38.       printf("   * *  \n");
39.  }
40.
41.  /*
42.   * Draws intersecting lines
43.   */
44.  void
45.  draw_intersect(void)
46.  {
47.       printf("  / \\  \n"); /* Use 2 \'s to print 1 */
48.       printf(" /    \\ \n");
49.       printf("/      \\\n");
50.  }
51.
```

(continued)

FIGURE 3.14   (continued)

```
52. /*
53.  * Draws a base line
54.  */
55. void
56. draw_base(void)
57. {
58.         printf("-------\n");
59. }
60.
61. /*
62.  * Draws a triangle
63.  */
64. void
65. draw_triangle(void)
66. {
67.         draw_intersect();
68.         draw_base();
69. }
```

If you look closely at function `draw_intersect`, you will notice that the symbol pair \\ represents a single backslash character in a format string. This convention enables C to differentiate the backslash character from the escape symbol (just \).

Program Style   *Use of Comments in a Program with Functions*

Figure 3.14 includes several comments. Each function begins with a comment that describes its purpose. If the function subprograms were more complex, we would include comments on each major algorithm step just as we do in function `main`. From now on throughout this text, the block comment and heading of each function definition are in color to help you locate functions in the program listing.

Order of Execution of Function Subprograms and Main Function

Because the prototypes for the function subprograms appear before the main function, the compiler processes the function prototypes before it translates the main function. The information in each prototype enables the compiler to correctly translate a call to that function. The compiler translates a function call statement as a transfer of control to the function.

After compiling the main function, the compiler translates each function subprogram. During translation, when the compiler reaches the end of a function body, it inserts a machine language statement that causes a *transfer of control* back from the function to the calling statement.

Figure 3.15 shows the main function and function `draw_circle` of the stick figure program in separate areas of memory. Although the C statements are shown in Fig. 3.15, it is actually the object code corresponding to each statement that is stored in memory.

When we run the program, the first statement in the main function is the first statement executed (the call to `draw_circle` in Fig. 3.15). When the computer executes a function call statement, it transfers control to the function that is referenced (indicated by the colored line in Fig. 3.15). The computer allocates any memory that may be needed for variables declared in the function and then performs the statements in the function body. After the last statement in function `draw_circle` is executed, control returns to the main function (indicated by the black line in Fig. 3.15), and the computer releases any memory that was allocated to the function. After the return to the main function, the next statement is executed (the call to `draw_triangle`).

Advantages of Using Function Subprograms

There are many advantages to using function subprograms. Their availability changes the way in which an individual programmer organizes the solution to a programming problem. For a team of programmers working together on a large program, subprograms make it easier to apportion programming tasks: Each programmer will be responsible for a particular set of functions. Finally, they simplify programming tasks because existing functions can be reused as the building blocks for new programs.

Procedural Abstraction   Function subprograms allow us to remove from the main function the code that provides the detailed solution to a subproblem. Because these details are provided in the function subprograms and not in the main function,

FIGURE 3.15

Flow of Control Between the main Function and a Function Subprogram

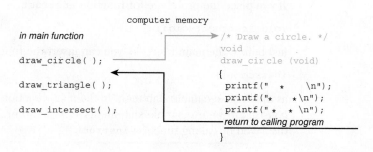

we can write the main function as a sequence of function call statements as soon as we have specified the initial algorithm and before we refine any of the steps. We should delay writing the function for an algorithm step until we have finished refining that step. With this approach to program design, called **procedural abstraction**, we defer implementation details until we are ready to write an individual function subprogram. Focusing on one function at a time is much easier than trying to write the complete program all at once.

procedural abstraction
a programming tech-nique in which a main function consists of a sequence of function calls and each function is implemented separately

Reuse of Function Subprograms   Another advantage of using function subprograms is that functions can be executed more than once in a program. For example, function `draw_intersect` is called twice in Fig. 3.14 (once by `draw_triangle` and once by the main function). Each time `draw_intersect` is called, the list of output statements shown in Fig. 3.14 is executed and a pair of intersecting lines is drawn. Without functions, the `printf` statements that draw the lines would be listed twice in the main function, thereby increasing the main function's length and the chance of error.

Finally, once you have written and tested a function, you can use it in other programs or functions. For example, the functions in the stick figure program could easily be reused in programs that draw other diagrams.

Displaying User Instructions

The simple functions introduced in this section have limited capability. Without the ability to pass information into or out of a function, we can use functions only to display multiple lines of program output, such as instructions to a program user or a title page or a special message that precedes a program's results.

EXAMPLE 3.4   Let's write a function (Fig. 3.16) that displays instructions to a user of the program that computes the area and the circumference of a circle (see Fig. 3.3). This simple function demonstrates one of the benefits of separating the statements that display user instructions from the main function body: Editing these instructions is simplified when they are separated from the code that performs the calculations.

If you place the prototype for function `instruct`

```
void instruct(void);
```

just before the main function, you can insert the function call statement

```
instruct();
```

as the first executable statement in the main function. The rest of the main function consists of the executable statements shown earlier. Figure 3.16 shows the output displayed by calling function `instruct`.

FIGURE 3.16   Function instruct and the Output Produced by a Call

```
1.  /*
2.   * Displays instructions to a user of program to compute
3.   * the area and circumference of a circle.
4.   */
5.  void
6.  instruct(void)
7.  {
8.        printf("This program computes the area\n");
9.        printf("and circumference of a circle.\n\n");
10.       printf("To use this program, enter the radius of\n");
11.       printf("the circle after the prompt: Enter radius>\n");
12. }
```

```
This program computes the area
and circumference of a circle.

To use this program, enter the radius of
the circle after the prompt: Enter radius>
```

EXERCISES FOR SECTION 3.4

Self-Check

1. Assume that you have functions print_h, print_i, print_m, and print_o, each of which draws a large block letter (for example, print_o draws a block letter o). What is the effect of executing the following main function?

```
int
main(void)
{
      print_h();
      print_i();
      printf("\n\n\n");
      print_m();
      print_o();
      print_m();

      return (0);
}
```

2. Draw a structure chart for a program with three function subprograms that displays DOLL in a vertical column of block letters.

Programming

1. Write a function `draw_parallel` that draws parallel lines and a function `draw_rectangle` that uses `draw_parallel` and `draw_base` to draw a rectangle.
2. Write a complete program for the problem described in Self-Check Exercise 2.
3. Rewrite the miles-to-kilometers conversion program shown in Fig. 2.1, so that it includes a function that displays instructions to its user.
4. Show the revised program that calls function `instruct` for the circle area and circumference problem.

3.5   Functions with Input Arguments

Programmers use functions like building blocks to construct large programs. Functions are more like Lego® blocks (Fig. 3.17) than the smooth-sided wooden blocks you might have used as a young child to demonstrate your potential as a budding architect. Your first blocks were big and did not link together, so buildings over a certain size would topple over. Legos, in contrast, have one surface with little protrusions and one surface with little cups. By placing the protrusions into the cups, you could build rather elaborate structures.

What does this have to do with programming? Simple functions like `draw_circle` and `instruct` are like wooden blocks. They can display information on the screen, but they are not particularly useful. To be able to construct more interesting programs, we must provide functions with "protrusions" and "cups" so they can be easily interconnected.

FIGURE 3.17

Lego® Blocks

The arguments of a function are used to carry information into the function subprogram from the main function (or from another function subprogram) or to return multiple results computed by a function subprogram. Arguments that carry information into the function subprogram are called **input arguments**; arguments that return results are called **output arguments**. We can also return a single result from a function by executing a `return` statement in the function body. We study functions with input arguments in this section and functions with output arguments in Chapter 6.

input arguments
arguments used to pass information into a function subprogram

output arguments
arguments used to return results to the calling function

The use of arguments is a very important concept in programming. Arguments make function subprograms more versatile because they enable a function to manipulate different data each time it is called. For example, in the statement

```
rim_area = find_area(edge_radius) - find_area(hole_radius);
```

each call to function `find_area` calculates the area of a circle with a different radius.

void Functions with Input Arguments

In the last section, we used `void` functions like `instruct` and `draw_circle` to display several lines of program output. Recall that a `void` function does not return a result. We can use a `void` function with an argument to "dress up" our program output by having the function display its argument value in a more attractive way.

EXAMPLE 3.5   Function `print_rboxed` (Fig. 3.18) displays the value of its argument, a real number, in a box. The real number is displayed on the third line starting at the position of the placeholder `%7.2f`. When function `print_rboxed` is called, the value

FIGURE 3.18   Function print_rboxed and Sample Run

```
1.  /*
2.   * Displays a real number in a box.
3.   */
4.
5.  void
6.  print_rboxed(double rnum)
7.  {
8.       printf("***********\n");
9.       printf("*         *\n");
10.      printf("* %7.2f *\n", rnum);
11.      printf("*         *\n");
12.      printf("***********\n");
13. }
```

(continued)

FIGURE 3.18   (continued)

```
***********
*         *
*  135.68 *
*         *
***********
```

of its **actual argument** (135.68) is passed into the function and substituted for its **formal parameter** rnum. Because rnum appears only in the third call to printf, the real number 135.68 is displayed once inside the box. Figure 3.19 shows the effect of the function call

```
print_rboxed(135.68);
```

Functions with Input Arguments and a Single Result

Next, we show how to write functions with input arguments that return a single result, as diagrammed in Fig. 3.20. We can call or reference these functions in expressions just like the library functions described in Section 3.2. For example, if we write our own function f that has two type double inputs, we can reference it in an expression such as w + f(2.5, 4.0). This expression means execute function f with a first argument of 2.5 and a second argument of 4.0. Add the function result to w.

Let's reconsider the problem of finding the area and circumference of a circle using functions with just one argument. Section 3.2 described functions find_circum and find_area, each of which has a single input argument (a circle radius) and returns a single result (the circle circumference or area). Figure 3.21 shows these functions.

FIGURE 3.19

Effect of Executing
print_rboxed
(135.68);

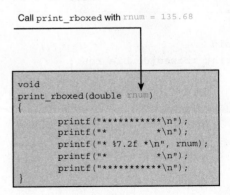

FIGURE 3.20

Function with
Input Arguments
and One Result

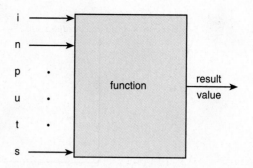

FIGURE 3.21   Functions find_circum and find_area

```
1.  /*
2.   * Computes the circumference of a circle with radius r.
3.   * Pre: r is defined and is > 0.
4.   *     PI is a constant macro representing an approximation of pi.
5.   */
6.  double
7.  find_circum(double r)
8.  {
9.      return (2.0 * PI * r);
10. }
11.
12. /*
13.  * Computes the area of a circle with radius r.
14.  * Pre: r is defined and is > 0.
15.  *     PI is a constant macro representing an approximation of pi.
16.  *     Library math.h is included.
17.  */
18. double
19. find_area(double r)
20. {
21.     return (PI * pow(r, 2));
22. }
```

Each function heading begins with the word `double`, indicating that the function result is a real number. Both function bodies consist of a single `return` statement. When either function executes, the expression in its `return` statement is evaluated and returned as the function result. If `PI` is the constant macro `3.14159`, calling function `find_circum` causes the expression `2.0 * 3.14159 * r` to be

FIGURE 3.22

Effect of Executing
`circum = find_circum(radius);`

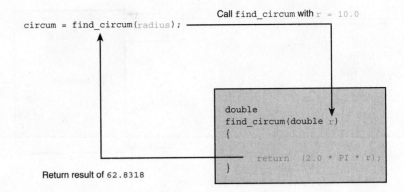

evaluated. To evaluate this expression, C substitutes the actual argument used in the function call for the formal parameter `r`.

For the function call below

```
radius = 10.0;
circum = find_circum(radius);
```

the actual argument, `radius`, has a value of `10.0`, so the function result is `62.8318` (`2.0 * 3.14159 * 10.0`). The function result is assigned to `circum`. Figure 3.22 illustrates the function execution.

The function call to `find_area`

```
area = find_area(radius);
```

causes C to evaluate the expression `3.14159 * pow(r, 2)`, where `pow` is a library function (part of `math.h`) that raises its first argument to the power indicated by its second argument (`pow(r, 2)` computes r^2). When `radius` is `10.0`, `pow` returns `100.0` and `find_area` returns a result of `314.59`, which is assigned to `area`. This example shows that a user-defined function can call a C library function.

Function Definition (Input Arguments and Single Result)

SYNTAX: *function interface comment*
            ftype
            fname (*formal parameter declaration list*)
            {
                    local variable declarations
                    executable statements

            }

                                                    (continued)

EXAMPLE:
```
/*
 * Finds the cube of its argument.
 * Pre: n is defined.
 */
int
cube(int n)
{
      return (n * n * n);
}
```

INTERPRETATION: The *function interface comment* is described in the next Program Style display. The next two lines are the function heading, which specifies the function name, *fname*, and the type of the result returned, *ftype*. It also indicates the names and types of the formal parameters in the *formal parameter declaration list*. Note that the lines of the heading do not end in semicolons. The braces enclose the function body. The type of any additional variables needed should be declared in the *local variable declarations*. The *executable statements* describe the data manipulation that the function performs on the parameters and local variables in order to compute the result value. Execution of a **return** statement causes the function to **return** control to the statement that called it. The function returns the value of the expression following **return** as its result.

Note: Use **void** as the *formal parameter declaration list* to indicate that a function has no arguments. The parentheses around the expression that follows **return** are not required.

Program Style   *Function Interface Comment*

The block comment and heading that begin each function in Fig. 3.21 contain all the information required in order to use the function. The function interface block comment begins with a statement of what the function does. Then the line

```
* Pre: n is defined.
```

describes the condition that should be true before the function is called; this condition is known as the **precondition**. You will also want to include a statement describing the condition that must be true after the function completes execution, if some details of this **postcondition** are not included in the initial statement of the function's purpose.

precondition
a condition assumed to be true before a function call

postcondition
a condition assumed to be true after a function executes

We recommend that you begin all function definitions in this way. The function interface comment combined with the heading (or prototype) provides valuable documentation to other programmers who might want to reuse your functions in a new program without reading the function code.

Functions with Multiple Arguments

Functions `find_area` and `find_circum` each have a single argument. We can also define functions with multiple arguments.

EXAMPLE 3.6   Function `scale` (Fig. 3.23) multiplies its first argument (a real number) by 10 raised to the power indicated by its second argument (an integer). For example, the function call

```
scale(2.5, 2)
```

returns the value `250.0` (2.5×10^2). The function call

```
scale(2.5, -2)
```

returns the value `0.025` (2.5×10^{-2}).

In function `scale`, the statement

```
scale_factor = pow(10, n);
```

calls function `pow` to raise 10 to the power specified by the second formal parameter n. Local variable `scale_factor`, defined only during the execution of the function, stores this value. The `return` statement defines the function result as the product of the first formal parameter, x, and `scale_factor`.

Figure 3.24 shows a very simple main function written to test function `scale`. The prototype for function `scale` is

```
double scale(double x, int n);
```

FIGURE 3.23   Function scale

```
1.  /*
2.   * Multiplies its first argument by the power of 10 specified
3.   * by its second argument.
4.   * Pre : x and n are defined and math.h is included.
5.   */
6.  double
7.  scale(double x, int n)
8.  {
9.      double scale_factor;    /* local variable */
10.     scale_factor = pow(10, n);
11.
12.     return (x * scale_factor);
13. }
```

FIGURE 3.24   Testing Function scale

```
1.  /*
2.   * Tests function scale.
3.   */
4.  #include <stdio.h>          /* printf, scanf definitions */
5.  #include <math.h>           /* pow definition */
6.
7.  /* Function prototype */
8.  double scale(double x, int n);
9.
10. int
11. main(void)
12. {
13.        double num_1;
14.        int num_2;
15.
16.        /* Get values for num_1 and num_2 */
17.        printf("Enter a real number> ");
18.        scanf("%lf", &num_1);
19.        printf("Enter an integer> ");
20.        scanf("%d", &num_2);
21.
22.        /* Call scale and display result. */
23.        printf("Result of call to function scale is %f\n",
24.               scale(num_1, num_2));          actual arguments
25.
26.        return (0);
27. }
28.                                              information flow
29.
30. double
31. scale(double x, int n)                       formal parameters
32. {
33.        double scale_factor;       /* local variable - 10 to power n */
34.
35.        scale_factor = pow(10, n);
36.
37.        return (x * scale_factor);
38. }

Enter a real number> 2.5
Enter an integer> -2
Result of call to function scale is 0.025
```

The `printf` statement calls function `scale` and displays the function result after it is returned. The arrows drawn in Fig. 3.24 show the information flow between the two actual arguments and formal parameters. To clarify the information flow, we omitted the function interface comment. The argument list correspondence is shown below.

Actual Argument	corresponds to	*Formal Parameter*
num_1		x
num_2		n

Argument List Correspondence

When using multiple-argument functions, you must be careful to include the correct number of arguments in the function call. Also, the order of the actual arguments used in the function call must correspond to the order of the formal parameters listed in the function prototype or heading.

Finally, if the function is to return meaningful results, assignment of each actual argument to the corresponding formal parameter must not cause any loss of information. Usually, you should use an actual argument of the same data type as the corresponding formal parameter, although this is not always essential. For example, the `<math.h>` library description indicates that both parameters of the function `pow` are of type `double`. Function `scale` calls `pow` with two actual arguments of type `int`. This call does not cause a problem because there is no loss of information when an `int` is assigned to a type `double` variable. If you pass an actual argument of type `double` to a formal parameter of type `int`, loss of the fractional part of the actual argument would likely lead to an unexpected function result. Next, we summarize these constraints on the **n**umber, **o**rder, and **t**ype (**not**) of input arguments.

Argument List Correspondence

- The **n**umber of actual arguments used in a call to a function must be the same as the number of formal parameters listed in the function prototype.
- The **o**rder of arguments in the lists determines correspondence. The first actual argument corresponds to the first formal parameter, the second actual argument corresponds to the second formal parameter, and so on.
- Each actual argument must be of a data **t**ype that can be assigned to the corresponding formal parameter with no unexpected loss of information.

The Function Data Area

Each time a function call is executed, an area of memory is allocated for storage of that function's data. Included in the function data area are storage cells for its formal parameters and any local variables that may be declared in the function. The function data area is always lost when the function terminates; it is recreated empty (all values undefined) when the function is called again.

FIGURE 3.25

Data Areas After
Call scale(num_1,
num_2);

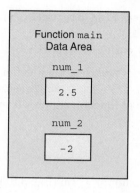

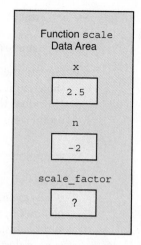

Figure 3.25 shows the main function data area and the data area for function scale when the function call scale(num_1, num_2) is executing. The values 2.5 and -2 are passed into the formal parameters x and n, respectively. The local variable, scale_factor, is initially undefined; the execution of the function body changes the value of this variable to 0.01.

The local variable scale_factor can be accessed only in function scale. Similarly, the variables num_1 and num_2 declared in function main can be accessed only in function main. If you want a function subprogram to use the value stored in num_1, you must provide num_1 as an actual argument when you call the function.

Testing Functions Using Drivers

driver a short function written to test another function by defining its arguments, calling it, and displaying its result

A function is an independent program module, and as such, it can be tested separately from the program that uses it. To run such a test, you should write a short **driver** function that defines the function arguments, calls the function, and displays the value returned. For example, the function main in Fig. 3.24 acts as a driver to test function scale.

EXERCISES FOR SECTION 3.5

Self-Check

1. Evaluate each of the following:

    a.   scale(3.14159, 3)
    b.   find_circum(5.0)

    c.   `print_rboxed(find_circum(5.0))`
    d.   `find_area(1.0)`
    e.   `scale(find_area(10.0), -2)`

2. Explain the effect of reversing the function arguments in the call to `scale` shown in Example 3.6—that is, `scale(num_2, num_1)`.

3. How does the use of function arguments make it possible to write larger, more useful programs?

Programming

1. Revise the flat-washer program (Fig. 3.5) to use function subprograms `find_area`, `find_rim_area`, `find_unit_weight`, and `instruct`. Show the complete program.

2. Write a function that computes the time one must leave in order to reach a certain destination by a designated time. You need to deal only with arrivals occurring later in the same day as the departure. Function inputs include the arrival time as an integer on a 24-hour clock (8:30 P.M. = 2030), the distance to the destination in kilometers, and the speed you plan to average in km/hr. The function result should be the required departure time (rounded to the nearest minute) as an integer on a 24-hour clock. Also, write a driver program to test your function.

3.6 Introduction to Computer Graphics (Optional)

text mode a display mode in which a C program displays only characters

graphics mode a display mode in which a C program draws graphics patterns and shapes in an output window

In normal computer display mode (called **text mode**), we use `printf` to display lines of characters to the standard output device, or console. In Section 3.3, we showed how to write C functions for drawing simple stick figures using text mode. In several optional sections beginning with this one, we discuss another display mode (called **graphics mode**) that enables a C program to draw pictures or graphical patterns in an output window. To write graphics programs, you must learn how to use special graphics functions that enable you to draw lines and various geometric shapes (for example, rectangles, circles, and ellipses) anywhere on your screen and color and shade them in different ways.

    Several programming languages include graphics libraries. Although there is no standard graphics library for C, several libraries have been developed for use with C. We will study a simple graphics library called WinBGIm, which is based on Borland Turbo Pascal Graphics, with the addition of mouse control. This library was developed by Professor Michael Main of the Computer Science Department, University of Colorado, Boulder. The principles we study will apply to other graphics libraries you may use in the future.

Composition of a Window

In text mode, you don't pay much attention to the position of each line of characters displayed on the screen. In graphics programming, you control the location of each line or shape that you draw in a window. Consequently, you must know your window size and how to reference the individual picture elements (called **pixels**) in a window.

pixel a picture element on a computer screen

You can visualize a window as an *x-y* grid of pixels. Assume that your window has the dimensions 400×300. Figure 3.26 shows the coordinates for the four pixels at the corners. The pixel at the top-left corner has *x-y* coordinates $(0, 0)$, and the pixel at the top-right corner has *x-y* coordinates $(400, 0)$.

Notice the pixels in the *y*-direction are numbered differently from how we are accustomed. The pixel $(0, 0)$ is at the top-left corner of the screen, and the *y*-coordinate values increase as we move down the screen. In a normal *x-y* coordinate system, the point $(0, 0)$ is at the bottom-left corner.

Some Common Graphics Functions

A graphics program is a sequence of statements that call graphics functions to do the work. Figure 3.27 is a program that uses several key functions. The functions `getmaxwidth` and `getmaxheight` return the position of the last pixel in the *X*- and *Y*-directions on your computer screen. Some typical screen dimensions are 640×480 for 14-inch screens and 1366×768 for 15-inch screens, but the largest window will be slightly smaller. Therefore, the statements

```
bigx = getmaxwidth();   /* get largest x-coordinate. */
bigy = getmaxheight();  /* get largest y-coordinate. */
initwindow(bigx, bigy,
   "Full screen window - press a character to close window");
```

FIGURE 3.26

Referencing Pixels in a Window

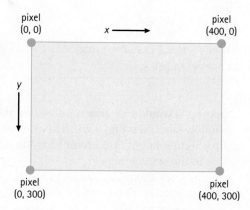

FIGURE 3.27   Drawing Intersecting Lines

```
1.  /* Displays screen size and draws intersecting lines */
2.
3.  #include <graphics.h>
4.
5.  int
6.  main(void)
7.  {
8.      int bigX;                        /* largest x-coordinate */
9.      int bigY;                        /* largest y-coordinate */
10.
11.     bigX = getmaxwidth();            /* get largest x-coordinate */
12.     bigY = getmaxheight();           /* get largest y-coordinate */
13.     initwindow(bigX, bigY,
14.               "Full screen window - press a key to close");
15.
16.     /* Draw intersecting lines */
17.     /* Draw white line from (0, 0) to (bigX, bigY) */
18.     line(0, 0, bigX, bigY);
19.     setcolor(BLUE);                  /* Change color to blue */
20.     /* Draw blue line from (bigX, 0) to (0, bigY) */
21.     line(bigX, 0, 0, bigY);
22.
23.     /* Display window size in console */
24.     printf("Window size is %d X %d", bigX, bigY);
25.
26.      /* Close screen when ready */
27.     getch();                         /* pause until user presses a key */
28.     closegraph();                    /* close the window */
29.
30.     return(0);
31. }
```

```
Window size is 1018 X 736
```

pop up a window of maximum width and height with the third argument as the window label (see Fig. 3.28). The window position is set by the optional fourth and fifth arguments. If they are missing, the top-left corner of the window is at $(0, 0)$.

In the statements

```
line(0, 0, bigX, bigY);  /* Draw white line from(0, 0) to
                               (bigX, bigY) */
setcolor(BLUE);          /* Change color to blue */
line(bigX, 0, 0, bigY);  /* Draw blue line from (bigX, 0) to (0, bigY) */
```

FIGURE 3.28

Window Drawn by
`lines.c`

the two calls to function `line` draw a pair of intersecting lines in this window. Method `setcolor` changes the drawing color from white (the default color) to blue for the second line. Then, the statements

```
getch();        /* pause until user presses a key */
closegraph();   /* close the window */
```

call the `getch` function (also part of `graphics.h`) to pause the program until the user presses a key. Once a key is pressed, or the user clicks on the close icon on the top right ☒, the `closegraph` function closes the window. Finally, the statement beginning with `printf` displays the window size in the console window as normal text output.

Program Style   *Camelback Notation*

In the optional graphics sections, we use *CamelBack* notation for variable names rather than the usual C naming convention. This means that we will capitalize the start of each new word in a variable name rather than use the underscore symbol between words. For example, `bigX` instead of `big_x` and `myLastName` instead of `my_last_name`.

Background Color and Foreground Color

In graphics mode, the computer displays all pixels continuously in one of 16 colors. The default color used to display a pixel is called the background color. Consequently, your initial display window appears empty because all its pixels are displayed in the **background color**. When you draw a line or a shape, the pixels it contains stand out because they are changed to the **foreground color**.

background color
the default color for all of the pixels in a display window

foreground color
the new color of pixels that are part of a graphics object in a display window

Black and white are the default values for the background and foreground colors, respectively. The statements

```
setbkcolor(GREEN);   /* GREEN is the background color. */
setcolor(RED);       /* RED is the foreground color. */
```

reset the background color to GREEN and the foreground color to RED where GREEN and RED are color constants defined in `graphics.h`. You select a color constant from the list shown in Table 3.2, using either the constant name or its numeric value as a parameter (for example, RED or 4). Once you change the foreground or background color, it retains its new value until you change it again.

Drawing Rectangles

We use function `rectangle` to draw a rectangle in a window. The statement

```
rectangle(x1, y1, x2, y2);
```

draws a rectangle that has one diagonal with end points (x1, y1) and (x2, y2).

EXAMPLE 3.7   The program in Fig. 3.29 draws a house (Fig. 3.30). The program begins by defining the corner points of the house, where the roof is a pair of lines intersecting

TABLE 3.2 Color Constants

Constant	Value	Constant	Value
BLACK	0	DARKGRAY	8
BLUE	1	LIGHTBLUE	9
GREEN	2	LIGHTGREEN	10
CYAN	3	LIGHTCYAN	11
RED	4	LIGHTRED	12
MAGENTA	5	LIGHTMAGENTA	13
BROWN	6	YELLOW	14
LIGHTGRAY	7	WHITE	15

FIGURE 3.29 Drawing a House

```
1.   /* Draws a house */
2.
3.   #include <graphics.h>
4.
5.   int
6.   main(void)
7.   {
8.      initwindow(640, 500,
                   "House - press a key to close", 100, 50);
9.
10.     /* Define corners of house */
11.     int x1 = 100; int y1 = 200;          /* top-left corner */
12.     int x2 = 300; int y2 = 100;              /* roof peak */
13.     int x3 = 500; int y3 = 200;          /* top-right corner */
14.     int x4 = 500; int y4 = 400;        /* bottom-right corner */
15.     int x5 = 325; int y5 = 400;   /* bottom-right corner of door */
16.     int x6 = 275; int y6 = 325;      /* top-left corner of door */
17.
18.     /* Draw roof. */
19.     line(x1, y1, x2, y2);   /* Draw line from (x1, y1) to (x2, y2) */
20.     line(x2, y2, x3, y3);   /* Draw line from (x2, y2) to (x3, y3) */
21.
22.     /* Draw rest of house. */
23.     rectangle(x1, y1, x4, y4);
24.
25.     /* Draw door. */
26.     rectangle(x5, y5, x6, y6);
27.
28.     getch();            /* pause until user presses a key */
29.     closegraph();       /* close the window */
30.
31.     return(0);
32.   }
```

at point (x2, y2). The first call to rectangle draws the rest of the house, and the second call to rectangle draws the door. We drew the house in a window of size 640 × 500, with the top-left corner of the window at point (100, 50) of the screen.

FIGURE 3.30

House Drawn by
`house.c`

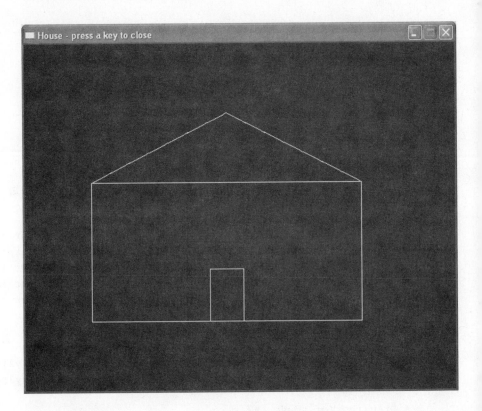

Drawing Circles, Ellipses, and Arcs

We use function `circle` to draw a circle. The function call statement

```
circle(x, y, radius);
```

draws a circle whose center is at `(x, y)`. The third parameter is the circle radius.

Function `arc` draws an arc, or part of a circle. To draw an arc, you must specify its starting angle and ending angle in degrees. The statement

```
arc(x, y, 0, 180, radius);
```

draws the top half of a circle with center at `(x, y)`. If you imagine a clock on the screen, 0 degrees is at 3 o'clock (horizontal direction), 30 degrees is at 2 o'clock, 60 degrees is at 1 o'clock, 90 degrees is at 12 o'clock (vertical direction), and function `ellipse` draws an ellipse or a portion of an ellipse: the third argument is the start angle, the fourth argument is the end angle, the fifth argument is the horizontal radius, and the sixth argument is the vertical radius. The statement

```
ellipse(x, y, 0, 360, radius, 2 * radius);
```

draws a complete ellipse that is twice as high as it is wide.

EXAMPLE 3.8　The program in Fig. 3.31 draws a happy face (Fig. 3.32). It begins by completing an outer circle (radius headRadius), then it draws three smaller circles (radius eyeNoseRadius) representing the eyes and nose. Finally, it draws the smile as an

FIGURE 3.31　Program to Draw a Happy Face

```
1.   /* Draws a happy face */
2.
3.   #include <graphics.h>
4.
5.   int
6.   main(void)
7.   {
8.      int midX, midY,               /* coordinates of center point */
9.          leftEyeX, rightEyeX, eyeY,  /* eye center points */
10.         noseX, noseY,             /* nose center point */
11.         headRadius,               /* head radius */
12.         eyeNoseRadius,            /* eye/nose radius */
13.         smileRadius,              /* smile radius */
14.         stepX, stepY;             /* x and y increments */
15.
16.     initwindow(500, 400,
17.              "Happy Face - press key to close", 200, 150);
18.
19.     /* draw head */
20.     midX = getmaxx() / 2;          /* center head in x-direction */
21.     midY = getmaxy() / 2;          /* center head in y-direction */
22.     headRadius = getmaxy() / 4;   /* head will fill half the window */
23.     circle(midX, midY, headRadius); /* draw head */
24.
25.     /* draw eyes */
26.     stepX = headRadius / 4;         /* x-offset for eyes */
27.     stepY = stepX;                  /* y-offset for eyes and nose */
28.     leftEyeX = midX - stepX;        /* x-coordinate for right eye */
29.     eyeY = midY - stepY;            /* y-coordinate for both eyes */
30.     eyeNoseRadius = headRadius / 10;
31.     circle(leftEyeX,  eyeY, eyeNoseRadius);   /* draw left eye. */
32.     circle(rightEyeX, eyeY, eyeNoseRadius);   /* draw right eye. */
33.
```

(continued)

FIGURE 3.31 (continued)

```
34.    /* draw nose */
35.    noseX = midX;              /* nose is centered in x direction. */
36.    noseY = midY + stepY;
37.    circle(noseX, noseY, eyeNoseRadius);
38.
39.    /* draw smile */
40.    smileRadius = (int)(0.75 * headRadius + 0.5);
41.    arc(midX, midY, 210, 330, smileRadius);
42.
43.    getch();
44.    closegraph();
45.
46.    return(0);
47. }
```

FIGURE 3.32

Happy Face Drawn
by happyFace.c

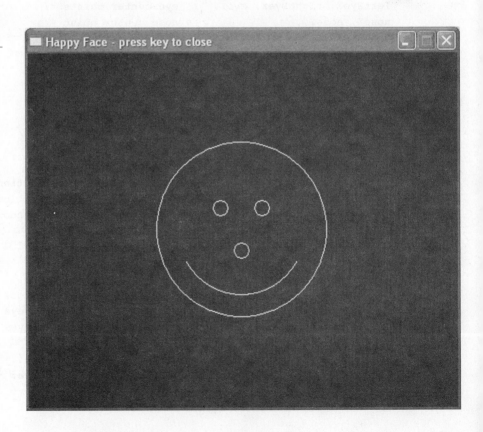

arc from 210 degrees (8 o'clock) to 330 degrees (4 o'clock). The arc has the same center as the outer circle, but its radius is 75% as large:

```
smileRadius = int(0.75 * headRadius + 0.5);
                            /* 3/4 of head radius */
arc(midX, midY, 210, 330, smileRadius);
```

Note that this program uses functions `getmaxx` and `getmaxy` to determine the width and height of the drawing window, instead of `getmaxwidth` and `getmaxheight`, which return the screen width and height. The statements

```
midX = getmaxx() / 2;       /* center head in x-direction */
midY = getmaxy() / 2;       /* center head in y-direction */
```

use these functions to find the coordinates of the center of the window.

Program Style   *Writing General Graphics Programs*

The program in Fig. 3.31 is general and bases the happy face position and dimensions on the window dimensions as determined by `getmaxx` and `getmaxy`. If you change the window dimensions, the happy face will expand or shrink to fit. Conversely, the size of the house drawn by the program in Fig. 3.29 is fixed and is independent of the window size. If the window is too small, part of the house may be missing. It is generally easier to draw figures with fixed dimensions; however, with a little practice you should be able to draw general graphics figures. To generalize the program in Fig. 3.29, you could base the coordinates of the house corners on the window dimensions as follows (see Self-Check Exercise 4).

```
x1 = getmaxx() / 4; y1 = getmaxy() / 2; /* top-left corner */
x2 = getmaxx() / 2; y2 = getmaxy() / 4; /* roof peak */
```

Drawing Filled Figures   So far, all our graphics figures have been line drawings. To fill in sections of the screen using different colors and patterns, you would use function `setfillstyle` to specify the pattern and color. The function call statement

```
setfillstyle(SLASH_FILL, RED);
```

sets the fill pattern to red slashes until you change it through another call to `setfillstyle`. Table 3.3 shows the options for the first parameter in a call to `setfillstyle`. Use either the constant name or its value (for example, `SLASH_FILL` or 4) and any color constant in Table 3.2 as the second parameter.

Use function `floodfill` to actually fill in a portion of a diagram. The function call statement

```
floodfill(x, y, WHITE);
```

TABLE 3.3 Fill Pattern Constants

Constant	Value	Fill Pattern	Constant	Value	Fill Pattern
EMPTY_FILL	0	Background color	LTBKSLASH_FILL	6	\ \ \ (light)
SOLID_FILL	1	Solid color	HATCH_FILL	7	Hatch (light)
LINE_FILL	2	---	XHATCH_FILL	8	Crosshatch
LTSLASH_FILL	3	/ / / (light)	INTERLEAVE_FILL	9	Interleaving line
SLASH_FILL	4	/// (heavy)	WIDE_DOT_FILL	10	Dots (light)
BKSLASH_FILL	5	\\\ (heavy)	CLOSE_DOT_FILL	11	Dots (heavy)

fills with the current fill pattern an area on the screen that contains the point (x, y) and is bounded by white lines. If the point (x, y) is outside an area bounded by white lines, the exterior of the bounded figure is filled.

The floodfill function sometimes gives unexpected results and is a bit inefficient. As an alternative to drawing a rectangle and then filling it, function bar draws a filled rectangle. The function call statement

```
setfillstyle(SOLID_FILL, GREEN);
bar(x1, y1, x2, y2);
```

draws a green rectangle that has a diagonal with end points (x1, y1) and (x2, y2).

EXAMPLE 3.9   We can insert the following program fragment at the end of the program in Fig. 3.29 to paint the house (Fig. 3.33).

```
/* Paint the house */
setfillstyle(HATCH_FILL, LIGHTGRAY);
floodfill(x2, y2 + 10, WHITE);          /* Paint the roof */
setfillstyle(LINE_FILL, WHITE);
floodfill(x2, y1 + 10, WHITE);          /* Paint the house front */
```

In the two calls to floodfill, we use x2, the midpoint in the X-direction, as the first parameter. The second parameter (the Y-coordinate) determines which section (roof or house front) to fill in. All boundary lines for the house are white (the default foreground color), so the third parameter is WHITE. The roof is painted in a gray hatch pattern, the house itself is painted in a white lined pattern.

The call to function bar below paints the door blue. It replaces the earlier call to function rectangle with the same arguments. Figure 3.34 shows the complete program.

```
setfillstyle(SOLID_FILL, BLUE);
bar(x5, y5, x6, y6);            /* Draw blue door */
```

FIGURE 3.33

Painted House
Drawn by
paintedHouse.c

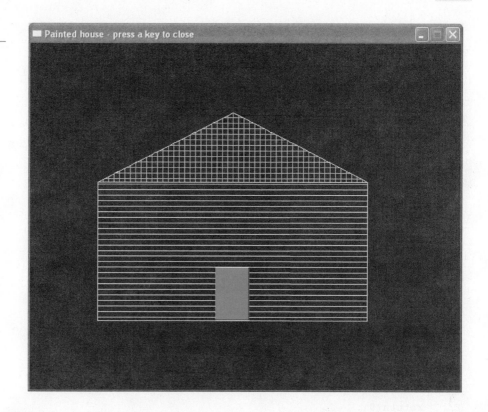

FIGURE 3.34   Program to Paint a House

```
 1.  /* Paints a house */
 3.  #include <graphics.h>
 4.
 5.  int
 6.  main(void)
 7.  {
 8.     /* Define corners of house */
 9.     int x1 = 100; int y1 = 200;          /* top-left corner */
10.     int x2 = 300; int y2 = 100;          /* roof peak */
11.     int x3 = 500; int y3 = 200;          /* top-right corner */
12.     int x4 = 500; int y4 = 400;          /* bottom-right corner */
13.     int x5 = 325; int y5 = 400;   /* bottom-right corner of door */
14.     int x6 = 275; int y6 = 325;          /* top-left corner of door */
15.
```

(continued)

FIGURE 3.34   (continued)

```
16.     initwindow(640, 500,
17.                 "Painted house - press a key to close", 100, 50);
18.
19.     /* Draw roof */
20.     line(x1, y1, x2, y2);
21.     line(x2, y2, x3, y3);
22.
23.     /* Draw rest of house */
24.     rectangle(x1, y1, x4, y4);
25.
26.     /* Paint the house */
27.     setfillstyle(HATCH_FILL, LIGHTGRAY);
28.     floodfill(x2, y2 + 10,  WHITE);        /* Paint the roof */
29.     setfillstyle(LINE_FILL, WHITE);
30.     floodfill(x2, y1 + 10, WHITE);         /* Paint the house */
31.
32.     setfillstyle(SOLID_FILL, BLUE);
33.     bar(x5, y5, x6, y6);                   /* Draw blue door */
34.
35.     getch();
36.     closegraph();
37.
38.     return(0);
39. }
```

Program Pitfall   Incorrect Order of Function Calls Draws over Earlier Results

The order of statement execution is critical in all programs, but an incorrect order can cause strange results in graphics program. If you call function `bar` to paint the door blue before calling `floodfill` to paint the house front, `floodfill` will change the color of the pixels in the door to white, and it will not appear in the window.

Pie Slices and Filled Ellipses

Function `pieslice` draws a filled pie slice (section of a circle) and `fillellipse` draws a filled ellipse or circle. Insert the statement below at the end of Fig. 3.31 to change the happy face smile to a frown (replaces the original call to function `arc`).

The last statement below calls `pieslice` to draw an eye patch over the pirate's right eye (Fig. 3.35).

```
arc(midX, midY + headRadius, 65, 115, smileRadius / 2);
                                /* Draw frown      */
setfillstyle(CLOSE_DOT_FILL, WHITE);
pieslice(midX, midY, 10, 60, smileRadius);
                                /* Draw eye patch */
```

The eye patch is a pie slice with radius `smileRadius` centered at point (`midX`, `midY`). The pie slice goes from 10 degrees to 60 degrees. The final program is shown in Fig. 3.36.

You can use the `pieslice` and `bar` functions to draw pie charts and bar graphs (see Programming Projects 16 and 17 at the end of the chapter). We describe how to display the message shown under the happy face next.

FIGURE 3.35

Pirate Drawn by `pirate.c`

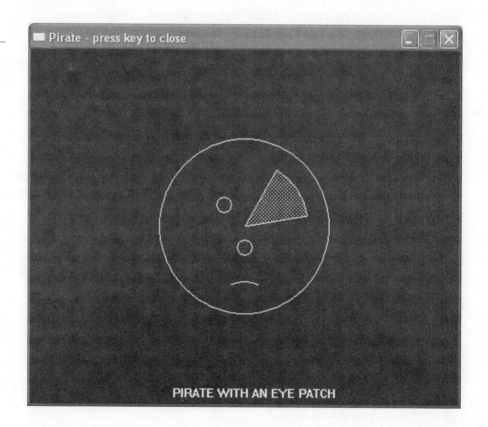

FIGURE 3.36 Program to Draw a Pirate

```
1.  /* Draws a pirate */
3.  #include <graphics.h>
4.
5.  int
6.  main(void)
7.  {
8.     int midX, midY;              /* coordinates of center point */
9.     int leftEyeX, rightEyeX, eyeY;    /* eye center points */
10.    int noseX, noseY;              /* nose center point */
11.    int headRadius;                /* head radius */
12.    int eyeNoseRadius;             /* eye/nose radius */
13.    int smileRadius;               /* smile radius */
14.    int stepX, stepY;              /* x and y increments */
15.
16.    initwindow(500, 400,
17.              "Pirate - press key to close", 200, 150);
18.
19.    /* Draw head. */
20.    midX = getmaxx() / 2;          /* center head in x-direction. */
21.    midY = getmaxy() / 2;          /* center head in y-direction. */
22.    headRadius = getmaxy() / 4;
23.    circle (midX, midY, headRadius);   /* draw head. */
24.
25.    /* Draw eyes. */
26.    stepX = headRadius / 4;         /* x-offset for eyes */
27.    stepY = stepX;                  /* y-offset for eyes and nose */
28.    leftEyeX = midX - stepX;        /* x-coordinate for left eye */
29.    rightEyeX = midX + stepX;       /* x-coordinate for right eye */
30.    eyeY = midY - stepY;            /* y-coordinate for both eyes */
31.    eyeNoseRadius = headRadius / 10;
32.    circle(leftEyeX,  eyeY, eyeNoseRadius);    /* draw left eye. */
33.    circle(rightEyeX, eyeY, eyeNoseRadius);    /* draw right eye. */
34.
35.    /* Draw nose. */
36.    noseX = midX;                   /* nose is centered in x direction. */
37.    noseY = midY + stepY;
38.    circle(noseX, noseY, eyeNoseRadius);
39.
40.    /* Draw smile -- use 3/4 of head radius. */
41.    smileRadius = (int)(0.75 * headRadius + 0.5);
```

(continued)

FIGURE 3.36 (continued)

```
42.    /* Draw frown */
43.    arc(midX, midY + headRadius, 65, 115, smileRadius / 2);
44.
45.    setfillstyle(CLOSE_DOT_FILL, WHITE);
46.    pieslice(midX, midY, 10, 60, smileRadius); /* Draw eye patch */
47.
48.    outtextxy(getmaxx() / 3, getmaxy() - 20,
49.            "PIRATE WITH AN EYE PATCH");
50.
51.    getch();
52.    closegraph();
53.
54.    return(0);
55. }
```

Adding Text to Drawings

In graphics mode, you cannot use `printf` to display characters, but you must instead draw characters just as you draw other shapes. Fortunately, the graphics library provides a function that does this. The function call statement

```
outtextxy(getmaxx() / 3, getmaxy() - 20,
                "PIRATE WITH AN EYE PATCH");
```

draws each character in a string (its third parameter) starting at the pixel whose X-Y coordinates are specified by its first two parameters (see Fig. 3.35). You may see a warning message associated with `outtextxy` during program compilation, but you can ignore it.

Table 3.4 shows the functions in the graphics library. With the exception of `label` (in `init`) and `textString` (in `outtextxy`), all arguments are type `int`. We will pass string "literals" as arguments corresponding to `label` and `textString`.

TABLE 3.4 Functions in Graphics Library

Function	Effect
arc(x, y, stAng, endAng, r)	Draws an arc from angle `stAng` to `endAng` with center at (x, y) and radius r
bar(x1, y1, x2, y2)	Draws a filled rectangle with a diagonal through points (x1, y1) and (x2, y2)

(continued)

Function	Effect
circle(x, y, r)	Draws a circle with center at (x, y) and radius r
closegraph()	Closes graphics mode
ellipse(x, y, stAng, endAng, xRad, yRad)	Draws an ellipse with center at (x, y) from stAng to endAng with xRad as horizontal radius and yRad as vertical radius
fillellipse(x, y, xRad, yRad)	Draws a filled ellipse with center at (x, y) with xRad as horizontal radius and yRad as vertical radius
floodfill(x, y, border)	Fills with the current fill pattern the figure containing the point (x, y) and bounded by lines with color border
getch()	Pauses the program until the user enters a character
getmaxheight()	Returns the position of the last pixel in the y-direction in the screen
getmaxwidth()	Returns the position of the last pixel in the x-direction in the screen
getmaxx()	Returns the window width in pixels
getmaxy()	Returns the window height in pixels
initgraph(x, y, label)	Displays a window x pixels wide and y pixels high with the given label and top-left corner at (0, 0)
initgraph(x, y, label, x0, y0)	Displays a window x pixels wide and y pixels high with the given label and top-left corner at (x0, y0)
line(x1, y1, x2, y2)	Draws a line with end points (x1, y1) and (x2, y2)
outtextxy(x, y, textString)	Draws the characters for textString starting at point (x, y)
pieslice(x, y, stAng, endAng, r)	Draws a filled pie slice with center at (x, y) from angle stAng to endAng with radius r
rectangle(x1, y1, x2, y2)	Draws a rectangle with a diagonal through points (x1, y1) and (x2, y2)
setbkcolor(backColor)	Sets the background color to backColor
setcolor(foreColor)	Sets the foreground color to foreColor
setfillstyle(filPat, filCol)	Sets the fill pattern to filPat and the fill color to filCol

EXERCISES FOR SECTION 3.6

Self-Check

1. In Fig. 3.36, what is the reason for basing the head radius on getmaxy and not getmaxx?

2. Describe or show the drawing produced by the following fragment. Assume a 640 × 480 window.

```
circle(200, 50, 25);
line(200, 75, 100, 100);
```

```
line(200, 75, 300, 100);
pieslice(200, 75, 245, 295, 100);
line(200, 150, 100, 250);
line(200, 150, 300, 250);
bar(50, 250, 350, 300);
```

3. Write statements to add two windows to the second floor of the house in Fig. 3.30.
4. Modify the program in Fig. 3.34 so that it draws the house in the center of the screen and with the same relative size regardless of the actual palette dimensions.

Programming

1. Write the statements to draw a tennis racket in the appropriate place in the figure for Self-Check Exercise 2. At the end of a thin bar, draw a circle and fill it with a green crosshatch pattern.
2. Write a graphics program that draws a rocket ship consisting of a triangle (the cone) on top of a rectangle (the body). Draw a pair of intersecting lines under the rectangle. Fill the cone with a blue hatch pattern and the body with a red solid pattern.
3. Write a program that draws a pair of nested rectangles at the center of the screen, filling the inner rectangle in red and the outer rectangle in white. The outer rectangle should have a width 1/4 of the X-dimension and a height 1/4 of the Y-dimension of the screen. The height and width of the inner rectangle should be half that of the outer rectangle.
4. Write a program that draws a male and a female stick figure side-by-side.

3.7 Common Programming Errors

Remember to use a #include preprocessor directive for every standard library from which you are using functions. Place prototypes for your own function subprograms in the source file preceding the main function; place the actual function definitions after the main function.

Syntax or run-time errors may occur when you use functions. The acronym **not** summarizes the requirements for argument list correspondence. Provide the required **n**umber of arguments and make sure the **o**rder of arguments is correct. Make sure that each function argument is the correct **t**ype or that conversion to the correct type will lose no information. For user-defined functions, verify that each argument list is correct by comparing it to the formal parameter list in the function heading or prototype.

Also, be careful in using functions that are undefined on some range of values. For example, if the argument for function sqrt, log, or log10 is negative, a run-time error will occur.

Chapter Review

1. Develop your program solutions from existing information. Use the system documentation derived from applying the software development method as the initial framework for the program.

   ▪ Edit the data requirements to obtain the main function declarations.
   ▪ Use the refined algorithm as the starting point for the executable statements in the main function.

2. If a new problem is an extension of a previous one, modify the previous program rather than starting from scratch.

3. Use C's library functions to simplify mathematical computations through the reuse of code that has already been written and tested. Write a function call (consisting of the function name and arguments) to activate a library function. After the function executes, the function result is substituted for the function call.

4. Use a structure chart to show subordinate relationships between subproblems.

5. Utilize modular programming by writing separate function subprograms to implement the different subproblems in a structure chart. Ideally, your main function will consist of a sequence of function call statements that activate the function subprograms.

6. You can write functions without arguments and results to display a list of instructions to a program user or to draw a diagram on the screen. Use a function call consisting of the function name followed by an empty pair of parentheses ( ) to activate such a function.

7. Write functions that have input arguments and that return a single result to perform computations similar to those performed by library functions. When you call such a function, each actual argument value is assigned to its corresponding formal parameter.

8. Place prototypes (similar to function headings) for each function subprogram before the main function, and place the function definitions after the main function in a source file. Use (void) to indicate that a function has no parameters.

NEW C CONSTRUCTS

Construct	Effect
Function Prototype (void function without arguments)	
`void star_line(void);`	Describes `star_line` as a function with no result and no arguments

(continued)

NEW C CONSTRUCTS (continued)

Construct	Effect
Function Prototype (function with arguments and a result)	
`double ave(int n, double sum);`	Describes `ave` as a function with a type `double` result and two arguments, one type `int` and one type `double`
Function Call Statement (void function without arguments)	
`star_line();`	Calls function `star_line` and causes it to begin execution
Function Call (function with arguments and a result)	
`money = ave(num_kids, funds);`	Calls function `ave` to compute a result that is stored in `money`
Function Definition (void function without arguments)	

`void`
`star_line(void)`
`{`
`    printf("*\n*\n*\n*\n");`
`}`
	Defines `star_line` as a function that prints a vertical line of four asterisks

Function Definition (function with arguments and a result)	

`/*`
` * Returns the quotient of`
` * its 2 arguments.`
` * Pre : sum and n are`
` *       defined, sum >= 0,`
` *       n > 0.`
` * Post: result is sum / n`
` */`
`double`
`ave(int n, double sum)`
`{`
`    return (sum / n);`
`}`
	Defines `ave` as a function that returns the result of dividing its second argument by its first argument

Quick-Check Exercises

1. Developing a program from its documentation means that every statement in the program has a comment. True or false?
2. A conversion of type `double` to type `int` will result in the loss of any fractional part. True or false?

3. Write this expression as a C assignment statement using functions `exp`, `log`, and `pow`:

$$x = e^{w + \log n} + r^2$$

4. What is the purpose of a function argument?

5. Each function is executed in the order in which it is defined in the source file. True or false?

6. How is a function in a C program executed?

7. What is a formal parameter?

8. Explain how a structure chart differs from an algorithm.

9. What does the following function print?

```
      void
shape(void)
{
      printf("###\n");
      printf("###\n");
      printf("###\n");
}
```

10. What does the following main function do?

```
      int
main(void)
{
      shape();
      shape();
      shape();
            shape();
      return (0);
}
```

11. What will happen if an actual argument that contains the addition of two type `double` variables is passed to a type `int` formal parameter? What will happen if it is passed to a type `double` formal parameter?

Answers to Quick-Check Exercises

1. False
2. True
3. `x = exp(w + log(n)) + pow(r, 2);`
4. A function argument is used to pass information into a function.
5. False
6. It is called into execution by a function call, that is, the function name followed by its arguments in parentheses.
7. A formal parameter is used in a function definition to represent a corresponding actual argument.

8. A structure chart shows the subordinate relationships between subproblems; an algorithm lists the sequence in which subproblem solutions are carried out.
9. It prints a square of hash marks.
10. It displays four squares of hash marks on top of each other.
11. In the first case, there will be a loss of precision. In the second case, there will be no loss of precision.

Review Questions

1. Define top-down design and structure charts.
2. What is a function prototype?
3. When is a function executed, and where should a function prototype and function definition appear in a source program?
4. What are three advantages of using functions?
5. Is the use of functions a more efficient use of the programmer's time or the computer's time? Explain your answer.
6. Write a program that prompts the user for the radius in degrees of a circle and makes use of the pow function to compute the area of the circle. Use the value of π as 3.14.
7. Write a program that draws a square made of a triple border of hash marks. Use two functions: `square_sides` and `square_lines`.
8. Draw a structure chart for the program described in Review Question 7.
9. Write the prototype for a function called `script` that has three input parameters. The first parameter will be the number of spaces to display at the beginning of a line. The second parameter will be the character to display after the spaces, and the third parameter will be the number of times to display the second parameter on the same line.

Programming Projects

1. You have saved $500 to use as a down payment on a car. Before beginning your car shopping, you decide to write a program to help you figure out what your monthly payment will be, given the car's purchase price, the monthly interest rate, and the time period over which you will pay back the loan. The formula for calculating your payment is

$$payment = \frac{iP}{1 - (1 + i)^{-n}}$$

where
   P = principal (the amount you borrow)
   i = monthly interest rate ($\frac{1}{12}$ of the annual rate)
   n = total number of payments

Your program should prompt the user for the purchase price, the down payment, the annual interest rate, and the total number of payments (usually 36, 48, or 60). It should then display the amount borrowed and the monthly payment including a dollar sign and two decimal places.

2. Write two functions, one that displays a circle and one that displays a trapezium. Use these functions to write a complete C program from the following outline:

```
int
main(void)
{
    /* Draw circle. */
    /* Draw trapezium */
    /* Display one blank line */
    /* Draw circle. */
    /* Draw trapezium */
}
```

3. Write a program that prompts the user to enter the radius of the circular base of a cone and the slant height of the cone. The program must compute the total surface area of a right circular cone and display it back to the user. (Hint: π will be used in the equation to calculate the total surface area and hence, you may have to use an appropriate value for it.)

4. For any integer $n > 0$, $n!$ is defined as the product $n \times n - 1 \times n - 2 \ldots \times 2 \times 1$. $0!$ is defined to be 1. It is sometimes useful to have a closed-form definition instead; for this purpose, an approximation can be used. R.W. Gosper proposed the following such approximation formula:

$$ n! \approx n^n e^{-n} \sqrt{\left(2n + \frac{1}{3} \right) \pi} $$

Create a program that prompts the user to enter an integer n, uses Gosper's formula to approximate $n!$, and then displays the result. The message displaying the result should look something like this:

```
5! equals approximately 119.97003
```

Your program will be easier to debug if you use some intermediate values instead of trying to compute the result in a single expression. If you are not getting the correct results, then you can compare the results of your intermediate values to what you get when you do the calculations by hand. Use at least two intermediate variables—one for $2n + \frac{1}{3}$ and one for $\sqrt{(2n + \frac{1}{3})\pi}$. Display each of these intermediate values to simplify debugging. Be sure to use a named constant for PI, and use the approximation 3.14159265. Test the program on nonnegative integers less than 8.

5. Given the value of the monthly payment obtained in Programming Project 1 and a certain hourly income of the student, write a program that calculates

how many hours the student will need to work so as to pay every month's payment towards the laptop.

6. Four track stars have entered the mile race at the Penn Relays. Write a program that scans in the race time in minutes (`minutes`) and seconds (`seconds`) for a runner and computes and displays the speed in feet per second (`fps`) and in meters per second (`mps`). (*Hints:* There are 5,280 feet in one mile, and one kilometer equals 3,282 feet.) Write and call a function that displays instructions to the program user. Run the program for each star's data.

Minutes	Seconds
3	52.83
3	59.83
4	00.03
4	16.22

7. In shopping for a new house, you must consider several factors. In this problem the initial cost of the house, the estimated annual fuel costs, and the annual tax rate are available. Write a program that will determine the total cost of a house after a five-year period and run the program for each of the following sets of data.

Initial House Cost	Annual Fuel Cost	Tax Rate
67,000	2,300	0.025
62,000	2,500	0.025
75,000	1,850	0.020

To calculate the house cost, add the initial cost to the fuel cost for five years, then add the taxes for five years. Taxes for one year are computed by multiplying the tax rate by the initial cost. Write and call a function that displays instructions to the program user.

8. A bullet train slows from a speed of 200 mi/hr to 150 mi/hr in one minute. Write a computer program that calculates the bullet train's constant rate of acceleration and determines how long the bullet train will take to come to rest, given an initial speed of 200 mi/hr. (*Hint:* Use the equation

$$a = \frac{v_f - v_i}{t}$$

where a is acceleration, t is time interval, v_i is initial velocity, and v_f is final velocity.) Write and call a function that displays instructions to the program user and a function that computes a, given t, v_f, and v_i.

9. An epidemic of a new strain of flu (i.e., one for which a vaccine is not available) begins with a single case on a college campus of 40,000 faculty, staff, and

students. Three days later a second case is reported, and in the following days the reported cases are as shown in the table below. The day of the initial case report is noted as day 0.

Day #	0	3	5	6	7	8	9	10	11
Total cases	1	2	3	4	5	7	9	11	15

A math professor observes that the number of cases seems to be increasing by about 28% per day and proposes the following model to predict the total number of cases by day number x:

$$Cases(x) = \frac{40000}{1 + 39999(e^{-0.24681})}$$

Write a function that implements this model. Test your function with a main function that prompts the user three times to enter a day number and then calculates and displays the number of cases predicted for each day number entered.

Sample run:

```
FLU EPIDEMIC PREDICTIONS BASED ON ELAPSED DAYS SINCE FIRST
CASE REPORT

Enter day number>> 7
By day 7, model predicts 5 cases total.

Enter day number>> 10
By day 10, model predicts 11 cases total.

Enter day number>> 20
By day 20, model predicts 138 cases total.
```

10. Write a program to take a depth (in kilometers) inside the earth as input data; compute and display the temperature at this depth in degrees Celsius and degrees Fahrenheit. The relevant formulas are

$$Celsius = 10\ (depth) + 20 \qquad \text{(Celsius temperature at depth in km)}$$
$$Fahrenheit = 1.8\ (Celsius) + 32$$

Include two functions in your program. Function `celsius_at_depth` should compute and return the Celsius temperature at a depth measured in kilometers. Function `fahrenheit` should convert a Celsius temperature to Fahrenheit.

11. The ratio between successive speeds of a six-speed gearbox (assuming that the gears are evenly spaced to allow for whole teeth) is

$$\sqrt[5]{M/m}$$

where M is the maximum speed in revolutions per minute and m is the minimum speed. Write a function `speeds_ratio` that calculates this ratio for any maximum and minimum speeds. Write a main function that prompts for maximum and minimum speeds (rpm), calls `speeds_ratio` to calculate the ratio, and displays the results in a sentence of the form

```
The ratio between successive speeds of a six-speed gearbox
with maximum speed _____ rpm and minimum speed _____
rpm is _____.
```

12. Write a program that calculates the speed of sound (a) in air of a given temperature T (°F). Formula to compute the speed in ft/sec:

$$a = 1086\sqrt{\frac{5T + 297}{247}}$$

Be sure your program does not lose the fractional part of the quotient in the formula shown. As part of your solution, write and call a function that displays instructions to the program user.

13. After studying the population growth of Gotham City in the last decade of the 20th century, we have modeled Gotham's population function as

$$P(t) = 52.966 + 2.184t$$

where t is years after 1990, and P is population in thousands. Thus, $P(0)$ represents the population in 1990, which was 52.966 thousand people. Write a program that defines a function named `population` that predicts Gotham's population in the year provided as an input argument. Write a program that calls the function and interacts with the user as follows:

```
Enter a year after 1990> 2015
Predicted Gotham City population for 2015 (in thousands):
107.566
```

Graphics Projects

14. Use graphics functions in programs that draw a rocket ship (triangle over rectangle over intersecting lines), a male stick figure (circle over rectangle over intersecting lines), and a female stick figure standing on the head of a male stick figure.

15. Write a graphics program that draws your first and last initials as block letters in different colors. Write separate functions that draw each letter. The position of each letter and its color should be function arguments.

16. Read in five values that represent the monthly amount spent on budget categories: food, clothing, transportation, entertainment, and rent. Write a program that displays a bar graph showing these values. In a bar graph, the height of each bar is proportional to the value it represents. Use a different color for each bar. (*Hint:* Multiply each value by the scale factor `getmaxy()/maxExpense,` where `maxExpense` is the largest possible expense.)

17. Redo Programming Project 16 using a pie chart. For the pie chart, the arc length of each section should be proportional to the amount it represents. Use a different fill pattern and color for each section.

18. Redo Programming Project 16 drawing a line graph. The first line should begin at the height representing the first budget category value and end at the height representing the second budget category value; the second line should begin at the height representing the second budget category value and end at the height representing the third budget category value; and so on.

Selection Structures: if and switch Statements

CHAPTER OBJECTIVES

- To become familiar with the three kinds of control structures: sequence, selection, and repetition
- To understand compound statements
- To learn how to compare numbers and characters
- To learn how to use the relational, equality, and logical operators to write expressions that are true or false
- To learn how to write selection statements that choose between two alternatives in a program using the if statement
- To learn how to implement decisions in algorithms using the if statement
- To understand how to select among more than two alternatives by nesting if statements
- To learn how to use the switch statement as another technique for selecting among multiple alternatives

This chapter begins your study of statements that control the flow of program execution. You will learn to use `if` and `switch` statements to select one statement group to execute from many alternatives. First, the chapter discusses conditions and logical expressions because the `if` statement relies on them.

The case studies in this chapter emphasize reusing solutions to prior problems to speed up the problem-solving process. You will also learn how to trace an algorithm or program to verify that it does what you expect.

4.1 Control Structures

control structure
a combination of individual instructions into a single logical unit with one entry point and one exit point

Control structures control the flow of execution in a program or function. The C control structures enable you to combine individual instructions into a single logical unit with one entry point and one exit point.

Instructions are organized into three kinds of control structures to control execution flow: *sequence, selection,* and *repetition.* Until now we have been using only sequential flow. A **compound statement**, written as a group of statements bracketed by `{` and `}`, is used to specify sequential flow.

compound statement
a group of statements bracketed by `{` and `}` that are executed sequentially

```
{
    statement₁;
    statement₂;
        .
        .
        .
    statementₙ;
}
```

Control flows from *statement₁* to *statement₂*, and so on. You have been using compound statements all along—a function body consists of a single compound statement.

selection control structure   a control structure that chooses among alternative program statements

This chapter describes the C control structures for selection, and Chapter 5 covers the control structures for repetition. Some problem solutions require steps with two or more alternative courses of action. A **selection control structure** chooses which alternative to execute.

4.2 Conditions

A program chooses among alternative statements by testing the value of key variables. For example, one indicator of the health of a person's heart is the resting heart rate. Generally, a resting rate of 75 beats per minute or less indicates a healthy heart, but a resting heart rate over 75 indicates a potential problem. A program that gets a person's resting heart rate as data should compare that value to 75 and display a warning message if the rate is over 75.

If `rest_heart_rate` is a type `int` variable, the expression

```
rest_heart_rate > 75
```

performs the necessary comparison and evaluates to 1 (true) when `rest_heart_rate` is over 75; the expression evaluates to 0 (false) if `rest_heart_rate` is not greater than 75. Such an expression is called a **condition** because it establishes a criterion for either executing or skipping a group of statements.

condition an expression that is either false (represented by 0) or true (usually represented by 1)

Relational and Equality Operators

Most conditions that we use to perform comparisons will have one of these forms:

variable	*relational-operator*	*variable*
variable	*relational-operator*	*constant*
variable	*equality-operator*	*variable*
variable	*equality-operator*	*constant*

Table 4.1 lists the relational and equality operators.

TABLE 4.1 Relational and Equality Operators

Operator	Meaning	Type
<	less than	relational
>	greater than	relational
<=	less than or equal to	relational
>=	greater than or equal to	relational
==	equal to	equality
!=	not equal to	equality

EXAMPLE 4.1   Table 4.2 shows some sample conditions in C. Each condition is evaluated assuming these variable and constant macro values:

x	power	MAX_POW	y	item	MIN_ITEM	mom_or_dad	num	SENTINEL
-5	1024	1024	7	1.5	-999.0	'M'	999	999

TABLE 4.2   Sample Conditions

Operator	Condition	English Meaning	Value
<=	x <= 0	x less than or equal to 0	1 (true)
<	power < MAX_POW	power less than MAX_POW	0 (false)
>=	x >= y	x greater than or equal to y	0 (false)
>	item > MIN_ITEM	item greater than MIN_ITEM	1 (true)
==	mom_or_dad == 'M'	mom_or_dad equal to 'M'	1 (true)
!=	num != SENTINEL	num not equal to SENTINEL	0 (false)

Logical Operators

With the three logical operators—&& (and), || (or), ! (not)—we can form more complicated conditions or **logical expressions**. Examples of logical expressions formed with these operators are

logical expression
an expression that uses one or more of the logical operators && (and), || (or), ! (not)

```
salary < MIN_SALARY  ||  dependents > 5
temperature > 90.0  &&  humidity > 0.90
n >= 0  &&  n <= 100
0 <= n  &&  n <= 100
```

The first logical expression determines whether an employee is eligible for special scholarship funds. It evaluates to 1 (true) if *either* the condition

```
salary < MIN_SALARY
```

or the condition

```
dependents > 5
```

is true. The second logical expression describes an unbearable summer day, with temperature and humidity both in the nineties. The expression evaluates to true only when *both* conditions are true. The last two expressions are equivalent and evaluate to true if n lies between 0 and 100 inclusive.

The third logical operator, ! (not), has a single operand and yields the **logical complement**, or **negation**, of its operand (that is, if the variable `positive` is nonzero (true), `!positive` is 0 (false) and vice versa). The logical expression

`!(0 <= n && n <= 100)`

is the complement of the last expression in the list above. It evaluates to 1 (true) when n does not lie between 0 and 100 inclusive.

Table 4.3 shows that the `&&` operator (and) yields a true result only when both its operands are true. Table 4.4 shows that the `||` operator (or) yields a false result only when both its operands are false. Table 4.5 shows the ! operator (not).

Tables 4.3 through 4.5 show that the result is always 0 or 1 when C evaluates a logical expression. However, C accepts *any nonzero value* as a representation of true. For now, we will always use the integer 1 when we need the value true, but knowing how C really views logical expressions will help you understand why some common mistakes that you may make will not be seen by the C compiler as syntax errors.

TABLE 4.3 The && Operator (and)

operand1	operand2	operand1 && operand2
nonzero (true)	nonzero (true)	1 (true)
nonzero (true)	0 (false)	0 (false)
0 (false)	nonzero (true)	0 (false)
0 (false)	0 (false)	0 (false)

TABLE 4.4 The || Operator (or)

operand1	operand2	operand1 || operand2
nonzero (true)	nonzero (true)	1 (true)
nonzero (true)	0 (false)	1 (true)
0 (false)	nonzero (true)	1 (true)
0 (false)	0 (false)	0 (false)

TABLE 4.5 The ! Operator (not)

operand1	!operand1
nonzero (true)	0 (false)
0 (false)	1 (true)

Operator Precedence

An operator's precedence determines its order of evaluation. Table 4.6 lists the precedence of all C operators so far, from highest to lowest.

unary operator an operator that has one operand

The table shows that function calls are evaluated first. The **unary operators**, ! (not), + (plus sign), – (minus sign), and & (address of), which have a single operand, are evaluated second. Next come all the binary operators in the sequence: arithmetic, relational, equality, and logical (&& and then ||). The assignment operator (=) is evaluated last. Notice that the precedence of operators + and – depends on whether they have one operand or two. In the expression

```
-x - y * z
```

the unary minus is evaluated first (-x), then *, and then the second –.

You can use parentheses to change the order of operator evaluation. In the expression

```
(x < y  ||  x < z)  &&  x > 0.0
```

C evaluates || before &&.

If you remove the parentheses from the expression, C would evaluate && before ||, thereby changing the meaning of the expression.

You can also use parentheses to clarify the meaning of expressions. If x, min, and max are type **double**, the C compiler will interpret the expression

```
x + y < min + max
```

correctly as

```
(x + y) < (min + max)
```

because + has higher precedence than <, but the second expression is clearer.

TABLE 4.6   Operator Precedence

Operator	Precedence
function calls	highest (evaluated first)
! + – & (unary operators)	
* / %	
+ –	
< <= >= >	
== !=	
&&	
||	
=	lowest (evaluated last)

EXAMPLE 4.2   Expressions 1 to 4 below contain different operands and operators. Each expression's value is given in the corresponding comment, assuming x, y, and z are type double, flag is type int, and the variables have the values

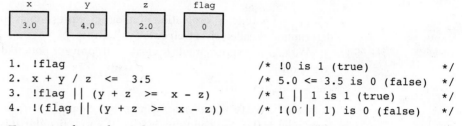

```
1.  !flag                           /* !0 is 1 (true)           */
2.  x + y / z  <=  3.5              /* 5.0 <= 3.5 is 0 (false)  */
3.  !flag || (y + z  >=  x - z)     /* 1 || 1 is 1 (true)       */
4.  !(flag || (y + z  >=  x - z))   /* !(0 || 1) is 0 (false)   */
```

Figure 4.1 shows the evaluation tree and step-by-step evaluation for expression 3.

Short-Circuit Evaluation

Although Fig. 4.1 shows the evaluation of the entire logical expression, C evaluates only part of the expression. An expression of the form *a* || *b* must be true if *a* is true. Consequently, C stops evaluating the expression when it determines that the value of !flag is 1 (true).

Similarly, an expression of the form *a* && *b* must be false if *a* is false, so C would stop evaluating such an expression if its first operand evaluates to 0. This

FIGURE 4.1

Evaluation Tree
and Step-by-Step
Evaluation for
!flag ||
(y + z >= x - z)

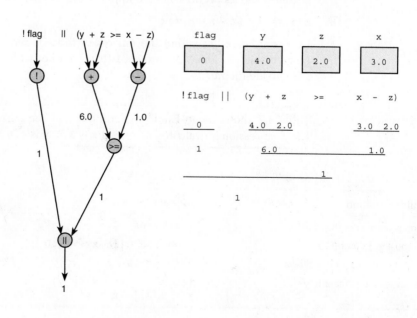

FIGURE 4.2

Range of True
Values for
min <= x &&
x <= max

min   max   x

**short-circuit
evaluation** stopping
evaluation of a logical
expression as soon
as its value can be
determined

technique of stopping evaluation of a logical expression as soon as its value can be determined is called **short-circuit evaluation**.

We can use short-circuit evaluation to prevent potential run-time errors. The condition

```
(num % div == 0)
```

tests whether `div` is a divisor of `num`. For example, if `num` is 6 and `div` is 2, the remainder is 0 so the condition is true. If `num` is 6 and `div` is 4, the remainder is 2 so the condition is false.

What if `div` is 0? In this case, the remainder calculation would cause a *division by zero* run-time error. However, we can prevent this error by using the revised condition

```
(div != 0 && (num % div == 0))
```

The remainder would not be calculated when `div` is 0 because `div != 0` is false.

Writing English Conditions in C

To solve programming problems, you must convert conditions expressed in English to C. Many algorithm steps require testing to see if a variable's value is within a specified range of values. For example, if `min` represents the lower bound of a range of values and `max` represents the upper bound (`min` is less than `max`), the expression

```
min <= x  &&  x <= max
```

tests whether `x` lies within the range `min` through `max`, inclusive. In Fig. 4.2 this range is shaded. The expression is 1 (true) if `x` lies within this range and 0 (false) if `x` is outside the range.

EXAMPLE 4.3   Table 4.7 shows some English conditions and the corresponding C expressions. Each expression is evaluated assuming `x` is `3.0`, `y` is `4.0`, and `z` is `2.0`.

TABLE 4.7   English Conditions as C Expressions

English Condition	Logical Expression	Evaluation
x and y are greater than z	x > z && y > z	1 && 1 is 1 (true)
x is equal to 1.0 or 3.0	x == 1.0 || x == 3.0	0 || 1 is 1 (true)
x is in the range z to y, inclusive	z <= x && x <= y	1 && 1 is 1 (true)
x is outside the range z to y	!(z <= x && x <= y) z > x || x > y	!(1 && 1) is 0 (false) 0 || 0 is 0 (false)

FIGURE 4.3

Range of True
Values for

z > x || x > y

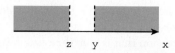

The first logical expression shows the C code for the English condition "x and y are greater than z." You may be tempted to write this as

```
x && y > z       /* invalid logical expression */
```

However, if we apply the precedence rules to this expression, we quickly see that it does not have the intended meaning. Also, the type `double` variable x is an invalid operand for the logical operator `&&`.

The third logical expression shows the C code for the mathematical relationship $z \leq x \leq y$. The boundary values, 2.0 and 4.0, are included in the range of x values that yield a true result.

The last table entry shows a pair of logical expressions that are true when x is outside the range bounded by z and y. We get the first expression in the pair by complementing the expression just above it. The second expression states that x is outside the range if z is larger than x or x is larger than y. In Fig. 4.3 the shaded areas represent the values of x that yield a true result. Both y and z are excluded from the set of values that yield a true result.

Comparing Characters

We can also compare characters in C using the relational and equality operators. Table 4.8 shows some examples of these comparisons.

The first three lines of Table 4.8 show that the digits, characters, and letters are ordered as expected (that is, '0'<'1'<'2'< ... <'8'<'9' and 'a'<'b'<'c'... <'y'<'z'). The next two lines show that the lowercase and uppercase form of

TABLE 4.8 Character Comparisons

Expression	Value
'9' >= '0'	1 (true)
'a' < 'e'	1 (true)
'B' <= 'A'	0 (false)
'Z' == 'z'	0 (false)
'a' <= 'A'	system dependent
'a' <= ch && ch <= 'z'	1 (true) if ch is a lowercase letter

the same letter have different values and their order is system dependent. The expression `'a' <= 'A'` is false for ASCII (see Table 2.7). The last entry shows an expression that is true if `ch` is a lowercase letter. (On some systems, this expression also will be true for some characters that are not lowercase letters.)

Logical Assignment

The simplest form of a logical expression in C is a single type `int` value or variable intended to represent the value true or false. We can use assignment statements to set such variables to true (a nonzero value) or false (0).

EXAMPLE 4.4   Given the declarations

```
int   age;            /* input - a person's age      */
char gender;          /* input - a person's gender    */
int   senior_citizen; /* logical - indicates senior status  */
```

Assume that a value of 1 for `senior_citizen` indicates that the person is a senior citizen (65 years old or over). You can use the assignment statement

```
senior_citizen = 1;    /* Set senior status */
```

to set `senior_citizen` to true.

A more likely scenario is to set the value of `senior_citizen` based on the value scanned into `age`:

```
scanf("%d", &age);                   /* Read the person's age */
senior_citizen = (age >= 65);        /* Set senior status */
```

In the assignment above, the condition in parentheses evaluates first. Its value is 1 (true) if the value scanned into `age` is 65 or greater. Consequently, the value of `senior_citizen` is true when `age` satisfies the condition and false otherwise.

The logical operators `&&`, `||`, and `!` can be applied to `senior_citizen`. The expression

```
!senior_citizen
```

is 1 (true) if the value of `age` is less than 65. Finally, the logical expression

```
senior_citizen  &&   gender == 'M'
```

is 1 (true) if `senior_citizen` is 1 (true) and the character in `gender` is M.

EXAMPLE 4.5

The following assignment statements assign values to two type int variables, in_range and is_letter. Variable in_range gets 1 (true) if the value of n is between –10 and 10 excluding the endpoints; is_letter gets 1 (true) if ch is an uppercase or a lowercase letter.

```
in_range = (n > -10  &&  n < 10);
is_letter = ('A' <= ch  &&  ch <= 'Z') ||
            ('a' <= ch  &&  ch <= 'z');
```

The expression in the first assignment statement is true if n satisfies both the conditions listed (n is greater than –10 and n is less than 10); otherwise, the expression is false.

The expression in the second assignment statement uses the logical operators &&, ||. The subexpression before || is true if ch is an uppercase letter; the subexpression after || is true if ch is a lowercase letter. Consequently, is_letter gets 1 (true) if either subexpression is true (that is, ch is a letter); otherwise, is_letter gets 0 (false). You can delete the parentheses without affecting the order of operator evaluation, since && has higher precedence than ||.

EXAMPLE 4.6

The statement below assigns the value 1 (true) to even (type int) if n is an even number:

```
even = (n % 2 == 0);
```

Because all even numbers are divisible by 2, the remainder of n divided by 2 (n % 2 in C) is 0 when n is an even number. The expression in parentheses compares the remainder to 0, so its value is 1 (true) when the remainder is 0 and its value is 0 (false) when the remainder is nonzero.

Complementing a Condition

You have seen how to complement a logical expression by preceding it with the symbol !. You can also complement a simple condition by just changing its operator.

EXAMPLE 4.7

Two forms of the complement of the condition

```
item == SENT
```

are

```
!(item == SENT)              item != SENT
```

The form on the right is obtained by changing the equality operator (that is, changing == to !=).

Usually, changing the equality or relational operator to complement a simple condition is easy to do. The relational operator <= should be changed to >, < should be changed to >=, and so on. Use the ! operator with more complicated expressions.

EXAMPLE 4.8   The condition

```
status == 'S'  &&  age > 25
```

is true for a single person over 25. The complement of this condition is

```
!(status == 'S'  &&  age > 25)
```

DeMorgan's Theorem   DeMorgan's theorem gives us a way of simplifying the logical expression above. DeMorgan's theorem states

- The complement of $expr_1$ && $expr_2$ is written as $comp_1$ || $comp_2$, where $comp_1$ is the complement of $expr_1$, and $comp_2$ is the complement of $expr_2$.
- The complement of $expr_1$ || $expr_2$ is written as $comp_1$ && $comp_2$, where $comp_1$ is the complement of $expr_1$, and $comp_2$ is the complement of $expr_2$.

Using DeMorgan's theorem, we can write the complement of

```
age > 25  &&  (status == 'S' || status == 'D')
```

as

```
age <= 25 || (status != 'S'  &&  status != 'D')
```

The original condition is true for anyone who is over 25, and is either single or divorced. The complement would be true for anyone who is 25 or younger, or for anyone who is currently married.

EXERCISES FOR SECTION 4.2

Self-Check

1. Assuming x is 15.0 and y is 25.0, what are the values of the following conditions?

    ```
    x != y
    x < x
    x >= y - x
    x == y + x - y
    ```

2. Evaluate each of the following expressions if a is 6, b is 9, c is 14, and flag is 1. Which parts of these expressions are not evaluated due to short-circuit evaluation?

a. `c == a + b  ||  !flag`
b. `a != 7  &&  flag  ||  c >= 6`
c. `!(b <= 12)  &&  a % 2 == 0`
d. `!(a > 5  ||  c < a + b)`

3. Show step-by-step evaluation of expression 4 in Example 4.2.
4. Complement each expression in Exercise 2. Use DeMorgan's theorem if applicable.
5. What value is assigned to the type int variable ans in this statement if the value of p is 100 and q is 50?

```
ans = (p > 95) + (q < 95);
```

This statement is not shown as an example of a reasonable assignment statement; rather, it is a sample of a statement that makes little sense to the reader. The statement is still legal and executable in C, however, because C uses integers to represent the logical values true and false.

Programming

1. Write an expression to test for each of the following relationships.

   a. age is from 18 to 21 inclusive.
   b. water is less than 1.5 and also greater than 0.1.
   c. year is divisible by 4. (*Hint:* Use %.)
   d. speed is not greater than 55.
   e. y is greater than x and less than z.
   f. w is either equal to 6 or not greater than 3.

2. Write assignment statements for the following:

   a. Assign a value of 0 to between if n is less than -k or greater than +k; otherwise, assign 1.
   b. Assign a value of 1 to divisor if digit is a divisor of num; otherwise, assign a value of 0.
   c. Assign a value of 1 to lowercase if ch is a lowercase letter; otherwise, assign a value of 0.

4.3 The if Statement

You now know how to write a C expression that is the equivalent of a question such as "Is resting heart rate more than 75 beats per minute?" Next, we need to investigate a way to use the value of the expression to select a course of action. In C, the if statement is the primary selection control structure.

if Statement with Two Alternatives

The `if` statement

```
if (rest_heart_rate > 75)
      printf("Keep up your exercise program!\n");
else
      printf("Your heart is doing well!\n");
```

selects one of the two calls to `printf`. It selects the statement following the parenthesized condition if the condition evaluates to `1` (true) (that is, if `rest_heart_rate` is greater than `75`), or it selects the statement following `else` if the condition evaluates to `0` (false) (if `rest_heart_rate` is not greater than `75`).

flowchart a diagram that shows the step-by-step execution of a control structure

Figure 4.4a is a **flowchart** of the preceding `if` statement. A flowchart is a diagram that uses boxes and arrows to show the step-by-step execution of a control structure. A diamond-shaped box in a flowchart represents a decision. There is always one path into a decision and there are two paths out (labeled true and false). A rectangular box represents an assignment statement or a process.

Figure 4.4a shows that the condition (`rest_heart_rate > 75`) is evaluated first. If the condition is true, program control follows the arrow labeled true, and the display statement on the right is executed. If the condition is false, program control follows the arrow labeled false, and the display statement on the left is executed.

Figure 4.5 shows a program that uses this `if` statement.

FIGURE 4.4 Flowcharts of if Statements with (a) Two Alternatives and (b) One Alternative

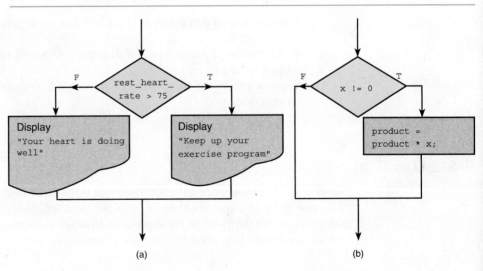

(a)   (b)

FIGURE 4.5 Program Using an if Statement for Selection

```
1.  /*
2.   * Displays message about heart rate.
3.   */
4.  #include <stdio.h>
5.
6.  int main(void)
7.  {
8.          int pulse;           /* resting pulse rate for 10 secs */
9.          int rest_heart_rate; /* resting heart rate for 1 minute */
10.
11.         /* Enter your resting pulse rate */
12.         printf("Take your resting pulse for 10 seconds.\n");
13.         printf("Enter your pulse rate and press return> ");
14.         scanf("%d", &pulse);
15.
16.         /* Calculate resting heart rate for  minute */
17.         rest_heart_rate = pulse * 6;
18.         printf("Your resting heart rate is %d.\n", rest_heart_rate);
19.
20.         /* Display message based on resting heart rate */
21.         if (rest_heart_rate > 75)
22.             printf("Keep up your exercise program!\n");
23.         else
24.             printf("Your heart is in doing well!\n");
25.
26.         return (0);
27. }
```

Sample Run 1
```
Take your resting pulse for 10 seconds.
Enter your pulse rate and press return> 13
Your resting heart rate is 78.
Keep up your exercise program!
```

Sample Run 2
```
Take your resting pulse for 10 seconds.
Enter your pulse rate and press return> 9
Your resting heart rate is 54.
Your heart is doing well!
```

if Statement with One Alternative

The `if` statement in the last section has two alternatives but executes only one for a given value of `rest_heart_rate`. You also can write `if` statements with a single alternative that executes only when the condition is true.

The `if` statement diagrammed in Fig. 4.4b

```
/* Multiply Product by a nonzero x */
if (x != 0.0)
    product = product * x;
```

has one alternative, which is executed only when `x` is not zero. It causes `product` to be multiplied by `x` and the new value to be saved in `product`, replacing the old value. If `x` is zero, the multiplication is not performed.

A Comparison of One and Two Alternative if Statements

EXAMPLE 4.9   The `if` statement below has two alternatives.

```
if (crsr_or_frgt == 'C')
    printf("Cruiser\n");
else
    printf("Frigate\n");
```

It displays either `Cruiser` or `Frigate`, depending on the character stored in the type `char` variable `crsr_or_frgt`.

EXAMPLE 4.10   The `if` statement that follows has one alternative; it displays the message `Cruiser` only when `crsr_or_frgt` has the value `'C'`. Regardless of whether `Cruiser` is displayed or not, the message `Combat ship` is displayed.

```
if (crsr_or_frgt == 'C')
    printf("Cruiser\n");
printf("Combat ship\n");
```

EXAMPLE 4.11   The program fragment

```
if crsr_or_frgt == 'C'        /* error - missing parentheses */
    printf("Cruiser\n");
printf("Combat ship\n");
```

is an incorrect version of the `if` statement in Example 4.10. The missing parentheses around the condition is a syntax error that will be detected (and possibly corrected) by the compiler.

The extra semicolon in the first line below

```
if (crsr_or_frgt == 'C');   /* error - improper placement of ;*/
      printf("Cruiser\n");
printf("Combat ship\n");
```

does not cause a violation of C syntax rules because the compiler translates the first line as a single-alternative `if` statement with an *empty statement* implying no action if the condition is true. The first `printf` loses its dependency on the value of the condition, so both calls to `printf` are executed unconditionally.

---

if Statement (One Alternative)

FORM: `if (` *condition* `)`
           statement$_T$`;`

EXAMPLE: `if (x > 0.0)`
           `pos_prod = pos_prod * x;`

INTERPRETATION: If *condition* evaluates to **true** (a nonzero value), then *statement$_T$* is executed; otherwise, *statement$_T$* is skipped.

---

if Statement (Two Alternatives)

FORM: `if (` *condition* `)`
           statement$_T$`;`
       `else`
           statement$_F$`;`

EXAMPLE: `if (x >= 0.0)`
           `printf("positive\n");`
       `else`
           `printf("negative\n");`

INTERPRETATION: If *condition* evaluates to **true** (a nonzero value), then *statement$_T$* is executed and *statement$_F$* is skipped; otherwise, *statement$_T$* is skipped and *statement$_F$* is executed.

Program Style   *Format of the if Statement*

All `if` statement examples in this text indent *statement$_T$* and *statement$_F$*. The word `else` is typed without indentation on a separate line. The format of the `if` statement makes its meaning apparent and is used solely to improve program readability; the format makes no difference to the compiler.

EXERCISES FOR SECTION 4.3

Self-Check

1. What do these statements display?

   a. ```
       if (12 < 12)
               printf("less");
       else
               printf("not less");
       ```
   b.  ```
       var1 = 25.12;
       var2 = 15.00;
       if (var1 <= var2)
               printf("less or equal");
       else
               printf("greater than");
       ```

2. What value is assigned to x when y is 10.0?

   a. ```
       x = 25.0;
       if (y != (x - 10.0))
               x = x - 10.0;
       else
               x = x / 2.0;
       ```
   b.  ```
       if (y < 15.0)
               if (y >= 0.0)
                       x = 5 * y;
               else
                       x = 2 * y;
       else
               x = 3 * y;
       ```
   c. ```
       if (y < 15.0 && y >= 0.0)
               x = 5 * y;
       else
               x = 2 * y;
       ```

Programming

1. Write C statements to carry out the following steps.

   a. If item is nonzero, then multiply product by item and save the result in product; otherwise, skip the multiplication. In either case, print the value of product.

   b. Store the absolute difference of x and y in y, where the absolute difference is (x - y) or (y - x), whichever is positive. Do not use the abs or fabs function in your solution.
       ```

c. If x is 0, add 1 to `zero_count`. If x is negative, add x to `minus_sum`. If x is greater than 0, add x to `plus_sum`.

4.4 if Statements with Compound Statements

This section describes `if` statements having compound statements after the condition or the keyword `else`. When the symbol { follows the condition or `else`, the C compiler either executes or skips all statements through the matching }.

EXAMPLE 4.12

Suppose you are a biologist studying the growth rate of fruit flies. The `if` statement

```
if (pop_today > pop_yesterday) {
    growth = pop_today - pop_yesterday;
    growth_pct = 100.0 * growth / pop_yesterday;
    printf("The growth percentage is %.2f\n", growth_pct);
}
```

computes the population growth from yesterday to today as a percentage of yesterday's population. The compound statement after the condition executes only when today's population is larger than yesterday's. The first assignment computes the increase in the fruit fly population, and the second assignment converts it to a percentage of the original population, which is displayed.

EXAMPLE 4.13

As manager of a company's automobile fleet, you keep records of the safety ratings of the fleet cars. In the `if` statement that follows, the true task makes a record of an automobile (`auto_id`) whose crash test rating index (`ctri`) is at least as low (good) as the cutoff you have established for acceptably safe cars (`MAX_SAFE_CTRI`). The false task records an auto whose `ctri` does not meet your standard. In either case, an appropriate message is displayed, and one is added to the count of safe or unsafe cars. Both the true and false tasks are compound statements.

```
if (ctri <= MAX_SAFE_CTRI) {
    printf("Car #%d: safe\n", auto_id);
    safe = safe + 1;
} else {
    printf("Car #%d: unsafe\n", auto_id);
    unsafe = unsafe + 1;
}
```

If you omit the braces enclosing the compound statements, the `if` statement would end after the first `printf` call. The assignment to `safe` would be translated as an unconditional statement (always executed), and the compiler would mark the keyword `else` as an error because a statement cannot begin with `else`.

Program Style   *Writing if Statements with Compound True or False Statements*

We enclose a compound statement that is a true task or a false task in braces. The placement of the braces is a matter of personal preference. We use the form shown in Example 4.13. Some programmers prefer to type each brace on its own line and to align the braces:

```
if (condition)
{
        true task
}
else
{
        false task
}
```

Some programmers prefer to use braces around all true and false tasks whether compound or not, so that all `if` statements in a program have a consistent style. We recommend enclosing both the true and the false tasks in braces if either is a compound statement. Whichever style you choose, make sure you apply it consistently.

Tracing an if Statement

A critical step in program design is to verify that an algorithm or C statement is correct before you spend extensive time coding or debugging it. Often a few extra minutes spent in verifying the correctness of an algorithm saves hours of coding and testing time.

hand trace (desk check) step-by-step simulation of an algorithm's execution

A **hand trace**, or **desk check**, is a careful, step-by-step simulation on paper of how the computer executes the algorithm or statement. The results of this simulation should show the effect of each step's execution using data that are relatively easy to process by hand.

EXAMPLE 4.14   In many programming problems you must order a pair of data values in memory so that the smaller value is stored in one variable (say, `x`) and the larger value in another (say, `y`). The `if` statement in Fig. 4.6 rearranges any two values stored in

FIGURE 4.6 if Statement to Order x and y

```
1.  if (x > y) {              /* Switch x and y */
2.       temp = x;            /* Store old x in temp */
3.       x = y;               /* Store old y in x */
4.       y = temp;            /* Store old x in y */
5.  }
```

x and y so that the smaller number is in x and the larger number is in y. If the two numbers are already in the proper order, the compound statement is not executed.

Variables x, y, and temp should all be the same data type. Although the values of x and y are being switched, an additional variable, temp, is needed to store a copy of one of these values.

Table 4.9 traces the execution of this if statement when x is 12.5 and y is 5.0. The table shows that temp is initially undefined (indicated by ?). Each line of the table shows the part of the if statement that is being executed, followed by its effect. If any variable gets a new value, its new value is shown on that line. If no new value is shown, the variable retains its previous value. The last value stored in x is 5.0, and the last value stored in y is 12.5.

The trace in Table 4.9 shows that 5.0 and 12.5 are correctly stored in x and y when the condition is true. To verify that the if statement is correct, you would need to select other data that cause the condition to evaluate to false. Also, you should verify that the statement is correct for special situations. For example, what would happen if x were equal to y? Would the statement still provide the correct result? To complete the hand trace, you would need to show that the algorithm handles this special situation properly.

In tracing each case, you must be careful to execute the statement step-by-step exactly as the computer would execute it. Often programmers assume how a particular step will be executed and don't explicitly test each condition and trace each step. A trace performed in this way is of little value.

TABLE 4.9 Trace of if Statement

Statement Part	x	y	temp	Effect
	12.5	5.0	?	
if (x > y) {				12.5 > 5.0 is true.
temp = x;			12.5	Store old x in temp.
x = y;	5.0			Store old y in x.
y = temp;		12.5		Store old x in y.
}				

EXERCISES FOR SECTION 4.4

Self-Check

1. Insert braces where they are needed so the meaning matches the indentation.

    ```
    if (x > y)
          x = x + 10.0;
          printf("x Bigger\n");
    else
          printf("x Smaller\n");
          printf("y is %.2f\n", y);
    ```

2. Correct the following `if` statement; assume the indentation is correct.

    ```
    if (deduct < balance);
          balance = balance - deduct;
          printf("New balance is %.2f\n", balance);
    else;
          printf("Deduction of %.2f refused.\n", deduct);
          printf("Would overdraw account.\n");
    printf("Deduction = %.2f  Final balance = %.2f",
            deduct, balance);
    ```

3. Revise the style of the following `if` statement to improve its readability.

    ```
    if (engine_type == 'J') {printf("Jet engine");
    speed_category = 1;}
    else{printf("Propellers"); speed_category
    = 2;}
    ```

Programming

1. Write an `if` statement that might be used to compute and display the average of a set of *n* numbers whose sum is stored in variable `total`. This average should be found only if *n* is greater than 0; otherwise, an error message should be displayed.
2. Write an interactive program that contains an `if` statement that may be used to compute the area of a square (*area* = *side*^{2}) or a circle (*area* = $\pi \times$ *radius*^{2}) after prompting the user to type the first character of the figure name (S or C).

4.5 Decision Steps in Algorithms

decision step an algorithm step that selects one of several actions

Algorithm steps that select from a choice of actions are called **decision steps**. The algorithm in the next problem contains decision steps to compute and display a customer's water bill based on usage. The decision steps are coded as `if` statements.

CASE STUDY   Water Bill Problem

PROBLEM

Write a program that computes a customer's water bill. The bill includes a $35 water demand charge plus a consumption (use) charge of $1.10 for every thousand gallons used. Consumption is figured from meter readings (in thousands of gallons) taken recently and at the end of the previous quarter. If the customer's unpaid balance is greater than zero, a $2 late charge is assessed as well.

ANALYSIS

The total water bill is the sum of the demand and use charges, the unpaid balance, and a possible late charge. The demand charge is a program constant ($35), but the use charge must be computed. To do this, we must know the previous and current meter readings (the problem inputs). After obtaining these data, we can compute the use charge by multiplying the difference between the two meter readings by the charge for 1000 gallons, the problem constant $1.10. Next, we can determine the applicable late charge, if any, and finally compute the water bill by adding the four components. The data requirements and initial algorithm follow.

DATA REQUIREMENTS

Problem Constants

```
DEMAND_CHG 35.00      /* basic water demand charge          */
PER_1000_CHG 1.10     /* charge per thousand gallons used   */
LATE_CHG 2.00         /* surcharge on an unpaid balance     */
```

Problem Inputs

```
int previous   /* meter reading from previous quarter
                  in thousands of gallons                 */
int current    /* meter reading from current quarter      */
double unpaid  /* unpaid balance of previous bill         */
```

Problem Outputs

```
double bill          /* water bill                        */
double use_charge    /* charge for actual water use       */
double late_charge   /* charge for nonpayment of part
                        of previous balance               */
```

Relevant Formulas

water bill = demand charge + use charge + unpaid balance
*   + applicable late charge*

DESIGN

INITIAL ALGORITHM

1. Display user instructions.
2. Get data: unpaid balance, previous and current meter readings.
3. Compute use charge.
4. Determine applicable late charge.
5. Figure bill amount.
6. Display the bill amount and charges.

The structure chart in Fig. 4.7 includes *data flow* information that shows the inputs and the outputs of each individual algorithm step. The structure chart shows that step 2, "Get data," provides values for `unpaid`, `previous`, and `current` as its outputs (data flow arrow points up). Similarly, step 3, "Compute use charge," uses `previous` and `current` as its inputs (data flow arrow points down) and provides `use_charge` as its output. We will discuss the relevance of the data flow information after we complete the problem solution.

FIGURE 4.7   Structure Chart for Water Bill Problem

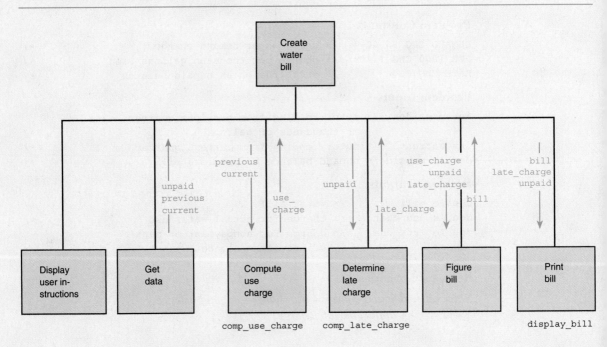

As shown in the structure chart, we use functions to implement all but steps 2 and 5. Each function name appears below the subproblem it solves. Next, we turn our attention to the function subprograms. We will discuss each function except `instruct_water`, which is straightforward.

ANALYSIS AND DESIGN OF COMP_USE_CHARGE

The structure chart shows that function `comp_use_charge` computes a value for `use_charge` based on data stored in `previous` and `current`. The data requirements and algorithm follow.

DATA REQUIREMENTS FOR COMP_USE_CHARGE

Input Parameters

```
int previous    /* meter reading from previous quarter
                   in thousands of gallons          */
int current     /* meter reading from current quarter */
```

Return Value

```
double use_charge /* charge for actual water use */
```

Program Variable

```
int used /* thousands of gallons used this quarter */
```

Relevant Formulas

$used = current\ meter\ reading - previous\ meter\ reading$

$use\ charge = used \times charge\ per\ thousand\ gallons$

ALGORITHM FOR COMP_USE_CHARGE

1. used is `current - previous`
2. `use_charge` is used `* PER_1000_CHG`

ANALYSIS AND DESIGN OF COMP_LATE_CHARGE

Function `comp_late_charge` returns a late charge of $2.00 or $0.00 depending on the unpaid balance. Consequently, it requires a decision step as shown in the algorithm that follows.

DATA REQUIREMENTS FOR COMP_LATE_CHARGE

Input Parameter

```
double unpaid /* unpaid balance of previous bill          */
```

Return Value

```
double late_charge /* charge for nonpayment of part
                      of previous balance                 */
```

ALGORITHM FOR COMP_LATE_CHARGE

1. if unpaid > 0

        assess late charge

    else

        assess no late charge

pseudocode
a combination of
English phrases and C
constructs to describe
algorithm steps

The decision step above is expressed in **pseudocode**, which is a mixture of English and C used to describe algorithm steps. The indentation and reserved words if and else show the logical structure of each decision step. Each decision step has a condition (following if) that can be written in English or C; similarly, the true and false tasks can be written in English or C.

ANALYSIS AND DESIGN OF DISPLAY_BILL

The void function display_bill displays the bill amount and the late charge and unpaid balance if any. The values of bill, late_charge, and unpaid are passed to the function as input arguments; display_bill displays these values on the screen.

DATA REQUIREMENTS FOR DISPLAY_BILL

Input Parameters

```
double late_charge      /* charge for nonpayment of
                           part of previous balance      */
double bill             /* bill amount                   */
double unpaid           /* unpaid balance                */
```

ALGORITHM FOR DISPLAY_BILL

1. if late_charge > 0

        display late charge and unpaid balance
2. Display the bill amount.

IMPLEMENTATION

Follow the approach described in Section 3.1 to write the program (Fig. 4.8). Begin by writing #define directives for the problem constants. In the main function, declare all variables from the problem data requirements that appear in the structure chart. Next, write each step of the initial algorithm as a comment in the main function body. To complete the main function, code each algorithm step in-line (as part of the main function code) or as a function call. For each function call, refer to the structure chart to determine the names of the input arguments and the variable receiving the function result.

Follow a similar approach to write each function subprogram (Fig. 4.8). Declare all identifiers listed in the function data requirements as either formal parameters

FIGURE 4.8 Program for Water Bill Problem

```
1.   /*
2.    * Computes and prints a water bill given an unpaid balance and previous and
3.    * current meter readings. Bill includes a demand charge of $35.00, a use
4.    * charge of $1.10 per thousand gallons, and a surcharge of $2.00 if there is
5.    * an unpaid balance.
6.    */
7.
8.   #include <stdio.h>
9.
10.  #define DEMAND_CHG   35.00    /* basic water demand charge                */
11.  #define PER_1000_CHG 1.10     /* charge per thousand gallons used         */
12.  #define LATE_CHG      2.00    /* surcharge assessed on unpaid balance     */
13.
14.  /* Function prototypes                                                     */
15.  void instruct_water(void);
16.
17.  double comp_use_charge(int previous, int current);
18.
19.  double comp_late_charge(double unpaid);
20.
21.  void display_bill(double late_charge, double bill, double unpaid);
22.
23.  int
24.  main(void)
25.  {
26.          int     previous;    /* input - meter reading from previous quarter
27.                                  in thousands of gallons                  */
28.          int     current;     /* input - meter reading from current quarter */
29.          double unpaid;       /* input - unpaid balance of previous bill    */
30.          double bill;         /* output - water bill                        */
31.          int     used;        /* thousands of gallons used this quarter     */
32.          double use_charge;   /* charge for actual water use                */
33.          double late_charge;  /* charge for nonpayment of part of previous
34.                                  balance                                  */
35.
36.          /* Display user instructions.                                     */
37.          instruct_water();
38.
39.          /* Get data: unpaid balance, previous and current meter
40.             readings.                                                      */
```

(continued)

FIGURE 4.8　(continued)

```
41.            printf("Enter unpaid balance> $");
42.            scanf("%lf", &unpaid);
43.            printf("Enter previous meter reading> ");
44.            scanf("%d", &previous);
45.            printf("Enter current meter reading> ");
46.            scanf("%d", &current);
47.
48.            /* Compute use charge.                                      */
49.            use_charge = comp_use_charge(previous, current);
50.
51.            /* Determine applicable late charge                         */
52.            late_charge = comp_late_charge(unpaid);
53.
54.            /* Figure bill.                                             */
55.            bill = DEMAND_CHG + use_charge + unpaid + late_charge;
56.
57.            /* Print bill.                                              */
58.            display_bill(late_charge, bill, unpaid);
59.
60.            return (0);
61.    }
62.
63.    /*
64.     * Displays user instructions
65.     */
66.    void
67.    instruct_water(void)
68.    {
69.            printf("This program figures a water bill ");
70.            printf("based on the demand charge\n");
71.            printf("($%.2f) and a $%.2f per 1000 ", DEMAND_CHG, PER_1000_CHG);
72.            printf("gallons use charge.\n\n");
73.            printf("A $%.2f surcharge is added to ", LATE_CHG);
74.            printf("accounts with an unpaid balance.\n");
75.            printf("\nEnter unpaid balance, previous ");
76.            printf("and current meter readings\n");
77.            printf("on separate lines after the prompts.\n");
78.            printf("Press <return> or <enter> after ");
79.            printf("typing each number.\n\n");
80.    }
81.
```

(continued)

FIGURE 4.8   (continued)

```
82.   /*
83.    * Computes use charge
84.    * Pre: previous and current are defined.
85.    */
86.   double
87.   comp_use_charge(int previous, int current)
88.   {
89.         int used;            /* gallons of water used (in thousands)        */
90.         double use_charge; /* charge for actual water use                   */
91.
92.         used = current - previous;
93.         use_charge = used * PER_1000_CHG;
94.
95.         return (use_charge);
96.   }
97.
98.   /*
99.    * Computes late charge.
100.   * Pre : unpaid is defined.
101.   */
102.  double
103.  comp_late_charge(double unpaid)
104.  {
105.        double late_charge; /* charge for nonpayment of part of previous balance */
106.
107.        if (unpaid > 0)
108.            late_charge = LATE_CHG; /* Assess late charge on unpaid balance.    */
109.        else
110.            late_charge = 0.0;
111.
112.        return (late_charge);
113.  }
114.
115.  /*
116.   * Displays late charge if any and bill.
117.   * Pre : late_charge, bill, and unpaid are defined.
118.   */
119.  void
120.  display_bill(double late_charge, double bill, double unpaid)
```

(continued)

FIGURE 4.8   (continued)

```
121.    {
122.            if (late_charge > 0.0) {
123.                    printf("\nBill includes $%.2f late charge", late_charge);
124.                    printf(" on unpaid balance of $%.2f\n", unpaid);
125.            }
126.            printf("\nTotal due = $%.2f\n", bill);
127.    }
```

FIGURE 4.9   Sample Run of Water Bill Program

```
This program figures a water bill based on the demand charge
($35.00) and a $1.10 per 1000 gallons use charge.

A $2.00 surcharge is added to accounts with an unpaid balance.

Enter unpaid balance, previous and current meter readings
on separate lines after the prompts.
Press <return> or <enter> after typing each number.

Enter unpaid balance> $71.50
Enter previous meter reading> 4198
Enter current meter reading> 4238

Bill includes $2.00 late charge on unpaid balance of $71.50

Total due = $152.50
```

or local variables, depending on how the identifier is used by the function. Make sure that the order of parameters in the function heading corresponds to the order of arguments in the function call. After you write each function heading, copy it into the function prototype area preceding function main.

TESTING

To test this program, run it with data sets that cause each branch of the two decision steps to execute. For example, one data set should have a positive unpaid balance, and another should have an unpaid balance of zero. Figure 4.9 shows a sample run.

Program Style   *Consistent Use of Names in Functions*

Notice that we use the same identifier, `late_charge`, to refer to the customer's late charge in the main function and in two function subprograms. We declare `late_charge` as a local variable in functions `main` and `comp_late_charge` and as a formal parameter in function `display_bill`. Although C does not require that we use the same name for the customer's late charge in all three functions, it is perfectly permissible to do so. Using the same name avoids the confusion that would result from using different names to reference the same information.

Program Style   *Cohesive Functions*

cohesive function
a function that performs a single operation

Function `comp_late_charge` only computes the late charge—it does not display it. That task is left to function `display_bill`. Functions that perform a single operation are called **cohesive functions**. Writing cohesive functions is good programming style, because cohesive functions are easier to read, write, debug, and maintain, and are more likely to be reusable.

Program Style   *Using Constant Macros to Enhance Readability and Ease Maintenance*

The function subprograms in Fig. 4.8 reference the constant macros `DEMAND_CHG`, `PER_1000_CHG`, and `LATE_CHG`. It is perfectly permissible to reference such names in any function body that appears in the same source file as the constant macro definitions.

We could just as easily have placed the values that these names represent (`35.00`, `1.10`, and `2.00`) directly in the statements where they are needed. The resulting statements would be

```
printf("This program figures a water bill ");
printf("based on the demand charge\n");
printf("($%.2f) and a $%.2f per 1000 ",
       35.00, 1.10);
printf("gallons use charge.\n\n");
printf("A $%.2f surcharge is added to ", 2.00);
printf("accounts with an unpaid balance.\n");
use_charge = used * 1.10;
late_charge = 2.00; /* Assess late charge on unpaid
                       balance. */
bill = 35.00 + use_charge + unpaid + late_charge;
```

However, use of constant macro names rather than actual values has two advantages. First, the original statements are easier to understand because they use the descriptive names `DEMAND_CHG`, `PER_1000_CHG`, and `LATE_CHG` rather than numbers, which have no intrinsic meaning. Second, a program written using constant macros is much easier to maintain than one written with constant values. For example, if we want to use different constant values in the water bill program in Fig. 4.8, we need to change only the constant macro definitions. However, if we inserted constant values directly in the statements, we would need to change any statements that manipulate the constant values.

EXERCISES FOR SECTION 4.5

Self-Check

1. Change the algorithm for function `comp_use_charge` assuming the fee is doubled for any gallons used in excess of 100,000. The basic fee is assessed for the first 100,000 gallons used.
2. Revise the flat-washer problem from Section 3.1 so that the user can compute the weight of a batch of circular or square washers. Give the algorithm with refinements. Draw a structure chart with data flow information for the new problem showing the relationship between the main program and its subproblems. Assume that the user can specify whether the washer type is circular or square.

Programming

1. Write function `comp_use_charge` described in Self-Check Exercise 1.

4.6 More Problem Solving

Data Flow Information in Structure Charts

In Fig. 4.7, the data flow information in the structure chart shows the inputs and outputs of each individual algorithm step. Data flow information is an important part of system documentation because it shows what program variables are processed by each step and the manner in which those variables are processed. If a step gives a new value to a variable, then the variable is considered an *output of the step*. If a step displays a variable's value or uses a variable in a computation without changing its value, the variable is considered an *input to the step*.

Figure 4.8 shows that a variable may have different roles for different subproblems in the algorithm. In the context of the original problem statement, `previous` and `current` are problem *inputs* (data supplied by the program user). However, in the context of the subproblem "Get data," the subproblem's task is to deliver values for `previous` and `current` to the main program; thus, `previous` and `current` are considered *outputs* from this step. In the context of the subproblem "Compute use charge," the subproblem's task is to use `previous` and `current` to compute `use_charge`, so they are *inputs* to this step. In the same way, the role of the other variables changes as we go from step to step in the problem.

Modifying a Program with Function Subprograms

Often what appears to be a new problem will turn out to be a variation of one that you have already solved. Consequently, an important skill in problem solving is the ability to recognize that one problem is similar to another solved earlier. As you progress through this course, you will start to build up your own personal library of programs and functions. Whenever possible, you should try to adapt or reuse parts of successful programs.

Writing programs that can be easily changed or modified to fit other situations is advisable; programmers and program users will often want to make slight improvements to a program after they use it. If the original program is well designed and modular, the programmer will be able to accommodate changing specifications with a minimum of effort. As you will find by working through the next problem, when changes are needed it may be possible to modify one or two functions rather than rewriting the entire program.

CASE STUDY   Water Bill with Conservation Requirements

PROBLEM

We need to modify the water bill program so that customers who fail to meet conservation requirements are charged for all their water use at twice the rate of customers who meet the guidelines. Residents of this water district are required to use no more than 95% of the amount of water they used in the same quarter last year in order to qualify for the lower use rate of $1.10 per thousand gallons.

ANALYSIS

This problem is a modification of the water bill problem solved in the last section. Customers who meet the conservation guidelines should be charged the basic use rate of $1.10 per thousand gallons; those who do not should be charged at twice this rate. We can solve this problem by adding the use figure from last year to our problem inputs and modifying function `comp_use_charge`. The additions to the data requirements and revised algorithm for function `comp_use_charge` follow.

ADDITIONS TO DATA REQUIREMENTS

Problem Constants

```
OVERUSE_CHG_RATE 2.0      /* double use charge as non-conservation
                             penalty                              */
CONSERV_RATE 95           /* percent of last year's use
                             allowed this year                    */
```

Problem Inputs

```
int use_last_year         /* use for same quarter
                             last year                            */
```

ALGORITHM FOR COMP_USE_CHARGE

1. used is current - previous
2. if guidelines are met
        use_charge is used * PER_1000_CHARGE
   else
        notify customer of overuse
        use_charge is used * overuse_chg_rate *
          PER_1000_CHG

Figure 4.10 shows the revised function. If the condition

```
(used <= CONSERV_RATE / 100.0 * use_last_year)
```

is true, the conservation guidelines are met and the use charge is computed as before; otherwise, the customer is notified of the overuse, and the overuse charge rate is factored into the computation of the use charge.

FIGURE 4.10   Function comp_use_charge Revised

```
1.  /*
2.   * Computes use charge with conservation requirements
3.   * Pre: previous, current, and use_last_year are defined.
4.   */
5.  double
6.  comp_use_charge(int previous, int current, int use_last_year)
7.  {
8.       int used;  /* gallons of water used (in thousands)        */
9.       double use_charge;  /* charge for actual water use        */
10.      used = current - previous;
11.      if (used <= CONSERV_RATE / 100.0 * use_last_year) {
12.          /* conservation guidelines met */
```

(continued)

FIGURE 4.10   (continued)

```
13.           use_charge = used * PER_1000_CHG;
14.      } else {
15.           printf("Use charge is at %.2f times ", OVERUSE_CHG_RATE);
16.           printf("normal rate since use of\n");
17.           printf("%d units exceeds %d percent ", used, CONSERV_RATE);
18.           printf("of last year's %d-unit use.\n", use_last_year);
19.           use_charge = used * OVERUSE_CHG_RATE * PER_1000_CHG;
20.      }
21.
22.      return (use_charge);
23. }
```

We must change the prototype for function comp_use_charge to match its heading and replace the call to function comp_use_charge in Fig. 4.8 with

```
use_charge = comp_use_charge(previous, current,
                             use_last_year);
```

To complete the program revision, change function instruct_water to display the new user instructions. Also, modify the main function to prompt for and get the value of use_last_year.

EXERCISES FOR SECTION 4.6

Programming

1.   Provide the complete program for the water bill problem with conservation requirements.

4.7   Nested if Statements and Multiple-Alternative Decisions

nested if statement
an if statement with
another if statement
as its true task or its
false task

Until now, we have used if statements to code decisions with one or two alternatives. In this section, we use **nested if statements** (one if statement inside another) to code decisions with multiple alternatives.

EXAMPLE 4.15   The following nested if statement has three alternatives. It increases one of three variables (num_pos, num_neg, or num_zero) by 1, depending on whether x is greater than zero, less than zero, or equal to zero, respectively. The boxes show the logical structure of the nested if statement: The second if statement is the false task (following else) of the first if statement.

`/* increment num_pos, num_neg, or num_zero depending on x */`

```
if (x > 0)
      num_pos = num_pos + 1;
else

      if (x < 0)
            num_neg = num_neg + 1;
      else /* x equals 0 */
            num_zero = num_zero + 1;
```

The execution of the nested `if` statement proceeds as follows: the first condition $(x > 0)$ is tested; if it is true, `num_pos` is incremented and the rest of the `if` statement is skipped. If the first condition is false, the second condition $(x < 0)$ is tested; if it is true, `num_neg` is incremented; otherwise, `num_zero` is incremented. It is important to realize that the second condition is tested *only* when the first condition is false. Table 4.10 traces the execution of this statement when x is -7. Because $x > 0$ is false, the second condition $(x < 0)$ is tested.

Comparison of Nested if and Sequence of ifs

Beginning programmers sometimes prefer to use a sequence of `if` statements rather than a single nested `if` statement. For example, the nested `if` statement in Example 4.15 is rewritten as a sequence of `if` statements.

```
if (x > 0)
      num_pos = num_pos + 1;
if (x < 0)
      num_neg = num_neg + 1;
if (x == 0)
      num_zero = num_zero + 1;
```

Although this sequence is logically equivalent to the original, it is neither as readable nor as efficient. Unlike the nested `if` statement, the sequence does not clearly show that exactly one of the three assignment statements is executed for a

TABLE 4.10 Trace of if Statement in Example 4.15 for x = −7

Statement Part	Effect
`if (x > 0)`	−7 > 0 is false.
`if (x < 0)`	−7 < 0 is true.
`num_neg = num_neg + 1`	Add 1 to **num_neg**.

particular x. It is less efficient because all three of the conditions are always tested. In the nested if statement, only the first condition is tested when x is positive.

Multiple-Alternative Decision Form of Nested if

Nested if statements can become quite complex. If there are more than three alternatives and indentation is not consistent, it may be difficult for you to determine the logical structure of the if statement. In situations like Example 4.15 in which each false task (except possibly the last) is followed by an if-then-else statement, you can code the nested if as the *multiple-alternative decision* described next.

Multiple-Alternative Decision

SYNTAX:
```
if (condition₁)
      statement₁
else if (condition₂)
      statement₂
         .
         .
         .
else if (conditionₙ)
      statementₙ
else
      statementₑ
```

EXAMPLE:
```
/* increment num_pos, num_neg, or num_zero depending
   on x */
if (x > 0)
      num_pos = num_pos + 1;
else if (x < 0)
      num_neg = num_neg + 1;
else /* x equals 0 */
      num_zero = num_zero + 1;
```

INTERPRETATION: The conditions in a multiple-alternative decision are evaluated in sequence until a true condition is reached. If a condition is true, the statement following it is executed, and the rest of the multiple-alternative decision is skipped. If a condition is false, the statement following it is skipped, and the next condition is tested. If all conditions are false, then *statementₑ* following the final else is executed.

Notes: In a multiple-alternative decision, the words else and if the next condition appear on the same line. All the words else align, and each dependent statement is indented under the condition that controls its execution.

EXAMPLE 4.16   Suppose you want to associate noise loudness measured in decibels with the effect of the noise. The following table shows the relationship between noise levels and human perceptions of noises.

Loudness in Decibels (db)	Perception
50 or lower	quiet
51–70	intrusive
71–90	annoying
91–110	very annoying
above 110	uncomfortable

The multiple-alternative decision in the following code fragment displays the perception of noise according to this table. If the noise were measured at 62 decibels, the last three conditions would be true if evaluated; however, the perception 62-decibel noise is intrusive. would be displayed because the first true condition is noise_db <= 70.

```
/* Display perception of noise loudness */

if (noise_db <= 50)
        printf("%d-decibel noise is quiet.\n", noise_db);
else if (noise_db <= 70)
        printf("%d-decibel noise is intrusive.\n", noise_db);
else if (noise_db <= 90)
        printf("%d-decibel noise is annoying.\n", noise_db);
else if (noise_db <= 110)
        printf("%d-decibel noise is very annoying.\n", noise_db);
else
        printf("%d-decibel noise is uncomfortable.\n", noise_db);
```

Order of Conditions in a Multiple-Alternative Decision

When more than one condition in a multiple-alternative decision is true, only the task following the first true condition executes. Therefore, the order of the conditions can affect the outcome.

Writing the decision as follows would be incorrect. All but the loudest sounds (above 110 db) would be categorized as "very annoying" because the first condition would be true and the rest would be skipped.

```
/* incorrect perception of noise loudness */

if (noise_db <= 110)
        printf("%d-decibel noise is very annoying.\n", noise_db);
else if (noise_db <= 90)
```

```
        printf("%d-decibel noise is annoying.\n",
               noise_db);
else if (noise_db <= 70)
        printf("%d-decibel noise is intrusive.\n",
               noise_db);
else if (noise_db <= 50)
        printf("%d-decibel noise is quiet.\n",
               noise_db);
else
        printf("%d-decibel noise is uncomfortable.\n", noise_db);
```

The order of conditions can also have an effect on program efficiency. If we know that loud noises are much more likely than soft ones, it would be more efficient to test first for noise levels above 110 db, next for levels between 91 and 110 db, and so on.

EXAMPLE 4.17   You could use a multiple-alternative if statement to implement a *decision table* that describes several alternatives. For instance, let's say you are an accountant setting up a payroll system based on Table 4.11, which shows five different ranges for salaries up to $150,000.00. Each table line shows the base tax amount (column 2) and tax percentage (column 3) for a particular salary range (column 1). Given a person's salary, you can calculate the tax due by adding the base tax to the product of the percentage times the excess salary over the minimum salary for that range.

For example, the second line of the table specifies that the tax due on a salary of $20,000.00 is $2,250.00 plus 18% of the excess salary over $15,000.00 (that is, 18% of $5000.00, or $900.00). Therefore, the total tax due is $2,250.00 plus $900.00, or $3,150.00.

The if statement in function comp_tax (Fig. 4.11) implements the tax table. If the value of salary is within the table range (0.00 to 150,000.00), exactly one of the statements assigning a value to tax will execute. Table 4.12 shows a trace of the if statement when salary is $25,000.00. You can see that the value assigned to tax, $4,050.00, is correct.

TABLE 4.11   Decision Table for Example 4.17

Salary Range ($)	Base Tax ($)	Percentage of Excess
0.00–14,999.99	0.00	15
15,000.00–29,999.99	2,250.00	18
30,000.00–49,999.99	5,400.00	22
50,000.00–79,999.99	11,000.00	27
80,000.00–150,000.00	21,600.00	33

FIGURE 4.11 Function comp_tax

```
1.  /*
2.   * Computes the tax due based on a tax table.
3.   * Pre : salary is defined.
4.   * Post: Returns the tax due for 0.0 <= salary <= 150,000.00;
5.   *        returns -1.0 if salary is outside the table range.
6.   */
7.  double
8.  comp_tax(double salary)
9.  {
10.     double tax;
11.
12.     if (salary < 0.0)
13.         tax = -1.0;
14.     else if (salary < 15000.00)              /* first range   */
15.         tax = 0.15 * salary;
16.     else if (salary < 30000.00)              /* second range  */
17.         tax = (salary - 15000.00) * 0.18 + 2250.00;
18.     else if (salary < 50000.00)              /* third range   */
19.         tax = (salary - 30000.00) * 0.22 + 5400.00;
20.     else if (salary < 80000.00)              /* fourth range  */
21.         tax = (salary - 50000.00) * 0.27 + 11000.00;
22.     else if (salary <= 150000.00)            /* fifth range   */
23.         tax = (salary - 80000.00) * 0.33 + 21600.00;
24.     else
25.         tax = -1.0;
26.
27.     return (tax);
28. }
```

TABLE 4.12 Trace of if Statement in Fig. 4.11 for salary = $25000.00

Statement Part	salary	tax	Effect
	25000.00	?	
if (salary < 0.0)			25000.0 < 0.0 is false.
else if (salary < 15000.00)			25000.0 < 15000.0 is false.
else if (salary < 30000.00)			25000.0 < 30000.0 is true.
tax = (salary - 15000.00)			Evaluates to 10000.00.
* 0.18			Evaluates to 1800.00.
+ 2250.00;		4050.00	Evaluates to 4050.00.

Program Style   *Validating the Value of Variables*

If you validate the value of a variable before using it in a computation, you can avoid processing invalid or meaningless data. Instead of computing an incorrect tax amount, function `comp_tax` returns −1.0 (an impossible tax amount) if the value of `salary` is outside the range covered by the table (0.0 to 150,000.00). The first condition sets `tax` to −1.0 if `salary` is negative. All conditions evaluate to false if `salary` is greater than $150,000.00, so the task following `else` also sets `tax` to −1.0. The function calling `comp_tax` should display an error message if the value returned to it is −1.0.

Nested if Statements with More Than One Variable

In most of our examples, we have used nested `if` statements to test the value of a single variable; consequently, we have been able to write each nested `if` statement as a multiple-alternative decision. If several variables are involved in the decision, we cannot always use a multiple-alternative decision. Example 4.18 contains a situation in which we can use a nested `if` statement as a "filter" to select data that satisfy several different criteria.

EXAMPLE 4.18   The Department of Defense would like a program that identifies single males between the ages of 18 and 26, inclusive. One way to do this is to use a nested `if` statement whose conditions test the next criterion only if all previous criteria tested were satisfied. In the following nested `if` statement, assume that all variables have values. The call to `printf` executes only when all conditions are true.

```
/* Print a message if all criteria are met. */
if (marital_status == 'S')
    if (gender == 'M')
        if (age >= 18  &&  age <= 26)
            printf("All criteria are met.\n");
```

An equivalent statement that uses a single `if` with a compound condition follows.

```
if (marital_status == 'S'  &&  gender == 'M'
    &&  age >= 18  &&  age <= 26)
        printf("All criteria are met.\n");
```

EXAMPLE 4.19   You are developing a program to control the warning signs at the exits of major tunnels. If roads are slick (`road_status` is `'S'`), you want to advise drivers that stopping times are doubled or quadrupled, depending on whether the roads are wet or icy. Your program will also have access to the current temperature in degrees Celsius (`temp`), so a check as to whether the temperature is above or below freezing would allow you to

FIGURE 4.12

Flowchart of Road
Sign Decision
Process

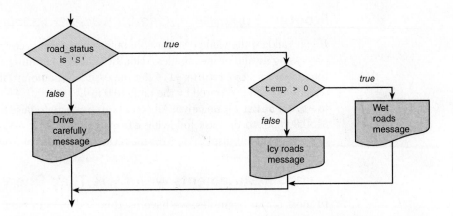

choose the correct message. The nested `if` statement below summarizes the decision process you should follow; the flowchart in Fig. 4.12 diagrams the process.

```
if (road_status == 'S')
        if (temp > 0) {
                printf("Wet roads ahead\n");
                printf("Stopping time doubled\n");
        } else {
                printf("Icy roads ahead\n");
                printf("Stopping time quadrupled\n");
        }
else
        printf("Drive carefully!\n");
```

To verify that the nested `if` statement in Example 4.19 is correct, we trace its execution for all possible combinations of road status values and temperatures. The flowchart's rightmost output is executed only when both conditions are true. The leftmost output is always executed when the condition involving `road_status` is false. The output in the middle occurs when the condition involving `road_status` is true but the condition involving `temp` is false.

When you are writing a nested `if` statement, you should know that C associates an `else` with the most recent incomplete `if`. For example, if the first `else` of the road sign decision were omitted, the following would be left:

```
/* incorrect interpretation of nested if */
if (road_status == 'S')
        if (temp > 0) {
                printf("Wet roads ahead\n");
                printf("Stopping time doubled\n");
        }
else
        printf("Drive carefully!\n");
```

Although the indentation would lead you to believe that the `else` remains the false branch of the first `if`, the C compiler actually sees it as the false branch of the second `if`. Indentation like this would match the actual meaning of the statement.

```
/* correct interpretation of nested if */
if (road_status == 'S')
        if (temp > 0) {
              printf("Wet roads ahead\n");
              printf("Stopping time doubled\n");
        } else
              printf("Drive carefully!\n");
```

To force the `else` to be the false branch of the first `if`, we place braces around the true task of this first decision.

```
/* interpretation with braces around first true task */
if (road_status == 'S') {
        if (temp > 0) {
              printf("Wet roads ahead\n");
              printf("Stopping time doubled\n");
        }
} else
        printf("Drive carefully!\n");
```

Note that we could not use a multiple-alternative decision statement to implement the flowchart in Fig. 4.12 because the second decision (`temp > 0`) falls on the true branch of the first decision. However, if we were to change the initial condition so the branches were switched, a multiple-alternative structure would work. We could do this simply by checking if the road is dry.

```
if (road_status == 'D') {
        printf("Drive carefully!\n");
} else if (temp > 0) {
        printf("Wet roads ahead\n");
        printf("Stopping time doubled\n");
} else {
        printf("Icy roads ahead\n");
        printf("Stopping time quadrupled\n");
}
```

The first condition is true only if the road is dry. The second condition is tested only when the first condition fails, so its dependent statement executes only when the road is not dry and the temperature is above freezing. Finally, the `else` clause executes only when the two conditions fail; then we know that the roads are not dry and the temperature is not above freezing.

EXERCISES FOR SECTION 4.7

Self-Check

1. Trace the execution of the nested `if` statement in Fig. 4.11 for a salary of $23,500.00.
2. What would be the effect of reversing the order of the first two conditions in the `if` statement in Fig. 4.11?
3. Write a nested `if` statement for the decision diagrammed in the accompanying flowchart. Use a multiple-alternative `if` for intermediate decisions where possible.

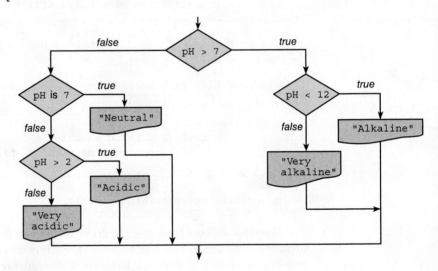

Programming

1. Rewrite the `if` statement for Example 4.16 using only the relational operator `>` in all conditions.
2. Implement the following decision table using a nested `if` statement. Assume that the grade point average is within the range 0.0 through 4.0.

Grade Point Average	Transcript Message
0.0–0.99	Failed semester—registration suspended
1.0–1.99	On probation for next semester
2.0–2.99	(no message)
3.0–3.49	Dean's list for semester
3.5–4.00	Highest honors for semester

3. Implement the following decision table using a multiple-alternative `if` statement. Assume that the wind speed is given as an integer.

Wind Speed (mph)	Category
below 25	not a strong wind
25–38	strong wind
39–54	gale
55–72	whole gale
above 72	hurricane

4. Write a multiple-alternative `if` statement to implement the following decision table that categorizes a systolic blood pressure reading (pressure as ventricles contract) as "normal," "prehypertension," or "hypertension." Assume that the systolic blood pressure has been input as an integer.

Systolic Blood Pressure	Category
140 and higher	hypertension
120–139	pre-hypertension
under 120	normal

4.8   The switch Statement

The `switch` statement may also be used in C to select one of several alternatives. The `switch` statement is especially useful when the selection is based on the value of a single variable or of a simple expression (called the *controlling expression*). The value of this expression may be of type `int` or `char`, but not of type `double`.

EXAMPLE 4.20

Figure 4.13 shows a program that reads a ship's serial number and displays the class of the ship. Each ship serial number begins with a letter indicating the class of the ship. The program first reads the first letter of a ship's serial number into the `char` variable `class` and then displays that character.

The `switch` statement displays a message indicating the class of the ship. It implements the following decision table.

Class ID	Ship Class
B or b	Battleship
C or c	Cruiser
D or d	Destroyer
F or f	Frigate

FIGURE 4.13   Program Using a `switch` Statement for Selection

```
1.  /*
2.   * Reads serial number and displays class of ship
3.   */
4.
5.  #include <stdio.h>
6.
7.  int
8.  main(void)
9.  {
10.      char class;      /* input - character indicating class of ship */
11.
12.      /* Read first character of serial number */
13.      printf("Enter ship serial number> ");
14.      scanf("%c", &class);           /* scan first letter */
15.
16.      /* Display first character followed by ship class */
17.      printf("Ship class is %c: ", class);
18.      switch (class) {
19.      case 'B':
20.      case 'b':
21.              printf("Battleship\n");
22.              break;
23.      case 'C':
24.      case 'c':
25.              printf("Cruiser\n");
26.              break;
27.      case 'D':
28.      case 'd':
29.              printf("Destroyer\n");
30.              break;
31.      case 'F':
32.      case 'f':
33.              printf("Frigate\n");
34.              break;
35.      default:
36.              printf("Unknown\n");
37.      }
38.
39.      return (0);
40.  }
```

(continued)

FIGURE 4.13 (continued)

```
Sample Run 1
Enter ship serial number> f3456
Ship class is f: Frigate

Sample Run 2
Enter ship serial number> P210
Ship class is P: Unknown
```

The `switch` statement displays a message that depends on the value of the controlling expression, that is, the value of the variable `class` (type `char`). First, this expression is evaluated; then, the list of `case` labels (`case 'B':`, `case 'b':`, `case 'C':`, etc.) is searched until one label that matches the value of the controlling expression is found. Statements following the matching `case` label are executed until a `break` statement is encountered. The `break` causes an exit from the `switch` statement, and execution continues with the statement that follows the closing brace of the `switch` statement body. If no `case` label matches the value of the `switch` statement's controlling expression, the statements following the `default` label are executed, if there is a `default` label. If not, the entire `switch` statement body is skipped.

Using a string such as `"Cruiser"` or `"Frigate"` as a case label is a common error. It is important to remember that type `int` and `char` values may be used as `case` labels, but strings and type `double` values cannot be used. Another common error is the omission of the `break` statement at the end of one alternative. In such a situation, execution "falls through" into the next alternative. We recommend using a blank line after each `break` statement to emphasize the fact that there is no "fall-through."

Forgetting the closing brace of the `switch` statement body is also easy to do. If the brace is missing and the `switch` has a `default` label, the statements following the `switch` statement become part of the default case.

The following syntax display shows the form of the `switch` statement as a multiple-alternative decision structure.

---

switch Statement

SYNTAX: `switch (`*controlling expression*`) {`
        *label set*₁
          *statements*₁
          `break;`

(continued)

```
              label set₂
                  statements₂
                  break;
                        •
                        •
                        •
              label setₙ
                  statementsₙ
                  break;

          default:
                  statements_d
          }
```

EXAMPLE:
```
/* Determine life expectancy in hours of an
   incandescent light bulb */
switch (watts) {
case 25:
        life = 2500;
        break;

case 40:
case 60:
        life = 1000;
        break;

case 75:
case 100:
        life = 750;
        break;

default:
        life = 0;
}
```

INTERPRETATION: The *controlling expression*, an expression with a value of type **int** or type **char**, is evaluated and compared to each of the case labels in the *label sets* until a match is found. A *label set* is made of one or more labels of the form **case** followed by a constant value and a colon. When a match between the value of the *controlling expression* and a **case** label value is found, the statements following the **case** label are executed until a **break** statement is encountered. Then the rest of the **switch** statement is skipped.

Notes: The *statements* following a **case** label may be one or more C statements, so you do not need to make multiple statements into a single compound statement using braces. If no **case** label value matches the controlling expression, the entire **switch** statement body is skipped unless it contains a **default** label. If so, the statements following the **default** label are executed when no other **case** label value matches the *controlling expression*.

Comparison of Nested if Statements and the switch Statement

You can use a nested `if` statement, which is more general than the `switch` statement, to implement any multiple-alternative decision. The `switch` as described in the syntax display is more readable in many contexts and should be used whenever practical. Case labels that contain type `double` values or strings are not permitted.

You should use the `switch` statement when each label set contains a reasonable number of `case` labels (a maximum of ten). However, if the number of values is large, use a nested `if` statement. You should include a `default` label in `switch` statements wherever possible. The discipline of trying to define a default will help you to consider what will happen if the value of your `switch` statement's controlling expression falls outside your set of `case` label values.

C IN FOCUS

The UNIX Connection

The language in which the fundamental components of UNIX systems are written and the base language for most other operating systems, C, is an outgrowth of the development of the first UNIX operating system created by Ken Thompson and Dennis Ritchie.

At the time of its development, UNIX was crucial to making computers more accessible. Until the late 1960s, only a few organizations had the luxury of owning computers, and even then, these computers were sprawling, monolithic systems like IBM's OS/360. It was not until the next generation of computers, mini-computers, that time-sharing made it possible for users to connect to and use a computer interactively via terminals. This interactive computer usage, pioneered by operating systems such as UNIX, made computers far more accessible.

When Thompson and Ritchie built the first UNIX system in 1969, they were inspired by the interactive feel of the Multics system, then being developed at MIT (as a joint project of MIT, General Electric, and Bell Laboratories). When the developers rewrote the UNIX kernel, the heart of the operating system, in 1973, they used the C language to do it. Ever since then, the UNIX system calls that programs use to request services from the kernel have been defined

as C functions. The use of these system calls made it very natural to write application programs in C, and later in C++. Many UNIX user programs also follow C's syntactic conventions.

The connection between C and UNIX runs in both directions. Any C program you may write is going to call upon functions in the C library either implicitly or explicitly. Even the simplest do-nothing program implicitly calls the **exit** function, which in turn calls upon the operating environment to terminate the program. Many of the other functions in the standard C library such as **getc** and **time** also require support from the operating system, and that support is modeled on UNIX. The code for those functions involves a request to the operating system for system services. Although there are many flavors of UNIX, they all include a "Programmer's Library" containing functions closely resembling the C library. Those functions are themselves defined in terms of a C interface.

In the other direction, many UNIX utilities that include programming facilities have borrowed C syntax and semantics. The best example is the "shell script" facility, usually just called the "shell." A simple shell script is a text file containing operating system commands to execute along with some logic to control the order of execution. A good example of C syntax in the shell is the use of the **&&** and **||** operators. In C, they perform short-circuit evaluation of a logical expression. In the shell, they behave similarly and can provide conditional execution of a program. Evaluating the shell expression **a && b**, where **a** and **b** are programs, executes the program **a**. If the execution succeeds, then **b** is executed; if it fails, **b** is not executed. Similarly, **a || b** executes **a** and then executes **b** only if the execution of **a** failed.

The connection between C and UNIX was more obvious to the average user in the days when most computer interfaces were text-based. The rise of graphical user interfaces has hidden the connection from most users, except systems programmers. With a graphical interface, user-level programs have very little syntax in the usual sense: most input is provided by moving and clicking a mouse rather than by typing text. The C syntax that manifests itself in many UNIX utilities is irrelevant to these programs.

Many of the user-level programs available under UNIX systems are now written in languages such as Perl, Python, and TCL/TK. These languages generally view the machine at a higher, more abstract level than C. They are not appropriate for lower-level programming such as the code required for the UNIX kernel, but they work very well for graphical programs.

Moreover, with the almost universal use of C and its derivative C++ for writing other operating systems and with the C and C++ compilers available for those systems, one can no longer assume that C code is being written for a UNIX environment. The universality of C and C++ as systems programming languages, paradoxically, has severed that half of the connection between C and UNIX. The result of all these developments is that the UNIX connection to C, while of great historical importance and still vital to systems programmers, is no longer as visible as it once was.

Many thanks to Paul Abrahams, author of *UNIX for the Impatient* and a past president of the Association for Computing Machinery, for contributing his UNIX insights to this article.

EXERCISES FOR SECTION 4.8

Self-Check

1. What will be printed by this carelessly constructed `switch` statement if the value of `color` is `'R'`?

```
switch (color) { /* break statements missing */
case 'R':
     printf("red\n");
case 'B':
     printf("blue\n");
case 'Y':
     printf("yellow\n");
}
```

2. Why can't we rewrite our multiple-alternative `if` statement code from Examples 4.16 and 4.17 using `switch` statements?

Programming

1. Write a `switch` statement that assigns to the variable `lumens` the expected brightness of an incandescent light bulb whose wattage has been stored in `watts`. Use this table:

Watts	Brightness (in Lumens)
15	125
25	215
40	500
60	880
75	1000
100	1675

Assign –1 to `lumens` if the value of `watts` is not in the table.

2. Write a nested `if` statement equivalent to the `switch` statement described in the first programming exercise.

4.9 Common Programming Errors

The fact that C relational and equality operators give a result of 1 for true and 0 for false means that C interprets some common mathematical expressions in a way that seems surprising at first. You would probably not anticipate the fact that the following `if` statement displays `Condition is true` for all values of `x`.

```
if (0 <= x <= 4)
    printf("Condition is true\n");
```

For example, let's consider the case when `x` is 5. The value of `0 <= 5` is 1, and 1 is certainly less than or equal to 4! In order to check if `x` is in the range 0 to 4, you should use the condition

```
(0 <= x  &&  x <= 4)
```

Remember that the C equality operator is `==`. If you slip up and use `=`, the mathematical equal sign, the compiler can detect this error only if the first operand is not a variable. Otherwise, your code will simply produce incorrect results. For example, the code fragment that follows always prints `x is 10`, regardless of the value of `x`.

```
if (x = 10)
    printf("x is 10");
```

The assignment operator stores the value 10 in `x`. The value of an assignment expression is the value assigned, so in this case, the value of the `if` condition of the statement is 10. Since 10 is nonzero, C views it as meaning true and executes the true task.

Don't forget to parenthesize the condition of an `if` statement and to enclose in braces a single-alternative `if` used as a true task within a double-alternative `if`.

The braces will force the else to be associated with the correct if. Also enclose in braces a compound statement used as a true task or false task. If the braces are missing, only the first statement will be considered part of the task. This can lead to a syntax error if the braces are omitted from the true task of a double-alternative if. Leaving out the braces on the false task of a double-alternative if or on the true task of a single-alternative if will not usually generate a syntax error; the omission will simply lead to incorrect results. In the example that follows, the braces around the true task are missing. The compiler assumes that the semicolon at the end of the assignment statement terminates the if statement.

```
if (x > 0)
      sum = sum + x;
      printf("Greater than zero\n");
else
      printf("Less than or equal to zero\n");
```

The compiler may generate an unexpected symbol syntax error when it reaches the reserved word else.

When writing a nested if statement, try to select the conditions so that you can use the multiple-alternative format shown in Section 4.7. When possible, the logic should be constructed so each intermediate condition falls on the false branch of the previous decision. If more than one condition can be true at the same time, place the most restrictive condition first.

Remember that the C compiler matches each else with the closest unmatched if. If you are not careful, you may get a pairing that is different from what you expect. This may not cause a syntax error, but it will affect the outcome.

In switch statements, make sure the controlling expression and case labels are of the same permitted type (int or char but not a string or type double). Remember to include a default case; otherwise the entire body of the switch statement will be skipped if the controlling expression value is not listed in any of the case labels.

Don't forget that the body of the switch statement is a single compound statement, enclosed in one set of braces. However, the statements of each alternative within the switch are not enclosed in braces; instead, each alternative is ended by a break statement. If you omit a break statement, your program "falls through" and executes the statements for the next case.

Chapter Review

1. Use control structures to control the flow of statement execution in a program. The compound statement is a control structure for sequential execution.
2. Use selection control structures to represent decisions in an algorithm and use pseudocode to write them in algorithms. Use the if statement or switch statement to code decision steps in C.

3. Expressions whose values indicate whether certain conditions are true can be written

- using the relational operators (<, <=, >, >=) and equality operators (==, !=) to compare variables and constants
- using the logical operators (&& (and), || (or), ! (not)) to form more complex conditions

4. Data flow information in a structure chart indicates whether a variable processed by a subproblem is used as an input or an output, or as both. An input provides data that are manipulated by the subproblem, and an output returns a value copied from an input device or computed by the subproblem. The same variable may be an input to one subproblem and an output from another.

5. Extending a solution is a problem-solving technique in which you solve a new problem by modifying the solution to an existing problem. Writing modular programs (with function subprograms) makes it easier to apply this technique.

6. A hand trace of an algorithm verifies whether it is correct. You can discover errors in logic by carefully hand tracing an algorithm. Hand tracing an algorithm before coding it as a program will save you time in the long run.

7. Nested if statements are common in C and are used to represent decisions with multiple alternatives. Programmers use indentation and the multiple-alternative decision form when applicable to enhance readability of nested if statements.

8. The switch statement implements decisions with several alternatives, where the alternative selected depends on the value of a variable or expression (the *controlling expression*). The controlling expression can be type int or char, but cannot be a string or type double.

NEW C CONSTRUCTS

Construct	Effect
if Statement	
One Alternative	
`if (x != 0.0)` `    product = product * x;`	Multiplies **product** by **x** only if **x** is nonzero.
Double-Alternative	

`if (temp > 32.0)`
`    printf("%.1f: above freezing",`
`          temp);`
`else`
`    printf("%.1f: freezing", temp);`
	If **temp** is greater than **32.0**, it is labeled as **above freezing**; otherwise, it is labeled as **freezing**.

(continued)

NEW C CONSTRUCTS (continued)

Construct	Effect

Multiple-Alternative

```
if (x < 0.0) {
        printf("negative");
        absx = -x;
} else if (x == 0.0) {
        printf("zero");
        absx = 0.0;
} else {
        printf("positive");
        absx = x;
}
```

Displays one of three messages depending on whether **x** is negative, positive, or zero. Sets **absx** to represent the absolute value or magnitude of **x**.

switch Statement

```
switch (next_ch) {
case 'A':
case 'a':
        printf("Excellent");
        break;

case 'B':
case 'b':
        printf("Good");
        break;

case 'C':
case 'c':
        printf("O.K.");
        break;

case 'D':
case 'd':
case 'F':
case 'f':
        printf("Poor, student is ");
        printf("on probation");
        break;

default:
        printf("Invalid letter grade");
}
```

Displays one of five messages based on the value of **next_ch** (type **char**). If **next_ch** is **'D'**, **'d'**, or **'F'**, **'f'**, the student is put on probation. If **next_ch** is not listed in the **case** labels, displays an error message.

Quick-Check Exercises

1. An `if` statement implements _____ execution.
2. What is a compound statement?
3. A `switch` statement is often used instead of _____.
4. What can be the values of an expression with a relational operator?
5. The relational operator `<=` means _____.
6. A hand trace is used to verify that a(n) _____ is correct.
7. List the three types of control structures.
8. Correct the syntax errors.

```
if {m >= 10} {
    n = m;
else {
    n = n - 5
}
```

9. What value is assigned to `remaining` by the `if` statement when price is 60?

```
if (price> 200)
    remaining= 5000;
else if (price> 40)
    remaining = 2000;
else if (price> 60)
    remaining = 1000;
```

10. Answer Exercise 9 for the `if` statement that follows. Which `if` statement seems reasonable?

```
if (price> 60)
    remaining= 1000;
else if (price > 40)
    remaining = 2000;
else if (price> 200)
    remaining = 5000;
```

11. What output line(s) are displayed by the statements that follow when `choice` is 'c'? When `choice` is 'h'? When `choice` is 'f'?

```
switch (choice) {
case 'a':
price = 100;
break;

case 'b':
    price = 200;
    break;
```

```
case 'c':
        price = 300;
        break;

case 'd':
        price = 450;
        break;

case 'r':
case 'f':
case 'g':
        price = 1150;
}
if (price < 1000)
        printf("Within the range, Price = %d\n", price);
else
        printf("Too high! Outside the range\n");
```

12. Explain the difference between the statements on the left and the statements on the right. For each group of statements, give the final value of p if the initial value of p is 9.

```
if (p <= 10)                     if (p<= 10)
      p = p * 2;                         p = p * 2;
else if (p >= 15)                if (p >= 15)
      p = p- 1;                          p = p - 1;
```

13. a.   Evaluate the expression

```
1   &&   (30 % 10 >= 0)   &&   (30 % 10 <= 3)
```

   b.   Is either set of parentheses required?

   c.   Write the complement of the expression two ways. First, add one operator and one set of parentheses. For the second version, use DeMorgan's theorem.

Answers to Quick-Check Exercises

1. conditional
2. one or more statements surrounded by braces
3. nested if statements or a multiple-alternative if statement
4. 0 and 1
5. less than or equal to
6. algorithm
7. sequence, selection, repetition
8. Parenthesize if condition, add closing braces to the body, and add a semicolon to the assignment statement in the else condition.

9. 2000 (second condition is met)

10. 2000, the second `if` statement.

11. when `grade` is 'c':
> within the range, Price = 300

when `grade` is 'h':
> The `switch` statement is skipped so the output printed depends on the previous value of `price` (which may be garbage).

when `grade` is 'f':
> Too high! Outside the range.

12. A nested `if` statement is on the left; a sequence of `if` statements is on the right. On the left `p` becomes `18`; on the right `p` becomes `17`.

13. a. 1

b. no

c. `!(1  &&  (30 % 10 >= 0)  &&  (30 % 10 <= 3))`
    `0  ||  (30 % 10 < 0)  ||  (30 % 10 > 3)`

Review Questions

1. Making a decision between two alternative courses of action is usually implemented with a(n) _____ statement in C.

2. Trace the following program fragment; indicate which function will be called if a data value of `102` is entered.

```
printf("Enter the speed> ");
scanf("%d", &speed);
if (speed< 105)
      safe();
else
      unsafe();
```

3. Write a multiple-alternative `if` statement to display a message indicating the designation of an employee based on the employee's number of years of experience (0–3, under probation; 4–8, junior staff; 9–15, senior staff; more than 15, manager). Print a message to indicate bad data as well.

4. Write a `switch` statement to select an operation based on the value of `incentive`. Increment `total_annual` by `annual_incentive` if incentive is 'A' or 'B'; increment `total_monthly` by `monthly_incentive` if incentive is 'D', 'C', or 'M'; increment `total_weekly` by `weekly_incentive` if incentive is 'E' or 'F'. Do nothing if incentive is 'X'. Display an error message if the value of `incentive` is not one of these eight letters.

5. Write an `if` statement that displays an acceptance message for an astronaut candidate if the person's weight is between the values of `opt_min` and `opt_max`

FIGURE 4.14 Flowchart for Review Question 6

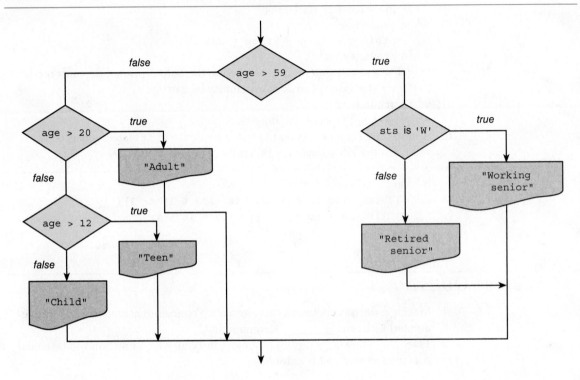

inclusive, the person's age is between `age_min` and `age_max` inclusive, and the person is a nonsmoker (`smoker` is false).

6. Implement the flowchart in Fig. 4.14 using a nested `if` structure.

Programming Projects

1. The Students' Corner Store in a university needs a program to implement its students' discount policy. The program is to prompt the user to enter the purchase total and to indicate whether the purchaser is a student. Students are eligible to receive a 20% discount on all their purchases. The discount calculation, however, must be done before addition of the 5% sales tax. This is done to ensure that the discount is not applied to the sales tax. Here are two sample output files—one for a student purchaser and one for a nonstudent purchaser.

Total purchases	$122.00
Student's discount (20%)	24.40
Discounted total	97.60
Sales tax (5%)	4.88
Total	$102.48

Total purchases	$ 24.90
Sales tax (5%)	1.25
Total	$ 26.15

Note: to display a % sign, place two % signs in the format string:

```
printf("%d%%", SALES_TAX);
```

2. Write a program that calculates the user's body mass index (BMI) and categorizes it as underweight, normal, overweight, or obese, based on the following table from the United States Centers for Disease Control:

BMI	Weight Status
Below 18.5	Underweight
18.5–24.9	Normal
25.0–29.9	Overweight
30.0 and above	Obese

To calculate BMI based on weight in pounds (*wt_lb*) and height in inches (*ht_in*), use this formula (rounded to tenths):

$$\frac{703 \times wt\_lb}{ht\_in^2}$$

Prompt the user to enter weight in pounds and height in inches.

3. Review the "C in Focus" article entitled "The UNIX Connection" on 221–222. Then write a C program that demonstrates C's short-circuit evaluation of the && and || operators. Include two user-defined functions, fun1 and fun2. Function fun1 should prompt the user to enter "T" for true or "F" for false. If the user input is "T," fun1 should return 1; otherwise it should return 0. Function fun2 should simply display "fun2 executed" and then return 1. Function main should include two conditional statements: one that displays "Test of && complete" if the && of function calls to fun1 and fun2 is true. The second conditional statement should display "Test of || complete" if the || of function calls to fun1 and fun2 is true (of course, this display will occur on every run since fun2 always returns 1). Before the first conditional statement, display "Testing &&," and before the second, "Testing ||." Then test your program four times with inputs of T T, T F, F T, and F F. Predict the output of each run before running it to verify your understanding of the short-circuit evaluation of these two operators.

4. Write a program that reports the contents of a compressed-gas cylinder based on the first letter of the cylinder's color. The program input is a character representing the observed color of the cylinder: "Y" or "y" for yellow, "O" or "o" for orange, and so on. Cylinder colors and associated contents are as follows:

orange   ammonia
brown   carbon monoxide
yellow   hydrogen
green   oxygen

Your program should respond to input of a letter other than the first letters of the given colors with the message, Contents unknown.

5. An Internet Service Provider charges its subscribers every month based on the information provided in the following table:

Data Usage (n), Gbs	Charges
$0.0 < n \le 1.0$	250
$1.0 < n \le 2.0$	500
$2.0 < n \le 5.0$	1000
$5.0 < n \le 10.0$	1500
$n > 10.0$	2000

Given the amount of data used by the subscriber (i.e. n), write a program to calculate the charges to be paid by the subscriber. Print a message to indicate bad data as well.

6. Write a program that takes the x–y coordinates of a point in the Cartesian plane and prints a message telling either an axis on which the point lies or the quadrant in which it is found.

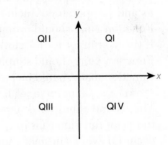

Sample lines of output:

```
(-1.0, -2.5) is in quadrant III
(0.0, 4.8) is on the y-axis
```

7. Write a program that determines the day number (1 to 366) in a year for a date that is provided as input data. As an example, January 1, 1994, is day 1. December 31, 1993, is day 365. December 31, 1996, is day 366, since 1996 is a leap year. A year is a leap year if it is divisible by four, except that any year divisible by 100 is a leap year only if it is divisible by 400. Your program should accept the month, day, and year as integers. Include a function leap that returns 1 if called with a leap year, 0 otherwise.

8. Write a program that interacts with the user like this:

```
(1) First Free Service

(2) Second Free Service

Enter the Free Service number>> 2

Enter number of Miles>> 3557

Vehicle must be serviced.
```

Use the table below to determine the appropriate message.

Free Services	Miles (k)
First Service	$1500 < k \leq 3000$
Second Service	$3001 < k \leq 4500$

9. Chatflow Wireless offers customers 600 weekday minutes for a flat rate of 39.99. Night (8 P.M. to 7 A.M.) and weekend minutes are free, but additional weekday minutes cost 0.40 each. There are taxes of 5.25% on all charges. Write a program that prompts the user to enter the number of weekday minutes, night minutes, and weekend minutes used, and calculates the monthly bill and average cost of a minute before taxes. The program should display with labels all the input data, the pretax bill and average minute cost, the taxes, and the total bill. Store all monetary values as whole cents (rounding the taxes and average minute cost), and divide by 100 for display of results.

10. Write a program to control a bread machine. Allow the user to input the type of bread as W for White and S for Sweet. Ask the user if the loaf size is double and if the baking is manual. The following table details the time chart for the machine for each bread type. Display a statement for each step. If the loaf size is double, increase the baking time by 50%. If baking is manual, stop after the loaf-shaping cycle and instruct the user to remove the dough for manual baking. Use functions to display instructions to the user and to compute the baking time.

BREAD TIME CHART

Operation	White Bread	Sweet Bread
Primary kneading	15 mins	20 mins
Primary rising	60 mins	60 mins
Secondary kneading	18 mins	33 mins
Secondary rising	20 mins	30 mins
Loaf shaping	2 seconds	2 seconds
Final rising	75 mins	75 mins
Baking	45 mins	35 mins
Cooling	30 mins	30 mins

11. The table below shows the normal boiling points of several substances. Write a program that prompts the user for the observed boiling point of a substance in °C and identifies the substance if the observed boiling point is within 5% of the expected boiling point. If the data input is more than 5% higher or lower than any of the boiling points in the table, the program should output the message `Substance unknown`.

Substance	Normal Boiling Point (°C)
Water	100
Mercury	357
Copper	1187
Silver	2193
Gold	2660

Your program should define and call a function `within_x_percent` that takes as parameters a reference value `ref`, a data value `data`, and a percentage value `x` and returns 1 meaning true if `data` is within $x\%$ of `ref`—that is, $(\text{ref} - x\% * \text{ref}) \leq \text{data} \leq (\text{ref} + x\% * \text{ref})$. Otherwise `within_x_percent` would return zero, meaning false. For example, the call `within_x_percent(357, 323, 10)` would return true, since 10% of 357 is 35.7, and 323 falls between 321.3 and 392.7.

Repetition and Loop Statements

CHAPTER OBJECTIVES

- To understand why repetition is an important control structure in programming
- To learn about loop control variables and the three steps needed to control loop repetition
- To learn how to use the C `for`, `while`, and `do-while` statements for writing loops and when to use each statement type
- To learn how to accumulate a sum or a product within a loop body
- To learn common loop patterns such as counting loops, sentinel-controlled loops, and flag-controlled loops
- To understand nested loops and how the outer loop control variable and inner loop control variable are changed in a nested loop
- To learn how to debug programs using a debugger
- To learn how to debug programs by adding diagnostic output statements

$\mathbf{I}$n your programs so far, the statements in the program body execute only once. However, in most commercial software that you use, you can repeat a process many times. For example, when using an editor program or a word processor, you can move the cursor to a program line and perform as many edit operations as you need to.

Repetition, you'll recall, is the third type of program control structure (*sequence, selection, repetition*), and the repetition of steps in a program is called a **loop**. In this chapter, we describe three C loop control statements: `while`, `for`, and `do-while`. In addition to describing how to write loops using each statement, we describe the advantages of each and explain when it is best to use each one. Like `if` statements, loops can be nested, and the chapter demonstrates how to write and use nested loops in your programs.

loop a control structure that repeats a group of steps in a program

5.1 Repetition in Programs

Just as the ability to make decisions is an important programming tool, so is the ability to specify repetition of a group of operations. For example, a company that has seven employees will want to repeat the gross pay and net pay computations in its payroll program seven times, once for each employee. The **loop body** contains the statements to be repeated.

loop body the statements that are repeated in the loop

Writing out a solution to a specific case of a problem can be helpful in preparing you to define an algorithm to solve the same problem in general. After you solve the sample case, ask yourself some of the following questions to determine whether loops will be required in the general algorithm:

1. Were there any steps I repeated as I solved the problem? If so, which ones?
2. If the answer to question 1 is yes, did I know in advance how many times to repeat the steps?
3. If the answer to question 2 is no, how did I know how long to keep repeating the steps?

Your answer to the first question indicates whether your algorithm needs a loop and what steps to include in the loop body if it does need one. Your answers to the other questions will help you determine which loop structure to choose for your solution. Figure 5.1 diagrams the relationship between these questions and the type of loop you should choose. Table 5.1 defines each of the kinds of loops you may need and refers you to the sections(s) of this chapter where you will find implementations of these loops.

FIGURE 5.1

Flow Diagram
of Loop Choice
Process

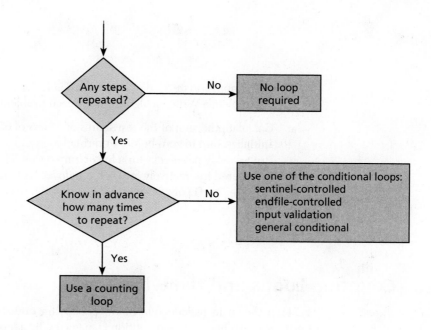

TABLE 5.1 Comparison of Loop Kinds

Kind	When Used	C Implementation Structures	Section Containing an Example
Counting loop	We can determine before loop execution exactly how many loop repetitions will be needed to solve the problem.	while for	5.2 5.4
Sentinel-controlled loop	Input of a list of data of any length ended by a special value	while, for	5.6
Endfile-controlled loop	Input of a single list of data of any length from a data file	while, for	5.6
Input validation loop	Repeated interactive input of a data value until a value within the valid range is entered	do-while	5.8
General conditional loop	Repeated processing of data until a desired condition is met	while, for	5.5

 EXERCISES FOR SECTION 5.1

Self-Check

1. Choose an appropriate kind of loop from Table 5.1 for solving each of the following problems. Write an algorithm for each problem.

   a. Calculate the sum of the test scores of a class of 35 students. (*Hint:* Initialize sum to zero before entering loop.)
   b. Print weekly paychecks for a list of employees. The following data are to be entered interactively for each employee: ID, hours worked, and hourly pay rate. An ID of zero marks the end of the data.
   c. Process a data file of Celsius temperatures. Count how many are above 100°C.

5.2 Counting Loops and the while Statement

counter-controlled loop (counting loop) a loop whose required number of iterations can be determined before loop execution begins

The loop shown in pseudocode below is called a **counter-controlled loop** (or **counting loop**) because its repetition is managed by a loop control variable whose value represents a count. A counter-controlled loop follows this general format:

Set *loop control variable* to an initial value of 0.
while *loop control variable* < *final value*

  . . .

  Increase *loop control variable* by 1.

We use a counter-controlled loop when we can determine prior to loop execution exactly how many loop repetitions will be needed to solve the problem. This number should appear as the *final value* in the `while` condition.

The while Statement

Figure 5.2 shows a program fragment that computes and displays the gross pay for seven employees. The loop body is the compound statement that starts on the third line. The loop body gets an employee's payroll data and computes and displays that employee's pay. After seven weekly pay amounts are displayed, the statement following the loop body executes and displays the message All employees processed.

The three color lines in Fig. 5.2 control the looping process. The first statement

```
count_emp = 0;    /* no employees processed yet */
```

stores an initial value of 0 in the variable count_emp, which represents the count of employees processed so far. The next line evaluates the condition count_emp < 7. If the condition is true, the compound statement representing the loop body is executed,

FIGURE 5.2   Program Fragment with a Loop

```
1.  count_emp = 0;                    /* no employees processed yet   */
2.  while (count_emp < 7) {           /* test value of count_emp      */
3.      printf("Hours> ");
4.      scanf("%d", &hours);
5.      printf("Rate> ");
6.      scanf("%lf", &rate);
7.      pay = hours * rate;
8.      printf("Pay is $%6.2f\n", pay);
9.      count_emp = count_emp + 1; /* increment count_emp          */
10. }
11. printf("\nAll employees processed\n");
```

causing a new pair of data values to be scanned and a new pay amount to be computed and displayed. The last statement in the loop body

```
count_emp = count_emp + 1; /* increment count_emp */
```

adds 1 to the current value of `count_emp`. After executing the last step in the loop body, control returns to the line beginning with `while` and the condition is reevaluated for the next value of `count_emp`. The loop body is executed once for each value of `count_emp` from 0 to 6. Eventually, `count_emp` becomes 7, and the condition evaluates to false (0). When this happens, the loop body is not executed and control passes to the display statement that follows the loop body. The expression following the reserved word `while` is called the **loop repetition condition**. The loop is repeated when this condition is true—that is, when its value is not 0. The *loop is exited* when this condition is false.

loop repetition condition   the condition that controls loop repetition

The flowchart in Fig. 5.3 summarizes what we have explained so far about `while` loops. In the flowchart, the expression in the diamond-shaped box is evaluated first. If that expression is true, the loop body is executed, and the process is repeated. The `while` loop is exited when the expression becomes false. If the loop repetition condition is false when it is first tested, then the loop body is not executed at all.

Make sure you understand the difference between the `while` statement in Fig. 5.3 and the following `if` statement:

```
if (count_emp < 7) {
    . . .
}
```

In an `if` statement, the compound statement after the parenthesized condition executes at most only once. In a `while` statement, the compound statement can execute more than once.

FIGURE 5.3

Flowchart for
a while Loop

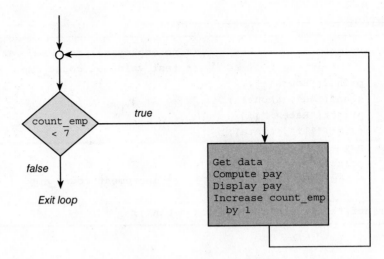

Syntax of the while Statement   In Fig. 5.2, the variable count_emp is called
the **loop control variable** because its value determines whether the loop body is
repeated. The loop control variable count_emp must be (1) initialized, (2) tested,
and (3) updated for the loop to execute properly. Each step is summarized next.

**loop control
variable**   the variable
whose value controls
loop repetition

- *Initialization.* count_emp is set to an initial value of 0 (*initialized to* 0) before
  the while statement is reached.
- *Testing.* count_emp is tested before the start of each loop repetition (called an
  iteration or a *pass*).
- *Updating.* count_emp is updated (its value increased by 1) during each iteration.

Similar steps must be performed for every while loop. Without the initialization, the initial test of count_emp is meaningless. The updating step ensures that the
program progresses toward the final goal (count_emp >= 7) during each repetition
of the loop. If the loop control variable is not updated, the loop will execute "forever." Such a loop is called an **infinite loop**.

infinite loop   a loop
that executes forever

---

while Statement

SYNTAX: while (*loop repetition condition*)
                 statement;

EXAMPLE: /* Display N asterisks. */
             count_star = 0;
             while (count_star < N) {
                 printf("*");
                 count_star = count_star + 1;
             }   *(continued)*

INTERPRETATION: The *loop repetition condition* (a condition to control the loop process) is tested; if it is true, the *statement* (loop body) is executed, and the *loop repetition condition* is retested. The *statement* is repeated as long as (`while`) the loop repetition condition is true. When this condition is tested and found to be false, the `while` loop is exited and the next program statement after the `while` statement is executed.

Note: If *loop repetition condition* evaluates to false the first time it is tested, *statement* is not executed.

EXERCISES FOR SECTION 5.2

Self-Check

1. Predict the output of this program fragment:

```
i = 0;
while (i <= 5) {
    printf("%3d %3d\n", i, 10 - i);
    i = i + 1;
}
```

2. What is displayed by this program fragment for an input of 8?

```
scanf("%d", &n);
ev = 0;
while (ev < n) {
    printf("%3d", ev);
    ev = ev + 2;
}
printf("\n");
```

Programming

1. Write a program fragment that produces this output:

```
0    1
1    2
2    4
3    8
4    16
5    32
6    64
```

5.3   Computing a Sum or a Product in a Loop

Loops often accumulate a sum or a product by repeating an addition or multiplication operation as demonstrated in Examples 5.1 and 5.2.

EXAMPLE 5.1	The program in Fig. 5.4 has a `while` loop similar to the loop in Fig. 5.2. Besides displaying each employee's pay, it computes and displays the company's total payroll. Prior to loop execution, the statements

```
total_pay = 0.0;
count_emp = 0;
```

initialize both `total_pay` and `count_emp` to 0, where `count_emp` is the counter variable. Here `total_pay` is an **accumulator** variable, and it accumulates the total payroll value. Initializing `total_pay` to 0 is critical; if you omit this step, your final total will be off by whatever value happens to be stored in `total_pay` when the program begins execution.

accumulator a variable used to store a value being computed in increments during the execution of a loop

In the loop body, the assignment statement

```
total_pay = total_pay + pay;      /* Add next pay. */
```

adds the current value of `pay` to the sum being accumulated in `total_pay`. Consequently, the value of `total_pay` increases with each loop iteration. Table 5.2 traces the effect of repeating this statement for the three values of `pay` shown in the sample run. Recall that iteration means a pass through the loop.

FIGURE 5.4 Program to Compute Company Payroll

```
1.   /* Compute the payroll for a company */
2.
3.   #include <stdio.h>
4.
5.   int
6.   main(void)
7.   {
8.        double total_pay;      /* company payroll        */
9.        int    count_emp;      /* current employee       */
10.       int    number_emp;     /* number of employees    */
11.       double hours;          /* hours worked           */
12.       double rate;           /* hourly rate            */
13.       double pay;            /* pay for this period    */
```

(continued)

FIGURE 5.4   (continued)

```
14.
15.         /* Get number of employees. */
16.         printf("Enter number of employees> ");
17.         scanf("%d", &number_emp);
18.
19.         /* Compute each employee's pay and add it to the payroll. */
20.         total_pay = 0.0;
21.         count_emp = 0;
22.         while (count_emp < number_emp) {
23.             printf("Hours> ");
24.             scanf("%lf", &hours);
25.             printf("Rate > $");
26.             scanf("%lf", &rate);
27.             pay = hours * rate;
28.             printf("Pay is $%6.2f\n\n", pay);
29.             total_pay = total_pay + pay;          /* Add next pay. */
30.             count_emp = count_emp + 1;
31.         }
32.         printf("All employees processed\n");
33.         printf("Total payroll is $%8.2f\n", total_pay);
34.
35.         return (0);
36.     }
```

```
Enter number of employees> 3
Hours> 50
Rate > $5.25
Pay is $262.50

Hours> 6
Rate > $5.00
Pay is $ 30.00

Hours> 15
Rate > $7.00
Pay is $105.00

All employees processed
Total payroll is $ 397.50
```

TABLE 5.2 Trace of Three Repetitions of Loop in Fig. 5.4

Statement	hours	rate	pay	total_pay	count_emp	Effect
	?	?	?	0.0	0	
count_emp < number_emp						true
scanf("%lf", &hours);	50.0					get hours
scanf("%lf", &rate);		5.25				get rate
pay = hours * rate;			262.5			find pay
total_pay = total_pay + pay;				262.5		add to total_pay
count_emp = count_emp + 1;					1	increment count_emp
count_emp < number_emp						true
scanf("%lf", &hours);	6.0					get hours
scanf("%lf", &rate);		5.0				get rate
pay = hours * rate;			30.0			find pay
total_pay = total_pay + pay;				292.5		add to total_pay
count_emp = count_emp + 1;					2	increment count_emp
count_emp < number_emp						true
scanf("%lf", &hours);	15.0					get hours
scanf("%lf", &rate);		7.0				get rate
pay = hours * rate;			105.0			find pay
total_pay = total_pay + pay;				397.5		add pay to total_pay
count_emp = count_emp + 1;					3	increment count_emp

Program Style   *Writing General Loops*

Because the loop in Fig. 5.2 uses the loop repetition condition count_emp < 7, it processes exactly 7 employees. The loop in Fig. 5.4 is more general. It uses the loop repetition condition count_emp < number_emp so it can process any number of employees. The number of employees to be processed must be scanned into variable number_emp before the while statement executes. The loop repetition condition compares the number of employees processed so far (count_emp) to the total number of employees (number_emp).

Multiplying a List of Numbers

In a similar way, we can use a loop to compute the product of a list of numbers as shown in the next example.

EXAMPLE 5.2

The loop that follows multiplies data items together as long as the product remains less than 10,000. It displays the product calculated so far before asking for the next data value. The product so far is updated on each iteration by executing the statement

```
product = product * item; /* Update product */
```

Loop exit occurs when the value of `product` is greater than or equal to 10,000. Consequently, the loop body does not display the last value assigned to `product`.

```
/* Multiply data while product remains less than 10000 */
product = 1;
while (product < 10000) {
    printf("%d\n", product); /* Display product so far */
    printf("Enter next item> ");
    scanf("%d", &item);
    product = product * item; /* Update product */
}
```

This loop is an example of the general conditional loop presented in Table 5.1, whose pseudocode is shown below.

1. Initialize *loop control variable.*
2. As long as exit condition hasn't been met
     3. Continue processing.

The product-computation loop's loop control variable is `product`, which is initialized to 1. Its exit condition is that `product` is greater than or equal to 10,000, and the steps of the loop body make up the processing mentioned in pseudocode step 3.

Compound Assignment Operators

We have seen several instances of assignment statements of the form

$$variable = variable \; op \; expression;$$

where *op* is a C arithmetic operator. These include increments and decrements of loop counters

```
count_emp = count_emp + 1;
time = time - 1;
```

TABLE 5.3 Compound Assignment Operators

Statement with Simple Assignment Operator	Equivalent Statement with Compound Assignment Operator
`count_emp = count_emp + 1;`	`count_emp += 1;`
`time = time - 1;`	`time -= 1;`
`total_time = total_time + times;`	`total_time += time;`
`product = product * item;`	`product *= item;`
`n = n * (x + 1);`	`n *= x + 1;`

as well as statements accumulating a sum or computing a product in a loop, such as

```
total_pay = total_pay + pay;
product = product * item;
```

C provides special assignment operators that enable a more concise notation for statements of this type. For the operations +, -, *, /, and %, C defines the compound *op*= assignment operators +=, -=, *=, /=, and %=. A statement of the form

$$\text{variable } op = expression;$$

is an alternative way of writing the statement

$$\text{variable } = \text{variable } op \ (expression);$$

Table 5.3 shows some examples using compound assignment operators. The last example demonstrates the relevance of the parentheses around *expression* in the definition of an assignment statement with a compound operator.

EXERCISES FOR SECTION 5.3

Self-Check

1. What output values are displayed by the following `while` loop for a data value of 5? Of 6? Of 7?

    ```
    printf("Enter an integer> ");
    scanf("%d", &x);
    product = x;
    count = 0;
    ```

```
while (count < 4) {
    printf("%d\n", product);
    product *= x;
    count += 1;
}
```

In general, for a data value of any number *n*, what does this loop display?

2. What values are displayed if the call to `printf` comes at the end of the loop instead of at the beginning?

3. The following segment needs some revision. Insert braces where they are needed and correct the errors. The corrected code should take five integers and display their sum.

```
count = 0;
while (count <= 5)
count += 1;
printf("Next number> ");
scanf("%d", &next_num);
next_num += sum;
printf("%d numbers were added; \n", count);
printf("their sum is %d.\n", sum);
```

4. Where possible, write equivalents for the following statements using compound assignment operators:

```
s = s / 5;
q = q * n + 4;
z = z - x * y;
t = t + (u % v);
```

Programming

1. Write a program segment that computes $1 + 2 + 3 + \ldots + (n - 1) + n$, where n is a data value. Follow the loop body with an `if` statement that compares this value to `(n * (n + 1)) / 2` and displays a message that indicates whether the values are the same or different. What message do you think will be displayed?

5.4 The for Statement

C provides the `for` statement as another form for implementing loops. The loops we have seen so far are typical of most repetition structures in that they have three loop control components in addition to the loop body:

- initialization of the *loop control variable,*
- test of the *loop repetition condition,* and
- change (update) of the *loop control variable.*

FIGURE 5.5   Using a for Statement in a Counting Loop

```
1.   /* Process payroll for all employees */
2.   total_pay = 0.0;
3.   for (count_emp = 0;                      /* initialization              */
4.        count_emp < number_emp;             /* loop repetition condition   */
5.        count_emp += 1) {                    /* update                      */
6.       printf("Hours> ");
7.       scanf("%lf", &hours);
8.       printf("Rate > $");
9.       scanf("%lf", &rate);
10.      pay = hours * rate;
11.      printf("Pay is $%6.2f\n\n", pay);
12.      total_pay = total_pay + pay;
13.  }
14.  printf("All employees processed\n");
15.  printf("Total payroll is $%8.2f\n", total_pay);
```

An important feature of the for statement in C is that it supplies a designated place for each of these three components. A for statement implementation of the loop from Fig. 5.4 is shown in Fig. 5.5.

The effect of this for statement is exactly equivalent to the execution of the comparable while loop section of the program in Fig. 5.4. Because the for statement's heading

```
for    (count_emp = 0;            /* initialization              */
        count_emp < number_emp;   /* loop repetition condition   */
        count_emp += 1) {          /* update                      */
```

combines the three loop control steps of initialization, testing, and update in one place, separate steps to initialize and update count_emp must not appear elsewhere. The for statement can be used to count up or down by any interval.

Program Style   *Formatting the for Statement*

For clarity, we usually place each expression of the for heading on a separate line. If all three expressions are very short, we may place them together on one line. Here is an example:

```
/* Display nonnegative numbers < max */
for (i = 0; i < max; i += 1)
    printf("%d\n", i);
```

---

for Statement

SYNTAX: `for` (*initialization expression*;
                  loop repetition condition;
                  update expression)
              statement;

EXAMPLE: `/* Display N asterisks. */`
            `for (count_star = 0;`
                 `count_star < N;`
                 `count_star += 1)`
              `printf("*");`

INTERPRETATION: First, the *initialization expression* is executed. Then, the *loop repetition condition* is tested. If it is true, the *statement* is executed, and the *update expression* is evaluated. Then the *loop repetition condition* is retested. The *statement* is repeated as long as the *loop repetition condition* is true. When this condition is tested and found to be false, the `for` loop is exited, and the next program statement after the `for` statement is executed.

Caution: Although C permits the use of fractional values for counting loop control variables of type **double**, we strongly discourage this practice. Counting loops with type **double** control variables will not always execute the same number of times on different computers.

The body of the `for` loop is indented. If the loop body is a compound statement or if we are using a style in which we bracket all loop bodies, we place the opening brace at the end of the `for` heading and terminate the statement by placing the closing brace on a separate line. This closing brace should be aligned with the "f" of the `for` that it is ending.

Increment and Decrement Operators

The counting loops that you have seen have all included assignment expressions of the form

`counter = counter + 1`

or

`counter += 1`

side effect a change
in the value of a
variable as a result
of carrying out an
operation

The increment operator ++ takes a single variable as its operand. The **side effect** of applying the ++ operator is that the value of its operand is incremented by one. Frequently, ++ is used just for this side effect, as in the following loop in which the variable `counter` is to run from 0 up to `limit`:

`for (counter = 0; counter < limit;  ++counter)`
    `. . .`

The *value* of the expression in which the ++ operator is used depends on the position of the operator. When the ++ is placed immediately in front of its operand (*prefix increment*), the value of the expression is the variable's value *after* incrementing. When the ++ comes immediately after the operand (*postfix increment*), the expression's value is the value of the variable *before* it is incremented. Compare the action of the two code segments in Fig. 5.6, given an initial value of 2 in i.

C also provides a decrement operator that can be used in either the prefix or postfix position. For example, if the initial value of n is 4, the code fragment on the left prints

```
3   3
```

and the one on the right prints

```
4   3
```

```
printf("%3d", --n);    printf("%3d", n--);
printf("%3d", n);      printf("%3d", n);
```

You should avoid using the increment and decrement operators in complex expressions in which the variables to which they are applied appear more than once. C compilers are expected to exploit the commutativity and associativity of various operators in order to produce efficient code. For example, this code fragment may assign y the value 13 (2 * 5 + 3) in one implementation and the value 18 (3 * 5 + 3) in another.

```
x = 5;
i = 2;
y = i * x + ++i;
```

A programmer must not depend on side effects that will vary from one compiler to another.

FIGURE 5.6

Comparison of Prefix and Postfix Increments

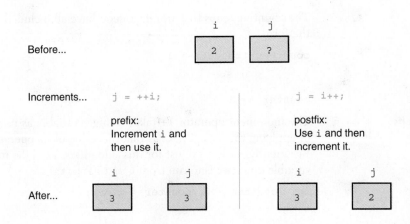

EXAMPLE 5.3   Function `factorial` (Fig. 5.7) computes the factorial of an integer represented by the formal parameter n. The loop body executes for decreasing values of i from n through 2, and each value of i is incorporated in the accumulating product. Loop exit occurs when i is 1.

Increments and Decrements Other Than 1

We have seen `for` statement counting loops that count up by one and down by one. Now we will use a loop that counts down by five to display a Celsius-to-Fahrenheit conversion table.

EXAMPLE 5.4   The table displayed by the program in Fig. 5.8 shows temperature conversions from 10 degrees Celsius to –5 degrees Celsius because of the values of the constant macros named CBEGIN and CLIMIT. Since the loop update step subtracts CSTEP (5) from celsius, the value of the counter celsius decreases by five after each repetition. Loop exit occurs when celsius becomes less than CLIMIT—that is, when celsius is -10. Table 5.4 uses the small circled numbers to trace the execution of this counting `for` loop.

FIGURE 5.7   Function to Compute Factorial

```
1.  /*
2.   * Computes n!
3.   * Pre: n is greater than or equal to zero
4.   */
5.  int
6.  factorial(int n)
7.  {
8.      int i,          /* local variables */
9.          product;    /* accumulator for product computation */
10.
11.     product = 1;
12.     /* Computes the product n x (n-1) x (n-2) x . . . x 2 x 1 */
13.     for (i = n; i > 1; --i) {
14.         product = product * i;
15.     }
16.
17.     /* Returns function result */
18.     return (product);
19. }
```

FIGURE 5.8   Displaying a Celsius-to-Fahrenheit Conversion Table

```
1.   /* Conversion of Celsius to Fahrenheit temperatures */
2.
3.   #include <stdio.h>
4.
5.   /* Constant macros */
6.   #define CBEGIN 10
7.   #define CLIMIT -5
8.   #define CSTEP 5
9.
10.  int
11.  main(void)
12.  {
13.        /* Variable declarations */
14.        int    celsius;
15.        double fahrenheit;
16.
17.        /* Display the table heading */
18.        printf("  Celsius  Fahrenheit\n");
19.
20.        /* Display the table */
21.  1     for  (celsius = CBEGIN;
22.  2           celsius >= CLIMIT;
23.  3           celsius -= CSTEP) {
24.  4        fahrenheit = 1.8 * celsius + 32.0;
25.  5        printf("%6c%3d%8c%7.2f\n", ' ', celsius, ' ', fahrenheit);
26.        }
27.
28.        return (0);
29.  }
       Celsius      Fahrenheit
           10           50.00
            5           41.00
            0           32.00
           -5           23.00
```

TABLE 5.4 Trace of Loop in Fig. 5.8

	Statement	celsius	fahrenheit	Effect
1	for (celsius = CBEGIN;	10	?	Initialize **celsius** to 10
2	celsius >= CLIMIT;			10 >= -5 is true
4	fahrenheit = 1.8 * celsius + 32.0;		50.0	Assign 50.0 to fahrenheit
5	printf ...			Display 10 and 50.0
	Update and test **celsius**			
3	... celsius -= CSTEP	5		Subtract 5 from **celsius**, giving 5
2	celsius >= CLIMIT;			5 >= -5 is true
4	fahrenheit = 1.8 * celsius + 32.0;		41.0	Assign 41.0 to fahrenheit
5	printf ...			Display 5 and 41.0
	Update and test **celsius**			
3	... celsius -= CSTEP	0		Subtract 5 from **celsius**, giving 0
2	celsius >= CLIMIT;			0 >= -5 is true
4	fahrenheit = 1.8 * celsius + 32.0;		32.0	Assign 32.0 to **fahrenheit**
5	printf ...			Display 0 and 32.0
	Update and test **celsius**			
3	... celsius -= CSTEP	-5		Subtract 5 from **celsius**, giving -5
2	celsius >= CLIMIT;			-5 >= -5 is true
4	fahrenheit = 1.8 * celsius + 32.0;		23.0	Assign 23.0 to **fahrenheit**
5	printf ...			Display -5 and 23.0
	Update and test **celsius**			
3	... celsius -= CSTEP	-10		Subtract 5 from **celsius**, giving -10
2	celsius >= CLIMIT;			-10 >= -5 is false, so exit loop

The trace in Table 5.4 shows that the loop control variable celsius is initialized to CBEGIN (10) when the for loop is reached. Since 10 is greater than or equal to CLIMIT (-5), the loop body is executed. After each loop repetition, CSTEP (5) is subtracted from celsius, and celsius is tested in the loop repetition condition to see whether its value is still greater than or equal to CLIMIT. If the condition is true, the loop body is executed again and the next value of fahrenheit is computed and displayed. If the condition is false, the loop is exited.

Because the structure of the `for` statement makes it easy for the reader of a program to identify the major loop control elements, we will use it often in the remainder of our study of repetition when a loop requires simple initialization, testing, and updating of a loop control variable.

Displaying a Table of Values

The program in Fig. 5.8 displays a table of output values. The `printf` call before the loop displays a string that forms the table heading. Within the loop body, the `printf` statement

```
printf("%6c%3d%8c%7.2f\n", ' ', celsius, ' ', fahrenheit);
```

displays a pair of output values each time it executes. Function `printf` substitutes the space character ' ' for the placeholders `%6c` and `%8c` in its format string, causing 6 blanks to precede the value of `celsius` and 8 blanks to separate the values of `celsius` and `fahrenheit`. The `\n` in the `printf` format string ends the line on which each pair of numbers appears, so the loop creates a table consisting of two columns of numbers.

EXERCISES FOR SECTION 5.4

Self-Check

1. Trace the execution of the loop that follows for n = 8. Show values of `odd` and `sum` after the update of the loop counter for each iteration.

    ```
    sum = 0;
    for  (odd = 1;
          odd < n;
          odd += 2)
       sum = sum + odd;

    printf("Sum of positive odd numbers less than %d is %d.\n", n,
           sum);
    ```

2. Given the constant macro definitions of Fig. 5.8 (repeated here)

    ```
    #define CBEGIN 10
    #define CLIMIT -5
    #define CSTEP 5
    ```

    indicate what values of `celsius` would appear in the conversion table displayed if the `for` loop header of Fig. 5.8 were rewritten as shown:

    a. `for  (celsius = CLIMIT;`
                     `celsius <= CBEGIN;`
                     `celsius += CSTEP)`

    b. `for  (celsius = CLIMIT;`
                     `celsius >= CBEGIN;`
                     `celsius += CSTEP)`

```
c.  for  (celsius = CSTEP;
          celsius >= CBEGIN;
          celsius += CLIMIT)
d.  for  (celsius = CLIMIT;
          celsius <= CSTEP;
          celsius += CBEGIN)
```

3. What is the least number of times that the body of a `while` loop can be executed? Answer the question for the body of a `for` loop.

4. What values are assigned to `n`, `m`, and `p`, given these initial values?

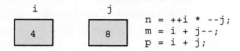

5. Rewrite the code shown in Exercise 4 so the effect is equivalent but no increment/decrement operator appears in an expression with another arithmetic operator.

6. What errors do you see in the following fragment? Correct the code so it displays all multiples of 4 from 0 through 100.

```
for mult4 = 0;
mult4 < 100;
mult4 += 4;
printf("%d\n", mult4);
```

7. a. Trace the following program fragment:

```
j = 10;
for (i = 1; i <= 5; ++i) {
    printf("%d %d\n", i, j);
    j -= 2;
}
```

   b. Rewrite the previous program fragment so that it produces the same output but uses 0 as the initial value of i.

Programming

1. Write a loop that displays a table of angle measures along with their sine and cosine values. Assume that the initial and final angle measures (in degrees) are available in `init_degree` and `final_degree` (type `int` variables), and that the change in angle measure between table entries is given by `step_degree` (also a type `int` variable). Remember that the math library's `sin` and `cos` functions take arguments that are in radians.

2. Write a program to display a centimeters-to-inches conversion table. The smallest and largest number of centimeters in the table are input values. Your table should give conversions in 10-centimeter intervals. One centimeter equals 0.3937 inch.

5.5   Conditional Loops

In many programming situations, you will not be able to determine the exact number of loop repetitions before loop execution begins. When we multiplied a list of numbers in Example 5.2, the number of repetitions depended on the data entered. Although we did not know in advance how many times the loop would execute, we were still able to write a condition to control the loop. Here is another case of this type of repetition. You want to continue prompting the user for a data value as long as the response is unreasonable.

> Print an initial prompting message.
> Get the number of observed values.
> while the number of values is negative
>> Print a warning and another prompting message.
>> Get the number of observed values.

Like the counting loops we considered earlier, such a conditional loop typically has three parts that control repetition: initialization, testing of a loop repetition condition, and an update. Let's analyze the algorithm for ensuring valid input. Clearly, the loop repetition condition is

$$number\ of\ values < 0$$

Because it makes no sense to test this condition unless *number of values* has a meaning, getting this value must be the initialization step. The update action—the statement that, if left out, would cause the loop to repeat infinitely—remains to be identified. Getting a new number of observed values within the loop body is just such a step. Since we have found these three essential loop parts, we can write this validating input loop in C by using a `while` statement:

```
printf("Enter number of observed values> ");
scanf("%d", &num_obs);          /* initialization    */
while (num_obs < 0) {
    printf("Negative number invalid; try again> ");
    scanf("%d", &num_obs);      /* update            */
}
```

At first, it may seem odd that the initialization and update steps are identical. In fact, this is very often the case for loops performing input operations in situations where the number of input values is not known in advance.

EXAMPLE 5.5   The program in Fig. 5.9 is designed to assist in monitoring the gasoline supply in a storage tank at the Super Oil Company refinery. The program is to alert the supervisor when the supply of gasoline in the tank falls below 10% of the tank's 80,000-barrel storage capacity. Although the supervisor always deals with the contents of the tank in terms of a number of *barrels*, the pump that is used to fill tanker trucks gives its measurements in *gallons*. The barrel used in the petroleum industry equals 42 U.S. gallons.

FIGURE 5.9   Program to Monitor Gasoline Storage Tank

```
1.  /*
2.   * Monitor gasoline supply in storage tank. Issue warning when supply
3.   * falls below MIN_PCT % of tank capacity.
4.   */
5.
6.  #include <stdio.h>
7.
8.  /* constant macros */
9.  #define CAPACITY      80000.0  /* number of barrels tank can hold     */
10. #define MIN_PCT       10       /* warn when supply falls below this   */
11.                                percent of capacity                    */
12. #define GALS_PER_BRL 42.0      /* number of U.S. gallons in one barrel */
13.
14. /* Function prototype */
15. double monitor_gas(double min_supply, double start_supply);
16.
17. int
18. main(void)
19. {
20.         double start_supply, /* input - initial supply in barrels      */
21.                min_supply,   /* minimum number of barrels left without  */
22.                                 warning                                  */
23.                current;      /* output - current supply in barrels      */
24.
25.         /* Compute minimum supply without warning */
26.         min_supply = MIN_PCT / 100.0 * CAPACITY;
27.
28.         /* Get initial supply */
29.         printf("Number of barrels currently in tank> ");
30.         scanf("%lf", &start_supply);
31.
32.         /* Subtract amounts removed and display amount remaining
33.            as long as minimum supply remains.                           */
34.         current = monitor_gas(min_supply, start_supply);
35.
36.         /* Issue warning                                                */
37.         printf("only %.2f barrels are left.\n\n", current);
38.         printf("*** WARNING ***\n");
```

(continued)

FIGURE 5.9 (continued)

```
39.          printf("Available supply is less than %d percent of tank's\n",
40.                  MIN_PCT);
41.          printf("%.2f-barrel capacity.\n", CAPACITY);
42.
43.          return (0);
44.   }
45.
46.   /*
47.    * Computes and displays amount of gas remaining after each delivery
48.    * Pre : min_supply and start_supply are defined.
49.    * Post: Returns the supply available (in barrels) after all permitted
50.    *       removals. The value returned is the first supply amount that is
51.    *       less than min_supply.
52.    */
53.   double
54.   monitor_gas(double min_supply, double start_supply)
55.   {
56.          double remov_gals, /* input - amount of current delivery      */
57.                 remov_brls, /*            in barrels and gallons        */
58.                 current;    /* output - current supply in barrels      */
59.
60.          for  (current = start_supply;
61.                current >= min_supply;
62.                current -= remov_brls) {
63.             printf("%.2f barrels are available.\n\n", current);
64.             printf("Enter number of gallons removed> ");
65.             scanf("%lf", &remov_gals);
66.             remov_brls = remov_gals / GALS_PER_BRL;
67.
68.             printf("After removal of %.2f gallons (%.2f barrels),\n",
69.                     remov_gals, remov_brls);
70.          }
71.
72.          return (current);
73.   }
```

```
Number of barrels currently in tank> 8500.5
8500.50 barrels are available.
```

(continued)

FIGURE 5.9   (continued)

```
Enter number of gallons removed> 5859.0
After removal of 5859.00 gallons (139.50 barrels),
8361.00 barrels are available.

Enter number of gallons removed> 7568.4
After removal of 7568.40 gallons (180.20 barrels),
8180.80 barrels are available.

Enter number of gallons removed> 8400.0
After removal of 8400.00 gallons (200.00 barrels),
only 7980.80 barrels are left.

*** WARNING ***
Available supply is less than 10 percent of tank's
80000.00-barrel capacity.
```

The main function first prompts the operator for the amount of gasoline currently stored in the tank. Next, it calls function `monitor_gas` to monitor the removal of gasoline and to stop removals as soon as the current supply falls below the minimum supply level. After gasoline is pumped into each tanker, the operator enters the number of gallons removed and function `monitor_gas` updates the number of barrels still available (`current`). When the supply drops below the 10% limit, loop exit occurs and `monitor_gas` returns the value of `current` to the main function, which issues a warning.

A counting loop would not be appropriate in this program because we do not know in advance how many tanker deliveries will need to be processed before the warning is issued. However, the `for` statement is still a good choice because we do have initialization, testing, and update steps.

Let's take a close look at the loop in function `monitor_gas`. Logically, we want to continue to record amounts of gasoline removed as long as the supply in the tank does not fall below the minimum. The loop repetition condition, the second expression in the `for` loop heading, states that we stay in the loop as long as

```
current >= min_supply
```

Since `min_supply` does not change, `current` is the variable that controls the loop. Therefore, the first and third expressions of the `for` statement's heading handle the initialization and update of this variable's value.

Tracing this program with the data shown, we come first to the assignment statement that computes a value for `min_supply` of 8000.0, based on the tank capacity and minimum percentage. The call to `printf` just before the call to `scanf` generates the prompting message for entering the tank's initial supply. Next, the starting supply entered by the program operator is scanned into variable `start_supply` and the main function calls `monitor_gas`.

In `monitor_gas`, the initialization expression of the `for` statement copies the starting supply into `current`, the loop control variable, giving `current` the value `8500.5`. When the loop repetition condition

```
current >= min_supply
```

is first tested, it evaluates to true, causing the loop body (the compound statement in braces) to execute. The current supply is displayed followed by a prompting message. A value is obtained for gallons removed (`5859.0`), the value is converted to barrels, and this amount is displayed. When execution of the loop body is complete, the update expression of the `for` statement

```
current -= remov_brls
```

is executed, subtracting from the current supply the amount removed. The loop repetition condition is retested with the new value of `current` (`8361.00`). Since `8361.00` > `8000.0` is true, the loop body once again displays the current supply and processes a delivery of `7568.4` gallons, or `180.20` barrels. The value of `current` is then updated to `8180.80` barrels, which is still not below the minimum, so the loop body executes a third time, processing removal of `200.00` barrels. This time execution of the `for` statement update expression brings the value of `current` to `7980.80`. The loop repetition condition is tested again: Since `7980.8 >= 8000.0` is false, loop exit occurs, and the statements following the closing brace of the loop body are executed.

Just as in the counting loop shown in Fig. 5.5, there are three critical steps in Fig. 5.9 that involve the loop control variable `current`.

- `current` is *initialized* to the starting supply in the `for` statement initialization expression.
- `current` is *tested* before each execution of the loop body.
- `current` is *updated* (by subtraction of the amount removed) during each iteration.

Remember that steps similar to these appear in virtually every loop you write. The C `for` statement heading provides you with a designated place for each of the three steps.

Program Style *Performing Loop Processing in a Function Subprogram*

In Fig. 5.9, function `monitor_gas` contains a `for` loop that performs the major program task—monitoring gasoline deliveries. The function result is the final value of the loop control variable, `current`. This program structure is fairly common and quite effective. Placing all loop processing in a function subprogram simplifies the main function.

EXERCISES FOR SECTION 5.5

Self-Check

1. Give an example of data the user could enter for the storage tank monitoring program that would cause function `monitor_gas` to return without executing the body of the `for` loop.
2. Correct the syntax and logic of the code that follows so that it prints all multiples of 4 from 0 through 100:

```
for sum = 0;
    sum < 100;
    sum += 4;
printf("%d\n", sum);
```

3. What output is displayed if this list of data is used for the program in Fig. 5.9?

```
8350.8
7581.0
7984.2
```

4. How would you modify the program in Fig. 5.9 so that it also determines the number of deliveries (`count_deliv`) made before the gasoline supply drops below the minimum? Which is the loop control variable, `current` or `count_deliv`?

Programming

1. There are 9,870 people in a town whose population increases by 10% each year. Write a loop that displays the annual population and determines how many years (`count_years`) it will take for the population to surpass 30,000.
2. Rewrite the payroll program (Fig. 5.5), moving the loop processing into a function subprogram. Return the total payroll amount as the function result.

5.6 Loop Design

Being able to analyze the operation of a loop is one thing; designing your own loops is another. In this section, we will consider the latter. The comment that precedes the call to function `monitor_gas` in Fig. 5.9 is a good summary of the purpose of the loop in this function.

```
/* Subtract amounts removed and display amount remaining
   as long as minimum supply remains.                        */
```

Let's see how the problem-solving questions suggested in Sections 1.5 and 5.1 can help us formulate a valid loop structure. As always, the columns labeled "Answer" and "Implications . . ." in Table 5.5 represent an individual problem solver's thought processes and are not offered as the "one and only true path" to a solution.

Sentinel-Controlled Loops

Many programs with loops input one or more additional data items each time the loop body is repeated. Often we don't know how many data items the loop should process when it begins execution. Therefore, we must find some way to signal the program to stop reading and processing new data.

One way to do this is to instruct the user to enter a unique data value, called a **sentinel value**, after the last data item. The loop repetition condition tests each data item and causes loop exit when the sentinel value is read. Choose the sentinel value carefully; it must be a value that could not normally occur as data.

sentinel value   an end marker that follows the last item in a list of data

TABLE 5.5   Problem-Solving Questions for Loop Design

Question	Answer	Implications for the Algorithm
What are the inputs?	Initial supply of gasoline (barrels). Amounts removed (gallons).	Input variables needed: `start_supply` `remov_gals` Value of `start_supply` must be input once, but amounts removed are entered many times.
What are the outputs?	Amounts removed in gallons and barrels, and the current supply of gasoline.	Values of `current` and `remov_gals` are echoed in the output. Output variable needed: `remov_brls`
Is there any repetition?	Yes. One repeatedly 1. gets amount removed 2. converts the amount to barrels 3. subtracts the amount removed from the current supply 4. checks to see whether the supply has fallen below the minimum.	Program variable needed: `min_supply`
Do I know in advance how many times steps will be repeated?	No.	Loop will not be controlled by a counter.
How do I know how long to keep repeating the steps?	As long as the current supply is not below the minimum.	The loop repetition condition is `current >= min_supply`

A loop that processes data until the sentinel value is entered has the form

1. Get a line of data.
2. while the sentinel value has not been encountered
   3. Process the data line.
   4. Get another line of data.

Note that this loop, like other loops we have studied, has an *initialization* (step 1), a *loop repetition condition* (step 2), and an *update* (step 4). Step 1 gets the first line of data; step 4 gets all the other data lines and then tries to obtain one more line. This attempted extra input permits entry (but not processing) of the sentinel value. For program readability, we usually name the sentinel by defining a constant macro.

EXAMPLE 5.6

A program that calculates the sum of a collection of exam scores is a candidate for using a sentinel value. If the class is large, the instructor may not know the exact number of students who took the exam being graded. The program should work regardless of class size. The loop below uses sum as an accumulator variable and score as an input variable.

Sentinel Loop
1. Initialize sum to zero.
2. Get first score.
3. while score is not the sentinel
   4. Add score to sum.
   5. Get next score.

One is tempted to try the following algorithm that reverses the order of steps 4 and 5 so as to be able to omit the duplication of step 5 in step 2.

Incorrect Sentinel Loop
1. Initialize sum to zero.
2. while score is not the sentinel
   3. Get score.
   4. Add score to sum.

There are two problems associated with this strategy. First, with no initializing input statement, you will have no value for score on which to judge the loop repetition condition when it is first tested. Second, consider the last two iterations of the loop. On the next-to-last iteration, the last data value is copied into score and added to the accumulating sum; on the last iteration, the attempt to get another score obtains the sentinel value. However, this fact will not cause the loop to exit until the loop repetition condition is tested again. Before exit occurs, the sentinel is added to sum. For these reasons, it is important to set up sentinel-controlled loops using the recommended structure: one input to get the loop going (the *initialization* input), and a second to keep it going (the *updating* input). The following program uses a

FIGURE 5.10   Sentinel-Controlled while Loop

```
1.  /* Compute the sum of a list of exam scores. */
2.
3.  #include <stdio.h>
4.
5.  #define SENTINEL -99
6.
7.  int
8.  main(void)
9.  {
10.       int sum = 0,    /* output - sum of scores input so far   */
11.           score;      /* input - current score                */
12.
13.       /* Accumulate sum of all scores.                        */
14.       printf("Enter first score (or %d to quit)> ", SENTINEL);
15.       scanf("%d", &score);        /* Get first score.         */
16.       while (score != SENTINEL) {
17.           sum += score;
18.           printf("Enter next score (%d to quit)> ", SENTINEL);
19.           scanf("%d", &score);  /* Get next score.            */
20.       }
21.       printf("\nSum of exam scores is %d\n", sum);
22.
23.       return (0);
24.  }
```

while loop to implement the sentinel-controlled loop (Fig. 5.10). It also shows that the declaration of a variable may include an initialization.

The following sample dialogue would be used to enter the scores 55, 33, and 77:

```
Enter first score (or -99 to quit)> 55
Enter next score (-99 to quit)> 33
Enter next score (-99 to quit)> 77
Enter next score (-99 to quit)> -99

Sum of exam scores is 165
```

It is usually instructive (and often necessary) to question what happens when there are no data items to process. In this case, the sentinel value would be entered at the first prompt. Loop exit would occur right after the first and only test of the loop repetition condition, so the loop body would not be executed—that is, it is a loop with zero iterations. The variable sum would correctly retain its initial value of zero.

Using a for Statement to Implement a Sentinel Loop

Because the for statement combines the initialization, test, and update in one place, some programmers prefer to use it to implement sentinel-controlled loops. The for statement form of the while loop in Fig. 5.10 follows.

```
/* Accumulate sum of all scores.                                  */
printf("Enter first score (or %d to quit)> ", SENTINEL);
for  (scanf("%d", &score);
      score != SENTINEL;
      scanf("%d", &score)) {
    sum += score;
    printf("Enter next score (%d to quit)> ", SENTINEL);
}
```

Endfile-Controlled Loops

In Section 2.7, we discussed writing programs to run in batch mode using data files. A data file is always terminated by an endfile character that can be detected by the scanf function. Therefore, you can write a batch program that processes a list of data of any length without requiring a special sentinel value at the end of the data.

To write such a program, you must set up your input loop so it notices when scanf encounters the endfile character. So far we have discussed only the effect scanf has on the variables passed to it as arguments. However, scanf also returns a result value just like the functions we studied in Section 3.2. When scanf is successfully able to fill its argument variables with values from the standard input device, the result value that it returns is the number of data items it actually obtained. For example, successful execution of the scanf in the following statement gets values for the variables in its input list, part_id, num_avail, and cost, and returns a result of 3, which is assigned to input_status:

```
input_status = scanf("%d%d%lf", &part_id, &num_avail, &cost);
```

However, if scanf runs into difficulty with invalid or insufficient data (for instance, if it comes across the letter 'o' instead of a zero when trying to get a decimal integer), the function returns as its value the number of data items scanned before encountering the error or running out of data. This means that for the example shown, a nonnegative value less than 3 returned by scanf indicates an error. The third situation scanf can encounter is detecting the endfile character before getting input data for any of its arguments. In this case, scanf returns as its result the value of the standard constant EOF (a negative integer).

It is possible to design a repetition statement very similar to the sentinel-controlled loop that uses the status value returned by the scanning function to control repetition rather than using the values scanned. Here is the pseudocode for an endfile-controlled loop:

1. Get the first *data value* and save *input status*
2. while *input status* does not indicate that end of file has been reached
    3. Process *data value*
    4. Get next *data value* and save *input status*

An example of such a loop is shown in Fig. 5.11, which is a batch version of the exam scores program in Fig. 5.10. The loop repetition condition

```
input_status != EOF
```

causes loop exit after the endfile character is reached. The data file `scores.txt` contains the three numbers shown in the sample run.

Infinite Loops on Faulty Data

The behavior of the `scanf` function when it encounters faulty data can quickly make infinite loops of the `while` statements in Figs. 5.10 and 5.11. For example, let's assume the user responds to the prompt

```
Enter next score (-99 to quit)>
```

in Fig. 5.10 with the faulty data 7o (the second character is the letter `'o'` rather than a zero). The function `scanf` would stop at the letter `'o'`, storing just the value 7 in `score` and leaving the letter `'o'` unprocessed. On the next loop iteration, there would be no wait for the user to respond to the prompt, for `scanf` would find the letter `'o'` awaiting processing. However, since this letter is not part of a valid integer, the `scanf` function would then leave the variable `score` unchanged and the letter `'o'` unprocessed, returning a status value of zero as the result of the function call. Because the sentinel-controlled loop of Fig. 5.10 does not use the value returned by `scanf`, the printing of the prompt and the unsuccessful attempt to process the letter `'o'` would repeat over and over.

Even though the loop of the batch program in Fig. 5.11 does use the status value returned by `scanf`, it too would go into an infinite loop on faulty data. The only status value that causes this loop to exit is the negative integer meaning `EOF`. However, the endfile-controlled loop could be easily modified to exit when encountering the end of file or faulty data. Changing the loop repetition condition to

```
input_status == 1
```

would cause the loop to exit on either the end of file (`input_status` negative) or faulty data (`input_status` zero). We would also need to add an `if` statement after the loop to decide whether to simply print the results or to warn of bad input. The

FIGURE 5.11   Batch Version of Sum of Exam Scores Program

```
1.  /*
2.   *    Compute the sum of the list of exam scores stored in the
3.   *    file scores.txt
4.   */
5.  #include <stdio.h>
6.
7.  int
8.  main(void)
9.  {
10.       int sum = 0,        /* sum of scores input so far */
11.           score,          /* current score  */
12.           input_status; /* status value returned by scanf */
13.
14.       printf("Scores\n");
15.
16.       input_status = scanf("%d", &score);
17.       while (input_status != EOF) {
18.               printf("%5d\n", score);
19.               sum += score;
20.               input_status = scanf("%d", &score);
21.       }
22.
23.       printf("\nSum of exam scores is %d\n", sum);
24.
25.       return (0);
26.  }

Scores
    55
    33
    77
Sum of exam scores is 165
```

false task in the following `if` statement gets and displays the bad character when input_status is not EOF.

```
if (input_status == EOF) {
        printf("Sum of exam scores is %d\n", sum);
} else {
        scanf("%c", &bad_char);
        printf("*** Error in input: %c ***\n", bad_char);
}
```

▨▨▨▨ **EXERCISES FOR SECTION 5.6**

Self-Check

1. Identify these three steps in the pseudocode that follows: the initialization of the loop control variable, the loop repetition condition, and the update of the loop control variable.

    a. Get a value for n.
    b. Give p the value 1.
    c. while n is positive
            d. Multiply p by n.
        e. Subtract 1 from n.
    f. Print p with a label.

2. What would be the behavior of the loop in Fig. 5.11 if the braces around the loop body were omitted?

Programming

1. Translate the pseudocode from Exercise 1 using a `while` loop. Which of these three labels would it make sense to print along with the value of p?

    `n*i =`   `n! =`   `n to the ith power =`

2. Modify the loop in Fig. 5.4 so that it is a sentinel-controlled loop. Get an input value for `pay` as both the initialization and update steps of the loop. Use the value `-99` as the sentinel.
3. Rewrite the program in Fig. 5.4 to run in batch mode with an endfile-controlled loop.
4. Write a program segment that allows the user to enter values and prints out the number of whole numbers and the number of values with fractional parts entered. Design this segment as a sentinel-controlled loop using zero as the sentinel value.

5.7 Nested Loops

Loops may be nested just like other control structures. Nested loops consist of an outer loop with one or more inner loops. Each time the outer loop is repeated, the inner loops are reentered, their loop control expressions are reevaluated, and all required iterations are performed.

EXAMPLE 5.7   The program in Fig. 5.12 contains a sentinel loop nested within a counting loop. This structure is being used to tally by month the local Audubon Club members'

FIGURE 5.12   Program to Process Bald Eagle Sightings for a Year

```
1.  /*
2.   * Tally by month the bald eagle sightings for the year. Each month's
3.   * sightings are terminated by the sentinel zero.
4.   */
5.
6.  #include <stdio.h>
7.
8.  #define SENTINEL    0
9.  #define NUM_MONTHS 12
10.
11. int
12. main(void)
13. {
14.
15.         int month,        /* number of month being processed        */
16.             mem_sight,  /* one member's sightings for this month  */
17.             sightings;  /* total sightings so far for this month  */
18.
19.         printf("BALD EAGLE SIGHTINGS\n");
20.         for (month = 1;
21.              month <= NUM_MONTHS;
22.              ++month) {
23.             sightings = 0;
24.             scanf("%d", &mem_sight);
25.             while (mem_sight != SENTINEL) {
26.                 if (mem_sight >= 0)
27.                     sightings += mem_sight;
28.                 else
29.                     printf("Warning, negative count %d ignored\n",
30.                             mem_sight);
31.                 scanf("%d", &mem_sight);
32.             }   /* inner while */
33.
34.             printf(" month %2d: %2d\n", month, sightings);
35.         }   /* outer for */
36.
37.         return (0);
38. }

Input data
2 1 4 3 0
1 2 0
```

(continued)

FIGURE 5.12 (continued)

```
0
5  4  -1  1  0
. . .


Results
BALD EAGLE SIGHTINGS
   month   1: 10
   month   2:  3
   month   3:  0
Warning, negative count -1 ignored
   month   4: 10
. . .
```

sightings of bald eagles for the past year. The data for this program consist of a group of integers followed by a zero, then a second group of integers followed by a zero, then a third group, and so on, for 12 groups of numbers. The first group of numbers represents sightings in January, the second represents sightings in February, and so on, for all 12 months.

The outer `for` loop repeats twelve times (value of NUM_MONTHS). The first statement in the outer loop sets the accumulator variable `sightings` to zero. The number of repetitions of the inner `while` loop depends on the data and may be zero (e.g., month 3 of the sample). The `if` statement nested in the inner loop adds a positive count of eagles to `sightings` and displays a warning message for negative counts. After exit from the inner loop, the outer loop displays the total sightings for the current month.

EXAMPLE 5.8 Figure 5.13 shows a sample run of a program with two nested counting loops. The outer loop is repeated three times (for `i` = 1, 2, and 3). Each time the outer loop is repeated, the statement

```
printf("Outer %6d\n", i);
```

displays the string `"Outer"` and the value of `i` (the outer loop control variable). Next, the inner loop is entered, and its loop control variable `j` is reset to `0`. The number of times the inner loop is repeated depends on the current value of `i`. Each time the inner loop is repeated, the statement

```
printf("    Inner %9d\n", j);
```

displays the string `"   Inner  "` and the value of `j`.

FIGURE 5.13   Nested Counting Loop Program

```
1.  /*
2.   * Illustrates a pair of nested counting loops
3.   */
4.
5.  #include <stdio.h>
6.
7.  int
8.  main(void)
9.  {
10.       int i, j;    /* loop control variables */
11.
12.       printf("          i      j\n");             /* prints column labels        */
13.
14.       for (i = 1;  i < 4;  ++i) {                 /* heading of outer for loop    */
15.           printf("Outer %6d\n", i);
16.           for  (j = 0;  j < i;  ++j) {            /* heading of inner loop        */
17.               printf("Inner %9d\n", j);
18.           }    /* end of inner loop */
19.       }  /*  end of outer loop */
20.
21.       return (0);
22.  }
```

```
                    i    j
Outer               1
    Inner                0
Outer               2
    Inner                0
    Inner                1
Outer               3
    Inner                0
    Inner                1
    Inner                2
```

The outer loop control variable, i, appears in the condition that determines the number of repetitions of the inner loop. Although this is perfectly valid, you cannot use the same variable as the loop control variable of both an outer and an inner for loop in the same nest.

 **EXERCISES FOR SECTION 5.7**

Self-Check

1. What is displayed by the following program segments, assuming m is 3 and n is 5?

   a.
   ```
   for   (i = 1;   i <= n;   ++i) {
           for   (j = 0;   j < i;   ++j) {
               printf("*");
           }
           printf("\n");
   }
   ```

   b.
   ```
   for   (i = n;   i > 0;   --i) {
           for   (j = m;   j > 0;   --j) {
               printf("*");
           }
           printf("\n");
   }
   ```

2. Show the output displayed by these nested loops:

   ```
   for   (i = 0;   i < 3;   ++i) {
           printf("Outer %4d\n", i);
           for (j = 0;   j < 2;   ++j) {
               printf("  Inner%3d%3d\n", i, j);
           }
           for (k = 2;   k > 0; --k) {
               printf("  Inner%3d%3d\n", i, k);
           }
   }
   ```

Programming

1. Write a program that displays the multiplication table for numbers 0 to 9.
2. Write nests of loops that cause the following output to be displayed:

   ```
   0
   0 1
   0 1 2
   0 1 2 3
   0 1 2 3 4
   0 1 2 3 4 5
   0 1 2 3 4
   0 1 2 3
   0 1 2
   0 1
   0
   ```

5.8   The do-while Statement and Flag-Controlled Loops

Both the `for` statement and the `while` statement evaluate a loop repetition condition before the first execution of the loop body. In most cases, this pretest is desirable and prevents the loop from executing when there may be no data items to process or when the initial value of the loop control variable is outside its expected range. There are some situations, generally involving interactive input, when we know that a loop must execute at least one time. We write the pseudocode for an input validation loop as follows:

1. Get a *data value*.
2. If *data value* isn't in the acceptable range, go back to step 1.

C provides the `do-while` statement to implement such loops as shown next.

EXAMPLE 5.9   The loop

```
do {
    printf("Enter a letter from A through E> ");
    scanf("%c", &letter_choice);
} while (letter_choice < 'A' || letter_choice > 'E');
```

prompts the user to enter one of the letters A through E. After `scanf` gets a data character, the loop repetition condition tests to see whether `letter_choice` contains one of the letters requested. If so, the repetition condition is false, and the next statement after the loop executes. If `letter_choice` contains some other letter, the condition is true and the loop body is repeated. Since we know the program user must enter at least one data character, the `do-while` is an ideal statement to use to implement this loop.

---

do-while Statement

SYNTAX: **do**

        statement;
    while (*loop repetition condition*);

EXAMPLE: `/* Find first even number input */`
    do

        `status = scanf("%d", &num);`
    while `(status > 0    &&    (num % 2) != 0);`

(continued)

> INTERPRETATION: First, the *statement* is executed. Then, the *loop repetition condition* is tested, and if it is true, the *statement* is repeated and the *condition* retested. When this condition is tested and found to be false, the loop is exited and the next statement after the `do-while` is executed.
>
> *Note:* If the loop body contains more than one statement, the group of statements must be surrounded by braces.

Flag-Controlled Loops for Input Validation

Sometimes a loop repetition condition becomes so complex that placing the full expression in its usual spot is awkward. In many cases, the condition may be simplified by using a flag. A **flag** is a type int variable used to represent whether or not a certain event has occurred. A flag has one of two values: 1 (true) and 0 (false).

flag a type int variable used to represent whether or not a certain event has occurred

---

EXAMPLE 5.10   Function `get_int` (Fig. 5.14) returns an integer value that is in the range specified by its two arguments (n_min through n_max, inclusive). The loop repeatedly prompts the user for a value in the desired range. The outer `do-while` structure implements the stated purpose of the function. The type int variable `error` acts as a program flag to signal whether an error has been detected. It is initialized to 0 (false) at the beginning of the outer loop and is changed to 1 (true) when an error is detected by the `if` statement that validates the data scanned into `in_val`. Execution of the outer loop continues as long as `error` is true. The inner `do-while` skips any characters remaining on a data line by repeatedly scanning a character and checking to see whether it is the newline character `'\n'`.

Execution of the function call

`next_int = get_int(10, 20);`

proceeds as follows, assuming that the user responds to the first prompt by mistyping the number 20 as @20. Because the first character is @, `scanf` returns 0 to `status`, `error` is set to 1, the first error message is displayed, and the inner `do-while` skips the rest of the data line. When the outer loop repeats, the user enters 2o. When `scanf` encounters the o, it stops scanning, stores the 2 in `in_val`, and returns the result 1 to `status`. Because the number 2 is less than n_min (10), `error` is set to 1, the second error message is displayed, and the inner `do-while` skips the rest of the data line. Because `error` is 1, the outer loop is repeated. After the user responds to the last prompt below by entering 20, the outer loop is exited and 20 is returned as the result and stored in `next_int`.

FIGURE 5.14 Validating Input Using do-while Statement

```
1.  /*
2.   * Returns the first integer between n_min and n_max entered as data.
3.   * Pre : n_min <= n_max
4.   * Post: Result is in the range n_min through n_max.
5.   */
6.  int
7.  get_int (int n_min, int n_max)
8.  {
9.        int    in_val,               /* input - number entered by user  */
10.              status;                /* status value returned by scanf  */
11.       char   skip_ch;              /* character to skip                */
12.       int    error;               /* error flag for bad input         */
13.       /* Get data from user until in_val is in the range.             */
14.       do {
15.            /* No errors detected yet. */
16.            error = 0;
17.            /* Get a number from the user. */
18.            printf("Enter an integer in the range from %d ", n_min);
19.            printf("to %d inclusive> ", n_max);
20.            status = scanf("%d", &in_val);
21.
22.            /* Validate the number. */
23.            if (status != 1) { /* in_val didn't get a number */
24.                 error = 1;
25.                 scanf("%c", &skip_ch);
26.                 printf("Invalid character >>%c>>. ", skip_ch);
27.                 printf("Skipping rest of line.\n");
28.            } else if (in_val < n_min || in_val > n_max) {
29.                 error = 1;
30.                 printf("Number %d is not in range.\n", in_val);
31.            }
32.
33.            /* Skip rest of data line. */
34.            do
35.                 scanf("%c", &skip_ch);
36.            while (skip_ch != '\n');
37.       } while (error);
38.
39.       return (in_val);
40.  }
```

```
Enter an integer in the range from 10 to 20 inclusive> @20
Invalid character >>@>>. Skipping rest of line.
Enter an integer in the range from 10 to 20 inclusive> 2o
Number 2 is not in range.
Enter an integer in the range from 10 to 20 inclusive> 20
```

The do-while is often the structure to choose when checking for valid input. As soon as the input loop of Fig. 5.14 receives a status code from scanf indicating an error, the loop body explicitly scans and echoes the bad character, skips the rest of the input line, and sets the error flag so the loop will execute again, permitting fresh (and hopefully valid) input. The do-while used in Fig. 5.14 also prevents an infinite input loop in the event the user types an invalid character.

EXERCISES FOR SECTION 5.8

Self-Check

1. Which of the following code segments is a better way to implement a sentinel-controlled loop? Why?

```
scanf("%d", &num);            do {
while (num != SENT) {             scanf("%d", &num);
    /* process num */            if (num != SENT) {
    scanf("%d", &num);               /* process num */}
}                             } while (num != SENT);
```

2. Rewrite the following code using a do-while statement with no decisions in the loop body:

```
sum = 0;
for (odd = 1; odd < n; odd = odd + 2)
    sum = sum + odd;
printf("Sum of the positive odd numbers less than %d is %d\n",
        n, sum);
```

In what situations will the rewritten code print an incorrect sum?

Programming

1. Design an interactive input loop that scans pairs of integers until it reaches a pair in which the first integer evenly divides the second.

5.9 Iterative Approximations

Numerical analysis is the branch of mathematics and computer science that develops algorithms for solving computational problems. Problems from numerical analysis include finding solutions to sets of equations, performing operations on matrices,

FIGURE 5.15

Six Roots for the
Equation $f(x) = 0$

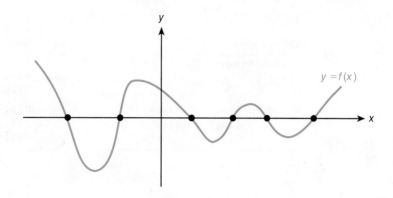

root (zero of a
function) a function
argument value that
causes the function
result to be zero

finding roots of equations, and performing mathematical integration. The next case study illustrates a method for iteratively approximating a root of an equation.

Many real-world problems can be solved by finding roots of equations. A value k is a **root** of an equation, $f(x) = 0$, if $f(k)$ equals zero. If we graph the function $f(x)$, as shown in Fig. 5.15, the roots of the equation are those points where the x-axis and the graph of the function intersect. The roots of the equation $f(x) = 0$ are also called the *zeros* of the function $f(x)$.

The *bisection method* is one way of approximating a root of the equation $f(x) = 0$. This method repeatedly generates approximate roots until a true root is discovered or until an approximation is found that differs from a true root by less than *epsilon,* where *epsilon* is a very small constant (for example, 0.0001). The approximation can be found if we can isolate the true root and the approximate root within the same interval whose length is less than *epsilon.* In our next case study, we develop a function to implement this method of iterative approximation.

Function Parameters

Although we could develop a bisection function to find roots of one specified function, our bisection routine would be far more useful if we could call it to find a root of any function, just by specifying the name of the function in the call. To do this, we must be able to include a function in the parameter list of another function. Declaring a function parameter is accomplished by simply including a prototype of the function in the parameter list. For example, if you want to write a function `evaluate` that evaluates another function at three different points and displays the results, write `evaluate` as shown in Fig. 5.16. Then you can call `evaluate` either with library functions that take a type `double` argument and return a type `double` result or with your own function that meets these criteria. Table 5.6 shows two calls to `evaluate` along with the output generated.

TABLE 5.6   Calls to Function evaluate and the Output Produced

Call to Evaluate	Output Produced

`evaluate(sqrt, 0.25, 25.0, 100.0);`	`f(0.25000) = 0.50000`
	`f(25.00000) = 5.00000`
	`f(100.00000) = 10.00000`

`evaluate(sin, 0.0, 3.14159,`
`            0.5 * 3.14159);`
	`f(0.00000) = 0.00000`
	`f(3.14159) = 0.00000`
	`f(1.57079) = 1.00000`

FIGURE 5.16   Using a Function Parameter

```
1.   /*
2.    * Evaluate a function at three points, displaying results.
3.    */
4.   void
5.   evaluate(double f(double f_arg), double pt1, double pt2, double pt3)
6.   {
7.        printf("f(%.5f) = %.5f\n", pt1, f(pt1));
8.        printf("f(%.5f) = %.5f\n", pt2, f(pt2));
9.        printf("f(%.5f) = %.5f\n", pt3, f(pt3));
10.  }
```

CASE STUDY   Bisection Method for Finding Roots

PROBLEM

Develop a function `bisect` that approximates a root of a function `f` on an interval that contains an odd number of roots.

ANALYSIS

A program that is to call function `bisect` should first tabulate function values to find an appropriate interval in which to search for a root. If a change of sign occurs on an interval, that interval must contain an odd number of roots. Figure 5.17 shows two such intervals. If there is no change of sign, the interval may contain no roots. Let us assume that $[x_{left}, x_{right}]$ (`x_left` to `x_right`) is an interval on which a change of sign does occur and in which there is exactly one root. Furthermore,

FIGURE 5.17

Change of Sign
Implies an Odd
Number of Roots

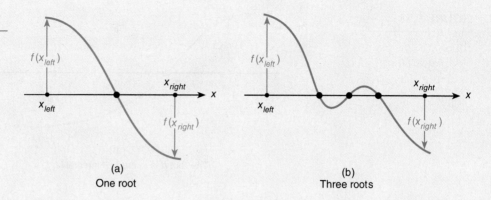

(a)
One root

(b)
Three roots

assume that the function $f(x)$ is continuous on this interval. If we bisect this interval
by computing its midpoint x_{mid}, using the formula

$$x_{mid} = \frac{x_{left} + x_{right}}{2.0}$$

there are three possible outcomes: the root is in the lower half of the interval,
$[x_{left}, x_{mid}]$; the root is in the upper half of the interval, $[x_{mid}, x_{right}]$; or $f(x_{mid})$ is zero.
Figure 5.18 shows these three possibilities graphically.

A fourth possibility is that the length of the interval is less than *epsilon*. In this
case, any point in the interval is an acceptable root approximation.

DATA REQUIREMENTS

Problem Inputs

```
double x_left        /* left endpoint of interval               */
double x_right       /* right endpoint of interval              */
double epsilon       /* error tolerance                         */
double f(double farg) /* function whose root is sought          */
```

Problem Outputs

```
double root          /* approximate root of f                   */
```

DESIGN

The initial interval on which to search for a root is defined by the input parameters
`x_left` and `x_right`. Before searching this interval, we must verify that it contains
an odd number of roots. If it does, we need to repeatedly bisect the interval, searching the half containing an odd number of roots until we find a true root or until the
length of the interval to search is less than `epsilon`.

FIGURE 5.18

Three Possibilities
That Arise When
the Interval [x_{left},
x_{right}] Is Bisected

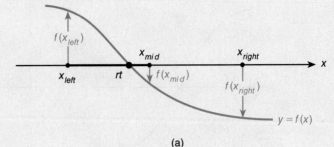

(a)

The root *rt* is in the half interval [x_{left}, x_{mid}].

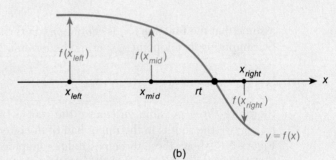

(b)

The root *rt* is in the half interval [x_{mid}, x_{right}].

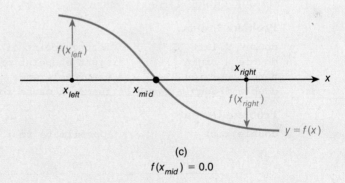

(c)

$f(x_{mid}) = 0.0$

INITIAL ALGORITHM

1. if the interval contains an even number of roots
    2. Display "no root" message.
    3. Return NO_ROOT and exit the function.
4. repeat as long as interval is greater than tolerance and a root is not found
    5. Compute the function value at the midpoint of the interval.
    6. if the function value at midpoint is zero
        7. Set root to the midpoint.
    else
        8. Choose the left or right half of the interval and
           continue the search.
9. Return the midpoint of the final interval as the root.

PROGRAM VARIABLES

```
int root_found    /* whether or not root is found */
double x_mid      /* interval midpoint */
double f_left,    /* values of function at left and */
       f_mid,     /* right endpoints and at midpoint */
       f_right    /* of interval */
```

Refinement of Step 1

1.1 `f_left = f(x_left)`
1.2 `f_right = f(x_right)`
1.3 if signs of `f_left` and `f_right` are the same (i.e., if their product is nonnegative)

Refinement of Step 4

4.1 while `x_right - x_left > epsilon` and `!root_found`

Refinement of Step 8

8.1 if root is in left half of interval (`f_left * f_mid < 0.0`)
    8.2 Change right end to midpoint
else
    8.3 Change left end to midpoint

IMPLEMENTATION

Figure 5.19 shows an implementation of this algorithm. We have added some calls to `printf` to make function `bisect` self-tracing. Two functions (`g` and `h`) whose roots will be found are shown at the end of the program listing.

FIGURE 5.19   Finding a Function Root Using the Bisection Method

```
1.   /*
2.    *   Finds roots of the equations
3.    *        g(x) = 0    and     h(x) = 0
4.    *   on a specified interval [x_left, x_right] using the bisection method.
5.    */
6.
7.   #include <stdio.h>
8.   #include <math.h>
9.
10.  #define FALSE 0
11.  #define TRUE  1
12.  #define NO_ROOT -99999.0
13.
14.  double bisect(double x_left, double x_right, double epsilon,
15.                double f(double farg));
16.  double g(double x);
17.  double h(double x);
18.
19.
20.  int
21.  main(void)
22.  {
23.        double x_left, x_right, /* left, right endpoints of interval  */
24.               epsilon,          /* error tolerance          */
25.               root;
26.
27.        /*  Get endpoints and error tolerance from user          */
28.        printf("\nEnter interval endpoints> ");
29.        scanf("%lf%lf", &x_left, &x_right);
30.        printf("\nEnter tolerance> ");
31.        scanf("%lf", &epsilon);
32.
33.        /*  Use bisect function to look for roots of g and h       */
34.        printf("\n\nFunction g");
35.        root = bisect(x_left, x_right, epsilon, g);
36.        if (root != NO_ROOT)
37.              printf("\n   g(%.7f) = %e\n", root, g(root));
38.
```

(continued)

FIGURE 5.19 (continued)

```
39.          printf("\n\nFunction h");
40.          root = bisect(x_left, x_right, epsilon, h);
41.          if (root != NO_ROOT)
42.                  printf("\n    h(%.7f) = %e\n", root, h(root));
43.
44.          return (0);
45. }
46.
47. /*
48.  *  Implements the bisection method for finding a root of a function f.
49.  *  Returns a root if signs of fp(x_left) and fp(x_right) are different.
50.  *  Otherwise returns NO_ROOT.
51.  */
52. double
53. bisect(double x_left,          /* input  - endpoints of interval in */
54.        double x_right,         /*                which to look for a root */
55.        double epsilon,         /* input  - error tolerance           */
56.        double f(double farg))  /* input  - the function              */
57. {
58.      double x_mid,      /* midpoint of interval */
59.             f_left,     /* f(x_left)            */
60.             f_mid,      /* f(x_mid)             */
61.             f_right;    /* f(x_right)           */
62.
63.      int    root_found;  /* flag to indicate whether root is found */
64.
65.      /* Computes function values at initial endpoints of interval  */
66.      f_left = f(x_left);       f_right = f(x_right);
67.
68.      /* If no change of sign occurs on the interval there is not a
69.         unique root. Exit function and return NO_ROOT */
70.      if (f_left * f_right > 0) {      /* same sign */
71.          printf("\nMay be no root in [%.7f, %.7f]", x_left, x_right);
72.          return NO_ROOT;
73.      }
74.
75.      /*  Searches as long as interval size is large enough
76.          and no root has been found                              */
```

(continued)

FIGURE 5.19   (continued)

```
77.        root_found = FALSE;    /* no root found yet */
78.        while (fabs(x_right - x_left) > epsilon  &&  !root_found)
79.        {
80.            /* Computes midpoint and function value at midpoint */
81.            x_mid = (x_left + x_right) / 2.0;
82.            f_mid = f(x_mid);
83.
84.            if (f_mid == 0.0) {                /* Here's the root    */
85.                root_found = TRUE;
86.            } else if (f_left * f_mid < 0.0) {/* Root in [x_left,x_mid]*/
87.                x_right = x_mid;
88.            } else {                           /* Root in [x_mid,x_right]*/
89.                x_left = x_mid;
90.            }
91.
92.
93.            /* Trace loop execution - print root location or new interval */
94.            if (root_found)
95.                printf("\nRoot found at x = %.7f, midpoint of [%.7f, %.7f]",
96.                        x_mid, x_left, x_right);
97.            else
98.                printf("\nNew interval is [%.7f, %.7f]",
99.                        x_left, x_right);
100.        }
101.
102.        /*  If there is a root, it is the midpoint of [x_left, x_right]      */
103.        return ((x_left + x_right) / 2.0);
104. }
105.
106. /*  Functions for which roots are sought                          */
107.
108. /*    3      2
109.  *  5x   - 2x  + 3
110.  */
111. double
112. g(double x)
113. {
114.      return (5 * pow(x, 3.0) - 2 * pow(x, 2.0) + 3);
115. }
```

(continued)

FIGURE 5.19   (continued)

```
116.
117. /*     4       2
118.  *   x   - 3x   - 8
119.  */
120. double
121. h(double x)
122. {
123.         return (pow(x, 4.0) - 3 * pow(x, 2.0) - 8);
124. }
```

TESTING

The C program shown in Fig. 5.19 looks for approximate roots for the equations $g(x) = 0$ and $h(x) = 0$ on the interval [x_left, x_right]. The left and right endpoints, x_left and x_right, and the tolerance, epsilon, are inputs from the user. The main function gets these three inputs, calls function bisect, and displays the results. Each call to bisect passes a function name as the fourth argument. Because the bisection method as implemented in Fig. 5.19 can be applied to any function that both returns a type double value and takes a single type double argument, we can test bisect on multiple functions in a single program run. When bisect is executing as a result of function main's statement

```
root = bisect(x_left, x_right, epsilon, g);
```

the statement

```
f_left = f(x_left);
```

is equivalent to

```
f_left = g(x_left);
```

However, when bisect executes as a result of the call statement

```
root = bisect(x_left, x_right, epsilon, h);
```

the same statement means

```
f_left = h(x_left);
```

Figure 5.20 shows the results of one run of the program in Fig. 5.19.

FIGURE 5.20   Sample Run of Bisection Program with Trace Code Included

```
Enter interval endpoints> -1.0   1.0
Enter tolerance> 0.001

Function g
New interval is [-1.0000000,  0.0000000]
New interval is [-1.0000000, -0.5000000]
New interval is [-0.7500000, -0.5000000]
New interval is [-0.7500000, -0.6250000]
New interval is [-0.7500000, -0.6875000]
New interval is [-0.7500000, -0.7187500]
New interval is [-0.7343750, -0.7187500]
New interval is [-0.7343750, -0.7265625]
New interval is [-0.7304688, -0.7265625]
New interval is [-0.7304688, -0.7285156]
New interval is [-0.7294922, -0.7285156]
   g(-0.7290039) = -2.697494e-05

Function h
May be no root in [-1.0000000, 1.0000000]
```

EXERCISES FOR SECTION 5.9

Self-Check

1. Find endpoints of an interval one unit long in which a root of $h(x) = 0$ is found for function h from Fig. 5.19.
2. It is unusual for a program to use equality comparison of two type `double` values as in

   ```
   if (f_mid == 0.0)
   ```

   Find a function and an interval that would cause this test to evaluate to 1 (true).

Programming

1. Revise the program in Fig. 5.19 so that if the user enters an interval longer than one unit, the program checks one-unit segments of the interval until a subinterval is found with different signs for the values of function f. The program should then call `bisect` with this subinterval and function f.

5.10 How to Debug and Test Programs

In Section 2.8, we described the three general categories of errors: syntax errors, run-time errors, and logic errors. Sometimes the cause of a run-time error or the source of a logic error is apparent and the error can be fixed easily. Often, however, the error is not obvious and you may spend considerable time and energy locating it.

The first step in locating a hidden error is to examine the program output to determine which part of the program is generating incorrect results. Then you can focus on the statements in that section of the program to determine which are at fault. We describe two ways to do this next.

Using Debugger Programs

A *debugger program* can help you find defects in a C program. The debugger program lets you execute your program one statement at a time (*single-step execution*). Through single-step execution, you can trace your program's execution and observe the effect of each C statement on variables you select. With single-step execution you can validate that loop control variables and other important variables (e.g., accumulators) are incremented as expected during each iteration of a loop. You can also check that input variables contain the correct data after each scan operation.

If your program is very long, you can separate your program into segments by setting *breakpoints* at selected statements. A breakpoint is like a fence between two segments of a program. You should set a breakpoint at the end of each major algorithm step. Then instruct the debugger to execute all statements from the last breakpoint up to the next breakpoint. When the program stops at a breakpoint, you can examine the values of selected variables to determine whether the program segment has executed correctly. If it has, you will want to execute through to the next breakpoint. If it has not, you may want to set more breakpoints in that segment or perhaps perform single-step execution through that segment.

Debugging Without a Debugger

If you cannot use a debugger, insert extra *diagnostic calls* to `printf` that display intermediate results at critical points in your program. For example, you should display the values of variables affected by each major algorithm step before and after the step executes. By comparing these results at the end of a run, you may be able to determine which segment of your program contains bugs.

Once you have determined the likely source of an error, you should insert additional diagnostic calls to `printf` to trace the values of critical variables in the "buggy" segment. For example, if the loop in Fig. 5.10 is not computing the correct sum, the conditional call to `printf`, shown in color below, will display each value of `score` and `sum` when the value of `DEBUG` is nonzero. The asterisks highlight the diagnostic output in the debugging runs and the diagnostic calls to `printf` in the source program.

```
while (score != SENTINEL) {
    sum += score;
    if   (DEBUG)
        printf("***** score is %d, sum is %d\n", score, sum);
    printf("Enter next score (%d to quit)> ", SENTINEL);
    scanf("%d", &score);   /* Get next score.                 */
}
```

By making all diagnostic calls to `printf` dependent on a constant such as `DEBUG`, you can turn your diagnostics on by inserting

```
#define DEBUG 1
```

in a region of your program that you expect may contain bugs. Insertion of

```
#define DEBUG 0
```

will turn your diagnostics off.

We usually include a `\n` at the end of every `printf` format string. It is especially critical that you do this in diagnostic calls to `printf` so that your output will be displayed immediately; otherwise, if a run-time error occurs before a `\n` is encountered in another format string, you may never see the diagnostic message.

Be careful when you insert diagnostic calls to `printf`. Sometimes you must add braces if a single statement inside an `if` or a `while` statement becomes a compound statement when you add a diagnostic `printf`.

Off-by-One Loop Errors

A fairly common logic error in programs with loops is a loop that executes one more time or one less time than required. If a sentinel-controlled loop performs an extra repetition, it may erroneously process the sentinel value along with the regular data.

If a loop performs a counting operation, make sure that the initial and final values of the loop control variable are correct and that the loop repetition condition is right. For example, the following loop body executes n + 1 times instead of n times. If you want the loop body to execute exactly n times, change the loop repetition condition to count < n.

```
for   (count = 0;   count <= n;   ++count)
    sum += count;
```

loop boundaries
initial and final values
of the loop control
variable

Often you can determine whether a loop is correct by checking the **loop boundaries**—that is, the initial and final values of the loop control variable. For a counting `for` loop, carefully evaluate the expression in the initialization step, substitute this value everywhere the counter variable appears in the loop body, and verify that it makes sense as a beginning value. Then choose a value for the counter that still causes the loop repetition condition to be true, but that will make this condition false after one more evaluation of the update expression. Check the validity of this boundary value wherever the counter variable appears. As an example, in the `for` loop,

```
sum = 0;
k = 1;
for    (i = -n;    i < n - k;    ++i)
    sum += i * i;
```

check that the first value of the counter variable `i` is supposed to be `-n` and that the last value should be `n - 2`. Next, check that the assignment statement

```
sum += i * i;
```

is correct at these boundaries. When `i` is `-n`, `sum` gets the value of n^2. When `i` is `n - 2`, the value of $(n - 2)^2$ is added to the previous value of `sum`. As a final check, pick some small value of `n` (for example, `2`) and trace the loop execution to see that it computes `sum` correctly for this case.

Testing

After all errors have been corrected and the program appears to execute as expected, the program should be tested thoroughly to make sure that it works. For a simple program, make enough test runs to verify that the program works properly for representative samples of all possible data combinations.

EXERCISES FOR SECTION 5.10

Self-Check

1. For the first counting loop in the subsection "Off-by-One Loop Errors," add debugging statements to show the value of the loop control variable at the start of each repetition. Also, add debugging statements to show the value of `sum` at the end of each loop repetition.
2. Repeat Exercise 1 for the second loop in the same subsection.

C IN FOCUS: TEAM PROGRAMMING

Since real-world C software is typically developed by teams of programmers, some instructors like to have students work as teams even in early computer science courses. Beginning in this chapter, we have marked some projects with the icon (shown in the left margin) to indicate that these are potentially good team projects, but many of the other projects could also be solved in this manner.

Many volumes have been written on design methodologies for team creation of software. Your instructor

© *Picture-Factory for Fotolia*

may have a preferred methodology for teams to follow. Naturally, in an educational setting, some of the goals of team projects are different from the goals in an industrial setting. Both professional and student teams desire to create readable defect-free programs with intuitive user interfaces, but in a class, it is also important to give every student an opportunity to understand, practice, and learn from failures in all facets of the software development process. Here are some tips to help you learn the most from your earliest team projects.

1. In your initial meeting, discuss answers to the following questions:
    a. Is the statement of the assigned problem complete, or is there more we need to know about the requirements than what we've been given?
    b. Are there any constants that need to be named? Choose meaningful names for them.
    c. What data is coming in from the outside world? What structures and names will we use for these?
    d. What results will be displayed? Will we need additional variables to store these internally?
    e. Can we break the larger problem into smaller ones to solve separately? If so, choose names for the pieces and for the data going into and coming out of each piece.
    f. What control structures will we need? If there are decisions to be made, do they lend themselves more naturally to if-else structures or switch structures? If there is repetition, what loops seem most appropriate?

2. At the end of the first meeting, choose a couple of members to take the team's answers to the questions above and work on the formal design

and pseudocode. A couple of other members should prepare scenarios and data sets for testing the program along with predicted results. You will likely want to pick a time for your next meeting and designate a manager who will check on everyone's progress.

3.   At the second meeting, try hand tracing the pseudocode on the prepared data sets. Verify that the results obtained are correct. Discuss whether the data sets test all boundary conditions, and create additional test cases if needed. Always predict the correct results for a data set. Have the pair of members who designed the test data begin the implementation of the pseudocode: the one typing is the "driver" and the observer is the "navigator," who is watching out for typos, logic errors, and flaws in readability. The two should switch roles frequently. This "pair programming" technique has been demonstrated to produce more reliable and readable code than solo coding. Moreover, having people other than the primary designers do the initial implementation brings fresh (and skeptical) eyes to the design, helping to guard against the natural human inclination to believe that our design does indeed do what we intended it to do. If the project divides naturally into multiple sections, your team could have more than one pair working on coding. As soon possible, run small tests on the completed portions of code.

4.   When your program seems to be approaching completion, run all the data sets prepared above and verify that the results produced are correct. Then as a team try testing the code on some *unreasonable* data and discuss whether or not you have the programming tools yet to make the code robust enough to trap these data and provide an error message rather than allowing the program to abort with a system error message or to run to completion with incorrect results. Write a summary for your instructor of each of these scenarios and your reasons for allowing your program to handle them as it does.

It is unlikely that your team will consist of members with uniform programming and communication skills. Working with a team can make software development more fun, but initially students may find it time-consuming and frustrating to work with others. If you are a student with more programming experience or aptitude than other members of the team, we encourage you to recognize that novices can help you identify areas in which you may have developed a style that is hard for others to read or a tendency to rush into coding without considering design options. It really is worth everyone's time to have to explain clearly to one another why you feel certain design choices are better than others. If you find that one or two students are dominating the program creation process and you are feeling lost, it is important to speak up and insist that team members discuss their reasoning until the team can reach consensus that the best design/code/test plan has been created. As you work together you will come to recognize each individual's strengths and be better able to take advantage of these in future projects.

5.11   Loops in Graphics Programs (Optional)

You can form many interesting geometric patterns on your screen by using a loop in a graphics program to repeatedly draw similar shapes. Each shape can have a different size, color, fill pattern, and position. Using a loop, you can also draw a sequence of frames to move an object across the screen.

EXAMPLE 5.11   The program in Fig. 5.22 draws a "quilt" consisting of nested filled rectangles (see Figure 5.21). It first draws a large black bar, which fills the output window. Each subsequent bar is centered inside the previous one, overwriting its pixels in a new color, so only a border from the previous rectangle remains on the screen.

Before switching to graphics mode, the program prompts the user to specify the number of bars. The statements

```
stepX = width / (2 * numBars);    /* x increment */
stepY = height / (2 * numBars);   /* y increment */
```

define the change in x and y values for the corners of each bar and are computed so that there will be room to display all the bars.

In the `for` loop, the statements

```
foreColor = i % 16;                   /* 0 <= foreColor <= 15 */
setcolor(foreColor);
setfillstyle(i % 12, foreColor);      /* set fill style. */
bar(x1, y1, x2, y2);                  /* draw a bar.     */
```

FIGURE 5.21

Nested Rectangles
for a Quilt Pattern

FIGURE 5.22   Program to Draw a Quilt

```
1.   /*
2.    * Display a pattern for a quilt -- a set of nested rectangles
3.    */
4.   #include <graphics.h>
5.   #include <stdio.h>
6.
7.   int
8.   main(void)
9.   {
10.      int x1, y1, x2, y2;        /* coordinates of corner points */
11.      int stepX, stepY;          /* change in coordinate values */
12.      int foreColor;             /* foreground color */
13.      int numBars;               /* number of bars */
14.      int width, height;         /* screen width and height */
15.
16.      printf("Enter number of bars> ");
17.      scanf("%d", &numBars);
18.
19.      width = getmaxwidth();
20.      height = getmaxheight();
21.
22.      initwindow(width, height, "Quilt");
23.
24.      /* set corner points of outermost bar
25.         and increments for inner bars */
26.      x1 = 0;            y1 = 0;             /* top left corner */
27.      x2 = width;        y2 = height;        /* bottom right corner */
28.      stepX = width / (2 * numBars);         /* x increment */
29.      stepY = height / (2 * numBars);        /* y increment */
30.
31.      for (int i = 1; i <= numBars; ++i)
32.      {
33.         foreColor = i % 16;                 /* 0 <= foreColor <= 15 */
34.         setcolor(foreColor);
35.         setfillstyle(i % 12, foreColor);    /* Set fill style */
36.         bar(x1, y1, x2, y2);                /* Draw a bar */
37.         x1 = x1 + stepX;  y1 = y1 + stepY;  /* Change top left corner */
38.         x2 = x2 - stepX;  y2 = y2 - stepY;  /* Change bottom right */
39.      }
40.
41.      getch();           /* pause for user */
42.      closegraph();
43.      return (0);
44.   }
```

set the foreground color to one of 16 colors, based on the value of loop control variable i. Similarly, function setfillstyle sets the fill pattern to one of 12 possible patterns. After each bar is drawn, the statements

```
x1 = x1 + stepX;    y1 = y1 + stepY;   /* change top left */
x2 = x2 - stepX;    y2 = y2 - stepY;   /* change bottom right */
```

change the top-left corner (point x1, y1) and the bottom-right corner (point x2, y2) for the next bar, moving them closer together. For interesting effects, try running this program with different values assigned to stepX and stepY.

Animation

graphics animation motion achieved by displaying series of frames with object in a slightly different position from one frame to the next

Loops are used in graphics programs to create animation. In **graphics animation**, motion is achieved by displaying a series of frames in which the object is in a slightly different position from one frame to another, so it appears that the object is moving. Each frame is displayed for a few milliseconds. This is analogous to the flip-books you may have seen in which objects are drawn in slightly different positions on each page of the book. As you flip the pages, the object moves.

The program in Fig. 5.23 draws a ball that moves around the screen like the ball in a pong game. It starts moving down the screen and to the right until it reaches a

FIGURE 5.23 Program to Draw a Moving Ball

```
1.  /*
2.   * Draw a ball that moves around the screen
3.   */
4.  #include <graphics.h>
5.  #define TRUE   1
6.
7.  int
8.  main(void)
9.  {
10.     const int PAUSE = 20;           /* delay between frames */
11.     const int DELTA = 5;            /* change in x or y value */
12.     const int RADIUS = 30;          /* ball radius */
13.     const int COLOR = RED;
14.
15.     int width;                      /* width of screen */
16.     int height;                     /* height of screen */
17.     int x; int y;                   /* center of ball */
18.     int stepX;                      /* increment for x */
19.     int stepY;                      /* increment for y */
```

(continued)

FIGURE 5.23   (continued)

```
20.
21.     /* Open a full-screen window with double buffering */
22.      width = getmaxwidth();
23.      height = getmaxheight();
24.      initwindow(width, height,
25.                     "Pong - close window to quit", 0, 0, TRUE);
26.      x = RADIUS;  y = RADIUS;        /* Start ball at top-left corner */
27.      stepX = DELTA;  stepY = DELTA; /* Move down and to the right */
28.
29.      /* Draw the moving ball */
30.      while (TRUE)     /* Repeat forever */
31.      {
32.          /* Clear the old frame and draw the new one. */
33.          clearviewport();
34.          setfillstyle(SOLID_FILL, COLOR);
35.          fillellipse(x, y, RADIUS, RADIUS);  /* Draw the ball */
36.
37.          /* After drawing the frame, swap the buffers */
38.          swapbuffers();
39.          delay(PAUSE);
40.
41.          /* If ball is too close to window edge, change direction      */
42.          if (x <= RADIUS)                /* Is ball too close to left edge? */
43.             stepX = DELTA;               /* Move right                 */
44.          else if (x >= width - RADIUS)  /* Is ball too close to right edge? */
45.             stepX = -DELTA;              /* Move left                  */
46.
47.          if (y <= RADIUS)                /* Is ball too close to top?  */
48.             stepY = DELTA;               /* Move down                  */
49.          else if (y >= height - RADIUS) /* Is ball too close to bottom? */
50.             stepY = -DELTA;              /* Move up                    */
51.
52.
53.          /* Move the ball */
54.          x = x + stepX;
55.          y = y + stepY;
56.      }
57.
58.      closegraph();
59.      return (0);
60.  }
```

"wall" (a window edge) and then reverses its *x*- or *y*-direction depending on which wall it hit.

Animation programs use a technique called double buffering to reduce the screen flicker and make the motion seem smoother. In **single buffering** (the default situation), a single memory area (or **buffer**) is used to hold the frame that will be shown next on the screen. After the buffer is filled, its bytes are sent to the graphics hardware for display. When done, the bytes for the next frame are loaded into the buffer. In **double buffering**, while the bytes in the first buffer are being sent to the graphics display, the second buffer is being filled with the bytes for the next frame. Then, the contents of the second buffer are sent to the graphics hardware, while the first buffer is being filled. The extra buffer enables the screen display to be refreshed more frequently, resulting in less flicker between transitions. In `graphics.h`, double buffering is turned on by setting the sixth argument for `initwindow` to `TRUE`.

> **single buffering**   the default case in which only one memory area is allocated
>
> **buffer**   an area of memory where data to be displayed or printed is temporarily stored
>
> **double buffering**   a technique used in graphics programming to reduce display flicker by allocating two buffers: the second buffer is filled while the contents of the first buffer is displayed and then the roles of the buffers are reversed

```
initwindow(width, height,
           "Pong - close window to quit", 0, 0, TRUE);
```

Because the `while` loop condition is `TRUE`, the loop executes "forever," or until the user closes the window. The loop begins by clearing the window for the new frame (function `clearviewport`). Next, it draws the ball in the new frame (stored in the second buffer). Then the buffers are swapped (function `swapbuffers`) and there is a delay of 10 milliseconds while the ball is displayed in its new position.

```
swapbuffers();
delay(PAUSE);
```

The `if` statements change the direction of motion when the ball reaches an edge. For example, in the statement below, the first condition is true if the current `x` position is closer to the left edge than the radius of the ball. In that case, the ball should move to the right (`stepX` is positive).

```
if (x <= RADIUS)              /* Is ball too close to left edge? */
   stepX = DELTA;             /* Move right */
else if (x >= width - RADIUS) /* Is ball too close to right edge? */
   stepX = -DELTA;            /* Move left */
```

The second condition is true if the `x` position of the ball is too close to the right edge, so the ball should move to the left (`stepX` is negative). The assignment statements at the end of the loop compute the position of the ball for the next frame.

Figure 5.24 shows a trace of the ball as it bounces around the screen. This was obtained by removing the call to `clearviewport`. In the actual display, only one ball would be drawn at a time. Table 5.7 shows the new graphics functions introduced in this section.

FIGURE 5.24

Trace of the
Moving Ball

EXERCISES FOR SECTION 5.11

Self-Check

1. What would be drawn by the following fragment?

```
radius = 20;
x = radius;        y = getmaxy() / 2;
for (int i = 1; i <= 10; ++i)
{
    color = i % 16;
```

TABLE 5.7   Functions in Graphics Library

Function Prototype	Effect
void clearviewport()	Clears the active viewport. The current window is the default viewport.
void delay(int)	The program pauses for the number of milliseconds specified by its argument.
swapbuffers()	Swaps the buffers if double buffering is turned on.

```
        setcolor(color);
        setfillstyle(HATCH_FILL, color);
        fillellipse(x, y, radius, radius);
        x = x + radius;
        getch();        /* pause for user entry */
    }
```

2. Experiment with the animation program by removing the call to `clearview-port`. What happens? Also what happens if you eliminate double buffering by removing the call to `swapbuffers`? How does changing the value of PAUSE affect the animation?

Programming

1. Write a program that draws an archery target with alternating black and white circles.
2. Modify the program in Self-Check Exercise 1 so the ball moves continuously back and forth in a horizontal direction.

5.12 Common Programming Errors

Beginners sometimes confuse `if` and `while` statements because both statements contain a parenthesized condition. Always use an `if` statement to implement a decision step and a `while` or `for` statement to implement a loop.

The syntax of the `for` statement header is repeated.

```
for (initialization expression;
      loop repetition condition;
      update expression)
```

Remember to end the initialization expression and the loop repetition condition with semicolons. Be careful not to put a semicolon before or after the closing parenthesis of the `for` statement header. A semicolon after this parenthesis would have the effect of ending the `for` statement without making execution of the loop body dependent on its condition.

Another common mistake in using `while` and `for` statements is to forget that the structure assumes that the loop body is a single statement. Remember to use braces around a loop body consisting of multiple statements. Some C programmers always use braces around a loop body, whether it contains one or many statements. Keep in mind that your compiler ignores indentation, so the loop below (without braces around the loop body)

```
while (x > xbig)
        x -= 2;
        ++xbig;
/* intended end of while loop */
```

really executes as

```
while (x > xbig)
        x -= 2; /* only this statement is repeated */
++xbig;
```

The C compiler can easily detect that there is something wrong with a program fragment in which a closing brace has been omitted in a compound statement. However, the error message noting the symbol's absence may be far from the spot where the brace belongs, and other error messages often appear as a side effect of the omission. When compound statements are nested, the compiler will associate the first closing brace encountered with the innermost structure. Even if it is the terminator for this inner structure that is left out, the compiler may complain about the outer structure. In the example that follows, the body of the while statement is missing a brace. However, the compiler will associate the closing brace before else with the body of the while loop and then proceed to mark the else as improper.

```
printf("Experiment successful? (Y/N)> ");
scanf("%c", &ans);
if (ans == 'Y') {
    printf("Enter one number per line (Enter %d to quit)\n> ",
           SENT);
    scanf("%d", &data);
    while (data != SENT) {
        sum += data;
        printf("> ");
        scanf("%d", &data);
                            /* <- missing } */
} else {
    printf("Try it again tomorrow.\n");
    printf("Now follow correct shutdown procedure.\n");
}
```

Be careful when you use tests for inequality to control the repetition of a loop. The following loop is intended to process all transactions for a bank account while the balance is positive:

```
scanf("%d%lf", &code, &amount);
while (balance != 0.0) {
    . . .
    scanf("%d%lf", &code, &amount);
}
```

If the bank balance goes from a positive to a negative amount without being exactly 0.0, the loop will not terminate (an infinite loop). This loop is safer:

```
scanf("%d%lf", &code, &amount);
while (balance > 0.0) {
    . . .
    scanf("%d%lf", &code, &amount);
}
```

Be sure to verify that a loop's repetition condition will eventually become false (0); otherwise, an infinite loop may result. If you use a sentinel-controlled loop, remember to provide a prompt that tells the program's user what value to enter as the sentinel. Make sure that the sentinel value cannot be confused with a normal data item.

One common cause of a nonterminating loop is the use of a loop repetition condition in which an equality test is mistyped as an assignment operation. Consider the following loop that expects the user to type the number 0 (actually any integer other than 1) to exit:

```
do {
    . . .
    printf("One more time? (1 to continue/0 to quit)> ");
    scanf("%d", &again);
}   while (again = 1); /* should be: again == 1 */
```

The value of the loop repetition condition will always be 1, never 0 (false), so this loop will not exit on an entry of zero or of any other number.

A do-while always executes at least once. Use a do-while only when there is no possibility of zero loop iterations. If you find yourself adding an if statement to patch your code with a result like this

```
if (condition₁)
    do {
        . . .
    } while (condition₁);
```

replace the segment with a while or for statement. Both these statements automatically test the loop repetition condition *before* executing the loop body.

Do not use increment, decrement, or compound assignment operators as subexpressions in complex expressions. At best, such usage leads to expressions that are difficult to read; at worst, to expressions that produce varying results in different implementations of C.

Remember the parentheses that are assumed to be around any expression that is the second operand of a compound assignment operator. Since the statement

```
a *= b + c;
```

is equivalent to

```
a = a * (b + c);
```

there is no shorter way to write

```
a = a * b + c;
```

Be sure that the operand of an increment or decrement operator is a variable and that this variable is referenced after executing the increment or decrement operation. Without a subsequent reference, the operator's side effect of changing the value of the variable is pointless. Do not use a variable twice in an expression in which it is incremented/decremented. Applying the increment/decrement operators to constants or expressions is illegal.

Chapter Review

1. Use a loop to repeat steps in a program. Two kinds of loops occur frequently in programming: counting loops and sentinel-controlled loops. For a counting loop, the number of iterations required can be determined before the loop is entered. For a sentinel-controlled loop, repetition continues until a special data value is scanned. The pseudocode for each loop form follows.

   Counter-Controlled Loop
   Set *loop control variable* to an initial value of 0.
   While *loop control variable* < *final value*
       . . .
          Increase *loop control variable* by 1.

   Sentinel-Controlled Loop
   Get a line of data.
   While the sentinel value has not been encountered
       Process the data line.
       Get another line of data.

2. We also introduced pseudocode forms for three other kinds of loops:

   Endfile-Controlled Loop
   Get first *data value* and save *input status*.
   While *input status* does not indicate that end of file has been reached
       Process *data value*.
       Get next *data value* and save *input status*.

   Input Validation Loop
   Get a *data value*.
   If *data value* isn't in the acceptable range,
       go back to first step.

   General Conditional Loop
   Initialize *loop control variable*.
   As long as exit condition hasn't been met,
       continue processing.

3. C provides three statements for implementing loops: `while`, `for`, and `do-while`. Use the `for` to implement counting loops and the `do-while` to implement loops that must execute at least once, such as data validation loops for interactive programs. Depending on which implementation is clearer, code other conditional loops using `for` or `while` statements.

4. In designing a loop, focus on both loop control and loop processing. For loop processing, make sure that the loop body contains steps that perform the operation that must be repeated. For loop control, you must provide steps that initialize, test, and update the loop control variable. Make sure that the initialization step leads to correct program results when the loop body is not executed (zero-iteration loop).

5. A function can take another function as a parameter.
6. Numerical analysis is the branch of mathematics and computer science that develops algorithms for mathematical computation. We demonstrated how to use the bisection method, a technique for iterative approximation of a root of a function.

NEW C CONSTRUCTS

Construct	Effect
Counting for Loop	
| ```c
for (num = 0;
     num < 26;
     ++num) {
   square = num * num;
   printf("%5d %5d\n", num,
          square);
}
``` | Displays 26 lines, each containing an integer from 0 to 25 and its square. |
| **Counting for Loop with a Negative Step** | |
| ```c
for (volts = 20;
     volts >= -20;
     volts -= 10) {
   current = volts / resistance;
   printf("%5d %8.3f\n", volts,
          current);
}
``` | For values of **volts** equal to 20, 10, 0, −10, −20, computes value of **current** and displays **volts** and **current**. |
| **Sentinel-Controlled while Loop** | |
| ```c
product = 1;
printf("Enter %d to quit\n",
       SENVAL);
printf("Enter first number> ");
scanf("%d", &dat);
while (dat != SENVAL) {
    product *= dat;
    printf("Next number> ");
    scanf("%d", &dat);
}
``` | Computes the product of a list of numbers. The product is complete when the user enters the sentinel value (**SENVAL**). |
| **Endfile-Controlled while Loop** | |
| ```c
sum = 0;
status = scanf("%d", &n);
while (status == 1) {
   sum += n;
   status =
      scanf("%d", &n);
}
``` | Accumulates the sum of a list of numbers input from a file. The sum is complete when **scanf** detects the endfile character or encounters erroneous data. |

(continued)

NEW C CONSTRUCTS (continued)

Construct	Effect
do-while Loop	

<pre>do {
    printf("Positive number < 10> ");
    scanf("d%, &num");
} while (num < 1 || num >= 10);</pre>
	Repeatedly displays prompts and stores a number in **num** until user enters a number that is in range.

Increment / Decrement	
`z = ++j * k--;`	Stores in **z** the product of the incremented value of **j** and the current value of **k**. Then **k** is decremented.
Compound Assignment	
`ans *= a - b;`	Assigns to **ans** the value of `ans * (a - b)`.

Quick-Check Exercises

1. A loop that continues to process input data until a special value is entered is called a _____ -controlled loop.
2. Some `for` loops cannot be rewritten in C using a `while` loop. True or false?
3. It is an error if the body of a `for` loop never executes. True or false?
4. In an endfile-controlled `while` loop, the initialization and update expressions typically include calls to the function _____.
5. In a typical counter-controlled loop, the number of loop repetitions may not be known until the loop is executing. True or false?
6. During execution of the following program segment, how many lines of hash marks are displayed?

```
for (m = 9; m > 0; - -m)
    for (n = 6; n > 1; - -n)
        printf("########\n");
```

7. During execution of the following program segment:
   a. How many times does the first call to `printf` execute?
   b. How many times does the second call to `printf` execute?
   c. What is the last value displayed?

```
for   (m = 10;   m > 0;   - -m) {
    for   (n = m;   n > 1;   - -n)
        printf("%d", m + n);
    printf("\n");
}
```

8. If the value of n is 4 and m is 5, is the value of the following expression 21?

```
++(n * m)
```

Explain your answer.

9. What are the values of x, y, and z after execution of this three-statement fragment?

m	n
9	6

```
x = m- - + - -n;
y = ++m — n++;
z = m++ + n- -;
```

10. What are the values of p, q, and r after execution of this three-statement fragment?

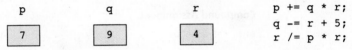

p	q	r
7	9	4

```
p += q * r;
q -= r + 5;
r /= p * r;
```

11. What does the following code segment display? Try each of these inputs: 12, 9, 3. Then, describe the action of the code.

```
printf("\nEnter a positive integer> ");
scanf("%d", &num);
while (num > 0) {
        if(num % 2 == 0)
                printf("%d\t", num);
num--;
} printf("\n");
```

Answers to Quick-Check Exercises

1. sentinel
2. false
3. false
4. scanf
5. false
6. 45
7. a.   9 + 8 + 7 + 6 + 5 + 4 + 3 + 2 + 1 = 45
   b.   10
   c.   4
8. No. The expression is illegal. The increment operator cannot be applied to an expression such as (n * m).
9. x = 14, y = 4, z = 15
10. p = 43, q = 0 , r = 0

11. Enter a positive integer> 12
```
12      10      8       6       4       2
```
Enter a positive integer> 9
```
8       6       4       2
```
Enter a positive integer> 3
```
2
```

The code displays all the even numbers separated by spaces that are less than or equal to the integer entered by the user.

Review Questions

1. In what ways are the initialization, repetition test, and update steps alike for a sentinel-controlled loop and an endfile-controlled loop? How are they different?
2. Write a program that computes and displays the product of a collection of even numbers entered interactively until a sentinel value of 99 is entered.
3. Hand trace the program that follows given the following data:

```
4 2 8 4    1 4 2 1    9 3 3 1    -22 10 8 2    3 3 4 5

#include <stdio.h>
#define SPECIAL_SLOPE    0.0

int
main(void)
{
        double slope, y2, y1, x2, x1;

        printf("Enter 4 numbers separated by spaces.");
        printf("\nThe last two numbers cannot be the ");
        printf("same, but\nthe program terminates if ");
        printf("the first two are.\n");
        printf("\nEnter four numbers> ");
        scanf("%lf%lf%lf%lf", &y2, &y1, &x2, &x1);

        for (slope = (y2 - y1) / (x2 - x1);
             slope != SPECIAL_SLOPE;
             slope = (y2 - y1) / (x2 - x1)) {
           printf("Slope is %5.2f.\n", slope);
           printf("\nEnter four more numbers> ");
           scanf("%lf%lf%lf%lf", &y2, &y1, &x2, &x1);
        }
        return (0);
}
```

4. Rewrite the program in Review Question 3 so that it uses a while loop.

5. Rewrite the program segment that follows, using a `for` loop:

```
product = 1;
i = 0;
while (i < n) {
            scanf("%d", &a);
            if (a != i)
        product *= a;
            ++i;

}
```

6. Rewrite this `do-while` loop, adding any missed semicolons.

```
do {
    printf("Number = %d\n.", num);
    num-- } while (num > 0)
```

7. Write a `do-while` loop that repeatedly prompts for and takes input until a value in the range 0 through 15 inclusive is input. Include code that prevents the loop from executing forever on input of a wrong data type.

Programming Projects

1. An integer n is divisible by 9 if the sum of its digits is divisible by 9. Develop a program to display each digit, starting with the rightmost digit. Your program should also determine whether or not the number is divisible by 9. Test it on the following numbers:

```
n = 154368
n = 621594
n = 123456
```

Hint: Use the % operator to get each digit; then use / to remove that digit. So 154368 % 10 gives 8 and 154368 / 10 gives 15436. The next digit extracted should be 6, then 3 and so on.

2. Redo programming project 1 by reading each digit of the number to be tested into a type char variable `digit`. Display each digit and form the sum of the numeric values of the digits. Hint: The numeric value of `digit` is

```
(int) digit - (int) '0'
```

 3. Write a program to create an output file containing a customized loan amortization table. Your program will prompt the user to enter the amount borrowed (the *principal*), the annual interest rate, and the number of payments (n). To calculate the monthly payment, it will use the formula from Programming

Project 1 in Chapter 3. This payment must be rounded to the nearest cent. After the payment has been rounded to the nearest cent, the program will write to the output file *n* lines showing how the debt is paid off. Each month part of the payment is the monthly interest on the principal balance, and the rest is applied to the principal. Because the payment and each month's interest are rounded, the final payment will be a bit different and must be calculated as the sum of the final interest payment and the final principal balance. Here is a sample table for a $1,000 loan borrowed at a 9% annual interest rate and paid back over 6 months.

| Principal | | $1,000.00 | Payment | $171.07 |
| Annual interest | | 9.0% | Term | 6 months |

Payment	Interest	Principal	Principal Balance
1	7.50	163.57	836.43
2	6.27	164.80	671.63
3	5.04	166.03	505.60
4	3.79	167.28	338.32
5	2.54	168.53	169.79
6	1.27	169.79	0.00
Final payment	$171.06		

4. a. Write a program that will count the number of odd values and the number of even values in a collection of *N* numbers. Get the value of *N* before scanning each value in the collection of *N* numbers.

   b. Modify your program to compute and display each of the following in a collection of *N* numbers: the sum of odd values, the sum of even values, the square of the sum of odd values, and the square of the sum of even values.

5. The greatest common divisor (gcd) of two integers is the product of the integers' common factors. Write a program that inputs two numbers and implements the following approach to finding their gcd. We will use the numbers −252 and 735. Working with the numbers' absolute values, we find the remainder of one divided by the other.

$$
\begin{array}{r}
0 \\
735\overline{)\,252} \\
0 \\
\hline
252
\end{array}
$$

Now we calculate the remainder of the old divisor divided by the remainder found.

$$\begin{array}{r} 2 \\ 252\overline{)735} \\ 504 \\ \hline 231 \end{array}$$

We repeat this process until the remainder is zero.

$$\begin{array}{r} 1 \\ 231\overline{)252} \\ 231 \\ \hline 21 \end{array} \qquad \begin{array}{r} 11 \\ 21\overline{)231} \\ 21 \\ \hline 21 \\ 21 \\ \hline 0 \end{array}$$

The last divisor (21) is the gcd.

6. The Environmental Awareness Club of BigCorp International is proposing that the company subsidize at $.08 per passenger-kilometer the commuting costs of employees who form carpools that meet a prescribed minimum passenger efficiency. Passenger efficiency P (in passenger-kilometers per liter) is defined as

$$P = \frac{ns}{l}$$

where n is the number of passengers, s is the distance traveled in kilometers, and l is the number of liters of gasoline used.

Write a program that processes an input file of data on existing carpools (carpool.txt), creating an output file effic.txt containing a table of all carpools that meet the passenger efficiency minimum. The input file begins with a number that is the minimum passenger efficiency. Each carpool is represented by a data line containing three numbers: the number of people in the carpool, the total commuting distance per five-day week, and the number of liters of gasoline consumed in a week of commuting. The data file ends with a line of zeros. Write your results with this format:

CARPOOLS MEETING MINIMUM PASSENGER EFFICIENCY OF 25 PASSENGER KM/L

Passengers	Weekly Commute (km)	Gasoline Consumption(L)	Efficiency (pass km/L)	Weekly Subsidy($)
4	75	11.0	27.3	24.00
2	60	4.5	26.7	19.60

. . .

7. a.   Write a program to process a collection of the speeds of vehicles. Your program should count and print the number of vehicles moving at a high speed (90 miles/hour or higher), the number of vehicles moving at a medium speed (50–90 miles/hour), and the number of vehicles moving at a slow speed (less than 50 miles/hour). It should also display the category of each vehicle. Test your program on the following data:

Speed of vehicles (in miles): 43   23   54   57   68   67   51   90   33   22   11   88   34   52   75   12   78   32   89   14   65   67   97   53   10   47   34

b.   Modify your program to display the average speed of a vehicle (a real number) at the end of the run.

8. Write a program to process weekly employee time cards for all employees of an organization. Each employee will have three data items: an identification number, the hourly wage rate, and the number of hours worked during a given week. Each employee is to be paid time and a half for all hours worked over 40. A tax amount of 3.625% of gross salary will be deducted. The program output should show the employee's number and net pay. Display the total payroll and the average amount paid at the end of the run.

9. Suppose you own a beer distributorship that sells Piels (ID number 1), Coors (ID number 2), Bud (ID number 3), and Iron City (ID number 4) by the case. Write a program to

a.   Get the case inventory for each brand for the start of the week.
b.   Process all weekly sales and purchase records for each brand.
c.   Display out the final inventory.

Each transaction will consist of two data items. The first item will be the brand ID number (an integer). The second will be the amount purchased (a positive integer value) or the amount sold (a negative integer value). For now you may assume that you always have sufficient foresight to prevent depletion of your inventory for any brand. (*Hint:* Your data entry should begin with four values representing the case inventory, followed by the transaction values.)

10. The pressure of a gas changes as the volume and temperature of the gas vary. Write a program that uses the Van der Waals equation of state for a gas,

$$\left(P + \frac{an^2}{V^2}\right)(V - bn) = nRT$$

to create a file that displays in tabular form the relationship between the pressure and the volume of n moles of carbon dioxide at a constant absolute temperature (T). P is the pressure in atmospheres and V is the volume in liters. The Van der Waals constants for carbon dioxide are $a = 3.592$ L$^2 \cdot$ atm/mol^2 and $b = 0.0427$ L/mol. Use 0.08206 L $\cdot$ atm/mol $\cdot$ K for the gas constant R. Inputs to the program include n, the Kelvin temperature, the initial and final volumes in milliliters, and the volume increment between lines of the table. Your program will output a table that varies the volume of the gas from the initial to the final volume in steps prescribed by the volume increment. Here is a sample run:

```
Please enter at the prompts the number of moles of carbon
dioxide, the absolute temperature, the initial volume in
milliliters, the final volume, and the increment volume
between lines of the table.

Quantity of carbon dioxide (moles)> 0.02
Temperature (kelvin)> 300
Initial volume (milliliters)> 400
Final volume (milliliters)> 600
Volume increment (milliliters)> 50
```

Output File

```
0.0200 moles of carbon dioxide at 300 kelvin

Volume (ml)     Pressure (atm)

    400             1.2246
    450             1.0891
    500             0.9807
    550             0.8918
    600             0.8178
```

11. A concrete channel to bring water to Crystal Lake is being designed. It will have vertical walls and be 15 feet wide. It will be 10 feet deep, have a slope of .0015 feet/foot, and a roughness coefficient of .014. How deep will the water be when 1000 cubic feet per second is flowing through the channel?

To solve this problem, we can use Manning's equation

$$Q = \frac{1.486}{N} A R^{2/3} S^{1/2}$$

where Q is the flow of water (cubic feet per second), N is the roughness coefficient (unitless), A is the area (square feet), S is the slope (feet/foot), and R is the hydraulic radius (feet).

The hydraulic radius is the cross-sectional area divided by the wetted perimeter. For square channels like the one in this example,

Hydraulic radius = depth × width/(2.0 × depth + width)

To solve this problem, design a program that allows the user to guess a depth and then calculates the corresponding flow. If the flow is too little, the user should guess a depth a little higher; if the flow is too high, the user should guess a depth a little lower. The guessing is repeated until the computed flow is within 0.1% of the flow desired.

To help the user make an initial guess, the program should display the flow for half the channel depth. Note the example run:

```
At a depth of 5.0000 feet, the flow is 641.3255 cubic
feet per second.

Enter your initial guess for the channel depth
when the flow is 1000.0000 cubic feet per second
Enter guess> 6.0

Depth: 6.0000 Flow: 825.5906 cfs Target: 1000.0000 cfs
Difference: 174.4094 Error: 17.4409 percent
Enter guess> 7.0

Depth: 7.0000 Flow: 1017.7784 cfs Target: 1000.0000 cfs
Difference: -17.7784 Error: -1.7778 percent

Enter guess> 6.8
```

12. The table below lists approximations in meters of the longest wavelengths in each region of the electromagnetic spectrum. The final column gives these lengths as they would be represented in C scientific notation. You can see that the "E" would be read as "times 10 to the power." Numbers in this format can be used as constants. They can be scanned in using the %lf placeholder. However, to output a number in scientific notation, use the %e placeholder. Note that visible light makes up a tiny fraction of the full spectrum. Write a program that repeatedly prompts the user to enter a wavelength in scientific notation (or zero to quit) and displays for each entry the wavelength and the region of the spectrum into which it falls. Note that zero is used as a sentinel, so no region should be displayed when the user enters zero.

Regions of the Electromagnetic Spectrum

	Longest Wavelength	C Scientific Notation
gamma ray	3×10^{-11} m	3E-11
X-ray	3×10^{-9} m	3E-9
ultraviolet	4×10^{-7} m	4E-7
visible	7×10^{-7} m	7E-7
infrared	1.4×10^{-5} m	1.4E-5
microwave	0.1 m	1.0E-1
radio wave	longer	

13. A baseball player's batting average is calculated as the number of hits divided by the official number of at-bats. In calculating official at-bats, walks, sacrifices, and occasions when hit by the pitch are not counted. Write a program that takes an input file containing player numbers and batting records. Trips to the plate are coded in the batting record as follows: H—hit, O—out, W—walk, S—sacrifice, and P—hit by pitch. The program should output for each player the input data followed by the batting average. (*Hint*: Each batting record is followed by a newline character.)

    Sample input file:
    ```
    12 HOOOWSHHOOHPWWHO
    4 OSOHHHWWOHOHOOO
    7 WPOHOOHWOHHOWOO
    ```

    Corresponding output:
    ```
    Player 12's record: HOOOWSHHOOHPWWHO
    Player 12's batting average: 0.455

    Player 4's record: OSOHHHWWOHOHOOO
    Player 4's batting average: 0.417

    Player 7's record: WPOHOOHWOHHOWOO
    Player 7's batting average: 0.364
    ```

14. The rate of decay of a radioactive isotope is given in terms of its half-life H, the time lapse required for the isotope to decay to one-half of its original mass. The isotope cobalt-60 (^{60}Co) has a half-life of 5.272 years. Compute and print in table form the amount of this isotope that remains after each year for five years, given the initial presence of an amount in grams. The value of *amount* should be provided interactively. The amount of ^{60}Co remaining can be computed by using the following formula:

$$r = amount \times C^{(y/H)}$$

    where *amount* is the initial amount in grams, C is expressed as $e^{-0.693}$ ($e = 2.71828$), y is the number of years elapsed, and H is the half-life of the isotope in years.

15. The value for π can be determined by the series equation:

$$\pi = 4 \times \left(1 - \frac{1}{3} + \frac{1}{5} - \frac{1}{7} + \frac{1}{9} - \frac{1}{11} + \frac{1}{13} - \ldots\right)$$

    Write a program that prompts the user to enter the number of iterations to be executed to determine the value of π.

16. In this chapter, we studied the bisection method for finding a root of an equation. Another method for finding a root, Newton's method, usually converges

FIGURE 5.25

Geometric
Interpretation of
Newton's Method

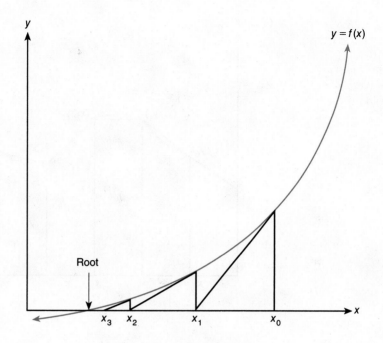

to a solution even faster than the bisection method, if it converges at all.
Newton's method starts with an initial guess for a root, x_0, and then generates
successive approximate roots $x_1, x_2, \ldots, x_j, x_{j+1}, \ldots$, using the iterative formula

$$x_{j+1} = x_j - \frac{f(x_j)}{f'(x_j)}$$

where $f'(x)$ is the derivative of function f evaluated at $x = x_j$. The formula generates a new guess, x_{j+1}, from a previous one, x_j. Sometimes Newton's method
will fail to converge to a root. In this case, the program should terminate after
many trials, perhaps 100.

Figure 5.25 shows the geometric interpretation of Newton's method
where x_0, x_1, and x_2 represent successive guesses for the root. At each point
x_j, the derivative, $f'(x_j)$, is the slope of the tangent to the curve, $f(x)$. The next
guess for the root, x_{j+1}, is the point at which the tangent crosses the x-axis.

From geometry, we get the equation

$$\frac{y_{j+1} - y_j}{x_{j+1} - x_j} = m$$

FIGURE 5.26

Approximating
the Area Under
a Curve with
Trapezoids

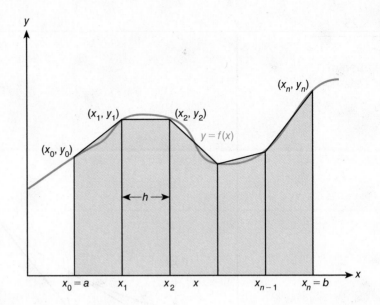

where m is the slope of the line between points (x_{j+1}, y_{j+1}) and (x_j, y_j). In Fig. 5.23, we see that y_{j+1} is zero, y_j is $f(x_j)$, and m is $f'(x_j)$; therefore, by substituting and rearranging terms, we get

$$- f(x_j) = f'(x_j) \times (x_{j+1} - x_j)$$

leading to the formula shown at the beginning of this problem.

Write a program that uses Newton's method to approximate the nth root of a number to six decimal places. If $x^n = c$, then $x^n - c = 0$. Finding a root of the second equation will give you $\sqrt[n]{c}$. Test your program on $\sqrt{2}$, $\sqrt[3]{7}$, and $\sqrt[3]{-1}$. Your program could use $c/2$ as its initial guess.

17. You would like to find the area under the curve

$$y = f(x)$$

between the lines $x = a$ and $x = b$. One way to approximate this area is to use line segments as approximations of small pieces of the curve and then to sum the areas of trapezoids created by drawing perpendiculars from the line segment endpoints to the x-axis, as shown in Fig. 5.26. We will assume that $f(x)$ is non-negative over the interval $[a,b]$. The trapezoidal rule approximates this area T as

$$T = \frac{h}{2} \left(f(a) + f(b) + 2\sum_{i=1}^{n-1} f(x_i) \right)$$

for n subintervals of length h:

$$h = \frac{b - a}{n}$$

Write a function `trap` with input parameters `a`, `b`, `n`, and `f` that implements the trapezoidal rule. Call `trap` with values for n of 2, 4, 8, 16, 32, 64, and 128 on functions

$$g(x) = x^2 \sin x \quad (a = 0, b = 3.14159)$$

and

$$h(x) = \sqrt{4 - x^2} \quad (a = -2, b = 2)$$

Function h defines a half-circle of radius 2. Compare your approximation to the actual area of this half-circle.

Note: If you have studied calculus, you will observe that the trapezoidal rule is approximating

$$\int_a^b f(x)dx$$

Graphics Projects

18. Draw a series of circles along one diagonal of a window. The circles should be different colors and each circle should touch the ones next to it.

19. Redo Programming Project 18 but this time draw a series of squares along the other diagonal as well.

20. Draw a simple stick figure and move it across the screen.

21. Redo Programming Project 18 but this time draw a single circle that moves down a diagonal.

22. Redo Programming Project 19 with a single circle and square moving along each diagonal.

Pointers and Modular Programming

CHAPTER OBJECTIVES

- To learn about pointers and indirect addressing
- To see how to access external data files in a program and to be able to read from input files and write to output files using file pointers
- To learn how to return function results through a function's arguments
- To understand the differences between call-by-value and call-by-reference
- To understand the distinction between input, inout, and output parameters and when to use each kind
- To learn how to modularize a program system and pass information between system modules (functions)
- To understand how to document the flow of information using structure charts
- To learn testing and debugging techniques appropriate for a program system with several modules

T his chapter begins with a discussion of pointers and highlights some of their uses in C. We will see how pointers can be used to store a memory cell address and access or modify the contents of this cell through indirect reference. We will also learn how to use file pointers to enable a program to access input and output files.

In Chapter 3, you learned how to write the separate modules—functions—of a program. The functions correspond to the individual steps in a problem solution. You also learned how to provide inputs to a function and how to return a single output. In this chapter, you learn how to write functions that can return multiple outputs. You will also learn how to write programs that use several functions to build modular program systems.

6.1 Pointers and the Indirection Operator

The declaration

```
float *p;
```

pointer or pointer variable a memory cell that stores the address of a data item.

identifies p as a **pointer variable** of type "pointer to `float`." This means that we can store the *memory address* of a type `float` variable in p.

Pointer Type Declaration

SYNTAX: *type* *variable;

EXAMPLE: `float *p;`

INTERPRETATION: The value of the pointer variable p is a memory address. A data item whose address is stored in this variable must be of the specified *type*.

EXAMPLE 6.1   The declaration statements

```
int m = 25;
int *itemp;        /* a pointer to an integer */
```

allocate storage for an `int` variable (m) and a pointer variable (`itemp`). The following statement stores the memory address of m in pointer `itemp`. It applies the

FIGURE 6.1

Referencing a
Variable Through a
Pointer

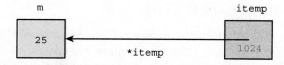

unary address-of operator `&` to variable `m` to get its address, which is then stored in `itemp`.

```
itemp = &m;        /* Store address of m in pointer itemp */
```

This is the same `&` operator that we have applied to variables in the input list of a `scanf` statement.

Figure 6.1 is a diagram of the situation that results after the above assignment assuming that variable `m` is associated with memory cell 1024. Because it makes no difference to a program which memory cell is used, we represent the address in a pointer by drawing an arrow from the pointer (`itemp`) to the variable (`m`) that it points to.

Indirect Reference

indirect reference
accessing the contents
of a memory cell
through a pointer
variable that stores its
address

The label below the arrow in Fig. 6.1 shows that we can use `*itemp` to reference the cell selected by pointer `itemp`. When the unary indirection operator `*` is applied to a pointer variable, it has the effect of following the pointer referenced by its operand. This provides an **indirect reference** to the cell that is selected by the pointer variable. Table 6.1 shows the values of some pointer references for Fig. 6.1.

EXAMPLE 6.2

For the declarations shown earlier, the statement

```
*itemp = 35;
```

stores 35 in the variable `m` that is pointed to by `itemp`. The statement

```
printf("%d", *itemp);
```

displays the new value of `m` (35). The statement

```
*itemp = 2 * (*itemp);
```

doubles the value currently stored in `m`, the variable pointed to by `itemp`. Note that the parentheses are inserted for clarity but are not needed.

TABLE 6.1 References with Pointers

Reference	Cell Referenced	Cell Type (Value)
itemp	gray shaded cell	pointer (1024)
*itemp	cell in color	int (25)

Pointers to Files

As an alternative to input/output redirection, C allows a program to explicitly name a file from which the program will take input or write output. To use files in this way, we must declare pointer variables of type `FILE *`. The statements

```
FILE *inp;     /* pointer to input file */
FILE *outp;    /* pointer to output file */
```

declare that file pointer variables `inp` and `output` will hold information allowing access to the program's input and output files, respectively.

The operating system must prepare a file for input or output before permitting access. This preparation is the purpose of the calls to function `fopen` in the statements

```
inp = fopen("distance.txt", "r");
outp = fopen("distout.txt", "w");
```

The first assignment statement *opens* (prepares for access) file `distance.txt` as a source of program input and stores the necessary access value in the file pointer variable `inp`. The `"r"` in the first call to `fopen` indicates that we wish to read (scan) data from the file opened. Because the second assignment statement includes a `"w"`, indicating our desire to write to `distout.txt`, `outp` is initialized as an output file pointer.

The next two statements demonstrate the use of the functions `fscanf` and `fprintf`, file equivalents of functions `scanf` and `printf`.

```
fscanf(inp, "%lf", &item);
fprintf(outp, "%.2f\n", item);
```

Function `fscanf` must first be given an input file pointer like `inp`. The remainder of a call to `fscanf` is identical to a call to `scanf`: It includes a format string and an input list. Similarly, function `fprintf` differs from function `printf` only in its requirement of an output file pointer like `outp` as its first argument. Like `scanf`, function `fscanf` returns either the number of items read or a negative value (`EOF`) if the end of file character is detected.

When a program has no further use for its input and output files, it *closes* them by calling function `fclose` with the file pointers.

```
fclose(inp);
fclose(outp);
```

Figure 6.2 shows a program that inputs a collection of numbers from a file `indata.txt` and writes each number rounded to two decimal places on a separate line of file `outdata.txt`. We show a sample file `indata.txt` and the resulting file `outdata.txt` after the program.

FIGURE 6.2 Program Using File Pointers

```
1.   /* Inputs each number from an input file and writes it
2.    * rounded to 2 decimal places on a line of an output file.
3.    */
4.   #include <stdio.h>
5.
6.   int
7.   main(void)
8.   {
9.         FILE *inp;           /* pointer to input file */
10.        FILE *outp;          /* pointer to ouput file */
11.        double item;
12.        int input_status;  /* status value returned by fscanf */
13.
14.        /* Prepare files for input or output */
15.        inp = fopen("indata.txt", "r");
16.        outp = fopen("outdata.txt", "w");
17.
18.        /* Input each item, format it, and write it */
19.        input_status = fscanf(inp, "%lf", &item);
20.        while (input_status == 1) {
21.            fprintf(outp, "%.2f\n", item);
22.            input_status = fscanf(inp, "%lf", &item);
23.        }
24.
25.        /* Close the files */
26.        fclose(inp);
27.        fclose(outp);
28.
29.        return (0);
30.   }
```

File indata.txt
```
344 55 6.3556 9.4
43.123 47.596
```

File outdata.txt
```
344.00
55.00
6.36
9.40
43.12
47.60
```

EXERCISES FOR SECTION 6.1

Self-Check

1. Trace the execution of the following fragment.

```
int m = 10, n = 5;
int *mp, *np;
mp = &m;
np = &n;
*mp = *mp + *np;
*np = *mp - *np;
printf("%d %d\n%d %d\n", m, *mp, n, *np);
```

2. Given the declarations

```
int m = 25, n = 77;
char c = '*';
int *itemp;
```

describe the errors in each of the following statements.

```
m = &n;
itemp = m;
*itemp = c;
*itemp = &c;
```

Programming

1. Add statements to Fig. 6.2 that count the number of items input and write the count (an integer) as the last line of the output file. Why can't you write the count as the first item of the output file?

6.2 Functions with Output Parameters

Argument lists provide the communication links between the main function and its function subprograms. Arguments make functions more versatile because they enable a function to manipulate different data each time it is called. So far, we know how to pass inputs to a function and how to use the `return` statement to send back one result value from a function. This section describes how programmers use output parameters to return multiple results from a function.

When a function call executes, the computer allocates memory space in the function data area for each formal parameter. The value of each actual parameter is stored in the memory cell allocated to its corresponding formal parameter. Or, we can use the address-of operator (`&`) to store the actual parameter's address, that is, a pointer to the actual parameter instead of its value. Next, we discuss how a function uses pointers and the indirection operator (`*`) to return results to the function that calls it.

FIGURE 6.3   Function Separate

```
1.   /*
2.    * Separates a number into three parts: a sign (+, -, or blank),
3.    * a whole number magnitude, and a fractional part.
4.    */
5.   void
6.   separate(double   num,      /* input - value to be split           */
7.            char    *signp,   /* output - sign of num                 */
8.            int     *wholep, /* output - whole number magnitude of num */
9.            double  *fracp)  /* output - fractional part of num       */
10.  {
11.        double magnitude; /* local variable - magnitude of num        */
12.
13.        /* Determines sign of num */
14.        if (num < 0)
15.            *signp = '-';
16.        else if (num == 0)
17.            *signp = ' ';
18.        else
19.            *signp = '+';
20.
21.        /* Finds magnitude of num (its absolute value) and
22.           separates it into whole and fractional parts           */
23.        magnitude = fabs(num);
24.        *wholep = floor(magnitude);
25.        *fracp = magnitude - *wholep;
26.  }
```

EXAMPLE 6.3   Function `separate` in Fig. 6.3 finds the sign, whole number magnitude, and fractional parts of its first parameter. In our previous examples, all the formal parameters of a function represent inputs to the function from the calling function. In function `separate`, however, only the first formal parameter, `num`, is an input; the other three formal parameters—`signp`, `wholep`, and `fracp`—are output parameters, used to carry multiple results from function `separate` back to the function calling it. Note that output parameters are declared as pointers. Figure 6.4 illustrates the function as a box with one input and three outputs.

FIGURE 6.4

Diagram of
Function separate
with Multiple
Results

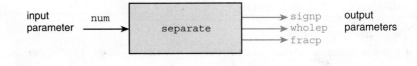

Let's focus for a moment on the heading of the function in Fig. 6.3.

```
void
separate(double  num,     /* input - value to be split           */
         char    *signp,  /* output - sign of num                */
         int     *wholep, /* output - whole number magnitude
                              of num                              */
         double  *fracp)  /* output - fractional part of num      */
```

The actual argument value passed to the formal parameter num is used to determine the values to be sent back through signp, wholep, and fracp. Notice that in Fig. 6.3 the declarations of these output parameters in the function heading have asterisks before the parameter names denoting that they are pointers. The assignment statements in the function use indirect reference to send back the function results. The function type is void as it is for functions returning no result, and the function body does not include a return statement to send back a single value, as we saw in earlier functions.

The declaration char *signp tells the compiler that output parameter signp will contain the *address* of a type char variable. Another way to express the idea that signp is the address of a type char variable is to say that the parameter signp is a pointer to a type char variable. Similarly, the output parameters wholep and fracp are pointers to variables of types int and double. We have chosen names for these output parameters that end in the letter "p" because they are all pointers.

Figure 6.5 shows a complete program including a brief function main that calls function separate. Function separate is defined as it was in Fig. 6.3,

FIGURE 6.5   Program That Calls a Function with Output Arguments

```
1.  /*
2.   * Demonstrates the use of a function with input and output parameters.
3.   */
4.
5.  #include <stdio.h>
6.  #include <math.h>
```

(continued)

FIGURE 6.5   (continued)

```
7.  void separate(double num, char *signp, int *wholep, double *fracp);
8.
9.  int
10. main(void)
11. {
12.       double value; /* input - number to analyze                      */
13.       char sn;       /* output - sign of value                         */
14.       int whl;       /* output - whole number magnitude of value       */
15.       double fr;     /* output - fractional part of value              */
16.
17.       /* Gets data                                                     */
18.       printf("Enter a value to analyze> ");
19.       scanf("%lf", &value);
20.
21.       /* Separates data value into three parts                         */
22.       separate(value, &sn, &whl, &fr);
23.
24.       /* Prints results                                                */
25.       printf("Parts of %.4f\n sign: %c\n", value, sn);
26.       printf(" whole number magnitude: %d\n", whl);
27.       printf(" fractional part: %.4f\n", fr);
28.
29.       return (0);
30. }
31.
32. /*
33.  * Separates a number into three parts: a sign (+, -, or blank),
34.  * a whole number magnitude, and a fractional part.
35.  * Pre: num is defined; signp, wholep, and fracp contain addresses of memory
36.  *       cells where results are to be stored
37.  * Post: function results are stored in cells pointed to by signp, wholep, and
38.  *       fracp
39.  */
40. void
41. separate(double   num,      /* input - value to be split               */
42.          char    *signp,    /* output - sign of num                    */
43.          int     *wholep,   /* output - whole number magnitude of num  */
44.          double  *fracp)    /* output - fractional part of num         */
45. {
46.       double magnitude;    /* local variable - magnitude of num        */
```

(continued)

FIGURE 6.5 (continued)

```
47.          /* Determines sign of num */
48.          if (num < 0)
49.                  *signp = '-';
50.          else if (num == 0)
51.                  *signp = ' ';
52.          else
53.                  *signp = '+';
54.
55.          /* Finds magnitude of num (its absolute value) and separates it into
56.             whole and fractional parts                                        */
57.          magnitude = fabs(num);
58.          *wholep = floor(magnitude);
59.          *fracp = magnitude - *wholep;
60.  }


Enter a value to analyze> 35.817
Parts of 35.8170
  sign: +
  whole number magnitude: 35
  fractional part: 0.8170
```

but pre- and postconditions have been added to its block comment. The calling function must declare variables in which function separate can store the multiple results it computes. Function main in our example declares three variables to receive these results—a type char variable sn, a type int variable whl, and a type double variable fr. Notice that no values are placed in these variables prior to the call to function separate, for it is the job of separate to define their values.

Figure 6.6 shows the data areas of main and separate as they are set up by the function call statement

```
separate(value, &sn, &whl, &fr);
```

This statement causes the number stored in the actual argument value to be copied into the input parameter num and the addresses of the arguments sn, whl, and fr to be stored in the corresponding output parameters signp, wholep, and fracp. The small numbers in color represent possible actual addresses in memory. Since it makes no difference to our program which specific cells are used, we draw an arrow from signp to sn. Note that the use of the address-of operator & on the actual arguments sn, whl, and fr is essential. If the operator & were omitted, we would be passing to separate the *values* of sn, whl, and fr, information that is worthless from the perspective of separate. The only way separate can store values in sn,

FIGURE 6.6

Parameter
Correspondence
for separate(value,
&sn, &whl, &fr);

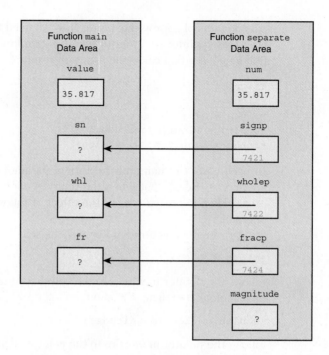

whl, and fr is if it knows where to find them in memory. The purpose of separate with regard to its second, third, and fourth arguments is comparable to the purpose of the library function scanf with regard to all of its arguments except the first (the format string).

In addition to the fact that the *values* of the actual output arguments in the call to separate are useless, these values are also of data types that do not match the types of the corresponding formal parameters. Table 6.2 shows the effect of the address-of operator & on the data type of a reference. You see that in general if a reference x is of type "whatever-type," the reference &x is of type "pointer to whatever-type," that is, "whatever-type *."

So far, we have examined how to declare simple output parameters in a function prototype and how to use the address-of operator & in a function call statement to

TABLE 6.2 Effect of & Operator on the Data Type of a Reference

Declaration	Data Type of x	Data Type of &x
char x	char	char * (pointer to char)
int x	int	int * (pointer to int)
double x	double	double * (pointer to double)

pass pointers of appropriate types. Now we need to study how the function manipulates these pointers in order to send back multiple results. The statements in function `separate` that cause the return of results follow.

```
*signp = '-';
*signp = ' ';
*signp = '+';
*wholep = floor(magnitude);
*fracp = magnitude - *wholep;
```

In each case, the name of the formal parameter is preceded by the indirection operator `*`. Recall that when the unary `*` operator is applied to a reference that is of some pointer type, it has the effect of following the pointer referenced by its operand.

For the data pictured in Fig. 6.6, the statement

```
*signp = '+';
```

follows the pointer in `signp` to the cell that function `main` calls `sn` and stores in it the character `'+'`. The statement

```
*wholep = floor(magnitude);
```

follows the pointer in `wholep` to the cell called `whl` by `main` and stores the integer 35 there. Similarly, the statement

```
*fracp = magnitude - *wholep;
```

uses two indirect references: One accesses the value in `main`'s local variable `whl` through the pointer `wholep`, and another accesses `fr` of `main` through the pointer `fracp` to give the final output argument the value `0.817`.

Meanings of * Symbol

We have now seen three distinct meanings of the symbol `*`. In Chapter 2, we studied its use as the binary operator meaning multiplication. Function `separate` introduces two additional meanings. The `*`'s in the declarations of the function's formal parameters are part of the names of the parameters' data types. These `*`'s should be read as "pointer to." Thus the declaration

```
char *signp;
```

tells the compiler that the type of parameter `signp` is "pointer to `char`."

The `*` has a completely different meaning when it is used as the unary indirection operator in the function body. Here it means "follow the pointer." Thus, when used in a reference, `*signp` means follow the pointer in `signp`. Notice that the data type of the reference `*signp` is `char`, the data type of `*wholep` is `int`, and the data type of `*fracp` is `double`.

EXERCISES FOR SECTION 6.2

Self-Check

1. Write a prototype for a function `sum_n_avg` that has three type `double` input parameters and two output parameters.

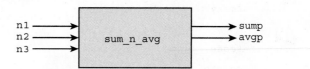

   The function computes the sum and the average of its three input arguments and relays its results through two output parameters.

2. The following code fragment is from a function preparing to call `sum_n_avg` (see Exercise 1). Complete the function call statement.

```
{
    double one, two, three, sum_of_3, avg_of_3;
    printf("Enter three numbers> ");
    scanf("%lf%lf%lf", &one, &two, &three);
    sum_n_avg(_____);
    . . .
}
```

3. Given the memory setup shown, fill in the chart by indicating the data type and value of each reference as well as the name of the function in which the reference would be legal.

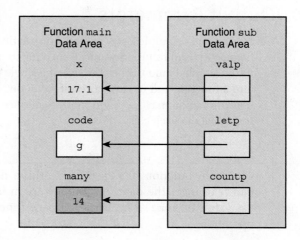

Describe pointer values by referring to cell attributes. For example, the value of `valp` would be "pointer to color-shaded cell," and the value of `&many` would be "pointer to gray-shaded cell."

Reference	Where Legal	Data Type	Value
valp	sub	double *	pointer to color-shaded cell
&many			
code			
&code			
countp			
*countp			
*valp			
letp			
&x			

Programming

1. Define the function `sum_n_avg` whose prototype you wrote in Self-Check Exercise 1. The function should compute both the sum and the average of its three input parameters and relay these results through its output parameters.

6.3 Multiple Calls to a Function with Input/Output Parameters

In previous examples, we passed information into a function through its input parameters and returned results from a function through its output parameters. Our next example demonstrates the use of a single parameter both to bring a data value into a function and to carry a result value out of the function. It also demonstrates how a function may be called more than once in a given program and process different data in each call.

sorting rearranging data in a particular sequence (increasing or decreasing)

EXAMPLE 6.4

The main function in Fig. 6.7 gets three data values, `num1`, `num2`, and `num3`, and rearranges the data so that they are in increasing sequence with the smallest value in `num1`. The three calls to function `order` perform this **sorting** operation.

FIGURE 6.7   Program to Sort Three Numbers

```
1.  /*
2.   * Tests function order by ordering three numbers
3.   */
4.  #include <stdio.h>
5.
6.  void order(double *smp, double *lgp);
7.
8.  int
9.  main(void)
10. {
11.         double num1, num2, num3; /* three numbers to put in order     */
12.
13.         /* Gets test data                                             */
14.         printf("Enter three numbers separated by blanks> ");
15.         scanf("%lf%lf%lf", &num1, &num2, &num3);
16.
17.         /* Orders the three numbers                                    */
18.         order(&num1, &num2);
19.         order(&num1, &num3);
20.         order(&num2, &num3);
21.
22.         /* Displays results                                           */
23.         printf("The numbers in ascending order are: %.2f %.2f %.2f\n",
24.                 num1, num2, num3);
25.
26.         return (0);
27. }
28.
29. /*
30.  * Arranges arguments in ascending order.
31.  * Pre:    smp and lgp are addresses of defined type double variables
32.  * Post:   variable pointed to by smp contains the smaller of the type
33.  *         double values; variable pointed to by lgp contains the larger
34.  */
35. void
36. order(double *smp, double *lgp)     /* input/output */
37. {
38.         double temp; /* temporary variable to hold one number during swap    */
```

(continued)

FIGURE 6.7   (continued)

```
39.          /* Compares values pointed to by smp and lgp and switches if necessary    */
40.          if (*smp > *lgp) {
41.                temp = *smp;
42.                *smp = *lgp;
43.                *lgp = temp;
44.          }
45.  }
```

```
Enter three numbers separated by blanks> 7.5 9.6 5.5
The numbers in ascending order are: 5.50 7.50 9.60
```

Each time function `order` executes, the smaller of its two argument values is stored in its first actual argument and the larger is stored in its second actual argument. Therefore, the function call

```
order(&num1, &num2);
```

stores the smaller of `num1` and `num2` in `num1` and the larger in `num2`. In the sample run shown, `num1` is `7.5` and `num2` is `9.6`, so these values are not changed by the function execution. However, the function call

```
order(&num1, &num3);
```

switches the values of `num1` (initial value is `7.5`) and `num3` (initial value is `5.5`). Table 6.3 traces the main function execution.

The body of function `order` is based on the `if` statement from Fig. 4.6. The function heading

```
void
order(double *smp, double *lgp)    /* input/output */
```

TABLE 6.3   Trace of Program to Sort Three Numbers

Statement	num1	num2	num3	Effect
`scanf("...", &num1, &num2, &num3);`	7.5	9.6	5.5	Enters data
`order(&num1, &num2);`				No change
`order(&num1, &num3);`	5.5	9.6	7.5	Switches num1 and num3
`order(&num2, &num3);`	5.5	7.5	9.6	Switches num2 and num3
`printf("...", num1, num2, num3);`				Displays 5.5 7.5 9.6

identifies `smp` and `lgp` as *input/output parameters* because the function uses the current actual argument values as inputs and may return new values.

During the execution of the second call

```
order(&num1, &num3);
```

the formal parameter `smp` contains the address of the actual argument `num1`, and the formal parameter `lgp` contains the address of the actual argument `num3`. Testing the condition

```
(*smp > *lgp)
```

causes both of these pointers to be followed, resulting in the condition

```
(7.5 > 5.5)
```

which evaluates to true. Executing the first assignment statement in the true task,

```
temp = *smp;
```

causes the `7.5` to be copied into the local variable `temp`. Figure 6.8 shows us a snapshot of the values in memory immediately after execution of this assignment statement.

Execution of the next assignment statement,

```
*smp = *lgp;
```

would cause the `7.5` in the variable pointed to by `smp` to be replaced by `5.5`, the value of the variable pointed to by `lgp`. The final assignment statement,

```
*lgp = temp;
```

copies the contents of the temporary variable (`7.5`) into the variable pointed to by `lgp`. This completes the swap of values.

FIGURE 6.8

Data Areas After
`temp = *smp;`
During Call
`order(&num1,`
`&num3);`

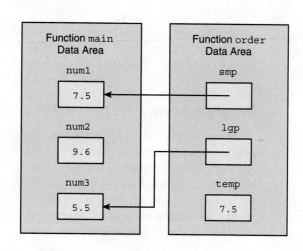

TABLE 6.4 Different Kinds of Function Subprograms

Purpose	Function Type	Parameters	To Return Result
To compute or obtain as input a single numeric or character value.	Same as type of value to be computed or obtained.	Input parameters hold copies of data provided by calling function.	Function code includes a `return` statement with an expression whose value is the result.
To produce printed output containing values of numeric or character arguments.	`void`	Input parameters hold copies of data provided by calling function.	No result is returned.
To compute multiple numeric or character results.	`void`	Input parameters hold copies of data provided by calling function. Output parameters are pointers to actual arguments.	Results are stored in the calling function's data area by indirect assignment through output parameters. No `return` statement is required.
To modify argument values.	`void`	Input/output parameters are pointers to actual arguments. Input data is accessed by indirect reference through parameters.	Results are stored in the calling function's data area by indirect assignment through output parameters. No `return` statement is required.

So far we have seen four kinds of functions, and we have studied how formal parameters are used in all of them. Table 6.4 compares the various kinds of functions and indicates the circumstances when each kind should be used.

Program Style   *Preferred Kinds of Functions*

Although all the kinds of functions in Table 6.4 are useful in developing program systems, we recommend that you use the first kind whenever it is possible to do so. Functions that return a single value are the easiest functions for a program reader to deal with. You will note that all the mathematical functions we discussed in Section 3.2 are of this variety. Since such functions take only input arguments, the programmer is not concerned with using such complexities as indirect referencing in the function definition or applying the address-of operator in the function call. If the value returned by the function is to be stored in a variable, the reader sees an assignment statement in the code of the calling function. If a function subprogram has a meaningful name, the reader can often get a good idea of what is happening in the calling function without reading the function subprogram's code.

EXERCISES FOR SECTION 6.3

Self-Check

1. What would be the effect of the following sequence of calls to function `order`? (*Hint:* Trace the calls for `num1 = 8, num2 = 12, num3 = 10`.)

```
order(&num3, &num2);
order(&num2, &num1);
order(&num3, &num2);
```

2. Show the table of values for x, y, and z that is the output displayed by the following program. You will notice that the function `sum` does not follow the suggestion in the last Program Style segment of Section 6.3. You can improve this program in the programming exercise that follows.

```
#include <stdio.h>

void sum(int a, int b, int *cp);

int
main(void)
{
        int x, y, z;

        x = 7; y = 2;

        printf("    x    y    z\n\n");

        sum(x, y, &z);
        printf("%4d%4d%4d\n", x, y, z);

        sum(y, x, &z);
        printf("%4d%4d%4d\n", x, y, z);

        sum(z, y, &x);
        printf("%4d%4d%4d\n", x, y, z);

        sum(z, z, &x);
        printf("%4d%4d%4d\n", x, y, z);
```

```
                            sum(y, y, &y);
                            printf("%4d%4d%4d\n", x, y, z);

                            return (0);
                    }

                    void
                    sum(int a, int b, int *cp)
                    {
                            *cp = a + b;
                    }
```

Programming

1. Rewrite the sum function in Self-Check Exercise 2 as a function that takes just two input arguments. The sum computed should be returned as the function's type int result. Also, write an equivalent function main that calls your sum function.

6.4 Scope of Names

scope of a name the region in a program where a particular meaning of a name is visible

The **scope of a name** refers to the region of a program where a particular meaning of a name is visible or can be referenced. Let's consider the names in the program outline shown in Fig. 6.9. The names MAX and LIMIT are defined as constant macros and their scope begins at their definition and continues to the end of the source file. This means that all three functions can access MAX and LIMIT.

FIGURE 6.9 Outline of Program for Studying Scope of Names

```
1.   #define MAX 950
2.   #define LIMIT 200
3.
4.   void one(int anarg, double second);    /* prototype 1 */
5.
6.   int fun_two(int one, char anarg);       /* prototype 2 */
7.
8.   int
9.   main(void)
10.  {
11.          int localvar;
```

(continued)

FIGURE 6.9   (continued)

```
12.            . . .
13.  } /* end main */
14.
15.
16.  void
17.  one(int anarg, double second)        /* header 1    */
18.  {
19.          int onelocal;                /* local 1     */
20.          . . .
21.  } /* end one */
22.
23.
24.  int
25.  fun_two(int one, char anarg)          /* header 2    */
26.  {
27.          int localvar;                /* local 2     */
28.          . . .
29.  } /* end fun_two */
```

The scope of the function subprogram name `fun_two` begins with its prototype and continues to the end of the source file. This means that function `fun_two` can be called by functions `one`, `main`, and itself. The situation is different for function `one` because `one` is used as a formal parameter name in function `fun_two`. Therefore, function `one` can be called by the main function and itself but not by function `fun_two`.

All of the formal parameters and local variables in Fig. 6.9 are visible only from their declaration to the closing brace of the function in which they are declared. For example, from the line that is marked with the comment `/* header 1 */` to the line marked `/* end one */` the identifier `anarg` means an integer variable in the data area of function `one`. From the line with the comment `/* header 2 */` through the line marked `/* end fun_two */` this name refers to a character variable in the data area of `fun_two`. In the rest of the file, the name `anarg` is not visible.

Table 6.5 shows which identifiers are visible within each of the three functions.

TABLE 6.5   Scope of Names in Fig. 6.9

Name	Visible in one	Visible in fun_two	Visible in main
MAX	yes	yes	yes
LIMIT	yes	yes	yes
main	yes	yes	yes
localvar (in main)	no	no	yes
one (the function)	yes	no	yes
anarg (int)	yes	no	no
second	yes	no	no
onelocal	yes	no	no
fun_two	yes	yes	yes
one (formal parameter)	no	yes	no
anarg (char)	no	yes	no
localvar (in fun_two)	no	yes	no

6.5 Formal Output Parameters as Actual Arguments

So far, all of our actual arguments in calls to functions have been either local variables or input parameters of the calling function. However, sometimes a function needs to pass its own output parameter as an argument when it calls another function. In Fig. 6.10, which we have left incomplete, we write a function that scans a data line representing a common fraction of the form

numerator / denominator

where *numerator* is an integer and *denominator* is a positive integer. The / symbol is a separator. The function is based on function get_int (see Fig. 5.14). Its outer loop repeats until a valid fraction is scanned, and its inner loop skips any characters at the end of the data line.

Function scan_fraction has two output parameters, nump and denomp, through which it returns the numerator and denominator of the fraction scanned. Function scan_fraction needs to pass its output parameters to library function scanf, which gets the needed numerator and denominator values. In all other calls to scanf, we applied the address-of operator & to each variable to be filled. However, because nump and denomp are pointers and already store addresses, we can use them directly in the call to scanf:

```
status = scanf("%d %c%d", nump, &slash, denomp);
```

FIGURE 6.10 Function scan_fraction (incomplete)

```
1.  /*
2.   * Gets and returns a valid fraction as its result
3.   * A valid fraction is of this form: integer/positive integer
4.   * Pre : none
5.   */
6.  void
7.  scan_fraction(int *nump, int *denomp)
8.  {
9.          char slash;     /* character between numerator and denominator    */
10.         int  status;    /* status code returned by scanf indicating
11.                            number of valid values obtained                 */
12.         int error;      /* flag indicating presence of an error           */
13.         char discard;   /* unprocessed character from input line          */
14.         do {
15.             /* No errors detected yet                                      */
16.             error = 0;
17.
18.             /* Get a fraction from the user                               */
19.             printf("Enter a common fraction as two integers separated ");
20.             printf("by a slash> ");
21.             status = scanf("%d %c%d",_____, _____, _____);
22.
23.             /* Validate the fraction                                       */
24.             if (status < 3) {
25.                     error = 1;
26.                     printf("Invalid-please read directions carefully\n");
27.             } else if (slash != '/') {
28.                     error = 1;
29.                     printf("Invalid-separate numerator and denominator");
30.                     printf(" by a slash (/)\n");
31.             } else if (*denomp <= 0) {
32.                     error = 1;
33.                     printf("Invalid—denominator must be positive\n");
34.             }
35.
36.             /* Discard extra input characters                             */
37.             do {
38.                 scanf("%c", &discard);
39.             } while (discard != '\n');
40.         } while (error);
41.  }
```

FIGURE 6.11

Data Areas for
scan_fraction and
Its Caller

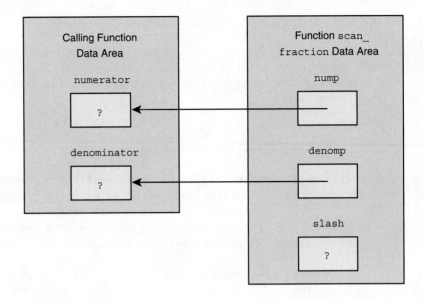

The statement

```
status = scanf("%d %c%d", nump, &slash, denomp);
```

stores the first number scanned in the variable whose address is in `nump`, the slash character (possibly preceded by blanks) in local variable `slash`, and the second number scanned in the variable whose address is in `denomp`. The `if` statement validates the fraction, setting the flag `error` to `1` (true) if the data entry was unsuccessful.

Figure 6.11 shows the data areas for `scan_fraction` and the function calling it. For the situation shown, `scanf` stores the two numbers scanned in variables `numerator` and `denominator`. The slash character is stored in local variable `slash`.

When you pass an output parameter of function a to function b, you need to carefully consider how it will be used in function b. You may find it helpful to sketch the data areas as we did in Fig. 6.11. Table 6.6 gives you guidelines for function arguments of type `int`, `double`, and `char`.

EXERCISES FOR SECTION 6.5

Self-Check

1. Box models of functions `onef` and `twof` follow. Do not try to define the complete functions; write only the portions described.

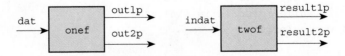

TABLE 6.6   Passing an Argument x to Function some_fun

Actual Argument Type	Use in Calling Function	Purpose in Called Function (some_fun)	Formal Parameter Type	Call to some_fun	Example
`int` `char` `double`	local variable or input parameter	input parameter	`int` `char` `double`	`some_fun(x)`	Fig. 6.5, `main`: `separate(value,` `&sn, &whl, &fr);` (1st argument)
`int` `char` `double`	local variable	output or input/ output parameter	`int *` `char *` `double *`	`some_fun(&x)`	Fig. 6.5, `main`: `separate(value,` `&sn, &whl, &fr);` (2nd–4th arguments)
`int *` `char *` `double *`	output or input/ output parameter	output or input/ output parameter	`int *` `char *` `double *`	`some_fun(x)`	Fig. 6.10 completed, `scanf(. . .,nump,` `&slash, denomp);` (2nd and 4th arguments)
`int *` `char *` `double *`	output or input/ output parameter	input parameter	`int` `char` `double`	`some_fun(*x)`	Self-Check Ex. 2 in Section 6.6, `trouble: double_` `trouble(y, *x);` (2nd argument)

Assume that these functions are concerned only with integers, and write headings for `onef` and `twof`. Begin the body of function `onef` with a declaration of an integer local variable `tmp`. Show a call from `onef` to `twof` in which the input argument is `dat`, and `tmp` and `out2p` are the output arguments. Function `onef` intends for `twof` to store one integer result in `tmp` and one in the variable pointed to by `out2p`.

2. a. Classify each formal parameter of `double_trouble` and `trouble` as input, output, or input/output.

    b. What values of x and y are displayed by this program? (*Hint:* Sketch the data areas of `main`, `trouble`, and `double_trouble` as the program executes.)

```
void double_trouble(int *p, int y);
void trouble(int *x, int *y);

int
main(void)

{
    int x, y;
```

```
                        trouble(&x, &y);
                        printf("x = %d, y = %d\n", x, y);
                        return (0);
            }

            void
            double_trouble(int *p, int y)
            {
                        int x;
                        x = 10;
                        *p = 2 * x - y;
            }

            void
            trouble(int *x, int *y)
            {
                        double_trouble(x, 7);
                        double_trouble(y, *x);
            }
```

    c. What naming convention introduced in Section 6.2 is violated in the formal parameter list of `trouble`?

6.6 Problem Solving Illustrated

In this section, we examine two programming problems that illustrate many of the concepts discussed in this chapter. The *top-down design* process will be demonstrated in solving each programming problem. Each program will be implemented in a stepwise manner, starting with a list of major algorithm steps and continuing to add detail through refinement until the program and its function subprogram can be written. The first problem uses files and file pointers. The second problem implements a set of functions for manipulating fractions.

CASE STUDY Collecting Area for Solar-Heated House

PROBLEM

An architect needs a program that can estimate the appropriate size for the collecting area of a solar-heated house. Determining collecting area size requires consideration of several factors, including the average number of heating degree days for the coldest month of a year (the product of the average difference between inside and outside temperatures and the number of days in the month), the heating requirement per square foot of floor space, the floor space, and the efficiency of the collection method. The program will have access to two data files. File hdd.txt contains numbers representing the average heating degree days in the construction location for each of 12 months. File solar.txt contains the average solar insolation (rate in BTU/day at which solar radiation falls on one square foot of a given location) for each month. The first entry in each file represents data for January, the second, data for February, and so on.

ANALYSIS

The formula for approximating the desired collecting area (A) is

$$A = \frac{heat\ loss}{energy\ resource}$$

In turn, *heat loss* is computed as the product of the heating requirement, the floor space, and the heating degree days. We compute the necessary *energy resource* by multiplying the efficiency of the collection method by the average solar insolation per day and the number of days.

In all of our previous programs, data for program inputs have come from the same source—either the keyboard or a file. In this program, we will use three input sources: the two data files and the keyboard. We can now identify the problem's data requirements and develop an algorithm.

DATA REQUIREMENTS

Problem Inputs

Average heating degree days file
Average solar insolation file

```
heat_deg_days /* average heating degree days for coldest month   */
coldest_mon   /* coldest month (number 1 .. 12)                   */
solar_insol   /* average daily solar insolation (BTU/ft^2)for
                 coldest month                                    */
heating_req   /* BTU/degree day ft^2 for planned type construction*/
efficiency    /* % of solar insolation converted to usable heat   */
floor_space   /* square feet */
```

Program Variables

```
energy_resrc  /* usable solar energy available in coldest month
                 (BTUs obtained from 1 ft^2 of collecting area)   */
```

Problem Outputs

```
heat_loss     /* BTUs of heat lost by structure in coldest month  */
collect_area  /* approximate size (ft^2) of collecting area needed*/
```

DESIGN

Initial Algorithm

1. Determine the coldest month and the average heating degree days for this month.
2. Find the average daily solar insolation per ft² for the coldest month.
3. Get from the user the other problem inputs: `heating_req`, `efficiency`, and `floor_space`.
4. Estimate the collecting area needed.
5. Display results.

As shown in the structure chart (Fig. 6.12), we will design step 2 as a separate function. Function `nth_item` will find the value in file solar.txt that corresponds to the coldest month. Steps 3 and 5 are quite straightforward, so only steps 1 and 4 call for refinement here.

FIGURE 6.12

Structure Chart for Computing Solar Collecting Area Size

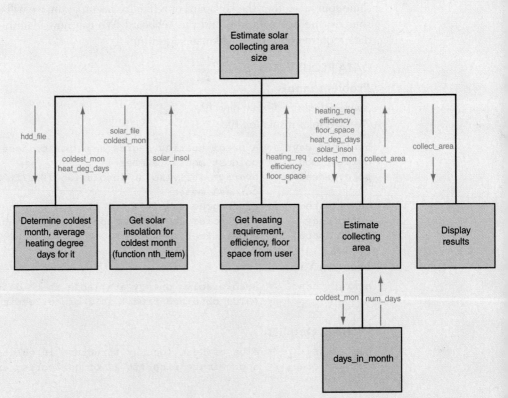

STEP 1 REFINEMENT

We will introduce three new variables to use in our refinement—a counter, ct, to keep track of our position in the heating degree days file, an integer variable to record file status, and an integer variable next_hdd to hold each heating degree days value in turn.

Additional Program Variables

```
ct                 /* position in file */
status             /* input status */
next_hdd           /* one heating degree days value */
```

1.1 Scan first value from heating degree days file into heat_deg_days, and initialize coldest_mon to 1.
1.2 Initialize ct to 2.
1.3 Scan a value from the file into next_hdd, saving status.
1.4 As long as no faulty data or not at end of file, repeat
    1.5 if next_hdd is greater than heat_deg_days
        1.6 Copy next_hdd into heat_deg_days.
        1.7 Copy ct into coldest_mon.
    1.8 Increment ct.
    1.9 Scan a value from the file into next_hdd, saving status.

STEP 4 REFINEMENT

4.1 Calculate heat_loss as the product of heating_req, floor_space, and heat_deg_days.
4.2 Calculate energy_resrc as the product of efficiency (converted to hundredths), solar_insol, and the number of days in the coldest month.
4.3 Calculate collect_area as heat_loss divided by energy_resrc. Round result to nearest whole square foot.

We will develop a separate function for finding the number of days in a month, a value needed in step 4.2 (see Fig. 6.12).

Functions

Functions nth_item and days_in_month are quite simple, so we will show only their implementation. Figure 6.13 is an implementation of the entire program for approximating the necessary size of a solar collecting area for solar heating a certain structure in a given geographic area.

Input file hdd.txt

```
995 900 750 400 180 20 10 10 60 290 610 1051
```

Input file solar.txt

```
500 750 1100 1490 1900 2100 2050 1550 1200 900 500 500
```

FIGURE 6.13 Program to Approximate Solar Collecting Area Size

```
1.   /*
2.    * Estimate necessary solar collecting area size for a particular type of
3.    * construction in a given location.
4.    */
5.   #include <stdio.h>
6.
7.   int days_in_month(int);
8.   int nth_item(FILE *, int);
9.
10.  int main(void)
11.  {
12.     int heat_deg_days, /* average for coldest month */
13.         solar_insol,   /* average daily solar radiation per
14.                            ft^2 for coldest month */
15.         coldest_mon,   /* coldest month: number in range 1..12 */
16.         heating_req,   /* BTU / degree day ft^2 requirement for
17.                            given type of construction     */
18.         efficiency,    /* % of solar insolation converted to
19.                            usable heat */
20.         collect_area,  /* ft^2 needed to provide heat for
21.                            coldest month */
22.         ct,            /* position in file */
23.         status,        /* file status variable */
24.         next_hdd;      /* one heating degree days value */
25.     double floor_space,    /* ft^2 */
26.            heat_loss,   /* BTUs lost in coldest month */
27.            energy_resrc; /* BTUs heat obtained from 1 ft^2
28.                            collecting area in coldest month */
29.     FILE *hdd_file;    /* average heating degree days for each
30.                            of 12 months */
31.     FILE *solar_file;  /* average solar insolation for each of
32.                            12 months */
33.
34.     /* Get average heating degree days for coldest month from file */
35.     hdd_file = fopen("hdd.txt", "r");
36.     fscanf(hdd_file, "%d", &heat_deg_days);
37.     coldest_mon = 1;
38.     ct = 2;
39.     status = fscanf(hdd_file, "%d", &next_hdd);
40.     while (status == 1) {
```

(continued)

FIGURE 6.13 (continued)

```
41.          if (next_hdd > heat_deg_days) {
42.              heat_deg_days = next_hdd;
43.              coldest_mon = ct;
44.          }
45.
46.          ++ct;
47.          status = fscanf(hdd_file, "%d", &next_hdd);
48.      }
49.      fclose(hdd_file);
50.
51.      /* Get corresponding average daily solar insolation from other file */
52.      solar_file = fopen("solar.txt", "r");
53.      solar_insol = nth_item(solar_file, coldest_mon);
54.      fclose(solar_file);
55.
56.      /* Get from user specifics of this house */
57.      printf("What is the approximate heating requirement (BTU / ");
58.      printf("degree day ft^2)\nof this type of construction?\n=> ");
59.      scanf("%d", &heating_req);
60.      printf("What percent of solar insolation will be converted ");
61.      printf("to usable heat?\n=> ");
62.      scanf("%d", &efficiency);
63.      printf("What is the floor space (ft^2)?\n=> ");
64.      scanf("%lf", &floor_space);
65.
66.      /* Project collecting area needed */
67.      heat_loss = heating_req * floor_space * heat_deg_days;
68.      energy_resrc = efficiency * 0.01 * solar_insol *
69.          days_in_month(coldest_mon);
70.      collect_area = (int)(heat_loss / energy_resrc + 0.5);
71.
72.      /* Display results */
73.      printf("To replace heat loss of %.0f BTU in the ", heat_loss);
74.      printf("coldest month (month %d)\nwith available ", coldest_mon);
75.      printf("solar insolation of %d BTU / ft^2 / day,", solar_insol);
76.      printf(" and an\nefficiency of %d percent,", efficiency);
77.      printf(" use a solar collecting area of %d", collect_area);
78.      printf(" ft^2.\n");
79.
80.      return (0);
81. }
```

(continued)

FIGURE 6.13 (continued)

```
82.
83.  /*
84.   * Given a month number (1 = January, 2 = February, …,
85.   * 12 = December ), return the number of days in the month
86.   * (nonleap year).
87.   * Pre: 1 <= monthNumber <= 12
88.   */
89.  int days_in_month( int month_number )
90.  {
91.
92.      int ans;
93.
94.      switch (month_number) {
95.      case 2: ans = 28; /* February */
96.            break;
97.
98.      case 4: /* April */
99.      case 6: /* June */
100.     case 9: /* September */
101.     case 11: ans = 30; /* November */
102.            break;
103.
104.     default: ans = 31;
105.     }
106.
107.     return ans;
108. }
109.
110. /*
111.  * Finds and returns the nth integer in a file.
112.  * Pre: data_file accesses a file of at least n integers (n >= 1).
113.  */
114. int nth_item(FILE *data_file, int n)
115. {
116.     int i, item;
117.
118.     for (i = 1; i <= n; ++i)
119.         fscanf(data_file, "%d", &item);
120.
```

(continued)

FIGURE 6.13   (continued)

```
121.    return item;
122.  }
```

Sample Run
What is the approximate heating requirement (BTU / degree day ft^2)
of this type of construction?
=> 9
What percent of solar insolation will be converted to usable heat?
=> 60
What is the floor space (ft^2)?
=> 1200
To replace heat loss of 11350800 BTU in the coldest month (month 12)
with available solar insolation of 500 BTU / ft^2 / day, and an
efficiency of 60 percent, use a solar collecting area of 1221 ft^2.

Functions for Common Fractions

In our next case study, we manipulate numeric data of a type not provided as one
of C's base types. In order to do this, we must write our own functions to perform
operations on common fractions that we take for granted when using types int
and double.

CASE STUDY   Arithmetic with Common Fractions

PROBLEM

You are working problems in which you must display your results as integer ratios;
therefore, you need to be able to perform computations with common fractions and get
results that are common fractions in reduced form. You want to write a program that
will allow you to add, subtract, multiply, and divide several pairs of common fractions.

ANALYSIS

Because the problem specifies that results are to be in reduced form, we will need
to include a fraction-reducing function in addition to the computational functions. If
we break the problem into small enough chunks, there should be an opportunity to
reuse code by calling the same function multiple times. The in-depth analysis of the
problem is actually distributed through the development of these functions.

DATA REQUIREMENTS

Problem Inputs

```
int n1, d1    /* numerator, denominator of first fraction    */
int n2, d2    /* numerator, denominator of second fraction   */
char op       /* arithmetic operator + - * or /              */
char again    /* y or n depending on user's desire to continue */
```

Problem Outputs

```
int n_ans    /* numerator of answer     */
int d_ans    /* denominator of answer   */
```

DESIGN

As we develop an algorithm through stepwise refinement, we will look for instances in which a definition of a new function would simplify the design.

INITIAL ALGORITHM

1. Repeat as long as user wants to continue.
   2. Get a fraction problem.
   3. Compute the result.
   4. Display problem and result.
   5. Check if user wants to continue.

Step 2 Refinement

2.1 Get first fraction.
2.2 Get operator.
2.3 Get second fraction.

Step 3 Refinement

3.1 Select a task based on operator:
'+': 3.1.1 Add the fractions.
'−': 3.1.2 Add the first fraction and the negation of the second.
'*': 3.1.3 Multiply the fractions.
'/': 3.1.4 Multiply the first fraction and the reciprocal of the second.
3.2 Put the result fraction in reduced form.

Step 3.2 Refinement

3.2.1 Find the greatest common divisor (gcd) of the numerator and denominator.
3.2.2 Divide the numerator and denominator by the gcd.

The structure chart in Fig. 6.14 shows the data flow among the steps we have identified.

FIGURE 6.14

Structure Chart for
Common Fraction
Problem

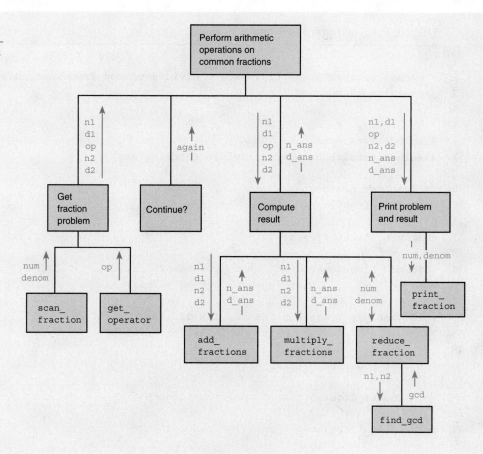

IMPLEMENTATION

stub a skeleton
function that consists
of a header and
statements that display
trace messages and
assign values to output
parameters; enables
testing of the flow
of control among
functions before this
function is completed

For steps 2.1, and 2.3, we will use function `scan_fraction` from Fig. 6.10. We
will write new function subprograms for `get_operator` (step 2.2), `add_frac-
tions` (steps 3.1.1 and 3.1.2), `multiply_fractions` (steps 3.1.3 and 3.1.4),
`reduce_fraction` (step 3.2), `find_gcd` (step 3.2.1), and `print_fraction` (part
of step 4). As a result, coding function `main` is quite straightforward. Figure 6.15
shows most of the program; however, the functions `multiply_fractions` and
`find_gcd` have been left as exercises. In their places, we have inserted **stubs**,
skeleton functions that have complete comments and headers but merely
assign values to their output parameters to allow testing of the partial system.
Debugging and testing the system will be explained in Section 6.7.

FIGURE 6.15 Program to Perform Arithmetic Operations on Common Fractions

```
1.   /*
2.    * Adds, subtracts, multiplies and divides common fractions, displaying
3.    * results in reduced form.
4.    */
5.
6.   #include <stdio.h>
7.   #include <stdlib.h>    /* provides function abs */
8.
9.   /* Function prototypes */
10.  void scan_fraction(int *nump, int *denomp);
11.
12.  char get_operator(void);
13.
14.  void add_fractions(int n1, int d1, int n2, int d2,
15.                     int *n_ansp, int *d_ansp);
16.
17.  void multiply_fractions(int n1, int d1, int n2, int d2,
18.                          int *n_ansp, int *d_ansp);
19.
20.  int find_gcd (int n1, int n2);
21.
22.  void reduce_fraction(int *nump, int *denomp);
23.
24.  void print_fraction(int num, int denom);
25.
26.  int
27.  main(void)
28.  {
29.         int n1, d1;    /* numerator, denominator of first fraction       */
30.         int n2, d2;    /* numerator, denominator of second fraction      */
31.         char op;       /* arithmetic operator + - * or /                 */
32.         char again;    /* y or n depending on user's desire to continue  */
33.         int n_ans, d_ans; /* numerator, denominator of answer            */
34.
35.         /* While the user wants to continue, gets and solves arithmetic
36.            problems with common fractions                                */
37.         do {
38.            /* Gets a fraction problem                                     */
39.            scan_fraction(&n1, &d1);
40.            op = get_operator();
```

(continued)

FIGURE 6.15 (continued)

```
40.              scan_fraction(&n2, &d2);
41.
42.          /* Computes the result */
43.          switch (op) {
44.          case '+':
45.              add_fractions(n1, d1, n2, d2, &n_ans, &d_ans);
46.              break;
47.
48.          case '-':
49.              add_fractions(n1, d1, -n2, d2, &n_ans, &d_ans);
50.              break;
51.
52.          case '*':
53.              multiply_fractions(n1, d1, n2, d2, &n_ans, &d_ans);
54.              break;
55.
56.          case '/':
57.              multiply_fractions(n1, d1, d2, n2, &n_ans, &d_ans);
58.          }
59.          reduce_fraction(&n_ans, &d_ans);
60.
61.          /* Displays problem and result                              */
62.          printf("\n");
63.          print_fraction(n1, d1);
64.          printf(" %c ", op);
65.          print_fraction(n2, d2);
66.          printf(" = ");
67.          print_fraction(n_ans, d_ans);
68.
69.          /* Asks user about doing another problem                    */
70.          printf("\nDo another problem? (y/n)> ");
71.          scanf(" %c", &again);
72.      } while (again == 'y' || again == 'Y');
73.      return (0);
74. }
75. /* Insert function scan_fraction from Fig. 6.10 here. */
76.
77. /*
78.  * Gets and returns a valid arithmetic operator. Skips over newline
79.  * characters and permits reentry of operator in case of error.
```

(continued)

FIGURE 6.15 (continued)

```
80.  */
81.  char
82.  get_operator(void)
83.  {
84.      char op;
85.
86.      printf("Enter an arithmetic operator (+,-,*, or /)\n> ");
87.      for (scanf("%c", &op);
88.           op != '+' && op != '-' &&
89.           op != '*' && op != '/';
90.           scanf("%c", &op)) {
91.         if (op != '\n')
92.            printf("%c invalid, reenter operator (+,-, *,/)\n> ", op);
93.      }
94.      return (op);
95.  }
96.
97.   /*
98.    * Adds fractions represented by pairs of integers.
99.    * Pre:  n1, d1, n2, d2 are defined;
100.  *       n_ansp and d_ansp are addresses of type int variables.
101.  * Post: sum of n1/d1 and n2/d2 is stored in variables pointed
102.  *       to by n_ansp and d_ansp. Result is not reduced.
103.  */
104. void
105. add_fractions(int      n1, int      d1, /* input - first fraction */
106.               int      n2, int      d2, /* input - second fraction */
107.               int *n_ansp, int *d_ansp) /* output - sum of 2 fractions*/
108. {
109.      int denom,       /* common denominator used for sum (may not be least)  */
110.          numer,       /* numerator of sum                                     */
111.          sign_factor; /* -1 for a negative, 1 otherwise                       */
112.
113.      /* Finds a common denominator                                           */
114.      denom = d1 * d2;
115.
116.      /* Computes numerator                                                   */
117.      numer = n1 * d2 + n2 * d1;
118.
119.      /* Adjusts sign (at most, numerator should be negative)                 */
```

(continued)

FIGURE 6.15   (continued)

```
120.        if (numer * denom >= 0)
121.              sign_factor = 1;
122.        else
123.              sign_factor = -1;
124.
125.        numer = sign_factor * abs(numer);
126.        denom = abs(denom);
127.
128.        /* Returns result                                                */
129.        *n_ansp = numer;
130.        *d_ansp = denom;
131. }
132.
133. /*
134. ***** STUB *****
135. * Multiplies fractions represented by pairs of integers.
136. * Pre:  n1, d1, n2, d2 are defined;
137. *       n_ansp and d_ansp are addresses of type int variables.
138. * Post: product of n1/d1 and n2/d2 is stored in variables pointed
139. *       to by n_ansp and d_ansp. Result is not reduced.
140. */
141. void
142. multiply_fractions(int     n1, int   d1, /* input - first fraction      */
143.                    int     n2, int   d2, /* input - second fraction     */
144.                    int *n_ansp,           /* output -                    */
145.                    int *d_ansp)           /* product of 2 fractions      */
146. {
147.       /* Displays trace message                                         */
148.       printf("\nEntering multiply_fractions with\n");
149.       printf("n1 = %d, d1 = %d, n2 = %d, d2 = %d\n", n1, d1, n2, d2);
150.       /* Defines output arguments                                       */
151.       *n_ansp = 1;
152.       *d_ansp = 1;
153. }
154.
155. /*
156. ***** STUB *****
157. * Finds greatest common divisor of two integers
158. */
159. int
```

(continued)

FIGURE 6.15   (continued)

```
160. find_gcd (int n1, int n2) /* input - two integers                                */
161. {
162.      int gcd;
163.
164.      /* Displays trace message                                                    */
165.      printf("\nEntering find_gcd with n1 = %d, n2 = %d\n", n1, n2);
166.
167.      /* Asks user for gcd                                                          */
168.      printf("gcd of %d and %d?> ", n1, n2);
169.      scanf("%d", &gcd);
170.
171.      /* Displays exit trace message                                               */
172.      printf("find_gcd returning %d\n", gcd);
173.      return (gcd);
174. }
175.
176. /*
177.  * Reduces a fraction by dividing its numerator and denominator by their
178.  * greatest common divisor.
179.  */
180. void
181. reduce_fraction(int *nump,    /* input/output -                                  */
182.                 int *denomp) /* numerator and denominator of fraction           */
183. {
184.      int gcd;      /* greatest common divisor of numerator & denominator         */
185.
186.      gcd = find_gcd(*nump, *denomp);
187.      *nump = *nump / gcd;
188.      *denomp = *denomp / gcd;
189. }
190.
191. /*
192.  * Displays pair of integers as a fraction.
193.  */
194. void
195. print_fraction(int num, int denom) /* input - numerator & denominator            */
196. {
197.      printf("%d/%d", num, denom);
198. }
```

TESTING

We have chosen to leave portions of our fraction system for you to write, but we would still like to test the functions that are complete. We have inserted a stub for each function not yet completed. Each stub prints an identification message and assigns values to its output parameters. For testing purposes, we made the `find_gcd` stub interactive so the program tester can enter a correct greatest common divisor and see if this leads to correct results.

Figure 6.16 shows a run of the program in its present form. Notice that when we choose operator + and enter a correct greatest common divisor interactively, the result is correct. However, when we choose operator *, although the program continues execution by calling the stubs, the result is incorrect because the stub for function `multiply_fractions` always returns a numerator and denominator value of 1.

FIGURE 6.16 Sample Run of a Partially Complete Program Containing Stubs

```
Enter a common fraction as two integers separated by a slash> 3/-4
Invalid—denominator must be positive
Enter a common fraction as two integers separated by a slash> 3/4
Enter an arithmetic operator (+,-,*, or /)
> +
Enter a common fraction as two integers separated by a slash> 5/8
Entering find_gcd with n1 = 44, n2 = 32
gcd of 44 and 32?> 4
find_gcd returning 4

3/4 + 5/8 = 11/8
Do another problem? (y/n)> y
Enter a common fraction as two integers separated by a slash> 1/2
Enter an arithmetic operator (+,-,*, or /)
> 5
5 invalid, reenter operator (+,-,*,/)
> *
Enter a common fraction as two integers separated by a slash> 5/7
Entering multiply_fractions with
n1 = 1, d1 = 2, n2 = 5, d2 = 7
Entering find_gcd with n1 = 1, n2 = 1
gcd of 1 and 1?> 1
find_gcd returning 1

1/2 * 5/7 = 1/1
Do another problem? (y/n)> n
```

Self-Check

1. Why are pointer types used for the parameters of `scan_fraction`?
2. Why was it not necessary to include a default case in the `switch` statement that calls `add_fractions` and `multiply_fractions`?

Programming

1. Implement the following algorithm as the `find_gcd` function needed in the common fraction system of Fig. 6.15. Your function will find the greatest common divisor (that is, the product of all common factors) of integers `n1` and `n2`.

    1. Put the absolute value of `n1` in `q` and of `n2` in `p`.
    2. Store the remainder of `q` divided by `p` in `r`.
    3. while `r` is not zero
        4. Copy `p` into `q` and `r` into `p`.
        5. Store the remainder of `q` divided by `p` in `r`.
    6. `p` is the `gcd`.

2. Write the function `multiply_fractions`. If your result has a zero denominator, display an error message and change the denominator to `1`.

6.7　Debugging and Testing a Program System

We have seen that testing is the process of exercising a program or part of a program under controlled conditions and verifying that the results are as expected. The purpose of testing is to detect program defects after all syntax errors have been removed and the program compiles successfully. The more thorough the testing, the greater the likelihood that the defects will be found. However, no amount of testing can guarantee the absence of defects in sufficiently complex programs. The number of test cases required to test all possible inputs and states in which each function may execute can quickly become prohibitively large. That is one reason why commercial software products have successive versions or patches that the user must install. Version n typically corrects the errors that were discovered in version $n - 1$.

Testing is generally done at the following levels:

- **Unit testing** refers to testing the smallest testable piece of the software, a single function. To perform a unit test, we write a short driver function to call the function tested. The driver function begins by giving values to all input and input/output parameters. Next comes the call to the function being tested. After calling the function, the driver should display the function results. Fig. 6.17 shows a driver to use in a unit test of function `scan_fraction`.

FIGURE 6.17   Driver for Function scan_fraction

```
1.  /* Driver for scan_fraction */
2.
3.  int
4.  main(void)
5.  {
6.        int num, denom;
7.        printf("To quit, enter a fraction with a zero numerator\n");
8.        scan_fraction(&num, &denom);
9.        while (num != 0) {
10.             printf("Fraction is %d/%d\n", num, denom);
11.             scan_fraction(&num, &denom);
12.       }
13.
14.       return (0);
15. }
```

- **Integration testing** involves testing the interactions among functions. In a large system, testing functions that are dependent on other functions whose unit tests may not yet be complete requires an ability to have a temporary function take the place of the function still being tested. The replacement for a function that has not yet been implemented or unit tested is called a stub. A stub such as function `multiply_fractions` shown in Fig. 6.18 has the same header as the function it replaces, but its body displays only a message indicating that the stub was called and provides temporary values for any output arguments or data returned.
- **System testing** is the testing of the whole program in the context in which it will be used. A program is generally part of a collection of other programs and hardware, called a system. Sometimes a program will work correctly until some other software is loaded onto the system, and then it will fail for no apparent reason.
- **Acceptance testing** is system testing designed to show that the program meets its functional requirements. It typically involves use of the system in the real environment or in a close approximation to the real environment.

Testing Tips for Program Systems

A list of suggestions for removing defects from a program system follows.

1. Carefully document each function parameter and local variable using comments as you write the code. Also, describe the function's purpose using comments.
2. Create a trace of execution by displaying the function name as you enter it.

FIGURE 6.18   Stub for Function multiply_fractions

```
1.    /*
2.     ***** STUB *****
3.     * Multiplies fractions represented by pairs of integers.
4.     * Pre: n1, d1, n2, d2 are defined;
5.     *      n_ansp and d_ansp are addresses of type int variables.
6.     * Post: product of n1/d1 and n2/d2 is stored in variables pointed
7.     *       to by n_ansp and d_ansp. Result is not reduced.
8.     */
9.    void
10.   multiply_fractions(int     n1, int d1, /* input - first fraction      */
11.                      int     n2, int d2, /* input - second fraction     */
12.                      int *n_ansp,        /* output -                     */
13.                      int *d_ansp)        /* product of 2 fractions       */
14.   {
15.         /* Displays trace message                                       */
16.         printf("\nEntering multiply_fractions with\n");
17.         printf("n1 = %d, d1 = %d, n2 = %d, d2 = %d\n", n1, d1, n2, d2);
18.
19.         /* Defines output arguments                                     */
20.         *n_ansp = 1;
21.         *d_ansp = 1;
22.   }
```

3. Trace or display the values of all input and input/output parameters upon entry to a function. Check that these values make sense.

4. Trace or display the values of all function outputs after returning from a function. Verify that these values are correct by hand computation. Make sure you declare all input/output and output parameters as pointer types.

5. Make sure that a function stub assigns a value to the variable pointed to by each output parameter and returns a value if the function type is not void.

If you are using a debugger, you may be able to specify whether you want to execute a function as if it were a single statement or whether you want to step through the individual statements of a function. Initially, execute the function as a single statement and trace the values of all input and output parameters (tips 3 and 4 above). If the function results are incorrect, step through its individual statements.

If you are not using a debugger, you should plan for debugging as you write each function rather than waiting until after you finish the whole program. Include the display statements (mentioned in debugging tips 2 through 4) in the original C code for the function. When you are satisfied that the function works correctly, remove the debugging statements. One simple approach is to change them to comments by enclosing them within the symbols /*, */; if you have a problem later, you can remove these symbols, thereby changing the comments back to executable statements.

6.8   Common Programming Errors

Many opportunities for error arise when you use functions with parameter lists, so be extremely careful. Proper use of parameters is difficult for new programmers to master, but it is an essential skill. One obvious pitfall is not ensuring that the actual argument list has the same number of items as the formal parameter list. Each actual input argument must be of a type that can be assigned to its corresponding formal parameter. An actual output argument must be of the same pointer data type as the corresponding formal parameter.

It is easy to introduce errors in a function that produces multiple results. If an output parameter is not of a pointer type or if the calling function neglects to send a correct variable address, the function results will be incorrect.

The C scope rules determine where a name is visible and can, therefore, be referenced. If an identifier is referenced outside its scope, an `undeclared symbol` syntax error will result.

Chapter Review

1. A program can declare pointers to variables of a specified type. For example, `int *mp` declares `mp` as a pointer to an integer. The statement `mp = &p;` stores the address of `p` (type `int`) in `mp`. The unary indirection operator `*` enables indirect access through a pointer. The statement `n1 = *mp;` stores the value of `p` in `n1` where `*mp` means follow the pointer in `mp`. The statement `*mp = n2;` stores the value of `n2` (type `int`) in the variable `p`.
2. The declaration `FILE *inp;` declares `inp` as a pointer to a type `FILE` variable. The function `fopen` is used to prepare a file for access by a C program. The function `fscanf` (`fprintf`) is used to read (write) data from (to) a file. The function `fclose` is used to close or disconnect a file.
3. Parameters enable a programmer to pass data to functions and to return multiple results from functions. The parameter list provides a highly visible communication path between a function and its calling program. Using parameters enables a function to process different data each time it executes, thereby making it easier to reuse the function in other programs.
4. Parameters may be used for input to a function, for output or sending back results, and for both input and output. An input parameter is used only for passing data into a function. The parameter's declared type is the same as the

type of the data. Output and input/output parameters must be able to access variables in the calling function's data area so they are declared as pointers to the result data types. The actual argument corresponding to an input parameter may be an expression or a constant; the actual argument corresponding to an output or input/output parameter must be the address of a variable.

5. A function can use parameters declared as pointers to return values. Use &x in a function call to pass the address of x to an output parameter or to an input/output parameter. In the function called, use *xp = . . . to assign a value to the actual argument associated with formal parameter xp.

6. The scope of an identifier dictates where it can be referenced. A parameter or local variable can be referenced anywhere in the function that declares it. A function name is visible from its declaration (the function prototype) to the end of the source file except within functions that have local variables of the same name. The same rule applies for a constant macro: It is visible from its #define directive.

NEW C CONSTRUCTS

Construct	Effect
File Open	
`inp = fopen("num.txt", "r");` `outp = fopen("out.txt", "w");`	Opens num.txt as an input file, storing file pointer in inp. Opens out.txt as an output file, storing file pointer in outp.
Calls to Input/Output Functions	
`fscanf(inp, "%d%d", &mid, &low);`	Copies input data from file num.txt into the type int variables mid and low.
`fprintf(outp, "%5d %5d %5d\n",` `        high, mid, low);`	Stores in the file out.txt a line containing the values of high, mid, and low.
File Close	
`fclose(inp);` `fclose(outp);`	Closes input file num.txt and newly created file out.txt.
Function That Returns Multiple Results	

`void`
`make_change(double change,        /* input */`
`           double token_val,     /* input */`
`           int    *num_tokenp,   /* output*/`
`           double *leftp)        /* output*/`
`{`
`    *num_tokenp = floor(change /`
`                        token_val);`
`    *leftp = change - *num_tokenp *`
`                        token_val;`
`}`
	Determines how many of a certain bill or coin (token_val) should be included in change amount. This number is sent back through the output parameter num_tokenp. The amount of change remaining to be made is sent back through the output parameter leftp. The following call assigns a 3 to num_twenties and 11.50 to remaining_change.
	`int    num_twenties;`
	`double remaining_change;`
	`    . . .`
	`make_change(71.50, 20.00,`
	`            &num_twenties,`
	`            &remaining_change);`

(continued)

NEW C CONSTRUCTS (continued)

Construct	Effect

Function with Input/Output Parameters
`void`
`correct_fraction(int *nump,    /* input/ */`
`              int *denomp)  /* output */`
`{`
`     if ((*nump * *denomp) > 0)`
`         *nump = abs(*nump);`
`     else`
`         *nump = -abs(*nump);`
`     *denomp = abs(*denomp);`
`}`
	The following call corrects the form of a common fraction so the denominator is always positive (e.g., −5/3 rather than 5/−3).
	
	`int num, denom;`
	
	`num = 5;`
	`denom = -3;`
	`correct_fraction(&num, &denom);`

Quick-Check Exercises

1. The items passed in a function call are the _____ _____. The corresponding _____ _____ appear in the function prototype and heading.
2. Constants and expressions can be actual arguments corresponding to formal parameters that are _____ parameters.
3. When a program has no further use for its input and output files, it closes them by calling _____.
4. Which level of testing is used to test the smallest piece of software?
5. Which of the following is used to test program flow in a partially complete system: A driver or a stub?
6. The part of a program where an identifier can be referenced is called the _____ of the identifier.
7. What are the values of main function variables a and b at the point marked /* values here */ in the following program?

```
/* experimental */
void trail(float a);
int main(void)

{
        float a, b;

        a = 1.8; b = 2.1;

        trail(a);

        trail(b);    /* values here */

        ....

}
```

```
void trail(float a)

{

        float b;

        b = a * 1.1;

        a += 2.0;

}
```

8. Let's make some changes in our experimental program. What are main's a and b at /* values here */ in the following version?

```
/* experimental */
void trail(float *a);
int main(void)

{

        float a, b;

        a = 1.8; b = 2.1;

        trail(&a);

        trail(&b);  /* values here */

        .....

}
void trail(float *a)

{

        float b;

        b = *a * 1.1;

        *a = *a + 2.0;

}
```

Answers to Quick-Check Exercises

1. actual arguments; formal parameters
2. input
3. fclose
4. unit testing
5. stub
6. scope
7. a = 2.1, b = 1.8
8. a = 3.8, b = 4.1

Review Questions

1. Write a function called `letter_grade` that has a type `int` input parameter called `points` and returns through an output parameter `gradep` the appropriate letter grade using a straight scale (90–100 is an A, 80–89 is a B, and so on). Return through a second output parameter (`just_missedp`) an indication of whether the student just missed the next higher grade (true for 89, 79, and so on).
2. Why would you choose to write a function that computes a single numeric or character value as a nonvoid function that returns a result through a `return` statement rather than to write a `void` function with an output parameter?
3. Explain the allocation of memory cells when a function is called. What is stored in the function data area for an input parameter? Answer the same question for an output parameter.
4. Which of the functions in the following program outline *can* call the function `grumpy`? All function prototypes and declarations are shown; only executable statements are omitted.

```
int grumpy(int dopey);

char silly(double grumpy);

double happy(int goofy, char greedy);

int
main(void)
{
        double p, q, r;
        . . .
}

int
grumpy(int dopey)
{
        double silly;
        . . .
}

char
silly(double grumpy)
{
        double happy;
        . . .
}
```

```
double
happy(int goofy, char greedy)
{
        char grumpy;
        . . .
}
```

5. Sketch the data areas of functions main and trail as they appear immediately before the return from the first call to trail in Quick-Check
Exercise 8.
6. Present arguments against these statements:
    a. Using parameters enables a function to process different data each time
        it executes, thereby making it difficult to reuse the function in other
        programs.
    b. Parameters may be used for input to a function or to obtain an output
        from a function, but not for both.

Programming Projects

1. Write a program that counts the number of odd digits and even digits in an
integer. The user should enter the desired integer and the program counts
the number of odd digits and even digits in that integer. Write a function that
determines the number of odd digits and even digits and displays the same to
the user.

2. A hospital supply company wants to market a program to assist with the calculation of intravenous rates. Design and implement a program that interacts
with the user as follows:

```
INTRAVENOUS RATE ASSISTANT

Enter the number of the problem you wish to solve.
    GIVEN A MEDICAL ORDER IN                        CALCULATE RATE IN
(1) ml/hr & tubing drop factor                      drops / min
(2) 1 L for n hr                                     ml / hr
(3) mg/kg/hr & concentration in mg/ml               ml / hr
(4) units/hr & concentration in units/ml            ml / hr
(5) QUIT

Problem> 1
Enter rate in ml/hr=> 150
Enter tubing's drop factor(drops/ml)=> 15
The drop rate per minute is 38.
```

```
Enter the number of the problem you wish to solve.
     GIVEN A MEDICAL ORDER IN              CALCULATE RATE IN
(1)  ml/hr & tubing drop factor           drops / min
(2)  1 L for n hr                         ml / hr
(3)  mg/kg/hr & concentration in mg/ml    ml / hr
(4)  units/hr & concentration in units/ml ml / hr
(5)  QUIT


Problem=> 2
Enter number of hours=> 8
The rate in milliliters per hour is 125.


Enter the number of the problem you wish to solve.
     GIVEN A MEDICAL ORDER IN              CALCULATE RATE IN
(1)  ml/hr & tubing drop factor           drops / min
(2)  1 L for n hr                         ml / hr
(3)  mg/kg/hr & concentration in mg/ml    ml / hr
(4)  units/hr & concentration in units/ml ml / hr
(5)  QUIT


Problem=> 3
Enter rate in mg/kg/hr=> 0.6
Enter patient weight in kg=> 70
Enter concentration in mg/ml=> 1
The rate in milliliters per hour is 42.


Enter the number of the problem you wish to solve.
     GIVEN A MEDICAL ORDER IN              CALCULATE RATE IN
(1)  ml/hr & tubing drop factor           drops / min
(2)  1 L for n hr                         ml / hr
(3)  mg/kg/hr & concentration in mg/ml    ml / hr
(4)  units/hr & concentration in units/ml ml / hr
(5)  QUIT


Problem=> 4
Enter rate in units/hr=> 1000
Enter concentration in units/ml=> 25
The rate in milliliters per hour is 40.


Enter the number of the problem you wish to solve.
     GIVEN A MEDICAL ORDER IN              CALCULATE RATE IN
(1)  ml/hr & tubing drop factor           drops / min
(2)  1 L for n hr                         ml / hr
(3)  mg/kg/hr & concentration in mg/ml    ml / hr
(4)  units/hr & concentration in units/ml ml / hr
(5)  QUIT
```

`Problem=> 5`

Implement the following functions:

`get_problem`—Displays the user menu, then inputs and returns as the function value the problem number selected.

`get_rate_drop_factor`—Prompts the user to enter the data required for problem 1, and sends this data back to the calling module via output parameters.

`get_kg_rate_conc`—Prompts the user to enter the data required for problem 3, and sends this data back to the calling module via output parameters.

`get_units_conc`—Prompts the user to enter the data required for problem 4, and sends this data back to the calling module via output parameters.

`fig_drops_min`—Takes rate and drop factor as input parameters and returns drops/min (rounded to nearest whole drop) as function value.

`fig_ml_hr`—Takes as an input parameter the number of hours over which one liter is to be delivered and returns ml/hr (rounded) as function value.

`by_weight`—Takes as input parameters rate in mg/kg/hr, patient weight in kg, and concentration of drug in mg/ml and returns ml/hr (rounded) as function value.

`by_units`—Takes as input parameters rate in units/hr and concentration in units/ml, and returns ml/hr (rounded) as function value.

(*Hint:* Use a sentinel-controlled loop. Call `get_problem` once before the loop to initialize the problem number and once again at the end of the loop body to update it.)

3. Write a program to display the following and find the area of a given shape:
```
Enter the number of the problem you wish to solve.
(1) Area of a parallelogram     (4) Area of a circle
(2) Area of a triangle          (5) QUIT
(3) Area of a trapezoid
```

4. The table below summarizes three commonly used mathematical models of nonvertical straight lines.

Mode	Equation	Given
Two-point form	$m = \dfrac{y_2 - y_1}{x_2 - x_1}$	$(x_1, y_1), (x_2, y_2)$
Point-slope form	$y - y_1 = m(x - x_1)$	$m, (x_1, y_1)$
Slope-intercept form	$y = mx + b$	m, b

Design and implement a program that permits the user to convert either two-point form or point-slope form into slope-intercept form. Your program should interact with the user as follows:

```
Select the form that you would like to convert to slope-intercept
form:
1) Two-point form (you know two points on the line)
2) Point-slope form (you know the line's slope and one point)
=> 2

Enter the slope=> 4.2
Enter the x-y coordinates of the point separated by a space=> 1 1

Point-slope form
   y - 1.00 = 4.20(x - 1.00)

Slope-intercept form
   y = 4.20x - 3.20

Do another conversion (Y or N)=> Y

Select the form that you would like to convert to slope-intercept
form:
1) Two-point form (you know two points on the line)
2) Point-slope form (you know the line's slope and one point)
=> 1

Enter the x-y coordinates of the first point separated by a
space=> 4 3
Enter the x-y coordinates of the second point separated by a
space=> -2 1

Two-point form
      (1.00 - 3.00)
m = ---------------
      (-2.00 - 4.00)

Slope-intercept form
y = 0.33x + 1.66

Do another conversion (Y or N)=> N
```

Implement the following functions:

get_problem—Displays the user menu, then inputs and returns as the function value the problem number selected.

get2_pt—Prompts the user for the x-y coordinates of both points, inputs the four coordinates, and returns them to the calling function through output parameters.

get_pt_slope—Prompts the user for the slope and x-y coordinates of the point, inputs the three values, and returns them to the calling function through output parameters.

`slope_intcpt_from2_pt`—Takes four input parameters, the *x-y* coordinates of two points, and returns through output parameters the slope (*m*) and *y*-intercept (*b*).

`intcpt_from_pt_slope`—Takes three input parameters, the *x-y* coordinates of one point and the slope, and returns as the function value the *y*-intercept.

`display2_pt`—Takes four input parameters, the *x-y* coordinates of two points, and displays the two-point line equation with a heading.

`display_pt_slope`—Takes three input parameters, the *x-y* coordinates of one point and the slope, and displays the point-slope line equation with a heading.

`display_slope_intcpt`—Takes two input parameters, the slope and *y*-intercept, and displays the slope-intercept line equation with a heading.

5. Given a list of positive integers, perform the following tasks:

   a. Reverse a given number.
   b. Check whether the given number is prime or not.
   c. Check whether the given number is a palindrome or not.

   You should write each of the above as a separate program with functions that send back the answers to these three questions. Some sample input data might be:

   323   12242   09   463   678   8679

6. Develop a collection of functions to solve simple conduction problems using various forms of the formula

$$H = \frac{kA(T_2 - T_1)}{X}$$

where *H* is the rate of heat transfer in watts, *k* is the coefficient of thermal conductivity for the particular substance, *A* is the cross-sectional area in m² (square meters), T_2 and T_1 are the kelvin temperatures on the two sides of the conductor, and *X* is the thickness of the conductor in meters.

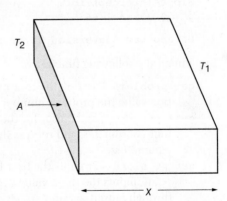

Define a function for each variable in the formula. For example, function `calc_h` would compute the rate of heat transfer, `calc_k` would figure the coefficient of thermal conductivity, `calc_a` would find the cross-sectional area, and so on.

Develop a driver function that interacts with the user in the following way:

```
Respond to the prompts with the data known. For the
unknown quantity, enter a question mark (?).
Rate of heat transfer (watts) >> 755.0
Coefficient of thermal conductivity (W/m-K) >> 0.8
Cross-sectional area of conductor (m^2) >> 0.12
Temperature on one side (K) >> 298
Temperature on other side (K) >> ?
Thickness of conductor (m) >> 0.003
            kA (T2 - T1)
    H = ----------------
              X
Temperature on the other side is 274 K.
H = 755.0 W                T2 = 298 K
k = 0.800 W/m-K            T1 = 274 K
A = 0.120 m^2             X = 0.0003 m
```

(*Hint:* Input of the question mark when looking for a number will cause `scanf` to return a value of 0. Be sure to check for this, and then scan the question mark into a character variable before proceeding with the remaining prompts.)

7. The square root of a number N can be approximated by repeated calculation using the formula

$$NG = 0.5(LG + N/LG)$$

where NG stands for next guess and LG stands for last guess. Write a function that calculates the square root of a number using this method.

The initial guess will be the starting value of LG. The program will compute a value for NG using the formula given. The difference between NG and LG is checked to see whether these two guesses are almost identical. If they are, NG is accepted as the square root; otherwise, the next guess (NG) becomes the last guess (LG) and the process is repeated (another value is computed for NG, the difference is checked, and so on). The loop should be repeated until the difference is less than 0.005. Use an initial guess of 1.0.

Write a driver function and test your square root function for the numbers 4, 120.5, 88, 36.01, 10,000, and 0.25.

8. InternetLite Corporation is an Internet service provider that charges customers a flat rate of $7.99 for up to 10 hours of connection time. Additional hours or partial hours are charged at $1.99 each. Write a function `charges` that computes the total charge for a customer based on the number of hours

of connection time used in a month. The function should also calculate the average cost per hour of the time used (rounded to the nearest cent), so use two output parameters to send back these results. Write a second function round_money that takes a real number as an input argument and returns as the function value the number rounded to two decimal places. Write a main function that takes data from an input file usage.txt and produces an output file charges.txt. The data file format is as follows:

Line 1: current month and year as two integers

Other lines: customer number (a five-digit number) and number of hours used

Here is a sample data file and the corresponding output file:

Data file usage.txt
```
10 2009
15362   4.2
42768   11.1
11111   9.9
```

Output file charges.txt
```
Charges for 10/2009
```

Customer	Hours used	Charge per hour	Average cost
15362	4.2	7.99	1.90
42768	11.1	11.97	1.08
11111	9.9	7.99	0.81

9. When an aircraft or an automobile is moving through the atmosphere, it must overcome a force called *drag* that works against the motion of the vehicle. The drag force can be expressed as

$$F = \frac{1}{2} CD \times A \times \rho \times V^2$$

where F is the force (in newtons), CD is the drag coefficient, A is the projected area of the vehicle perpendicular to the velocity vector (in m²), ρ is the density of the gas or fluid through which the body is traveling (kg/m³), and V is the body's velocity. The drag coefficient CD has a complex derivation and is frequently an empirical quantity. Sometimes the drag coefficient has its own dependencies on velocities: For an automobile, the range is from approximately 0.2 (for a very streamlined vehicle) through about 0.5. For simplicity, assume a streamlined passenger vehicle is moving through air at sea level (where $\rho = 1.23$ kg/m³). Write a program that allows a user to input A and CD interactively and calls a function to compute and return the drag force. Your program should call the drag force function repeatedly and display a table showing the drag force for the input shape for a range of velocities from 0 m/s to 40 m/s in increments of 5 m/s.

10. Write a program to calculate $n!$ for a given number n and perform the simple calculator operations. The valid operations of the calculator are:

```
+    add
-    sub
*    mul
/    div
```

The program must contain a function `fact` with one input parameter that returns the factorial of a number, a function `add` that performs the addition of two numbers, a function `sub` that performs the subtraction of two numbers, a function `mul` that performs the multiplication of two numbers, a function `div` that performs the division of two numbers. The program must also check for bad input data.

Output must be displayed as follows:

```
1: Addition
2: Subtraction
3: Multiplication
4: Division
5: Factorial
6: Quit
Enter the choice => 1
Enter two numbers => 2, 3
Sum => 5
```

11. After studying gross revenues of PQR Production Company over a 25-year period, you model the company's revenue as a function of time:

$$R(t) = 471.621 \times (1.063)^t$$

where R is in thousands of dollars and t is the years since 1990. Create the following C functions to implement this model:

`annual_revenue`—calculates and returns R for an input parameter of t.

`predict_year`—predicts the year in which revenues (in thousands) will first equal or exceed the value of the input parameter. For example, `predict_year(450)` would return 1990.

Write a main function that calls `predict_year` to determine when revenues will likely exceed $1 billion. Then create an output file that contains a table of estimated revenues (in thousands of dollars) for all the years from 1990 through the year when revenues should exceed $1 billion. Round revenue estimates to three decimal places.

12. Since communications channels are often noisy, numerous ways have been devised to ensure reliable data transmission. One successful method uses a checksum. A checksum for a message can be computed by summing the integer codes of the characters in the message and finding the remainder of this sum divided by 64. The integer code for a space character is added to this result to obtain the checksum. Since this value is within the range of the displayable characters, it is displayed as a character as well. Write a program that accepts single-line messages ending with a period and displays the checksum character for each message. Your program should continue displaying checksums until the user enters a line with only a period.

13. A finite state machine (FSM) consists of a set of states, a set of transitions, and a string of input data. In the FSM of Fig. 6.19, the named ovals represent states, and the arrows connecting the states represent transitions. The FSM is designed to recognize a list of C identifiers and nonnegative integers, assuming that the items are ended by one or more blanks and that a period marks the end of all the data. The following table traces how the diagrammed machine would process a string composed of one blank, the digits 9 and 5, two blanks, the letter K, the digit 9, one blank, and a period. The machine begins in the start state.

FIGURE 6.19

Finite State
Machine for
Numbers and
Identifiers

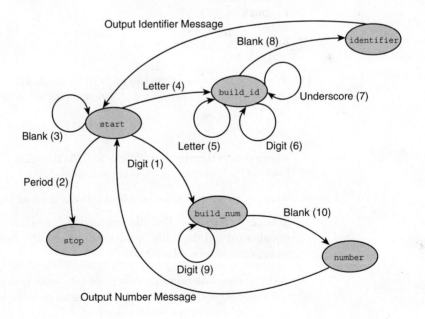

Trace of Fig. 6.19 FSM on data " 95 K9 ."

State	Next Character	Transition
start	' '	3
start	'9'	1
build_num	'5'	9
build_num	' '	10
number		Output number message
start	' '	3
start	'K'	4
build_id	'9'	6
build_id	' '	8
identifier		Output identifier message
start	'.'	2
stop		

Write a program that uses an enumerated type to represent the names of the states. Your program should process a correctly formatted line of data, identifying each data item. Here is a sample of correct input and output.

Input:
```
rate   R2D2 48    2 time     555666
```

Output:
```
rate — Identifier
R2D2 — Identifier
48 — Number
2 — Number
time — Identifier
555666 — Number
```

Use the following code fragment in `main`, and design function `transition` to return the next state for all the numbered transitions of the finite state machine. If you include the header file `ctype.h`, you can use the library function `isdigit`, which returns 1 if called with a digit character, 0 otherwise. Similarly, the function `isalpha` checks whether a character is a letter. When your program correctly models the behavior of the FSM shown, extend the FSM and your program to allow optional signs and optional fractional parts (i.e., a decimal point followed by zero or more digits) in numbers.

```
        current_state = start;
        do {
            if (current_state == identifier) {
                printf(" - Identifier\n");
                current_state = start;
            } else if (current_state == number) {
                printf(" - Number\n");
                current_state = start;
            }
            scanf("%c", &transition_char);
            if (transition_char != ' ')
                printf("%c", transition_char);
            current_state = transition(current_state, transition_char);
        } while (current_state != stop);
```

14. Harlan A. Brothers and John A. Knox discovered that as the value of x gets larger, the value of the expression $\left(\dfrac{2x + 1}{2x - 1}\right)^x$ gets closer and closer to e. Write a program that evaluates this expression for $x = 1, 2, 3$, and so on until the absolute difference between the expression's value and the value of e calculated by the library function exp is less than 0.000001. Display the value of x that causes your loop to exit along with both the final approximation of e and the value of e calculated by the exp function. Show seven decimal places.

Array Pointers

CHAPTER OBJECTIVES

- To learn how to declare and use arrays for storing collections of values of the same type
- To understand that C implements arrays as pointers
- To understand how to use a subscript to reference the individual values in an array
- To learn how to process the elements of an array in sequential order using loops
- To understand how to pass individual array elements and entire arrays through function arguments
- To learn a method for searching an array
- To learn a method for sorting an array
- To learn how to use multidimensional arrays for storing tables of data
- To understand the concept of parallel arrays
- To learn how to declare and use your own data types

imple data types use a single memory cell to store a variable. To solve many programming problems, it is more efficient to group data items together in main memory than to allocate an individual memory cell for each variable. A program that processes exam scores for a class, for example, would be easier to write if all the scores were stored in one area of memory and were able to be accessed as a group. C allows a programmer to group such related data items together into a single composite **data structure**. In this chapter, we look at one such data structure: the **array**.

data structure a composite of related data items stored under the same name

array a collection of data items of the same type

7.1 Declaring and Referencing Arrays

array element a data item that is part of an array

An array is a collection of two or more adjacent memory cells, called **array elements**, that are associated with a particular symbolic name. To set up an array in memory, we must declare both the name of the array and the number of cells associated with it.

The declaration

```
double x[8];
```

instructs the compiler to associate eight memory cells with the name x; these memory cells will be adjacent to each other in memory. Each element of array x may contain a single type `double` value, so a total of eight such numbers may be stored and referenced using the array name x. C implements arrays using pointers. The value of x declared above is the address of the initial array element, and x's type is pointer to `double`.

subscripted variable a variable followed by a subscript in brackets, designating an array element

array subscript a value or expression enclosed in brackets after the array name, specifying which array element to access

To process the data stored in an array, we reference each individual element by specifying the array name and identifying the element desired (for example, element 3 of array x). The **subscripted variable** x[0] (read as x sub zero) may be used to reference the initial or 0th element of the array, x, x[1] the next element, and x[7] the last element. The integer enclosed in brackets is the **array subscript**, and its value must be in the range from 0 to one less than the number of memory cells in the array.

EXAMPLE 7.1

Let x be the array shown in Fig. 7.1. Notice that x[1] is the second array element and x[7], not x[8], is the last array element. A sequence of statements that manipulate this array is shown in Table 7.1. The contents of array x after execution of these statements are shown after Table 7.1. Only x[2] and x[3] are changed.

FIGURE 7.1

The Eight Elements
of Array x

```
double x[8];
```

Array x

x[0]	x[1]	x[2]	x[3]	x[4]	x[5]	x[6]	x[7]
16.0	12.0	6.0	8.0	2.5	12.0	14.0	-54.5

TABLE 7.1   Statements That Manipulate Array x

Statement	Explanation
`printf("%.1f", x[0]);`	Displays the value of `x[0]`, which is `16.0`.
`x[3] = 25.0;`	Stores the value `25.0` in `x[3]`.
`sum = x[0] + x[1];`	Stores the sum of `x[0]` and `x[1]`, which is `28.0` in the variable `sum`.
`sum += x[2];`	Adds `x[2]` to `sum`. The new `sum` is `34.0`.
`x[3] += 1.0;`	Adds `1.0` to `x[3]`. The new `x[3]` is `26.0`.
`x[2] = x[0] + x[1];`	Stores the sum of `x[0]` and `x[1]` in `x[2]`. The new `x[2]` is `28.0`.

Array x

x[0]	x[1]	x[2]	x[3]	x[4]	x[5]	x[6]	x[7]
16.0	12.0	28.0	26.0	2.5	12.0	14.0	-54.5

EXAMPLE 7.2   You can declare more than one array in a single type declaration. The statements

```
double cactus[5], needle, pins[6];
int    factor[12], n, index;
```

declare cactus and pins to be arrays with five and six type double elements, respectively. The variable factor is an array with 12 type int elements. In addition, individual memory cells will be allocated for storage of the simple variables needle, n, and index.

Array Initialization

We can initialize a simple variable when we declare it:

```
int sum = 0;
```

We can also initialize an array in its declaration. We can omit the size of an array that is being fully initialized since the size can be deduced from the initialization list. For example, in the following statement, we initialize a 25-element array with the prime numbers less than 100. Array element `prime_lt_100[24]` is 97.

```
int prime_lt_100[] = {2, 3, 5, 7, 11, 13, 17, 19, 23, 29, 31, 37,
                      41, 43, 47, 53, 59, 61, 67, 71, 73, 79, 83,
                      89, 97};
```

Array Declaration

SYNTAX: *element-type aname* [*size*];   /* uninitialized */
           element-type aname [*size*] = {*initialization list*}; /* initialized */

EXAMPLE: `#define A_SIZE 5`

           `. . .`

           `double a[A_SIZE];`
           `char vowels[] = {'A', 'E', 'I', 'O', 'U'};`

INTERPRETATION: The general uninitialized array declaration allocates storage space for array *aname* consisting of *size* memory cells. Each memory cell can store one data item whose data type is specified by *element-type* (i.e., **double**, **int**, or **char**). The individual array elements are referenced by the subscripted variables *aname*[0], *aname*[1], . . . , *aname*[*size* −1]. A constant expression of type **int** is used to specify an array's *size*.

   In the initialized array declaration shown, the *size* shown in brackets is optional since the array's size can also be indicated by the length of the *initialization list*. The *initialization list* consists of constant expressions of the appropriate *element-type* separated by commas. Element 0 of the array being initialized is set to the first entry in the *initialization list*, element 1 to the second, and so forth.

Storing a String in an Array of Characters

The previous syntax display shows that you can store individual characters in an array by writing each character in the initialization list. If the list is long, you can do this more easily by using a string instead of an initialization list.

```
char vowels[] = "This is a long string";
```

In this case, `vowels[0]` stores the character `'T'`, `vowels[]` stores the character `'h'`, and so on. We will discuss this further in Sections 8.1 and 8.2.

EXERCISES FOR SECTION 7.1

Self-Check

1. What is the difference in meaning between `x3` and `x[3]`?
2. For the declaration

   ```
   int list[8];
   ```

   how many memory cells are allocated for data storage? What type of data can be stored there? How does one refer to the initial array element? To the final array element?
3. Declare one array for storing the square roots of the integers from 0 through 10 and a second array for storing the cubes of the same integers.

7.2 Array Subscripts

We use a subscript to differentiate between the individual array elements and to specify which array element is to be manipulated. We can use any expression of type `int` as an array subscript. However, to create a valid reference, the value of this subscript must lie between 0 and one less than the declared size of the array.

EXAMPLE 7.3

Understanding the distinction between an array subscript value and an array element value is essential. The original array `x` from Fig. 7.1 follows. The subscripted variable `x[i]` references a particular element of this array. If `i` has the value `0`, the subscript value is `0`, and `x[0]` is referenced. The value of `x[0]` in this case is `16.0`. If `i` has the value `2`, the subscript value is `2`, and the value of `x[i]` is `6.0`. If `i` has the value `8`, the subscript value is `8`, and we cannot predict the value of `x[i]` because the subscript value is out of the allowable range.

Array x

x[0]	x[1]	x[2]	x[3]	x[4]	x[5]	x[6]	x[7]
16.0	12.0	6.0	8.0	2.5	12.0	14.0	-54.5

EXAMPLE 7.4

Table 7.2 lists some sample statements involving the array `x` above. The variable `i` is assumed to be of type `int` with value `5`. Make sure you understand each statement.

TABLE 7.2 Code Fragment That Manipulates Array x

Statement	Explanation
`i = 5;`	
`printf("%d %.1f\n", 4, x[4]);`	Displays 4 and 2.5 (value of `x[4]`)
`printf("%d %.1f\n", i, x[i]);`	Displays 5 and 12.0 (value of `x[5]`)
`printf("%.1f\n", x[i] + 1);`	Displays 13.0 (value of `x[5]` plus 1)
`printf("%.1f\n", x[i] + i);`	Displays 17.0 (value of `x[5]` plus 5)
`printf("%.1f\n", x[i + 1]);`	Displays 14.0 (value of `x[6]`)
`printf("%.1f\n", x[i + i]);`	Invalid. Attempt to display `x[10]`
`printf("%.1f\n", x[2 * i]);`	Invalid. Attempt to display `x[10]`
`printf("%.1f\n", x[2 * i - 3]);`	Displays −54.5 (value of `x[7]`)
`printf("%.1f\n", x[(int)x[4]]);`	Displays 6.0 (value of `x[2]`)
`printf("%.1f\n", x[i++]);`	Displays 12.0 (value of `x[5]`); then assigns 6 to `i`
`printf("%.1f \n", x[--i]);`	Assigns 5 (6 − 1) to `i` and then displays 12.0 (value of `x[5]`)
`x[i - 1] = x[i];`	Assigns 12.0 (value of `x[5]`) to `x[4]`
`x[i] = x[i + 1];`	Assigns 14.0 (value of `x[6]`) to `x[5]`
`x[i] - 1 = x[i];`	Illegal assignment statement

The two attempts to display element `x[10]`, which is not in the array, may result in a run-time error, but they are more likely to print incorrect results. Consider the call to `printf` that uses `(int)x[4]` as a subscript expression. Since this expression evaluates to 2, the value of `x[2]` (*not* `x[4]`) is printed. If the value of `(int)x[4]` were outside the range 0 through 7, its use as a subscript expression would not reference a valid array element.

Array Subscripts

SYNTAX: *aname* [*subscript*]

EXAMPLE: `b[i + 1]`

INTERPRETATION: The *subscript* may be any expression of type `int`. Each time a subscripted variable is encountered in a program, the subscript is evaluated and its value determines which element of array *aname* is referenced.

> *Note:* It is the programmer's responsibility to verify that the *subscript* is within the declared range. If the subscript is in error, an invalid reference will be made. Although occasionally a run-time error message will be printed, more often an invalid reference will cause a side effect whose origin is difficult for the programmer to pinpoint. The side effect can also lead to incorrect program results.

EXERCISES FOR SECTION 7.2

Self-Check

1. Show the contents of array x after executing the valid statements in Table 7.2.
2. For the new array derived in Exercise 1, describe what happens when the valid statements in Table 7.2 are executed for i = 2.

7.3 Using for Loops for Sequential Access

Very often, we wish to process the elements of an array in sequence, starting with element zero. An example would be scanning data into the array or printing its contents. In C, we can accomplish this processing easily using an *indexed* **for** loop, a counting loop whose loop control variable runs from 0 to one less than the array size. Using the loop counter as an array *index* (subscript) gives access to each array element in turn.

EXAMPLE 7.5   The following array `square` will be used to store the squares of the integers 0 through 10 (e.g., `square[0]` is 0, `square[10]` is 100). We assume that the name `SIZE` has been defined to be 11.

```
int square[SIZE], i;
```

The for loop

```
for  (i = 0; i < SIZE; ++i)
    square[i] = i * i;
```

initializes this array, as shown.

Array square

[0]	[1]	[2]	[3]	[4]	[5]	[6]	[7]	[8]	[9]	[10]
0	1	4	9	16	25	36	49	64	81	100

Statistical Computations Using Arrays

One common use of arrays is for storage of a collection of related data values. Once the values are stored, we can perform some simple statistical computations. In Fig. 7.2, we use the array x for this purpose.

FIGURE 7.2 Program to Print a Table of Differences

```
1.   /*
2.    * Computes the mean and standard deviation of an array of data and displays
3.    * the difference between each value and the mean.
4.    */
5.
6.   #include <stdio.h>
7.   #include <math.h>
8.
9.   #define MAX_ITEM 8    /* maximum number of items in list of data          */
10.
11.  int
12.  main(void)
13.  {
14.        double x[MAX_ITEM],    /* data list                                  */
15.               mean,           /* mean (average) of the data                 */
16.               st_dev,         /* standard deviation of the data             */
17.               sum,            /* sum of the data                            */
18.               sum_sqr;        /* sum of the squares of the data             */
19.        int    i;
20.
21.        /* Gets the data                                                     */
22.        printf("Enter %d numbers separated by blanks or <return>s\n> ",
23.              ·   MAX_ITEM);
24.        for   (i = 0; i < MAX_ITEM; ++i)
25.            scanf("%lf", &x[i]);
26.
27.        /* Computes the sum and the sum of the squares of all data           */
28.        sum = 0;
29.        sum_sqr = 0;
30.        for   (i = 0;   i < MAX_ITEM; ++i) {
31.            sum += x[i];
32.            sum_sqr += x[i] * x[i];
33.        }
```

(continued)

FIGURE 7.2   (continued)

```
34.          /* Computes and prints the mean and standard deviation              */
35.          mean = sum / MAX_ITEM;
36.          st_dev = sqrt(sum_sqr / MAX_ITEM - mean * mean);
37.          printf("The mean is %.2f.\n", mean);
38.          printf("The standard deviation is %.2f.\n", st_dev);
39.
40.          /* Displays the difference between each item and the mean            */
41.          printf("\nTable of differences between data values and mean\n");
42.          printf("Index        Item        Difference\n");
43.          for  (i = 0; i < MAX_ITEM; ++i)
44.              printf("%3d%4c%9.2f%5c%9.2f\n", i, ' ', x[i], ' ', x[i] - mean);
45.
46.          return (0);
47. }
```

```
Enter 8 numbers separated by blanks or <return>s
>  16  12  6  8  2.5  12  14  -54.5
The mean is 2.00.
The standard deviation is 21.75.

Table of differences between data values and mean
Index        Item        Difference
   0         16.00           14.00
   1         12.00           10.00
   2          6.00            4.00
   3          8.00            6.00
   4          2.50            0.50
   5         12.00           10.00
   6         14.00           12.00
   7        -54.50          -56.50
```

The program in Fig. 7.2 uses three for loops to process the array x. The constant macro MAX_ITEM determines the size of the array. The variable i is used as the loop control variable and array subscript in each loop.

The first for loop,

```
for  (i = 0; i < MAX_ITEM; ++i)
    scanf("%lf", &x[i]);
```

stores one input value into each element of array x (the first item is placed in x[0], the next in x[1], and so on). The call to scanf is repeated for each value of i from 0 to 7; each repetition gets a new data value and stores it in x[i]. The subscript i determines which array element receives the next data value.

The second `for` loop accumulates (in `sum`) the sum of all values stored in the array. The loop also accumulates (in `sum_sqr`) the sum of the squares of all element values. This loop implements the formulas

$$sum = \mathtt{x[0]} + \mathtt{x[1]} + \cdots + \mathtt{x[6]} + \mathtt{x[7]} = \sum_{i=0}^{\mathtt{MAX\_ITEM}-1} \mathtt{x[i]}$$

$$sum\_sqr = \mathtt{x[0]}^2 + \mathtt{x[1]}^2 + \cdots + \mathtt{x[6]}^2 + \mathtt{x[7]}^2 = \sum_{i=0}^{\mathtt{MAX\_ITEM}-1} \mathtt{x[i]}^2$$

This loop will be discussed in detail later.

The last `for` loop,

```
for  (i = 0; i < MAX_ITEM; ++i)
    printf("%3d%4c%9.2f%5c%9.2f\n", i, ' ', x[i], ' ',
           x[i] - mean);
```

displays a table. Each line of the table displays an array subscript, an array element, and the difference between that element and the mean, `x[i] - mean`. Notice that the placeholders in the format string of the call to `printf` cause each column of values in the output table to be lined up under its respective column heading.

Now that we have seen the entire program, we will take a closer look at the computation `for` loop:

```
/* Computes the sum and the sum of the squares of all data */
sum = 0;
sum_sqr = 0;
for  (i = 0; i < MAX_ITEM; ++i) {
    sum += x[i];
    sum_sqr += x[i] * x[i];
}
```

This loop accumulates the sum of all eight elements of array `x` in the variable `sum`. Each time the loop body executes, the next element of array `x` is added to `sum`. Then this array element value is squared, and its square is added to the sum being accumulated in `sum_sqr`. We trace the execution of this program fragment in Table 7.3 for the first three repetitions of the loop.

The *standard deviation* of a set of data is a measure of the spread of the data values around the mean. A small standard deviation indicates that the data values are all relatively close to the average value. For `MAX_ITEM` data items, if we assume that `x` is an array whose lowest subscript is 0, the standard deviation is given by the formula

$$standard\ deviation = \sqrt{\dfrac{\displaystyle\sum_{i=0}^{\mathtt{MAX\_ITEM}-1} \mathtt{x[i]}^2}{\mathtt{MAX\_ITEM}} - mean^2}$$

TABLE 7.3   Partial Trace of Computing for Loop

Statement	i	x[i]	sum	sum_sqr	Effect
sum = 0; sum_sqr = 0;			0.0	0.0	Initializes sum Initializes sum_sqr

for (i = 0;
  i < MAX_ITEM;
  ++i)
	0	16.0			Initializes i to 0
					which is less than 8

sum += x[i]; sum_sqr += x[i] * x[i];			16.0	256.0	Adds x[0] to sum Adds 256.0 to sum_sqr
increment and test i sum += x[i];	1	12.0	28.0		1 < 8 is true Adds x[1] to sum
sum_sqr += x[i] * x[i];				400.0	Adds 144.0 to sum_sqr
increment and test i sum += x[i];	2	6.0	34.0		2 < 8 is true Adds x[2] to sum
sum_sqr += x[i] * x[i];				436.0	Adds 36.0 to sum_sqr

In Fig. 7.2, this formula is implemented by the statement

```
st_dev = sqrt(sum_sqr / MAX_ITEM - mean * mean);
```

Program Style   *Using Loop Control Variables as Array Subscripts*

In Fig. 7.2, the variable i, which is the counter of each indexed for loop, determines which array element is manipulated during each loop repetition. The use of the loop control variable as an array subscript is common, because it allows the programmer to specify easily the sequence in which the elements of an array are to be manipulated. Each time the value of the loop control variable is increased, the next array element is automatically selected. Note that the same loop control variable is used in all three loops. This reuse is not necessary, but is permitted since the loop control variable is always initialized at loop entry. Thus, i is reset to 0 when each loop is entered.

  EXERCISES FOR SECTION 7.3

Self-Check

1. Write an indexed for loop to fill the arrays described in Exercise 3 at the end of Section 7.1. Each array element should be assigned the value specified for it.

Programming

1. Write an indexed `for` loop to fill an array `prime` such that element `prime[0]` contains the first prime number, `prime[1]` the second prime number, and so on. The prime numbers will be provided as data. Also, write a loop that calculates the sum of all the prime numbers stored.

7.4 Using Array Elements as Function Arguments

Figure 7.2 uses `x[i]` as an argument for functions `scanf` and `printf`. The actual array element referenced depends on the value of `i`. The call

```
printf("%3d%4c%9.2f%5c%9.2f\n", i, ' ', x[i], ' ',
       x[i] - mean);
```

uses array element `x[i]` as an input argument to function `printf`. When `i` is 3, the value of `x[3]` or `8.0` is passed to `printf` and displayed.

The call

```
scanf("%lf", &x[i]);
```

uses array element `x[i]` as an output argument of `scanf`. When `i` is 4, a pointer to array element `x[4]` is passed to `scanf`, and `scanf` stores the next value scanned (`2.5`) in element `x[4]`.

You can also pass array elements as arguments to functions that you write. Each array element must correspond to a formal parameter that is the same simple type as the array element.

EXAMPLE 7.6

The function prototype below shows one type `double` input parameter (`arg_1`) and two type `double *` output parameters (`arg2_p` and `arg3_p`).

```
void do_it (double arg_1, double *arg2_p, double *arg3_p);
```

If `p`, `q`, and `r` are declared as type `double` variables in the calling module, the statement

```
do_it (p, &q, &r);
```

passes the value of `p` to function `do_it` and returns the function results to variables `q` and `r`. If `x` is declared as an array of type `double` elements in the calling module, the statement

```
do_it(x[0], &x[1], &x[2]);
```

uses the first three elements of array `x` as actual arguments. Array element `x[0]` is an input argument and `x[1]` and `x[2]` are output arguments (see Fig. 7.3). In function `do_it`, you can use statements like

```
*arg2_p = ...
*arg3_p = ...
```

FIGURE 7.3

Data Area for
Calling Module
and Function do_it

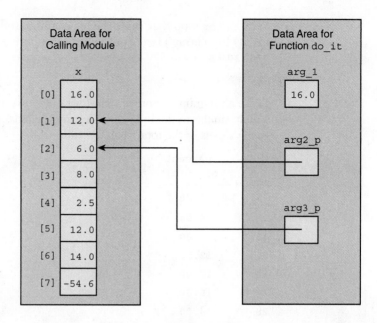

to return values to the calling module. These statements use indirection to follow the pointers `arg2_p` and `arg3_p` to send the function results back to the calling module. Because the function parameters `arg2_p` and `arg3_p` contain addresses of array elements `x[1]` and `x[2]`, the function execution changes the values of those elements.

 EXERCISES FOR SECTION 7.4

Self-Check

1. Write a statement that assigns to `seg_len` the length of a line segment from $x_i y_i$ to $x_{i+1} y_{i+1}$ using the formula

$$\sqrt{(x_{i+1} - x_i)^2 + (y_{i+1} - y_i)^2}$$

Assume that x_i represents the ith element of array `x`, y_i represents the ith element of array `y`, and the minimum `i` is `0`.

2. Write a `for` loop that sums the odd values from the `LIST_SIZE` element array `list`. For example, the sum for this list would be `113` (`51 + 17 + 45`).

Array `list`

list[0]	list[1]	list[2]	list[3]	list[4]	list[5]
30	12	51	17	45	62

3. Write a `for` loop that sums the even-numbered elements (elements 0, 2, and 4) from array `list`. For the list shown in Exercise 2, the sum would be 126 (30 + 51 + 45).

Programming

1. Write a program to store an input list of ten integers in an array; then display a table similar to the following, showing each data value and what percentage each value is of the total of all ten values.

n	percent of total
8	4.00
12	6.00
18	9.00
25	12.50
24	12.00
30	15.00
28	14.00
22	11.00
23	11.50
10	5.00

7.5 Array Arguments

Besides passing individual array elements to functions, we can write functions that have arrays as arguments. Such functions can manipulate some, or all, of the elements corresponding to an actual array argument.

Formal Array Parameters

We have seen that an array name with no subscript is a pointer, so when an array name with no subscript appears in the argument list of a function call, what is actually stored in the function's corresponding formal parameter is the address of the initial array element. In the function body, we can use subscripts with the formal parameter to access the array's elements. However, the function manipulates the original array, not its own personal copy, so an assignment to one of the array elements by a statement in the function changes the contents of the original array.

EXAMPLE 7.7   Figure 7.4 shows a function that stores the same value (`in_value`) in all elements of the array corresponding to its formal array parameter `list`. The statement

```
list[i] = in_value;
```

stores `in_value` in element `i` of its actual array argument.

FIGURE 7.4 Function fill_array

```
1.  /*
2.   * Sets all elements of its array parameter to in_value.
3.   * Pre: n and in_value are defined.
4.   * Post: list[i] = in_value, for 0 <= i < n.
5.   */
6.  void
7.  fill_array (int list[],     /* output - list of n integers        */
8.              int n,          /* input - number of list elements    */
9.              int in_value)   /* input - initial value              */
10. {
11.
12.      int i;               /* array subscript and loop control      */
13.
14.      for  (i = 0; i < n; ++i)
15.          list[i] = in_value;
16. }
```

In function `fill_array`, the array parameter is declared as

```
int list[]
```

Notice that the parameter declaration does not indicate how many elements are in list. Because C does not allocate space in memory for a copy of the actual array, the compiler does not need to know the size of the array parameter. In fact, since we do not provide the size, we have the flexibility to pass to the function an array of any number of integers.

Argument Correspondence for Array Parameters

To call function `fill_array`, you must specify the actual array argument, the number of array elements, and the value to be stored in the array. If y is an array with ten type int elements, the function call

```
fill_array(y, 10, num);
```

stores the value of num in the ten elements of array y. If x is a five-element array of type int values, the statement

```
fill_array(x, 5, 1);
```

causes function `fill_array` to store 1 in all elements of array x.

Figure 7.5 shows the data areas just before the return from the function call

```
fill_array(x, 5, 1);
```

FIGURE 7.5

Data Areas Before
Return from
`fill_array`
`(x, 5, 1);`

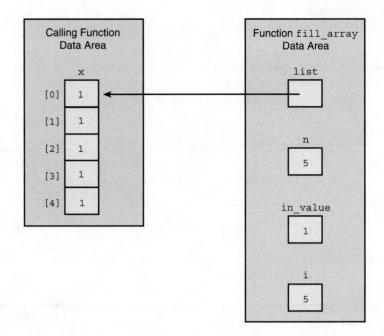

Notice that C stores the address of the type `int` variable `x[0]` in `list`. In fact, the call

```
fill_array(&x[0], 5, 1);
```

would execute exactly like the call above. However, this call may lead the reader of the code to expect that `fill_array` may be using only the array element `x[0]` as an output argument. For readability, you should use the name of an array (with no subscript) when you call a function that processes the list the array represents.

Use of `*list` Instead of `list[]` in a Formal Parameter List
In the declaration for function `fill_array`, we can use either parameter declaration:

```
int list[]
int *list
```

The first tells us that the actual argument is an array. However, because C implements arrays using pointers, the second declaration would be equally valid for an integer array parameter. In this text, we will usually use the first form to declare a parameter representing an array, saving the second form to represent simple output parameters. You should take care, however, to remember that a formal parameter of the form

$type_1$ `*param`

is compatible with an actual argument that is an array of $type_1$ values.

Arrays as Input Arguments

ANSI C provides a qualifier that we can include in the declaration of the array formal parameter in order to notify the C compiler that the array is only an input to the function and that the function does not intend to modify the array. The qualifier const allows the compiler to mark as an error any attempt to change an array element within the function.

EXAMPLE 7.8   Function get_max in Fig. 7.6 can be called to find the largest value in an array. It uses the variable list as an array input parameter. If x is a five-element array of type int values, the statement

```
x_large = get_max(x, 5);
```

causes function get_max to search array x for its largest element; this value is returned and stored in x_large. As in the call to function fill_array shown in Fig. 7.5, formal parameter list actually contains the address of the type int variable x[0].

FIGURE 7.6   Function to Find the Largest Element in an Array

```
1.  /*
2.   * Returns the largest of the first n values in array list
3.   * Pre: First n elements of array list are defined and n > 0
4.   */
5.  int
6.  get_max(const int list[], /* input - list of n integers          */
7.          int       n)      /* input - number of list elements to examine  */
8.  {
9.      int i,
10.         cur_large;       /* largest value so far                 */
11.
12.     /* Initial array element is largest so far.                 */
13.     cur_large = list[0];
14.
15.     /* Compare each remaining list element to the largest so far;
16.        save the larger                                          */
17.     for  (i = 1; i < n; ++i)
18.         if (list[i] > cur_large)
19.             cur_large = list[i];
20.
21.     return (cur_large);
22.  }
```

Array Input Parameter

SYNTAX: `const` *element-type array-name* `[ ]`
or
`const` *element-type *array-name*

EXAMPLE:

```
int
get_min_sub(const double data[], /* input - array
                                       of numbers   */
            int          data_size) /* input -
                                    number of elements   */
{
    int    i,
           small_sub; /* subscript of smallest value
                           so far                      */
    small_sub = 0;    /* Assume first element is
                          smallest.                    */
    for (i = 1; i < data_size; ++i)
        if (data[i] < data[small_sub])
            small_sub = i;
    return (small_sub);
}
```

INTERPRETATION: In a formal parameter list, the reserved word **const** indicates that the array variable declared is strictly an input parameter and will not be modified by the function. This fact is important because the value of the declared formal parameter will be the address of the actual argument array; if **const** were omitted, modification of the argument would be possible. The data type of an array element is indicated by *element-type*. The [ ] after *array_name* means that the corresponding actual argument will be an array. What is actually stored in the formal parameter when the function is called is the address of the initial element of the actual argument array. Since this value is a pointer to a location used to store a value of type *element-type*, the second syntax option is equivalent to the first.

Returning an Array Result

In C, it is not legal for a function's return type to be an array; therefore, defining a function of the variety modeled in Fig. 7.7 requires use of an output parameter to send the result array back to the calling module.

In Section 6.2, we saw that when we use simple output parameters, the calling function must declare variables into which the function subprogram will store its results. Similarly, a function returning an array result depends on its caller to provide

FIGURE 7.7

Diagram of a
Function That
Computes an
Array Result

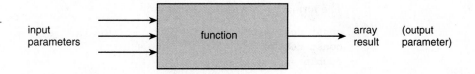

an array variable into which the result can be stored. We have already seen an example of a function with an array output parameter (function `fill_array` in Fig. 7.4). The next example shows a function with two input array parameters and an output array parameter that returns an array result.

EXAMPLE 7.9   Function `add_arrays` in Fig. 7.8 adds two arrays. The sum of arrays `ar1` and `ar2` is defined as `arsum` such that `arsum[i]` is equal to `ar1[i] + ar2[i]` for each subscript `i`. The last parameter, `n`, specifies how many corresponding elements are summed.

FIGURE 7.8   Function to Add Two Arrays

```
1.  /*
2.   * Adds corresponding elements of arrays ar1 and ar2, storing the result in
3.   * arsum. Processes first n elements only.
4.   * Pre: First n elements of ar1 and ar2 are defined. arsum's corresponding
5.   *      actual argument has a declared size >= n (n >= 0)
6.   */
7.  void
8.  add_arrays(const double ar1[],    /* input -                                */
9.             const double ar2[],    /* arrays being added                     */
10.            double       arsum[],  /* output - sum of corresponding
11.                                      elements of ar1 and ar2                 */
12.            int          n)        /* input - number of element
13.                                      pairs summed                           */
14. {
15.      int i;
16.
17.      /* Adds corresponding elements of ar1 and ar2                          */
18.      for  (i = 0; i < n; ++i)
19.          arsum[i] = ar1[i] + ar2[i];
20. }
```

The formal parameter list declaration

```
const double ar1[],
const double ar2[],
double      arsum[],
int         n
```

indicates that formal parameters `ar1`, `ar2`, and `arsum` are pointers to actual argument arrays whose elements are of type `double` and that `ar1` and `ar2` are strictly input parameters, as is n. The function can process type `double` arrays of any size as long as the preconditions stated in the initial block comment are met.

If we assume that a calling function has declared three five-element arrays x, y, and x_plus_y and has filled x and y with data, the call

```
add_arrays(x, y, x_plus_y, 5);
```

would lead to the memory setup pictured in Fig. 7.9.

FIGURE 7.9

Function Data Areas for add_arrays(x, y, x_plus_y, 5);

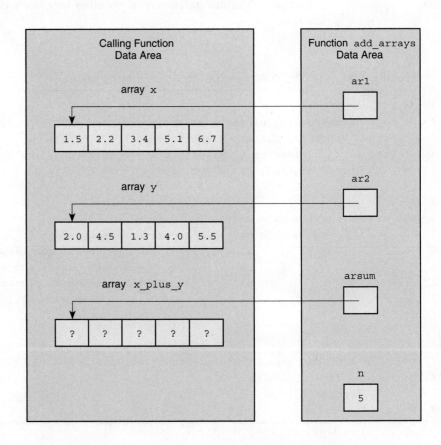

After execution of the function, x_plus_y[0] will contain the sum of x[0] and y[0], or 3.5; x_plus_y[1] will contain the sum of x[1] and y[1], or 6.7; and so on. Input argument arrays x and y will be unchanged; output argument array x_plus_y will have these new contents:

x_plus_y after call to add_arrays

3.5	6.7	4.7	9.1	12.2

Address-of Operator Not Used

Note carefully that in the *call* to add_arrays there is no notational difference between the references to input argument arrays x and y and the reference to output argument array x_plus_y. Specifically, the & (address-of) operator is *not* applied to the name of the output array argument. We discussed earlier the fact that C always passes whole arrays used as arguments by storing the *address* of the initial array element in the corresponding formal parameter. Since the output parameter arsum is declared with no const qualifier, function add_arrays automatically has access and authority to change the corresponding actual array argument.

Partially Filled Arrays

Frequently, a program will need to process many lists of similar data; these lists may not all be the same length. In order to reuse an array for processing more than one data set, the programmer often declares an array large enough to hold the largest data set anticipated. This array can be used for processing shorter lists as well, provided that the program keeps track of how many array elements are actually in use.

EXAMPLE 7.10 The purpose of function fill_to_sentinel is to fill a type double array with data until the designated sentinel value is encountered in the input data. Figure 7.10 shows both the input parameters that fill_to_sentinel requires and the results that are communicated through its output parameters.

When we use an array that may be only partially filled (such as dbl_arr in Fig. 7.10), we must deal with *two* array sizes. One size is the array's declared size, represented by the input parameter dbl_max, shown in Fig. 7.10. The other is the size counting only

FIGURE 7.10

Diagram of Function fill_to_sentinel

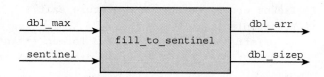

the elements in use, represented by the output parameter `dbl_sizep`. The declared size is only of interest at the point in a program where the array is being filled, for it is important not to try to store values beyond the array's bounds. However, once this input step is complete, the array size relevant in the rest of the processing is the number of elements actually filled. Figure 7.11 shows an implementation of function `fill_to_sentinel`.

FIGURE 7.11   Function Using a Sentinel-Controlled Loop to Store Input Data in an Array

```
1.  /*
2.   * Gets data to place in dbl_arr until value of sentinel is encountered in
3.   * the input.
4.   * Returns number of values stored through dbl_sizep.
5.   * Stops input prematurely if there are more than dbl_max data values before
6.   * the sentinel or if invalid data is encountered.
7.   * Pre:   sentinel and dbl_max are defined and dbl_max is the declared size
8.   *         of dbl_arr
9.   */
10. void
11. fill_to_sentinel(int     dbl_max,      /* input - declared size of dbl_arr    */
12.                  double sentinel,      /* input - end of data value in
13.                                           input list                          */
14.                  double dbl_arr[],     /* output - array of data              */
15.                  int    *dbl_sizep)    /* output - number of data values
16.                                           stored in dbl_arr                   */
17. {
18.      double data;
19.      int    i, status;
20.
21.      /* Sentinel input loop                                                   */
22.      i = 0;
23.      status = scanf("%lf", &data);
24.      while (status == 1 && data != sentinel && i < dbl_max) {
25.          dbl_arr[i] = data;
26.          ++i;
27.          status = scanf("%lf", &data);
28.      }
29.
30.      /* Issues error message on premature exit                                */
31.      if (status != 1) {
32.          printf("\n*** Error in data format ***\n");
33.          printf("*** Using first %d data values ***\n", i);
```

(continued)

FIGURE 7.11 (continued)

```
34.        } else if (data != sentinel) {
35.              printf("\n*** Error: too much data before sentinel ***\n");
36.              printf("*** Using first %d data values ***\n", i);
37.        }
38.
39.        /* Sends back size of used portion of array                    */
40.        *dbl_sizep = i;
41. }
```

Figure 7.12 shows a main function that calls `fill_to_sentinel`. The main function is using batch mode; it issues no prompting message, but it does echo print its input data. Notice that after the call to `fill_to_sentinel`, the expression used as the upper bound on the subscripting variable in the loop that echo prints the data is not the array's declared size, `A_SIZE`. Rather, it is the variable `in_use` that designates how many elements of `arr` are currently filled.

In the call to `fill_to_sentinel` in Fig. 7.12, we see another example of the difference between the way an array output argument is passed to a function and the way

FIGURE 7.12 Driver for Testing fill_to_sentinel

```
1. /* Driver to test fill_to_sentinel function */
2.
3. #define A_SIZE 20
4. #define SENT -1.0
5.
6. int
7. main(void)
8. {
9.        double arr[A_SIZE];
10.        int    in_use,      /* number of elements of arr in use */
11.               i;
12.
13.        fill_to_sentinel(A_SIZE, SENT, arr, &in_use);
14.
15.        printf("List of data values\n");
16.        for  (i = 0; i < in_use; ++i)
17.            printf("%13.3f\n", arr[i]);
18.
19.        return (0);
20. }
```

a simple output argument is passed. Both `arr` and `in_use` are output arguments, but the address-of operator `&` is applied only to the simple variable `in_use`. Since `arr` is an array name with no subscript, it already represents an address, the address of the initial array element.

Stacks

A stack is a data structure in which only the top element can be accessed. To illustrate, the plates stored in the spring-loaded device in a buffet line perform like a stack. A customer always takes the top plate; when a plate is removed, the plate beneath it moves to the top.

The following diagram shows a stack of three characters. The letter C, the character at the top of the stack, is the only one we can access. We must remove C from the stack in order to access the symbol +. Removing a value from a stack is called **popping the stack**, and storing an item in a stack is called **pushing it onto the stack**.

pop   remove the top element of a stack

push   insert a new element at the top of the stack

```
C
+
2
```

Figure 7.13 shows functions `pop` and `push`. The formal parameter `top` points to the variable that stores the subscript of the element at the top of the stack. Each push operation increments the value pointed to by `top` before storing the new item at the top of the stack (i.e., in element `stack[*top]`). Each pop operation returns the item currently at the top of the stack and then decrements the value pointed to by `top`. The `if` condition in `push` checks that there is room on the stack before storing a new item. The `if` condition in `pop` checks that the stack is not empty before popping it. If the stack is empty, `STACK_EMPTY` (a previously defined constant macro) is returned instead.

We can use the array `s` declared next to store a stack of up to `STACK_SIZE` characters where `s_top` stores the subscript of the element at the top of the stack. Giving `s_top` an initial value of `-1` ensures that the first item pushed onto the stack will be stored in the stack element `s[0]`.

```
char s[STACK_SIZE];    /* a stack of characters */
int  s_top = -1;       /* stack s is empty       */
```

The statements

```
push(s, '2', &s_top, STACK_SIZE);
push(s, '+', &s_top, STACK_SIZE);
push(s, 'C', &s_top, STACK_SIZE);
```

create the stack shown earlier where the last character pushed (C) is at the top of the stack (array element `s[2]`).

FIGURE 7.13 Functions push and pop

```
1.  void
2.  push(char stack[],      /* input/output - the stack */
3.       char item,         /* input - data being pushed onto the stack */
4.       int  *top,         /* input/output - pointer to top of stack */
5.       int  max_size)     /* input - maximum size of stack */
6.  {
7.       if (*top < max_size-1) {
8.           ++(*top);
9.           stack[*top] = item;
10.      }
11. }
12.
13. char
14. pop(char stack[],       /* input/output - the stack */
15.     int *top)           /* input/output - pointer to top of stack */
16. {
17.      char item;         /* value popped off the stack */
18.
19.      if (*top >= 0) {
20.          item = stack[*top];
21.          --(*top);
22.      } else {
23.          item = STACK_EMPTY;
24.      }
25.
26.      return (item);
27. }
```

EXERCISES FOR SECTION 7.5

Self-Check

1. When is it better to pass an entire array of data to a function rather than individual elements?
2. Assume a main function contains declarations for three type double arrays—c, d, and e, each with six elements. Also, assume that values have been stored in all array elements. Explain the effect of each valid call to add_arrays (see Fig. 7.8). Explain why each invalid call is invalid.

   a. add_arrays(ar1, ar2, c, 6);
   b. add_arrays(c[6], d[6], e[6], 6);

c. `add_arrays(c, d, e, 6);`
d. `add_arrays(c, d, e, 7);`
e. `add_arrays(c, d, e, 5);`
f. `add_arrays(c, d, 6, 3);`
g. `add_arrays(e, d, c, 6);`
h. `add_arrays(c, c, c, 6);`
i. `add_arrays(c, d, e, c[1]);` (if c[1] is 4.3? if c[1] is 91.7?)
j. `add_arrays(&c[2], &d[2], &e[2], 4);`

3. Modify function `fill_to_sentinel` from Fig. 7.11 so its return type is `int` rather than `void`. Have the function return the value 1 if no error conditions occur and 0 if there is an error. In all other respects, leave the function's purpose unchanged.

4. Can you think of a way to combine the following two statements from the body of the `while` loop of function `fill_to_sentinel` into just one statement?

```
dbl_arr[i] = data;
++i;
```

5. Assume stack `s` is a stack of `MAX_SIZE` characters and `s_top` is the subscript of the element at the top of stack `s`. Perform the following sequence of operations. Indicate the result of each operation and the new stack if it is changed. Rather than draw the stack each time, use the notation `|2+C/` to represent a stack of four characters, where the last symbol on the right (`/`) is at the top of the stack.

```
/* Start with an empty stack. */
s_top = -1;
push(s, '$', &s_top, MAXSIZE);
push(s, '-', &s_top, MAXSIZE);
ch = pop(s, &s_top);
```

Programming

1. Define a function `multiply` that computes and returns the product of the type `int` elements of its array input argument. The function should have a second input argument telling the number of array elements to use.

2. Define a function `abs_table` that takes an input array argument with type `double` values and displays a table of the data and their absolute values like the table shown below.

x	|x|
38.4	38.4
−101.7	101.7
−2.1	2.1

. . .

3. Write a function that negates the type `double` values stored in an array. The first argument should be the array (an input/output parameter), and the second should be the number of elements to negate.

4. Write a function that takes two type `int` array input arguments and their effective size and produces a result array containing the sums of corresponding elements. For example, for the three-element input arrays `5 -1 7` and `2 4 -2`, the result would be an array containing `7 3 5`.

5. Rewrite operators `push` and `pop` for a stack of integers. Also, write a new function `retrieve` that accesses the element at the top of the stack without removing it.

7.6 Searching and Sorting an Array

This section discusses two common problems in processing arrays: *searching* an array to determine the location of a particular value and *sorting* an array to rearrange the array elements in numerical order. As an example of an array search, we might want to search an array of student exam scores to determine which student, if any, got a particular score. An example of an array sort would be rearranging the array elements so that they are in increasing order by score. Sorting an array would be helpful if we wanted to display the list in order by score or if we needed to locate several different scores in the array.

Array Search

In order to search an array, we need to know the array element value we are seeking, or the search *target*. Then, we can perform the search by examining in turn each array element using a loop and by testing whether the element matches the target. The search loop should be exited when the target value is found; this process is called a *linear search*. The following algorithm for linear search sets a flag (for loop control) when the element being tested matches the target.

ALGORITHM

1.   Assume the target has not been found.
2.   Start with the initial array element.
3.   repeat while the target is not found and there are more array elements
4.   if the current element matches the target
5.   Set a flag to indicate that the target has been found.
      else
6.   Advance to the next array element.
7.   if the target was found
8.   Return the target index as the search result.
   else
9.   Return `-1` as the search result.

Figure 7.14 shows a function that implements this algorithm. This function returns the index of the target if it is present in the array; otherwise, it returns -1. The local variable i (initial value 0) selects the array element that is compared to the target value.

FIGURE 7.14   Function That Searches for a Target Value in an Array

```
1.   #define NOT_FOUND -1     /* Value returned by search function if target not
2.                             found                                              */
3.
4.   /*
5.    * Searches for target item in first n elements of array arr
6.    * Returns index of target or NOT_FOUND
7.    * Pre:  target and first n elements of array arr are defined and n>=0
8.    */
9.   int
10.  search(const int arr[],   /* input - array to search               */
11.         int       target,  /* input - value searched for            */
12.         int       n)       /* input - number of elements to search  */
13.  {
14.       int i,
15.           found = 0,      /* whether or not target has been found   */
16.           where;          /* index where target found or NOT_FOUND  */
17.
18.       /* Compares each element to target                            */
19.       i = 0;
20.       while (!found && i < n) {
21.           if (arr[i] == target)
22.               found = 1;
23.           else
24.               ++i;
25.       }
26.
27.       /* Returns index of element matching target or NOT_FOUND      */
28.       if (found)
29.           where = i;
30.       else
31.           where = NOT_FOUND;
32.
33.       return (where);
34.  }
```

The type int variable found is used to represent the logical concept of whether the target has been found yet and is tested in the loop repetition condition. The variable is initially set to 0 for false (the target is certainly not found before we begin searching for it) and is reset to 1 for true only if the target is found. After found becomes true or the entire array has been searched, the loop is exited, and the decision statement following the loop defines the value returned.

If array ids is declared in the calling function, the assignment statement

```
index = search(ids, 4902, ID_SIZE);
```

calls function search to search the first ID_SIZE elements of array ids for the target ID 4902. The subscript of the first occurrence of 4902 is saved in index. If 4902 is not found, then index is set to -1.

Sorting an Array

Many programs execute more efficiently if the data they process are sorted before processing begins. For example, a check-processing program executes more quickly if all checks are in order by checking account number. Other programs produce more understandable output if the information is sorted before it is displayed. For example, your university might want your instructor's grade report sorted by student ID number. In this section, we describe one simple sorting algorithm from among the many that have been studied by computer scientists.

The *selection sort* is a fairly intuitive (but not very efficient) sorting algorithm. To perform a selection sort of an array with n elements (subscripts 0 through n-1), we locate the smallest element in the array and then switch the smallest element with the element at subscript 0, thereby placing the smallest element in the first position. Then we locate the smallest element remaining in the subarray with subscripts 1 through n-1 and switch it with the element at subscript 1, thereby placing the second smallest element in the second position. Then we locate the smallest element remaining in the subarray with subscripts 3 through n-1 and switch it with the element at subscript 3, and so on.

ALGORITHM FOR SELECTION SORT

1. for each value of fill from 0 to n-2
    2. Find index_of_min, the index of the smallest element in the unsorted subarray list[fill] through list[n-1].
    3. if fill is not the position of the smallest element (index_of_min)
        4. Exchange the smallest element with the one at position fill.

Figure 7.15 traces the operation of the selection sort algorithm on an array of length 4. The first array shown is the original array. Then we show each step

FIGURE 7.15

Trace of Selection
Sort

	[0]	[1]	[2]	[3]
	74	45	83	16

fill is 0. Find the smallest element in subarray
list[1] through list[3] and swap it with list[0].

	[0]	[1]	[2]	[3]
	16	45	83	74

fill is 1. Find the smallest element in subarray
list[1] through list[3] —no exchange needed.

	[0]	[1]	[2]	[3]
	16	45	83	74

fill is 2. Find the smallest element in subarray
list[2] through list[3] and swap it with list[2].

	[0]	[1]	[2]	[3]
	16	45	74	83

as the next smallest element is moved to its correct position. Each array diagram
has two parts: a subarray that is sorted (in color) and a subarray that has not yet
been sorted. After each pass through the array, the sorted subarray contains an
additional element. Notice that, at most, n-1 exchanges will be required to sort an
array with n elements.

We will use function get_min_range to perform step 2. Function select_
sort in Fig. 7.16 performs a selection sort on the array represented by parameter
list, which is an input/output parameter. Notice that its declaration is of the same
form as the output parameter arrays discussed in the previous section. Local variable index_of_min holds the index of the smallest value found so far in the current subarray. At the end of each pass, if index_of_min and fill are not equal,
the statements

```
temp = list[index_of_min];
list[index_of_min] = list[fill];
list[fill] = temp;
```

exchange the array elements with subscripts fill and index_of_min. After function
select_sort executes, the values in its corresponding array argument will form
an increasing sequence. See Programming Exercise 1 for a description of function
get_min_range.

FIGURE 7.16   Function select_sort

```
1.  /*
2.   * Finds the position of the smallest element in the subarray
3.   * list[first] through list[last].
4.   * Pre: first < last and elements 0 through last of array list are defined.
5.   * Post: Returns the subscript k of the smallest element in the subarray;
6.   *        i.e., list[k] <= list[i] for all i in the subarray
7.   */
8.  int get_min_range(int list[], int first, int last);
9.
10.
11.  /*
12.   * Sorts the data in array list
13.   * Pre: first n elements of list are defined and n >= 0
14.   */
15.  void
16.  select_sort(int list[],  /* input/output - array being sorted       */
17.               int n)      /* input - number of elements to sort      */
18.  {
19.        int fill,          /* index of first element in unsorted subarray  */
20.            temp,          /* temporary storage                       */
21.            index_of_min;  /* subscript of next smallest element      */
22.
23.        for (fill = 0; fill < n-1; ++fill) {
24.            /* Find position of smallest element in unsorted subarray */
25.            index_of_min = get_min_range(list, fill, n-1);
26.
27.            /* Exchange elements at fill and index_of_min */
28.            if (fill != index_of_min) {
29.                temp = list[index_of_min];
30.                list[index_of_min] = list[fill];
31.                list[fill] = temp;
32.            }
33.        }
34.  }
```

EXERCISES FOR SECTION 7.6

Self-Check

1. For the search function in Fig. 7.14, what happens if:

   a. the last ID stored matches the target?
   b. several IDs match the target?

2. Trace the execution of the selection sort on the following two lists:

   8 53 32 54 74 3   7 18 28 37 42 42

   Show the arrays after each exchange occurs. How many exchanges are required to sort each list? How many comparisons?
3. How could you modify the selection sort algorithm to get the scores in descending order (largest score first)?

Programming

1. Write function `get_min_range` based on function `get_min_sub` in the syntax display for array input parameter (see page 412). Function `get_min_range` returns the subscript of the smallest value in a portion of an array containing type `int` values. It has three arguments: an array, the first subscript in the sub-array, and the last subscript in the subarray.
2. Another method of performing the selection sort is to place the largest value in position $n-1$, the next largest in position $n-2$, and so on. Write this version.
3. Modify the heading and declarations of function `select_sort` so it would sort an array of type `double` values. Be careful—some variables should still be of type `int`!

7.7 Parallel Arrays and Enumerated Types

parallel arrays two or more arrays with the same number of elements used for storing related information about a collection of data objects

In this section, we discuss a collection of arrays called **parallel arrays** that have the same number of elements. If there are n elements, these parallel arrays contain data for n objects of the same kind. Further, all array elements at subscript i contain data for the ith object in this group of n objects.

EXAMPLE 7.11   We declare two parallel arrays for a student records program as follows:

```
int    id[NUM_STUDENTS];
double gpa[NUM_STUDENTS];
```

Here we assume that NUM_STUDENTS has already appeared in a #define directive such as

```
#define NUM_STUDENTS 50
```

The arrays id and gpa each have 50 elements. Each element of array id can be used to store an integer value; each element of array gpa can be used to store a value of type double. If you use these declarations in a problem to assess the range and distribution of grade point averages, you can store the first student's ID in id[0], and store the same student's gpa in gpa[0]. Samples of these arrays are shown next.

id[0]	5503	gpa[0]	2.71
id[1]	4556	gpa[1]	3.09
id[2]	5691	gpa[2]	2.98
	. . .		. . .
id[49]	9146	gpa[49]	1.92

Figure 7.17 shows a simple program that reads data into these two parallel arrays and displays the information stored. We show just the output for the first two elements of each array.

FIGURE 7.17 Student Data in Parallel Arrays

```
1.  /* Read data for parallel arrays and echo stored data.                    */
2.
3.  #include <stdio.h>
4.  #define NUM_STUDENTS 50
5.
6.  int
7.  main(void)
8.  {
9.      int id[NUM_STUDENTS];
10.     double gpa[NUM_STUDENTS];
11.     int i;
12.
13.     for (i = 0; i < NUM_STUDENTS; ++i) {
14.         printf("Enter the id and gpa for student %d: ", i);
15.         scanf("%d%lf", &id[i], &gpa[i]);
16.         printf("%d   %4.2f\n", id[i], gpa[i]);
17.     }
```

(continued)

FIGURE 7.17 (continued)

```
18.
19.    return (0);
20. }
```

```
Enter the id and gpa for student 0: 5503 2.71
5503    2.71
Enter the id and gpa for student 1: 4556 3.09
4556    3.09
```

Enumerated Types

Good solutions to many programming problems require new data types. For example, in a budget program you might distinguish among the following categories of expenses: entertainment, rent, utilities, food, clothing, automobile, insurance, and miscellaneous. ANSI C allows you to associate a numeric code with each category by creating an **enumerated type** that has its own list of meaningful values.

enumerated type a data type whose list of values is specified by the programmer in a type declaration

For example, the enumerated type `expense_t` has eight possible values:

```
typedef enum
      {entertainment, rent, utilities, food, clothing,
       automobile, insurance, miscellaneous}
expense_t;
```

Our new type name `expense_t` is used just as we would use a standard type such as `int` or `double`. Here is a declaration of variable `expense_kind`:

```
expense_t expense_kind;
```

enumeration constant an identifier that is one of the values of an enumerated type

Defining type `expense_t` as shown causes the **enumeration constant** entertainment to be represented as the integer 0, constant `rent` to be represented as integer 1, `utilities` as 2, and so on. Variable `expense_kind` and the eight enumeration constants can be manipulated just as one would handle any other integers. Figure 7.18 shows a program that scans an integer representing an expense code and calls a function that uses a `switch` statement to display the code meaning.

The scope rules for identifiers (see Section 6.4) apply to enumerated types and enumeration constants. Enumeration constants must be identifiers; they cannot be numeric, character, or string literals (e.g., `"entertainment"` cannot be a value for an enumerated type). We recommend that you place type definitions immediately after any `#define` and `#include` directives (see Fig. 7.18) so that you can use the types throughout all parts of your program. The reserved word `typedef` can be used to name many varieties of user-defined types. We will study some of these uses in Chapters 10 and 13.

FIGURE 7.18   Enumerated Type for Budget Expenses

```c
1.  /* Program demonstrating the use of an enumerated type */
2.
3.  #include <stdio.h>
4.
5.  typedef enum
6.        {entertainment, rent, utilities, food, clothing,
7.         automobile, insurance, miscellaneous}
8.  expense_t;
9.
10. void print_expense(expense_t expense_kind);
11.
12. int
13. main(void)
14. {
15.      expense_t expense_kind;
16.
17.      printf("Enter an expense code between 0 and 7>>");
18.      scanf("%d", &expense_kind);
19.      printf("Expense code represents ");
20.      print_expense(expense_kind);
21.      printf(".\n");
22.
23.      return (0);
24. }
25.
26. /*
27.  * Display string corresponding to a value of type expense_t
28.  */
29. void
30. print_expense(expense_t expense_kind)
31. {
32.      switch (expense_kind) {
33.      case entertainment:
34.          printf("entertainment");
35.          break;
36.
37.      case rent:
38.          printf("rent");
39.          break;
40.
```

(continued)

FIGURE 7.18   (continued)

```
40.       case utilities:
41.             printf("utilities");
42.             break;
43.
44.       case food:
45.             printf("food");
46.             break;
47.
48.       case clothing:
49.             printf("clothing");
50.             break;
51.
52.       case automobile:
53.             printf("automobile");
54.             break;
55.
56.       case insurance:
57.             printf("insurance");
58.             break;
59.
60.       case miscellaneous:
61.             printf("miscellaneous");
62.             break;
63.
64.       default:
65.             printf("\n*** INVALID CODE ***\n");
66.       }
67. }
```

Enumerated Type Definition

SYNTAX: **typedef enum**
                {identifier_list}
          enum_type;

EXAMPLE: **typedef enum**
                {monday, tuesday, wednesday, thursday,
                 friday, saturday, sunday}
          day_t;

> INTERPRETATION: A new data type named *enum_type* is defined. The valid values of this type are the identifiers of *identifier_list*. The first identifier is represented by the integer 0, the second by the integer 1, and so on.
>
> *Note:* A particular identifier can appear in only one *identifier_list* in a given scope.

    * An identifier cannot appear in more than one enumerated type definition. For example, the definition

```
typedef enum
        {monday, tuesday, wednesday, thursday, friday}
weekday_t;
```

could not be used with the type `day_t` shown in the Syntax Display.

    Relational, assignment, and even arithmetic operators can be used with enumerated types, just as with other integers. For type `day_t`, the following relations are true:

```
sunday < monday
wednesday != friday
tuesday >= sunday
```

We can combine the use of arithmetic operators and casts to find enumeration constants that follow and precede a current value.

EXAMPLE 7.12   If `today` and `tomorrow` are type `day_t` variables, the following `if` statement assigns the value of `tomorrow` based on the value of `today`:

```
if (today == sunday)
        tomorrow = monday;
else
        tomorrow = (day_t)(today + 1);
```

Because the days of a week are cyclical, `tomorrow` should be set to `monday` when `today` is `sunday`. The last value (`saturday`) in type `day_t` is treated separately, because adding 1 to its integer representation yields a result not associated with a valid `day_t` value.

Because C handles enumerated type values just as it handles other integers, C provides no range checking to verify that the value stored in an enumerated type variable is valid. For example, this assignment statement will not cause a run-time error even though it is clearly invalid.

```
today = saturday + 3;
```

We have seen that an enumerated type variable can be used as the controlling expression of a switch statement. Such a variable can also be used as a loop counter:

```
for (today = monday; today <= friday; ++today) {
    . . .
}
```

This loop will execute for each value of today from monday through friday.

Array with Enumerated Type Subscript

The next example uses an array with an enumerated type subscript.

EXAMPLE 7.13

The #define directives and type and variable declaration sections for a grading program follow:

```
#define NUM_QUEST      10  /* number of questions on daily quiz */
#define NUM_CLASS_DAYS 5   /* number of days in a week of class */

typedef enum
        {monday, tuesday, wednesday, thursday, friday}
weekday_t;

. . .

char answer[NUM_QUEST];      /* correct answers for one quiz */
int score[NUM_CLASS_DAYS];   /* one student's quiz scores for each
                                day */
```

Array answer is declared with ten elements; each element can store a single character. We can use this array to store the ten answers for a true–false quiz (e.g., answer[0] is 'T', answer[1] is 'F'). Array score has five elements corresponding to the five class days listed in the weekday_t type declaration. Since the enumeration constants monday through friday are represented by the integers 0 through 4, we can use them as subscripts on array score. Sample arrays are illustrated in Fig. 7.19.

For array score the assignment statements

```
score[monday] = 9;
score[tuesday] = 7;
score[wednesday] = 5;
score[thursday] = 3;
score[friday] = 1;
```

assign the values shown in Fig. 7.19 to score. Assuming that today is type weekday_t and ascore is type int, the following statements have the same effect.

FIGURE 7.19

Arrays answer and
score

answer[0]	T	score[monday]	9
answer[1]	F	score[tuesday]	7
answer[2]	F	score[wednesday]	5
	. . .	score[thursday]	3
answer[9]	T	score[friday]	1

```
ascore = 9;
for  (today = monday; today <= friday; ++today) {
    score[today] = ascore;
    ascore -= 2;
}
```

EXERCISES FOR SECTION 7.7

Self-Check

1. Evaluate each of the following expressions, assuming before each operation
   that the value of variable `today` (type `day_t`) is `thursday`.
   a. `(int)monday`
   b. `(int)today`
   c. `today < tuesday`
   d. `(day_t)(today + 1)`
   e. `(day_t)(today - 1)`
   f. `today >= thursday`

2. Indicate whether each of the following type definition groups is valid or invalid. Explain the flaws in invalid definitions.
   a. ```
      typedef enum
            {int, double, char}
      type_t;
      ```
   b. ```
      typedef enum
            {p, q, r}
      letters_t;
      typedef enum
            {o, p}
      more_letters_t;
      ```
   c. ```
      typedef enum
            {'X', 'Y', 'Z'}
      alpha_t;
      ```

3. Declare parallel arrays for storing information about 10 employees. One array
   will store the hours each person worked for a week and a second array will
   store each person's hourly pay rates.
      ```

Programming

1. Declare an enumerated type `month_t` and rewrite the following `if` statement, assuming that `cur_month` is type `month_t` instead of type `int`. Also, write the equivalent `switch` statement.

```
if (cur_month == 1)
      printf("Happy New Year\n");
else if (cur_month == 6)
      printf("Summer begins\n");
else if (cur_month == 9)
      printf("Back to school\n");
else if (cur_month == 12)
      printf("Happy Holidays\n");
```

2. Write a function `print_day` for enumerated type `day_t` that displays its argument as a string.

```
void print_day(day_t day);
```

    Hint: Use a `switch` statement to select the appropriate `printf` statement.

3. Write a program fragment that fills the two arrays in Self-Check Exercise 3 with data and then calculates and displays each person's salary for the week.

7.8   Multidimensional Arrays

multidimensional array   an array with two or more dimensions

In this section, we introduce **multidimensional arrays**, that is, arrays with two or more dimensions. We will use two-dimensional arrays to represent tables of data, matrices, and other two-dimensional objects. A two-dimensional object that many are familiar with is a tic-tac-toe board. The array declaration

```
char tictac[3][3];
```

allocates storage for a two-dimensional array (`tictac`) with three rows and three columns. This array has nine elements, each of which must be referenced by specifying a row subscript (`0`, `1`, or `2`) and a column subscript (`0`, `1`, or `2`). Each array element contains a character value. The array element `tictac[1][2]` marked in Fig. 7.20 is in row 1, column 2 of the array; the element contains the character `o`. The diagonal line consisting of array elements `tictac[0][0]`, `tictac[1][1]`, and `tictac[2][2]` represents a win for player `x` because each cell contains the character `x`.

FIGURE 7.20

A Tic-tac-toe Board
Stored as Array
tictac

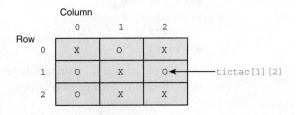

JRE 7.21 Function to Check Whether Tic-tac-toe Board Is Filled

```
Checks whether a tic-tac-toe board is completely filled.            */
it
illed(char ttt_brd[3][3])   /* input - tic-tac-toe board            */
{
        int r, c, /* row and column subscripts   */
            ans;  /* whether or not board filled */

        /* Assumes board is filled until blank is found             */
        ans = 1;

        /* Resets ans to zero if a blank is found                   */
        for (r = 0; r < 3; ++r)
           for  (c = 0; c < 3; ++c)
              if (ttt_brd[r][c] == ' ')
                    ans = 0;

        return (ans);
}
```

EXAMPLE 7.15   Function `filled` checks whether a tic-tac-toe board is completely filled (see Fig. 7.21). If the board contains no cells with the value ' ', the function returns 1 for true; otherwise, it returns 0 for false.

Initialization of Multidimensional Arrays

You can initialize multidimensional arrays in their declarations just like you initialize one-dimensional arrays. However, instead of listing all table values in one list, the values are usually grouped by rows. For example, the following statement would declare a tic-tac-toe board and initialize its contents to blanks.

```
char tictac[3][3] = { {' ', ' ', ' '}, {' ', ' ', ' '},
                      {' ', ' ', ' '} };
```

Arrays with Several Dimensions

The array `enroll` declared here

```
int enroll[MAXCRS][5][4];
```
           ↗   ↑   ↖
        course | *year*
           campus

and pictured in Fig. 7.22 is a three-dimensional array that may be used to store the enrollment data for a college. We will assume that the college offers 100 (`MAXCRS`)

A function that takes a tic-tac-toe board as a pa.
similar to this in its prototype:

```
char tictac[][3]
```

multidimensional array parameter declaration only the first dimension can be omitted:
`char tictac[][3]`

In the declaration of a multidimensional array parameter, o.
the number of rows, can be omitted. Including both dimensio.
Because tic-tac-toe boards do not vary in size, using the decla
would probably make more sense.

```
char tictac[3][3]
```

Multidimensional Array Declaration

SYNTAX: *element-type aname* [*size*$_1$] [*size*$_2$] ... [*size*$_n$]; /*   storage
                                                                allocation   */

element-type aname [ ] [*size*$_2$] ... [*size*$_n$]   /* parameter in
                                                                prototype   */

EXAMPLES: `double table[NROWS][NCOLS];`/* storage allocation   */

```
void
process_matrix(int in[][4],  /* input parameter    */
               int out[][4], /* output parameter   */
               int nrows);   /* input - number of
                                rows               */
```

INTERPRETATION: The first form shown allocates storage space for an array *aname* consisting of *size*$_1$ × *size*$_2$ × ... × *size*$_n$ memory cells. Each memory cell can store one data item whose data type is specified by *element-type*. The individual array elements are referenced by the subscripted variables *aname*[0][0]...[0] through *aname*[*size*$_1$−1][*size*$_2$−1]...[*size*$_n$−1]. An integer constant expression is used to specify each *size*$_i$.

The second declaration form shown is valid when declaring a multidimensional array parameter in a function prototype. The size of the first dimension (the number of rows) is the only size that can be omitted. As for one-dimensional arrays, the value actually stored in an array formal parameter is the address of the initial element of the actual argument.

Note: ANSI C requires that an implementation allow multidimensional arrays of at least six dimensions.

EXAMPLE 7.14

The array `table`

```
double table[7][5][6];
```

consists of three dimensions: The first subscript may take on values from 0
second, from 0 to 4; and the third, from 0 to 5. A total of 7 × 5 × 6, or 210, typ
values may be stored in the array `table`. All three subscripts must be specifi
reference to array `table` in order to access a single number (e.g., `table[2]`

FIGURE 7.22
_____

Three-Dimensional
Array enroll

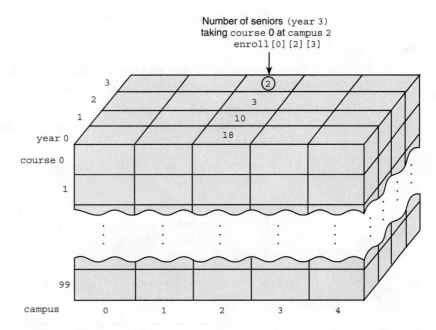

Number of seniors (year 3)
taking course 0 at campus 2
enroll[0][2][3]

courses at five different campuses. In keeping with C's practice of starting array subscripts with zero, we will number the freshman year 0, the sophomore year 1, and so on. Thus, enroll[1][4][3] represents the number of seniors taking course 1 at campus 4.

Array enroll is composed of a total of 2000 (100 × 5 × 4) elements. A potential pitfall exists when you are dealing with multidimensional arrays: Memory space can be used up rapidly if several multidimensional arrays are declared in the same program. You should be aware of the amount of memory space required by each large array in a program.

We can answer many different questions by processing the data in Fig. 7.22. We can determine the total number of students taking a particular course, the number of juniors in course 2 at all campuses, and so on. The type of information desired determines the order in which we must reference the array elements.

EXAMPLE 7.16

The program fragment that follows finds and displays the total number of students in each course.

```
/*  Finds and displays number of students in each course */
for  (course = 0; course < MAXCRS; ++course) {
    crs_sum = 0;
    for  (campus = 0; campus < 5; ++campus) {
        for  (cls_rank = 0; cls_rank < 4; ++cls_rank) {
            crs_sum += enroll[course][campus][cls_rank];
        }
    }
```

```
    printf("Number of students in course %d is %d\n", course,
           crs_sum);
}
```

Since we are displaying the number of students in each course, the loop control variable for the outermost indexed loop is the subscript that denotes the course.

The program fragment that follows displays the number of students at each campus. This time the loop control variable for the outermost indexed loop is the subscript that denotes the campus.

```
/* Finds and displays number of students at each campus      */
for  (campus = 0; campus < 5; ++campus) {
    campus_sum = 0;
    for  (course = 0; course < MAXCRS; ++course) {
        for  (cls_rank = 0; cls_rank < 4; ++cls_rank) {
            campus_sum += enroll[course][campus][cls_rank];
        }
    }
    printf("Number of students at campus %d is %d\n",
           campus, campus_sum);
}
```

EXERCISES FOR SECTION 7.8

Self-Check

1. Redefine MAXCRS as 5, and write and test program segments that perform the following operations:
   a. Enter the enrollment data.
   b. Find the number of juniors in all classes at all campuses. Students will be counted once for each course in which they are enrolled.
   c. Write a function that has three input parameters: the enrollment array, a class rank, and a course number. The function is to find the number of students of the given rank who are enrolled in the given course on all campuses. Try using your function to find the number of sophomores (rank = 1) on all campuses who are enrolled in course 2.
   d. Compute and display the number of upperclass students in all courses at each campus, as well as the total number of upperclass students enrolled on all campuses. (Upperclass students are juniors and seniors—ranks 2 and 3.) Again, students will be counted once for each course in which they are enrolled.

Programming

1. Write a function that displays the values on the diagonal of its 10 × 10 matrix parameter.

7.9 Array Processing Illustrated

The next problem illustrates two common ways of selecting array elements for processing. Sometimes we need to manipulate many or all elements of a table in some uniform manner (for example, display them all). In such situations, it makes sense to process the table rows or columns in sequence (*sequential access*), starting with the first and ending with the last.

At other times, the order in which the array elements are accessed depends either on the order of the problem data or the nature of the formula that is the basis of the processing. In these situations, access to element i+1 of an array does not necessarily occur right after access to element i. Thus, we are not using sequential access, but rather *random access*.

CASE STUDY   Summary of Hospital Revenue

PROBLEM

The chief financial officer of a regional medical center needs software to track revenue by unit and by quarter. The program will input all revenue transactions from a text file. The data for each transaction will be the unit number (0—Emergency, 1—Medicine, 2—Oncology, 3—Orthopedics, and 4—Psychiatry), the quarter in which the revenue was credited, and the revenue amount. These transactions are in no particular order. After scanning all revenue items, the program should display a table in the form shown in Fig. 7.23, which shows quarterly totals by unit along with annual unit totals and quarterly hospital totals rounded to the nearest thousand dollars.

ANALYSIS

You will need separate arrays to hold the revenue table, the unit totals (row sums) and the hospital quarterly totals (column sums).

FIGURE 7.23

```
                            REVENUE SUMMARY
                            ---------------

  Unit        Summer          Fall           Winter          Spring         TOTAL*
  -----------------------------------------------------------------------------------
  Emerg     12701466.16     12663532.66     12673191.41     11965595.94      50004
  Medic     12437354.59     11983744.61     12022200.48     11067640.00      47511
  Oncol     16611825.25     16996019.70     15976592.83     15391817.42      64976
  Ortho     16028467.82     15635498.54     15675941.06     15175890.29      62516
  Psych      6589558.39      6356869.38      5860253.24      6196157.30      25003
  -----------------------------------------------------------------------------------
  TOTALS*      64369           63636           62208           59797
```

*In thousands of dollars.

DATA REQUIREMENTS

New Types

```
quarter_t   {fall, winter, spring, summer}
unit_t      {emerg, medic, oncol, ortho, psych}
```

Problem Constants

```
NUM_UNITS     5
NUM_QUARTERS  4
```

Problem Inputs

Revenue transactions file
```
double revenue[NUM_UNITS][NUM_QUARTERS] /* revenue data array */
```

Problem Outputs

```
double unit_totals[NUM_UNITS];          /* Totals for
                                     each row of table */
double quarter_totals[NUM_QUARTERS];  /* Totals for
                                     each column */
```

DESIGN

INITIAL ALGORITHM

1. Scan revenue data, posting by unit and quarter, and returning a value to show success or failure of the data scan.
2. If the data scan proceeded without error:
   3. Compute unit totals (row sums).
   4. Compute quarterly totals (column sums).
   5. Display the revenue table along with the row and column sums.

IMPLEMENTATION

Coding Function main

We will call functions for steps 1, 3, 4, and 5. After introducing a program variable status to record the success or failure of the data scan, we can code function main directly from our initial algorithm pseudocode. Figure 7.24 shows the main function along with the necessary preprocessor directives and type definitions.

FIGURE 7.24 Hospital Revenue Summary Main Function

```
1.  /*
2.   * Scans revenue figures for one year and stores them in a table organized
3.   * by unit and quarter. Displays the table and the annual totals for each
4.   * unit and the revenue totals for each quarter
5.   */
6.
7.  #include <stdio.h>
8.
9.  #define REVENUE_FILE "revenue.txt"    /* name of revenue data file    */
10. #define NUM_UNITS     5
11. #define NUM_QUARTERS  4
12.
13. typedef enum
14.      {summer, fall, winter, spring}
15. quarter_t;
16.
17. typedef enum
18.      {emerg, medic, oncol, ortho, psych}
19. unit_t;
20.
21. int  scan_table(double revenue[][NUM_QUARTERS], int num_rows);
22. void sum_rows(double row_sum[], double revenue[][NUM_QUARTERS], int num_rows);
23. void sum_columns(double col_sum[], double revenue[][NUM_QUARTERS], int num_rows);
24. void display_table(double revenue[][NUM_QUARTERS], const double unit_totals[],
25.                  const double quarter_totals[], int num_rows);
26. /* Insert function prototypes for any helper functions. */
27.
28. int
29. main(void)
30. {
31.      double revenue[NUM_UNITS][NUM_QUARTERS]; /* table of revenue */
32.      double unit_totals[NUM_UNITS];           /* row totals */
33.      double quarter_totals[NUM_QUARTERS];     /* column totals */
34.      int    status;
35.
36.      status = scan_table(revenue, NUM_UNITS);
37.      if (status == 1) {
38.           sum_rows(unit_totals, revenue, NUM_UNITS);
39.           sum_columns(quarter_totals, revenue, NUM_UNITS);
40.           display_table(revenue, unit_totals, quarter_totals,
41.                      NUM_UNITS);
42.      }
43.      return (0);
44. }
```

Coding Function scan_table

Function `scan_table` (Fig. 7.25) scans in the data from the file `revenue.txt` one line at a time until end of file or an error is encountered. The unit and quarter values are input as `int` data, since types `unit_t` and `quarter_t` are strictly for the internal use of the program. Because C represents enumeration types as integers, an array with enumeration type subscripts can be accessed using either an enumeration type subscript or the associated integers. Within the loop body, `scan_table` checks the range of both the unit and the quarter of the current transaction. If the data are valid, the statement

```
revenue[trans_unit][quarter] += trans_revenue;
```

adds the current revenue amount to the total being accumulated for the unit indicated by `trans_unit` (row subscript) and `quarter` (column subscript). Because the data are in no particular order, the elements of array revenue are accessed randomly. Before beginning the data scan, the function must initialize all the elements of the revenue array to zero. This is the purpose of the call to `initialize`. The implementation of function `initialize` is also shown in Fig. 7.25. Because `initialize` must change the value of every element of revenue, it accesses the elements sequentially, using nested `for` loops. The outer `for` loop provides row subscripts of type `unit_t` running from `emerg` to `psych`, and the inner loop provides column subscripts of type `quarter_t` running from `summer` through `spring`.

FIGURE 7.25   Function scan_table and Helper Function Initialize

```
1.   /*
2.    * Scans the revenue data from REVENUE_FILE and computes and stores the
3.    * revenue results in the revenue table. Flags out-of-range data and data
4.    * format errors.
5.    * Post:  Each entry of revenue represents the revenue total for a
6.    *        particular unit and quarter.
7.    *        Returns 1 for successful table scan, 0 for error in scan.
8.    * Calls: initialize to initialize table to all zeros
9.    */
10.  int
11.  scan_table(double revenue[][NUM_QUARTERS], /* output */
12.             int num_rows)                   /* input  */
13.  {
14.       double   trans_amt;      /* transaction amount */
15.       int      trans_unit;     /* unit number        */
16.       int      quarter;        /* revenue quarter    */
17.       FILE     *revenue_filep; /* file pointer to revenue file */
18.       int      valid_table = 1;/* data valid so far  */
```

(continued)

FIGURE 7.25 (continued)

```
19.        int      status;           /* input status        */
20.        char     ch;               /* one character in bad line */
21.
22.        /* Initialize table to all zeros */
23.        initialize(revenue, num_rows, 0.0);
24.
25.        /* Scan and store the valid revenue data */
26.        revenue_filep = fopen(REVENUE_FILE, "r");
27.        for  (status = fscanf(revenue_filep, "%d%d%lf", &trans_unit,
28.                             &quarter, &trans_amt);
29.              status == 3 && valid_table;
30.              status = fscanf(revenue_filep, "%d%d%lf", &trans_unit,
31.                          &quarter, &trans_amt)) {
32.           if (summer <= quarter && quarter <= spring &&
33.               trans_unit >= 0 && trans_unit < num_rows) {
34.                 revenue[trans_unit][quarter] += trans_amt;
35.           } else {
36.                 printf("Invalid unit or quarter -- \n");
37.                 printf("  unit is ");
38.                 display_unit(trans_unit);
39.                 printf(", quarter is ");
40.                 display_quarter(quarter);
41.                 printf("\n\n");
42.                 valid_table = 0;
43.           }
44.        }
45.
46.        if (!valid_table) {           /* error already processed */
47.             status = 0;
48.        } else if (status == EOF) {   /* end of data without error */
49.             status = 1;
50.        } else {                      /* data format error */
51.             printf("Error in revenue data format. Revise data.\n");
52.             printf("ERROR HERE >>> ");
53.             for  (status = fscanf(revenue_filep, "%c", &ch);
54.                   status == 1 && ch != '\n';
55.                   status = fscanf(revenue_filep, "%c", &ch))
56.                printf("%c", ch);
57.             printf(" <<<\n");
58.             status = 0;
59.        }
```

(continued)

FIGURE 7.25   (continued)

```
60.        return (status);
61.  }
62.  /*
63.   * Stores value in all elements of revenue.
64.   * Pre: value is defined and num_rows is the number of rows in
65.   *      revenue.
66.   * Post: All elements of revenue have the desired value.
67.   */
68.  void
69.  initialize(double revenue[][NUM_QUARTERS], /* output */
70.             int    num_rows,                /* input  */
71.             double value)                   /* input  */
72.  {
73.       int       row;
74.       quarter_t quarter;
75.
76.       for  (row = 0; row < num_rows; ++row)
77.            for  (quarter = summer; quarter <= spring; ++quarter)
78.                 revenue[row][quarter] = value;
79.  }
```

Coding Functions sum_rows and sum_columns

The design and implementation of functions sum_rows and sum_columns are left as an exercise for you. Function sum_rows will need nested loops similar to those in function initialize. Full execution of the inner loop should add up the values in one row of sales. After exiting the inner loop, the accumulated sum should be stored in the element of row_sum corresponding to the current row. Function sum_columns will need a revision of the nested loops that allows the column subscript to remain constant while the row subscript varies.

Coding Function display_table

You should display the information in a two-dimensional array in the same way that humans visualize it: as a table whose rows correspond to the array's first dimension and whose columns correspond to the array's second dimension. To accomplish this, access and display the array elements row by row.

Function display_table (Fig. 7.26) displays the data in the revenue table in the form shown in Fig. 7.23. Since the display represents thousands of dollars, the values must be divided by 1000 and rounded, the purpose of helper function whole_thousands, whose code is also shown in Fig. 7.26. In addition to the array data (first parameter), the function also displays in whole thousands the unit totals (second parameter) and the quarterly totals (third parameter). The column headings are displayed by repeated calls to function display_quarter, whose code is also part of Fig. 7.26. The row labels require a similar function display_unit, which is left as an exercise for you.

FIGURE 7.26 Function display_table and Helper Functions display_quarter and whole_thousands

```
1.   /*
2.    * Displays the revenue table data (rounded to whole thousands) in table
3.    * form along with the row and column sums (also rounded).
4.    * Pre:  revenue, unit_totals, quarter_totals, and num_rows are defined.
5.    * Post: Values stored in the three arrays are displayed rounded to
6.    * whole thousands.
7.    */
8.   void
9.   display_table(double        revenue[][NUM_QUARTERS], /* input */
10.                 const double unit_totals[],            /* input */
11.                 const double quarter_totals[],         /* input */
12.                 int          num_rows)                 /* input */
13.  {
14.       unit_t    unit;
15.       quarter_t quarter;
16.
17.       /* Display heading */
18.       printf("%34cREVENUE SUMMARY\n%34c---------------\n\n", ' ', ' ');
19.       printf("%4s%11c", "Unit", ' ');
20.       for  (quarter = summer; quarter <= spring; ++quarter){
21.            display_quarter(quarter);
22.            printf("%8c", ' ');
23.       }
24.       printf("TOTAL*\n");
25.       printf("----------------------------------------");
26.       printf("----------------------------------------\n");
27.
28.       /* Display table */
29.       for  (unit = emerg; unit <= psych; ++unit) {
30.            display_unit(unit);
31.          printf(" ");
```

(continued)

FIGURE 7.26   (continued)

```
32.              for  (quarter = summer; quarter <= spring; ++quarter)
33.                  printf("%14.2f", revenue[unit][quarter]);
34.              printf("%13d\n", whole_thousands(unit_totals[unit]));
35.          }
36.          printf("----------------------------------------");
37.          printf("---------------------------------------\n");
38.          printf("TOTALS*");
39.          for  (quarter = summer; quarter <= spring; ++quarter)
40.              printf("%14d", whole_thousands(quarter_totals[quarter]));
41.          printf("\n\n*in thousands of dollars\n");
42. }
43. /*
44.  * Display an enumeration constant of type quarter_t
45.  */
46. void
47. display_quarter(quarter_t quarter)
48. {
49.          switch (quarter) {
50.          case summer:  printf("Summer");
51.                        break;
52.
53.          case fall:    printf("Fall ");
54.                        break;
55.
56.          case winter:  printf("Winter");
57.                        break;
58.
59.          case spring:  printf("Spring");
60.                        break;
61.
62.          default:      printf("Invalid quarter %d", quarter);
63.          }
64. }
65.
66. /*
67.  * Return how many thousands are in number
68.  */
69. int whole_thousands(double number)
70. {
71.      return (int)((number + 500)/1000.0);
72. }
```

TESTING

To test the revenue summary program, create four sample data files. In one, place only correct data. In the second, include a unit number >= NUM_UNITS. In the third, include a quarter number >= NUM_QUARTERS. In the fourth file, place a data format error such as a letter where a number belongs. Check that your correct data file produces reasonable results: The sum of the unit totals should match the sum of the quarterly totals. Verify that the program produces the correct error message for each erroneous file.

EXERCISES FOR SECTION 7.9

Self-Check

1. For each fragment, which array locations are displayed and in what order?

   a.
   ```
   for (next_quarter = summer;
           next_quarter <= spring;
           ++next_quarter)
        printf("%14.2f", revenue[oncol][next_quarter]);
   ```
   b.
   ```
   for (next_unit = emerg;
           next_unit <= psych;
           ++next_unit)
        printf("%14.2f", revenue[next_unit][spring]);
   ```
   c.
   ```
   for (next_quarter = fall;
            next_quarter < spring;
            ++next_quarter) {
        for (next_unit = emerg;
             next_unit <= psych;
             ++next_unit)
         printf("%14.2f", revenue[next_unit][next_quarter]);
        printf("\n");
   }
   ```

Programming

1. Write functions sum_rows and sum_columns called from function main in Fig. 7.24. Write function display_unit called from function display_table in Fig. 7.26.
2. Write a function that determines who has won a game of tic-tac-toe. The function should first check all rows to see whether one player occupies all the cells

in one row, next check all columns, and then check the two diagonals. The function should return a value from the enumerated type {no_winner, x_wins, o_wins}.

7.10   Graphics Programs with Arrays (Optional)

In this section, we use arrays in graphics programs to draw a polygon and also to draw a grid or a two-dimensional table. We begin by drawing a polygon.

Drawing a Polygon

Rectangles and squares have four sides, but there are times when you want to draw a triangle (three sides) or a closed figure that has more than four sides. The graphics.h library has two functions that do this: drawpoly and fillpoly. Both functions require an array argument that stores the points to be displayed. The coordinates of each point are stored in consecutive elements of the array. For drawpoly, the polygon must be closed; that is, the first point should be repeated as the last point.

EXAMPLE 7.17   In Fig. 3.30, a house was drawn as a rectangle on top of a square. We can draw the outline of a house as a polygon using the following statements.

```
/*                (x,   y)                              */
int poly[12] = { 100, 200,    /* top-left corner      */
                 300, 100,    /* roof peak            */
                 500, 200,    /* top-right corner     */
                 500, 400,    /* bottom-right corner  */
                 100, 400,    /* bottom-left corner   */
                 100, 200     /* top-left corner      */
               };
drawpoly(6, poly);
```

The first argument for drawpoly is the number of points to draw. The array size is 12 because there are two elements for each point. For example, poly[0], poly[1] are the x, y coordinates for the first point.

The program in Fig. 7.27 draws a painted house by calling fillpoly instead of drawpoly. Each time the user presses a key, the fill pattern and color changes. Figure 7.28 shows one example.

The sentinel-controlled while loop repeats until the user types in q or Q. The pattern and color are randomly selected. We explain the role of functions rand and srand next.

FIGURE 7.27   Drawing and Filling a Polygon

```
1.  /* Draw and fill a polygon that is shaped like a house.
2.   * The color and fill pattern are selected randomly.
3.   */
4.  #include <graphics.h>
5.  #include <stdlib.h>
6.  #include <time.h>
7.
8.  int main()
9.  {
10.     /*                (x ,   y)                        */
11.     int poly[12] = { 100, 200, /* top-left corner     */
12.                      300, 100, /* roof peak           */
13.                      500, 200, /* top-right corner    */
14.                      500, 400, /* bottom-right corner */
15.                      100, 400, /* bottom-left corner  */
16.                      100, 200, /* top-left corner     */
17.                    };
18.     char ch;
19.     int color;   /* color of house */
20.     int fill;    /* fill pattern of house */
21.     char message[] =
22.             "Press a key to repaint house - press Q to quit";
23.     initwindow(640, 500, "House");
24.     outtextxy(100, 450, message);
25.
26.     srand(time(NULL));
27.     ch = '*';
28.     while (!(ch == 'q' || ch == 'Q')) {
29.        color = rand() % 16;
30.        fill = rand() % 12;
31.        setfillstyle(fill, color);
32.        fillpoly(6, poly);
33.        ch = getch();
34.     }
35.
36.     closegraph();        /* close the window */
37.  }
```

FIGURE 7.28

A Painted House

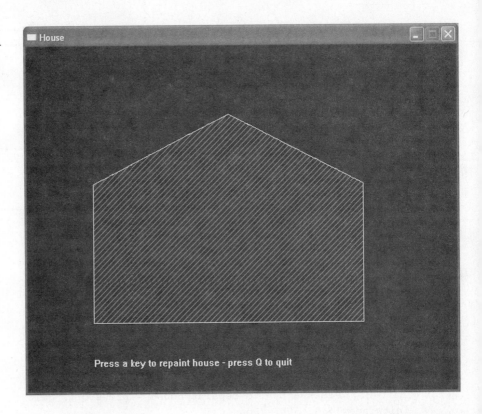

Program Style   *Using an Array of Characters to Store a Prompt*

Method `outtextxy` in the graphics library expects a character array as its third argument. That is the reason you may see the warning message: `deprecated conversion from string constant to char*` when you use a literal string as the third argument. You can avoid this warning if you store the literal string in an array of characters and then pass the name of this array as an argument to `outtextxy`.

```
char message[] =
    "Press a key to repaint house - press Q to quit");
outtextxy (100, 450, message);
```

Generating Random Numbers

Library `stdlib` provides a function `rand` that generates a pseudo-random integer. (They are called pseudo-random numbers because the sequence of numbers generated will eventually repeat, but they are certainly random enough for our purposes.)

In the statement below, function `rand` generates a random integer and the `%` operator yields a random value between 0 and 15.

```
color = rand() % 16;
```

Seeding the Random Number Generator

seed seed for a
random number
generator. An initial
value used in the
computation of the first
random number

The sequence of numbers that is generated depends on an integer value that **seeds** the random number generator, or provides it with a starting value for the computation of random numbers. If no starting value is provided by the programmer, a constant default value is used, so the sequence of numbers will be the same each time the program runs. To seed the random number generator with a different starting value each time, your program should execute the statement

```
srand(time(NULL));
```

before the first call to function `rand` where function `time` (defined in library `time.h`) returns an integer value representing the system clock. (The predefined value `NULL` is discussed in Section 13.2.) Because the system clock is always changing, the random number generator will use a different starting value each time the program runs, thereby generating a different sequence of random numbers. In Fig. 7.27, the call to `srand` should be placed before the `while` loop in the main function.

Drawing a Grid

In game programs, we often need to draw a two-dimensional grid pattern to show the current state of the game and record the position of a new move. Figure 7.29 is a program that draws the grid shown in Fig. 7.30. The program constants can be changed to allow different size grids and cells. In the main function, the two-dimensional array `gridArray` stores the color values to be displayed in each cell, starting with row 0, which happens to have all black cells (color value is 0). This array is passed to function `drawGrid`.

The body of function `drawGrid` contains a pair of nested loops to access each element of `gridArray`. For element `gridArray [r] [c]`, the statements

```
color = gridArray[r][c] % 16;                 /* cell color */
setfillstyle(SOLID_FILL, color);
bar(c*CELL_SIZE, r*CELL_SIZE,    /* top-left corner    */
    c*CELL_SIZE + CELL_SIZE,     /* bottom-right       */
    r*CELL_SIZE + CELL_SIZE);    /*    corner          */
```

draws a bar (filled rectangle) at row r, column c of the array. The x-coordinates of the pixels in the rectangle's sides depend on the value of c—the larger c is, the further to the right the rectangle is positioned. Adding `CELL_SIZE` to the x-coordinate of the left side gives the x-coordinate of the rectangle's right side. The y-coordinate values for the rectangle depend on the value of r and are calculated in a similar

FIGURE 7.29   Program to Draw a Two-Dimensional Grid

```
1.  /* Draws a grid and displays the row, column
2.   * of a selected cell
3.   */
4.  #include <graphics.h>
5.  #include <stdio.h>
6.
7.  #define NUM_ROWS  5
8.  #define NUM_COLS  6
9.  #define CELL_SIZE 50 /* dimensions of a square cell */
10.
11. void drawGrid(int gridArray[][NUM_COLS]);
12. void reportResult(int *row, int *column, int *color);
13. void recolor(int r, int c, int color, int pattern);
14.
15. int main(void)
16. {
17.     int gridArray[NUM_ROWS][NUM_COLS] =
18.                         { {0, 0, 0, 0, 0, 0},
19.                           {2, 4, 2, 4, 2, 4},
20.                           {1, 2, 3, 4, 5, 6},
21.                           {2, 3, 4, 15, 6, 7},
22.                           {5, 5, 5, 5, 5, 5}
23.                                 };
24.
25.     int width = CELL_SIZE * NUM_COLS;
26.     int height = CELL_SIZE * NUM_ROWS + 100;
27.     int row, column;   /* row, column of cell clicked */
28.     int color;              /* color of cell clicked */
29.     char message[100] = "Select a cell by clicking it";
30.
31.     initwindow(width, height, "Grid");
32.     outtextxy(100, height - 50, message);
33.
34.     drawGrid(gridArray);   /* Draw and color the grid */
35.
36.     /* Get position and color of cell clicked */
37.     reportResult(&row, &column, &color);
38.     printf("You clicked the cell in row %d, column %d\n",
39.            (row + 1), (column + 1));
40.
```

(continued)

FIGURE 7.29 (continued)

```
41.      /* Draw hatch pattern in cell clicked */
42.      recolor(row, column, color, HATCH_FILL);
43.
44.      getch();
45.      closegraph();
46.  }
47.
48.
49.  /* Draw the grid corresponding to the color values in gridArray
50.   * Pre:      Array gridArray is defined
51.   * Post:     A two-dimensional grid is drawn with the same number
52.   *           rows and columns as gridArray. The cell at row r,
53.   *           column c has the color value of gridArray[r][c].
54.   */
55.  void drawGrid(int gridArray[][NUM_COLS])
56.  {
57.      int color;                              /* color of cell */
58.      int r, c;                     /* row and column subscripts */
59.      /* Draw a grid cell for each array element */
60.      for (r = 0; r < NUM_ROWS; ++r) {
61.         for (c = 0; c < NUM_COLS; ++c) {
62.            /* Fill the cell */
63.            color = gridArray[r][c] % 16;     /* cell color */
64.            setfillstyle(SOLID_FILL, color);
65.            bar(c*CELL_SIZE, r*CELL_SIZE, /* top-left corner */
66.                c*CELL_SIZE + CELL_SIZE,      /* bottom-right */
67.                r*CELL_SIZE + CELL_SIZE);     /*    corner    */
68.
69.            /* Draw cell border */
70.            setcolor(WHITE);                    /* border color */
71.            rectangle(c*CELL_SIZE, r*CELL_SIZE, /* top-left corner */
72.                    c*CELL_SIZE + CELL_SIZE,      /* bottom-right */
73.                    r*CELL_SIZE + CELL_SIZE);     /*    corner    */
74.         }
75.      }
76.  }
77.
78.
79.  /* Report the results of a mouse click by the user.
80.   * Pre:     The grid is displayed
```

(continued)

FIGURE 7.29   (continued)

```
81.    * Post:    The row, column, and color of the cell
82.    *          clicked are returned through row and column.
83.    */
84.   void reportResult(int *row, int *column, int *color)
85.   {
86.       int x, y;     /* (x, y) position of mouse click */
87.
88.       clearmouseclick(WM_LBUTTONDOWN);
89.       while (!ismouseclick(WM_LBUTTONDOWN)) {
90.           delay(100);
91.       }
92.       getmouseclick(WM_LBUTTONDOWN, x, y);
93.
94.       /* Convert x (y) pixel position to row (column) */
95.       *row = y / CELL_SIZE;
96.       *column = x / CELL_SIZE;
97.       *color = getpixel(x, y);       /* get pixel color */
98.   }
99.
100.  /* Recolors a selected grid cell with a new color and pattern.
101.   * Pre:    The cell position, color,
102.   *         and pattern are defined.
103.   * Post:   The selected cell is filled with pattern
104.   */
105.  void recolor(int r, int c, int color, int pattern)
106.  {
107.      setfillstyle(pattern, color);
108.      bar(c*CELL_SIZE, r*CELL_SIZE,     /* top-left corner */
109.          c*CELL_SIZE + CELL_SIZE,      /* bottom-right */
110.          r*CELL_SIZE + CELL_SIZE);     /*     corner    */
111.  }
```

manner. The rectangle has the color value stored in grid [r][c]. Next, a white rectangular border is drawn around each bar.

After the grid is drawn, the main function prompts the user to select a cell by clicking in it. Method reportResult determines the cell that was clicked and returns its coordinates. The first statement below

```
clearmouseclick(WM_LBUTTONDOWN);
while (!ismouseclick(WM_LBUTTONDOWN)) {
    delay(100);
}
```

FIGURE 7.30

Two-Dimensional
Grid

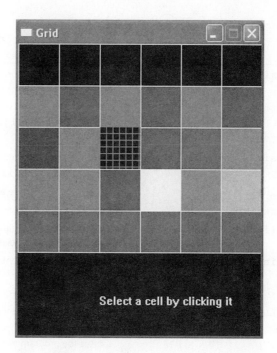

clears any left mouse button clicks that may have occurred in the past. The
`while` loop executes until the user clicks the left mouse button. The function call
`delay(100)` causes the program to pause for 100 milliseconds. Passing the predefined graphics constant `WM_LBUTTONDOWN` to the functions that process mouse clicks
causes these functions to respond to the left mouse button.

After the mouse click occurs, the statement

```
getmouseclick(WM_LBUTTONDOWN, x, y);
```

stores in (x, y) the coordinates of the pixel clicked. The statements

```
*row = y / CELL_SIZE;
*column = x / CELL_SIZE;
```

convert the pixel coordinates to row and column values, which are returned to the
main function. The `graphics` function `getpixel` returns an integer representing
the color value of the cell that was selected.

```
*color = getpixel (x, y); /* get pixel color */
```

The values of `color`, `row`, and `column` are outputs of `reportResult`.

After the return from `reportResult`, the main function adds 1 to `row` and
`column` before displaying the cell's grid position because non-programmers tend to
think of the first row of a grid as row 1 and not row 0. The following line appears in
the console window:

```
You clicked the cell in row 3, column 3
```

TABLE 7.4 Functions in `graphics` Library

Function	Effect
`drawpoly(int size, int poly[])`	Draws a closed polygon with `size` vertices. `poly[0]`, `poly[1]` are (x, y) for the first point, `poly[2]`, `poly[3]` are (x, y) for the second point, and so on. The last pair of array elements, `poly[size-2]` and `poly[size-1]`, should be the same as `poly[0]` and `poly[1]`.
`fillpoly(int size, int poly[])`	Fills the specified polygon with color and fill style as specified in the previous call to `setfillstyle`.
`int getpixel(int x, int y)`	Returns the color value at pixel (x, y).
`clearmouseclick(int)`	Clears any pending events for the argument.
`getmouseclick(int, int&, int&)`	Returns the (x, y) position of the mouse through its second and third arguments when the event specified by its first argument occurs.
`ismouseclick(int)`	Returns true if the event specified by its first argument occurs; otherwise, returns false.
`int rand()`	Returns a random integer.
`srand(time(NULL))`	Seeds the random number generator with a value based on the system clock.
`delay(int)`	Causes the program to pause for the number of milliseconds specified by the argument.

Next, the main function calls function `recolor` to draw a HATCH_FILL pattern of the same color in the cell that was clicked. Fig. 7.30 shows the grid after the user clicks the cell in row 3, column 3.

Table 7.4 shows the new functions.

 EXERCISES FOR SECTION 7.10

Self-Check

1. Sketch the polygon corresponding to the following array.

   {100, 200, 300, 400, 200, 500, 50, 300, 250, 400, 100, 200}

2. What changes would be needed to draw a grid with 10 rows and 20 columns whose cells are twice as high as they are wide?

Programming

1. Draw a polygon that is a six-sided star.
2. Draw a polygon that resembles the shape of a horse.

3. Write and test the program for Self-Check Exercise 2.
4. Modify function `drawGrid` to display a tic-tac-toe board. Use the color value RED to represent moves for player X, GREEN for player O, and the background color for unfilled cells. The moves for player X are in the middle of the first row, in the first and third cells in the second row, and in the third cell in the third row. Player O should be in the first cell in the first row, the middle cell in the second row, and in the first cell in the third row.
5. In Fig. 7.29, the main function specifies the array element values for `gridArray` when it is declared. Change the declaration so that the array values are not specified. Write and call a function `loadGrid` that loads the array by reading its element values from a data stream.

7.11 Common Programming Errors

The most common error in using arrays is a subscript-range error. An out-of-range reference occurs when the subscript value used is outside the range specified by the array declaration. For the array `celsius`,

```
int celsius[100];
```

a subscript-range error occurs when `celsius` is used with a subscript that has a value less than 0 or greater than 99. If the value of `i` is 150, a reference to the subscripted variable `celsius[i]` may cause an error message such as

```
access violation at line no. 28
```

In many situations, however, no run-time error message will be produced—the program will simply produce incorrect results. In ANSI C, the prevention of subscript-range errors is entirely the responsibility of the programmer. Subscript-range errors are not syntax errors; consequently, they will not be detected until program execution, and often not even then. They are most often caused by an incorrect subscript expression, a loop counter error, or a nonterminating loop. Before spending considerable time in debugging, you should check all suspect subscript calculations carefully for out-of-range errors. View the successive values of a subscripting variable in a debugger program, or insert diagnostic output statements that print subscript values that are of concern.

If a subscript-range error occurs inside an indexed loop, verify that the subscript is in range for both the initial and the final values of the loop control variable. If these values are in range, it is likely that all other subscript references in the loop are in range as well.

If a subscript-range error occurs in a loop controlled by a variable other than the array subscript, check that the loop control variable is being updated as required. If it is not, the loop may be repeated more often than expected, causing the subscript-range error. This error could happen if the control variable update step was inside a condition or was inadvertently omitted.

When using arrays as arguments to functions, be careful not to apply the address-of operator to the array name even if the array is an output argument. However, do remember to use the & on an array *element* that is being passed as an output argument.

Be sure to use the correct forms for declaring array input and output parameters in function prototypes. Remember when reading C code that a pointer parameter declared as

```
int *z
```

could represent a single integer output parameter or an integer array parameter. Comment your own prototypes carefully and use the alternate declaration form

```
int z[]
```

for array parameters to assist readers of your code.

If you are working on a computer system with very limited memory, you may find that some correct C programs generate run-time error messages indicating an access violation. The use of arrays can cause a program to require large amounts of memory for function data areas. The portion of memory set aside for function data areas is called the *stack*. You may need to tell your operating system that an increased stack size is necessary in order to be able to run programs using large arrays.

When you define enumerated types, remember that only identifiers can appear in the list of values (enumeration constants) for the type. Be careful not to reuse one of these identifiers in another type or as a variable name in a function that needs your type definition. Keep in mind that there is no built-in facility for input/output of the identifiers that are the valid values of an enumerated type. You must either scan and display the underlying integer representation or write your own input/output functions. Remember that C does not verify the validity of integers stored in enumerated type variables—that is the programmer's responsibility.

Chapter Review

1. A data structure is a grouping of related data items in memory.
2. An array is a data structure used to store a collection of data items of the same type.
3. An individual array element is referenced by placing immediately after the array name a square-bracketed subscript for each dimension.
4. The initial element of a one-dimensional array x is referenced as x[0]. If x has *n* elements, the final element is referenced as x[n-1].
5. An indexed `for` loop whose counter runs from 0 to one less than an array's size enables us to reference all the elements of a one-dimensional array in sequence by using the loop counter as the array subscript. Nested `for` loops provide sequential access to multidimensional array elements.

6. For an array declared as a local variable, space is allocated in the function data area for all the array elements.
7. For an array declared as a function parameter, space is allocated in the function data area for only a pointer to the initial element of the actual argument passed.
8. The name of an array with no subscript always refers to the address of the initial array element: that is, it is a pointer.
9. A function that creates an array result should require the calling module to pass an output argument array in which to store the result.
10. Defining an enumerated type requires listing the identifiers that are the values of the type. Each value is represented by an integer. Using enumerated types makes programs more readable because the type's values are meaningful for a particular application.

NEW C CONSTRUCTS

Example	Effect
Array Operations	
Local Variables	
```double data[30];``` ```int matrix[2][3];```	Allocates storage for 30 type `double` items in array `data` (`data[0]`, `data[1]`, ..., `data[29]`), and six type `int` items (2 rows of 3 columns) in two-dimensional array `matrix` (`matrix[0][0]`, `matrix[0][1]`, `matrix[0][2]`, `matrix[1][0]`, `matrix[1][1]`, `matrix[1][2]`).
Initialization	
```char vowels[5] =``` ``` {'A', 'E', 'I', 'O', 'U'};```	Allocates storage for five type `char` items in array `vowels` and initializes the array contents: `vowels[0]='A'`, `vowels[1]='E'`, ... `vowels[4]='U'`.
```int id[2][2] =``` ``` { {1, 0}, {0, 1} };```	Allocates four locations for the 2 × 2 matrix `id`, initializing the storage so `id[0][0]=1`, `id[0][1]=0`, `id[1][0]=0`, and `id[1][1]=1`.
Input Parameter	

```void```
```print_alpha(const char alpha[],```
```   const int m[],```
```   int   a_size,```
```   int   m_size)```
```   or```
```. . . (const char *alpha, . . .```
	States that function `print_alpha` uses arrays `alpha` and `m` as input parameters only— `print_alpha` will not change their contents.

(continued)

NEW C CONSTRUCTS (continued)

Example	Effect

Output or Input/Output Parameter
`void`
`fill(int nums[], int n)`
or
`fill(int *nums, int n)`
	States that function `fill` can both look at and modify the actual argument *array* passed to `nums`.

Array References `if (data[0] < 39.8)`	Compares value of initial element of array `data` to `39.8`.
`for  (i = 0; i < 30; ++i)` `    data[i] /= 2.0;`	Divides each element of array `data` by 2, changing the array contents.

`for  (i = 0; i < 2; ++i) {`
`    for (j = 0; j < 3; ++j)`
`        printf("%6d", matrix[i] [j]);`
`    printf("\n");`
`}`
	Displays contents of `matrix` in 2 rows with 3 columns.

Enumerated Type Definition
`typedef enum`
`    {keyboard, mouse, microphone,`
`     laser, scanner, synthesizer}`
`periph_t;`
	An enumerated type `periph_t` is defined with values `keyboard`, `mouse`, `microphone`, `laser`, `scanner`, and `synthesizer`. Values will be represented by integers 0 (`keyboard`) through 5 (`synthesizer`).

Enumeration Variable Declaration and Assignment
`periph_t peripheral;`
`peripheral = scanner;`
	Variable `peripheral` can represent any of the `periph_t` enumeration constants. Integer 4 is stored in `peripheral`, representing value `scanner`.

Quick-Check Exercises

1. What is a data structure?

2. Of what data type are array subscripting expressions?

3. Can two elements of the same array be of different data types?

4. If an array is declared to have ten elements, must the program use all ten?

5. The two methods of array access are called _____ and _____.

6. A(n) _____ loop allows us to access easily the elements of an array in _____ order.

7. What is the difference in the use of array b that is implied by these two prototypes?

```
int fun_one(int b[], n)    ;
int fun_two(const int b[], n);
```

8. Look again at the prototypes in Exercise 7. Why does neither array declaration indicate a size?

9. Let nums be an array of 5 type int locations. Describe how the following loop works.

```
product = 1;  i = 0;
for (value = scanf("%d", &n);
      value  == 1  && i < 5;
      value = scanf("%d", &n))
  product *= value; nums[i++] = product;
```

10. How many elements does array p have? Show how you would reference each one.

```
int p[3][2];
```

11. If p is an array declared

```
double p[100];
```

and you see a function call such as

```
sort_items(p, 100);
```

can you tell what operations would be performed on p?

12. Consider this enumerated type definition:

```
typedef enum
        {variables, keywords, constants, headers, loops}
class_t;
```

What is the value of each of the following?

a.   (class_t)4
b.   (int)variables
c.   (class_t)(7 - (int)headers)

What is displayed by this code fragment?

```
for (class = loops; class > variables; --class)
    printf("%d ", class);
printf("\t");
```

Answers to Quick-Check Exercises

1. A data structure is a grouping of related values in main memory.
2. type `int`
3. no
4. no
5. sequential, random
6. indexed, sequential
7. In `fun_one`, `b` can be used as an output parameter or as an input/output parameter. In `fun_two`, `b` is strictly an input parameter array.
8. The size of `b` is not needed because the function does not allocate storage for copying parameter arrays. Only the starting address of the actual argument array will be stored in the formal parameter.
9. As long as `scanf` continues to return a value of 1, unless the subscript i is >5, the loop body will update the product variable, and store the value of the product in the next element of `nums`, and will increment the loop counter. The loop exits on EOF (`scanf` returns a negative value e), on invalid data, or on i no longer being less than 5.
10. p has six elements: `p[0][0]`, `p[0][1]`, `p[1][0]`, `p[1][1]`, `p[2][0]`, `p[2][1]`.
11. By looking at the function call `sort_items`, you can tell that the items of the array will be sorted as the offset of the array and the size of the array have been passed as arguments in the function call.
12. a. `loops`
    b. `0`
    c. `loops`

    `4 3 2 1 0`

Review Questions

1. Identify an error in the following C statements:

```
int p[12], i;
for  (i = 12; i > 0; --i)
    p[i] = i * i;
```

Will the error be detected? If so, when?

2. Declare an array of type `integer` values called `months` that can be referenced by using any month of the year as a subscript, where 0 represents January, 1 represents February, and so on.

3. The statement marked /* this one */ in the following code is valid. True or false?

```
int counts[20], i;
/* Prompt the user for the even integer */
printf("Enter an even integer between 1 and 20> ");
scanf("%d", &i);
counts[20] = i; /* this one */
counts[i] = 1;
```

4. What are the two common ways of selecting array elements for processing?

5. Write a C program segment to display the index of the smallest and the largest numbers in an array x of 20 integers. Assume array x already has values assigned to each element.

6. Write a C function called reverse that takes an array named x as an input parameter and an array named y as an output parameter. A third function parameter is n, the number of values in x. The function should copy the integers in x into y but in reverse order (i.e., y[0] gets x[n - 1], ... y[n - 1] gets x[0]).

7. Write a program segment to display the sum of the values in each row of a 5×3 type double array named table. How many row sums will be displayed? How many elements are included in each sum?

8. Answer Review Question 7 for the column sums.

9. Write a function for displaying (as a string) a value of enumerated type season_t:

```
typedef enum
       {winter, spring, summer, fall}
season_t;
```

Programming Projects

1. Write a program to grade an n-question multiple-choice exam (for n between 5 and 50) and provide feedback about the most frequently missed questions. Your program will take data from the file examdat.txt. The first line of the file contains the number of questions on the exam followed by a space and then an n-character string of the correct answers. Write a function fgetAnswers that inputs the answers from an open input file. Each of the lines that follow contain an integer student ID followed by a space and then that student's answers. Function fgetAnswers can also be called to input a student's answers. Your program is to produce an output file, report.txt, containing the answer key, each student's ID, and each student's score as a percentage,

and then information about how many students missed each question. Here are short sample input and output files.

examdat.txt
```
5 dbbac
111 dabac
102 dcbdc
251 dbbac
```

report.txt
```
          Exam Report
Question  1 2 3 4 5
Answer    d b b a c

 ID   Score(%)
111      80
102      60
251     100

Question  1 2 3 4 5
Missed by 0 2 0 1 0
```

2. If n points are connected to form a closed polygon as shown below, the area A of the polygon can be computed as

$$A = \frac{1}{2} \left| \sum_{i=0}^{n-2} \left(x_{i+1} + x_i \right) \left(y_{i+1} - y_i \right) \right|$$

Notice that although the illustrated polygon has only six distinct corners, n for this polygon is 7 because the algorithm expects that the last point, (x_6, y_6), will be a repeat of the initial point, (x_0, y_0).

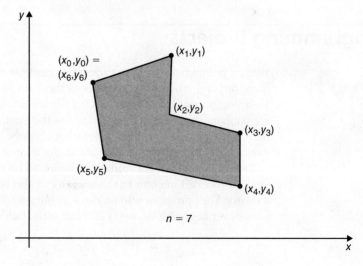

Represent the (x, y) coordinates of the connected points as two arrays of at most 20 type double values. For one of your tests, use the following data set, which defines a polygon whose area is 25.5 square units.

x	y
4	0
4	7.5
7	7.5
7	3
9	0
7	0
4	0

Implement the following functions:

get_corners—Takes as parameters an input file, arrays x and y, and the arrays' maximum size. Fills the arrays with data from the file (ignoring any data that would overflow the arrays) and returns as the function value the number of (x, y) coordinates stored in the arrays.

output_corners—Takes as parameters an output file and two type double arrays of the same size and their actual size, and outputs to the file the contents of the two arrays in two columns.

polygon_area—Takes as parameters two arrays representing the (x, y) coordinates of the corners of a closed polygon and their actual size and returns as the function value the area of the closed polygon.

3. A point mass consists of a 3-D location and an associated mass, such as

Location: $(6, 0, -2)$ Mass: 3g

In a system of point masses, let $p_1, p_2,...p_n$ be the n 3-D points and $m_1, m_2,...m_n$ be their associated masses. If m is the sum of the masses, the center of gravity C is calculated as

$$C = \frac{1}{m}(m_1p_1 + m_2p_2 + \cdots + m_np_n)$$

Write a program that repeatedly inputs point-mass system data sets from an input file until an input operation fails. For each data set, display the location matrix, the mass vector, n, and the center of gravity.

Each data set includes a location matrix (a matrix in which each row is a point), a one-dimensional array of masses, and the number of point masses, n.

Allow *n* to vary from 3 to 10.

Sample Data File

```
4
5    -4    3    2
4     3   -2    5
-4   -3   -1    2
-9    8    6    1
```

This sample should be stored as:

```
location   5   -4    3
           4    3   -2
          -4   -3   -1
          -9    8    6
mass       2
           5
           2
           1
n          4
```

Your main function should repeatedly input and process data sets from an input file until end of file is encountered. For each point-mass system data set, display the location matrix, the mass vector, *n*, and the center of gravity. Implement at least the following functions:

fget_point_mass: Takes an open input file and a maximum value for *n* as parameters and fills a two-dimensional array output parameter with a location matrix and a one-dimensional array output parameter with a mass vector from the data file. Returns as function value the actual value of *n*.

center_grav: Takes a location matrix, mass vector, and *n* value as parameters, and calculates and returns as the function value the center of gravity of the system.

fwrite_point_mass: Takes an open output file and the location matrix, mass vector, and *n* value of a point-mass system as parameters and writes the system to the file with meaningful labels.

4. There are several different types of searching algorithms, but each one has its own specific application and may not be equally suitable for other applications. The size of the array on which the search is to be performed also matters when choosing an appropriate searching algorithm. Which is the most efficient method of searching for an element when the array size is very small? Write a C program for using the same method to search for an element from a very small array of integers. Make up your own data, and be sure to test your program on at least one data set. If the element being searched for is not found in the array, display an appropriate message to the user.

5. A barcode scanner for Universal Product Codes (UPCs) verifies the 12-digit code scanned by comparing the code's last digit (called a *check digit*) to its own computation of the check digit from the first 11 digits as follows:

1. Calculate the sum of the digits in the odd-numbered positions (the first, third, …, eleventh digits) and multiply this sum by 3.

2. Calculate the sum of the digits in the even-numbered positions (the second, fourth, …, tenth digits) and add this to the previous result.

3. If the last digit of the result from step 2 is 0, then 0 is the check digit. Otherwise, subtract the last digit from 10 to calculate the check digit.

4. If the check digit matches the final digit of the 12-digit UPC, the UPC is assumed correct.

Write a program that prompts the user to enter the 12 digits of a barcode separated by spaces. The program should store the digits in an integer array, calculate the check digit, and compare it to the final barcode digit. If the digits match, output the barcode with the message "validated." If not, output the barcode with the message "error in barcode." Also, output with labels the results from steps 1 and 2 of the check-digit calculations. Note that the "first" digit of the barcode will be stored in element 0 of the array. Try your program on the following barcodes, three of which are valid. For the first barcode, the result from step 2 is 79 $(0 + 9 + 0 + 8 + 4 + 0) * 3 + (7 + 4 + 0 + 0 + 5)$.

```
0 7 9 4 0 0 8 0 4 5 0 1
0 2 4 0 0 0 1 6 2 8 6 0
0 1 1 1 1 0 8 5 6 8 0 7
0 5 1 0 0 0 1 3 8 1 0 1
```

6. Write a C program that prints the following output:

	6	7	8	9	10
6	36	42	48	54	60
7	42	49	56	63	70
8	48	56	64	72	80
9	54	63	72	81	90
10	60	70	80	90	100

7. You are creating software to assist the State Justice Department in calculating the recidivism rate of adult offenders. This rate is calculated as the percent of offenders re-arrested within three years (36 months) of their date of release from prison. You are to create a `recidivism` function that takes as input parameters five parallel arrays containing offender IDs (numeric), the release dates represented as month and year numbers, and rearrest dates represented as month and year numbers or as zeros if the offender has not been re-arrested. The function's sixth input parameter is the number of offender records in the arrays. For example, if your function received the data from the table below, it

would report a recidivism rate of 28.6%. Although three of the seven offenders were rearrested, only two were rearrested within the 3-year period counted in this statistic.

Offender ID	Month of Release	Year of Release	Month of Rearrest	Year of Rearrest
91152	10	2009	11	2012
83347	2	2012	0	0
60291	7	2011	9	2011
55520	8	2013	0	0
48275	6	2010	7	2013
36925	3	2009	0	0
76477	4	2013	0	0

Your main function should prompt the user to enter the name of a file containing the offender records. It should open the file and call a function to load the data into the five arrays, call a second function to display the data entered, and then call the recidivism function. Display the rate returned as a percentage with one decimal place. You may assume there are no more than 20 offender records, but use a constant macro to represent this number so it would be easy to modify your program to accommodate a far larger database.

8. Generate a table that indicates the rainfall for the city of Plainview and compares the current year's rainfall for the city with the rainfall from the previous year. Display some summary statistics that will indicate both the annual rainfall for each year and the average monthly rainfall for each year. The input data will consist of 12 pairs of numbers. The first number in each pair will be the current year's rainfall for a month, and the second number will be what fell during the same month the previous year. The first data pair will represent January, the second will be February, and so forth. If you assume the data begin

```
3.2    4      (for January)
2.2    1.6    (for February)
```

the output should resemble the following:

```
                Table of monthly rainfall
                  January       February      March . . .
This year           3.2           2.2
Last year           4.0           1.6
Total rainfall this year:       35.7
Total rainfall last year:       42.8
Average monthly rainfall for this year:    3.6
Average monthly rainfall for last year:    4.0
```

9. Write an interactive program that plays a game of hangman. Store the word to be guessed in successive elements of an array of individual characters called word. The player must guess the letters belonging to word. The program should terminate when either all letters have been guessed correctly (the player wins) or a specified number of incorrect guesses have been made (the computer wins). *Hint:* Use another array, guessed, to keep track of the solution so far. Initialize all elements of guessed to the '*' symbol. Each time a letter in word is guessed, replace the corresponding '*' in guessed with that letter.

10. The results from the mayor's race have been reported by each precinct as follows:

Precinct	Candidate A	Candidate B	Candidate C	Candidate D
1	192	48	206	37
2	147	90	312	21
3	186	12	121	38
4	114	21	408	39
5	267	13	382	29

Write a program to do the following:

a. Display the table with appropriate labels for the rows and columns.

b. Compute and display the total number of votes received by each candidate and the percentage of the total votes cast.

c. If any one candidate received over 50% of the votes, the program should display a message declaring that candidate the winner.

d. If no candidate received 50% of the votes, the program should display a message declaring a runoff between the two candidates receiving the highest number of votes; the two candidates should be identified by their letter names.

e. Run the program once with the data shown and once with candidate C receiving only 108 votes in Precinct 4.

11. Write a function that will merge the contents of two sorted (ascending order) arrays of type double values, storing the result in an array output parameter (still in ascending order). The function should not assume that both its input parameter arrays are the same length but can assume that one array does not contain two copies of the same value. The result array should also contain no duplicate values.

Hint: When one of the input arrays has been exhausted, do not forget to copy the remaining data in the other array into the result array. Test your function with cases in which (1) the first array is exhausted first, (2) the second array

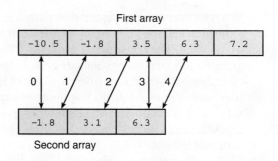

is exhausted first, and (3) the two arrays are exhausted at the same time (i.e., they end with the same value). Remember that the arrays input to this function *must already be sorted*.

12. The *binary search* algorithm that follows may be used to search an array when the elements are in order. This algorithm is analogous to the following approach for finding a name in a telephone book.

a.   Open the book in the middle, and look at the middle name on the page.

b.   If the middle name isn't the one you're looking for, decide whether it comes before or after the name you want.

c.   Take the appropriate half of the section of the book you were looking in and repeat these steps until you land on the name.

ALGORITHM FOR BINARY SEARCH

1. Let `bottom` be the subscript of the initial array element.
2. Let `top` be the subscript of the last array element.
3. Let `found` be false.
4. Repeat as long as `bottom` isn't greater than `top` and the target has not been found
    5.   Let `middle` be the subscript of the element halfway between `bottom` and `top`.
    6.   if the element at `middle` is the target
            7.   Set `found` to true and `index` to `middle`.
         else if the element at `middle` is larger than the target
            8.   Let `top` be `middle - 1`.
         else
            9.   Let `bottom` be `middle + 1`.

Write and test a function `binary_srch` that implements this algorithm for an array of integers. When there is a large number of array elements, which function do you think is faster: `binary_srch` or the linear search function of Fig. 7.14?

13. The *selection sort* is one of several techniques for sorting an array. A selection sort compares every element of an array with all the other elements of the array and exchanges their values if they are out of order. After the first pass of a selection sort, the first array element is in the correct position; after the second pass the first two elements of the array are in the correct position, and so on. Thus, after each pass of a selection sort, the unsorted portion of the array contains one less element. Write and test a function that implements this sorting method.

14. A C program can represent a real polynomial $p(x)$ of degree n as an array of the real coefficients $a_0, a_1, \ldots, a_n$ ($a_n \neq 0$).

$$p(x) = a_0 + a_1 x + a_2 x^2 + \cdots + a_n x^n$$

Write a program that inputs a polynomial of maximum degree 8 and then evaluates the polynomial at various values of x. Include a function `get_poly` that fills the array of coefficients and sets the degree of the polynomial, and a function `eval_poly` that evaluates a polynomial at a given value of x. Use these function prototypes:

```
void get_poly( double coeff[], int* degreep );
double eval_poly( const double coeff[], int degree,
                  double x );
```

15. Peabody Public Utilities tracks the status of its power service throughout the city with a 3 × 4 grid in which each cell represents power service in one sector. When power is available everywhere, all grid values are 1. A grid value of 0 indicates an outage somewhere in the sector.

   Write a program that inputs a grid from a file and displays the grid. If all grid values are 1, display the message

```
Power is on throughout grid.
```

Otherwise, list the sectors that have outages:

```
Power is off in sectors:
     (0,0)
     (1,2)
```

Include in your program functions `get_grid`, `display_grid`, `power_ok`, and `where_off`. Function `power_ok` returns true (1) if power is on in all sectors, false (0) otherwise. Function `where_off` should display the message regarding sectors experiencing outages.

16. Use matrix subtraction to calculate how much longer was the life expectancy of black and white women than men of the same races in each decade from year 1950 to year 2000. There is no need to store the year data in your matrices—just provide the years in the output. Input each matrix from a separate data file, calculate the matrix difference by calling a function you write called `matrix_diff` that will subtract any two 6-by-2 matrices, producing a third 6-by-2 matrix.

Display all three matrices with appropriate labels. Your function should calculate the matrix difference by subtracting each element of the second matrix from the corresponding element of the first.

United States Life Expectancy at Birth by Sex and Race

	Female			Male	
Year	Black	White	Year	Black	White
1950	62.9	72.2	1950	59.1	66.5
1960	66.3	74.1	1960	61.1	67.4
1970	68.3	75.6	1970	60.0	68.0
1980	72.5	78.1	1980	63.8	70.7
1990	73.6	79.4	1990	64.5	72.7
2000	75.2	80.1	2000	68.3	74.9

Source: National Center for Health Statistics

Strings

CHAPTER OBJECTIVES

- To understand how a string constant is stored in an array of characters

- To learn about the placeholder `%s` and how it is used in `printf` and `scanf` operations

- To learn some of the operations that can be performed on strings such as copying strings, extracting substrings, and joining strings using functions from the library `string`

- To understand the buffer overflow dangers inherent in some string library functions

- To learn how C compares two strings to determine their relative order

- To see some of the operations that can be performed on individual characters using functions from the library `ctype`

- To learn how to write your own functions that perform some of the basic operations of a text editor program

- To understand basic principles of defensive programming

So far, we have seen limited use of character data because most applications that process character data deal with a grouping of characters, a data structure called a *string*. Because C implements the string data structure using arrays of type `char`, we could not explore strings until we had a foundational understanding of arrays.

Strings are important in computer science because many computer applications are concerned with the manipulation of textual data rather than numerical data. Computer-based *word processing systems* enable a user to compose letters, term papers, newspaper articles, and even books at a computer instead of at a typewriter. Storing the text in the computer's memory allows us to modify the text, check the spelling electronically, move whole paragraphs, and then print a fresh copy without mistakes or erasures.

Strings play an important role in science as well. The chemist works with elements and compounds whose names often combine alphabetic and numeric characters (e.g., $C_{12}H_{22}O_{11}$)—data easily represented by a string. Molecular biologists identify amino acids by name and map our DNA with strings of amino acid abbreviations. Many mathematicians, physicists, and engineers spend more time modeling our world with equations (strings of character and numeric data) than they do crunching numbers. In subsequent chapters, we will meet other representations of some of these concepts that are more easily manipulated than the string model; however, we will still need strings as the vehicle for communication between the computer system and the human user.

In the sections that follow, we will introduce some fundamental operations that can be performed on character data. We will investigate selected functions from the standard string and ctype libraries that provide most of C's facilities for working with character strings.

8.1 String Basics

We have already used string constants extensively in our earlier work. Indeed, every one of our calls to `scanf` or `printf` used a string constant as the first argument. Consider this call:

```
printf("Average = %.2f", avg);
```

The first argument is the string constant `"Average = %.2f"`, a string of 14 characters. Notice that the blanks in the string are characters just as valid as those requiring ink! Like other constant values, a string constant can be associated with a symbolic name using the `#define` directive.

```
#define ERR_PREFIX    "*****Error - "
#define INSUFF_DATA   "Insufficient Data"
```

Declaring and Initializing String Variables

As we mentioned earlier, a string in C is implemented as an array, so declaring a string variable is the same as declaring an array of type `char`. In

```
char string_var[30];
```

the variable `string_var` will hold strings from 0 to 29 characters long. It is C's handling of this varying length characteristic that distinguishes the string data structure from other arrays. C permits initialization of string variables using a string constant as shown in the following declaration of `str`.

```
char str[20] = "Initial value";
```

Let's look at `str` in memory after this declaration with initialization.

[0]				[4]					[9]					[14]					[19]
I	n	i	t	i	a	l		v	a	l	u	e	\0	?	?	?	?	?	?

null character
character '\0' that
marks the end of a
string in C

Notice that `str[13]` contains the character `'\0'`, the **null character** that marks the end of a string. Using this marker allows the string's length within the character array to vary from 0 to one less than the array's declared size. All of C's string-handling functions simply ignore whatever is stored in the cells following the null character. The following diagram shows `str` holding a string that is the longest it can represent—19 characters plus the null character.

[0]				[4]					[9]					[14]					[19]
n	u	m	b	e	r	s		a	n	d		s	t	r	i	n	g	s	\0

Arrays of Strings

Because one string is an array of characters, an array of strings is a two-dimensional array of characters in which each row is one string. The following are statements to declare an array to store up to 30 names, each of which is less than 25 characters long.

```
#define NUM_PEOPLE 30
#define NAME_LEN 25
    . . .
char names[NUM_PEOPLE][NAME_LEN];
```

We can initialize an array of strings at declaration in the following manner:

```
char month[12][10] = {"January", "February", "March", "April",
                      "May", "June", "July", "August",
                      "September", "October", "November",
                      "December"};
```

Input/Output with printf and scanf

Both `printf` and `scanf` can handle string arguments as long as the placeholder `%s` is used in the format string:

```
printf("Topic: %s\n", string_var);
```

The `printf` function, like other standard library functions that take string arguments, depends on finding a null character in the character array to mark the end of the string. If `printf` were passed a character array that contained no `'\0'`, the function would first interpret the contents of each array element as a character and display it. Then `printf` would continue to display as characters the contents of memory locations following the array argument until it encountered a null character or until it attempted to access a memory cell that was not assigned to the program, causing a run-time error. When we write our own string-building functions, we must be sure that a null character is inserted at the end of every string. This inclusion of the null character is automatic for constant strings.

The `%s` placeholder in a `printf` format string can be used with a minimum field width as shown.

```
printf ("***%8s***%3s***\n", "Short", "Strings");
```

The first string is displayed right-justified in a field of eight columns. The second string is longer than the specified field width, so the field is expanded to accommodate it exactly with no padding. We are more accustomed to seeing lists of strings printed left-justified rather than right-justified. Consider the two lists in Fig. 8.1.

Placing a minus sign prefix on a placeholder's field width causes left justification of the value displayed. If `president` is a string variable, repeated execution of this call to `printf` will produce a left-justified list.

```
printf("%-20s\n", president);
```

The `scanf` function can be used for input of a string. However, when we call `scanf` with a string variable as an argument, we must remember that array output arguments are *always* passed to functions by sending the address of the initial array element. Therefore, we do not apply the address-of operator to a string argument passed to `scanf` or to any other function. In Fig. 8.2, we see a brief main function performing string I/O with `scanf` and `printf`. In this program, the user is expected to type in a string representing an academic department, an integer course code, a

FIGURE 8.1

Right and Left
Justification of
Strings

Right-Justified	Left-Justified
George Washington	George Washington
John Adams	John Adams
Thomas Jefferson	Thomas Jefferson
James Madison	James Madison

string abbreviation for the days of the week the course meets, and an integer that gives the meeting time of the class.

The approach `scanf` takes to string input is very similar to its processing of numeric input. As shown in Fig. 8.3, when it scans a string, `scanf` skips leading whitespace characters such as blanks, newlines, and tabs. Starting with the first nonwhitespace character, `scanf` copies the characters it encounters into successive memory cells of its character array argument. When it comes across a whitespace

FIGURE 8.2 String Input/Output with scanf and printf

```
1.  #include <stdio.h>
2.
3.  #define STRING_LEN   10
4.
5.  int
6.  main(void)
7.  {
8.       char dept[STRING_LEN];
9.       int  course_num;
10.      char days[STRING_LEN];
11.      int  time;
12.
13.      printf("Enter department code, course number, days and ");
14.      printf("time like this:\n> COSC 2060 MWF 1410\n> ");
15.      scanf("%s%d%s%d", dept, &course_num, days, &time);
16.      printf("%s %d meets %s at %d\n", dept, course_num, days, time);
17.
18.      return (0);
19.  }

Enter department code, course number, days and time like this:
> COSC 2060 MWF 1410
> MATH 1270 TR 800
MATH 1270 meets TR at 800
```

FIGURE 8.3

Execution of `scanf`
(`"%s"`, `dept`);

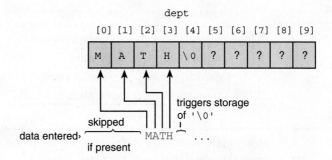

character, scanning stops, and `scanf` places the null character at the end of the string in its array argument.

Because of the way `scanf` treats whitespace, the values could be spaced on the data lines in many ways that would result in variables `dept`, `course_num`, `days`, and `time` receiving correct values upon execution of the `scanf` call in Fig. 8.2. For example, the data could have been entered one value per line with extra whitespace:

```
>      MATH
 1270
    TR
                        1800
```

or two values per line:

```
> MATH 1270
  TR 1800
```

Function `scanf` would have difficulty if some essential whitespace between values were omitted or if a nonwhitespace separator were substituted. For example, if the data were entered as

```
> MATH1270 TR 1800
```

`scanf` would store the eight-character string `"MATH1270"` in `dept` and would then be unable to convert `T` to an integer for storage using the next parameter. The situation would be worse if the data were entered as

```
> MATH,1270,TR,1800
```

Then the `scanf` function would store the entire 17-character string plus `'\0'` in the `dept` array, causing characters to be stored in eight locations not allocated to `dept`, as shown in Fig. 8.4.

buffer overflow
more data is stored
in an array than its
declared size allows

This is an example of a **buffer overflow** error, a very dangerous condition that is unlikely to be flagged as an error by either the compiler or the run-time system.

For easy input of predictable-length strings that have no internal blanks, `scanf` with the `%s` placeholder works well. However, in an environment in which the

FIGURE 8.4 Execution of `scanf("%s%d%s%d", dept, &course_num, days, &time);` on Entry of Invalid Data

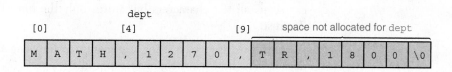

proper data entry format may not be observed or where even an occasional program fault is critical, a more robust string input function should be used. We will write one such function in Section 8.3.

EXAMPLE 8.1

Earlier in this chapter, we declared an array of strings suitable for holding 30 names (a two-dimensional array of type `char` values). Let's see how to use `scanf` and `printf` to fill this array and echo print it.

You will recall from our study of arrays that no address-of operator is needed when an array is passed as an output argument. Because each element `names[i]` of an array of strings represents a kind of array, it is passed as an output argument without using the `&` operator. The following code segment fills parallel arrays `names` and `ages` with data. In the call to `scanf`, note the contrasting application of the `&` operator to elements of the `ages` array since these elements are simple output arguments of type `int`.

```c
#define NUM_PEOPLE 30
#define NAME_LEN 25
   . . .
char names[NUM_PEOPLE][NAME_LEN];

for (i = 0;   i < NUM_PEOPLE;   ++i) {
    scanf("%s%d", names[i], &ages[i]);
    printf("%-35s %3d\n", names[i], ages[i]);
}
```

EXERCISES FOR SECTION 8.1

Self-Check

1. When the `scanf` function is scanning a string, if there is more input data (with no blanks) than will fit in the array output argument, `scanf` _____ (choose one).

    a. copies in only the characters that will fit and ignores the rest.

    b. copies in the whole string overflowing the output argument because `scanf` has no way of knowing the array's declared size.

    c. scans all the characters but stores only the ones that fit, discarding the rest.

2. When `printf` is given a string argument to print using a `%s` placeholder, how does it know how many characters to print?

3. Declare a 30-character array, and initialize it at declaration to a string of 29 blanks.

Programming

1. Write a program that takes a word less than 25 characters long and prints a statement like this:

```
fractal starts with the letter f
```

Have the program process words until it encounters a "word" beginning with the character `'9'`.

8.2 String Library Functions: Assignment and Substrings

We have become accustomed to using the assignment operator = to copy data into a variable. Although we do use the assignment symbol in a declaration of a string variable with initialization, this context is the *only* one in which the operator means to copy the string that is the right operand into the variable that is the left operand. We have seen that an array name with no subscript is an address, a pointer to the initial array element. This address is constant and cannot be changed through assignment, so the following code fragment will cause a compiler error message such as `Invalid target of assignment`:

```
char one_str[20];
one_str = "Test string";      /* Does not work */
```

    C provides the string assignment operation in the same way that it provides square root and absolute value operations—through library functions. Along with assignment functions, the library `string.h` provides functions for substring, concatenation, string length, string comparison, and whole line input operations, to name a few. Table 8.1 summarizes selected functions from `string.h`, and Appendix B presents the complete library. Notice that the data type of the value returned by each string-building function is the pointer type `char *`. As always, an array is being represented by a pointer, the address of its initial value.

TABLE 8.1 Some String Library Functions from string.h

Function	Purpose: Example	Parameters	Result Type	
strcpy	Makes a copy of source, a string, in the character array accessed by dest: strcpy(s1, "hello");	char *dest const char *source	char *	`h e l l o \0 ? ? ...`
strncpy	Makes a copy of up to n characters from source in dest: strncpy(s2, "inevitable", 5) stores the first five characters of the source in s1 and does NOT add a null character.	char *dest const char *source size_t n	char *	`i n e v i ? ? ...`
strcat	Appends source to the end of dest: strcat(s1, "and more");	char *dest const char *source	char *	`h e l l o a n d m o r e \0`
strncat	Appends up to n characters of source to the end of dest, adding the null character if necessary: strncat(s1, "and more", 5);	char *dest const char *source size_t n	char *	`h e l l o a n d m \0 ?`
strcmp	Compares s1 and s2 alphabetically; returns a negative value if s1 should precede s2, a zero if the strings are equal, and a positive value if s2 should precede s1 in an alphabetized list: if (strcmp(name1, name2) == 0)	const char *s1 const char *s2	int	
strncmp	Compares the first n characters of s1 and s2 returning positive, zero, and negative values as does strcmp: if (strncmp(n1, n2, 12) == 0)	const char *s1 const char *s2 size_t n	int	
strlen	Returns the number of characters in s, not counting the terminating null: strlen("what") returns 4.	const char *s	size_t	
strtok	Breaks parameter string source into tokens by finding groups of characters separated by any of the delimiter characters in delim. First call must provide both source and delim. Subsequent calls using NULL as the source string find additional tokens in original source. Alters source by replacing first delimiter following a token by '\0'. When no more delimiters remain, returns rest of source. For example, if s1 is "Jan.12,1842", strtok(s1,".,") returns "Jan", then strtok (NULL,".,") returns "12" and strtok(NULL,".,") returns "1842". The memory in the right column shows the altered s1 after the three calls to strtok. Return values are pointers to substrings of s1 rather than copies.	const char *source const char *delim	char *	`J a n \0 1 2 \0 1 8 4 2 \0`

size_t is an unsigned integer

Functions whose names are in color change a string value, but do not take a parameter indicating the size of the destination string or the size of the string to copy, and therefore do not provide the programmer with a means of preventing buffer overflow.

String Assignment

Function `strcpy` copies the string that is its second argument into its first argument. To carry out the desired assignment shown in our faulty code above, we would write

```
strcpy(one_str, "Test String");
```

Like a call to `scanf` with a `%s` placeholder, a call to `strcpy` can easily overflow the space allocated for the destination variable (`one_str` in the example given). Variable `one_str` has room for up to 19 characters plus the null character. This call to `strcpy`

```
strcpy(one_str, "A very long test string");
```

would overflow `one_str`, storing the final characters `'i'`, `'n'`, `'g'`, and `'\0'` in memory allocated for other variables. The values of these other variables would seem to change spontaneously. On rare occasions, such overflow would generate a run-time error message.

The string library provides another string-copying function named `strncpy` that takes an argument specifying the number of characters to copy (call this number n). If the string to be copied (the source string) is shorter than n characters, the remaining characters stored are null. For example,

```
strncpy(one_str, "Test string", 20);
```

would give `one_str` the value:

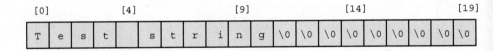

The net effect is the same as the call

```
strcpy(one_str, "Test string");
```

since any characters after the first null are ignored. However, when the source string is longer than n characters, only the first n characters are copied.

```
strncpy(one_str, "A very long test string", 20);
```

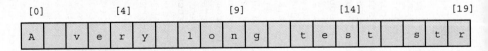

Notice that although this call to `strncpy` has prevented overflow of destination string `one_str`, it has not stored a valid string in `one_str`: There is no terminating

'\0'. In general, one can assign as much as will fit of a source string (source) to a destination (dest) of length dest_len by using these two statements:

```
strncpy(dest, source, dest_len - 1);
dest[dest_len - 1] = '\0';
```

Both strcpy and strncpy mimic the assignment operator in that the value they return is the string assigned (specifically, the copy that is in the destination variable). The calling function actually has two ways of referencing the results: It can either use the first argument from the call or use the function result. This characteristic is typical of string-building functions in the string library.

Substrings

substring a fragment of a longer string

We frequently need to reference a **substring** of a longer character string. For example, we might want to examine the "Cl" in the string "NaCl", or the "30" in the string "Jan. 30, 1996". We have already seen that function strncpy can be used to extract the first *n* characters of a string. Considering how strncpy works will give us insight into how we could also use this function to copy a middle or an ending portion of a string. Assuming that the prototype of strncpy is

```
char *strncpy(char *dest, const char *source, size_t n);
```

Fig. 8.5 depicts the data areas of strncpy and the calling function just before the return from the call to strncpy in this code fragment:

```
char result[10], s1[15] = "Jan. 30, 1996";
strncpy(result, s1, 9);
result[9] = '\0';
```

FIGURE 8.5

Execution of
strncpy(result,
s1, 9);

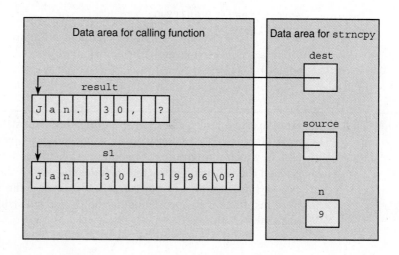

FIGURE 8.6

Execution of
`strncpy(result,`
`&s1[5], 2);`

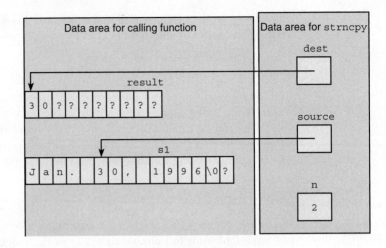

This figure reminds us that an array reference with no subscript (such as `result` and `s1`) actually represents the address of the initial array element. If we wish to use `strncpy` to extract a middle substring, we must call the function with the address of the first character to copy. For example, given the same value of `s1`, this code fragment would extract the substring `"30"`

```
strncpy(result, &s1[5], 2);
result[2] = '\0';
```

as shown in Fig. 8.6.

To extract the final characters of a source string, we can use `strcpy` as in this call to copy the `1996` at the end of `s1`.

```
strcpy(result, &s1[9]);
```

Function `strcpy` always copies characters beginning with the initial character of a source string and continuing until a `'\0'` has been encountered (and copied).

EXAMPLE 8.2   Here are two approaches to extracting three substrings of the string stored in `pres`. In the first version we use string library copy functions. Notice the only case in which a programmer need not explicitly assign a `'\0'` to end a substring is when the substring extracted includes the end of the source string. We see this case in the extraction of `"Quincy"`. Of course, if the space allocated for `middle` were insufficient to accommodate the copied substring, `strcpy` would overflow `middle`.

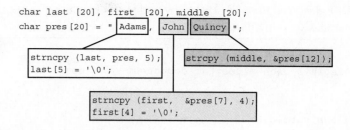

In our second version, we view Adams, John, and Quincy as tokens separated by delimiters comma and blank. We extract the three substrings by calls to string library function `strtok`. (See Table 8.1.) In the first call we provide both the source string `pres_copy` and the string of delimiters `", "`. Since the first argument in the second and third calls to `strtok` is `NULL`, `strtok` continues to search and change `pres_copy`. In this version, `first`, `middle`, and `last` are pointers to pieces of the original string in `pres_copy` rather than new copies. The fact that `strtok` alters its source string is the reason we copy `pres` into `pres_copy` before extracting the tokens.

```
char *last, *first, *middle;
char pres[20] = "Adams, John Quincy";
char pres_copy[20];
strcpy(pres_copy, pres);
```

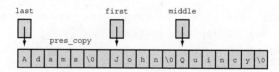

```
last = strtok(pres_copy, ", ");
first = strtok(NULL, ", ");
middle = strtok(NULL, ", ");
```

EXAMPLE 8.3   The program in Fig. 8.7 breaks compounds into their elemental components, assuming that each element name begins with a capital letter and that our implementation is using the ASCII character set. For example, this program would break `"NaCl"` into `"Na"` and `"Cl"`. The `if` statement in the `for` loop tests whether the character at position `next` is uppercase. If so, `strncpy` copies into `elem` all characters from the last capital letter (at position `first`) up to (but not including) the capital letter at position `next`.

FIGURE 8.7 Program Using strncpy and strcpy Functions to Separate Compounds into Elemental Components

```
1.   /*
2.    * Displays each elemental component of a compound
3.    */
4.
5.   #include <stdio.h>
6.   #include <string.h>
7.
8.   #define CMP_LEN 30   /* size of string to hold a compound  */
9.   #define ELEM_LEN 10  /* size of string to hold a component */
10.
11.  int
12.  main(void)
13.  {
14.       char compound[CMP_LEN];  /* string representing a compound */
15.       char elem[ELEM_LEN];     /* one elemental component        */
16.       int  first, next;
17.
18.       /* Gets data string representing compound               */
19.       printf("Enter a compound> ");
20.       scanf("%s", compound);
21.
22.       /* Displays each elemental component. These are identified
23.          by an initial capital letter.                        */
24.       first = 0;
25.       for (next = 1; next < strlen(compound); ++next)
26.          if (compound[next] >= 'A'  &&  compound[next] <= 'Z') {
27.                strncpy(elem, &compound[first], next - first);
28.                elem[next - first] = '\0';
29.                printf("%s\n", elem);
30.                first = next;
31.          }
32.
33.       /* Displays the last component                          */
34.       printf("%s\n", strcpy(elem, &compound[first]));
35.
36.       return (0);
37.  }
```

```
Enter a compound> H2SO4
H2
S
O4
```

The statement

```
printf("%s\n", strcpy(elem, &compound[first]));
```

following the loop is used to display the last component. Notice that this final call to printf takes advantage of the fact that strcpy returns as its value the starting address of the string it has just stored in elem. Because this final call to strcpy has extracted a complete string (i.e., a string ending in '\0'), we can avoid writing two statements

```
strcpy(elem, &compound[first]);
printf("%s\n", elem);
```

by simply calling strcpy right at the spot where the value it computes is needed, that is, in the argument list for printf.

Also, check carefully the use of CMP_LEN and strlen(compound). In this program, we see again the use of part of an array. As we studied in Chapter 7, in situations like this, the declared size of the array is no longer the effective size once data have been stored in the array. The **string length** as found by the strlen function is the number of characters in the string up to (but not including) the null character. This length may be less or greater than the array's declared size, but the only valid lengths are from 0 to one less than the declared size. We call a string of length zero the **empty string**. The type of the value returned by strlen is size_t, an unsigned integer type.

string length   in a character array, the number of characters before the first null character

empty string   a string of length zero: the first character of the string is the null character

EXERCISES FOR SECTION 8.2

Self-Check

1. Given the string variables pres, first, and last as defined in Example 8.2, show what would be displayed by this code fragment.

    ```
    strncpy(first, pres, 2);
    first[2] = '\0';
    printf("%s", first);
    printf(" %s", strcpy(last, &pres[7]));

    strncpy(first, &pres[7], 2);
    first[2] = '\0';
    strncpy(last, &pres[14], 2);
    last[2] = '\0';
    printf(" %s%s\n", first, last);
    ```

2. Given these declarations,

    ```
    char socsec[12] = "123-45-6789";
    char ssnshort[7], ssn1[4], ssn2[3], ssn3[5];
    ```

write statements to accomplish the following:

a.   Store in ssnshort as much of socsec as will fit.
b.   Store in ssn1 the first three characters of socsec.
c.   Store in ssn2 the middle two-digit portion of socsec.
d.   Store in ssn3 the final four digits of socsec.

Be sure your statements store valid strings in each variable.

Programming

1.   Write a program to take a product code from Millie's Mail-Order Catalog (MMOC) and separate it into its component parts. An MMOC product code begins with one or more letters identifying the warehouse where the product is stored. Next come the one or more digits that are the product ID. The final field of the string starts with a capital letter and represents qualifiers such as size, color, and so on. For example, ATL1203S14 stands for product 1203, size 14, in the Atlanta warehouse. Write a program that takes a code, finds the position of the first digit and of the first letter after the digits, and uses strcpy and strncpy to display a report such as the following:

```
Warehouse: ATL
Product: 1203
Qualifiers: S14
```

2.   Complete function trim_blanks whose purpose is to take a single string input parameter (to_trim) and return a copy of the string with leading and trailing blanks removed. Use strncpy in trim_blanks.

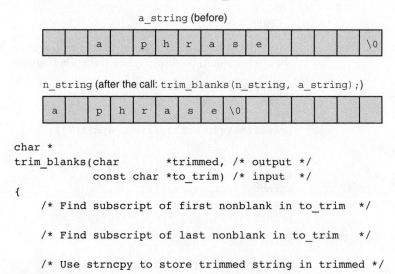

a_string (before)

n_string (after the call: trim_blanks(n_string, a_string);)

```
char *
trim_blanks(char        *trimmed, /* output */
            const char *to_trim) /* input  */
{
    /* Find subscript of first nonblank in to_trim */

    /* Find subscript of last nonblank in to_trim  */

    /* Use strncpy to store trimmed string in trimmed */
}
```

8.3 Longer Strings: Concatenation and Whole-Line Input

concatenation
joining of two strings

In this section we will study two library functions that let us join (**concatenate**) two strings to form a longer string. We also present functions that allow us to scan a full line of character data from the keyboard or from a file.

Concatenation

String library functions `strcat` and `strncat` modify their first string argument by adding all or part of their second string argument at the end of the first argument. Both functions assume that sufficient space is allocated for the first argument to allow addition of the extra characters.

EXAMPLE 8.4   Consider this code fragment:

```
#define STRSIZ 15
char f1[STRSIZ] = "John ", f2[STRSIZ] = "Jacqueline ",
     last[STRSIZ] = "Kennedy";

strcat(f1, last);
strcat(f2, last);        /* invalid overflow of f2 */
```

The first call to `strcat` copies the string `"Kennedy"` at the end of `f1`, creating the string `"John Kennedy"`, which has 12 characters plus the null character, a string that fits in the 15-character array `f1`. However, the second call to `strcat` creates the 19-character (including `'\0'`) string `"Jacqueline Kennedy"`, a string that overflows `f2` and could have the side effect of changing `last` if `last` is allocated immediately after `f2`. As an alternative to the second call to `strcat`, we could write

```
strncat(f2, last, 3);
```

This statement adds onto `"Jacqueline"` the portion of `"Kennedy"` that will fit at the end of `f2` without overflow, creating the string `"Jacqueline Ken"`.

When writing a string-manipulating program, one usually does not know in advance the sizes of the strings used as data. Fortunately, the string library provides function `strlen`, which returns the length of the value of its string argument, not counting the `'\0'` character. For example, this code fragment displays the numbers 8 and 16 followed by the phrase `Jupiter Symphony`.

```
#define STRSIZ 20
char s1[STRSIZ] = "Jupiter ",
     s2[STRSIZ] = "Symphony";
printf("%d %d\n", strlen(s1), strlen(strcat(s1, s2)));
printf("%s\n", s1);
```

Notice that the blank at the end of the initial value of s1 is counted in s1's length. Also, take note that the call to strcat modifies the value of s1 even when embedded in other function calls. Both strcat and strncat return as the function value the modified first argument. If s1 and s2 are both character strings declared to hold STRSIZ characters, the following decision statement would concatenate the full strings, if possible without overflow, and would concatenate only as much of the second string as would fit otherwise.

```
if (strlen(s1) + strlen(s2) < STRSIZ)
    strcat(s1, s2);
else
    strncat(s1, s2, STRSIZ - strlen(s1) - 1);
```

The condition correctly verifies that the sum of the lengths of s1 and s2 is strictly *less than* STRSIZ; if the sum *equaled* STRSIZ, then the '\0' that strcat places at the end of its result would overflow s1.

You can see from our examples of the use of strcpy, strncpy, strcat, and strncat that there are two critical questions that must always be in the mind of a C programmer who is manipulating strings:

- Is there enough space in the output parameter for the entire string being created?
- Does the created string end in '\0'?

Distinction Between Characters and Strings

When using strcat, one may be tempted to supply a single character as one of the two strings to join. A type char value is *not* a valid argument for a function with a corresponding parameter of type char *. Note the difference internally between the representations of the character 'Q' and the string "Q".

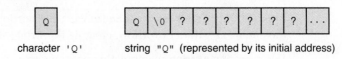

character 'Q'   string "Q" (represented by its initial address)

If you wish to add a single character at the end of a string, you should view the string as an array and use assignment to subscripted elements for access. Be sure to include the null character at the end of the string.

Scanning a Full Line

Although blanks are natural separators to place between numeric data values, viewing them as delimiters (as do functions scanf and fscanf) when processing strings may not make sense since a blank is a perfectly valid character element of a string.

For interactive input of one complete line of data, the `stdio` library provides the function `gets`. Consider this code fragment:

```
char line[80];
printf("Type in a line of data.\n> ");
gets(line);
```

If the user responds to the prompt as follows,

```
Type in a line of data.
> Here is a short sentence.
```

the value stored in line would be

| H | e | r | e | | i | s | | a | | s | h | o | r | t | | s | e | n | t | e | n | c | e | . | \0 | . . . |

The \n character representing the \<return\> or \<enter\> key pressed at the end of the sentence is *not* stored. Like `scanf`, `gets` can overflow its string argument if the user enters a longer data line than will fit.

The stdio library's file version of `gets`, `fgets`, behaves somewhat differently. Function `fgets` takes three arguments—the output parameter string, a maximum number of characters to store (n), and the file pointer to the data source. Function `fgets` will never store more than $n - 1$ characters from the data file, and the final character stored will always be `'\0'`. However, the next to last character may or may not be `'\n'`. If `fgets` has room to store the entire line of data, it will include `'\n'` before `'\0'`. If the line is truncated, no `'\n'` is stored. Like other string-building functions we have studied, `fgets` stores the string created in its first argument and returns this string argument (i.e., its address) as its value. When a call to `fgets` encounters the end of file, the value returned is the address 0, which is considered the *null pointer*. Since `fgets` prevents buffer overflow, some programmers use it in place of `gets` for interactive input, providing `stdin` (the standard input pointer associated with the keyboard) as the file pointer and adding extra code to replace the `'\n'` by `'\0'` if the newline character is unwanted. The C in Focus article on Evolving Standards (see p. 606) discusses how revisions of the original ANSI C standard have addressed some of these buffer overflow issues. Figure 8.8 shows a program that uses fgets to scans a data file one line at a time and creates a new double-spaced version with the lines numbered.

FIGURE 8.8 Demonstration of Whole-Line Input

```
1.  /*
2.   *   Numbers and double spaces lines of a document. Lines longer than
3.   *   LINE_LEN - 1 characters are split on two lines.
4.   */
5.
```

FIGURE 8.8   (continued)

```
 6.  #include <stdio.h>
 7.  #include <string.h>
 8.
 9.  #define LINE_LEN 80
10.  #define NAME_LEN 40
11.
12.  int
13.  main(void)
14.  {
15.        char line[LINE_LEN], inname[NAME_LEN], outname[NAME_LEN];
16.        FILE *inp, *outp;
17.        char *status;
18.        int i = 0;
19.
20.        printf("Name of input file> ");
21.        scanf("%s", inname);
22.        printf("Name of output file> ");
23.        scanf("%s", outname);
24.
25.        inp = fopen(inname, "r");
26.        outp = fopen(outname, "w");
27.
28.        for (status = fgets(line, LINE_LEN, inp);
29.             status != 0;
30.             status = fgets(line, LINE_LEN, inp)) {
31.          if (line[strlen(line) - 1] == '\n')
32.                line[strlen(line) - 1] = '\0';
33.          fprintf(outp, "%3d>> %s\n\n", ++i, line);
34.        }
35.      return (0);
36.  }
```

File used as input

In the early 1960s, designers and implementers of operating
systems were faced with a significant dilemma. As people's
expectations of modern operating systems escalated, so did
the complexity of the systems themselves. Like other
programmers solving difficult problems, the systems
programmers desperately needed the readability and
modularity of a powerful high-level programming language.

(continued)

FIGURE 8.8   (continued)

Output file

```
1>> In the early 1960s, designers and implementers of operating
2>> systems were faced with a significant dilemma. As people's
3>> expectations of modern operating systems escalated, so did
4>> the complexity of the systems themselves. Like other
5>> programmers solving difficult problems, the systems
6>> programmers desperately needed the readability and
7>> modularity of a powerful high-level programming language.
```

 EXERCISES FOR SECTION 8.3

Self-Check

1. Given the string pres (value is "Adams, John Quincy") and the 40-character temporary variables tmp1 and tmp2, what string is displayed by the following code fragment?

```
strncpy(tmp1, &pres[7], 4);
tmp1[4] = '\0';
strcat(tmp1, " ");
strncpy(tmp2, pres, 5);
tmp2[5] = '\0';
printf("%s\n", strcat(tmp1, tmp2));
```

2. There is an error in the last line of the following code fragment. What is the error? Why is it wrong? How would you correctly achieve the intent of this call?

```
strcpy(tmp1, &pres[12]);
strcat(tmp1, " ");
strcat(tmp1, pres[7]);
```

Programming

1. Write a function bracket_by_len that takes a word as an input argument and returns the word bracketed to indicate its length. Words less than five characters long are bracketed with << >>, words five to ten letters long are bracketed with (* *), and words over ten characters long are bracketed with /+ +/. Your function should require the calling function to provide as the first argument, space for the result, and as the third argument, the amount of space available. Consider the expected results of these calls to the function.

```
bracket_by_len(tmp, "insufficiently", 20)    →
        "/+insufficiently+/"
bracket_by_len(tmp, "the", 20)        →       "<<the>>"
```

8.4 String Comparison

In earlier chapters, we studied the fact that characters are represented by numeric codes, and we used relational and equality operators to compare characters. For example, the conditions

```
crsr_or_frgt == 'C'
```

and

```
ch1 < ch2
```

were used to test character variables in decision statements. Unfortunately, these operators cannot be used for comparison of strings because of C's representation of strings as arrays.

Because an array name used with no subscript represents the address of the initial array element, if `str1` and `str2` are string variables, the condition

```
str1 < str2
```

is *not* checking whether `str1` precedes `str2` alphabetically. However, the comparison *is* legal, for it determines whether the place in memory where storage of `str1` begins precedes the place in memory where `str2` begins.

The standard string library provides the `int` function `strcmp` for comparison of two strings that we will refer to as `str1` and `str2`. Function `strcmp` separates its argument pairs into three categories as shown in Table 8.2.

In this table, we are using the expression "less than" as a string generalization of the "less than" comparison of characters. We have seen that for character variables `ch1` and `ch2`, `ch1 < ch2` is true if the numeric character code value of `ch1` is less than the code in `ch2`. ANSI C extends this concept to strings by stating the following two conditions to define "less than:"

1. If the first n characters of `str1` and `str2` match and `str1[n]`, `str2[n]` are the first nonmatching corresponding characters, `str1` is less than `str2` if `str1[n] < str2[n]`.

    ```
    str1 t h r i l l          str1 e n e r g y
    str2 t h r o w            str2 f o r c e
                 °                    °
    First 3 letters match.    First 0 letters match.
    str1[3] < str2[3]         str1[0] < str2[0]
       'i' < 'o'                  'e' < 'f'
    ```

2. If `str1` is shorter than `str2` and all the characters of `str1` match the corresponding characters of `str2`, `str1` is less than `str2`.

    ```
    str1    j o y
    str2    j o y o u s
    ```

TABLE 8.2 Possible Results of strcmp(str1, str2)

Relationship	Value Returned	Example
str1 is less than str2	negative integer	str1 is "marigold" str2 is "tulip"
str1 equals str2	zero	str1 and str2 are both "end"
str1 is greater than str2	positive integer	str1 is "shrimp" str2 is "crab"

The string library also provides an analogous function strncmp that bases its comparison on only the first n characters of the two strings, where n is the third argument. For example, if str1 is "joyful" and str2 is "joyous", the function calls strncmp(str1, str2, 1), strncmp(str1, str2, 2), and strncmp(str1, str2, 3) all return the value 0 because "j" matches "j", "jo" matches "jo", and "joy" matches "joy". However, strncmp(str1, str2, 4) would return a negative integer, indicating that "joyf" precedes "joyo" alphabetically.

EXAMPLE 8.5   String comparisons are essential when alphabetizing a list. To alphabetize a list of words made up of either all uppercase or all lowercase letters, we could use the selection sort algorithm we developed in Section 7.6. Figure 8.9 compares the numeric and string versions of code that compares list elements in the search for the index of the smallest (or alphabetically first). It also shows the numeric and string versions of a code fragment that exchanges two array elements. In the string versions we see the use of the string library functions strcmp and strcpy. The string exchange code assumes that temp is a local string variable with sufficient space to hold a copy of any string in list.

FIGURE 8.9 Numeric and String Versions of Portions of Selection Sort That Compare and Exchange Elements

Comparison (in function that finds index of "smallest" remaining element)

Numeric
```
if (list[i] < list[first])
    first = i;
```

String
```
if (strcmp(list[i], list[first]) < 0)
    first = i;
```

Exchange of elements
```
temp = list[index_of_min];
list[index_of_min] = list[fill];
list[fill] = temp;
```
```
strcpy(temp, list[index_of_min]);
strcpy(list[index_of_min], list[fill]);
strcpy(list[fill], temp);
```

FIGURE 8.10   Sentinel-Controlled Loop for String Input

```
1.  printf("Enter list of words on as many lines as you like.\n");
2.  printf("Separate words by at least one blank.\n");
3.  printf("When done, enter %s to quit.\n", SENT);
4.
5.  for (scanf("%s", word);
6.      strcmp(word, SENT) != 0;
7.      scanf("%s", word)) {
8.      /* process word */
9.      . . .
10. }
```

EXAMPLE 8.6   When we process a list of string data interactively, we often do not know in advance how much data will be entered. In this situation, we can use a sentinel-controlled loop, prompting the user to type in the sentinel value when entry of the data is complete. Figure 8.10 outlines such a loop, using `strcmp` to check for entry of the sentinel (represented by the constant macro `SENT`).

 EXERCISES FOR SECTION 8.4

Self-Check

1. Write C code to accomplish each of the following goals.

    a. Write a message indicating whether `name1` and `name2` match.
    b. Store in the string variable `word` the value either of `w1` or of `w2`. Choose the value that comes first alphabetically.
    c. Store in `mtch` matching initial portions of `s1` and `s2`. For example, if `s1` is `"placozoa"` and `s2` is `"placement"`, `mtch` becomes `"plac"`. If `s1` is `"joy"` and `s2` is `"sorrow"`, `mtch` becomes the empty string.

Programming

1. Write the string selection sort function described in Example 8.5.

C IN FOCUS

Defensive Programming

Most of us are familiar with the notion of "defensive driving," and we all hope that any driver training course will go beyond covering the mechanics of vehi- cle operation and the laws that govern the roadways to teach the novice driver how to avoid collisions by anticipating dangerous situations arising from adverse weather conditions and other drivers' mistakes due to impaired judgment, unfamiliarity with local roads,

© ambrozinio for Fotolia

distraction by cell phones or children, or a host of other unexpected conditions. Just as a driver who assumes that everyone will follow all the rules of the road is an accident waiting to happen, software designed assuming that it will always be translated by a standards-compliant compiler, run under "reasonable" conditions, and used in the same context for which it was originally designed is on the fast track to system failure. **Defensive programming** is software design with the "standards-compliant compiler, reasonable execution conditions, and original context" assumptions thrown out the window. Defensive programming is a topic on which numerous books exist, so here we can merely introduce you to some of its basic ideas. You will note that indeed you have already met several of these.

The first characteristic of defensive programming is that it creates **readable** code. Any large project should have style rules that all participants will follow in order to enable groups of coders to more easily audit each other's code sections. These style guidelines include naming conventions for variables, functions, and constants, indentation rules for each control structure, use of braces and parentheses in contexts where they are optional, and quantity, positioning, and form of comments. Some of these style rules will do more than aid in readability—they may promote reliable execution across a range of standards-noncompliant compilers. For example, if a project adopts the policy that it will fully parenthesize every expression so as to *never* depend on the standard operator precedence, this style choice will also reduce the possibility of different expression values with different compilers.

It is not an accident that this C in Focus article on defensive programming appears in the chapter on string processing, for we have already seen cases where standard C library functions can cause string overflow and consequently unpredictable behavior of even very simple C code. A second characteristic of defensive programming is that it insists on **predictable results** even in the presence of unreasonable input, and thus prohibits use of any function like `gets` or `sprintf`, replacing such functions by user-defined modules that do not permit overflow. It is our commitment to predictable results that leads us to discourage use of a type `double` loop control variable with a fractional update since variation in number representations can lead such loops to exit after a different number of iterations on different computers. Just as the fully parenthesized expression style mentioned above contributes to predictable results, so too would the expectation that all conversions from one type to another in expression evaluation be made explicit through use of casts. Another trait of defensive programming is **enforcement of function preconditions**. Rather than simply placing a comment in a function statement of purpose indicating the expected precondition, the function will itself verify that the precondition is met. Depending on the circumstances, the function may force the precondition (e.g., if provided data is too long, use only part of it) or may cause a premature abort of the program.

Defensive programming techniques are not without cost. For example, having every function enforce its own preconditions doubtless leads to evaluation of redundant tests, but it also increases the safety of reuse of this function in another context. We have all seen the dire outcomes and enormous monetary costs arising from faulty software, so it is critical that we learn and commit to consistent use of defensive programming.

8.5   Arrays of Pointers

In Section 8.4, we discussed how we might modify our numeric selection sort code to create a program that would alphabetize a list of strings composed of uppercase or lowercase letters. Let's look closely at the code that exchanges two strings in Fig. 8.11.

Figure 8.12 pictures the data area of `strcpy` and the data area of the calling function as the second call to `strcpy` begins. This figure reminds us that C represents every array by its starting address. Since each element of `list` is a reference to an array of characters, it is passed to a function as a pointer, that is, as the address of the array's element `0`. When we consider sorting a list of strings, we see a lot of copying of characters from one memory cell to another. We have three operations that copy an entire string for every exchange that the sort requires, and when the sort is complete, our original list is lost.

In fact, C's use of pointers to represent arrays presents us with an opportunity to develop an alternate approach to our sorting problem. Study the two arrays in Fig. 8.13.

Listing the values of the elements of `alphap`

`alphap[0]`	address of	`"daisy"`
`alphap[1]`	address of	`"marigold"`
`alphap[2]`	address of	`"petunia"`
`alphap[3]`	address of	`"rose"`
`alphap[4]`	address of	`"tulip"`

calls to our attention that daisy, marigold, petunia, rose, and tulip form an alphabetized list. Therefore, if we were to execute this loop,

```
for  (i = 0;  i < 5;  ++i)
    printf("%s\n", alphap[i]);
```

we would see displayed the contents of `original` in alphabetical order, just as if we had copied the strings into a new array and sorted them. When `printf` sees a `%s` specifier, it *always* expects to receive a pointer to a string as the corresponding input argument, so `alphap[i]` is just as legitimate an argument as `original[i]`.

How would we declare the array of pointers `alphap`? Each element is the address of a character string, and there are five elements, so the appropriate declaration is

```
char *alphap[5];
```

FIGURE 8.11   Exchanging String Elements of an Array

```
1.  strcpy(temp, list[index_of_min]);
2.  strcpy(list[index_of_min], list[fill]);
3.  strcpy(list[fill], temp);
```

FIGURE 8.12

Executing
`strcpy (list`
`[index_of_min],`
`list[fill]);`

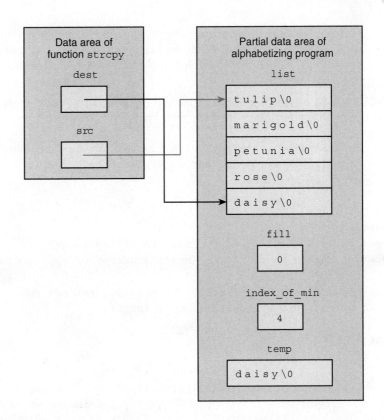

In our next example, we explore how to use an array of pointers to maintain two orderings of a list of strings while keeping only one copy of each string.

EXAMPLE 8.7 The Open School admits children to its kindergarten in the order in which they apply. However, most of the staff's use of the list of applicants is made easier if the

FIGURE 8.13

An Array
of Pointers

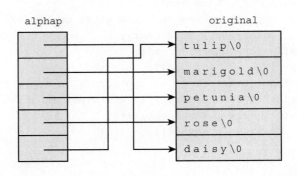

list is alphabetized. The program in Fig. 8.14 takes an input list of names reflecting the order in which applications were received and creates an array of pointers through which the list can be accessed in alphabetical order.

FIGURE 8.14 Two Orderings of One List Using an Array of Pointers

```
1.  /*
2.   *  Maintains two orderings of a list of applicants: the original
3.   *  ordering of the data, and an alphabetical ordering accessed through an
4.   *  array of pointers.
5.   */
6.
7.  #include <stdio.h>
8.  #define STRSIZ 30      /*      maximum string length */
9.  #define MAXAPP 50      /*      maximum number of applications accepted */
10.
11. int alpha_first(char *list[], int min_sub, int max_sub);
12. void select_sort_str(char *list[], int n);
13.
14. int
15. main(void)
16. {
17.      char applicants[MAXAPP][STRSIZ]; /* list of applicants in the
18.                                     order in which they applied        */
19.      char *alpha[MAXAPP];           /* list of pointers to
20.                                     applicants                         */
21.      int   num_app,                 /* actual number of applicants     */
22.            i;
23.      char  one_char;
24.
25.      /* Gets applicant list                                           */
26.      printf("Enter number of applicants (0 . . %d)\n> ", MAXAPP);
27.      scanf("%d", &num_app);
28.      do    /* skips rest of line after number */
29.         scanf("%c", &one_char);
30.      while (one_char != '\n');
31.
32.      printf("Enter names of applicants on separate lines of less than\n");
33.      printf(" 30 characters in the order in which they applied\n");
34.      for (i = 0; i < num_app; ++i)
35.         gets(applicants[i]);
36.
```

(continued)

FIGURE 8.14 (continued)

```
37.        /* Fills array of pointers and sorts                        */
38.        for (i = 0; i < num_app; ++i)
39.            alpha[i] = applicants[i]; /* copies ONLY address */
40.        select_sort_str(alpha, num_app);
41.
42.      /* Displays both lists                                        */
43.        printf("\n\n%-30s%5c%-30s\n\n", "Application Order", ' ',
44.                "Alphabetical Order");
45.        for (i = 0;  i < num_app;  ++i)
46.            printf("%-30s%5c%-30s\n", applicants[i], ' ', alpha[i]);
47.
48.        return(0);
49. }
50. /*
51.  *  Finds the index of the string that comes first alphabetically in
52.  *  elements min_sub..max_sub of list
53.  *  Pre: list[min_sub] through list[max_sub] are of uniform case;
54.  *       max_sub >= min_sub
55.  */
56. int
57. alpha_first(char *list[],        /* input - array of pointers to strings   */
58.             int   min_sub,       /* input - minimum and maximum subscripts  */
59.             int   max_sub)       /*  of portion of list to consider         */
60. {
61.     int first, i;
62.
63.     first = min_sub;
64.     for  (i = min_sub + 1;  i <= max_sub;  ++i)
65.         if (strcmp(list[i], list[first]) < 0)
66.             first = i;
67.
68.     return (first);
69. }
70.
71. /*
72.  * Orders the pointers in array list so they access strings
73.  * in alphabetical order
74.  * Pre:  first n elements of list reference strings of uniform case;
75.  *       n >= 0
76.  */
77. void
```

(continued)

FIGURE 8.14   (continued)

```
78.  select_sort_str(char *list[],   /* input/output - array of pointers being
79.                               ordered to access strings alphabetically */
80.                int n)          /* input - number of elements to sort      */
81.  {
82.
83.      int fill,            /* index of element to contain next string in order */
84.          index_of_min;    /* index of next string in order */
85.      char *temp;
86.
87.      for (fill = 0;  fill < n - 1;  ++fill) {
88.          index_of_min = alpha_first(list, fill, n - 1);
89.
90.          if (index_of_min != fill) {
91.              temp = list[index_of_min];
92.              list[index_of_min] = list[fill];
93.              list[fill] = temp;
94.          }
95.      }
96.  }
```

```
Enter number of applicants (0 . . 50)
> 5
Enter names of applicants on separate lines of less than
30 characters in the order in which they applied
SADDLER, MARGARET
INGRAM, RICHARD
FAATZ, SUSAN
GONZALES, LORI
KEITH, CHARLES


Application Order          Alphabetical Order


SADDLER, MARGARET          FAATZ, SUSAN
INGRAM, RICHARD            GONZALES, LORI
FAATZ, SUSAN               INGRAM, RICHARD
GONZALES, LORI             KEITH, CHARLES
KEITH, CHARLES             SADDLER, MARGARET
```

The array of pointers is initialized by assigning to each element the starting address of one of the strings in the `applicants` array. Then a selection sort is applied to the array of pointers. Although `strcmp` looks at the actual strings whose starting addresses are in the array of pointers, the element exchange code moves only the pointers.

Using an array of pointers to represent a second, or third, or fourth ordering of a list of strings has several benefits. First, a pointer (an integer address) requires less storage space than a full copy of a character string. Second, our sorting function executes faster when it copies only pointers and not complete arrays of characters. Finally, because the strings themselves are stored only once, a spelling correction made in the original list would automatically be reflected in the other orderings as well.

Arrays of String Constants

C also permits the use of an array of pointers to represent a list of string constants. Two alternatives for representing the list of month names we saw in Section 8.1 follow.

```c
char month[12][10] = {"January", "February", "March", "April",
                      "May", "June", "July", "August", "September",
                      "October", "November", "December"};
char *month[12] = {"January", "February", "March", "April", "May",
                   "June", "July", "August", "September",
                   "October", "November", "December"};
```

Actually, the number of rows (12) is optional in both of these declarations since the initialization list also implies this value.

EXERCISES FOR SECTION 8.5

Self-Check

1. Write two prototypes for a function that orders a list of strings according to string length—shortest to longest. In the first, the function should expect an input/output argument that is a two-dimensional array of characters in which strings have at most `STRSIZ` characters. In the second, the function should expect an input/output argument that is an array of pointers.
2. Consider the following valid call to `printf`. Is `strs` a two-dimensional array of characters or an array of pointers to strings?

   ```c
   printf("%s\n", strs[4]);
   ```

Programming

1. Write the function described in Exercise 1 using an array of pointers.

8.6   Character Operations

When we develop programs that involve string processing, often we must work with the individual characters that make up the string. C provides character input/output routines as part of the stdio library, and an extensive collection of facilities for character analysis and conversion is available in the library we `#include` as `<ctype.h>`.

Character Input/Output

The stdio library includes a routine named `getchar` that is used to get the next character from the standard input source, the same input source that `scanf` uses. Unlike `scanf`, `getchar` does not expect the calling module to pass as an argument the address of a variable in which to store the input character. Rather, `getchar` takes no arguments and returns the character as its result. Either of the following two expressions can be used to store the next available input character in `ch`.

```
scanf("%c", &ch)          ch = getchar()
```

There is, however, a difference between the two fragments, because the *values* of the expressions themselves are different. You will recall that `scanf` returns as its value an integer representing the number of values it took from the input stream for storage through its output parameters. When `scanf` encounters the end of the input file, it returns the value associated with `EOF`. In the expression that calls `getchar`, we have an assignment operator, so the value of the expression is the value assigned, namely the character that `getchar` found in standard input. What if there were no characters for `getchar` to take? What if `getchar` came across the end of the data? When we look up a full description of the `getchar` facility, we discover that the type of the value it returns is not `char` but `int`. This should not surprise us because we have already seen that in a computer, characters are represented by integer codes, and we can cast a `char` to an `int`.

Although character codes are, in fact, integers, in most C implementations the `char` data type is allotted only enough space to store the range of integers actually used by the implementation's character set. This range does not include the negative value associated with the name `EOF`. The data type `int` must be able to represent a much larger range of integers that includes both the full range of character codes and the `EOF` value. For this reason, we use a type `int` variable to store the result of a call to `getchar`, at least until we verify that `getchar` did not return `EOF`.

To get a single character from a file, use the facility `getc`. The call

```
getc(inp)
```

is comparable to a call to `getchar`, except that the character returned is obtained from the file accessed by file pointer `inp`.

EXAMPLE 8.8   In Fig. 8.15, we write a `scanline` function that uses `getchar`. Like the library function `gets`, our `scanline` function takes as its first argument the string variable in which to store the input line. Unlike `gets`, `scanline` also takes a second argument indicating the amount of space available. It stores in the output argument either the full input line or as much as will fit. Then it discards any characters remaining on the line until `'\n'` or `EOF` is encountered. We noted in Table 8.1 the fact that `gets` risks overflow of its string parameter. Our `scanline` is a safer function to accomplish whole-line input.

We could declare `scanline`'s first parameter as

```
char dest[]
```

since `dest` is an array of characters. We have chosen the notation shown so as to be consistent with declarations in the C standard string library. The `char *` declaration reminds us that like all arrays, `char` arrays are implemented in C as pointers.

FIGURE 8.15   Implementation of scanline Function Using getchar

```
1.  /*
2.   *  Gets one line of data from standard input. Returns an empty string on
3.   *  end of file. If data line will not fit in allotted space, stores
4.   *  portion that does fit and discards rest of input line.
5.   */
6.  char *
7.  scanline(char *dest,      /* output  - destination string            */
8.           int   dest_len) /* input   - space available in dest       */
9.  {
10.       int i, ch;
11.
12.       /*  Gets next line one character at a time.                      */
13.       i = 0;
14.       for (ch = getchar();
15.            ch != '\n'  &&  ch != EOF  &&  i < dest_len - 1;
16.            ch = getchar())
17.          dest[i++] = ch;
18.       dest[i] = '\0';
19.
20.       /* Discards any characters that remain on input line             */
21.       while (ch != '\n'  &&  ch != EOF)
22.          ch = getchar();
23.
24.       return (dest);
25.  }
```

The standard library's single-character output facilities are `putchar` (for display on the standard output device) and `putc` (for files). Both take as their first argument a type `int` character code. Because type `char` can always be converted to type `int` with no loss of information, we frequently call `putchar` and `putc` with arguments of type `char`:

```
putchar('a');                    putc('a', outp);
```

Character Analysis and Conversion

In many string-processing applications, we need to know if a character belongs to a particular subset of the overall character set. Is this character a letter? a digit? a punctuation mark? The library we `#include` as `<ctype.h>` defines facilities for answering questions like these and also provides routines to do common character conversions like uppercase to lowercase or lowercase to uppercase. Table 8.3 lists a number of these routines; each takes a single type `int` argument representing a

TABLE 8.3   Character Classification and Conversion Facilities in ctype Library

Facility	Checks	Example
`isalpha`	if argument is a letter of the alphabet	`if (isalpha(ch))` `printf("%c is a letter\n", ch);`
`isdigit`	if argument is one of the ten decimal digits	`dec_digit = isdigit(ch);`

`islower` `(isupper)`	if argument is a lowercase (or uppercase) letter of the alphabet	`if (islower(fst_let)) {`
		     `printf("\nError: sentence ");`
		     `printf("should begin with a ");`
		     `printf("capital letter.\n");`
		`}`

`ispunct`	if argument is a punctuation character, that is, a noncontrol character that is not a space, a letter of the alphabet, or a digit	`if (ispunct(ch))`
		     `printf("Punctuation mark: %c\n",`
		         `ch);`

`isspace`	if argument is a whitespace character such as a space, a newline, or a tab	`c = getchar();`
		`while (isspace(c) && c != EOF)`
		     `c = getchar();`

Facility	Converts	Example

`tolower` `(toupper)`	its lowercase (or uppercase) letter argument to the uppercase (or lower-case) equivalent and returns this equivalent as the value of the call	`if (islower(ch))`
		     `printf("Capital %c = %c\n",`
		         `ch, toupper(ch));`

character code. The *classification* routines (those whose names begin with `"is"`) return a nonzero value (not necessarily 1) if the condition checked is true. The example given for the `isspace` routine is a loop that can be used to advance to the next nonblank input character.

EXAMPLE 8.9   When we alphabetize a list of strings, we must frequently deal with words containing a mixture of uppercase and lowercase letters. In this situation, we cannot rely on `strcmp` to give useful results. This call to `strcmp`

```
strcmp("Ziegler", "aardvark")
```

will return a negative value indicating that `"Ziegler"` is less than `"aardvark"` if our system is using the ASCII character codes, since all capital letters have lower ASCII character codes than the lowercase letters have. On computers that use the EBCDIC character set, we also have difficulty handling a mixture of uppercase and lowercase letters because all *lowercase* letters have smaller character codes than uppercase letters (see Appendix D). Figure 8.16 shows a function `string_greater` that could be used to find out-of-order elements when alphabetizing a list of strings in a situation in which the case of the letters should be ignored. The function converts each of its arguments to all capital letters using `string_toupper` before comparing them. Since `str1` and `str2` are strictly input parameters of `string_greater`, their values must not be changed. However, `string_toupper` does change its parameter, so we first make copies of `str1` and `str2` in `s1` and `s2` and then send these copies to `string_toupper`.

FIGURE 8.16   String Function for a Greater-Than Operator That Ignores Case

```
1.  #include <string.h>
2.  #include <ctype.h>
3.
4.  #define STRSIZ 80
5.
6.  /*
7.   * Converts the lowercase letters of its string argument to uppercase
8.   * leaving other characters unchanged.
9.   */
10. char *
11. string_toupper(char *str) /* input/output - string whose lowercase
12.                              letters are to be replaced by uppercase    */
13. {
```

(continued)

FIGURE 8.16 (continued)

```
14.          int i;
15.          for (i = 0;  i < strlen(str);  ++i)
16.             if (islower(str[i]))
17.                   str[i] = toupper(str[i]);
18.
19.          return (str);
20.  }
21.
22.  /*
23.   * Compares two strings of up to STRSIZ characters ignoring the case of
24.   * the letters. Returns the value 1 if str1 should follow str2 in an
25.   * alphabetized list; otherwise returns 0
26.   */
27.  int
28.  string_greater(const char *str1, /* input -                          */
29.  const char *str2) /* strings to compare                             */
30.  {
31.          char s1[STRSIZ], s2[STRSIZ];
32.
33.          /* Copies str1 and str2 so string_toupper can modify copies    */
34.          strcpy(s1, str1);
35.          strcpy(s2, str2);
36.
37.          return (strcmp(string_toupper(s1), string_toupper(s2)) > 0);
38.  }
```

 EXERCISES FOR SECTION 8.6

Self-Check

1. What is wrong with the following statement? How would you rewrite it to accomplish its apparent purpose?

    ```
    if (isupper(strncpy(tmp, str, 1)))
        printf("%s begins with a capital letter\n", str);
    ```

Programming

1. Write a function scanstring that works basically like scanf with a %s placeholder—that is, it skips leading whitespace and then copies a string up to the next whitespace character—except that it uses getchar and takes an extra argument stating the amount of space available in the first argument. Unlike scanf, function scanstring should prevent overflow of its string argument.

2. Write a batch program that takes and echoes input data one character at a time until EOF is encountered and then prints a summary such as

```
The 14 lines of text processed contained 20 capital
letters, 607 lowercase letters, and 32 punctuation marks.
```

8.7 String-to-Number and Number-to-String Conversions

Some of the most common operations in a computer program are the conversion of a string like "3.14159" to the type double numeric value it represents and the conversion of a number like –36 from its internal representation in computer memory to the three-character string "-36" that is our usual picture of this number. Such conversions are constantly being carried out by the library functions scanf and printf. Tables 8.4 and 8.5 review some of the format string placeholders that we have used in earlier chapters to guide the conversion process. The characters that were scanned are in color. Table 8.5 also presents some new placeholders. The last example in Table 8.5 shows the use of a maximum field width. The %3.3s placeholder indicates output of a string using a minimum field width of 3 (3.3) and a maximum field width of 3 (3.3). As a result, only the first three characters of the string are printed.

TABLE 8.4   Review of Use of scanf

Declaration	Statement	Data (▌ means blank)	Value Stored
char t	scanf("%c", &t);	▌g	
		\n	\n
		A	A
int n	scanf("%d", &n);	▌32▌	32
		▌▌-8.6	-8
		▌+19▌	19
double x	scanf("%lf", &x);	▌▌▌4.32▌	4.32
		▌-8▌	-8.0
		▌1.76e-3▌	.00176
char str[10]	scanf("%s", str);	▌hello\n	hello\0
		overlengthy▌	overlengthy\0
			(overruns length of str)

TABLE 8.5 Placeholders Used with printf

Value	Placeholder	Output (▮ means blank)
`'a'`	`%c`	a
	`%3c`	▮▮a
	`%-3c`	a▮▮
-10	`%d`	-10
	`%2d`	-10
	`%4d`	▮-10
	`%-5d`	-10▮▮
49.76	`%.3f`	49.760
	`%.1f`	49.8
	`%10.2f`	▮▮▮▮▮49.76
	`%10.3e`	▮4.976e+01
`"fantastic"`	`%s`	fantastic
	`%6s`	fantastic
	`%12s`	▮▮▮fantastic
	`%-12s`	fantastic▮▮▮
	`%3.3s`	fan

The functions `printf` and `scanf` are such powerful string manipulators that sometimes we would like to directly control the strings on which they work. The stdio library gives us this ability through similar functions named `sprintf` and `sscanf`. The `sprintf` function requires space for a string as its first argument. Consider this call to `sprintf`; assume that s has been declared as `char s[100]`, and the values of type `int` variables `mon`, `day`, and `year` are as shown.

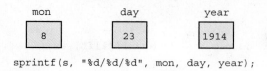

```
sprintf(s, "%d/%d/%d", mon, day, year);
```

Function `sprintf` substitutes values for placeholders just as `printf` does, but instead of printing the result, `sprintf` stores it in the character array accessed by its initial argument. Like function `scanf` with a `%s` placeholder and function `gets`, function `sprintf` risks overflowing its destination string.

```
          s
┌─────────────────────────────────────────────────┐
│ 8 / 2 3 / 1 9 1 4 \0                             │
└─────────────────────────────────────────────────┘
```

The sscanf function works exactly like scanf except that instead of taking the data values for its output parameters from the standard input device, it takes data from the string that is its first argument. For example, the illustration that follows shows how

sscanf(" 85 96.2 hello", "%d%lf%s", &num, &val, word);

stores values from the first string.

```
        num              val                word
    ┌─────────┐      ┌─────────┐      ┌─────────────────────────┐
    │   85    │      │  96.2   │      │ h  e  l  l  o \0         │
    └─────────┘      └─────────┘      └─────────────────────────┘
```

EXAMPLE 8.10   Because sscanf is available, we have the option of taking an entire data line as input and verifying that it conforms to the expected format before attempting to convert and store the line's values in memory. For example, if one line of data is expected to contain two nonnegative integers and then a string of up to 15 characters, one could write a validation function that would take the entire data line as an input argument and check the line one character at a time. The validation routine would look for optional whitespace characters followed by a group of digits, more whitespace, another group of digits, more whitespace, and then up to 15 non-whitespace characters. If the validation function discovered an error, it could print a message and return the position of the character where the error was detected. Otherwise, it could return a negative value. Figure 8.17 shows a program segment that assumes the availability of such a validation function and also of the scanline function defined in Fig. 8.15.

In our next example, we combine the power of sprintf/sscanf with the ability to directly access an array element to produce convenient functions for the conversion of one representation of a date to another.

EXAMPLE 8.11   The conversion of a date from a representation including a month name to a list of three numbers (12 January 1941 → 1 12 1941) and the reverse conversion are very common in everyday life. The program in Fig. 8.18 shows functions for both conversions and a driver program to test them. Arrays of pointers to strings are extremely useful for storing the constants needed in this type of conversion. Note

FIGURE 8.17   Program Segment That Validates Input Line Before Storing Data Values

```
1.  char data_line[STRSIZ], str[STRSIZ];
2.  int n1, n2, error_mark, i;
3.
4.  scanline(data_line, STRSIZ);
5.  error_mark = validate(data_line);
6.
7.  if (error_mark < 0) {
8.         /* Stores in memory values from correct data line    */
9.         sscanf(data_line, "%d%d%s", &n1, &n2, str);
10. } else {
11.        /* Displays line and marks spot where error detected */
12.        printf("\n%s\n", data_line);
13.        for (i = 0;   i < error_mark;   ++i)
14.           putchar(' ');
15.        putchar('/');
16. }
```

that we could change the representation of the date string to use an abbreviation (12 JAN 1941) or a different language (12 janvier 1941) merely by using a different initialization of our array. The conversion from a string including the month name to a group of three numbers involves a search of the list of month names using a function that is a string adaptation of the numeric linear search function we developed in Chapter 7.

FIGURE 8.18   Functions That Convert Representations of Dates

```
1.  /*
2.   * Functions to change the representation of a date from a string containing
3.   * day, month name and year to three integers (month day year) and vice versa
4.   */
5.
6.  #include <stdio.h>
7.  #include <string.h>
8.
9.  #define STRSIZ 40
10. char *nums_to_string_date(char *date_string, int month, int day,
11.                           int year, const char *month_names[]);
```

(continued)

FIGURE 8.18   (continued)

```
12.  int search(const char *arr[], const char *target, int n);
13.  void string_date_to_nums(const char *date_string, int *monthp,
14.                           int *dayp, int *yearp, const char *month_names[]);
15.
16.  /* Tests date conversion functions                                      */
17.  int
18.  main(void)
19.  {
20.      char *month_names[12] = {"January", "February", "March", "April", "May",
21.                               "June", "July", "August", "September", "October",
22.                               "November", "December"};
23.      int m, y, mon, day, year;
24.      char date_string[STRSIZ];
25.      for  (y = 1993;  y < 2010;  y += 10)
26.          for (m = 1; m <= 12; ++m) {
27.              printf("%s", nums_to_string_date(date_string,
28.                                   m, 15, y, month_names));
29.              string_date_to_nums(date_string, &mon, &day, &year, month_names);
30.              printf(" = %d/%d/%d\n", mon, day, year);
31.          }
32.
33.      return (0);
34.  }
35.
36.  /*
37.   * Takes integers representing a month, day and year and produces a
38.   * string representation of the same date.
39.   */
40.  char *
41.  nums_to_string_date(char       *date_string,        /* output - string
42.                                                          representation     */
43.                      int        month,               /* input -           */
44.                      int        day,                 /* representation     */
45.                      int        year,                /* as three numbers   */
46.                      const char *month_names[])      /* input - string representa-
47.                                                          tions of months    */
48.  {
49.      sprintf(date_string, "%d %s %d", day, month_names[month - 1], year);
50.      return (date_string);
51.  }
52.
```

(continued)

FIGURE 8.18   (continued)

```
53.  #define NOT_FOUND -1     /* Value returned by search function if target
54.                             not found                                      */
55.
56.  /*
57.   * Searches for target item in first n elements of array arr
58.   * Returns index of target or NOT_FOUND
59.   * Pre: target and first n elements of array arr are defined and n>0
60.   */
61.  int
62.  search(const char *arr[],        /* array to search              */
63.         const char *target,       /* value searched for           */
64.         int n)                    /* number of array elements to search */
65.  {
66.        int i,
67.            found = 0,     /* whether or not target has been found  */
68.            where;         /* index where target found or NOT_FOUND */
69.
70.        /* Compares each element to target                          */
71.        i = 0;
72.        while (!found && i < n) {
73.            if (strcmp(arr[i], target) == 0)
74.                  found = 1;
75.              else
76.                  ++i;
77.        }
78.
79.        /* Returns index of element matching target or NOT_FOUND */
80.        if (found)
81.              where = i;
82.        else
83.              where = NOT_FOUND;
84.        return (where);
85.  }
86.
87.  /*
88.   * Converts date represented as a string containing a month name to
89.   * three integers representing month, day, and year
90.   */
91.  void
```

(continued)

FIGURE 8.18   (continued)

```
 92. string_date_to_nums(const char *date_string,      /* input - date to convert  */
 93.                      int          *monthp,          /* output - month number    */
 94.                      int          *dayp,            /* output - day number      */
 95.                      int          *yearp,           /* output - year number     */
 96.                      const char *month_names[]) /* input - names used in
 97.                                                      date string             */
 98. {
 99.      char   mth_nam[STRSIZ];
100.      int    month_index;
101.
102.      sscanf(date_string, "%d%s%d", dayp, mth_nam, yearp);
103.
104.      /* Finds array index (range 0..11) of month name.                     */
105.      month_index = search(month_names, mth_nam, 12);
106.      *monthp = month_index + 1;
107. }


15 January 1993 = 1/15/1993
15 February 1993 = 2/15/1993
. . .
15 December 2003 = 12/15/2003
```

This date conversion application is one instance where C's required use of zero as the subscript of an initial array element is rather annoying. If we could have an array with row subscripts 1 . . . 12, the conversion from month number to name would be more direct. We have chosen to use a 12-string array and to correct the off-by-one error in the conversion functions. In `nums_to_string_date` we have

```
sprintf(date_string, "%d %s %d", day,
        month_names[month - 1], year);
```

and in `string_date_to_nums` we find the reference

```
*monthp = month_index + 1;
```

EXERCISES FOR SECTION 8.7

Self-Check

1. Consider the following call to `sscanf` from the `string_date_to_nums` function.

    ```
    sscanf(date_string, "%d%s%d", dayp, mth_name, yearp);
    ```

    Why is the address-of operator not applied to any of the arguments?

2. Write a code segment that uses an array of pointers to strings and `sprintf` to convert a type `double` monetary value less than `10.00` to a string for use on a check. For example, `4.83` would be converted to `"Four and 83/100 dollars"`.

Programming

1. Write a type `int` function `strtoint` and a type `double` function `strtodouble` that convert string representations of numbers to their numeric equivalents.

```
strtoint("-8")  →  -8
strtodouble("-75.812")  →  -75.812
```

8.8   String Processing Illustrated

You have been using a text editor to create and edit C programs. This is probably a fairly sophisticated program that uses special commands to move the cursor around the screen and to specify edit operations. Although you cannot develop such an editor yet, you can write a less sophisticated one that processes a single line of text.

CASE STUDY   Text Editor

PROBLEM

Design and implement a program to perform editing operations on a line of text. Your editor should be able to locate a specified target substring, delete a substring, and insert a substring at a specified location. The editor should expect source strings of less than 80 characters.

ANALYSIS

The editor's main function must get the source line to edit and then repeatedly scan and process editor commands until it receives the Q (Quit) command. We will allow strings of up to 99 characters, but we will not check for overflow.

DATA REQUIREMENTS

Problem Constant

```
MAX_LEN     100      /* maximum size of a string */
```

Problem Inputs

```
char source[MAX_LEN]      /* source string */
char command             /* edit command  */
```

Problem Output

```
char source[MAX_LEN]      /* modified source string */
```

DESIGN

INITIAL ALGORITHM

1. Scan the string to be edited into source.
2. Get an edit command.
3. while command isn't Q
   4. Perform edit operation.
   5. Get an edit command.

REFINEMENTS AND PROGRAM STRUCTURE

Step 4 is performed by function do_edit. A structure chart for the text editor is shown in Fig. 8.19; the local variables and algorithms for function do_edit follow.

Local Variables

```
char str[MAX_LEN]         /* string to find, delete, or insert */
int  index                /* position in source */
```

ALGORITHM FOR DO_EDIT

1. switch command

   'D': 2. Get the substring to be deleted (str).
        3. Find the position of str in source.
        4. if str is found, delete it.
   'I': 5. Get the substring to insert (str).
        6. Get position of insertion (index).
        7. Perform insertion of str at index position of source.
   'F': 8. Get the substring to search for (str).
        9. Find the position of str in source.
        10. Report position.
   Otherwise:
        11. Display error message.

FIGURE 8.19 Structure Chart for Text Editor Program

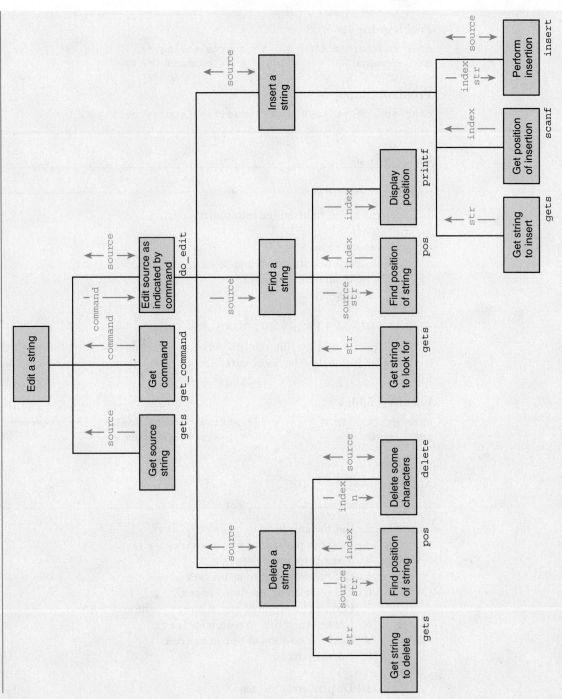

Function `do_edit` uses a function that finds the position of one string in another (`pos`) for steps 3 and 9, a function that deletes a certain number of characters from a string (`delete`) for step 4, and a function that inserts one string in another (`insert`) for step 7.

IMPLEMENTATION

Figure 8.20 shows a complete implementation of the text editor, and Fig. 8.21 shows a sample run. Read the helper functions `pos`, `insert`, and `delete` carefully as examples of functions that use C string library functions.

FIGURE 8.20 Text Editor Program

```
1.  /*
2.   * Performs text editing operations on a source string
3.   */
4.
5.  #include <stdio.h>
6.  #include <string.h>
7.  #include <ctype.h>
8.
9.  #define MAX_LEN 100
10. #define NOT_FOUND -1
11.
12. char *delete(char *source, int index, int n);
13. char *do_edit(char *source, char command);
14. char get_command(void);
15. char *insert(char *source, const char *to_insert, int index);
16. int  pos(const char *source, const char *to_find);
17.
18. int
19. main(void)
20. {
21.         char source[MAX_LEN], command;
22.         printf("Enter the source string:\n> ");
23.         gets(source);
24.
25.         for (command = get_command();
26.              command != 'Q';
27.              command = get_command()) {
28.             do_edit(source, command);
29.             printf("New source: %s\n\n", source);
```

(continued)

FIGURE 8.20   (continued)

```
30.          }
31.
32.          printf("String after editing: %s\n", source);
33.          return (0);
34. }
35.
36. /*
37.  * Returns source after deleting n characters beginning with source[index].
38.  * If source is too short for full deletion, as many characters are
39.  * deleted as possible.
40.  * Pre: All parameters are defined and
41.  *        strlen(source) - index - n < MAX_LEN
42.  * Post: source is modified and returned
43.  */
44. char *
45. delete(char *source,  /* input/output - string from which to delete part  */
46.        int   index,    /* input - index of first char to delete          */
47.        int   n)        /* input - number of chars to delete              */
48. {
49.          char rest_str[MAX_LEN]; /* copy of source substring following
50.                                     characters to delete */
51.
52.          /* If there are no characters in source following portion to
53.             delete, delete rest of string */
54.          if (strlen(source) <= index + n) {
55.                source[index] = '\0';
56.
57.          /* Otherwise, copy the portion following the portion to delete
58.             and place it in source beginning at the index position        */
59.          } else {
60.                strcpy(rest_str, &source[index + n]);
61.                strcpy(&source[index], rest_str);
62.          }
63.
64.          return (source);
65. }
66.
67. /*
68.  * Performs the edit operation specified by command
69.  * Pre: command and source are defined.
```

(continued)

FIGURE 8.20 (continued)

```
70.  * Post: After scanning additional information needed, performs a
71.  *        deletion (command = 'D') or insertion (command = 'I') or
72.  *        finds a substring ('F') and displays result; returns
73.  *        (possibly modified) source.
74.  */
75. char *
76. do_edit(char *source, /* input/output - string to modify or search */
77.         char command) /* input - character indicating operation    */
78. {
79.         char str[MAX_LEN]; /* work string */
80.         int index;
81.
82.         switch (command) {
83.         case 'D':
84.                 printf("String to delete> ");
85.                 gets(str);
86.                 index = pos(source, str);
87.                 if (index == NOT_FOUND)
88.                         printf("'%s' not found\n", str);
89.                 else
90.                         delete(source, index, strlen(str));
91.                 break;
92.
93.         case 'I':
94.                 printf("String to insert> ");
95.                 gets(str);
96.                 printf("Position of insertion> ");
97.                 scanf("%d", &index);
98.                 insert(source, str, index);
99.                 break;
100.
101.        case 'F':
102.                printf("String to find> ");
103.                gets(str);
104.                index = pos(source, str);
105.                if (index == NOT_FOUND)
106.                        printf("'%s' not found\n", str);
107.                else
108.                        printf("'%s' found at position %d\n", str, index);
109.                break;
```

(continued)

FIGURE 8.20   (continued)

```
110.
111.        default:
112.            printf("Invalid edit command '%c'\n", command);
113.        }
114.
115.        return (source);
116. }
117.
118. /*
119.  * Prompt for and get a character representing an edit command and
120.  * convert it to uppercase. Return the uppercase character and ignore
121.  * rest of input line.
122.  */
123. char
124. get_command(void)
125. {
126.        char command, ignore;
127.
128.        printf("Enter D(Delete), I(Insert), F(Find), or Q(Quit)> ");
129.        scanf(" %c", &command);
130.
131.        do
132.            ignore = getchar();
133.        while (ignore != '\n');
134.
135.        return (toupper(command));
136. }
137.
138. /*
139.  * Returns source after inserting to_insert at position index of
140.  * source. If source[index] doesn't exist, adds to_insert at end of
141.  * source.
142.  * Pre:  all parameters are defined, space available for source is
143.  *       enough to accommodate insertion, and
144.  *       strlen(source) - index - n < MAX_LEN
145.  * Post: source is modified and returned
146.  */
147. char *
148. insert(char       *source,      /* input/output - target of insertion */
149.        const char *to_insert,  /* input - string to insert           */
```

(continued)

FIGURE 8.20 (continued)

```
150.          int            index)      /* input - position where to_insert
151.                                            is to be inserted           */
152.  {
153.          char rest_str[MAX_LEN]; /* copy of rest of source beginning
154.                                  with source[index] */
155.
156.          if (strlen(source) <= index) {
157.                  strcat(source, to_insert);
158.          } else {
160.                  strcpy(rest_str, &source[index]);
161.                  strcpy(&source[index], to_insert);
162.                  strcat(source, rest_str);
163.          }
164.
165.          return (source);
166.  }
167.
168.  /*
169.   * Returns index of first occurrence of to_find in source or
170.   * value of NOT_FOUND if to_find is not in source.
171.   * Pre: both parameters are defined
172.   */
173.  int
174.  pos(const char *source,  /* input - string in which to look for to_find */
175.      const char *to_find) /* input - string to find                      */
176.
177.  {
178.          int i = 0, find_len, found = 0, position;
179.          char substring[MAX_LEN];
180.
181.          find_len = strlen(to_find);
182.          while (!found  &&  i <= strlen(source) - find_len) {
183.               strncpy(substring, &source[i], find_len);
184.               substring[find_len] = '\0';
185.
186.               if (strcmp(substring, to_find) == 0)
197.                     found = 1;
188.               else
189.                     ++i;
190.          }
191.
```

(continued)

FIGURE 8.20   (continued)

```
192.          if (found)
193.                  position = i;
194.          else
195.                  position = NOT_FOUND;
196.
197.          return (position);
198. }
```

TESTING

Choose test cases that check various boundary conditions as well as middle-of-the-road data. For example, to check the Delete command, try to delete the first few characters of source, the last few, and a substring in the middle of source. Also, try a substring that appears more than once to verify that only the first occurrence is deleted. Attempt two impossible deletions, one of a substring that does not resemble any part of source, and one of a substring that matches a part of source except for its last character. Also, test insertions at the beginning of source, exactly at the end of source, at a position several characters beyond the end of source, and in the middle of source. Use the Find command to look for all of source, single-letter pieces of source from the beginning, middle, and end, and multiple-character substrings from the beginning, middle, and end of the source string. Be sure to look for a substring not present in source, too.

FIGURE 8.21   Sample Run of Text Editor Program

```
Enter the source string:
> Internet use is growing rapidly.
Enter D(Delete), I(Insert), F(Find), or Q(Quit)> d
String to delete> growing
New source: Internet use is rapidly.

Enter D(Delete), I(Insert), F(Find), or Q(Quit)> F
String to find> .
'.' found at position 23
New source: Internet use is rapidly.

Enter D(Delete), I(Insert), F(Find), or Q(Quit)> I
String to insert> expanding
Position of insertion> 23

New source: Internet use is rapidly expanding.

Enter D(Delete), I(Insert), F(Find), or Q(Quit)> q
String after editing: Internet use is rapidly expanding.
```

8.9 Common Programming Errors

When manipulating string variables, the programmer must use great care in the allocation and management of memory. When we work with numeric values or single characters, we commonly compute a value of interest in a function, storing the result value temporarily in a local variable of the function until it is returned to the calling module using the return statement. One cannot use this approach in string functions, for such functions do not actually return a string *value* in the same way that an int function returns an integer value. Rather a string function returns a *pointer*, the address of the initial character of a string. If we were to use the same strategy in a string function as we do in many numeric functions, we would build our result string in a local variable and return the address of the new string as the function value. The problem with this approach is that the function's data area is deallocated as soon as the return statement is executed, so it is not valid to access from the calling module the string the function

FIGURE 8.22   Flawed scanline Returns Address of Deallocated Space

```
1.   /*
2.    * Gets one line of data from standard input. Returns an empty string on end
3.    * of file. If data line will not fit in allotted space, stores portion that
4.    * does fit and discards rest of input line.
5.    **** Error: returns address of space that is immediately deallocated.
6.    */
7.   char *
8.   scanline(void)
9.   {
10.        char dest[MAX_STR_LEN];
11.        int i, ch;
12.
13.        /* Get next line one character at a time.                          */
14.        i = 0;
15.        for (ch = getchar();
16.             ch != '\n'  &&  ch != EOF  &&  i < MAX_STR_LEN - 1;
17.             ch = getchar())
18.          dest[i++] = ch;
19.        dest[i] = '\0';
20.
21.        /* Discard any characters that remain on input line               */
22.        while (ch != '\n"  &&  ch != EOF)
23.             ch = getchar();
24.
25.        return (dest);
26.   }
```

constructed in its own local variable. Figure 8.22 shows a poor rewrite of the `scanline` function from Fig. 8.15. Rather than requiring the calling function to provide space in which to construct the function result as the earlier `scanline` did (and as is the practice of the functions in the C string library), this faulty `scanline` returns a string built in local storage. As a consequence, the string that the `printf` function tries to print is in a section of memory that neither `main` nor `printf` has any legitimate right to access and that may be overwritten with new values at any moment. What makes this type of error particularly grievous is that on some C implementations it will compile and pass unit testing without creating any error in the output.

To avoid creation of such "time-bomb" functions that do not "blow up" until system integration tests, follow the pattern of the C string library and have any string functions you write require the calling module to provide as the first argument a variable in which to build the string result. Some ANSI C compilers will flag the error illustrated in Fig. 8.22.

A second error that creeps into C programs with string use is the misuse or neglect of the `&` operator. The fact that this operator is *not* applied to strings or to any other whole arrays used as output arguments often leads beginning users of C to forget that the address-of operator must still be used on simple output arguments such as variables of type `int`, `char`, or `double`, as well as on single array elements of these types when used as output arguments.

Another problem that is common with string use is the overflow of character arrays allocated for strings. Since many string library functions just assume that the calling module has provided adequate space for whatever may need to be stored, calling these functions with inadequate storage causes errors that are really difficult to find. In Fig. 8.4, which is repeated here, we see such a situation.

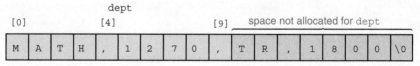

Execution of `scanf("%s%d%s%d", dept, &course_num, days, &time);` on Entry of Invalid Data

Whatever was stored in the cells following array `dept` has just been overwritten. If that memory was being used for other program variables, their values will appear to change spontaneously.

The `scanline` function that we wrote as an example protects the calling function from string overflow by requiring an input argument telling how much space is available for the string result. This function takes care to prevent storage of a string that is too long. We encourage you to use protective functions like this in your string programs.

A relatively minor error that can lead to difficult bugs is forgetting that all strings end with the null character. The programmer must remember the null character both when allocating space for a string and when building a string one character at a time.

It is easy to slip and use equality or relational operators when comparing strings or the assignment operator for copying them. Remember to use `strcmp` or `strncmp` for comparisons and library functions such as `strcpy` or `strncpy` for copying strings.

Chapter Review

1. Strings in C are arrays of characters ended by the null character `'\0'`.
2. String input is done using `scanf` and `fscanf` with `%s` descriptors for strings separated by whitespace, using `gets` and `fgets` for input of whole lines, and using `getchar` and `getc` for single character input.
3. String output is done using `printf` and `fprintf` with `%s` descriptors; `putchar` and `putc` do single-character output.
4. The string library provides functions for string assignment and extraction of substrings (`strcpy` and `strncpy`), for string length (`strlen`), for concatenation (`strcat` and `strncat`), and for alphabetic comparison (`strcmp` and `strncmp`).
5. The standard I/O library includes functions for string-to-number (`sscanf`) and number-to-string (`sprintf`) conversion.
6. String-building functions typically require the calling module to provide space for the new string as an output parameter, and they return the address of this parameter as the function result.
7. String manipulation in C requires the programmer to take great care to avoid overflow of string variables and creation of strings not ending in `'\0'`. For example, any string-building function that takes no parameter placing a size limitation on the string created (`scanf` with `%s`, `gets`, `strcat`, `sprintf` among others) risks overflow of the destination string.
8. Multiple orderings of a list of strings can be maintained by storing the strings once and creating arrays of pointers for additional orderings.
9. The ctype library provides functions for classification and conversion of single characters.

NEW C CONSTRUCTS

Statement	Effect
Declarations	
`char str[100];`	Allocates space for a string of up to 99 characters plus the null character.
`char str[11] = "          ";`	Allocates space for a string of up to ten characters plus the null and initializes it to all blanks.
`char *abbrevs[10];`	Declares an array of ten pointers to character strings.

`const char *arg1`
or
`const char arg1[]`
	Declares a string input parameter.

`char *out`
or
`char out[]`
	Declares a string output or input/output parameter.

(continued)

NEW C CONSTRUCTS (continued)

Statement	Effect
`char names[10][20];`	Allocates space for an array of ten strings, each of which has up to 19 characters plus the null character.

`char *weekdays[] =`
`    {"Mon", "Tue", "Wed",`
`    "Thu", "Fri"};`
	Declares and initializes an array of pointers to five strings.

`char list[][20]`	Declares a function parameter that is an array of strings in which each string has up to 19 characters plus the null.
`char *strs[]`	Declares a function parameter that is an array of pointers to strings.
Calls to I/O and Conversion Functions	
`gets(str1);`	Gets a line of data from the keyboard and stores it as a string in `str1` (without `'\n'`).
`c1 = getchar();`	Gets a character from the keyboard and stores its `int` character code in `c1`, or stores `EOF` in `c1` on end of file.
`putchar(c1);`	Displays character value of `c1`.
`sprintf(s, "%d + %d = %d", x,` `    y, x + y);`	If `x` is 3 and `y` is 4, builds and returns the string `"3 + 4 = 7"`.
`sscanf("14.3 -5", "%lf%d",` `    &p, &n);`	Stores `14.3` in `p` and `-5` in `n`.
Calls to Character Functions	
`if (islower(c1))` `    c1 = toupper(c1);`	If `c1`'s value is `'q'`, stores `'Q'` in `c1`.
`isdigit(c2)`	Returns 1 (true) if `c2` is one of the characters `'0'`, `'1'`, `'2'`, `'3'`, `'4'`, `'5'`, `'6'`, `'7'`, `'8'`, `'9'`.
Calls to String Library	
`strlen(a_string)`	Returns the number of characters in the string `a_string` up to but not including the null character.
`strcmp(str1, str2)`	Returns a negative integer if `str1` precedes `str2` alphabetically, a positive integer if `str2` precedes `str1`, and zero if `str1` and `str2` are equal.
`strncmp(str1, str2, 4)`	Compares first four characters of `str1` to first four characters of `str2`, returning a negative integer if the `str1` substring precedes the `str2` substring alphabetically, a positive integer if it follows, and zero if the substrings are equal.
`strcpy(str_result, str_src)`	Copies all the characters of `str_src` including the null character into `str_result`. Assumption is that `str_result` has enough room for all these characters.
`strncpy(str_result,` `    str_src, 10)`	Copies first ten characters of `str_src` into `str_result`. Assumption is that `str_result` has room for all ten. Characters stored include `'\0'` only if `strlen(str_src) < 10`.

(continued)

NEW C CONSTRUCTS   (continued)

Statement	Effect
Calls to String Library	
strcat(str_result, new)	Concatenates the complete value of **new** on the end of str_result. Assumption is that str_result has room enough for its own current value plus the added characters of **new**.
strncat(str_result, new, 10)	Concatenates the value of **new** at the end of str_result providing **new**'s length (not counting the null character) is less than or equal to ten. Otherwise, it concatenates the first ten characters of **new** on the end of str_result. It always adds a null character at the end, so at most 11 characters are added to str_result.

Quick-Check Exercises

1. For each of the following functions, explain its purpose, the type(s) of its output parameters, and the type(s) of its input parameter(s). Also, indicate if it is user-defined or if it is from the string library or from the ctype library.

   ```
   strcpy      strncpy     strncat
   islower     strcat      scanline
   isalpha     strlen      strcmp
   ```

2. Look at Appendix D, which lists three character sets. Which of the following expressions may yield different results on different computers?

   a. (char)45
   b. 'a' < 'A'
   c. 'A' < 'Z'
   d. ('A' <= ch && ch <= 'Z') && isalpha(ch)
   e. (int)'A'
   f. (int)'B' - (int)'A'

3. Which of the following strings could represent a formal parameter of any length? Which could represent a pointer to a string?

   ```
   char *s1[20]      char s2[]
   ```

4. A program you have written is producing incorrect results on your second data set, although it runs fine on the first. As you debug, you discover that the value of one of your strings is spontaneously changing from "blue" to "al" in the following code segment. What could be wrong?

   ```
   . . .
   printf("%s\n", s1);      /*    displays "blue" */
   scanf("%s", s2);
   printf("%s\n", s1);      /*    displays "al"   */
   . . .
   ```

5. Declare a variable `str` with as little space as would be reasonable given that `str` will hold each of the values below in turn.

```
March        June        May        July
```

6. What is the value of `s1` after execution of these statements if the value of `s2` is `"C Programming"`?

```
strncpy(s1, &s2[8], 3); s1[2] = '\0';
```

7. The action of joining two strings is called _____.

8. Write a statement that assigns to `s1` the end of the string value of `s2` starting with the fourth character (i.e., `s2[3]`).

9. Write statements that take a whole data line as input and display all the upper-case letters in the line.

10. What is the value of the following expression?

```
strncat("C", "Programming", 7)
```

11. What does this program fragment display?

```
char title[20] = "Program Design in C";
char *one, *two, *three, *four;
one = strtok(title, " ");
two = strtok(NULL, " ");
three = strtok(NULL, " "); four = strtok(NULL, " ");
printf("%s\t%s\n%s\n%s\n", one, two, three, four);
```

12. After execution of the fragment in Exercise 11, what is the value stored in the title?

Answers to Quick-Check Exercises

1.

Function's Purpose	Output Parameter Types	Input Parameter Types	Where Defined
`strcpy` copies one string into another.	`char *` (string result)	`const char *` (input string)	string
`islower` checks whether its argument is the character code for a lowercase character.	none	`int`	ctype
`isalpha` determines if its argument is the character code for a letter of the alphabet.	none	`int`	ctype

(continued)

Function's Purpose	Output Parameter Types	Input Parameter Types	Where Defined
strncpy copies *n* characters of one string into another.	char * (string result)	const char * (source string) int	string
strcat concatenates one string on the end of another.	char * (input/output argument — first source string and string result)	const char * (second source string)	string
strlen finds the length of its argument, counting the letters that precede the null character.	none	const char * (source string)	string
strncat concatenates two arguments by adding up to *n* characters from the second argument to the end of the first argument.	char * (input/output argument — first source string and string result)	const char * (second source string) int (maximum number of characters to copy from second string)	string
scanline takes one line of input as a string, stores as much as will fit in its output argument, and discards the rest.	char * (string result)	int (space available in result string)	user
strcmp compares arguments and returns a negative integer if first is less than second, zero if they are equal, and a positive integer otherwise.	none	const char * (two input strings)	string

2. Results differ for a, b, e.
3. parameter: s2; pointer: s1
4. The call to scanf may be getting a string too long to fit in s2, and the extra characters could be overwriting memory allocated to s1.
5. char str[6]. The longest value ("March") has five characters, and one more is needed for the null character.
6. "mm"
7. concatenation
8. strcpy(s1, &s2[3]);
9. gets(line);
   for (i = 0; i < strlen(line); ++i)
   if (isupper(line[i]))
         putchar(line[i]);

10. `CProgram`
11. `Program    Design`
    `in`
    `C`
12. program

Review Questions

Refer to these declarations when determining the effect of the statements in Questions 1–4.

```
char s5[5], s10[10], s20[20];
char aday[7] = "Sunday";
char another[9] = "Saturday";
```

1. `strncpy(s5, another, 4); s5[4] = '\0';`
2. `strcpy(s10, &aday[3]);`
3. `strlen(another)`
4. `strcpy(s20, aday); strcat(s20, another);`
5. Write a function that pads a variable-length string with blanks to its maximum size. For example, if `s10` is a ten-character array currently holding the string `"screen"`, `blank_pad` would add three blanks (one of which would overwrite the null character) and finish the string with the null character. Be sure your function would work if no blank padding were necessary.
6. Write a function that would return a copy of its string argument with the first occurrence of a specified letter in uppercase.
7. Write functions `isvowel` and `isconsonant` that return true if their type `int` argument is the character code for a vowel (or consonant). *Hint:* Use a `switch` statement in `isvowel`.
8. Which one of the following would call `itstricky` only if the string value of character array `a` preceded the string value of character array `b`?

    a. `if (a > b)`
       `itstricky();`

    b. `if (strcmp(a, b) < 0)`
       `itstricky();`

    c. `if (a[] > b[])`
       `itstricky();`

    d. `if (strcmp(a, b) > 0)`
       `itstricky();`

9. What does this program fragment display?

```
char x[80] = "Divide";
char y[80] = "Question";
printf("%s%s\n", x, y);
strcpy(x, y);
```

   a. Divide Question
   b. DivideQuestion
   c. Divide Divide
   d. Question Question

10. What does this program fragment display?

```
char x[80] = "Divide";
char y[80] = "Question";
printf("%s%s\n", x, y);
strcpy(x, y);

printf("%s %s\n", x, y);
int n = strlen(x);
if (strcmp(x, y) == 0)

printf("STRLEN = %d\n", n);
```

Programming Projects

1. Write a program that loads from a data file a list of hurricanes making landfall in the U.S. along with the year they occurred and the states affected before the storm was downgraded. Place each hurricane's data on a separate line of the file. Allow the user to select whether the hurricanes should be sorted by year of occurrence or by name. Display the data in the order selected, with the year in the first column, the hurricane name in the second, and the affected states in the third. Be sure to design your sort functions to keep the year list and affected states list parallel with the hurricane names. Allow for a maximum of 30 hurricanes, but use a constant macro for this number to permit easy future expansion of the database. Sample output sorted by year:

```
U.S. Hurricanes by Year of Occurrence

Year    Name       States
----    -------    --------
1960    Donna      FL,   NC
1969    Camille    MS
1972    Agnes      FL    ...
```

Hurricane Data for 1960-2012 from the National Hurricane Center

1960	Donna	FL, NC	2004	Ivan	AL
1969	Camille	MS	2004	Jeanne	FL
1972	Agnes	FL	2005	Dennis	FL, AL
1983	Alicia	TX	2005	Katrina	FL, LA, MS
1989	Hugo	SC, NC	2005	Rita	TX, LA
1992	Andrew	FL, LA	2005	Wilma	FL
1995	Opal	FL, AL	2008	Ike	TX
1999	Floyd	NC	2009	Ida	MS
2003	Isabel	NC, VA	2011	Irene	NC, NJ, MA, VT
2004	Charley	FL, SC, NC	2012	Isaac	LA
2004	Frances	FL			

2. A resistor is a circuit device designed to have a specific resistance value between its ends. Resistance values are expressed in ohms (Ω) or kilo-ohms (kΩ). Resistors are frequently marked with colored bands that encode their resistance values, as shown in Fig. 8.23. The first two bands are digits, and the third is a power-of-ten multiplier.

The table below shows the meanings of each band color. For example, if the first band is green, the second is black, and the third is orange, the resistor has a value of $50 \times 10^3 \Omega$ or 50 kΩ. The information in the table can be stored in a C program as an array of strings.

```c
char COLOR_CODES[10][7] = {"black", "brown", "red",
    "orange", "yellow", "green", "blue", "violet", "gray",
    "white"};
```

Notice that "red" is COLOR_CODES[2] and has a digit value of 2 and a multiplier value of 10^2. In general, COLOR_CODES[n] has digit value n and multiplier value $10n$.

FIGURE 8.23

Bands Encoding the Resistance Value of a Resistor

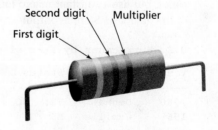

Second digit   Multiplier

First digit

Color Codes for Resistors*

Color	Value as Digit	Value as Multiplier
Black	0	1
Brown	1	10
Red	2	10^2
Orange	3	10^3
Yellow	4	10^4
Green	5	10^5
Blue	6	10^6
Violet	7	10^7
Gray	8	10^8
White	9	10^9

*Adapted from *Sears and Zemansky's University Physics*, 10th ed., edited by Hugh D. Young and Roger A. Freedman (Boston: Addison-Wesley, 2000), p. 807.

Write a program that prompts for the colors of Band 1, Band 2, and Band 3, and then displays the resistance in kilo-ohms. Include a helper function `search` that takes three parameters—the list of strings, the size of the list, and a target string, and returns the subscript of the list element that matches the target or returns –1 if the target is not in the list. Here is a short sample run:

```
Enter the colors of the resistor's three bands, beginning with
the band nearest the end. Type the colors in lowercase letters
only, NO CAPS.

Band 1 => green
Band 2 => black
Band 3 => yellow
Resistance value: 500 kilo-ohms
Do you want to decode another resistor?
=> y
Enter the colors of the resistor's three bands, beginning with
the band nearest the end. Type the colors in lowercase letters
only, NO CAPS.
Band 1 => brown
Band 2 => vilet
Band 3 => gray
Invalid color: vilet
Do you want to decode another resistor?
=> n
```

3. Write a function `fact_calc` that takes a string output argument and an integer input argument *n* and returns a string showing the calculation of *n!*. For example, if the value supplied for *n* were 6, the string returned would be "6! = 6 × 5 × 4 × 3 × 2 × 1 = 720". Write a program that repeatedly prompts the user for an integer between 0 and 9, calls `fact_calc` and outputs the resulting string in a box of asterisks of the right size to surround the result. If the user inputs an invalid value, the program should display an error message and reprompt for valid input. Input of the sentinel -1 should cause the input loop to exit. Sample run:

```
Enter an integer between 0 and 9 or -1 to quit => 6
**************************************
* 6! = 6 x 5 x 4 x 3 x 2 x 1 = 720 *
**************************************
Enter an integer between 0 and 9 or -1 to quit => 12
Invalid entry
Enter an integer between 0 and 9 or -1 to quit => 0
************
* 0! = 1 *
************
Enter an integer between 0 and 9 or -1 to quit => -1
```

4. Write a C program that reverses the input data, as shown below:

Input	Output
32023	32023
teacher	rehcaet

5. Write a program that takes verbs and forms their past tense on the basis of these rules:

   a. If verb ends in "e", add "d".
   b. If verb ends in "ss" or "gh", add "ed".
   c. In all other cases, inform the user that the verb may have an irregular past tense.

Print each verb and its past tense. Try the following data:

```
smile   discuss   confess   declare   laugh   run   cough   teach   buy
```

6. Write a program that stores lists of names (the last name first) and ages in parallel arrays and sorts the names into alphabetical order keeping the ages with the correct names. Sample output:

```
Original list
-----------------------------
    Ryan, Elizabeth        62
    McIntyre, Osborne      84
    DuMond, Kristin        18
    Larson, Lois           42
    Thorpe, Trinity        15
    Ruiz, Pedro            35

Alphabetized list
-----------------------------
    DuMond, Kristin        18
    Larson, Lois           42
    McIntyre, Osborne      84
    Ruiz, Pedro            35
    Ryan, Elizabeth        62
    Thorpe, Trinity        15
```

7. Write a C program that prompts the user to input exactly two strings. The program must offer an output whether the second string entered by the user is a part of the first string entered by the user or not. If so, the program must also print the total number of times the second string appears in the first string. The program must distinguish between lowercase and uppercase characters. Check the program for the following input:

   `Input 1: String 1 — Madam, String 2 — Mad`

8. Write a C program that displays the total number of vowels and consonants in the sentence (string) given as an input by the user. Check the program for the following input:

   `Welcome to C Programming`

9. Write a program that processes a data file of names in which each name is on a separate line of at most 80 characters. Here are two sample names:

   Hartman-Montgomery, Jane R.
   Doe, J. D.

   On each line the surname is followed by a comma and a space. Next comes the first name or initial, then a space and the middle initial. Your program should scan the names into three arrays—surname, first, and middle_init. If the surname is longer than 15 characters, store only the first 15. Similarly, limit the first name to ten characters. Do not store periods in the first and middle_init arrays. Write the array's contents to a file, aligning the contents of each column:

```
Hartman-Montgom     Jane     R
Doe                 J        D
```

10. You are developing software to use in a smartphone app to assist health care providers applying Advanced Cardiac Life Support (ACLS) algorithms in treating patients with moderate to severe cardiac problems. Your program should load a data file containing the names of the recommended drugs and the instructions for their administration. Each drug has a single line in the text data file (even though amiodarone appears to extend over 3 lines, you may assume there is no \n until after the semi-colon following "18 hrs.") Your program should scan the drug names into an array of strings and should store the accompanying dosing instructions in a second array of strings (maximum string length 120 characters). In this second array, replace all semicolons by \n characters. Thus, display of the string of instructions associated with amiodarone would appear as:

```
Dose 1: 300 mg IV push
Dose 2: 150 mg IV push
Infusion 1: 1 mg/min for 6 hrs
Infusion 2: 0.5 mg/min for 18 hrs
```

After loading the drugs and instructions, instruct the user to enter only the first three characters of a desired drug. Then repeatedly prompt the user to enter drugs (or q to quit), search for the requested drug, and display the full drug name and dosing instructions.

Data file:

```
amiodarone Dose 1: 300 mg IV push;Dose 2: 150 mg IV push;
Infusion 1: 1 mg/min for 6 hrs; Infusion 2: 0.5 mg/min for
18 hrs;
adenosine Dose 1: 6 mg rapid IV push;Dose 2: 12 mg rapid IV
push;
atropine 0.5 mg IV push every 3-5 min;max 3 mg;
dopamine Infusion 2-10 mcg/kg/min;
epinephrine 1 mg IV push every 3-5 min;Infusion: 2-10 mcg/min
magnesium Infusion: 1-2g over 5 to 20 min;
vasopressin 40 units IV push;
```

Recursion

CHAPTER OBJECTIVES

- To understand how recursion is used as a problem solving tool
- To learn how to write and trace recursive functions
- To see how to implement mathematical functions with recursive definitions as C functions
- To learn how to use recursion to solve problems involving arrays and strings
- To learn how to write a recursive sort function
- To understand a recursive solution to the Towers of Hanoi Problem

recursive function
function that calls itself
or that is part of a cycle
in the sequence of
function calls

A function that calls itself is said to be **recursive**. A function `f1` is also recursive if it calls a function `f2`, which under some circumstances calls `f1`, creating a cycle in the sequence of calls. The ability to invoke itself enables a recursive function to be repeated with different parameter values. You can use recursion as an alternative to iteration (looping). Generally, a recursive solution is less efficient than an iterative solution in terms of computer time due to the overhead for the extra function calls; however, in many instances, the use of recursion enables us to specify a very natural, simple solution to a problem that would otherwise be very difficult to solve. For this reason, recursion is an important and powerful tool in problem solving and programming.

9.1 The Nature of Recursion

Problems that lend themselves to a recursive solution have the following characteristics:

simple case problem
case for which a
straightforward solution
is known

- One or more **simple cases** of the problem have a straightforward, nonrecursive solution.
- The other cases can be redefined in terms of problems that are closer to the simple cases.
- By applying this redefinition process every time the recursive function is called, eventually the problem is reduced entirely to simple cases, which are relatively easy to solve.

The recursive algorithms that we write will generally consist of an `if` statement with the following form:

if this is a simple case
  solve it
else
  redefine the problem using recursion

Figure 9.1 illustrates this approach. Let's assume that for a particular problem of size n, we can split the problem into a problem of size 1, which we can solve (a simple case), and a problem of size $n - 1$. We can split the problem of size $n - 1$ into another problem of size 1 and a problem of size $n - 2$, which we can split further. If we split the problem $n - 1$ times, we will end up with n problems of size 1, all of which we can solve.

FIGURE 9.1   Splitting a Problem into Smaller Problems

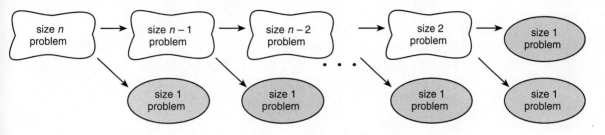

EXAMPLE 9.1   As a simple example of this approach, let's consider how we might solve the problem of multiplying 6 by 3, assuming we know our addition tables but not our multiplication tables. We do know, however, that any number multiplied by 1 gives us the original number, so if we ever come across this simple case, we'll just solve it. The problem of multiplying 6 by 3 can be split into the two problems:

1. Multiply 6 by 2.
2. Add 6 to the result of problem 1.

Because we know our addition tables, we can solve problem 2 but not problem 1. However, problem 1 is closer to the simple case than the original problem was. We can split problem 1 into the following two problems, 1.1 and 1.2, leaving us three problems to solve, two of which are additions.

1. Multiply 6 by 2.
    1.1 Multiply 6 by 1.
    1.2 Add 6 to the result of problem 1.1.
2. Add 6 to the result of problem 1.

Problem 1.1 is one of the simple cases we were looking for. By solving problem 1.1 (the answer is 6) and problem 1.2, we get the solution to problem 1 (the answer is 12). Solving problem 2 gives us the final answer (18).

Figure 9.2 implements this approach to doing multiplication as the recursive C function `multiply` that returns the product m × n of its two arguments. The body of function `multiply` implements the general form of a recursive algorithm shown earlier. The simplest case is reached when the condition n == 1 is true. In this case, the statement

```
ans = m;    /* simple case */
```

executes, so the answer is m. If n is greater than 1, the statement

```
ans = m + multiply(m, n - 1);    /* recursive step */
```

FIGURE 9.2   Recursive Function Multiply

```
1.  /*
2.   * Performs integer multiplication using + operator.
3.   * Pre:    m and n are defined and n > 0
4.   * Post:   returns m * n
5.   */
6.  int
7.  multiply(int m, int n)
8.  {
9.      int ans;
10.
11.     if (n == 1)
12.           ans = m;     /* simple case */
13.     else
14.           ans = m + multiply(m, n - 1); /* recursive step */
15.
16.     return (ans);
17. }
```

executes, splitting the original problem into the two simpler problems:

- multiply m by n-1
- add m to the result

The first of these problems is solved by calling multiply again with n-1 as its second argument. If the new second argument is greater than 1, there will be additional calls to function multiply.

At first, it may seem odd that we must rely on the function multiply before we have even finished writing it! However, this approach is the key to developing recursive algorithms. In order to solve a problem recursively, first we must trust our function to solve a simpler version of the problem. Then we build the solution to the whole problem on the result from the simpler version.

For now, you will have to take our word that function multiply performs as desired. We will see how to trace the execution of a recursive function in the next section.

One group of problems for which recursive solutions seem very natural are problems involving varying-length lists. Since a string is a varying-length list of characters, this chapter contains numerous examples of recursive functions that process strings.

EXAMPLE 9.2 We need to develop a function to count the number of times a particular character appears in a string. For example,

```
count('s', "Mississippi sassafrs")
```

should return the value 8. Of course, we could set up a loop to count the s's, but instead we will look for a recursive solution. Since recursion requires breaking a problem into a combination of simpler problems, our initial reaction to a problem should be something like, "This whole problem is entirely too hard. Maybe I can do a little bit of this problem, but I will definitely need help to do the whole problem." We then need to arrange things so the "help" needed is actually in solving a simpler version of the same problem. When dealing with a list of elements as we are in this problem, a recursive solution usually explicitly processes only the first list element. The recursive problem solver's thought process is illustrated in Fig. 9.3.

Looking back at the `if` statement that is our "generic" recursion algorithm,

if this is a simple case
> *solve it*

else
> *redefine the problem using recursion*

we see that the thought process shown in Fig. 9.3 fits into our generic `else` clause. We have redefined the problem "Count s's in `Mississippi sassafras`" as "Count s's in `ississippi sassafras` and add one more if the first letter is an s." Our redefinition of the general problem "Count a letter in a string" is recursive, since part of the solution is still to count a letter in a string. What has changed is that the new string is shorter. We still need to identify the simplest case of the problem, which must involve a *very* short string. Although it would be fairly easy to count a certain character in a string with only one character element, we would still need to do a comparison. If the string had *no* characters at all, we would know immediately that there were zero occurrences of the character being counted. Now that we have a simple case and a way to redefine more complex cases using recursion, we can write a recursive function `count`. Because the "rest of the string" to be processed by the recursive call will be examined by `count`, but

FIGURE 9.3

Thought Process of Recursive Algorithm Developer

Counting occurrences of `'s'` in

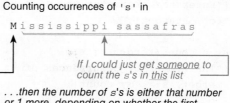

M i s s i s s i p p i   s a s s a f r a s

If I could just get *someone* to count the s's in *this* list

. . .then the number of s's is either that number or 1 more, depending on whether the *first letter* is an s.

not modified by it, we do not even need to copy the substring containing all but the first letter of `str`.

Our implementation of function `count` at the bottom of Fig. 9.4 simply calls `count` with `ch` and `&str[1]` as its arguments. Therefore, the string processed in the next call to function `count` will be the substring starting at position 1 of the string in the previous call. Figure 9.4 shows a main function that calls `count` after reading in a string to process and a target character to count. A sample run is also shown.

In our first example, we saw how a recursive `multiply` function broke a size n multiplication problem into n size 1 addition problems. Similarly, the effect of our recursive `count` function is to split the problem of analyzing a length n string into n problems of comparing single characters.

FIGURE 9.4   Counting Occurrences of a Character in a String

```
1.  /*
2.   * Counting occurrences of a letter in a string.
3.   */
4.
5.  #include <stdio.h>
6.
7.  int count(char ch, const char *str);
8.
9.  int
10. main(void)
11. {
12.         char str[80];        /* string to be processed */
13.         char target;         /* character counted */
14.         int my_count;
15.
16.         printf("Enter up to 79 characters.\n");
17.         gets(str);           /* read in the string */
18.
19.         printf("Enter the character you want to count: ");
20.         scanf("%c", &target);
21.
22.         my_count = count(target, str);
23.         printf("The number of occurrences of %c in\n\"%s\"\nis %d\n",
24.                 target, str, my_count);
25.
```

(continued)

FIGURE 9.4   (continued)

```
26.        return (0);
27.  }
28.
29.  /*
30.   * Counts the number of times ch occurs in string str.
31.   * Pre:  Letter ch and string str are defined.
32.   */
33.  int
34.  count(char ch, const char *str)
35.  {
36.        int ans;
37.
38.        if (str[0] == '\0')                      /* simple case */
39.            ans = 0;
40.        else                 /* redefine problem using recursion */
41.            if (ch == str[0]) /* first character must be counted */
42.                ans = 1 + count(ch, &str[1]);
43.            else                 /* first character is not counted */
44.                ans = count(ch, &str[1]);
45.
46.        return (ans);
47.  }
48.
```

```
Enter up to 79 characters.
this is the string I am testing
Enter the character you want to count: t
The number of occurrences of t in
"this is the string I am testing" is 5
```

EXERCISES FOR SECTION 9.1

Self-Check

1. Using diagrams similar to those in Fig. 9.1, show the specific problems that are generated by the following calls.

    a.   `multiply(5, 4)`
    b.   `count('d', "dad")`

Programming

1. Write a recursive function `count_digits` that counts all the digits in a string.
2. Write a recursive function `add` that computes the sum of its two integer parameters. Assume `add` does not know general addition tables but does know how to add or subtract 1.

9.2 Tracing a Recursive Function

Hand tracing an algorithm's execution provides us with valuable insight into how that algorithm works. We can trace the execution of a recursive function, and now we will illustrate how to do this by first studying the execution of a recursive function that returns a value, and then studying the execution of a recursive `void` function.

Tracing a Recursive Function That Returns a Value

In Section 9.1, we wrote the recursive function `multiply` (see Fig. 9.2). We can trace the execution of the function call

```
multiply(6, 3)
```

activation frame
representation of one
call to a function

by drawing an **activation frame** corresponding to each call of the function. An activation frame shows the parameter values for each call and summarizes the execution of the call.

The three activation frames generated to solve the problem of multiplying 6 by 3 are shown in Fig. 9.5. The part of each activation frame that executes before the next recursive call is in color; the part that executes after the return from the next call is in gray. The darker the color of an activation frame, the greater the depth of recursion.

The value returned from each call is shown alongside each black arrow. The return arrow from each call points to the operator + because the addition is performed just after the return.

Figure 9.5 shows three calls to function `multiply`. Parameter m has the value 6 for all three calls; parameter n has the values 3, 2, and, finally, 1. Since n is 1 in the third call, the value of m (6) is assigned to `ans` and is returned as the result of the third and last call. After returning to the second activation frame, the value of m is added to this result, and the sum (12) is returned as the result of the second call. After returning to the first activation frame, the value of m is added to this result, and the sum (18) is returned as the result of the original call to function `multiply`.

Tracing a void Function That Is Recursive

Hand tracing a `void` function is somewhat simpler than tracing a function that returns a value. For both types of functions, we use activation frames to track each function call.

FIGURE 9.5

Trace of Function
Multiply

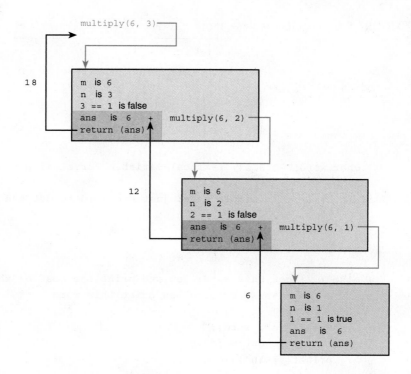

EXAMPLE 9.3   Function `reverse_input_words` in Fig. 9.6 is a recursive module that takes n
words of input and prints them in reverse order. If this function call statement

```
reverse_input_words(5)
```

is executed, the five words entered at the keyboard are printed in reverse order. If
the words entered are

```
the
course
of
human
events
```

the program output will be

```
events
human
of
course
the
```

FIGURE 9.6   Function reverse_input_words

```
1.   /*
2.    * Take n words as input and print them in reverse order on separate lines.
3.    * Pre: n > 0
4.    */
5.   void
6.   reverse_input_words(int n)
7.   {
8.          char word[WORDSIZ]; /* local variable for storing one word          */
9.
10.      if (n <= 1) { /* simple case: just one word to get and print          */
11.
12.          scanf("%s", word);
13.          printf("%s\n", word);
14.
15.      } else { /* get this word; get and print the rest of the words in
16.                  reverse order; then print this word                        */
17.
18.          scanf("%s", word);
19.          reverse_input_words(n - 1);
20.          printf("%s\n", word);
21.      }
22.   }
```

terminating condition   a condition that is true when a recursive algorithm is processing a simple case

Like most recursive modules, the body of function reverse_input_words consists of an if statement that evaluates a **terminating condition**, n <= 1. When the terminating condition is true, the function is dealing with one of the problem's simple cases—printing in reverse order a list of just one word. Since reversing word order has no effect on a single-word list, for the simple case when n is less than or equal to one, we just get the word using scanf and print it.

If the terminating condition is false (n > 1), the recursive step (following else) is executed. This group of statements transfers the current input word into memory, gets "someone" (i.e., reverse_input_words) to take and reverse print the remaining n - 1 words of interest, and then prints the current word.

Figure 9.7 shows a trace of the function call

```
reverse_input_words(3)
```

assuming that the words "bits" "and" "bytes" are entered as data. The trace shows three separate activation frames for function reverse_input_words. Each activation

FIGURE 9.7   Trace of reverse_input_words(3) When the Words Entered Are "bits" "and" "bytes"

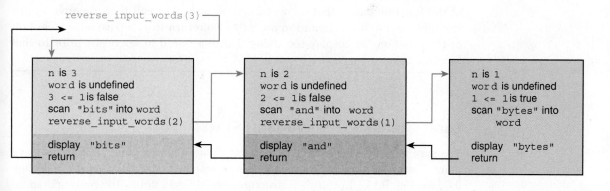

frame begins with a list of the initial values of n and word for that frame. The value of n is passed into the function when it is called; the value of the local variable word is initially undefined.

The statements that are executed for each frame are shown next. The statements in color in the activation frames are recursive function calls and result in new activation frames, as indicated by the colored arrows. A void function's return occurs when the closing brace of the function body is encountered, indicated by the word return and a black arrow that points to the statement in the calling frame to which the function returns. Tracing the colored arrows and then the black arrows in Fig. 9.7 gives us the sequence of events listed in Fig. 9.8. To help you understand this list, all the statements for a particular activation frame are indented to the same column.

FIGURE 9.8

Sequence of Events for Trace of reverse_input_words(3)

Call reverse_input_words with n equal to 3.
    Scan the first word ("bits") into word.
    Call reverse_input_words with n equal to 2.
        Scan the second word ("and") into word.
        Call reverse_input_words with n equal to 1.
            Scan the third word ("bytes") into word.
            Display the third word ("bytes").
            Return from third call.
        Display the second word ("and").
        Return from second call.
    Display the first word ("bits").
    Return from original call.

As shown, there are three calls to function `reverse_input_words`, each with a different parameter value. The function returns always occur in the reverse order of the function calls—that is, we return from the last call first, then we return from the next to last call, and so on. After we return from a particular execution of the function, we display the string that was stored in `word` just prior to that function call.

Parameter and Local Variable Stacks

stack a data structure in which the last data item added is the first data item processed

You may be wondering how C keeps track of the values of `n` and `word` at any given point. C uses the **stack** data structure that we implemented with an array in Section 9.5 (see Fig. 9.14). In this data structure, we add data items (the push operation) and remove them (the pop operation) from the same end of the list, so the last item stored is the first processed.

When executing a call to `reverse_input_words`, the system pushes the parameter value associated with the call on top of the parameter stack, and pushes a new undefined cell on top of the stack maintained for the local variable `word`. A return from `reverse_input_words` pops each stack, removing the top value.

As an example, let's look at the two stacks as they appear right after the first call to `reverse_input_words`. One cell is on each stack, as shown.

After first call to `reverse_input_words`

```
     n              word

  |  3  |         |  ?  |
```

The word `"bits"` is stored in `word` just before the second call to `reverse_input_words`.

```
     n              word

  |  3  |         |  bits  |
```

After the second call to `reverse_input_words`, the number 2 is pushed on the stack for `n`, and the top of the stack for `word` becomes undefined again, as shown next. The value in color is at the top of each stack.

After second call to `reverse_input_words`

```
        n                    word
      ┌─────┐              ┌─────┐
      │  2  │              │  ?  │
      │  3  │              │bits │
      └─────┘              └─────┘
```

The word `"and"` is scanned and stored in `word` just before the third call to `reverse_input_words`.

```
        n                    word
      ┌─────┐              ┌─────┐
      │  2  │              │ and │
      │  3  │              │bits │
      └─────┘              └─────┘
```

However, `word` becomes undefined again right after the third call.

After third call to `reverse_input_words`

```
        n                    word
      ┌─────┐              ┌─────┐
      │  1  │              │  ?  │
      │  2  │              │ and │
      │  3  │              │bits │
      └─────┘              └─────┘
```

During this execution of the function, the word `"bytes"` is scanned and stored in `word`, and `"bytes"` is echo printed immediately because `n` is 1 (a simple case).

```
        n                    word
      ┌─────┐              ┌─────┐
      │  1  │              │bytes│
      │  2  │              │ and │
      │  3  │              │bits │
      └─────┘              └─────┘
```

The function return pops both stacks, as shown next.

After first return

```
        n                    word
      ┌─────┐              ┌─────┐
      │  2  │              │ and │
      │  3  │              │bits │
      └─────┘              └─────┘
```

Because control is returned to a `printf` call, the value of `word` (`"and"`) at the top of the stack is then displayed. Another return occurs, popping the stacks again.

After second return

n	word
3	bits

Again, control is returned to a `printf` statement, and the value of `word` (`"bits"`) at the top of the stack is displayed. The third and last return exits the original function call, so there is no longer any memory allocated for `n` and `word`.

A stack is a data structure that you can implement and manipulate yourself using arrays. However, C automatically handles all the stack manipulation associated with function calls, so we can write recursive functions without needing to worry about the stacks.

Implementation of Parameter Stacks in C

system stack area of memory where parameters and local variables are allocated when a function is called and deallocated when the function returns

For illustrative purposes, we have used separate stacks for each parameter in our discussion; however, the compiler actually maintains a single **system stack**. Each time a call to a function occurs, all its parameters and local variables are pushed onto the stack along with the memory address of the calling statement. This address gives the computer the return point after execution of the function. Although multiple copies of a function's parameters may be saved on the stack, only one copy of the function body is in memory.

When and How to Trace Recursive Functions

Doing a trace by hand of multiple calls to a recursive function is helpful in understanding how recursion works but less useful when trying to develop a recursive algorithm. During algorithm development, it is best to trace a specific case simply by trusting any recursive call to return a correct value based on the function purpose. Then the hand trace can check whether this value is manipulated properly to produce a correct function result for the case under consideration.

However, if a recursive function's implementation is flawed, tracing its execution is an essential part of identifying the error. The function can be made to trace itself by inserting debugging print statements showing entry to and exit from the function. Figure 9.9 shows a self-tracing version of function `multiply` as well as output generated by the call

```
multiply(8, 3)
```

FIGURE 9.9   Recursive Function multiply with Print Statements to Create Trace and Output from multiply(8, 3)

```
1.   /*
2.    * *** Includes calls to printf to trace execution ***
3.    * Performs integer multiplication using + operator.
4.    * Pre: m and n are defined and n > 0
5.    * Post: returns m * n
6.    */
7.   int
8.   multiply(int m, int n)
9.   {
10.        int ans;
11.
12.      printf("Entering multiply with m = %d, n = %d\n", m, n);
13.
14.        if (n == 1)
15.              ans = m; /* simple case */
16.        else
17.              ans = m + multiply(m, n - 1); /* recursive step */
18.      printf("multiply(%d, %d) returning %d\n", m, n, ans);
19.
20.        return (ans);
21.   }
22.
23.   Entering multiply with m = 8, n = 3
24.   Entering multiply with m = 8, n = 2
25.   Entering multiply with m = 8, n = 1
26.   multiply(8, 1) returning 8
27.   multiply(8, 2) returning 16
28.   multiply(8, 3) returning 24
```

EXERCISES FOR SECTION 9.2

Self-Check

1. Trace the contents of stack representations of m, n, and ans for the evaluation of multiply(6,3) whose activation frames are shown in Fig. 9.5.
2. Draw activation frames showing the evaluation of count('B',"BOB"), assuming that count is defined as shown in Fig. 9.4.

Programming

1. Rewrite function `count` from Fig. 9.4, adding calls to `printf` to make `count` self-tracing. Then show the output produced by the call `count('l', "lull")`.

9.3 Recursive Mathematical Functions

Many mathematical functions can be defined recursively. An example is the factorial of a number n ($n!$), a function that we defined iteratively in Chapter 5.

- 0! is 1
- $n!$ is $n \times (n - 1)!$, for $n > 0$

Thus 4! is $4 \times 3!$, which means $4 \times 3 \times 2 \times 1$, or 24. Implementing this definition as a recursive function in C is quite straightforward.

EXAMPLE 9.4   Function `factorial` in Fig. 9.10 computes the factorial of its argument n. The recursive step

```
ans = n * factorial(n - 1);
```

implements the second line of the factorial definition just shown. Thus, the result of the current call (argument n) is computed by multiplying by n the result of the call `factorial(n - 1)`.

FIGURE 9.10   Recursive Factorial Function

```
1.  /*
2.   * Compute n! using a recursive definition
3.   * Pre: n >= 0
4.   */
5.  int
6.  factorial(int n)
7.  {
8.        int ans;
9.
10.       if (n == 0)
11.             ans = 1;
12.       else
13.             ans = n * factorial(n - 1);
14.
15.       return (ans);
16. }
```

FIGURE 9.11

Trace of fact =
factorial(3);

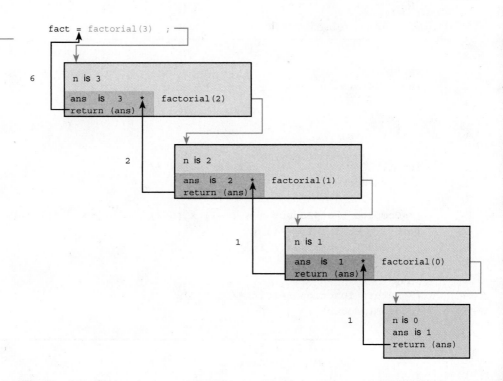

A trace of

```
fact = factorial(3);
```

is shown in Fig. 9.11. The value returned from the original call, `factorial(3)`, is 6, and this value is assigned to `fact`. Be careful when using the factorial function, as its value increases very rapidly and could lead to an integer overflow error (e.g., 8! is 40,320).

Although the recursive implementation of function `factorial` follows naturally from its definition, we saw in Chapter 5 that this function can also be implemented easily using iteration. The iterative version we developed in that chapter is shown in Fig. 9.12.

Note that the iterative version contains a loop as its major control structure, whereas the recursive version contains an `if` statement. In the iterative version, the variable `product` is the target of repeated assignments, each of which brings its value closer to the result value. Compare this use of `product` to the purpose of the local variable `ans` in the recursive version. Variable `ans` holds the answer to the subproblem that is the reason for the current call to the function.

FIGURE 9.12 Iterative Function Factorial

```
1.  /*
2.   * Computes n!
3.   * Pre: n is greater than or equal to zero
4.   */
5.  int
6.  factorial(int n)
7.  {
8.      int i,                  /* local variables */
9.          product = 1;
10.
11.     /* Compute the product n x (n-1) x (n-2) x . . . x 2 x 1 */
12.     for (i = n; i > 1; --i) {
13.         product = product * i;
14.     }
15.
16.     /* Return function result */
17.     return (product);
18. }
```

EXAMPLE 9.5

The Fibonacci numbers are a sequence of numbers that have many varied uses. They were originally intended to model the growth of a rabbit colony. Although we will not go into the details of the model here, the Fibonacci sequence 1, 1, 2, 3, 5, 8, 13, 21, 34, . . . certainly seems to increase rapidly enough. The fifteenth number in the sequence is 610 (that's a lot of rabbits!). The Fibonacci sequence is defined as

- Fibonacci$_1$ is 1
- Fibonacci$_2$ is 1
- Fibonacci$_n$ is Fibonacci$_{n-2}$ + Fibonacci$_{n-1}$, for $n > 2$

Verify for yourself that the sequence of numbers just shown is correct.

A recursive function that computes the nth Fibonacci number is shown in Fig. 9.13. Although easy to write, this version of `fibonacci` is not very efficient because each recursive step generates two calls to function `fibonacci`, and these calls duplicate many computations. Programming Exercise 2 at the end of this section describes an efficient (though more complicated) recursive algorithm for computing Fibonacci numbers.

FIGURE 9.13 Recursive Function fibonacci

```
1.   /*
2.    * Computes the nth Fibonacci number
3.    * Pre: n > 0
4.    */
5.   int
6.   fibonacci(int n)
7.   {
8.          int ans;
9.
10.         if (n == 1 || n == 2)
11.                 ans = 1;
12.         else
13.                 ans = fibonacci(n - 2) + fibonacci(n - 1);
14.
15.         return (ans);
16.  }
```

EXAMPLE 9.6

In a programming exercise for Section 6.5, we presented an iterative algorithm for finding the greatest common divisor of two integers. Euclid's algorithm for finding the gcd can be defined recursively as shown. You recall that the *greatest common divisor* of two integers is the largest integer that divides them both evenly.

- gcd(m,n) is n if n divides m evenly
- gcd(m,n) is gcd(n, remainder of m divided by n) otherwise

This algorithm states that the gcd is n if n divides m evenly. If n does not divide m with a zero remainder, the answer is obtained by finding the gcd of n and the remainder of m divided by n. One of the elegant features of this definition is that it does not matter whether m or n is the larger number. If m is greater than n, the computation seems to proceed more directly to a solution; if it is not, the first application of the recursive step has the effect of exchanging m and n. This exchange is a result of the fact that when m is less than n, the remainder of m divided by n is m. The declaration and use of a recursive gcd function is shown in Fig. 9.14.

FIGURE 9.14   Program Using Recursive Function gcd

```
1.   /*
2.    * Displays the greatest common divisor of two integers
3.    */
4.
5.   #include <stdio.h>
6.
7.   /*
8.    * Finds the greatest common divisor of m and n
9.    * Pre: m and n are both > 0
10.   */
11.  int
12.  gcd(int m, int n)
13.  {
14.       int ans;
15.
16.       if (m % n == 0)
17.            ans = n;
18.       else
19.            ans = gcd(n, m % n);
20.
21.       return (ans);
22.  }
23.  int
24.  main(void)
25.  {
26.       int n1, n2;
27.
28.       printf("Enter two positive integers separated by a space> ");
29.       scanf("%d%d", &n1, &n2);
30.       printf("Their greatest common divisor is %d\n", gcd(n1, n2));
31.
32.       return (0);
33.  }
34.
35.  Enter two positive integers separated by a space> 24 84
36.  Their greatest common divisor is 12
```

EXERCISES FOR SECTION 9.3

Self-Check

1. Complete the following recursive function that calculates the value of a number (`base`) raised to a power. Assume that `power` is a nonnegative integer.

```
int
power_raiser(int base, int power)
{
      int ans;
      if (power == _____)
            ans = _____;
      else
            ans = _____ * _____;
      return (ans);
}
```

2. What is the output of the following program? What does function `strange` compute when called with a positive integer?

```
#include <stdio.h>

int strange(int n);
int
main(void)
{
      printf("%d\n", strange(7));
}
int
strange(int n)
{
      int ans;

      if (n == 1)
            ans = 0;
      else
            ans = 1 + strange(n / 2);

      return (ans);
}
```

3. Explain what would happen if the terminating condition for function `fibonacci` were just (n == 1).

Programming

1. Write a recursive function `find_sum` that calculates the sum of successive integers starting at 1 and ending at n (i.e., `find_sum(n)` = (1 + 2 + ... + (n - 1) + n).

2. Write a recursive function `fast_fib` to compute a pair of Fibonacci numbers, F(n + 1) and F(n). Function `fast_fib` should make only one recursive call.

    Algorithm

    if n is 1
    >   The pair to send back is 1, 1.

    else
    >   Use `fast_fib` to compute F(n) and F(n – 1).
    >   The pair to send back is [F(n) + F(n – 1)], F(n).

9.4 Recursive Functions with Array and String Parameters

In this section, we will examine two problems and will implement recursive functions to solve them. Both problems involve processing of some type of array.

CASE STUDY   Finding Capital Letters in a String

PROBLEM

Form a string containing all the capital letters found in another string.

ANALYSIS

Just as in the problem of counting occurrences of a particular letter in a string, recursion will allow us to solve this problem by simply working out what to do with the string's first letter and then combining this processing with a recursive call handling the rest of the string. For instance, if the string in question were `"Franklin Delano Roosevelt"`, finding capital letters in `"ranklin Delano Roosevelt"` would give us the string `"DR"`. It is a simple matter to combine this string with the capital `'F'` to form the full result. Of course, the simplest string in which to look for *anything* is the empty string, so checking for this simple case gives us the necessary terminating condition.

DATA REQUIREMENTS

Problem Input

```
char *str    /* a string from which to extract capital letters  */
```

Problem Output

```
char *caps    /* the capital letters from str                   */
```

FIGURE 9.15   Recursive Function to Extract Capital Letters from a String

```
1.   /*
2.    * Forms a string containing all the capital letters found in the input
3.    * parameter str.
4.    * Pre: caps has sufficient space to store all caps in str plus the null
5.    */
6.   char *
7.   find_caps(char        *caps,    /* output - string of all caps found in str   */
8.             const char *str)      /* input - string from which to extract caps  */
9.   {
10.         char restcaps[STRSIZ]; /* caps from reststr */
11.
12.         if (str[0] == '\0')
13.               caps[0] = '\0'; /* no letters in str => no caps in str          */
14.         else
15.               if (isupper(str[0]))
16.                     sprintf(caps, "%c%s", str[0], find_caps(restcaps, &str[1]));
17.               else
18.                     find_caps(caps, &str[1]);
19.
20.         return (caps);
21.   }
```

DESIGN

Algorithm

1. if str is the empty string
   2. Store empty string in caps (a string with no letters has no capitals).
   else
   3. if initial letter of str is a capital letter
   4. Store in caps this letter and the capital letters from the rest of str.
   else
   5. Store in caps the capital letters from the rest of str.

Function find_caps in Fig. 9.15 implements the recursive algorithm.

TESTING

Given this #define directive and declaration,

```
#define STRSIZ 50
. . .
char caps[STRSIZ];
```

and the statement

```
printf("Capital letters in JoJo are %s\n",
       find_caps(caps, "JoJo"));
```

five calls to `find_caps` will be executed, as shown in Fig. 9.16. The string sent back from each function call is shown to the left of the arrow coming from the `return` statement.

FIGURE 9.16 Trace of Call to Recursive Function find_caps

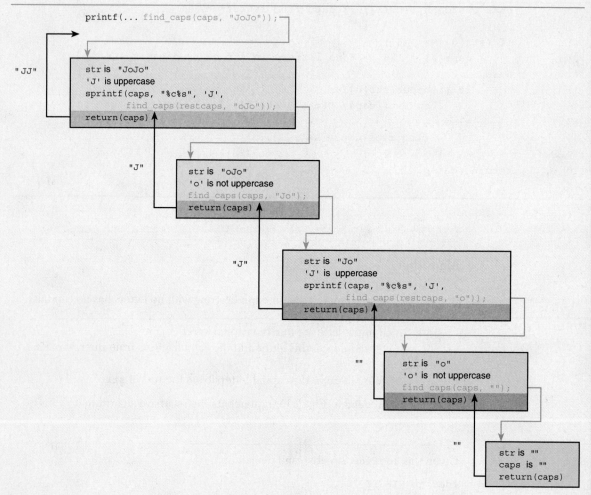

FIGURE 9.17 Sequence of Events for Trace of Call to find_caps from printf Statements

Call `find_caps` with input argument `"JoJo"` to determine value to print.
>Since `'J'` is a capital letter,
>prepare to use `sprintf` to build a string with `'J'`
>and the result of calling `find_caps` with input argument `"oJo"`.
>>Since `'o'` is not a capital letter,
>>call `find_caps` with input argument `"Jo"`.
>>>Since `'J'` is a capital letter,
>>>prepare to use `sprintf` to build a string with `'J'`
>>>and the result of calling `find_caps` with input argument `"o"`.
>>>>Since `'o'` is not a capital letter,
>>>>call `find_caps` with input argument `""`.
>>>>>Return `""` from fifth call.
>>>>Return `""` from fourth call.
>>>Complete execution of `sprintf` combining `'J'` and `""`.
>>>Return `"J"` from third call.
>>Return `"J"` from second call.
>Complete execution of `sprintf` combining `'J'` and `"J"`.
>Return `"JJ"` from original call.
Complete call to `printf` to print `Capital letters in JoJo are JJ`.

Figure 9.17 shows the sequence of events that results from following first the colored arrows and then the black arrows of Fig. 9.16. There are five calls to function `find_caps`, each with a different input argument. The desired string of capital letters is constructed one character at a time as the function returns cause the recursion to unwind.

CASE STUDY   Recursive Selection Sort

In Chapters 7 and 8, we studied an iterative selection sort algorithm. In this section we develop a recursive version of the algorithm that fills the array from the bottom up.

PROBLEM

Sort an array in ascending order using a selection sort.

FIGURE 9.18

Trace of Selection
Sort

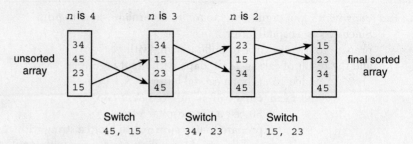

ANALYSIS

To perform a selection sort of an array with n elements (subscripts $0 \ldots n - 1$), we locate the largest element in the array and then switch the largest element with the element at subscript $n - 1$, thereby placing the largest element in the final array position. We then locate the largest element remaining in the subarray with subscripts $0 \ldots n - 2$, and switch it with the element at subscript $n - 2$, thereby placing the second largest element in the next to last position $n - 2$. We continue this process until the whole array is sorted.

Figure 9.18 traces the operation of this version of the selection sort algorithm. The diagram on the left shows the original array. Each subsequent diagram shows the array after the next largest element is moved to its final position in the array. The subarray in the darker color represents the portion of the array that is sorted after each exchange occurs. Note that it will require, at most, $n - 1$ exchanges to sort an array with n elements.

DESIGN

Because the selection sort can be viewed as a sort accomplished by first placing one element and then sorting a subarray, it is a good candidate for a recursive solution.

Recursive Algorithm for Selection Sort

1. if n is 1
    2. The array is sorted.
  else
    3. Place the largest array value in last array element.
    4. Sort the subarray which excludes the last array element
        (`array[0] .. array[n-2]`).

IMPLEMENTATION

Figure 9.19 shows an implementation of our recursive algorithm that uses a function place_largest to perform step 3 and a recursive function select_sort that carries out the overall procedure. The recursive function is slightly simpler to understand than the original iterative version because it contains a single if statement rather than a loop. The recursive function typically executes more slowly, however, because of the extra overhead due to the recursive function calls.

FIGURE 9.19 Recursive Selection Sort

```
 1.  /*
 2.   * Finds the largest value in list array[0]..array[n-1] and exchanges it
 3.   * with the value at array[n-1]
 4.   * Pre: n > 0 and first n elements of array are defined
 5.   * Post: array[n-1] contains largest value
 6.   */
 7.  void
 8.  place_largest(int array[],   /* input/output - array in which to place largest */
 9.                int n)          /* input - number of array elements to
10.                                   consider                                        */
11.  {
12.      int temp,          /* temporary variable for exchange                        */
13.          j,             /* array subscript and loop control                       */
14.          max_index;     /* index of largest so far                                */
15.
16.      /* Save subscript of largest array value in max_index                        */
17.      max_index = n - 1;    /* assume last value is largest                         */
18.      for (j = n - 2; j >= 0; --j)
19.          if (array[j] > array[max_index])
20.              max_index = j;
21.
22.      /* Unless largest value is already in last element, exchange
23.         largest and last elements                                                 */
24.      if (max_index != n - 1) {
25.          temp = array[n - 1];
26.          array[n - 1] = array[max_index];
27.          array[max_index] = temp;
28.      }
29.  }
```

(continued)

FIGURE 9.19 (continued)

```
30.
31.  /*
32.   * Sorts n elements of an array of integers
33.   * Pre: n > 0 and first n elements of array are defined
34.   * Post: array elements are in ascending order
35.   */
36.  void
37.  select_sort(int array[], /* input/output - array to sort              */
38.              int n)       /* input - number of array elements to sort   */
39.  {
40.
41.      if (n > 1) {
42.              place_largest(array, n);
43.              select_sort(array, n - 1);
44.      }
     }
```

Notice that the logic of the `select_sort` function does not exactly match our original algorithm or our generic recursive algorithm. If you look back at the initial algorithm, you will see that if we are at the simplest case (an array of one element), no action is necessary. Rather than explicitly making the test for the simple case and having an empty true branch, we have chosen to negate the test for the simplest case so that all the actions are on the true branch of the decision. Notice that if `n == 1`, the selection sort function returns without doing anything. This behavior is correct because a one-element array is always sorted.

EXERCISES FOR SECTION 9.4

Self-Check

1. Using activation frames, hand trace the execution of the `find_caps` function on the string `"DoD"`.
2. Trace the execution of the recursive `select_sort` function on an array that has the integers 2, 12, 15, 1 stored in consecutive elements.

Programming

1. Modify the `find_caps` function to create a `find_digits` function that returns a string consisting of all digit characters in the source string.

9.5   Problem Solving with Recursion

Since C does not have a built-in representation of a set data structure, we would like to develop an implementation of a group of set operations using strings as our sets.

CASE STUDY   Operations on Sets

PROBLEM

Develop a group of functions to perform the ∈ (is an element of), ⊆ (is a subset of), and ∪ (union) operations on sets of characters. Also, develop functions to check that a certain set is valid (that is, it contains no duplicate characters), to check for the empty set, and to print a set in standard set notation.

ANALYSIS

Character strings provide a fairly natural representation of sets of characters. Like sets, strings can be of varying sizes and can be empty. If a character array that is to hold a set is declared to have one more than the number of characters in the universal set (to allow room for the null character), then set operations should never produce a string that will overflow the array.

DESIGN

This problem is naturally divided into subproblems, each of which corresponds to a single function. Since these functions are all basic set utilities, their individual algorithms are quite straightforward. We will develop pseudocode for the simplest functions first and will refer to these functions in the more complex solutions. Since one goal of this case study is to demonstrate the use of recursion, we will ignore the existence of looping constructs for the time being.

Algorithm for `is_empty(set)`

1. Is initial character `'\0'`?

Algorithm for `is_element(ele, set)`

```
1.  if is_empty(set)                              /* simple case 1   */
        2.   Answer is false.
    else if initial character of set matches ele  /* simple case 2   */
        3.   Answer is true.
    else
        4.   Answer depends on whether ele
             is in the rest of set.               /* recursive step  */
```

Algorithm for `is_set(set)`

1. if `is_empty(set)`   /* simple case 1   */
    2.   Answer is true.
    else if `is_element`(initial set character,
                              rest of set)   /* simple case 2   */
        3.   Answer is false.
    else
        4.   Answer depends on whether rest of `set` is a
              valid `set`.   /* recursive step   */

Algorithm for `is_subset(sub, set)`

1. if `is_empty(sub)`   /* simple case 1   */
    2.   Answer is true.
    else if initial character of sub is not an element of `set` /* simple case 2   */
        3.   Answer is false.
    else
        4.   Answer depends on whether rest of `sub` is a
              subset of `set`.   /* recursive step   */

Algorithm for union of `set1` **and** `set2`

1. if `is_empty(set1)`   /* simple case   */
    2.   Result is `set2`.
    else if initial character of `set1` is also an element
        of `set2`   /* recursive steps   */
        3.   Result is the union of the rest of `set1` with
              `set2`.   /* case 1   */
    else   /* case 2   */
        4.   Result includes initial character of `set1` and the union of the rest of
              `set1` with `set2`.

Algorithm for `print_set(set)`

1. Output a {.
2. if set is not empty, print elements separated by commas.
3. Output a }.

Algorithm for `print_with_commas(set)`

1. if set has exactly one element
    2.   Print it.
    else
        3.   Print initial element and a comma.
        4.   `print_with_commas` the rest of `set`.

IMPLEMENTATION

Every recursive function in the collection of functions we have designed references "the rest of the set" for some set, that is, all but the first letter of the set. In all of these functions, this "rest of the set" is passed as an input argument only—the function called looks at it, but does not modify it. Since this particular substring includes all the characters of the original string from the substring's starting point right through the original string's null character, we can use &set[1] to reference the rest of the set. Figure 9.20 shows our implementation of all the set operations along with a main program that demonstrates the functions.

You will notice that the name of our function that forms the union of two sets is set_union. We could not use the name union because this is a reserved word in C. In the implementation of set_union, we could not use the variable result as the output argument for both the call to set_union and the call to sprintf because sprintf does not guarantee correct results if there is overlap between its input and output arguments.

FIGURE 9.20   Recursive Set Operations on Sets Represented as Character Strings

```
1.   /*
2.    * Functions to perform basic operations on sets of characters
3.    * represented as strings. Note: "Rest of set" is represented as
4.    * &set[1], which is indeed the address of the rest of the set excluding
5.    * the first element. This efficient representation, which does not
6.    * recopy the rest of the set, is an acceptable substring reference in
7.    * these functions only because the "rest of the set" is always passed
8.    * strictly as an input argument.
9.    */
10.
11.  #include <stdio.h>
12.  #include <string.h>
13.  #include <ctype.h>
14.
15.  #define SETSIZ 65 /* 52 uppercase and lowercase letters, 10 digits,
16.                             {, }, and '\0'                           */
17.  #define TRUE 1
18.  #define FALSE 0
19.
20.  int is_empty(const char *set);
21.  int is_element(char ele, const char *set);
```

(continued)

FIGURE 9.20   (continued)

```
22.  int is_set(const char *set);
23.  int is_subset(const char *sub, const char *set);
24.  char *set_union(char *result, const char *set1, const char *set2);
25.  void print_with_commas(const char *str);
26.  void print_set(const char *set);
27.  char *get_set(char *set);
28.  /*
29.   * Tries out set operation functions.
30.   */
31.  int
32.  main(void)
33.  {
34.        char ele, set_one[SETSIZ], set_two[SETSIZ], set_three[SETSIZ];
35.
36.        printf("A set is entered as a string of up to %d letters\n",
37.                    SETSIZ - 3);
38.        printf("and digits enclosed in {} ");
39.        printf("(no duplicate characters)\n");
40.        printf("For example, {a, b, c} is entered as {abc}\n");
41.
42.        printf("Enter a set to test validation function> ");
43.        get_set(set_one);
44.        putchar('\n');
45.        print_set(set_one);
46.        if (is_set(set_one))
47.              printf(" is a valid set\n");
48.        else
49.              printf(" is invalid\n");
50.
51.        printf("Enter a single character, a space, and a set> ");
52.        while(isspace(ele = getchar())); /* gets first character after
53.                                          whitespace                    */
54.        get_set(set_one);
55.        printf("\n%c ", ele);
56.        if (is_element(ele, set_one))
57.              printf("is an element of ");
58.        else
59.              printf("is not an element of ");
60.        print_set(set_one);
61.
```

(continued)

FIGURE 9.20   (continued)

```
62.        printf("\nEnter two sets to test set_union> ");
63.        get_set(set_one);
64.        get_set(set_two);
65.        printf("\nThe union of ");
66.        print_set(set_one);
67.        printf(" and ");
68.        print_set(set_two);
69.        printf(" is ");
70.        print_set(set_union(set_three, set_one, set_two));
71.        putchar('\n');
72.
73.        return (0);
74.  }
75.
76.  /*
77.   * Determines if set is empty. If so, returns 1; if not, returns 0.
78.   */
79.  int
80.  is_empty(const char *set)
81.  {
82.        return (set[0] == '\0');
83.  }
84.
85.  /*
86.   * Determines if ele is an element of set.
87.   */
88.  int
89.  is_element(char       ele,    /* input - element to look for in set          */
90.             const char *set)   /* input - set in which to look for ele         */
91.  {
92.        int ans;
93.
94.        if (is_empty(set))
95.              ans = FALSE;
96.        else if (set[0] == ele)
97.              ans = TRUE;
98.        else
99.              ans = is_element(ele, &set[1]);
100.
101.        return (ans);
102.  }
```

(continued)

FIGURE 9.20 (continued)

```
103.
104. /*
105.  * Determines if string value of set represents a valid set (no duplicate
106.  * elements)
107.  */
108. int
109. is_set (const char *set)
110. {
111.     int ans;
112.
113.     if (is_empty(set))
114.          ans = TRUE;
115.     else if (is_element(set[0], &set[1]))
116.          ans = FALSE;
117.     else
118.          ans = is_set(&set[1]);
119.     return (ans);
120. }
121.
122. /*
123.  * Determines if value of sub is a subset of value of set.
124.  */
125. int
126. is_subset(const char *sub, const char *set)
127. {
128.     int ans;
129.
130.     if (is_empty(sub))
131.          ans = TRUE;
132.     else if (!is_element(sub[0], set))
133.          ans = FALSE;
134.     else
135.          ans = is_subset(&sub[1], set);
136.
137.     return (ans);
138. }
139.
140. /*
141.  * Finds the union of set1 and set2.
```

(continued)

FIGURE 9.20   (continued)

```
142.    * Pre: size of result array is at least SETSIZ;
143.    *      set1 and set2 are valid sets of characters and digits
144.    */
145.   char *
146.   set_union(char    *result,    /* output - space in which to store
147.                                     string result                        */
148.            const char *set1, /* input - sets whose                       */
149.            const char *set2) /* union is being formed                    */
150.   {
151.          char temp[SETSIZ];    /* local variable to hold result of call
152.                                 to set_union embedded in sprintf call */
153.
154.          if (is_empty(set1))
155.                strcpy(result, set2);
156.          else if (is_element(set1[0], set2))
157.                set_union(result, &set1[1], set2);
158.          else
159.                sprintf(result, "%c%s", set1[0],
160.                      set_union(temp, &set1[1], set2));
161.
162.          return (result);
163.   }
164.
165.   /*
166.    * Displays a string so that each pair of characters is separated by a
167.    * comma and a space.
168.    */
169.   void
170.   print_with_commas(const char *str)
171.   {
172.          if (strlen(str) == 1) {
173.                putchar(str[0]);
174.          } else {
175.                printf("%c, ", str[0]);
176.                print_with_commas(&str[1]);
177.          }
178.   }
179.
180.   /*
181.    * Displays a string in standard set notation.
```

(continued)

FIGURE 9.20   (continued)

```
182.   * e.g. print_set("abc") outputs {a, b, c}
183.   */
184.  void
185.  print_set(const char *set)
186.  {
187.          putchar('{');
188.          if (!is_empty(set))
189.                  print_with_commas(set);
190.          putchar('}');
191.  }
192.
193.  /*
194.   * Gets a set input as a string with brackets (e.g., {abc})
195.   * and strips off the brackets.
196.   */
197.  char *
198.  get_set(char *set)     /* output - set string without brackets {}         */
199.  {
200.          char inset[SETSIZ];
201.
202.          scanf("%s", inset);
203.          strncpy(set, &inset[1], strlen(inset) - 2);
204.          set[strlen(inset) - 2] = '\0';
205.          return (set);
206.  }
```

TESTING

We have added one function to our group of set functions to make it easier to write a driver function for testing. The function `get_set` takes an input string representing a set and strips off the brackets {} that the driver program asks the user to place around the set entered. These brackets make it easy for the user to enter the empty set.

When testing this group of functions, choose data that check boundary conditions. For instance, test `is_set` with valid sets, including the empty set, and with invalid sets that have duplicate letters in various parts of the set string. For `is_element`, test an element found at the beginning of the set string, an element in the middle, an element at the end, and an element not in the string. Also, try the empty set as the second argument. With `is_subset`, test using empty sets for sub and/or set, and try various orderings of letters in sub. Try a case where the sets are equal as well. When testing `set_union`, test equal sets, disjoint sets, and partially overlapping sets with various orderings of the elements. In addition, try the empty set as the first argument, then as the second; then call `set_union` using the empty set for both arguments.

Self-Check

1. Imagine that we add calls to `printf` of the type shown in Fig. 9.9 to functions `is_element` and `is_subset`. Show the tracing output that would be produced for the function call `is_subset("bc", "cebf")`.

Programming

1. Define a recursive `intersection` function that computes `set1 ∩ set2`. Then, define an iterative version of the same function.
2. Define a very short `set_equal` function that calls the `intersection` function from Programming Exercise 1.

9.6 A Classic Case Study in Recursion: Towers of Hanoi

The Towers of Hanoi problem involves moving a specified number of disks that are all different sizes from one tower (or peg) to another. Legend has it that the world will come to an end when the problem is solved for 64 disks.

PROBLEM

Move *n* disks from peg A to peg C using peg B as needed. The following conditions apply:

1. Only one disk at a time may be moved, and this disk must be the top disk on a peg.
2. A larger disk can never be placed on top of a smaller disk.

ANALYSIS

The version of the problem shown in Fig. 9.21 has five disks (numbered 1 through 5) and three towers or pegs (lettered A, B, and C). The goal is to move the five disks

FIGURE 9.21

Towers of Hanoi

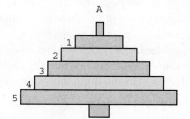

FIGURE 9.22

Towers of Hanoi
After Steps 1 and 2

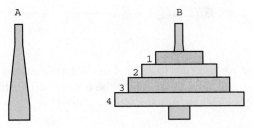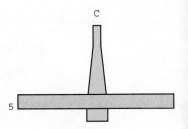

from peg A to peg C. The simplest cases of the problem involve moving one disk only (e.g., move disk 2 from peg A to peg C). A simpler problem than the original would be to move four disks subject to the conditions given or three disks, and so on. Therefore, we want to split the original five-disk problem into several simpler problems, each of which involves fewer disks. Let's consider splitting the original problem into the following three problems:

1. Move four disks from peg A to peg B.
2. Move disk 5 from peg A to peg C.
3. Move four disks from peg B to peg C.

In step 1, we move all disks but the largest to peg B, an auxiliary peg not mentioned in the original problem. In step 2, we move the largest disk to C, the goal peg. Then, in step 3, we move the remaining disks from B to the goal peg, where they will be placed on top of the largest disk. Let's assume that we will be able to perform step 1 and step 2 (a simple case). Fig. 9.22 shows the status of the three pegs after completing these steps. At this point, it should be clear that we will indeed solve the original five-disk problem if we can complete step 3.

Unfortunately, we still don't know how to perform step 1 or step 3. However, both of these steps involve four disks instead of five, so they are easier than the original problem. We should be able to split each of these steps into simpler problems in the same way that we split the original problem. Step 3 involves moving four disks from peg B to peg C, so we can split this step into the following two three-disk problems and one one-disk problem:

3.1 Move three disks from peg B to peg A.
3.2 Move disk 4 from peg B to peg C.
3.3 Move three disks from peg A to peg C.

Figure 9.23 shows the status of the pegs after completing step 3.1 and step 3.2. We now have the two largest disks on peg C. Once we complete step 3.3, all five disks will be on peg C as required.

By splitting each n-disk problem into two problems involving $n - 1$ disks and a third problem involving only one disk, we will eventually divide our original problem into many one-disk problems. These simple cases are ones we already know how to solve.

FIGURE 9.23

Towers of Hanoi
After Steps 1, 2,
3.1, and 3.2

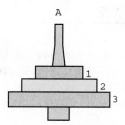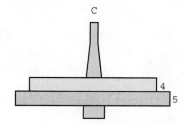

The solution to the Towers of Hanoi problem consists of a printed list of individual disk moves. We need a recursive function that can be used to print instructions for moving any number of disks from one peg to another using the third peg as an auxiliary.

DATA REQUIREMENTS

Problem Inputs

```
int n            /* the number of disks to be moved    */
char from_peg    /* the from peg                        */
char to_peg      /* the to peg                          */
char aux_peg     /* the auxiliary peg                   */
```

Problem Outputs

A list of individual disk moves.

DESIGN

Algorithm

1. if *n* is 1 then
   2. Move disk 1 from the *from* peg to the *to* peg
   else
   3. Move *n* − 1 disks from the *from* peg to the *auxiliary* peg using the *to* peg.
   4. Move disk *n* from the *from* peg to the *to* peg.
   5. Move *n* − 1 disks from the *auxiliary* peg to the *to* peg using the *from* peg.

If *n* is 1, we have a simple case that we can solve immediately. If *n* is greater than 1, the recursive step (the step following else) splits the original problem into three smaller subproblems, one of which is another simple case. Each simple case displays a move instruction. Verify that the recursive step generates the three problems listed below in Fig. 9.22, when *n* is 5, the *from* peg is A, and the *to* peg is C.

FIGURE 9.24 Recursive Function Tower

```
1.   /*
2.    * Displays instructions for moving n disks from from_peg to to_peg using
3.    * aux_peg as an auxiliary. Disks are numbered 1 to n (smallest to
4.    * largest). Instructions call for moving one disk at a time and never
5.    * require placing a larger disk on top of a smaller one.
6.    */
7.   void
8.   tower(char from_peg,       /* input - characters naming    */
9.         char to_peg,         /*          the problem's       */
10.        char aux_peg,        /*          three pegs          */
11.        int n)               /* input - number of disks to move  */
12.  {
13.       if (n == 1) {
14.            printf("Move disk 1 from peg %c to peg %c\n", from_peg, to_peg);
15.       } else {
16.            tower(from_peg, aux_peg, to_peg, n - 1);
17.            printf("Move disk %d from peg %c to peg %c\n", n, from_peg, to_peg);
18.            tower(aux_peg, to_peg, from_peg, n - 1);
19.       }
20.  }
```

The implementation of this algorithm is shown as function `tower` in Fig. 9.24. Function `tower` has four input parameters. The function call statement

```
tower('A', 'C', 'B', 5);
```

solves the problem that was posed earlier of moving five disks from peg A to peg C using B as an auxiliary (see Fig. 9.21).

In Fig. 9.24, when the terminating condition is true, a call to `printf` displays an instruction regarding moving disk 1. Each recursive step consists of two recursive calls to `tower` with a call to `printf` sandwiched between them. The first recursive call solves the problem of moving $n - 1$ disks to the *auxiliary* peg. The call to `printf` displays a message to move the remaining disk to the *to* peg. The second recursive call solves the problem of moving the $n - 1$ disks from the *auxiliary* peg to the *to* peg.

TESTING

The function call statement

```
tower('A', 'C', 'B', 3);
```

solves a simpler three-disk problem: Move three disks from peg A to peg C. Its execution is traced in Fig. 9.25 and the output generated is shown in Fig. 9.26. Verify for yourself that this list of steps does indeed solve the three-disk problem.

FIGURE 9.25

Trace of tower
('A', 'C', 'B', 3);

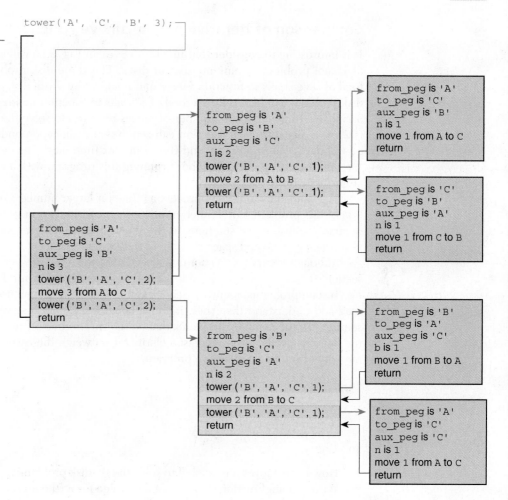

FIGURE 9.26

Output Generated
by tower
('A', 'C', 'B', 3);

```
Move disk 1 from A to C
Move disk 2 from A to B
Move disk 1 from C to B
Move disk 3 from A to C
Move disk 1 from B to A
Move disk 2 from B to C
Move disk 1 from A to C
```

Comparison of Iterative and Recursive Functions

It is interesting to consider that function `tower` in Fig. 9.26 will solve the Towers of Hanoi problem for any number of disks. The three-disk problem results in a total of seven calls to function `tower` and is solved by seven disk moves. The five-disk problem would result in a total of 31 calls to function `tower` and is solved in 31 moves. In general, the number of moves required to solve the n-disk problem is $2^n - 1$. Because each function call requires the allocation and initialization of a local data area in memory and the computer time increases exponentially with the problem size, be careful about running this program with a value of n that is larger than 10.

The dramatic increase in processing time for larger numbers of disks is a function of this problem, not a function of recursion. However, in general, if there are recursive and iterative solutions to the same problem, the recursive solution will require more time and space because of the extra function calls.

Although recursion was not really needed to solve the simpler problems in this section, it was extremely useful in formulating an algorithm for Towers of Hanoi. For certain problems, recursion leads naturally to solutions that are much easier to read and understand than their iterative counterparts. To researchers developing solutions to the complex problems that are at the frontiers of their research areas, the benefits gained from increased clarity far outweigh the extra cost in time and memory of running a recursive program.

 EXERCISES FOR SECTION 9.6

Self-Check

1. How many moves are needed to solve the six-disk problem?
2. Write a main function that takes a data value for n (the number of disks) and calls function `tower` to move n disks from A to B.

9.7 Common Programming Errors

The most common problem with a recursive function is that it may not terminate properly. For example, if the terminating condition is not correct or is incomplete, the function may call itself indefinitely or until all available memory is used up. Frequently, a run-time error message noting stack overflow or an access violation is an indicator that a recursive function is not terminating. Make sure that you identify all simple cases and provide a terminating condition for each one. Also, be sure that each recursive step redefines the problem in terms of arguments that are closer to simple cases so that repeated recursive calls will eventually lead to simple cases only.

In our examples of recursive functions that return a value, we have always used a local variable (or, in the case of string functions, an output parameter) into which the function result is placed by the function's decision structure. Then we have ended the function's code with a `return` statement. Since C permits the use of the `return` statement anywhere in the function code, a module like `is_set` from Fig. 9.20 could also have been written as follows.

```
int
is_set(const char *set)
{
        if (is_empty(set))
                return (TRUE);
        else if (is_element(set[0], &set[1]))
                return (FALSE);
        else
                return (is_set(&set[1]));
}
```

You should be aware that it is critical that every path through a nonvoid function lead to a `return` statement. In particular, the `return` statement to return the value of the recursive call to `is_set` is just as important as the other two `return` statements. However, it is easy to inadvertently omit one of these necessary `return` statements when a multiple `return` style is adopted.

The recopying of large arrays or other data structures can quickly consume all available memory. Such copying should be done inside a recursive function only when absolutely essential for data protection. If only a single copy is necessary, a nonrecursive function can be created that makes the necessary copy, passes the copy and the other arguments to the recursive function, and returns the result computed.

It is also a good idea to introduce a nonrecursive function to handle preliminaries and call the recursive function when there is error checking. Checking for errors inside a recursive function is extremely inefficient if the error is of the type that would be detected on the very first call. In such a situation, repeated checks in recursive calls are a waste of computer time.

Sometimes, it is difficult to observe the output produced when running recursive functions that you have made self-tracing as described in Section 9.2. If each recursive call generates two or more output lines and there are many recursive calls, the output will scroll down the screen more quickly than it can be read. On most systems, pressing a control character sequence (e.g., control-s) will temporarily stop output to the screen. If this is not possible, you can stop your output temporarily by printing a prompting message followed by a call to `getchar`. Your program will resume execution when you enter a data character.

Chapter Review

1. A recursive function either calls itself or initiates a sequence of function calls in which it may be called again.
2. Designing a recursive solution involves identifying simple cases that have straightforward solutions and then redefining more complex cases in terms of problems that are closer to simple cases.
3. Recursive functions depend on the fact that for each call to a function, space is allocated on the stack for the function's parameters and local variables.

Quick-Check Exercises

1. Explain the use of a stack in recursion.
2. Which is generally more efficient, recursion or iteration?
3. Which control statement do you typically find in a recursive function?
4. How would you improve the efficiency of the following factorial function?

```
int
fact(int n)
{
    int ans;
    if (n < 0 || n > 10) {
            printf("\nInvalid argument to fact: %d\n", n);
            ans = n;
    } else if (n == 0) {
            ans = 1;
    } else {
            ans = n * fact(n - 1);
    }
    return (ans);
}
```

5. When might a programmer conceptualize a problem solution using recursion but implement it using iteration?
6. What problem do you notice in the following recursive function? Show two possible ways to correct the problem.

```
int
trial(int a)
{
    if (a <= 1)
            return (1);
```

```
        else if (a + 2 == 0)
                else
                int b = trial(a * 2);
                return b;
}
```

7. What is a common cause of a stack overflow error?
8. What can you say about a recursive algorithm that has the following form?

for (i = 0;i < 1;i++)
  Perform recursive step.

Answers to Quick-Check Exercises

1. The stack is used to hold all parameter and local variable values along with the return point for each execution of a recursive function.
2. Iteration is generally more efficient than recursion.
3. `if` statement
4. Write as two functions so error checking occurs only once.

```
int
factorial(int n)
{
        int ans;
        if (n == 0)
                ans = 1;
        else
                ans = n * factorial(n - 1);
        return (ans);
}

int
fact(int n)
{
        int ans;

        if (n < 0 || n > 10) {
                printf("\nInvalid argument to fact: %d\n", n);
                ans = n;
        } else {
                ans = factorial(n);
        }
        return (ans);
}
```

5. When a problem's solution is much easier to conceptualize using recursion but a recursive implementation would be too inefficient.
6. One path through the function does not encounter a `return` statement. Either place a `return` statement in the `else` if

   ```
   return (a);
   ```

   or assign each result to a local variable, and place that variable in a `return` statement at the end of the function.
7. Too many recursive calls.
8. The recursive step is executed at least once.

Review Questions

1. Why does recursion make it easier to conceptualize a solution to a problem?
2. Discuss the efficiency of recursive functions.
3. Differentiate between a simple case and a terminating condition.
4. Write a recursive C function that accumulates the product of the values in an *n*-element array.
5. Write a recursive C function that counts the number of vowels in a string. You may wish to call the `is_element` function defined in Section 9.5.
6. The sequence 2, 6, 18, 54, 162, ... is *geometric* because each term divided by its predecessor yields the same result, 3. The number 3 is the *common ratio* of the sequence. Write the recursive helper function `check_geometric` that assists function `main` in carrying out its purpose.

   ```c
   /*
    * Determines if an input list forms a geometric
    * sequence, a sequence in which each term is the
    * product of the previous term and the common
    * ratio. Displays the message "List forms a geometric
    * sequence" if this is the case. Otherwise, stops
    * input and prints the messages "Input halted at
    * <incorrect term value>. List does not form a
    * geometric sequence"
    */
   int
   main(void)
   {
         double term1, term2,
                 ratio;     /* common ratio of a geometric sequence
                                whose first two terms are term1 and
                                term2                            */
   ```

```
            printf("Data: \n");
            scanf("%lf", &term1);
            printf("%.2f ", term1);
            scanf("%lf", &term2);
            printf("%.2f ", term2);

            ratio = term2 / term1;
            check_geometric(ratio, term2); /* gets and checks rest of
                    input list, considering ratios equal if they differ
                    by less than .001                                  */

            return (0);
    }
```

7. Write a recursive function that returns the position of the last nonblank character of a string. You may assume that you are working with a disposable copy of the string.

Programming Projects

1. Develop a program to count pixels (picture elements) belonging to an object in a photograph. The data are in a two-dimensional grid of cells, each of which may be empty (value 0) or filled (value 1). The filled cells that are connected form a blob (an object). Figure 9.27 shows a grid with three blobs. Include in your program a function **blob_check** that takes as parameters the grid and the x-y coordinates of a cell and returns as its value the number of cells in the blob to which the indicated cell belongs.

   Function **blob_check** must test whether the cell specified by its arguments is filled. There are two simple cases: The cell (**x, y**) may not be on the

FIGURE 9.27

Grid with Three Blobs

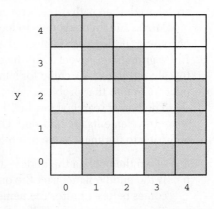

grid, or the cell (x, y) may be empty. In either of these cases, the value returned by blob_check is 0. If the cell is on the grid and filled, then the value returned is 1 plus the sizes of the blobs containing each of its eight neighbors. To avoid counting a filled cell more than once, mark a cell as empty once you have counted it.

2. A palindrome consists of a word or deblanked, unpunctuated phrase that is spelled exactly the same when the letters are reversed. Write a recursive function that returns a value of 1 if its string argument is a palindrome. Notice that in palindromes such as level, deed, sees, and Madam I'm Adam (madamimadam), the first letter matches the last, the second matches the next-to-last, and so on.

3. Write and test a recursive function that returns the value of the following recursive definition:

$$\begin{aligned} f(x) &= 0 && \text{if } x \leq 0 \\ f(x) &= f(x-1) + 2 && \text{otherwise} \end{aligned}$$

What set of numbers is generated by this definition?

4. Write recursive functions that list all of the one-element, two-element, and three-element subsets of a given set of letters. For example,

one_ele_subs ("ACEG")	two_ele_subs ("ACEG")	three_ele_subs ("ACEG")
{A}	{A, C}	{A, C, E}
{C}	{A, E}	{A, C, G}
{E}	{A, G}	{A, E, G}
{G}	{C, E}	{C, E, G}
	{C, G}	
	{E, G}	

5. Write a function that accepts an 8 by 8 array of characters that represents a maze. Each position can contain either an X or a blank. Starting at position (0,1), list any path through the maze to get to location (7,7). Only horizontal and vertical moves are allowed. If no path exists, write a message indicating there is no path.

   Moves can be made only to locations that contain a blank. If an X is encountered, that path is blocked and another must be chosen. Use recursion.

6. In Programming Project 12 at the end of Chapter 7, we described an iterative algorithm for searching for a target value in a sorted list. Here again is the introduction to that problem.

   The binary search algorithm that follows may be used to search an array when the elements are in order. This algorithm is analogous to the following approach to finding a name in a telephone book.

   a. Open the book in the middle and look at the middle name on the page.
   b. If the middle name isn't the one you're looking for, decide whether it comes before or after the name you want.
   c. Take the appropriate half of the section of the book you were looking in, and repeat these steps until you land on the name.

ITERATIVE ALGORITHM FOR BINARY SEARCH

1. Let bottom be the subscript of the initial array element.
2. Let top be the subscript of the last array element.
3. Let found be false.
4. Repeat as long as bottom isn't greater than top and the target has not been found.
5. Let middle be the subscript of the element halfway between bottom and top.
6. If the element at middle is the target
   7. Set found to true and index to middle.
   else if the element at middle is larger than the target
   8. Let top be middle − 1.
   else
   9. Let bottom be middle + 1.

Develop a recursive binary search algorithm, and write and test a function `binary_srch` that implements the algorithm for an array of integers.

7. Write a recursive function that displays all the binary (base 2) numbers represented by a string of `x`s, `0`s, and `1`s. The `x`s represent digits that can be either `0` or `1`. For example, the string `1x0x` represents the numbers `1000, 1001, 1100, 1101`. The string `xx1` represents `001, 011, 101, 111`. *Hint:* Write a helper function `replace_first_x` that builds two strings based on its input argument. In one, the first `x` is replaced by a `0`, and in the other by a `1`. The set function `is_element` may be useful too.

8. The version of the selection sort that we studied in Chapter 7 places the smallest value in the initial array element, the second smallest in the next element, and so on. Implement this version recursively.

9. In Chapter 5 we studied the bisection method of approximating a root of a function on an interval that contains an odd number of roots. Write a recursive function `find_root` that could be called by function `bisect` of Fig. 5.19 to handle any nonerror case, that is, any case involving an interval that definitely contains an odd number of roots. This problem lends itself to a recursive solution because there are two clearly defined simple cases: (a) when the function's value at the midpoint of the interval is actually zero, and (b) when the length of the interval is less than epsilon. Moreover, in all other cases the problem is naturally redefined as a simpler version of itself—a search within a shorter interval. Test your function by running a revised version of the program in Fig. 5.19. Simply replace the `while` loop of `bisect` by a call to `find_root`, and return its result as the value of `bisect`.

10. Write and test a merge function that uses a recursive algorithm to merge two sorted arrays of integers. Neither list contains duplicates, and the resulting list should not contain duplicates either. *Hint*: You may want to call a helper function from merge.

Structure and Union Types

CHAPTER OBJECTIVES

- To learn how to declare a `struct` data type which consists of several data fields, each with its own name and data type
- To understand how to use a `struct` to store data for a structured object or record
- To learn how to use dot notation to process individual fields of a structured object
- To learn how to use `structs` as function parameters and to return function results
- To see how to create a `struct` data type for representing complex numbers and how to write functions that perform arithmetic operations on complex numbers
- To understand the relationship between parallel arrays and arrays of structured objects
- To learn about `union` data types and how they differ from `structs`

In previous chapters, we have seen how to represent in C numbers, characters, words, other strings, and lists (arrays) of these objects. But surely there is more to the world we live in than words and lists of numbers! Every day the role of computers in this complex universe widens, and a programming language must be able to model not only numbers and names, but also protozoa, people, and planets.

In this chapter, we will study how to broaden the modeling facilities of C by defining our own data types that represent structured collections of data pertaining to particular objects. Unlike an array, a structure can have individual components that contain data of different types. A single variable of a composite type designed for planets can store a planet's name, diameter, number of moons, the number of years to complete one solar orbit, and the number of hours to make one rotation on its axis. Each of these data items is stored in a separate component of the structure and can be referenced by using the component name.

10.1 User-Defined Structure Types

record a collection of information about one data object

A *database* is a collection of information stored in a computer's memory or in a disk file. A database is subdivided into **records**, which normally contain information regarding specific data objects. The structure of the record is determined by the structure of the object's data type.

Structure Type Definition

Before a structured data object can be created or saved, the format of its components must be defined. Although C provides several ways to define structures, we will explore just one approach—defining a new data type for each category of structured objects.

EXAMPLE 10.1

As part of a project for our local observatory, we are developing a database of the planets in our solar system. For each planet, we need to represent information like the following:

Name: Jupiter
Diameter: 142,800 km
Moons: 16

Orbit time: 11.9 years
Rotation time: 9.925 hours

structure type a data type for a record composed of multiple components

We can define a **structure type** `planet_t` to use in declaring a variable in which to store this information. There must be five *components* in the structure type, one for each data item. We must specify the name of each component and the type of information stored in each component. We choose the names in the same way we choose all other identifiers: The names describe the nature of the information represented. The contents of each component determine the appropriate data type. For example, the planet's name should be stored in a component that is an array of characters.

The structure type `planet_t` has five distinct components. One is an array of characters; one is an `int`. The other three are of type `double`.

```
#define STRSIZ 10

typedef struct {
        char    name[STRSIZ];
        double diameter;            /* equatorial diameter in km   */
        int     moons;              /* number of moons             */
        double orbit_time,          /* years to orbit sun once     */
                rotation_time;      /* hours to complete one
                                       revolution on axis          */
} planet_t;
```

This type definition is a template that describes the format of a planet structure and the name and type of each component. A name chosen for a component of one structure may be the same as the name of a component of another structure or the same as the name of a variable. We will see that the approach C takes to referencing these components will rule out confusion of matching names used in these different contexts.

The `typedef` statement itself allocates no memory. A variable declaration is required to allocate storage space for a structured data object. The variables `current_planet` and `previous_planet` are declared next, and the variable `blank_planet` is declared and initialized.

```
{
        planet_t current_planet,
                previous_planet,
                blank_planet = {"", 0, 0, 0, 0};
    . . .
```

The structured variables `current_planet`, `previous_planet`, and `blank_planet` all have the format specified in the definition of type `planet_t`. Thus, the memory allocated for each consists of storage space for five distinct values. The variable `blank_planet` is pictured as it appears after initialization.

Variable `blank_planet`, a structure of type `planet_t`

.name	`\0 ? ? ? ? ? ? ? ? ?`
.diameter	0.0
.moons	0
.orbit_time	0.0
.rotation_time	0.0

A user-defined type like `planet_t` can be used to declare both simple and array variables and to declare components in other structure types. A structure containing components that are data structures (arrays or `struct`s) is sometimes called a **hierarchical structure**. The following definition of a structure type includes a component that is an array of planets.

hierarchical structure
a structure containing components that are structures

```
typedef struct {
    double    diameter;
    planet_t  planets[9];
    char      galaxy[STRSIZ];
} solar_sys_t;
```

Structure Type Definition

SYNTAX:
```
typedef struct {
        type₁ id_list₁;
        type₂ id_list₂;
            .
            .
            .
        typeₙ id_listₙ;
    } struct_type;
```

EXAMPLE:
```
typedef struct { /* complex number structure */
        double real_pt,
               imag_pt;
    } complex_t;
```

(continued)

INTERPRETATION: The identifier *struct_type* is the name of the structure type being defined. Each *id_list*ᵢ is a list of one or more component names separated by commas; the data type of each component in *id_list*ᵢ is specified by *type*ᵢ.

NOTE: *type*ᵢ can be any standard or previously specified user-defined data type.

Manipulating Individual Components of a Structured Data Object

direct component selection operator a period placed between a structure type variable and a component name to create a reference to the component

We can reference a component of a structure by using the **direct component selection operator**, which is a period. The period is preceded by the name of a structure type variable and is followed by the name of a component.

EXAMPLE 10.2

Figure 10.1 shows as an example the manipulation of the components of the variable `current_planet` listed at the beginning of Example 10.1. The statements in the figure store in the variable the data pictured earlier.

Once data are stored in a record, they can be manipulated in the same way as other data in memory. For example, the statement

FIGURE 10.1

Assigning Values to Components of Variable current_planet

```
strcpy(current_planet.name, "Jupiter");
current_planet.diameter = 142800;
current_planet.moons = 16;
current_planet.orbit_time = 11.9;
current_planet.rotation_time = 9.925;
```

Variable `current_planet`, a structure of type `planet_t`

.name	J u p i t e r \0 ? ?
.diameter	142800.0
.moons	16
.orbit_time	11.9
.rotation_time	9.925

```
printf("%s's equatorial diameter is %.1f km.\n",
       current_planet.name, current_planet.diameter);
```

displays the sentence

```
Jupiter's equatorial diameter is 142800.0 km.
```

Review of Operator Precedence

With the addition of the direct component selection operator to our repertory of operators, we will take a moment to see how this operator fits into our overall scheme of precedence rules. Table 10.1 not only shows operator precedence answering the question: In an expression with two operators, which is applied first? It also lists operator associativity answering the question: In an expression containing two of these operators in sequence, which is applied first?

In a generic expression containing two of the same operators in sequence,

$$operand_1 \quad op \quad operand_2 \quad op \quad operand_3$$

TABLE 10.1 Precedence and Associativity of Operators Seen So Far

Precedence	Symbols	Operator Names	Associativity
highest	`a[j]  f( ... )  .`	Subscripting, function calls, direct component selection	left
	`++  --`	Postfix increment and decrement	left
	`++  --  !` `-  +  &  *`	Prefix increment and decrement, logical not, unary negation and plus, address of, indirection	right
	`( type name )`	Casts	right
	`*  /  %`	Multiplicative operators (multiplication, division, remainder)	left
	`+  -`	Binary additive operators (addition and subtraction)	left
	`<  >  <=  >=`	Relational operators	left
	`==  !=`	Equality/inequality operators	left
	`&&`	Logical and	left
	`||`	Logical or	left
lowest	`=  +=  -=` `*=  /=  %=`	Assignment operators	right

if *op* has left associativity, the expression is evaluated as

(*operand*$_1$ *op* *operand*$_2$) *op* *operand*$_3$

whereas, if *op* has right associativity, the implied order of evaluation is

operand$_1$ *op* (*operand*$_2$ *op* *operand*$_3$)

Manipulating Whole Structures

The name of a structure type variable used with no component selection operator refers to the entire structure. A new copy of a structure's value can be made by simply assigning one structure to another as in the following statement:

```
previous_planet = current_planet;
```

We will see other instances of the manipulation of whole structures in the next section when we study the use of structures as input and output parameters of functions and as function result types.

Program Style   *Naming Convention for Types*

When we write programs that define new types, it is easy to confuse type names and variable names. To help reduce confusion, in this text we choose user-defined type names that use lowercase letters and end in the suffix **_t** (a practice recommended in some industrial software design environments).

EXERCISES FOR SECTION 10.1

Self-Check

1. Define a type named `long_lat_t` that would be appropriate for storing longitude or latitude values. Include components named `degrees` (an integer), `minutes` (an integer), and `direction` (one of the characters `'N'`, `'S'`, `'E'`, or `'W'`).

2. The following are a type to represent a geographic location and a variable of this hierarchical structure type. We will assume that `STRSIZ` means `20`.

```
typedef struct {
      char       place[STRSIZ];
      long_lat_t longitude,
                 latitude;
} location_t;

location_t resort;
```

Given that the values shown have been stored in `resort`, complete the following table to check your understanding of component selection.

Variable `resort`, a structure of type `location_t`

.place	H a w a i i \0 ?? ...		
.longitude	158	0	W
.latitude	21	30	N

Reference	Data Type of Reference	Value
resort.latitude	long_lat_t	21 30 'N'
resort.place	_____	_____
resort.longitude.direction	_____	_____
_____	int	30
resort.place[3]	_____	_____

3. A catalog listing for a textbook consists of the authors' names, the title, the publisher, and the year of publication. Declare a structure type `catalog_entry_t` and a variable `book`, and write statements that store the relevant data for this textbook in `book`.

10.2   Structure Type Data as Input and Output Parameters

When a structured variable is passed as an input argument to a function, all of its component *values* are copied into the components of the function's corresponding formal parameter. When such a variable is used as an output argument, the address-of operator must be applied in the same way that we would pass output arguments of the standard types `char`, `int`, and `double`.

EXAMPLE 10.3   Our observatory program from Example 10.1 and Example 10.2 frequently needs to output as a unit all of the descriptive data about a planet. Figure 10.2 shows a function to do this.

To display the value of our structure `current_planet`, we would use the call statement

```
print_planet(current_planet);
```

FIGURE 10.2   Function with a Structured Input Parameter

```
1.  /*
2.   * Displays with labels all components of a planet_t structure
3.   */
4.  void
5.  print_planet(planet_t pl) /* input - one planet structure */
6.  {
7.        printf("%s\n", pl.name);
8.        printf("   Equatorial diameter: %.0f km\n", pl.diameter);
9.        printf("   Number of moons: %d\n", pl.moons);
10.       printf("   Time to complete one orbit of the sun: %.2f years\n",
11.              pl.orbit_time);
12.       printf("   Time to complete one rotation on axis: %.4f hours\n",
13.              pl.rotation_time);
14. }
```

Having an output function like `print_planet` helps us to view the planet object as a concept at a higher level of abstraction rather than as an ad hoc collection of components.

Another function that would help us think of a planet as a data object is a function that would perform an equality comparison of two planets. Although C permits copying of a structure using the assignment operator, the equality and inequality operators cannot be applied to a structured type as a unit. Figure 10.3 shows a `planet_equal` function that takes two planets as input arguments and returns 1 or 0 depending on whether all components match.

FIGURE 10.3   Function Comparing Two Structured Values for Equality

```
1.  #include <string.h>
2.
3.  /*
4.   * Determines whether or not the components of planet_1 and planet_2 match
5.   */
6.  int
7.  planet_equal(planet_t planet_1, /* input - planets to          */
8.               planet_t planet_2) /*          compare            */
9.  {
```

(continued)

FIGURE 10.3   (continued)

```
10.          return (strcmp(planet_1.name, planet_2.name) == 0    &&
11.                  planet_1.diameter == planet_2.diameter        &&
12.                  planet_1.moons == planet_2.moons              &&
13.                  planet_1.orbit_time == planet_2.orbit_time    &&
14.                  planet_1.rotation_time == planet_2.rotation_time);
15.   }
```

A planet input function would also help us to process `current_planet` as `planet_t` data. Figure 10.4 shows the function `scan_planet` that resembles `scanf` in that it takes an output argument and returns the value `1` if its single output argument is successfully filled, returns the value `0` if there is an error, and returns the negative value `EOF` if the end of the file is encountered.

As you can see from this example, manipulating a structured output argument using operators `*` and `.` really requires you to keep C's operator-precedence rules straight. In order to use `scanf` to store a value in one component of the structure whose address is in `plnp`, we must carry out the following steps (in order):

1. Follow the pointer in `plnp` to the structure.
2. Select the component of interest.
3. Unless this component is an array (e.g., component `name` in Fig. 10.4), get its address to pass to `scanf`.

When we check our precedence chart (see Table 10.1), we find that this reference

`&*plnp.diameter`

would attempt step 2 before step 1. For this reason, the function in Fig. 10.4 overrides the default operator precedence by parenthesizing the application of the indirect referencing (pointer-following) operator, the unary `*`. Figure 10.5 shows the data areas of functions `main` and `scan_planet` during execution of the following statement in `main`:

`status = scan_planet(&current_planet);`

indirect component selection operator
the character sequence `->` placed between a pointer variable and a component name creates a reference that follows the pointer to a structure and selects the component

We are assuming that the assignment statement of `scan_planet` calling `scanf` has just finished executing and that it has successfully obtained input values for all components of the output argument structure.

In Table 10.2, we analyze the reference `&(*plnp).diameter` from our function `scan_planet`. C also provides a single operator that combines the functions of the indirection and component selection operators. This **indirect component selection**

FIGURE 10.4 Function with a Structured Output Argument

```
1.  /*
2.   * Fills a type planet_t structure with input data. Integer returned as
3.   * function result is success/failure/EOF indicator.
4.   *      1 => successful input of one planet
5.   *      0 => error encountered
6.   *      EOF => insufficient data before end of file
7.   * In case of error or EOF, value of type planet_t output argument is
8.   * undefined.
9.   */
10. int
11. scan_planet(planet_t *plnp) /* output - address of planet_t structure
12.                                         to fill                       */
13. {
14.      int result;
15.
16.      result = scanf("%s%lf%d%lf%lf", (*plnp).name,
17.                                       &(*plnp).diameter,
18.                                       &(*plnp).moons,
19.                                       &(*plnp).orbit_time,
20.                                       &(*plnp).rotation_time);
21.      if (result == 5)
22.           result = 1;
23.      else if (result != EOF)
24.           result = 0;
25.
26.      return (result);
27. }
```

operator is represented by the character sequence -> (a minus sign followed by a greater-than symbol). Thus, these two expressions are equivalent.

```
(*structp).component    structp->component
```

If we rewrite the `scan_planet` function of Fig. 10.4 using the -> operator, the assignment to `result` will be

```
result = scanf("%s%lf%d%lf%lf", plnp->name,
                                &plnp->diameter,
                                &plnp->moons,
                                &plnp->orbit_time,
                                &plnp->rotation_time);
```

FIGURE 10.5

Data Areas of main
and scan_planet
During Execution
Of status =
scan_planet
(&current_
planet);

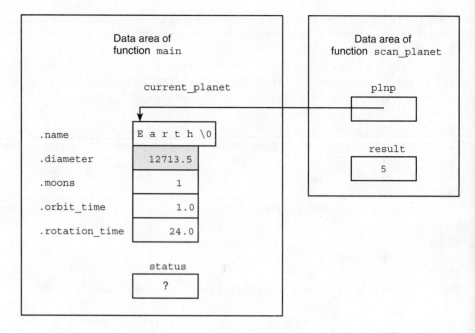

In the next section, we see how to write a function that fills up a `planet_t` structure with input data and returns this structure as the function value. This alternative way of approaching input of structures avoids the need for indirect referencing, but it cannot return a status indicator as the function value in the same way `scan_planet` does.

TABLE 10.2   Step-by-Step Analysis of Reference &(*plnp).diameter

Reference	Type	Value
`plnp`	`planet_t *`	address of structure that `main` refers to as `current_planet`
`*plnp`	`planet_t`	structure that `main` refers to as `current_planet`
`(*plnp).diameter`	`double`	12713.5
`&(*plnp).diameter`	`double *`	address of colored component of structure that `main` refers to as `current_planet`

EXERCISES FOR SECTION 10.2

Self-Check

1. Write functions `print_long_lat`, `long_lat_equal`, and `scan_long_lat` to perform output, equality comparison, and input of type `long_lat_t` data (see Self-Check Exercise 1 at the end of Section 10.1).

2. Assume that you have a function `verify_location` that manipulates a structured input/output argument of type `location_t` (see Self-Check Exercise 2 at the end of Section 10.1). The figure that follows shows the data areas of functions `main` and `verify_location` during execution of the call

```
code = verify_location(&resort);
```

Complete the table following the figure with references appropriate for use in `verify_location` (if such references were needed).

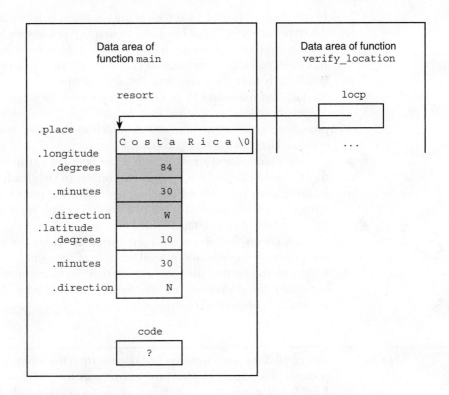

Reference in verify_location	Type of Reference	Value of Reference
locp	location_t *	address of the structure that main refers to as resort
_____	_____	the structure that main refers to as resort
_____	_____	"Costa Rica"
_____		address of the colored component of the structure that main refers to as resort
	_____	84

10.3   Functions Whose Result Values Are Structured

In our study so far, we have seen many situations in which user-defined structured data types are treated just like C's own simple types, yet we have seen only one situation in which structures are handled differently, namely, in equality comparisons. In Chapters 7 and 8, we saw that C's processing of the array data structure differs significantly from its handling of simple data types. One of the many differences is the fact that the values of an entire array cannot be returned as a function result. Rather, functions computing array results typically require the calling module to provide an array output argument in which to store the result and then return this array's address as the function value.

Since arrays and structure types are both data *structures,* one might expect that C would handle them in a similar fashion. In fact, learning C is greatly assisted by doing away with this expectation, because C's approach to processing structure types closely resembles its facilities for working with simple data types, but is very different from its handling of arrays.

A function that computes a structured result can be modeled on a function computing a simple result. A local variable of the structure type can be allocated, filled with the desired data, and returned as the function result. The function does not return the *address* of the structure as it would with an array result; rather it returns the *values* of all components.

EXAMPLE 10.4   In Fig. 10.6, we see a function that obtains from the input device values for all components of a planet_t structure and returns the structure as the function result. Like function getchar, our function get_planet requires no arguments. If we assume entry of correct data, the statement

```
current_planet = get_planet();
```

FIGURE 10.6   Function get_planet Returning a Structured Result Type

```
1.   /*
2.    * Gets and returns a planet_t structure
3.    */
4.   planet_t
5.   get_planet(void)
6.   {
7.         planet_t planet;
8.
9.         scanf("%s%lf%d%lf%lf", planet.name,
10.                               &planet.diameter,
11.                               &planet.moons,
12.                               &planet.orbit_time,
13.                               &planet.rotation_time);
14.         return (planet);
15.  }
```

has the same effect as

```
scan_planet(&current_planet);
```

However, the assumption of correct data entry format is frequently unjustified, so scan_planet with its ability to return an integer error code is the more generally useful function.

EXAMPLE 10.5   Before performing a potentially dangerous or costly experiment in the laboratory, we can often use a computer program to simulate the experiment. In computer simulations, we need to keep track of the time of day as the experiment progresses. Normally, the time of day is updated after a certain period has elapsed. Assuming a 24-hour clock, the structure type time_t is defined as follows:

```
typedef struct {
      int hour, minute, second;
} time_t;
```

Function new_time in Fig. 10.7 returns as its value an updated time based on the original time of day and the number of seconds that have elapsed since the previous update. If time_now were 21:58:32 and secs had the value 97, the result returned by the call

```
new_time(time_now, secs)
```

FIGURE 10.7   Function to Compute an Updated Time Value

```
1.   /*
2.    * Computes a new time represented as a time_t structure
3.    * and based on time of day and elapsed seconds.
4.    */
5.   time_t
6.   new_time(time_t time_of_day,    /* input - time to be
7.                                       updated                        */
8.            int     elapsed_secs)  /* input - seconds since last update  */
9.   {
10.       int new_hr, new_min, new_sec;
11.
12.       new_sec = time_of_day.second + elapsed_secs;
13.       time_of_day.second = new_sec % 60;
14.       new_min = time_of_day.minute + new_sec / 60;
15.       time_of_day.minute = new_min % 60;
16.       new_hr = time_of_day.hour + new_min / 60;
17.       time_of_day.hour = new_hr % 24;
18.
19.       return (time_of_day);
20.   }
```

would be 22:00:09. Because new_time's variable time_of_day is strictly an input parameter, the value of time_now will not be affected by the call to new_time. If the intent is to update time_now, an assignment statement is used:

```
time_now = new_time(time_now, secs);
```

Figure 10.8 traces the assignment statement just mentioned showing the structured time_t value used as an input argument and the type time_t function value.

C IN FOCUS

Evolving Standards

The original standard for the C programming language was published by the American National Standards Institute in 1989. This version is typically referred to as ANSI C or C89. The following year the Organization for International Standardization (ISO) adopted this standard as well, so sometimes the original standard may be called C90. In 1999 ISO published a C standard that incorporated some new

features including variable-length arrays, additional data types, and a single-line comment format, among other additions. C99, as this standard was called informally, was not widely implemented, so C textbooks have continued to emphasize ANSI C.

In 2011, ISO adopted yet another standard for C. Much of its focus is on providing greater safety in C, so it removes the whole-line input function gets, providing instead the bounds-checking alternative gets_s. Although C11 has not removed other risky functions such as `strcat` and `strcpy`, it does provide bounds-checking versions `strcat_s` and `strcpy_s` alongside the originals. C11 also offers a new version of `fopen` plus numerous new features such as anonymous `struct`s and `union`s, a standard multithreading library, a means of declaring a function that does not return, the ability to control memory alignment, support for Unicode, and static assertions that are evaluated later in the translation process than traditional preprocessor directives. Many of these features are beyond the scope of an introductory course, but if the compiler you are using is C11-compliant, it would be wise at the very least to adopt the habit of using the bounds-checking string functions rather than their overflow-prone C89 cousins.

EXERCISES FOR SECTION 10.3

Self-Check

1. Why does function `new_time`'s assignment of new values to the `second`, `minute`, and `hour` components of its formal parameter `time_of_day` have no effect on the components of actual argument `time_now` in the call `new_time(time_now, secs)`?

FIGURE 10.8

Structured Values as a Function Input Argument and as a Function Result

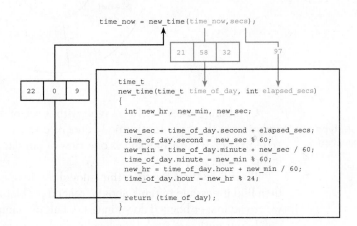

2. Could you modify function `get_planet` so that it would still have a type `planet_t` result and also indicate input success or failure to the calling function?

Programming

1. Define a structure type to represent a common fraction. Write a program that gets a fraction and displays both the fraction and the fraction reduced to lowest terms using the following code fragment:

```
frac = get_fraction();
print_fraction(frac);
printf(" = ");
print_fraction(reduce_fraction(frac));
```

10.4   Problem Solving with Structure Types

When we solve problems using C's standard data types, we take for granted the fact that C provides us with all the basic operations we need to manipulate our data. However, when we work with a problem whose data objects are more complex, we find that defining our own data types is just the first step in building a tool with which to attack the problem. In order to be able to think about the problem on the basis of our own data types, we must also provide basic operations for manipulating these types.

FIGURE 10.9

Data Type
planet_t and Basic
Operations

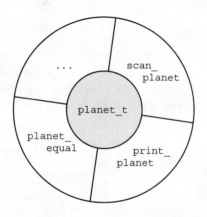

**abstract data type
(ADT)** a data type
combined with a set of
basic operations

Combining a user-defined type with a set of basic operations that allow one truly to see the type as a unified concept creates what is called an **abstract data type (ADT)**. Figure 10.9 shows one view of our data type `planet_t` combined with its operations.

If we take the time to define enough basic operations for a structure type, we then find it possible to think about a related problem at a higher level of abstraction; we are no longer bogged down in the details of manipulating the type's components.

In our next case study, we develop such a group of basic operations for processing complex numbers.

CASE STUDY   A User-Defined Type for Complex Numbers

PROBLEM

We are working on an engineering project that uses complex numbers for modeling of electrical circuits. We need to develop a user-defined structure type and a set of operations that will make complex arithmetic virtually as straightforward as arithmetic on C's built-in numeric types.

ANALYSIS

A complex number is a number with a real part and an imaginary part. For example, the complex number $a + bi$ has a real part a and an imaginary part b, where the symbol i represents $\sqrt{-1}$. We will need to define functions for complex I/O as well as for the basic arithmetic operations (addition, subtraction, multiplication, and division) and for finding the absolute value of a complex number.

DESIGN

The two major aspects of our solution to this problem are defining the structure of the user-defined type and describing the function name, parameters, and purpose of each operation. Each function purpose then forms a subproblem to be solved separately. The details of these subproblems will be of interest to us as we develop our operations. However, once this group of functions is complete, we will be concerned only with *what* each function does, not with *how* it does it. In the same way, when we use C's built-in multiplication operator, we are interested only in the fact that * does multiplication, not caring in the least *how* it manages to accomplish this.

As soon as the specification is complete, our coworkers on the circuit modeling project can begin designing algorithms that assume the availability of these operations. Then, when our implementation is complete, our code can either be added to their programs or packaged for inclusion in a way we will describe in Chapter 12.

Figure 10.10 shows a partial implementation of our specification together with a driver function. Functions `multiply_complex` and `divide_complex` have been left as an exercise. Notice that the definition of type `complex_t` is placed immediately after our preprocessor directives so that it is visible throughout the entire program. Function `abs_complex` uses the following formula to compute the absolute value of a complex number:

$$\left|a + bi\right| = \sqrt{(a+bi)(a-bi)} = \sqrt{a^2 + b^2}$$

This result always has an imaginary part of zero, so `print_complex` will display the result as a real number.

Specification of Type complex_t and Associated Operations

STRUCTURE: A complex number is an object of type **complex_t** that consists of a pair of type **double** values.

OPERATORS:
```
/*
 * Complex number input function returns standard scanning
 * error code
 */
```

(continued)

```
int
scan_complex(complex_t *c)  /* output - address of complex
                                        variable to fill     */

/*
 * Complex output function displays value as a + bi or a - bi.
 * Displays only a if imaginary part is 0.
 * Displays only bi if real part is 0.
 */
void
print_complex(complex_t c)  /* input - complex number to
                                        display             */

/*
 * Returns sum of complex values c1 and c2
 */
complex_t
add_complex(complex_t c1, complex_t c2)          /* input */

/*
 * Returns difference c1 - c2
 */
complex_t
subtract_complex(complex_t c1, complex_t c2)     /* input */

/*
 * Returns product of complex values c1 and c2
 */
complex_t
multiply_complex(complex_t c1, complex_t c2)     /* input */

/*
 * Returns quotient of complex values (c1 / c2)
 */
complex_t
divide_complex(complex_t c1, complex_t c2)       /* input */

/*
 * Returns absolute value of complex number c
 */
complex_t
abs_complex(complex_t c)                          /* input */
```

FIGURE 10.10 Partial Implementation of Type and Operators for Complex Numbers

```
1.  /*
2.   * Operators to process complex numbers
3.   */
4.  #include <stdio.h>
5.  #include <math.h>
6.
7.  /*  User-defined complex number type */
8.  typedef struct {
9.        double real, imag;
10. } complex_t;
11.
12. int scan_complex(complex_t *c);
13. void print_complex(complex_t c);
14. complex_t add_complex(complex_t c1, complex_t c2);
15. complex_t subtract_complex(complex_t c1, complex_t c2);
16. complex_t multiply_complex(complex_t c1, complex_t c2);
17. complex_t divide_complex(complex_t c1, complex_t c2);
18. complex_t abs_complex(complex_t c);
19.
20. /* Driver                                                          */
21. int
22. main(void)
23. {
24.       complex_t com1, com2;
25.
26.       /* Gets two complex numbers                                  */
27.       printf("Enter the real and imaginary parts of a complex number\n");
28.       printf("separated by a space> ");
29.       scan_complex(&com1);
30.       printf("Enter a second complex number> ");
31.       scan_complex(&com2);
32.
33.       /* Forms and displays the sum                                */
34.       printf("\n");
35.       print_complex(com1);
36.       printf(" + ");
37.       print_complex(com2);
38.       printf(" = ");
39.       print_complex(add_complex(com1, com2));
40.
```

(continued)

FIGURE 10.10   (continued)

```
41.         /* Forms and displays the difference                           */
42.         printf("\n\n");
43.         print_complex(com1);
44.         printf(" - ");
45.         print_complex(com2);
46.         printf(" = ");
47.         print_complex(subtract_complex(com1, com2));
48.
49.         /*  Forms and displays the absolute value of the first number    */
50.         printf("\n\n|");
51.         print_complex(com1);
52.         printf("| = ");
53.         print_complex(abs_complex(com1));
54.         printf("\n");
55.
56.         return (0);
57. }
58.
59. /*
60.  * Complex number input function returns standard scanning error code
61.  * 1 => valid scan, 0 => error, negative EOF value => end of file
62.  */
63. int
64. scan_complex(complex_t *c) /* output - address of complex variable to
65.                                          fill                            */
66. {
67.     int status;
68.
69.     status = scanf("%lf%lf", &c->real, &c->imag);
70.     if (status == 2)
71.         status = 1;
72.     else if (status != EOF)
73.         status = 0;
74.
75.     return (status);
76. }
77.
```

(continued)

FIGURE 10.10 (continued)

```
78.  /*
79.   * Complex output function displays value as (a + bi) or (a - bi),
80.   * dropping a or b if they round to 0 unless both round to 0
81.   */
82.  void
83.  print_complex(complex_t c) /* input - complex number to display    */
84.  {
85.        double a, b;
86.        char   sign;
87.
88.        a = c.real;
89.        b = c.imag;
90.
91.        printf("(");
92.
93.        if (fabs(a) < .005   &&   fabs(b) < .005) {
94.              printf("%.2f", 0.0);
95.        } else if (fabs(b) < .005) {
96.              printf("%.2f", a);
97.        } else if (fabs(a) < .005) {
98.              printf("%.2fi", b);
99.        } else {
100.            if (b < 0)
101.                  sign = '-';
102.            else
103.                  sign = '+';
104.            printf("%.2f %c %.2fi", a, sign, fabs(b));
105.       }
109.
107.       printf(")");
108. }
109.
110. /*
111.  * Returns sum of complex values c1 and c2
112.  */
113. complex_t
114. add_complex(complex_t c1, complex_t c2) /* input - values to add    */
```

(continued)

FIGURE 10.10   (continued)

```
115. {
116.        complex_t csum;
117.
118.        csum.real = c1.real + c2.real;
119.        csum.imag = c1.imag + c2.imag;
120.        return (csum);
121. }
123.
124. /*
125.  * Returns difference c1 - c2
126.  */
127. complex_t
128. subtract_complex(complex_t c1, complex_t c2) /* input parameters   */
129. {
130.        complex_t cdiff;
131.        cdiff.real = c1.real - c2.real;
132.        cdiff.imag = c1.imag - c2.imag;
133.
134.        return (cdiff);
135. }
136.
137. /*  ** Stub **
138.  * Returns product of complex values c1 and c2
139.  */
140. complex_t
141. multiply_complex(complex_t c1, complex_t c2) /* input parameters   */
142. {
143.        printf("Function multiply_complex returning first argument\n");
144.        return (c1);
145. }
146.
147. /*  ** Stub **
148.  * Returns quotient of complex values (c1 / c2)
149.  */
150. complex_t
151. divide_complex(complex_t c1, complex_t c2) /* input parameters   */
152. {
153.        printf("Function divide_complex returning first argument\n");
154.        return (c1);
```

(continued)

FIGURE 10.10	(continued)

```
155. }
156.
157. /*
158.  * Returns absolute value of complex number c
159.  */
160. complex_t
161. abs_complex(complex_t c) /* input parameter                        */
162. {
163.     complex_t cabs;
164.
165.     cabs.real = sqrt(c.real * c.real + c.imag * c.imag);
166.     cabs.imag = 0;
167.
168.     return (cabs);
169. }
```

Enter the real and imaginary parts of a complex number
separated by a space> 3.5 5.2
Enter a second complex number> 2.5 1.2

(3.50 + 5.20i) + (2.50 + 1.20i) = (6.00 + 6.40i)

(3.50 + 5.20i) - (2.50 + 1.20i) = (1.00 + 4.00i)

|(3.50 + 5.20i)| = (6.27)

EXERCISES FOR SECTION 10.4

Self-Check

1. What does the following program segment display if the data entered are 6.5
   5.0 3.0 -4.0?

   ```
   complex_t a, b, c;

   scan_complex(&a);
   scan_complex(&b);

   print_complex(a);
   printf(" + ");
   print_complex(b);
   printf(" = ");
   print_complex(add_complex(a, b));
   ```

```
c = subtract_complex(a, abs_complex(b));
printf("\n\nSecond result = ");
print_complex(c);
printf("\n");
```

Programming

1. Write functions `multiply_complex` and `divide_complex` to implement
   the operations of multiplication and division of complex numbers defined as
   follows:

$$(a + bi) \times (c + di) = (ac - bd) + (ad + bc)i$$

$$\frac{(a + bi)}{(c + di)} + \frac{ac + bd}{c^2 + d^2} + \frac{bc - ad}{c^2 + d^2} i$$

10.5   Parallel Arrays and Arrays of Structures

Often a data collection contains items of different types or items that, although of
the same type, represent quite distinct concepts. For example, the data used to represent a list of students might consist of an integer identification number and a type
`double` gpa for each student. The data representing a polygon might be a list of the
(x, y) coordinates of the polygon's corners.

Parallel Arrays

In Section 7.7, we learned how to represent such data collections using *parallel
arrays* like these:

```
int    id[50];      /* id numbers and              */
double gpa[50];     /* gpa's of up to 50 students  */
double x[NUM_PTS],  /* (x,y) coordinates of        */
       y[NUM_PTS];  /*    up to NUM_PTS points     */
```

Arrays `id` and `gpa` are called parallel arrays because the data items with the same
subscript (for example, i) pertain to the same student (the ith student). Similarly,
the ith elements of arrays `x` and `y` are the coordinates of one point. A better way to
organize data collections like these is shown next.

Declaring an Array of Structures

A more natural and convenient organization of student data or polygon points
is to group the information pertaining to one student or to one point in a

structure whose type we define. Declarations of arrays whose elements are structures follow.

```
#define MAX_STU 50
#define NUM_PTS 10

typedef struct {
      int    id;
      double gpa;
} student_t;

typedef struct {
      double x, y;
} point_t;

. . .

{
      student_t stulist[MAX_STU];
      point_t   polygon[NUM_PTS];
```

A sample array `stulist` is shown in Fig. 10.11. The data for the first student are stored in the structure `stulist[0]`. The individual data items are `stulist[0].id` and `stulist[0].gpa`. As shown, `stulist[0].gpa` is `2.71`.

If a function `scan_student` is available for scanning a `student_t` structure, the following `for` statement can be used to fill the entire array `stulist` with data.

```
for  (i = 0;   i < MAX_STU;   ++i)
     scan_student(&stulist[i]);
```

This `for` statement would display all the `id` numbers:

```
for  (i = 0;   i < MAX_STU;   ++i)
     printf("%d\n", stulist[i].id);
```

In our next case study, we see how to use an array of descriptive information about units of measurement in order to make possible conversion of any measurement to any other unit of the same category.

FIGURE 10.11

An Array of Structures

Array `stulist`

	`.id`	`.gpa`	
`stulist[0]`	609465503	2.71	← `stulist[0].gpa`
`stulist[1]`	512984556	3.09	
`stulist[2]`	232415569	2.98	
. . .	. . .	. . .	
`stulist[49]`	173745903	3.98	

CASE STUDY   Universal Measurement Conversion

In a day when our computer software spell-checks text and looks up synonyms for words, it seems primitive to use printed tables for hand conversion of feet to meters, liters to quarts, and so on.

PROBLEM

We would like a program that takes a measurement in one unit (e.g., 4.5 quarts) and converts it to another unit (e.g., liters). For example, this conversion request

```
450 km miles
```

would result in this program output

```
Attempting conversion of 450.0000 km to miles . . .
450.0000km = 279.6247 miles
```

The program should produce an error message if a conversion between two units of different classes (e.g., liquid volume to distance) is requested. The program should take a database of conversion information from an input file before accepting conversion problems entered interactively by the user. The user should be able to specify units either by name (e.g., kilograms) or by abbreviation (e.g., kg).

ANALYSIS

This program's basic data objects are units of measurement. We need to define a structure type that groups all relevant attributes about one unit. We can then store a database of these structures in an array and look up conversion factors as needed. To convert a measurement, the user will need to provide the measurement as a number and a string (e.g., 5 kg or 6.5 inches). The user must also enter the name or abbreviation of the desired units.

The attributes of a unit include its name and abbreviation, its class (mass, distance, and so on), and a representation of the unit in terms of the chosen standard unit for its class. If we allow the actual unit name, class names, and standard units to be determined by the contents of the input file, the program will be usable for any class of measurements and for units in any language based on our character set.

DATA REQUIREMENTS

Structured Data Type

```
unit_t
   components:
   name       /* character string such as "milligrams"    */
   abbrev     /* shorter character string such as "mg"     */
   class      /* character string "liquid_volume",
                 "distance", or "mass"                     */
   standard   /* number of standard units that are
                 equivalent to this unit                   */
```

Problem Constants

```
NAME_LEN     30   /* storage allocated for a unit name     */
ABBREV_LEN   15   /* storage allocated for a unit
                     abbreviation                          */
CLASS_LEN    20   /* storage allocated for a
                     measurement class                     */
MAX_UNITS    20   /* maximum number of different units
                     handled                               */
```

Problem Inputs

```
unit_t units[MAX_UNITS]  /* array representing unit conversion
                            factors database              */
double quantity          /* value to convert              */
char old_units[NAME_LEN] /* name or abbreviation of units to be
                            converted                     */
char new_units[NAME_LEN] /* name or abbreviation of units to
                            convert to                    */
```

Problem Output

Message giving conversion.

DESIGN

ALGORITHM

1. Load units of measurement database.
2. Get value to convert and old and new unit names.
3. Repeat until data format error encountered.
    4. Search for old units in database.
    5. Search for new units in database.

      6.   if conversion is impossible
           7.   Issue appropriate error message.
     else
           8.   Compute and display conversion.
      9.   Get value to convert and old and new unit names.

The refinement of step 1 follows.

1.1   Open database file.
1.2   Initialize subscripting variable `i`.
1.3   Scan a unit structure from the database file.
1.4   Repeat until EOF, data format error, or attempted overflow of `units` list
      1.4.1   Store unit structure in `units` array.
      1.4.2   Update `i`.
      1.4.3   Scan next unit structure from file.
1.5   Close database file.

    We will develop separate functions for step 1 (`load_units`), for step 1.3 and step 1.4.3 (`fscan_unit`), for the search used in step 4 and step 5, and for the conversion aspect of step 8. We can base our `search` function on the linear search algorithm used in Fig. 7.14.

IMPLEMENTATION

Code that implements our universal conversion program is shown in Fig. 10.12. In the universal conversion program, it makes sense to use two sources of input. The database of units is taken from a file (`units.txt`) that can be created once and then used for many runs of the program. In contrast, the program expects that the conversion problems will be entered interactively.

TESTING

In addition to testing the conversion of units of liquid volume, distance, and mass using values whose conversions are easy to verify, we should also select test cases that exercise each of the error message facilities of the program. Figure 10.13 shows a small data file and one run of the conversion program. The database in this file assumes standard units of meters, liters, and kilograms. Note that all that is required by the program is that the database consistently use *some* standard units. It does not prescribe *what* units these must be.

FIGURE 10.12 Universal Measurement Conversion Program Using an Array of Structures

```
1.  /*
2.   * Converts measurements given in one unit to any other unit of the same
3.   * category that is listed in the database file, units.txt.
4.   * Handles both names and abbreviations of units.
5.   */
6.  #include <stdio.h>
7.  #include <string.h>
8.
9.  #define NAME_LEN    30        /* storage allocated for a unit name        */
10. #define ABBREV_LEN  15        /* storage allocated for a unit abbreviation */
11. #define CLASS_LEN   20        /* storage allocated for a measurement class */
12. #define NOT_FOUND   -1        /* value indicating unit not found          */
13. #define MAX_UNITS   20        /* maximum number of different units handled */
14.
15. typedef struct {              /* unit of measurement type                 */
16.      char   name[NAME_LEN];   /* character string such as "milligrams"    */
17.      char   abbrev[ABBREV_LEN];/* shorter character string such as "mg"   */
18.      char   class[CLASS_LEN];  /* character string such as "pressure",
19.                                  "distance", "mass"                       */
20.      double standard;         /* number of standard units equivalent
21.                                  to this unit                             */
22. } unit_t;
23.
24. int fscan_unit(FILE *filep, unit_t *unitp);
25. void load_units(int unit_max, unit_t units[], int *unit_sizep);
26. int search(const unit_t units[], const char *target, int n);
27. double convert(double quantity, double old_stand, double new_stand);
28.
29. int
30. main(void)
31. {
32.      unit_t units[MAX_UNITS];      /* units classes and conversion factors*/
33.      int    num_units;             /* number of elements of units in use  */
34.      char   old_units[NAME_LEN],   /* units to convert (name or abbrev)   */
35.             new_units[NAME_LEN];   /* units to convert to (name or abbrev)*/
36.      int    status;                /* input status                        */
37.      double quantity;              /* value to convert                    */
38.
```

(continued)

FIGURE 10.12   (continued)

```
39.      int    old_index,           /* index of units element where
40.                                      old_units found                    */
41.             new_index;            /* index where new_units found        */
42.
43.      /* Load units of measurement database                              */
44.      load_units(MAX_UNITS, units, &num_units);
45.
46.      /* Convert quantities to desired units until data format error
47.         (including error code returned when q is entered to quit)        */
48.      printf("Enter a conversion problem or q to quit.\n");
49.      printf("To convert 25 kilometers to miles, you would enter\n");
50.      printf("> 25 kilometers miles\n");
51.      printf(" or, alternatively,\n");
52.      printf("> 25 km mi\n> ");
53.
54.      for  (status = scanf("%lf%s%s", &quantity, old_units, new_units);
55.            status == 3;
56.            status = scanf("%lf%s%s", &quantity, old_units, new_units)) {
57.         printf("Attempting conversion of %.4f %s to %s . . .\n",
58.                quantity, old_units, new_units);
59.         old_index = search(units, old_units, num_units);
60.         new_index = search(units, new_units, num_units);
61.         if (old_index == NOT_FOUND)
62.              printf("Unit %s not in database\n", old_units);
63.         else if (new_index == NOT_FOUND)
64.              printf("Unit %s not in database\n", new_units);
65.         else if (strcmp(units[old_index].class,
66.                         units[new_index].class) != 0)
67.              printf("Cannot convert %s (%s) to %s (%s)\n",
68.                     old_units, units[old_index].class,
69.                     new_units, units[new_index].class);
70.         else
71.              printf("%.4f%s = %.4f %s\n", quantity, old_units,
72.                     convert(quantity, units[old_index].standard,
73.                             units[new_index].standard),
74.                     new_units);
75.         printf("\nEnter a conversion problem or q to quit.\n> ");
76.      }
77.
```

(continued)

FIGURE 10.12   (continued)

```
78.        return (0);
79. }
80.
81. /*
82.  * Gets data from a file to fill output argument
83.  * Returns standard error code: 1 => successful input, 0 => error,
84.  *                         negative EOF value => end of file
85.  */
86. int
87. fscan_unit(FILE   *filep,  /* input - input file pointer        */
88.            unit_t *unitp)  /* output - unit_t structure to fill */
89. {
90.      int status;
91.
92.      status = fscanf(filep, "%s%s%s%lf", unitp->name,
93.                                          unitp->abbrev,
94.                                          unitp->class,
95.                                          &unitp->standard);
96.
97.      if (status == 4)
98.           status = 1;
99.      else if (status != EOF)
100.          status = 0;
101.
102.     return (status);
103. }
104.
105. /*
106.  * Opens database file units.txt and gets data to place in units until end
107.  * of file is encountered. Stops input prematurely if there are more than
108.  * unit_max data values in the file or if invalid data is encountered.
109.  */
110. void
111. load_units(int        unit_max,   /* input - declared size of units     */
112.            unit_t     units[],    /* output - array of data             */
113.            int        *unit_sizep) /* output - number of data values
114.                                          stored in units               */
115. {
```

(continued)

FIGURE 10.12   (continued)

```
116.        FILE * inp;
117.        unit_t data;
118.        int i, status;
119.
120.        /* Gets database of units from file                       */
121.        inp = fopen("units.txt", "r");
123.        i = 0;
124.
125.        for (status = fscan_unit(inp, &data);
126.             status == 1 && i < unit_max;
127.             status = fscan_unit(inp, &data)) {
128.           units[i++] = data;
129.        }
130.        fclose(inp);
131.
132.        /* Issue error message on premature exit                  */
133.        if (status == 0) {
134.             printf("\n*** Error in data format ***\n");
135.             printf("*** Using first %d data values ***\n", i);
136.        } else if (status != EOF) {
137.             printf("\n*** Error: too much data in file ***\n");
138.             printf("*** Using first %d data values ***\n", i);
139.        }
140.
141.        /* Send back size of used portion of array                */
142.        *unit_sizep = i;
143. }
144.
145. /*
146.  * Searches for target key in name and abbrev components of first n
147.  *     elements of array units
148.  * Returns index of structure containing target or NOT_FOUND
149.  */
150. int
151. search(const unit_t units[],     /* array of unit_t structures to search   */
152.        const char *target,       /* key searched for in name and abbrev
153.                                      components                             */
154.        int        n)             /* number of array elements to search     */
155. {
```

(continued)

FIGURE 10.12   (continued)

```
156.        int i,
157.            found = 0,       /* whether or not target has been found      */
158.            where;           /* index where target found or NOT_FOUND     */
159.
160.        /* Compare name and abbrev components of each element to target    */
161.        i = 0;
162.        while (!found && i < n) {
163.            if (strcmp(units[i].name,    target) == 0 ||
164.                strcmp(units[i].abbrev,  target) == 0)
165.                    found = 1;
166.            else
167.                    ++i;
168.        }
169.        /* Return index of element containing target or NOT_FOUND          */
170.        if (found)
171.                where = i;
172.        else
173.                where = NOT_FOUND;
174.        return (where);
175. }
176.
177. /*
178.  * Converts one measurement to another given the representation of both
179.  * in a standard unit. For example, to convert 24 feet to yards given a
180.  * standard unit of inches: quantity = 24, old_stand = 12 (there are 12
181.  * inches in a foot), new_stand = 36 (there are 36 inches in a yard),
182.  * result is 24 * 12 / 36 which equals 8
183.  */
184. double
185. convert(double quantity,    /* value to convert                          */
186.         double old_stand,   /* number of standard units in one of
187.                                 quantity's original units                 */
188.         double new_stand)   /* number of standard units in 1 new unit    */
189. {
190.        return (quantity * old_stand / new_stand);
191. }
```

FIGURE 10.13   Data File and Sample Run of Measurement Conversion Program

Data file units.txt:

miles	mi	distance	1609.3
kilometers	km	distance	1000
yards	yd	distance	0.9144
meters	m	distance	1
quarts	qt	liquid_volume	0.94635
liters	l	liquid_volume	1
gallons	gal	liquid_volume	3.7854
milliliters	ml	liquid_volume	0.001
kilograms	kg	mass	1
grams	g	mass	0.001
slugs	slugs	mass	0.14594
pounds	lb	mass	0.43592

Sample run:

```
Enter a conversion problem or q to quit.
To convert 25 kilometers to miles, you would enter
> 25 kilometers miles
    or, alternatively,
> 25 km mi
> 450 km miles
Attempting conversion of 450.0000 km to miles . . .
450.0000km = 279.6247 miles

Enter a conversion problem or q to quit.
> 2.5 qt l
Attempting conversion of 2.5000 qt to l . . .
2.5000qt = 2.3659 l

Enter a conversion problem or q to quit.
> 100 meters gallons
Attempting conversion of 100.0000 meters to gallons . . .
Cannot convert meters (distance) to gallons (liquid_volume)

Enter a conversion problem or q to quit.
> 1234 mg g
Attempting conversion of 1234.0000 mg to g . . .
Unit mg not in database

Enter a conversion problem or q to quit.
> q
```

EXERCISES FOR SECTION 10.5

Self-Check

1. In function `main` of our universal conversion program, we see the statement

   ```
   load_units(MAX_UNITS, units, &num_units);
   ```

   Inside `load_units` we see the function call

   ```
   fscan_unit(inp, &data);
   ```

   Variables `units`, `num_units`, and `data` are all being used as output arguments in these statements. Why is the `&` applied to `num_units` and `data`, but not to `units`?

2. Write a code fragment that would add `0.2` to all the gpa's in `stulist` (see Fig. 10.11). If the addition of `0.2` would inflate a gpa past `4.0`, just set the gpa to `4.0`.

10.6 Union Types (Optional)

So far, all the variables we have seen of a particular structure type have had exactly the same components. However, sometimes we need structured types in which some components vary depending on the value of another component. For example, if we were to write a program to manipulate a variety of geometric figures, the data we would need to store would vary depending on the type of figure processed. In order to find the area and circumference of a circle, we would need to know the radius; to compute the area and perimeter of a square, we would need to know the length of a side; to figure the area and perimeter of other rectangles, we would need height and width.

union a data structure that overlays components in memory, allowing one chunk of memory to be interpreted in multiple ways

C provides a data structure called a **union** to deal with situations in which one needs a data object that can be interpreted in a variety of ways.

EXAMPLE 10.6

The following declaration defines a union structure to use as the type of one component of a person's physical description. If the person has hair, we would like to record the hair color. However, if the person is bald, we need to note whether or not this baldness is disguised by a wig.

```
typedef union {
      int   wears_wig;
      char  color[20];
} hair_t;
```

As you can see, the format of a union type definition exactly parallels a structure type definition. As before, our `typedef` statement allocates no memory. A later declaration

```
hair_t hair_data;
```

creates a variable `hair_data` built on the template of the type definition. This variable `hair_data` does not contain *both* `wears_wig` *and* `color` components. Rather, it has *either* a `wears_wig` component referenced by `hair_data.wears_wig` *or* a `color` component referenced by `hair_data.color`. When memory is allocated for `hair_data`, the amount of memory is determined by the largest component of the union.

In most cases, it is useful to be able to interpret a chunk of memory in more than one way only if it is possible to determine *which* way is currently the valid interpretation. For this reason, unions are most often used as types of portions of a larger structure, and the larger structure typically contains a component whose value indicates which interpretation of the union is correct at the present time. Such a structure containing a `hair_t` union component is the following:

```
typedef struct {
    int     bald;
    hair_t h;
} hair_info_t;
```

When we write code using a `hair_info_t` structure, we can base our manipulation of the union component `h` on the value of the `bald` component. This component indicates whether the subject is bald. For bald subjects, the `wears_wig` interpretation of component `h` is valid. For nonbald subjects, the `color` interpretation is valid and represents the color of the subject's hair. Figure 10.14 shows a function to display `hair_info_t` data.

In Fig. 10.15, we see the two possible interpretations of the `h` component of parameter `hair`, one that is conceptually valid when `hair.bald` is true, and one that applies when `hair.bald` is false. Referencing the appropriate union component is *always* the programmer's responsibility; C can do no checking of the validity of such a component reference.

EXAMPLE 10.7   In Fig. 10.16, we see a partial solution to the problem of finding the area and perimeter (circumference) of a geometric figure, the problem mentioned at the beginning of our discussion of union types. First, we define structure types for each figure of interest including components for the figure's area and perimeter or circumference, as well as components for those dimensions of the figure that are

FIGURE 10.14 Function That Displays a Structure with a Union Type Component

```
1.  void
2.  print_hair_info(hair_info_t hair) /* input - structure to display      */
3.  {
4.       if (hair.bald) {
5.           printf("Subject is bald");
6.           if (hair.h.wears_wig)
7.               printf(", but wears a wig.\n");
8.           else
9.               printf(" and does not wear a wig.\n");
10.      } else {
11.          printf("Subject's hair color is %s.\n", hair.h.color);
12.      }
13. }
```

FIGURE 10.15 Two Interpretations of Parameter hair

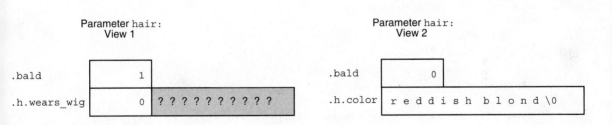

needed in computation of its area and perimeter. Then, we define a union type with a component for each figure type. Finally, we define a structure containing both a component of the union type and a component whose value denotes which is the correct interpretation of the union. Notice that all functions that process `figure_t` data contain `switch` statements to select the valid view of the `fig` component based on the value of the `shape` component. In function `compute_area`, the default case of the `switch` statement prints an error message. This message will never appear as long as the function's preconditions are met.

FIGURE 10.16 Program to Compute Area and Perimeter of Geometric Figures

```
1.   /*
2.    * Computes the area and perimeter of a variety of geometric figures.
3.    */
4.
5.   #include <stdio.h>
6.   #define PI 3.14159
7.
8.   /*  Types defining the components needed to represent each shape.        */
9.   typedef struct {
10.        double area,
11.               circumference,
12.               radius;
13.   } circle_t;
14.
15.   typedef struct {
16.        double area,
17.               perimeter,
18.               width,
19.               height;
20.   } rectangle_t;
21.
22.   typedef struct {
23.        double area,
24.               perimeter,
25.               side;
26.   } square_t;
27.
28.   /* Type of a structure that can be interpreted a different way for
29.      each shape                                                          */
30.   typedef union {
31.        circle_t    circle;
32.        rectangle_t rectangle;
33.        square_t    square;
34.   } figure_data_t;
35.
36.   /* Type containing a structure with multiple interpretations along with
37.    * a component whose value indicates the current valid interpretation   */
38.   typedef struct {
39.        char        shape;
40.        figure_data_t fig;
41.   } figure_t;
```

(continued)

FIGURE 10.16   (continued)

```
42.
43.  figure_t get_figure_dimensions(void);
44.  figure_t compute_area(figure_t object);
45.  figure_t compute_perim(figure_t object);
46.  void print_figure(figure_t object);
47.
48.  int
49.  main(void)
50.  {
51.       figure_t onefig;
52.
53.       printf("Area and Perimeter Computation Program\n");
54.
55.       for  (onefig = get_figure_dimensions();
56.             onefig.shape != 'Q';
57.             onefig = get_figure_dimensions()) {
58.          onefig = compute_area(onefig);
59.          onefig = compute_perim(onefig);
60.          print_figure(onefig);
61.       }
62.
63.       return (0);
64.  }
65.
66.  /*
67.   * Prompts for and stores the dimension data necessary to compute a
68.   * figure's area and perimeter. Figure returned contains a 'Q' in the
69.   * shape component when signaling end of data.
70.   */
71.  figure_t
72.  get_figure_dimensions(void)
73.  {
74.       figure_t object;
75.       printf("Enter a letter to indicate the object shape or Q to quit.\n");
76.       printf("C (circle), R (rectangle), or S (square)> ");
77.       object.shape = getchar();
78.
79.       switch (object.shape) {
80.       case 'C':
81.       case 'c':
```

(continued)

FIGURE 10.16   (continued)

```
82.             printf("Enter radius> ");
83.             scanf("%lf", &object.fig.circle.radius);
84.             break;
85.
86.         case 'R':
87.         case 'r':
88.             printf("Enter height> ");
89.             scanf("%lf", &object.fig.rectangle.height);
90.             printf("Enter width> ");
91.             scanf("%lf", &object.fig.rectangle.width);
92.             break;
93.
94.         case 'S':
95.         case 's':
96.             printf("Enter length of a side> ");
97.             scanf("%lf", &object.fig.square.side);
98.             break;
99.
100.        default: /* Error is treated as a QUIT */
101.             object.shape = 'Q';
102.        }
103.
104.        return (object);
105. }
106.
107. /*
108.  * Computes the area of a figure given relevant dimensions. Returns
109.  * figure with area component filled.
110.  * Pre:  value of shape component is one of these letters: CcRrSs
111.  *       necessary dimension components have values
112.  */
113. figure_t
114. compute_area(figure_t object)
115. {
116.        switch (object.shape) {
117.        case 'C':
118.        case 'c':
119.             object.fig.circle.area = PI * object.fig.circle.radius *
120.                                      object.fig.circle.radius;
121.             break;
```

(continued)

FIGURE 10.16   (continued)

```
122.
123.        case 'R':
124.        case 'r':
125.            object.fig.rectangle.area = object.fig.rectangle.height *
126.                                        object.fig.rectangle.width;
127.            break;
128.
129.        case 'S':
130.        case 's':
131.            object.fig.square.area = object.fig.square.side *
132.                                     object.fig.square.side;
133.            break;
134.
135.        default:
136.            printf("Error in shape code detected in compute_area\n");
137.        }
138.
139.        return (object);
140.    }
141.
142.    /* Code for compute_perim and print_figure goes here */
```

  EXERCISES FOR SECTION 10.6

Self-Check

1. Determine how many bytes are needed to store a structure of type `hair_info_t`, assuming two bytes for an integer and one byte for a character. How much of this space is actually in use when component `wears_wig` is true?

Programming

1. Write functions `compute_perim` and `print_figure` to complete the program in Fig. 10.16.

10.7   Common Programming Errors

When programmers manipulate structure types, their most common error is incorrect use of a component selected for processing. When using the direct selection operator (.), always be aware of the type of the component selected, and use the value in a manner consistent with its type. For example, if the component selected is an array, passing it to a function as an output argument does not require application of the address-of operator.

If a structure type output parameter is used in a function, one can avoid the operator precedence problems associated with combining the indirection (*) and direct component selection (.) operators by using the indirect component selection operator (->).

C allows the use of structure type values in assignment statements as function arguments and as function results, so one can easily forget that expressions of these types cannot be operands of equality comparators or arguments of printf and scanf. You can select simple components from a structure to use in these contexts, or you can write your own type-specific equality and I/O functions.

When you use a union type, referencing a component that is not currently valid is easy to do. It is helpful to place the union within another structure that contains a component whose value indicates which interpretation of the union is correct. Then all manipulation of the union can fall within if or switch statements that reference the union component based on the value of the associated structure component.

Chapter Review

1. C permits the user to define a type composed of multiple named components.
2. A component of a structure is referenced by placing the direct component selection operator (.) between the structure variable name and the component name.
3. A component of a structured output parameter is referenced by placing the indirect component selection operator (->) between the structure variable name and the component name.
4. User-defined structure types can be used in most situations where built-in types are valid: Structured values can be function arguments and function results and can be copied using the assignment operator; structure types are legitimate in declarations of variables, of structure components, and of arrays.
5. Structured values cannot be compared for equality using the == and != operators.

6. Structure types play an important role in data abstraction: You create an abstract data type (ADT) by implementing as functions all of the type's necessary operators.
7. In a union type variable, structure components are overlaid in memory.

NEW C CONSTRUCTS

Construct	Effect
Definition of a Structure Type	
```typedef struct { char name[20]; int quantity; double price; } part_t;```	A structure type **part_t** is defined with components that can store a string and two numbers, one of type **int** and one of type **double**.
Declaration of Variables to Hold One Structure or an Array of Structures	
```part_t nuts, bolts, parts_list[40]; part_t mouse = {"serial mouse", 30, 145.00};```	**nuts**, **bolts**, and **mouse** are structured variables of type **part_t**; **parts_list** is an array of 40 such structures. The three components of **mouse** are initialized in its declaration.
Component Reference	
```cost = nuts.quantity * nuts.price;```	Multiplies two components of type **part_t** variable **nuts**.
```printf("Part: %s\n", parts_list[i].name);```	Displays **name** component of **i**th element of **parts_list**.
Structure Copy	
```bolts = nuts;```	Stores in **bolts** a copy of each component of **nuts**.
Definition of a Union Type	
```typedef union { char str[4]; int intger; double real; } multi_t;```	A union type **multi_t** is defined allowing three interpretations of the contents of a type **multi_t** variable: The contents may be seen as a four-character string, as an integer, or as a type **double** number.

(continued)

NEW C CONSTRUCTS   (continued)

Construct	Effect
Definition of a Structure Type with a Union Component	
```typedef struct { char interp; multi_t val; } choose_t;```	A structure type `choose_t` is defined with a component `interp`, whose value ('S' for string, 'I' for integer, 'D' for `double`) indicates which interpretation of union component `val` is valid.

Quick-Check Exercises

1. What is the primary difference between a structure and an array? Which would you use to store the catalog description of a course? To store the names of students in the course?
2. How do you access a component of a structure type variable?

   Exercises 3–8 refer to the following type `student_t` and to variables `stu1` and `stu2`.

   ```
   typedef struct {
         char fst_name[20],
              last_name[20];
         int  score;
         char grade;
   } student_t;
   . . .
   student_t stu1, stu2;
   ```

3. Identify the following statements as possibly valid or definitely invalid. If invalid, explain why.

   a.   `student_t stulist[30];`
   b.   `printf("%s", stu1);`
   c.   `printf("%d %c", stu1.score, stu1.grade);`
   d.   `stu2 = stu1;`
   e.   `if (stu2.score == stu1.score)`
              `printf("Equal");`
   f.   `if (stu2 == stu1)`
              `printf("Equal structures");`

```
g.   scan_student(&stu1);
h.   stu2.last_name = "Martin";
```

4. Write a statement that displays the initials of stu1 (with periods).
5. How many components does variable stu2 have?
6. Write functions scan_student and print_student for type
   student_t variables.
7. Declare an array of 40 student_t structures, and write a code segment that
   displays on separate lines the names (*last name, first name*) of all the students
   in the list.
8. Identify the type of each of the following references:

   a.   stu1
   b.   stu2.score
   c.   stu2.fst_name[3]
   d.   stu1.grade

9. When should you use a union type component in a structured variable?

Answers to Quick-Check Exercises

1. A structure can have components of different types, but an array's elements
   must all be of the same type. Use a structure for the catalog item and an array
   of strings for the list of student names.
2. Components of structures are accessed using the direct selection operator followed by a component name.
3. a.   Valid
   b.   Invalid: printf does not accept structured arguments.
   c.   Valid
   d.   Valid
   e.   Valid
   f.   Invalid: Equality operators cannot be used with structure types.
   g.   Valid (assuming parameter type is student_t *)
   h.   Invalid: Cannot copy strings with = except in declaration (this case needs
        strcpy)
4. printf("%c.%c.", stu1.fst_name[0],
   stu1.last_name[0]);
5. four
6. int
   scan_student(student_t *stup) /* output - student structure to
                                              fill */
   {
           int status,
```
```

```
            char temp[4]; /* temporary storage for grade */
            status = scanf("%s%s%d%s", stu->fst_name,
                                       stu->last_name,
                                       &stu->score,
                                       temp);
        if (status == 4) {
            status = 1;
            (*stu).grade = temp[0];
        } else if (status != EOF) {
            status = 0;
        }
        return (status);
    }

    void
    print_student(student_t stu) /* input - student structure to
                                            display */
    {
        printf("Student: %s, %s\n", stu.last_name,
               stu.fst_name);
        printf("   Score: %d      Grade: %c\n", stu.score,
               stu.grade);
    }
```

7. `student_t students[40];`

```
   for  (i = 0;    i < 40;    ++i)
       printf("%s, %s\n", students[i].last_name,
              students[i].fst_name);
```

8. a.   `student_t`
   b.   `int`
   c.   `char`
   d.   `char`

9. Use a union type component in a structured variable when the needed structure components vary depending on the value of one component.

Review Questions

1. Define a structure type called `college_t` that contains the college name, `college_address`, and `number_of_programs` (i.e., how many courses the college offers).

2. Write a C program that scans data to fill the variable `college` declared below and then displays the contents of the structure with suitable labels.

```
#define STR_LENGTH 50

typedef struct {
      char college_name[STR_LENGTH],
            student_name[STR_LENGTH],
            country[STR_LENGTH];
      int code;
} university_t;

. . .

university_t college;
```

3. How would you call a function `scan_university` passing `college` as an output argument?

4. Identify and correct the errors in the following program:

```
typedef struct
      char    name[15],
              start_date[15],
      double hrs_worked,
summer_help_t;

/* prototype for function scan_sum_hlp goes here */

int
main(void)
{
      struct operator;

      scan_sum_hlp(operator);
      printf("Name: %s\nStarting date: %s\nHours worked:
            %.2f\n", operator);

      return(0);
}
```

5. Define a data structure to store the following employee data: salary, department, address (consisting of street address, city, state, zip), and work schedule (consisting of one week's work reports, each of which has description, time, and days components). Define whatever data types are needed.

Programming Projects

1. Define a structure type `auto_t` to represent an automobile. Include components for the make and model (strings), the odometer reading, the manufacture and purchase dates (use another user-defined type called `date_t`), and the gas tank (use a user-defined type `tank_t` with components for tank capacity and current fuel level, giving both in gallons). Write I/O functions `scan_date`, `scan_tank`, `scan_auto`, `print_date`, `print_tank`, and `print_auto`, and also write a driver function that repeatedly fills and displays an auto structure variable until `EOF` is encountered in the input file.

    Here is a small data set to try:

    ```
    Mercury Sable    99842 1 18 2001 5 30 1991 16    12.5
    Mazda    Navajo    123961 2 20 1993 6 15 1993 19.3 16.7
    ```

2. An iron manufacturing company maintains data about all of its employees, including every employee's name, unique ID, age, native city, contact number, the department to which she or he belongs, and gross salary. The company wants a program that can sort the employees based on their native city in order to easily trace how many employees belong to the same region. Write a C program module by using 'strcmp' to sort all the available names of cities in an ascending order.

3. A number expressed in scientific notation is represented by its mantissa (a fraction) and its exponent (an integer). Define a type `sci_not_t` that has separate components for these two parts. Define a function `scan_sci` that takes from the input source a string representing a positive number in scientific notation, and breaks it into components for storage in a `sci_not_t` structure. The mantissa of an input value (m) should satisfy this condition: `0.1 <= m < 1.0`. Also, write functions to compute the sum, difference, product, and quotient of two `sci_not_t` values. All these functions should have a result type of `sci_not_t` and should ensure that the result's mantissa is in the prescribed range. Define a `print_sci` function as well. Then, create a driver program to test your functions. Your output should be of this form:

    ```
    Values input:  0.25000e3  0.20000e1
    Sum:   0.25200e3
    Difference:   0.24800e3
    Product:   0.50000e3
    Quotient:   0.12500e3
    ```

4. Microbiologists estimating the number of bacteria in a sample that contains bacteria that do not grow well on solid media may use a statistical technique called the most probable number (MPN) method. Each of five tubes of nutrient medium receives 10 ml of the sample. A second set of five tubes receives 1 ml of sample per tube, and in each of a third set of five tubes, only 0.1 ml of sample is placed. Each tube in which bacterial growth is observed is recorded as a positive, and the numbers for the three groups are combined to create a triplet such as 5-2-1, which means that all five tubes receiving 10 ml of sample show bacterial growth, only two tubes in the 1-ml group show growth, and only one of the 0.1-ml group is positive. A microbiologist would use this combination-of-positives triplet as an index to a table like the table below to determine that the most probable number of bacteria per 100 ml of the sample

Table of Bacterial Concentrations for Most Probable Number Method

Combination of Positives	MPN Index/100 ml	95% Confidence Limits	
		Lower	Upper
4-2-0	22	9	56
4-2-1	26	12	65
4-3-0	27	12	67
4-3-1	33	15	77
4-4-0	34	16	80
5-0-0	23	9	86
5-0-1	30	10	110
5-0-2	40	20	140
5-1-0	30	10	120
5-1-1	50	20	150
5-1-2	60	30	180
5-2-0	50	20	170
5-2-1	70	30	210
5-2-2	90	40	250
5-3-0	80	30	250
5-3-1	110	40	300
5-3-2	140	60	360

[1]*Microbiology, An Introduction*, 7th ed. edited by Gerard J. Tortora, Berdell R. Funke, and Christine L. Case (San Francisco, California: Benjamin Cummings, 2001), p. 177.

is 70, and 95% of the samples yielding this triplet contain between 30 and 210 bacteria per 100 ml.

Define a structure type to represent one row of the MPN table. The structure will include one string component for the combination-of-positives triplet and three integer components in which to store the associated most probable number and the lower and upper bounds of the 95% confidence range. Write a program to implement the following algorithm for generating explanations of combination-of-positives triplets.

a. Load the MPN table from a file into an array of structures called `mpn_table`.

b. Repeatedly get from the user a combination-of-positives triplet, search for it in the combination-of-positives components of `mpn_table`, and then generate a message such as:

```
For 5-2-1, MPN = 70; 95% of samples contain between 30 and
210 bacteria/ml.
```

c. Define and call the following functions.

`load_Mpn_Table`—Takes as parameters the name of the input file, the `mpn_table` array and its maximum size. Function opens the file, fills the `mpn_table` array, and closes the file. Then it returns the actual array size as the function result. If the file contains too much data, the function should store as much data as will fit, display an error message indicating that some data has been ignored, and return the array's maximum size as its actual size.

`search`—Takes as parameters the `mpn_table` array, its actual size, and a target string representing a combination-of-positives triplet. Returns the subscript of the structure whose combination-of-positives component matches the target or −1 if not found.

5. Numeric addresses for computers on the international network Internet are composed of four parts, separated by periods, of the form

```
xx.yy.zz.mm
```

where `xx`, `yy`, `zz`, and `mm` are positive integers. Locally, computers are usually known by a nickname as well. You are designing a program to process a list of Internet addresses, identifying all pairs of computers from the same locality. Create a structure type called `address_t` with components for the four integers of an Internet address and a fifth component in which to store an associated nickname of ten characters. Your program should read a list of up to 100 addresses and nicknames terminated by a sentinel address of all zeros and a sentinel nickname.

Sample Data
```
111.22.3.44        platte
555.66.7.88        wabash
111.22.5.66        green
0.0.0.0            none
```

The program should display a list of messages identifying each pair of computers from the same locality, that is, each pair of computers with matching values in the first two components of the address. In the messages, the computers should be identified by their nicknames.

Example Message
```
Machines platte and green are on the same local network.
```

Follow the messages by a display of the full list of addresses and nicknames. Include in your program a `scan_address` function, a `print_address` function, and a `local_address` function. Function `local_address` should take two address structures as input parameters and return `1` (for true) if the addresses are on the same local network, and `0` (for false) otherwise.

6. Define a structure type to represent a word list. The structure will contain one string component for the language of the words (e.g., English, Japanese, Spanish), an integer component that keeps track of how many words are in the list, and an array of `MAX_WORDS` 20-character strings to hold the words. Define the following functions to work with word lists:

   a. `load_word_list`—Takes as parameters the name of an input file and a wordlist structure to be filled.

   b. `add_word`—Takes as parameters a word and a wordlist structure to modify. If the wordlist is already full, it displays the message "`List full,` *word* `not added.`" If the word is already in the list, it leaves the structure unchanged. Otherwise, it adds the word to the list and updates the list size. Do not bother keeping the list in order.

   c. `contains`—Takes as parameters a word and a wordlist. If the word matches one of the wordlist entries, the function returns true, otherwise false.

   d. `equal_lists`—Takes two wordlists as parameters and returns true if the lists are in the same language, have the same number of elements, and every element of one list is found in the other. (*Hint*: Call `contains` repeatedly.)

   e. `display_word_list`—Displays all the words of its wordlist structure parameter in four columns.

Write a program that fills a wordlist from a data file. Then prompt the user to enter a language and 12 words to add to a different list. Then ask the user to enter some words to search for in the first list using `contains`, and print a message indicating whether each is found. Use `equal_lists` to compare the two lists, printing an appropriate message. Finally, use `display_word_list` to output each list.

7. Design and implement a structure type to model an ideal transformer. If you have a single iron core with wire 1 coiled around the core N_1 times and wire 2 wound around the core N_2 times, and if wire 1 is attached to a source of alternating current, then the voltage in wire 1 (the input voltage V_1) is related to the voltage in wire 2 (the output voltage V_2) as

$$\frac{V_1}{V_2} = \frac{N_1}{N_2}$$

and the relationship between the input current I_1 and the output current I_2 is

$$\frac{I_1}{I_2} = \frac{N_1}{N_2}$$

A variable of type `transformer_t` should store N_1, N_2, V_1, and I_1. Also, define functions `v_out` and `i_out` to compute the output voltage and current of a transformer. In addition, define functions that set each of the transformer's components to produce a desired output voltage or current. For example, function `set_n1_for_v2` should take a desired output voltage as an input parameter and a transformer as an input/output parameter and should change the component representing N_1 to produce the desired current. Also, define `set_v1_for_v2`, `set_n2_for_v2`, and `set_n2_for_i2`. Include `scan_transformer` and `print_transformer` functions to facilitate I/O.

8. At a grocery store, certain categories of products sold have been established, and this information is to be computerized. Write a function to scan and store information in a structure variable whose data type is one you define—a type that includes a component that has multiple interpretations. Also, write an output function and a driver function to use in testing.

The data for each item consists of the item name (a string of less than 20 characters with no blanks), the unit cost in cents (an integer), and a character indicating the product category ('M' for meat, 'P' for produce, 'D' for dairy, 'C' for canned goods, and 'N' for nonfoods). The following additional data will depend on the product category.

Product Category	Additional Data
Meats	character indicating meat type ('R' for red meat, 'P' for poultry, 'F' for fish) date of packaging expiration date
Produce	character 'F' for fruit or 'V' for vegetable date received
Dairy	expiration date
Canned goods	expiration date (month and year only) aisle number (an integer) aisle side (letter 'A' or 'B')
Nonfoods	character indicating category ('C' for cleaning product, 'P' for pharmacy, 'O' for other) aisle number (an integer) aisle side (letter 'A' or 'B')

A data line for canned corn would be

```
corn    89C    11    2000    12B
```

The corn costs 89 cents, expires in November of 2000, and is displayed in aisle 12B.

9. Create a structure type to represent a battery. A `battery_t` variable's components will include the voltage, how much energy the battery is capable of storing, and how much energy it is currently storing (in joules). Define functions for input and output of batteries. Create a function called `power_device` that (a) takes the current of an electrical device (amps) and the time the device is to be powered by the battery (seconds) as input parameters and (b) takes a battery as an input/output parameter. The function first determines whether the battery's energy reserve is adequate to power the device for the prescribed time. If so, the function updates the battery's energy reserve by subtracting the energy consumed and then returns the value true (1). Otherwise, it returns the value false (0) and leaves the energy reserve unchanged. Also, define a function named `max_time` that takes a battery and the current of an electrical device as input parameters and returns the number of seconds the battery can operate the device before it is fully

discharged. This function does not change any of the battery's component values. Write a function `recharge` that sets to the maximum capacity the battery's component representing present energy reserve. Use the following equations in your design:

$$p = vi \qquad p = \text{power in watts (W)}$$
$$v = \text{voltage in volts (V)}$$
$$w = pt \qquad i = \text{current in amps (A)}$$
$$w = \text{energy in joules (J)}$$
$$t = \text{time in seconds (s)}$$

For this simulation, neglect any loss of energy in the transfer from battery to device.

Create a main function that declares and initializes a variable to model a 12-V automobile battery with a maximum energy storage of 5×10^6J. Use the battery to power a 4-A light for 15 minutes, and then find out how long the battery's remaining energy could power an 8-A device. After recharging the battery, recalculate how long it could operate an 8-A device.

10. You are writing software to create acknowledgement letters for gifts to a nonprofit organization. The program is designed to assist a data entry person who has a stack of envelopes containing donations. Your program will first load from the file `donors.txt` the name of the organization and the database of donors. Each donor is represented by separate lines containing last name, first name, line 1 of street address, line 2 of street address or a zero if there is no second line, city, two-character state abbreviation, five-digit zip code, and total donations so far this year. The file is sorted in ascending order by last name. After loading the database, the program will repeatedly prompt for the last name and first name of a donor and a donation amount. It will create and save to a file brief thank-you letters citing the donation amount and stating an updated total of donations received so far this year. Each thank-you should begin with a new page character (the form-feed character `\f`) followed by 10 newline characters so it will be positioned correctly on organization stationery. Your software will update the total-so-far field in the donor record of an existing donor or will prompt for additional information in order to add a donor record at the end of the list for new donors. When a donor last name of "q" is entered, the program will sort the updated donor list by last name of donor and output to the donor file the name of the organization and the updated donor list. You may assume for this project that a donor will occur only once in the list of interactively entered donor amounts, that there are no two donors with the same first and last names, and that the maximum number of donors is 100, including new donors. A sample donor file follows.

Donors.txt

The House	512 S Second Ave	Kansas City
Adams	Unit 14	KS
John	Mobile	66118
2707 Cancun Ct	AL	3500.00
0	36617	John
Grand Junction	25.00	2707
CO	Forrester	Cancun Ct
81506	Eric	0
1200.00	123 5th Ave	Grand Junction
Barnes	0	CO
Harry	New York	81506
1010 S 80th St	NY	1200.00
0	02721	McIntyre
Denver	1250.00	Osborne
CO	Geraldton	121 E First St
80235	Mark	Apt 2
50.00	25 E Hwy 50	Cumberland
Carlson	Suite 59	MD
Patricia	Rochester	21502
410 S Broadway	NY	5000.00
Apt 4	14607	Nelson
Denver	100.00	Jane
CO	Golden	241 E Fourth St
80234	Daniel	0
1350.00	801 Grand Ave	Frisco
Decker	0	CO
Diane	Springfield	80433
220 S St James Blvd	IL	650.00
0	62701	Ryan
Evansville	650.00	Myrtle
IN	Howard	501 S Marlin Ave
47714	Marla	Apt 110
430.00	2011 Butterfly Ct	Bradenton
Evans	0	FL
Charles		34205
	➙	➙ 200.00

11. Define a type named travel_data that would be appropriate for storing traveling information. Include components named destination (name), distance, time, and direction (one of the characters 'N', 'S', 'E', or 'W'). Write a C program module print_travel_data to provide output of type travel_data. Write C program modules for travel_data_compare and scan_travel_data to perform an equality comparison and input, respectively, of type travel_data.

Text and Binary File Pointers

CHAPTER 1

CHAPTER OBJECTIVES

- To learn about streams in C and their relationship to files and standard input and output devices
- To review how `scanf, fscanf` and `printf, fprintf` are used to read and write characters to text files
- To learn about escape sequences and their use in format strings
- To review file pointer variables and learn how to use functions that process them to make a backup copy of a text file
- To learn about binary files and understand the differences between binary and text files
- To see how to write a program that searches a database stored in a binary file

This chapter will explore in greater depth the use of standard input, standard output, and program-controlled text files. We also will introduce binary files and compare the advantages and disadvantages of text and binary files.

11.1 Input/Output Files: Review and Further Study

C can process two kinds of files, text files and binary files. We will study text files in this section and binary files later in this chapter. All the files you have created using an editor or word processor have been text files. A **text file** is a named collection of characters saved in secondary storage (e.g., on a disk). A text file has no fixed size. To mark the end of a text file, the computer places a special *end-of-file* character, which we will denote <eof>, after the last character in the file. As you create a text file using an editor program, pressing the <return> or <enter> key causes the newline character (represented by C as '\n') to be placed in the file.

text file a named collection of characters saved in secondary storage

The following lines represent a text file consisting of two lines of letters, blank characters, and the punctuation characters . and ! .

```
This is a text file!<newline>
It has two lines.<newline><eof>
```

Each line ends with the newline character, and the eof character follows the last newline in the file. For convenience in examining the file's contents, we listed each line of the file (through <newline>) as a separate line, although this would not be the case in the actual disk file. The disk file consists of a sequence of characters occupying consecutive storage locations on a track of the disk, as shown here:

```
This is a text file!<newline>It has two lines.<newline><eof>
```

The first character of the second line (I) follows directly after the last character of the first line (the newline character). Because all textual input and output data are actually a continuous stream of character codes, we sometimes refer to a data source or destination as an **input stream** or an **output stream**. These general terms can be applied to files, to the terminal keyboard and screen, and to any other sources of input data or destinations of output data.

input (output) stream continuous stream of character codes representing textual input (or output) data

The Keyboard and Screen as Text Streams

stdin system file pointer for keyboard's input stream

stdout, stderr system file pointers for screen's output stream

In interactive programming, C associates system names with the terminal keyboard and screen. The name **stdin** represents the keyboard's input stream. Two system streams, the "normal" output stream **stdout** and the "error" output stream **stderr**, are associated with the screen. All three streams can be treated like text files because their individual components are characters.

Normally at the keyboard, we enter one line of data at a time, pressing <return> or <enter> to indicate the end of a data line. Pressing one of these keys inserts the newline character in system stream **stdin**. Normally in interactive programming, we use a sentinel value to indicate the end of data rather than attempting to place the eof character in system stream **stdin**. However, the eof character could be used. No single key represents the eof character, so most systems use the control key followed by a letter. (For example, on computers running the UNIX operating system, the keystrokes <control-d> would be used.)

Writing characters to the streams **stdout** and **stderr** causes a display on the screen in an interactive program. We have studied the use of the **printf** function to write characters to the screen. Using a '\n' in the **printf** format string causes output of a newline character that moves the cursor to the start of the next line of the screen.

Newline and EOF

We have seen that C handles the special newline character differently than the eof character, even though they have similar purposes. The <newline> marks the end of a line of text, and the <eof> marks the end of the entire file. The <newline> can be processed like any other character: It can be input using **scanf** with the **%c** specifier, it can be compared to '\n' for equality, and it can be output using **printf**.

However, input of the special eof character is regarded as a failed operation, and the input function responsible returns as its value the negative integer associated with the identifier **EOF**. Because this special return value gives the calling function an indication that no more data are in the input file, the C run-time support system is under no obligation to provide an error message if the program ignores the warning value and continues to attempt to get input from the stream in question. The following is another example of the input loops that we studied that base their exit condition on the appearance of the **EOF** return value:

```
for  (status = scanf("%d", &num);
      status != EOF;
      status = scanf("%d", &num))
    process(num);
```

TABLE 11.1 Meanings of Common Escape Sequences

Escape Sequence	Meaning
'\n'	new line
'\t'	tab
'\f'	form feed (new page)
'\r'	return (go back to column 1 of current output line)
'\b'	backspace

Escape Sequences

The character '\n' is one of several escape sequences defined by C to represent special characters. Table 11.1 shows some of the most commonly used escape sequences. Because all the escape sequences begin with a backslash (\), to represent the actual backslash character in a C program, you must use two: '\\'. The '\r' sequence differs from the newline ('\n') in that it moves the cursor to the beginning of the *current* line of output, not to the beginning of the *next* line. Using '\r' gives a program the ability to create a file containing more than one character in one line position. For example, this call to printf displays a heading at the top of a new page, indented to the third tab stop and underlined.

```
printf("\f\t\t\tFinal Report\r\t\t\t_____\n");
```

Formatting Output with printf

In earlier chapters we have studied placeholders to include in printf format strings for integer, character, floating-point, and string values. Table 11.2 reviews these placeholders and presents additional placeholders that cause output of integers in octal (base 8) or hexadecimal (base 16) and that display floating-point numbers in scientific notation with either a lowercase or uppercase e just before the exponent. The notation calls for an exponent that will produce exactly one nonzero digit to the left of the decimal point. In the example shown in Table 11.2, 8.197000e+01 means 8.197000×10^1. The last entry in the table indicates that in order to display a single percent sign, you must place two of them (%%) in the format string.

Each of these placeholders can be combined with a numeric field width to prescribe the minimum number of columns occupied by the value displayed. If the field width number is positive, the value is right-justified in the field: That is, any blank padding is output *in front of* the displayed value. If the field width number is negative, the value is left-justified in the field: That is, any blank padding is output *following* the displayed value. If the field width is too small, printf simply uses the

TABLE 11.2 Placeholders for printf Format Strings

Placeholder	Used for Output of	Example	Output
%c	a single character	`printf("%c%c%c\n",` `'a', '\n', 'b');`	a b

%s	a string	`printf("%s%s\n",`
		`"Hi, how ",`
		`"are you?");`
			Hi, how are you?

%d	an integer (in base 10)	`printf("%d\n", 43);`	43
%o	an integer (in base 8)	`printf("%o\n", 43);`	53
%x	an integer (in base 16)	`printf("%x\n", 43);`	2b
%f	a floating-point number	`printf("%f\n", 81.97);`	81.970000
%e	a floating-point number in scientific notation	`printf("%e\n", 81.97);`	8.197000e+01
%E	a floating-point number in scientific notation	`printf("%E\n", 81.97);`	8.197000E+01
%%	a single % sign	`printf("%d%%\n", 10);`	10%

minimum-sized field that will accommodate the value. In the display of a floating-point value, you may specify both the total field width and the number of decimal digits to the right of the decimal point. The value will be rounded or padded with trailing zeros as necessary to comply with the prescribed precision. You should note that a decimal point occupies a full column of a field, and the precision specification can be used with or without a total field width. Table 11.3 gives examples of field-width use in format strings. In the "Output Produced" column, an individual blank is represented by the symbol ▌ for clarity.

File Pointer Variables

We saw in Chapter 6 that before using a nonstandard text file for input or output, we must declare a file pointer variable and give it a value, allowing us to access the desired file. The system must prepare the file for input or output before permitting access. This preparation is the purpose of the stdio library function fopen. The statements that follow declare and initialize the file pointer variables infilep and outfilep:

```
FILE *infilep;
FILE *outfilep;
infilep = fopen("data.txt", "r");
outfilep = fopen("results.txt", "w");
```

TABLE 11.3 Designating Field Width, Justification, and Precision in Format Strings

Example	Meaning of Highlighted Format String Fragment	Output Produced
`printf("%5d%4d\n", 100, 2);`	Display an integer right-justified in a field of five columns.	`  100   2`
`printf ("%2d with label\n", 5210);`	Display an integer in a field of two columns. Note: Field is too small.	`5210 with label`
`printf("%-16s%d\n", "Jeri R. Hanly", 28);`	Display a string left-justified in a field of 16 columns.	`Jeri R. Hanly   28`
`printf("%15f\n", 981.48);`	Display a floating-point number right-justified in a field of 15 columns.	`     981.480000`
`printf("%10.3f\n", 981.48);`	Display a floating-point number right-justified in a field of ten columns, with three digits to the right of the decimal point.	`   981.480`
`printf("%7.1f\n", 981.48);`	Display a floating-point number right-justified in a field of seven columns, with one digit to the right of the decimal point.	`  981.5`
`printf("%12.3e\n", 981.48);`	Display a floating-point number in scientific notation right-justified in a field of 12 columns, with three digits to the right of the decimal point and a lowercase e before the exponent.	`   9.815e+02`
`printf("%.5E\n", 0.098148);`	Display a floating-point number in scientific notation, with five digits to the right of the decimal point and an uppercase E before the exponent.	`9.81480E-02`

Notice that the data type of `infilep` and `outfilep` is `FILE*`. Remember that C is case sensitive, so you must use all capital letters when writing the type name `FILE`. It is possible to declare both `infilep` and `outfilep` in the same statement, but each must be immediately preceded by the asterisk denoting "pointer to," as shown here:

```
FILE *infilep, *outfilep;
```

We use the stdio library function `fopen` to open or create an additional text file. The `"r"` in the first call to `fopen` just shown indicates that we wish to use the text file opened as an input file from which we will read (scan) data. The `"w"` in the second call conveys that our intention is to write to the file—that is, to use it as an output destination. The first argument to `fopen` is a string that is the name of the text file to manipulate. The correct form of such a file name will vary from one operating system to another. The result returned by `fopen` is the file pointer to be used in all further operations on the file. This pointer is the address of a structure of type

FILE that contains the information necessary to access the file opened by fopen. The pointer must be saved in a variable of type FILE*. In a program containing the lines just shown, the variable infilep will be used to access the input file named "data.txt", and the variable outfilep will be used to access the newly created output file named "results.txt". The identifiers stdin, stdout, and stderr also name variables of type FILE*, variables initialized by the system prior to the start of a C program.

If the fopen function is unable to accomplish the requested operation, the file pointer that it returns is equal to the value associated with the identifier NULL by the stdio library. For example, if execution of this call to fopen

```
infilep = fopen("data.txt", "r");
```

were unsuccessful due to the nonexistence of a file named "data.txt", then execution of the following statement would display an appropriate error message:

```
if (infilep == NULL)
        printf("Cannot open data.txt for input\n");
```

null pointer pointer whose value is NULL

A pointer whose value equals NULL is called a **null pointer**. Take care not to confuse this concept with the *null character*, whose value is the character '\0'.

Using fopen with mode "w" to open for output a file that already exists usually causes loss of the contents of the existing file. However, if the computer's operating system automatically numbers file versions and creates a new version when it opens an output file, the contents of the existing file will not be lost.

Functions That Take File Pointer Arguments

Table 11.4 compares calls to printf and scanf with calls to analogous functions for input from the file accessed by infilep and for output to the file accessed by outfilep. In this table, we assume that infilep and outfilep have been initialized as shown earlier.

Line 1 shows input of a single integer value to be stored in num. The call to scanf obtains this value from the standard input stream, typically the keyboard. The call to fscanf obtains the integer value from "data.txt", the file accessed through the file pointer infilep. Like scanf, function fscanf returns as its result the number of input values it has successfully stored through its output arguments. Function fscanf also returns the negative EOF value when it encounters the end of the file accessed by its file pointer argument.

Similarly, the behavior of fprintf, getc, and putc is fully comparable to the behavior of the standard I/O equivalents—printf, getchar, and putchar—except that each takes a file pointer argument through which to access its input source or output destination. Observe carefully that this file pointer is provided as the first argument to fscanf, fprintf, and getc. In contrast, putc takes the file pointer as its second argument.

TABLE 11.4   Comparison of I/O with Standard Files and I/O with User-Defined File Pointers

Line	Functions That Access stdin and stdout	Functions That Can Access Any Text File
1	`scanf("%d", &num);`	`fscanf(infilep, "%d", &num);`
2	`printf ("Number = %d\n", num);`	`fprintf(outfilep, "Number = %d\n", num);`
3	`ch = getchar();`	`ch = getc(infilep);`
4	`putchar(ch);`	`putc(ch, outfilep);`

Closing a File

When a program has no further use for a file, it should *close* the file by calling the library function `fclose` with the file pointer. The following statement closes the file accessed through `infilep`:

```
fclose(infilep);
```

Function `fclose` disposes of the structure that was created to store file access information and carries out other "cleanup" operations.

If necessary, a program can create an output file and can then rescan the file. The file is first opened in `"w"` mode, and data are stored using a function such as `fprintf`. The file is then closed using `fclose` and reopened in `"r"` mode, allowing the data to be rescanned with a function such as `fscanf`.

EXAMPLE 11.1   For security reasons, having a backup or duplicate copy of a file is a good idea, in case the original is lost. Even though operating systems typically provide a command that will copy a file, we will write our own C program to do this. The program in Fig. 11.1 copies each character in one file to a backup file and allows the user to enter interactively both the name of the file to copy and the name of the backup file.

The program in Fig. 11.1 begins by displaying a prompting message on the screen using `printf`. Then `scanf` is executed to take the file name typed at the keyboard.

The repetition condition of the first `for` loop is

```
(inp = fopen(in_name, "r")) == NULL
```

The call to function `fopen` causes the system to try to open for input the file whose name is stored in `in_name`. If this attempt is successful, a file pointer is returned and assigned to `inp`. The value of this assignment will equal `NULL` only if the file

FIGURE 11.1   Program to Make a Backup Copy of a Text File

```
1.  /*
2.   * Makes a backup file. Repeatedly prompts for the name of a file to
3.   * back up until a name is provided that corresponds to an available
4.   * file. Then it prompts for the name of the backup file and creates
5.   * the file copy.
6.   */
7.
8.  #include <stdio.h>
9.  #define STRSIZ 80
10.
11. int
12. main(void)
13. {
14.        char  in_name[STRSIZ],    /* strings giving names              */
15.              out_name[STRSIZ];   /*    of input and backup files      */
16.        FILE *inp,                /* file pointers for input and       */
17.             *outp;               /*    backup files                   */
18.        char ch;                  /* one character of input file       */
19.
20.        /*  Get the name of the file to back up and open the file for input   */
21.        printf("Enter name of file you want to back up> ");
22.        for (scanf("%s", in_name);
23.           (inp = fopen(in_name, "r")) == NULL;
24.           scanf("%s", in_name)) {
25.        printf("Cannot open %s for input\n", in_name);
26.        printf("Re-enter file name> ");
27.        }
28.
29.        /*  Get name to use for backup file and open file for output   */
30.        printf("Enter name for backup copy> ");
31.        for  (scanf("%s", out_name);
32.              (outp = fopen(out_name, "w")) == NULL;
33.              scanf("%s", out_name)) {
34.           printf("Cannot open %s for output\n", out_name);
35.           printf("Re-enter file name> ");
36.        }
37.
38.        /*  Make backup copy one character at a time              */
39.        for  (ch = getc(inp); ch != EOF; ch = getc(inp))
40.             putc(ch, outp);
```

(continued)

FIGURE 11.1   (continued)

```
41.
42.        /*  Close files and notify user of backup completion              */
43.        fclose(inp);
44.        fclose(outp);
45.        printf("Copied %s to %s.\n", in_name, out_name);
46.
47.        return(0);
48.  }
```

could not be successfully opened; in this case, the user is asked to reenter the name of the file.

In the next program segment, a similar `for` loop is used to get the name of an output file and to open the file, storing the file pointer in `outp`.

The `for` loop that follows manipulates not the standard I/O streams but rather the input and output files accessed through the file pointers in `inp` and `outp`. Function `getc` is called repeatedly to take one character at a time from the input file, and `putc` echoes these characters to the output file. When the copy is complete, the calls to `fclose` release the two files after writing an <eof> on the output file.

Figure 11.2 shows the input and output streams used by the file backup program.

FIGURE 11.2

Input and Output Streams for File Backup Program

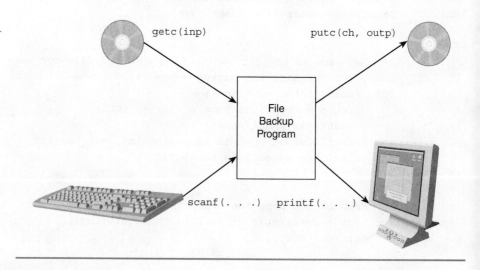

EXERCISES FOR SECTION 11.1

Self-Check

1. Assume these declarations for the problem that follows:

   ```
   double  x;
   int     n;
   char    ch, str[40];
   ```

   Indicate the contents of these variables after each of the following input operations is performed. Assume that the file accessed by `indatap` consists of the data given and that each lettered group of operations occurs at the beginning of a program, immediately following a statement that opens the file.

   ```
   123 3.145 xyz<newline>35 z<newline>
   ```

   a. `fscanf(indatap, "%d%lf%s%c", &n, &x, str, &ch);`
   b. `fscanf(indatap, "%d%lf", &n, &x);`
      `fscanf(indatap, "%s%c", str, &ch);`
   c. `fscanf(indatap, "%lf%d%c%s", &x, &n, &ch, str);`
   d. `fscanf(indatap, "%s%s%s%d%c%c", str, str, str, &n, &ch, &ch);`

2. List the library functions we have studied that require a file pointer argument.

3. The code for function `scan_complex` that we used in Chapter 10 to scan one complex number is shown with some blanks added. Fill in the blanks to create `fscan_complex`, a function that takes a file pointer argument in addition to the `complex_t` output argument. This function should scan a complex number from the file accessed by the file pointer.

   ```
   /*
    * Complex number _____ input function returns standard
    * scanning error code
    *    1 => valid scan, 0 => error, negative EOF value =>
    *    end of file
    */
   int
   fscan_complex(_____
                 complex_t *c) /* output - address of complex
                                          variable to fill */
   {
        int status;
        status = __scanf(_____,
                    "%lf%lf", &c->real, &c->imag;

        if (status == 2)
               status = 1;
   ```

```
                    else if (status != EOF)
                        status = 0;

                    return (status);
                }
```

Programming

1. Rewrite the file backup program in Fig. 11.1 so it uses a function with file pointer parameters to do the actual file copy.

11.2 Binary Files

When we use text files for storage of data, a program must expend a significant amount of effort to convert the stream of characters from an input file into the binary integers, type `double` mantissas and exponents, and character strings that are the representation in main memory of the same data. The program must again expend time in converting the internal data format back into a stream of characters for storage in an output file of text. In a C program, these conversions are carried out by functions such as `scanf` and `printf`.

Many programs produce output files that are used as input files for other programs. If there is no need for a human to read the file, it is a waste of computer time for the first program to convert its internal data format to a stream of characters, and then for the second program to have to apply an inverse conversion to extract the intended data from the stream of characters. We can avoid this unnecessary translation by using a binary file rather than a text file.

binary file   a file containing binary numbers that are the computer's internal representation of each file component

A **binary file** is created by executing a program that stores directly in the file the computer's internal representation of each file component. For example, the code fragment in Fig. 11.3 creates a binary file named `"nums.bin"`, which contains the even integers from 2 to 500.

You see in Fig. 11.3 that a binary file is declared in exactly the same way as a text file. The `fopen` and `fclose` functions are used just as they are for text files, except

FIGURE 11.3   Creating a Binary File of Integers

```
1.  FILE *binaryp;
2.  int    i;
3.
4.  binaryp = fopen("nums.bin", "wb");
5.
6.  for  (i = 2; i <= 500; i += 2)
7.      fwrite(&i, sizeof (int), 1, binaryp);
8.
9.  fclose(binaryp);
```

that the second argument to `fopen` is either `"wb"` (write binary) for output files or `"rb"` (read binary) for input files. However, a different stdio library function is used for copying values into the file: function `fwrite`, which has four input parameters. The first parameter is the *address* of the first memory cell whose contents are to be copied to the file. In Fig. 11.3, we want the contents of the variable `i` copied to the file, so we provide `fwrite` with the address of `i` (`&i`) as the first argument.

The second parameter of function `fwrite` is the number of bytes to copy to the file for one component. In Chapter 1, we noted that a memory cell is a collection of smaller units called *bytes* and that a byte is the amount of storage needed to represent one character. A C operator **sizeof** can be applied to any data type name to find the number of bytes that the current implementation uses for storage of the data type. For example, these statements will print a sentence indicating how many bytes are being occupied by one integer:

> **sizeof** operator that finds the number of bytes used for storage of a data type

```
printf("An integer requires %d bytes ", sizeof (int));
printf("in this implementation.\n");
```

The `sizeof` operator can be applied to both built-in and user-defined types.

The third parameter of `fwrite` is the number of values to write to the binary file. In our example, we are writing one integer at a time, so we provide the constant `1` as this argument. However, it is possible to save the contents of an entire array using just one call to `fwrite` by providing the array's size as the third argument. The final argument to `fwrite` is a file pointer to the file being created, a file previously opened in mode `"wb"` using function `fopen`. For example, if array `score` is an array of ten integers, the statement

```
fwrite(score, sizeof (int), 10, binaryp);
```

writes the entire array to the output file.

Writing the value of an integer variable `i` to a binary file using `fwrite` is faster than writing `i` to a text file. For example, if the value of `i` is `244`, the statement from the `for` loop

```
fwrite(&i, sizeof (int), 1, binaryp);
```

copies the internal binary representation of `i` from memory to the file accessed by `binaryp`. If your computer uses two bytes to store an `int` value, the byte that stores the highest order bits would contain all zeros, and the byte that stores the lowest order bits would contain the binary string `11110100` ($244 = 128 + 64 + 32 + 16 + 4$). Both bytes would be written to disk as the next file component.

Assuming `textp` is a pointer to a text output file, the statement

```
fprintf(textp, "%d ", i);
```

writes the value of `i` to the file using four characters (four bytes). The computer must first convert the binary number in `i` to the character string `"244"` and then write the binary codes for the characters 2, 4, 4, and blank to the file. Obviously, it takes more time to do the conversion and copy each character than it does to copy the internal binary representation to disk. Also, twice as much disk space is required to store four characters as to store the internal binary representation of the type int value (four bytes versus two).

Using a binary file has another advantage. Each time we write a type double value to a text file, the computer must convert this value to a character string whose precision is determined by the placeholder in the format string. A loss of precision may result.

There is a negative side to binary file usage, however. A binary file created on one computer is rarely readable on another type of computer. Since a binary file can be read only by a specialized computer program, a person cannot proofread the file by printing it out or by examining it in a word processor. Furthermore, a binary file cannot be created or modified in a word processor, so a program that expects binary file input cannot be tested until the program that produces the needed binary file is complete.

The stdio library includes an input function fread that is comparable to fwrite. Function fread also requires four arguments:

1. Address of first memory cell to fill.
2. Size of one value.
3. Maximum number of elements to copy from the file into memory.
4. File pointer to a binary file opened in mode "rb" using function fopen.

Function fread returns as its value an integer indicating how many elements it successfully copied from the file. This number will be less than the value of the third argument of fread if EOF is encountered prematurely.

It is very important not to mix file types. A binary file created (written) using fwrite must be read using fread. A text file created using fprintf must be read using a text file input function such as fscanf.

Table 11.5 compares the use of text and binary files for input and output of data of various types. The statements in both columns assume the following constant macros, type definition, and variable declarations.

```
#define STRSIZ   10
#define MAX      40
typedef struct {
     char    name[STRSIZ];
     double  diameter;       /* equatorial diameter in km        */
     int     moons;          /* number of moons                  */
     double  orbit_time,     /* years to orbit sun once          */
             rotation_time;  /* hours to complete one
                                revolution on axis               */
} planet_t;
     . . .
double nums[MAX], data;
planet_t a_planet;
int i, n, status;
FILE *plan_bin_inp, *plan_bin_outp, *plan_txt_inp, *plan_txt_outp;
FILE *doub_bin_inp, *doub_bin_outp, *doub_txt_inp, *doub_txt_outp;
```

TABLE 11.5 Data I/O Using Text and Binary Files

Example	Text File I/O	Binary File I/O	Purpose

1	`plan_txt_inp = fopen("planets.txt", "r");`
	
	`doub_txt_inp = fopen("nums.txt", "r");`
		`plan_bin_inp = fopen("planets.bin", "rb");`
		
		`doub_bin_inp = fopen("nums.bin", "rb");`
			Open for input a file of planets and a file of numbers, saving file pointers for use in calls to input functions.

2	`plan_txt_outp = fopen("pl_out.txt", "w");`
	
	`doub_txt_outp = fopen("nm_out.txt", "w");`
		`plan_bin_outp = fopen("pl_out.bin", "wb");`
		
		`doub_bin_outp = fopen("nm_out.bin", "wb");`
			Open for output a file of planets and a file of numbers, saving file pointers for use in calls to output functions.

3	`fscanf(plan_txt_inp, "%s%lf%d%lf%lf", a_planet.name, &a_planet.diameter, &a_planet.moons, &a_planet.orbit_time, &a_planet.rotation_time);`	`fread(&a_planet, sizeof (planet_t), 1, plan_bin_inp);`	Copy one planet structure into memory from the data file.
4	`fprintf(plan_txt_outp, "%s %e %d %e %e", a_planet.name, a_planet.diameter, a_planet.moons, a_planet.orbit_time, a_planet.rotation_time);`	`fwrite(&a_planet, sizeof (planet_t), 1, plan_bin_outp);`	Write one planet structure to the output file.

(continued)

663

TABLE 11.5 (continued)

Example	Text File I/O	Binary File I/O	Purpose
| 5 | ```
for (i = 0; i < MAX; ++i)
    fscanf(doub_txt_inp,
           "%lf", &nums[i]);
``` | ```
fread(nums, sizeof (double),
      MAX, doub_bin_inp);
``` | Fill array nums with type double values from input file. |
| 6 | ```
for (i = 0; i < MAX; ++i)
    fprintf(doub_txt_outp,
            "%e\n", nums[i]);
``` | ```
fwrite(nums, sizeof (double),
       MAX, doub_bin_outp);
``` | Write contents of array nums to output file. |
| 7 | ```
n = 0;
for (status =
        fscanf(doub_txt_inp,
               "%lf", &data);
     status != EOF &&
        n < MAX;
     status =
        fscanf(doub_txt_inp,
               "%lf", &data))
    nums[n++] = data;
``` | ```
n = fread(nums,
          sizeof (double),
          MAX, doub_bin_inp);
``` | Fill nums with data until EOF encountered, setting n to the number of values stored. |
| 8 | ```
fclose(plan_txt_inp);
fclose(plan_txt_outp);
fclose(doub_txt_inp);
fclose(doub_txt_outp);
``` | ```
fclose(plan_bin_inp);
fclose(plan_bin_outp);
fclose(doub_bin_inp);
fclose(doub_bin_outp);
``` | Close all input and output files. |

In Example 1 of Table 11.5, we use `fopen` to open our input files, and we store the file pointers returned by `fopen` in variables of type `FILE*`. Notice that the form of the call to `fopen` for opening a binary file differs from the call for opening a text file only in the value of the *mode* (second argument). In fact, even this difference is *optional*. Also, notice that the type of the file pointer does not vary. We see a similar situation in the opening of output files in Example 2. One consequence of this similarity is that the ability of the C compiler and run-time support system to detect misuse of a file pointer is severely limited. It is the programmer's responsibility to keep track of which type of file each file pointer accesses and to use the right I/O function at the right time.

In Examples 3 and 4 of Table 11.5, we compare input/output of a user-defined structure type as it is done with text and binary files. In Examples 5 and 6, we see input/output of an array of type `double` values. In the text file code, array elements are scanned or written one at a time in an indexed loop. When we use a binary file, we can fill the array from or copy it to the file using just one call to `fread` or `fwrite`. We see that the calls used to read/write array `nums` provide the size of one array element as the second argument to `fread` or `fwrite` and the number of array elements to process as the third argument. Example 7 demonstrates partially filling array `nums` and setting n to the number of elements filled. Example 8 shows that all files—binary or text, input or output—are closed in the same way.

EXERCISES FOR SECTION 11.2

Self-Check

1. Assume the environment shown, and complete the statements that follow so that they are valid:

```
#define NAME_LEN 50
#define SIZE     30

typedef struct {
     char    name[NAME_LEN];
     int     age;
     double  income;
} person_t;
 . . .
int      num_err[SIZE];
person_t exec;
FILE     *nums_inp, *psn_inp, *psn_outp, *nums_outp;
         /* binary files */
```

```
FILE    *nums_txt_inp, *psn_txt_inp, *psn_txt_outp;
        /* text files */

nums_inp = fopen("nums.bin", "rb");
nums_txt_inp = fopen("nums.txt", "r");
psn_inp = fopen("persons.bin", "rb");
psn_txt_inp = fopen("persons.txt", "r");
psn_outp = fopen("persout.bin", "wb");
psn_txt_outp = fopen("persout.txt", "w");
nums_outp = fopen("numsout.bin", "wb");
```

a.   fread(_____, sizeof (person_t), 1,
      _____);
b.   fscanf(psn_txt_____, "%s", _____);
c.   fwrite(&exec, _____, 1, psn_____);
d.   fwrite(num_err, _____, _____,
          nums_outp);
e.   fread(&num_err[3], _____, _____,
          nums_inp);
f.   fprintf(psn_txt_outp, "%s %d %f\n", _____,
          _____, _____);

Programming

1.   Write a function `fread_units` that is similar to the `load_units` function
     from the Universal Measurement Conversion Program (see Fig. 10.12)
     except it assumes that the unit conversion data have been stored as a
     binary file. The function should ask the user for the name of a binary file,
     open the file, and get up to `unit_max` type `unit_t` values to place in array
     `units`. Be sure to send back to the calling function the size of the used
     portion of the array.

11.3   Searching a Database

Computerized matching of data against a file of records is a common practice.
For example, many real estate companies maintain a large file of property list-
ings: A realtor can process the file to locate desirable properties for a client.
Similarly, mail-order firms purchase large files of information on potential
customers. These large files of data are called **databases**. In this section, we will
write a program that searches a database to find all records that match a proposed set of requirements.

database a vast
electronic file of
information that can be
quickly searched using
subject headings or
keywords

CASE STUDY   Database Inquiry

PROBLEM

Periphs Plus is a mail-order computer supply company that maintains its inventory as a computer file in order to facilitate answering questions regarding that database. Some questions of interest might be:

- What printer stands that cost less than $100 are available?
- What product has the code 5241?
- What types of data cartridges are available?

These questions and others can be answered if we know the correct way to ask them.

ANALYSIS

A database inquiry program has two phases: Setting the search parameters and searching for records that satisfy the parameters. In our program, we will assume that all the structure components can be involved in the search. The program user must enter low and high bounds for each field of interest. Let's illustrate how we might set the search parameters to answer the question, "What modems that cost less than $200 are available?"

Assuming that the price of any Periphs Plus product does not exceed $1,000, we can use the following menu-driven dialogue to set the search parameters.

```
Select by letter a search parameter to set, or enter q to
accept parameters shown.
        Search Parameter                        Current Value
[a]  Low bound for stock number                 1111
[b]  High bound for stock number                9999
[c]  Low bound for category                     aaaa
[d]  High bound for category                    zzzz
[e]  Low bound for technical description        aaaa
[f]  High bound for technical description       zzzz
[g]  Low bound for price                        $    0.00
[h]  High bound for price                       $1000.00


Selection> c
New low bound for category> modem

Select by letter a search parameter to set, or enter q to accept
parameters shown.
        Search Parameter                        Current Value
[a]  Low bound for stock number                 1111
[b]  High bound for stock number                9999
```

```
[c]  Low bound for category                     modem
[d]  High bound for category                    zzzz
[e]  Low bound for technical description        aaaa
[f]  High bound for technical description       zzzz
[g]  Low bound for price                        $  0.00
[h]  High bound for price                       $1000.00

Selection> d
New high bound for category> modem

Select by letter a search parameter to set, or enter q to accept
parameters shown.
        Search Parameter                        Current Value
[a]  Low bound for stock number                 1111
[b]  High bound for stock number                9999
[c]  Low bound for category                     modem
[d]  High bound for category                    modem
[e]  Low bound for technical description        aaaa
[f]  High bound for technical description       zzzz
[g]  Low bound for price                        $  0.00
[h]  High bound for price                       $1000.00

Selection> h
New high bound for price> 199.99

Select by letter a search parameter to set, or enter q to accept
parameters shown.
        Search Parameter                        Current Value
[a]  Low bound for stock number                 1111
[b]  High bound for stock number                9999
[c]  Low bound for category                     modem
[d]  High bound for category                    modem
[e]  Low bound for technical description        aaaa
[f]  High bound for technical description       zzzz
[g]  Low bound for price                        $  0.00
[h]  High bound for price                       $ 199.99

Selection> q
```

DATA REQUIREMENTS

Problem Inputs

```
search_params_t params;    /* search parameter
                              bounds                      */
char inv_filename[STR_SIZ] /* name of inventory file     */
```

FIGURE 11.4

Structure Chart for
Database Inquiry
Problem

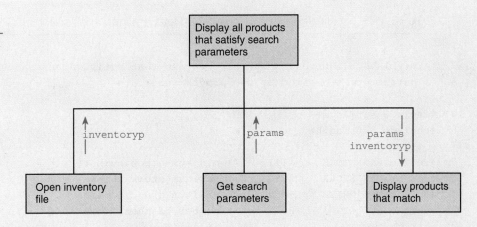

Problem Outputs

All products that satisfy the search.

DESIGN

INITIAL ALGORITHM

1. Open inventory file.
2. Get search parameters.
3. Display all products that satisfy the search parameters.

The structure chart for the database inquiry problem is shown in Fig. 11.4. The refinement of this design is distributed through the development of functions `get_params` and `display_match`.

IMPLEMENTATION

In Fig. 11.5, we see an outline of the database program's implementation including the full code of function `main`. Our design and implementation of the functions called by `main` and most of their helper functions follow this outline.

DESIGN OF THE FUNCTION SUBPROGRAMS

Function `get_params` must first initialize the search parameters to allow the widest search possible and then let the user change some parameters to narrow the search. The local variables and algorithm for `get_params` follow; the structure chart is in Fig. 11.6.

Local Variables for get_params

```
search_params_t params;    /* structure whose components
                              must be defined               */
char choice;               /* user's response to menu       */
```

FIGURE 11.5   Outline and Function main for Database Inquiry Program

```
1.   /*
2.    * Displays all products in the database that satisfy the search
3.    * parameters specified by the program user.
4.    */
5.   #include <stdio.h>
6.   #include <string.h>
7.
8.   #define MIN_STOCK    1111    /* minimum stock number                    */
9.   #define MAX_STOCK    9999    /* maximum stock number                    */
10.  #define MAX_PRICE    1000.00 /* maximum product price                   */
11.  #define STR_SIZ      80      /* number of characters in a string        */
12.
13.  typedef struct {            /* product structure type                  */
14.       int    stock_num;           /* stock number                       */
15.       char   category[STR_SIZ];
16.       char   tech_descript[STR_SIZ];
17.       double price;
18.  } product_t;
19.
20.  typedef struct {            /* search parameter bounds type            */
21.       int    low_stock, high_stock;
22.       char   low_category[STR_SIZ], high_category[STR_SIZ];
23.       char   low_tech_descript[STR_SIZ], high_tech_descript[STR_SIZ];
24.       double low_price, high_price;
25.  } search_params_t;
26.
27.  search_params_t get_params(void);
28.  void display_match(FILE *databasep, search_params_t params);
29.
30.  /* Insert prototypes of functions needed by get_params and display_match */
31.
32.  int
33.  main(void)
34.  {
35.       char            inv_filename[STR_SIZ];  /* name of inventory file   */
36.       FILE            *inventoryp;            /* inventory file pointer   */
37.       search_params_t params;                /* search parameter bounds  */
38.
39.       /*  Get name of inventory file and open it                         */
```

(continued)

FIGURE 11.5   (continued)

```
40.        printf("Enter name of inventory file> ");
41.        scanf("%s", inv_filename);
42.        inventoryp = fopen(inv_filename, "rb");
43.
44.        /*  Get the search parameters                              */
45.        params = get_params();
46.
47.        /*  Display all products that satisfy the search parameters   */
48.        display_match(inventoryp, params);
49.
50.        return(0);
51.  }
52.
53.  /*
54.   * Prompts the user to enter the search parameters
55.   */
56.  search_params_t
57.  get_params(void)
58.  {
59.      /* body of get_params to be inserted */
60.  }
61.  /*
62.   * Displays records of all products in the inventory that satisfy search
63.   * parameters.
64.   * Pre:  databasep accesses a binary file of product_t records that has
65.   *       been opened as an input file, and params is defined
66.   */
67.  void
68.  display_match(FILE            *databasep, /* input - file pointer to binary
69.                                                     database file
70.  */
71.            search_params_t params)   /* input - search parameter bounds
72.                                              */
73.  {
74.     /* body of display_match to be inserted */
75.  }
76.
77.  /* Insert functions needed by get_params and display_match */
```

FIGURE 11.6

Structure Chart for
get_params

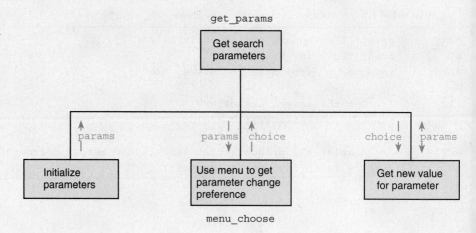

Algorithm for get_params

1. Initialize `params` to permit widest possible search.
2. Display menu and get response to store in choice.
3. Repeat while choice is not `'q'`
   4. Select appropriate prompt and get new parameter value.
   5. Display menu and get response to store in `choice`.
6. Return search parameters.

Function `display_match` must examine each file record with a stock number between the low and high bounds for stock numbers. If a record satisfies the search parameters, it is displayed. Function `display_match` will also print a message if no matches are found. The local variables, algorithm, and structure chart for the function follow (see Fig. 11.7).

Local Variables for display_match

```
product_t next_prod        /*  the current product          */
int no_matches             /*  a flag indicating whether or
                               not there are any matches     */
```

Algorithm for display_match

1. Initialize `no_matches` to true(1).
2. Advance to the first record whose stock number is within range.
3. while the current stock number is still in range repeat
   4. if the search parameters match
      5. Display the product and set `no_matches` to false(0).
   6. Get the next product record.

FIGURE 11.7

Structure Chart for
display_match

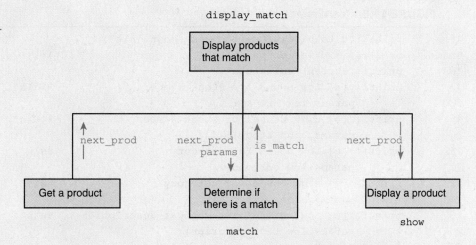

7. if there are no matches
    8. Print a `no products available` message.

IMPLEMENTATION OF THE FUNCTION SUBPROGRAMS

Figure 11.8 shows the code of functions `display_match`, `menu_choose`, and `match`, along with a stub for function `show`.

FIGURE 11.8   Functions display_match, menu_choose, and match

```
1.  /*
2.   * Displays a lettered menu with the current values of search parameters.
3.   * Returns the letter the user enters. A letter in the range a..h selects
4.   * a parameter to change; q quits, accepting search parameters shown.
5.   * Post: first nonwhitespace character entered is returned
6.   */
7.  char
8.  menu_choose(search_params_t params) /* input - current search parameter
9.                                                bounds                     */
10. {
11.     char choice;
12.
13.     printf("Select by letter a search parameter to set or enter");
```

(continued)

FIGURE 11.8 · (continued)

```
14.         printf("q to\naccept parameters shown.\n\n");
15.         printf("      Search parameter                     ");
16.         printf("Current value\n\n");
17.         printf("[a] Low bound for stock number             %4d\n",
18.                 params.low_stock);
19.         printf("[b] High bound for stock number            %4d\n",
20.                 params.high_stock);
21.         printf("[c] Low bound for category                 %s\n",
22.                 params.low_category);
23.         printf("[d] High bound for category                %s\n",
24.                 params.high_category);
25.         printf("[e] Low bound for technical description    %s\n",
26.                 params.low_tech_descript);
27.         printf("[f] High bound for technical description   %s\n",
28.                 params.high_tech_descript);
29.         printf("[g] Low bound for price                    $%7.2f\n",
30.                 params.low_price);
31.         printf("[h] High bound for price                   $%7.2f\n\n",
32.                 params.high_price);
33.
34.         printf("Selection> ");
35.         scanf(" %c", &choice);
36.
37.         return (choice);
38.  }
39.
40.  /*
41.   * Determines whether record prod satisfies all search parameters
43.   */
44.  int
45.  match(product_t        prod,        /* input - record to check        */
46.              search_params_t params)  /* input - parameters to satisfy   */
47.  {
48.          return (strcmp(params.low_category, prod.category) <= 0         &&
49.                  strcmp(prod.category, params.high_category) <= 0        &&
50.                  strcmp(params.low_tech_descript, prod.tech_descript) <= 0  &&
51.                  strcmp(prod.tech_descript, params.high_tech_descript) <= 0 &&
52.                  params.low_price <= prod.price                          &&
53.                  prod.price <= params.high_price);
54.  }
```

(continued)

FIGURE 11.8 (continued)

```
55.  /*
56.   * *** STUB ***
57.   * Displays each field of prod. Leaves a blank line after the product
58.   * display.
59.   */
60.  void
61.  show(product_t prod)
62.  {
63.      printf("Function show entered with product number %d\n",
64.             prod.stock_num);
65.  }
66.
67.  /*
68.   * Displays records of all products in the inventory that satisfy search
69.   * parameters.
70.   * Pre:  databasep accesses a binary file of product_t records that has
71.   *       been opened as an input file, and params is defined
72.   */
73.  void
74.  display_match(FILE          *databasep,   /* file pointer to binary
75.                                                database file              */
76.                search_params_t params)    /* input - search parameter bounds  */
77.  {
78.      product_t next_prod;               /* current product from database     */
79.      int      no_matches = 1;      /* flag indicating if no matches have
80.                                       been found                             */
81.      int status;                        /* input file status                 */
82.
83.      /*  Advances to first record with a stock number greater than or
84.          equal to lower bound.                                             */
85.      for  (status = fread(&next_prod, sizeof (product_t), 1, databasep);
86.            status == 1  && params.low_stock > next_prod.stock_num;
87.            status = fread(&next_prod, sizeof (product_t), 1, databasep)) {}
88.
89.      /*  Displays a list of the products that satisfy the search
90.          parameters                                                        */
91.      printf("\nProducts satisfying the search parameters:\n");
92.      while (next_prod.stock_num <= params.high_stock &&
93.             status == 1) {
```

(continued)

FIGURE 11.8   (continued)

```
 94.          if  (match(next_prod, params)) {
 95.              no_matches = 0;
 96.              show(next_prod);
 97.          }
 98.          status = fread(&next_prod, sizeof (product_t), 1, databasep);
 99.      }
100.
101.      /* Displays a message if no products found                        */
102.      if (no_matches)
103.          printf("Sorry, no products available\n");
104.  }
```

EXERCISES FOR SECTION 11.3

Self-Check

1. What values would you use as search parameter bounds to answer the questions listed at the beginning of this section?
2. Which function in our database search program determines whether a particular record matches the search parameters? Which one displays each matching record?
3. Why does function match not need to check a product's stock_num field?

Programming

1. Write the functions get_params and show described in the database inquiry problem. Since get_params calls function menu_choose, your implementation of algorithm step 4 for get_params must be sure to account for the fact that menu_choose does not validate the value the user enters.
2. Write a void function make_product_file that would convert a text file containing product information to a binary file of product_t structures. The function's parameters are file pointers to the text input and binary output files.

11.4   Common Programming Errors

File processing in any programming language has many pitfalls; C is no exception. Remember to declare a file pointer variable (type FILE*) for each file you want to process. Because C makes no type distinction between file pointers accessing text files and those accessing binary files, it is easy to use the wrong library function with a file pointer. In a program that manipulates both file types, choose names for your file pointers that remind you of the type of file accessed. For example, you could choose names containing "_txt_" for text file pointers and names containing "_bin_" for binary file pointers.

It is also critical that you remember that library functions fscanf, fprintf, getc, and putc must be used for text I/O only; functions fread and fwrite are applied exclusively to binary files. You should have the summary table in this chapter handy for reference when you are using these functions to help you keep straight the order of their arguments. The fact that fprintf, fscanf, and getc take the file pointer as their first argument while putc, fread, and fwrite take it as the last argument is definitely confusing at first.

If you are permitting the program user to enter the name of a file to process, you will have two variables identifying the file—one to hold its name (a character string) and one to hold the pointer for file access. It is essential to remember that the only file operation in which the file *name* is used is the call to fopen. Keep in mind that opening a file for output by calling fopen with a second argument of "w" or "wb" typically results in a loss of any existing file whose name matches the first argument.

It is easy to forget that binary files cannot be created, viewed, or modified using an editor or word processor program. Rather, they must be created and interpreted by a program that reads values into or writes values from variables of the same type as the binary file's elements.

Chapter Review

1. Text files are continuous streams of character codes that can be viewed as broken into lines by the newline character.
2. Processing text files requires the transfer of sequences of characters between main memory and disk storage.
3. In order to be processed as numbers, character strings taken as input from a text file must be converted to a different format such as int or double for storage in memory. Output of numeric values to a text file requires conversion of the internal formats back to a sequence of characters.
4. Binary files permit storage of information using a computer's internal data format: Neither time nor accuracy is lost through conversion of values transferred between main and secondary storage.
5. Binary files cannot be created using a word processor and are not meaningful when displayed on the screen or printed.

NEW C CONSTRUCTS

Statement	Effect
Declarations	
`char name_txt_in[50],` `    name_bin_out[50];`	Declares two string variables whose names imply that they may be used to hold names of a text file to be used for input and of a binary output file.
`FILE *text_inp, *text_outp,` `    *bin_inp, *bin_outp;`	Declares four file pointer variables.
Calls to stdio Library	

`text_inp = fopen(name_txt_in, "r");`
`text_outp = fopen("result.txt", "w");`
`bin_inp = fopen("data.bin", "rb");`
`bin_outp = fopen(name_bin_out, "wb");`
	Opens `"data.bin"` and the file whose name is the value of `name_txt_in` as input files; opens `"result.txt"` and the file whose name is the value of `name_bin_out` as output files. Pointers accessing the open files are stored in file pointer variables `text_inp`, `text_outp`, `bin_inp`, and `bin_outp`.

`fscanf(text_inp, "%s%d%lf", animal,` `        &age, &weight);`	Copies string, `int`, and `double` values from the *text* input file accessed by file pointer `text_inp`, storing the values in variables `animal`, `age`, and `weight`.
`fprintf(text_outp, "(%.2f, %.2f)",` `        x, y);`	Writes to the *text* output file accessed by file pointer `text_outp` a set of parentheses enclosing the values of `x` and `y` rounded to two decimal places.
`nextch = getc(text_inp);`	Stores in `nextch` the next character available in the *text* input file accessed by file pointer `text_inp`, or the integer `EOF` value if no characters remain.
`putc(ch, text_outp);`	Copies the value of `ch` into the *text* output file accessed by file pointer `text_outp`.
`fread(&var, sizeof (double), 1,` `    bin_inp);`	Copies into type `double` variable `var` the next value from the *binary* input file accessed by file pointer `bin_inp`.
`fwrite(&insect, sizeof (insect_t), 1,` `    bin_outp);`	Copies the value of type `insect_t` variable `insect` into the *binary* output file accessed by file pointer `bin_outp`.
`fclose(text_outp);`	Closes text file accessed by file pointer `text_outp` after writing the <eof> character.
`fclose(bin_inp);`	Closes binary file accessed by `bin_inp` so it is no longer available as an input source.

Quick-Check Exercises

1. A _____ file consists of a stream of character codes; a _____ file is a sequence of values of any type represented exactly as they would be in main memory.

2. For each of these library functions, indicate whether it is used in processing binary or text files.

   ```
   fread      putc
   fscanf     fwrite
   getc       fprintf
   ```

3. What file pointer name(s) does a C program associate with the keyboard? With the screen?

4. C makes no type distinction between file pointers accessing text files and those accessing binary files. True or false?

5. Write a prototype for a function `fscanf_student` that reads from a text input file the value of a structure of type `student_t`. The function does *not* open the input file; the function assumes the file is already open.

6. Write a prototype for a function `fread_student` that reads from a binary input file the value of a structure of type `student_t`. The function does *not* open the input file; the function assumes the file is already open.

7. The _____ character separates a _____ file into lines, and the _____ character appears at the end of a file.

8. What is the use of the `sizeof` operator?

9. Comment on the correctness of this statement: It is more efficient to use a text file because the computer knows that each component is a single character that can be copied into a single byte of main memory; with a binary file, however, the size of the components may vary.

10. Consider the following code segment, and then choose the correct "next" statement from the two options given. Indicate how you know which is the right choice. If you can't determine which is right, explain what additional information you would need in order to decide.

    ```
    FILE *inp;
    int   n;

    inp = fopen("data.in", "r");

    "next" option 1
        fread(&n, sizeof (int), 1, inp);

    "next" option 2
        fscanf(inp, "%d", &n);
    ```

Answers to Quick-Check Exercises

1. true
2. `fread`: binary; `fscanf`: text; `getc`: text; `putc`: text; `fwrite`: binary; `fprintf`: text
3. keyboard: `stdin`; screen: `stdout`, `stderr`
4. true
5. `void fscanf_ student(FILE *filep, student_t student);`
6. `void fread_ student(FILE *filep, student_t student);`
7. newline (or `'\n'`), text, eof
8. The `sizeof` operator is used to find the number of bytes used for storage of a data type.
9. The statement is not correct because no data conversions are necessary when you use binary files. Therefore, binary files are more efficient than text files.
10. The code segment shown could be followed by either statement. In order to choose one option, it would be necessary to know whether `data.in` was a text file or a binary file of integers. If one were certain that the code's author always used the mode `"rb"` when opening a binary file, then option 2 would be the expected next statement.

Review Questions

1. List the escape sequences and explain their meanings.
2. How would you modify the program in Fig. 11.1 so the data would be sent to the screen as well as written to the backup file?
3. Consider a file `empstat.txt` that contains employee records. The data for each employee consist of the employee's name (up to 20 characters), social security number (up to 11 characters), gross pay for the week (`double`), taxes deducted (`double`), and net pay (`double`) for the week. Each record is a separate text line in file `empstat.txt`. Write a program that will create a text file `report.txt` with the heading line

   ```
   NAME            SOC.SEC.NUM    GROSS        TAXES     NET
   ```

   followed by two blank lines and the pertinent information under each column heading. The program should also produce a binary file version of `empstat.txt` named `empstat.bin`.
4. What are the characteristics of a binary file?
5. Write a program that takes as input the file `empstat.bin` created in Review Question 3 and produces a binary file `ssngross.bin` containing only social security numbers and gross pay for each employee.

6. How is an actual backslash represented in a C program?
7. A sparse matrix is one in which a large number of the elements are zero. Write a `void` function `store_sparse` that writes to a binary file a compressed representation of a 50 × 50 sparse matrix of type `int`. The function's parameters are the file pointer and the matrix. The function will store only the nonzero matrix values, writing for each of these a record containing three components: Row subscript, column subscript, and value.
8. How would the prototype of function `store_sparse` be different if its purpose were to write the sparse matrix representation to a text file (see Review Question 7)? Discuss the implications of your answer.

Programming Projects

1. You are developing a database of measured meteorological data for use in weather and climate research. Define a structure type `measured_data_t` with components `site_id_num` (a four-digit integer), `wind_speed`, `day_of_month`, and `temperature`. Each site measures its data daily, at noon local time. Write a program that inputs a file of `measured_data_t` records and determines the site with the greatest variation in temperature (defined here as the biggest difference between extrema) and the site with the highest average wind speed for all the days in the file. You may assume that there will be at most ten sites. Test the program on the following July daily data collected over one week at three sites:

ID	Day	Wind Speed (knots)	Temperature (deg C)
2001	10	11	30
2001	11	5	22
2001	12	18	25
2001	13	16	26
2001	14	14	26
2001	15	2	25
2001	16	14	22
3345	10	8	29
3345	11	5	23
3345	12	12	23
3345	13	14	24
3345	14	10	24

ID	Day	Wind Speed (knots)	Temperature (deg C)
3345	15	9	22
3345	16	9	20
3819	10	17	27
3819	11	20	21
3819	12	22	21
3819	13	18	22
3819	14	15	22
3819	15	9	19
3819	16	12	18

2. Write a program that merges the contents of two text files in such a way that the contents of file 2 must be followed by the contents of file 1. Here is an example:

If the contents of file1 are

"A binary file is a file created by executing a program that stores directly in the file the computer's internal representation of each file component."

and the contents of file 2 are

"A pointer whose value equals NULL is called a null pointer."

the final output should be

"A pointer whose value equals NULL is called a null pointer.

A binary file is a file created by executing a program that stores directly in the file the computer's internal representation of each file component."

3. Develop a database inquiry program to search a binary file of aircraft data sorted in descending order by maximum cruise speed. Each aircraft record should include the name (up to 25 characters), maximum cruise speed (in km/h), wingspan and length (in m), the character M (for military) or C (for civilian), and a descriptive phrase (up to 80 characters). Your system should implement a menu-driven interface that allows the user to search on all components except the descriptive phrase. Here are three planes to start your database:

```
SR-71 Blackbird            (name)
3500                       (max cruise speed)
16.95 32.74 M              (wingspan, length, military/civilian)
high-speed strategic reconnaissance

EF-111A Raven
2280
19.21  23.16  M
electronic warfare
```

```
Concorde
2140
25.61   62.2   C
supersonic airliner
```

4. A sparse matrix is a two-dimensional array in which a large number of the elements are zero. A concise text file representation of a sparse matrix needs to store only the array dimensions on the first line and the number of nonzero elements on the second. Each of the remaining lines should contain three numbers—row subscript, column subscript, and value of one nonzero entry. Write a program that converts a text file containing a traditional matrix representation to a text file containing a compressed sparse matrix. The program should open the file containing the traditional representation (a line with dimensions followed by matrix contents a row at a time), call a function `scan_matrix` to input the matrix, open the output file, and call a function `write_sparse` to store the compressed representation. Write a second program that reverses the process—doing input of a sparse matrix file and creating a file containing the traditional representation. For the second program, write functions `scan_sparse` and `write_matrix`.

5. Write a program that reads the data from a text file and prints all the uppercase letters present in it into another text file. The program must generate an error message if necessary. Modify the same program to read a text file and print all the lines that start with letter "A" instead. This program too must generate an error message if necessary. (Hint: You may have to first create a file and then pass its name in fopen function).

6. Write a program that helps the user to consider a range of interest rates for a mortgage over 20, 25, and 30 years. Prompt the user to enter the amount of the loan and a minimum and maximum interest rate (in whole percentages). Then write a text file containing a table of the form,

	Loan Amount: $50,000.00		
Interest Rate	Duration (years)	Monthly Payment	Total Payment
10.00	20	_____	_____
10.00	25	_____	_____
10.00	30	_____	_____
10.25	20	_____	_____

The output file produced should contain payment information on a particular loan amount for interest rates from the minimum rate to the maximum rate in increments of 0.25%. The loan durations should be 20, 25, and 30 years. Output the monthly payment and total payment values rounded to two decimal places. You may neglect the fact that because the monthly payment must be rounded, the final payment will be slightly different. The formula for calculating monthly payment is given in Programming Project 1 of Chapter 3.

7. Develop a small airline reservation system. The database of flight information should be kept in a file of structures with the following components:

    a. Flight number (including airline code)
    b. City of departure
    c. Destination
    d. Date and time of departure
    e. Date and time of arrival
    f. Number of first-class seats still available
    g. Number of first-class seats sold
    h. Number of coach seats still available
    i. Number of coach seats sold

Include in your program separate functions for creation, deletion, and update of flight records. Also, implement `make_reservation` and `cancel_reservation` functions.

8. Cooking recipes can be stored on a computer and, with the use of files, can be quickly referenced.

    a. Write a function that will create a text file of recipes from information entered at the terminal. The format of the data to be stored is
        1. recipe type (dessert, meat, etc.)
        2. subtype (for dessert, use cake, pie, or cookies)
        3. name (e.g., German chocolate)
        4. number of lines in the recipe to follow
        5. the actual recipe
      Item 3 should be on a separate line.

    b. Write a function that will accept as parameters a file and a structured record of search parameter bounds, as was demonstrated in the Database Inquiry Case Study. The function should display all recipes satisfying the search parameters.

9. Write a program that prompts the user to enter the ASCII value of any one of the lowercase or uppercase characters. Once the user's input is taken, the program must print a table of ASCII values for all the lowercase or uppercase characters in a file called "`ascii.txt`" depending upon whether the user entered the ASCII value of a lowercase character or an uppercase character. If the ASCII value entered by the user does not represent any character, an appropriate error message must be displayed.

Programming in the Large

CHAPTER OBJECTIVES

- To learn how procedural abstraction helps the programmer separate concerns about what a function does from the details of how to code the function

- To understand how data abstraction enables us to describe what information is stored in an object and what operations we want to perform on the object without knowing the specifics of how the object's information is organized and represented

- To learn how to create your own personal library with a separate header file and implementation file and to understand what should be stored in each file

- To understand the purpose of different storage classes in C

- To learn how to use conditional compilation to prevent multiple declarations of the identifiers in a header file

- To learn how to use multidimensional arrays for storing tables of data

- To learn how to declare parameters for function main and how to pass data such as file names through command-line arguments

- To learn how to define macros with parameters and understand what happens when a macro is expanded

In this chapter, we examine the special difficulties associated with the development of large software systems. We explore how separating our expression of *what* we need to do from *how* we actually plan to accomplish it reduces the complexity of system development and maintenance (upkeep). This chapter introduces C's facilities for formalizing this separation of concerns.

We study how to define flexible macros that help to make a program more readable as well as easier to maintain. This chapter describes the storage classes of variables and functions we have been using along with some additional storage classes that may be useful in large program development. We also investigate how to build a library of reusable code from functions developed for specific contexts. We meet additional preprocessor directives that allow us to format libraries so they are easy to include in any combination.

12.1 Using Abstraction to Manage Complexity

Up to this point in your study of programming, you have been primarily concerned with writing relatively short programs that solve individual problems, but otherwise have little general use. In this chapter, we focus on the design and maintenance of large-scale programs. We discuss how to modularize a large project so that individual pieces can be implemented by different programmers at different times. We also see how to write software modules in ways that simplify their reuse in other projects.

Procedural Abstraction

When a team of programmers is assigned the task of developing a large software system, they must have a rational approach to breaking down the overall problem into solvable chunks. Abstraction is a powerful technique that helps problem solvers deal with complex issues in a piecemeal fashion. The dictionary defines *abstraction* as the process of separating the inherent qualities or properties of something from the actual physical object to which they belong. One example of the use of abstraction is the representation of a program variable (for example, `velocity`) by a storage location in memory. We don't have to know anything about the physical structure of memory in order to use such a variable in programming.

procedural abstraction
separation of *what* a function does from the details of *how* the function accomplishes its purpose

In this text, we have applied aspects of two types of abstraction to program development. First, we practiced **procedural abstraction**, which is the philosophy that function development should separate the concern of *what* is to be achieved by a function from the details of *how* it is to be achieved. In other words, you can specify what you expect a function to do and then use that function in the design of a problem solution before you know how to implement the function.

For example, in Chapter 11, when we tackled our database inquiry problem, our initial algorithm was one that could lead directly to an outline of a program fragment that identifies three functions representing the major steps of a solution. The following outline defers the details of parameter lists and use of function values.

Initial Algorithm	Program Outline
1. Open inventory file.	`fopen(. . .)`
2. Get the search parameters.	`get_params(. . .)`
3. Display all products that satisfy the search parameters.	`display_match(. . .)`

In this example of procedural abstraction, we see that *what* one of the functions must accomplish (i.e., open a file) corresponds to the purpose of a library function we have studied. Reuse of this existing function means that we *never* have to concern ourselves with the details of *how* this task is accomplished. Clearly, the availability of powerful libraries of functions is of significant benefit in reducing the complexity of large systems. As we have already seen, the use of such libraries is a fundamental feature of the C programming language.

In the example shown, the other two functions identified in this first level of procedural abstraction are excellent candidates for assignment to separate members of a program development team. Once the purpose and parameter lists of each function are spelled out, neither developer will have any need to be concerned about the details of *how* the other member carries out the assigned task.

Data Abstraction

data abstraction
separation of the logical view of a data object (*what* is stored) from the physical view (*how* the information is stored)

Data abstraction is another powerful tool we have seen for breaking down a large problem into manageable chunks. When we apply data abstraction to a complex problem, we initially specify the data objects involved and the operations to be performed on these data objects without being overly concerned with how the data objects will be represented and stored in memory. We can describe *what* information is stored in the data object without being specific as to *how* the information is organized and represented. This is the *logical view* of the data object as opposed to its *physical view,* the actual internal representation in memory. Once we understand the logical view, we can use the data object and its operators in our programs; however, we (or someone else) will eventually need to implement the data object and its operators before we can run any program that uses them.

One simple example of data abstraction is our use of the C data type `double`, which is an abstraction for the set of real numbers. The computer hardware limits the range of real numbers that can be represented, and not all real numbers within the specified range can be represented. Different computers use a variety of representation schemes for type `double`. However, we can generally use the data type `double` and its associated operators (+, -, *, /, =, ==, <, and so on) without being concerned with these details of its implementation. Another example of data abstraction is the definition of a data type and associated operators for complex numbers given in Chapter 10.

Information Hiding

One advantage of procedural abstraction and data abstraction is that they enable the designer to make implementation decisions in a piecemeal fashion. The designer can postpone making decisions regarding the actual internal representation of the data objects and the implementation of its operators. At the top levels of the design, the designer focuses on how to use a data object and its operators; at the lower levels of design, the designer works out the implementation details. In this way, the designer can hierarchically break down a large problem, controlling and reducing its overall complexity.

If the details of a data object's implementation are not known when a higher-level module is implemented, the higher-level module can access the data object only through its operators. This limitation is actually an advantage: It allows the designer to change his or her mind at a later date and possibly to choose a more efficient method of internal representation or implementation. If the higher-level modules reference a data object only through its operators, a change in the data object's representation will require no change in a higher-level module. The process of protecting the implementation details of a lower-level module from direct access by a higher-level module is called **information hiding**.

information hiding
protecting the implementation details of a lower-level module from direct access by a higher-level module

Reusable Code

One of the keys to productivity in software development is the writing of *reusable code*, code that can be reused in many different applications, preferably without having to be modified or recompiled. One way to facilitate reuse in C is to **encapsulate** a data object together with its operators in a personal library. Then we can use the `#include` preprocessor directive to give functions in a file access to this library.

encapsulate
packaging as a unit a data object and its operators

Encapsulation is a powerful concept in everyday life that can be applied very profitably to software design. For example, one encapsulated object that we are all familiar with is an aspirin. Our familiarity is based strictly on *what* the object does (relieves pain and reduces fever) when activated through the standard interface (swallowing). Only its producers and prescribers care *how* an aspirin does what it does (the effect of acetylsalicylic acid on inflammation and blood flow to the skin surface). By applying the principles of procedural and data abstraction, we can package the "bitter" details of a complex problem's solution in equally neat, easy-to-use capsules.

EXERCISES FOR SECTION 12.1

Self-Check

1. Describe how each of the following encapsulated objects allows the user to focus on *what* the object does with little or no concern for *how* it does it:

    microwave oven   television set   calculator

12.2 Personal Libraries: Header Files

We have seen how the availability of C's standard libraries simplifies program development. However, the standard libraries are not extensive enough to handle every programming need. Often we write a function that would be useful in a context other than the one for which it was originally written. Copying the code of functions into other programs to allow reuse is possible but cumbersome, especially when compared to the way we get access to standard libraries. In fact, one can use the C preprocessor directive #include to make available personal libraries as well. Since C permits source code files to be compiled separately and then linked prior to loading and execution, we can provide our personal libraries as object files; programs using our personal libraries need not first compile the functions in them. If we take another look at a diagram first presented in Chapter 1 and now repeated in Fig. 12.1, we are in a better position to understand the rectangle and arrow that are in color. Until now, the "other object files" that have been linked to our code have been the standard C libraries. When we learn to make our own library files, these files can also be provided to the linker as part of preparing our program for execution.

Header Files

header file   text file containing the interface information about a library needed by a compiler to translate a program system that uses the library or by a person to understand and use the library

To create a personal library, we must first make a **header file**—a text file containing all the information about a library needed by the compiler when compiling a program that uses the facilities defined in the library. Precisely this type of data is found in system header files such as stdio.h, math.h, and string.h. The form we recommend for a header file also provides all the information that a user of the library needs. Typical contents of a header file include:

1. a block comment summarizing the library's purpose
2. #define directives naming constant macros
3. type definitions
4. block comments stating the purpose of each library function and declarations of the form

    extern *prototype*

FIGURE 12.1   Preparing a Program for Execution

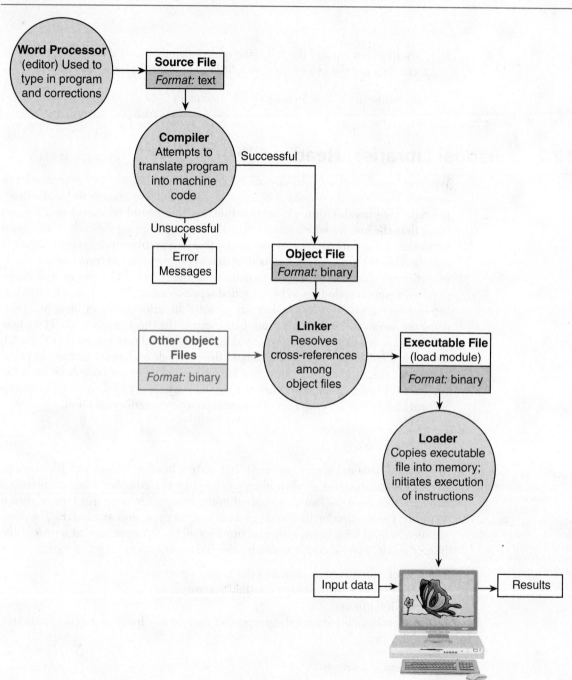

The use of the keyword `extern` in a function declaration notifies the compiler that the function's definition will be provided to the linker. Figure 12.2 shows a header file for our planet data type and operators from Chapter 10. In Fig. 12.3, we see the beginning of a source file that has need of facilities from this library. We are assuming here that the header file is named `planet.h`, and that it is located in the directory in which the preprocessor first looks for files whose names appear in quotation marks after a `#include`. This issue is system dependent, but, in many cases, the directory first searched would be the one in which the current source file resides.

FIGURE 12.2   Header File planet.h for Personal Library with Data Type and Associated Functions

```
1.  /* planet.h
2.   *
3.   * abstract data type planet
4.   *
5.   * Type planet_t has these components:
6.   *     name, diameter, moons, orbit_time, rotation_time
7.   *
8.   * Operators:
9.   *     print_planet, planet_equal, scan_planet
10.  */
11.
12. #define PLANET_STRSIZ 10
13.
14. typedef struct { /* planet structure */
15.       char name[PLANET_STRSIZ];
16.       double diameter;        /* equatorial diameter in km          */
17.       int    moons;           /* number of moons                    */
18.       double orbit_time,      /* years to orbit sun once            */
19.              rotation_time;   /* hours to complete one revolution on
20.                                  axis                               */
21. } planet_t;
22.
23. /*
24.  * Displays with labels all components of a planet_t structure
25.  */
26. extern void
27. print_planet(planet_t pl);   /* input - one planet structure       */
28.
```

(continued)

FIGURE 12.2   (continued)

```
29.  /*
30.   * Determines whether or not the components of planet_1 and planet_2
31.   * match
32.   */
33.  extern int
34.  planet_equal(planet_t planet_1,      /* input - planets to              */
35.               planet_t planet_2);     /*             compare             */
36.
37.  /*
38.   * Fills a type planet_t structure with input data. Integer returned as
39.   * function result is success/failure/EOF indicator.
40.   *      1 => successful input of planet
41.   *      0 => error encountered
42.   *      EOF => insufficient data before end of file
43.   * In case of error or EOF, value of type planet_t output argument is
44.   * undefined.
45.   */
46.  extern int
47.  scan_planet(planet_t *plnp); /* output - address of planet_t structure to fill */
```

In our programming so far, we have used angular brackets (<>), as in

```
#include <stdio.h>
```

to indicate to the preprocessor that a header file is to be found in a system directory. Quotes around the header file name, as in

```
#include "planet.h"
```

mark it as information about a library belonging to the programmer.

FIGURE 12.3   Portion of Program That Uses Functions from a Personal Library

```
 1.  /*
 2.   * Beginning of source file in which a personal library and system I/O library
 3.   * are used.
 4.   */
 5.
 6.  #include <stdio.h>       /* system's standard I/O functions                */
 7.
 8.  #include "planet.h"      /* personal library with planet_t data type and
 9.                                        operators                            */
10.  . . .
```

When revising a source file, the C preprocessor replaces each `#include` line with the contents of the header file it references.

In Chapters 3 and 6, when we first met user-defined functions, we emphasized the importance of the block comment placed at the beginning of the function and the importance of the function prototype and the comments on its parameters. When taken together, this prototype and its associated commentary provide the basic information needed by a programmer desiring to call the function: What the function does, what type of value it returns (if any), and what types of arguments it operates on. Notice that this is precisely the information placed in the header file.

An important aspect of dividing any problem into manageable chunks is defining the points at which the chunks of the solution come together to form the complete solution. The common boundary between two separate parts of a solution is called the *interface*. The header file's purpose is to define the interface between a library and any program that uses the library.

Cautionary Notes for Header File Design

You will notice that in our header file example, the constant macro defined (`PLANET_STRSIZ`) has a long name that begins with the library name. This naming strategy reduces the likelihood that the name associated with a constant in the header file will conflict with other constant macro names in the program.

In Section 12.3, we will see how to create an implementation file for a personal library. The header (interface) file and the implementation file are the two essential source files in a personal library.

EXERCISES FOR SECTION 12.2

Self-Check

1. How can the C preprocessor determine whether a header file name in an `#include` statement is the name of a system library or of a personal library?
2. A function's _____ and associated _____ are the collection of information that a programmer must know about the function in order to be able to use it.
3. A header (interface) file describes _____ the functions of a library do, not _____ they do it.

Programming

1. Look at the table of math library functions in Chapter 3 (Table 3.1). Define a header file `myops.h` that contains a full description of the interfaces of functions `fabs`, `sqrt`, and `pow`. Then add to this file information about the

`factorial` function (see Fig. 5.7). Would anything about your interface information for `factorial` require your implementation of the function to be iterative? Would anything require the implementation to be recursive?

12.3   Personal Libraries: Implementation Files

In Section 12.2, we saw how to create a library header file containing all the interface information needed by a program and programmer using the library. We created a header file for a planet library and studied a program that uses the `#include` directive in order to make this header a part of the program's code. In this section, we investigate how to create a library **implementation file**. The header file describes *what* the functions of the library do; the implementation file will show *how* the functions do it.

implementation file
file containing the C source code of a library's functions and any other information needed for compilation of these functions

A library's implementation file is a C source file that contains both the code of all the library functions and any other information needed for compilation of these functions. The elements of an implementation file are the same as the elements of any program and have many similarities with the elements of the library's header file. These elements are:

1. a block comment summarizing the library's purpose
2. `#include` directives for this library's header file and for other libraries used by the functions in this library
3. `#define` directives naming constant macros used only inside this library
4. type definitions used only inside this library
5. function definitions including the usual comments

It may seem odd that we `#include` the header file for the library we are implementing since the prototypes found in it are redundant. We do this to make maintenance and modification of the library more straightforward. Alternatively, we could simply restate the constant macro and type definitions from the header file in the implementation file. However, then a modification of one of these definitions would require changes in *two* files. Using the header file `#include` as shown, we would simply modify the header file; when the implementation file is recompiled, the change will be taken into account. Figure 12.4 shows an implementation file that might be associated with the header file `planet.h`.

Using a Personal Library

To use a personal library, one must complete these steps:

Creation

C1 Create a header file containing the interface information for a program needing the library.

C2 Create an implementation file containing the code of the library functions and other details of the implementation that are hidden from the user program.

FIGURE 12.4   Implementation File planet.c Containing Library with Planet Data Type and Operators

---

```
1.  /*
2.   *
3.   *      planet.c
4.   */
5.
6.  #include <stdio.h>
7.  #include <string.h>
8.  #include "planet.h"
9.
10. /*
11.  * Displays with labels all components of a planet_t structure
12.  */
13. void
14. print_planet(planet_t pl) /* input - one planet structure */
15. {
16.      printf("%s\n", pl.name);
17.      printf("  Equatorial diameter: %.0f km\n", pl.diameter);
18.      printf("  Number of moons: %d\n", pl.moons);
19.      printf("  Time to complete one orbit of the sun: %.2f years\n",
20.             pl.orbit_time);
21.      printf("  Time to complete one rotation on axis: %.4f hours\n",
22.             pl.rotation_time);
23. }
24.
25. /*
26.  * Determines whether or not the components of planet_1 and planet_2 match
27.  */
28. int
29. planet_equal(planet_t planet_1,    /* input - planets to            */
30.              planet_t planet_2)    /*          compare              */
31. {
32.      return (strcmp(planet_1.name, planet_2.name) == 0      &&
33.              planet_1.diameter == planet_2.diameter         &&
34.              planet_1.moons == planet_2.moons               &&
35.              planet_1.orbit_time == planet_2.orbit_time     &&
36.              planet_1.rotation_time == planet_2.rotation_time);
37. }
38.
39. /*
```

(continued)

FIGURE 12.4   (continued)

```
40.  *    Fills a type planet_t structure with input data. Integer returned as
41.  *    function result is success/failure/EOF indicator.
42.  *        1 => successful input of planet
43.  *        0 => error encountered
44.  *        EOF => insufficient data before end of file
45.  *    In case of error or EOF, value of type planet_t output argument is
46.  *    undefined.
47.  */
48.  int
49.  scan_planet(planet_t *plnp) /* output - address of planet_t structure to
50.                                          fill                              */
51.  {
52.       int result;
53.
54.       result = scanf("%s%lf%d%lf%lf", plnp->name,
55.                                       &plnp->diameter,
56.                                       &plnp->moons,
57.                                       &plnp->orbit_time,
58.                                       &plnp->rotation_time);
59.       if (result == 5)
60.            result = 1;
61.       else if (result != EOF)
62.            result = 0;
63.       return (result);
64.
65.  }
```

C3 Compile the implementation file. This step must be repeated any time either the header file or the implementation file is revised.

Use

U1 Include the library's header file in the user program through an #include directive.

U2 After compiling the user program, include both its object file and the object file created in C3 in the command that activates the linker.

EXERCISES FOR SECTION 12.3

Self-Check

1. Why do we openly define the constant macro PLANET_STRSIZ in the header file "planet.h" rather than protecting this name as one of the implementation details?

2. If you see the following `#include` directives in a program, what do you assume about libraries red and blue?

    ```
    #include <red.h>
    #include "blue.h"
    ```

Programming

1. Create a library named complex that defines the complex arithmetic operators from Section 10.4.

12.4   Storage Classes

C has five storage classes; so far we have seen three. Formal parameters and local variables of functions are variables that are *auto*matically allocated on the stack when a function is called and *auto*matically deallocated when the function returns; they are of storage class **auto**. In Chapter 6, we learned that the *scope* of these names—that is, the program region in which the name is visible—extends from the point of declaration to the end of the function in which the declaration appears.

The names of the functions themselves are of storage class **extern**, meaning that they will be available to the linker. If function prototypes precede any function definition, then these functions may be called by any other function in a program. The compiler needs to know the following vital information about a function in order to translate a call to it: Its return type, how many arguments it takes, and the data types of the arguments. Providing this information is the purpose of the

auto default storage class of function parameters and local variables; storage is automatically allocated on the stack at the time of a function call and deallocated when the function returns

extern storage class of names known to the linker

```
extern prototype
```

statement of which we have seen numerous examples in library header files. This statement *does not create* a function of storage class extern; it merely *notifies* the compiler that such a function exists and that the linker will know where to find it. Figure 12.5 shows the two storage classes, auto and extern. Names in color are of storage class auto; those in boldface black are of storage class extern.

The shaded area of Fig. 12.5 marks the program's *top level*. Class extern is the default storage class for all names declared at this level.

Global Variables

We have seen only declarations of functions at the top level of a program. However, it is also possible (though usually inadvisable) to declare variables at the top level. The scope of such a variable name extends from the point of declaration to the end of the source file, except in functions where the same name is declared as a formal parameter or local variable. If we need to reference a top-level variable in the region of its source file that precedes its declaration or in another source file, the compiler can be alerted to the variable's existence by placing a declaration of the variable that

FIGURE 12.5   Storage Classes auto and extern as Previously Seen

```
void
fun_one (int arg_one, int arg_two)
{
        int one_local;
        . . .
}

int
fun_two (int a2_one, int a2_two)
{
        int local_var;
        . . .
}

int
main (void)
{
        int num;
        . . .
}
```

begins with the keyword `extern` in the file prior to the first reference. Such a variable can be made accessible to *all* functions in a program and is therefore sometimes called a **global variable**. Figure 12.6 shows the declaration at the top level of `int` variable `global_var_x` of storage class `extern` in file `eg1.c` and an `extern` statement in `eg2.c` that makes the global variable accessible throughout this file as well. Only the *defining declaration,* the one in `eg1.c`, allocates space for `global_var_x`. A declaration beginning with the keyword `extern` allocates no memory; it simply provides information for the compiler.

Although there are applications in which global variables are unavoidable, such unrestricted access to a variable is generally regarded as detrimental to a program's readability and maintainability. Global access conflicts with the principle

global variable   a variable that may be accessed by many functions in a program

FIGURE 12.6

Declaration of a Global Variable

```
/* eg1.c */

int global_var_x;

void
afun(int n)
   . . .
```

```
/* eg2.c */

extern int global_var_x;

int
bfun(int p)
   . . .
```

that functions should have access to data on a need-to-know basis only, and then strictly through the documented interface as represented by the function prototype. However, one context in which a global variable can be used without reducing program readability is when the global represents a constant. We have been using globally visible macro constants throughout this text, and they have been a help, not a hindrance, in clarifying the meaning of a program. In Fig. 12.7, we see two global names that represent constant data structures. Because we plan to initialize these memory blocks and never change their values, there is no harm in letting our whole program access them. We include the `const` type qualifier in our declarations that define the globals as well as in the `extern` declarations that give additional functions access to the globals. This qualifier notifies the compiler that the program can look at, but not modify, these locations.

Figure 12.7 also shows another storage class that we have met before, namely, `typedef`. Including `typedef` in the set of storage classes is merely a notational convenience. As we saw in Chapter 10 , a `typedef` statement does not allocate storage space!

FIGURE 12.7

Use of Variables
of Storage Class
extern

```
/* fileone.c */

typedef struct {
        double real,
                imag;
} complex_t;

/* Defining declarations of
   global structured constant
   complex_zero and of global
   constant array of month
   names */
const complex_t complex_zero
        = {0, 0};
const char *months[12] =
     {"January", "February",
      "March", "April", "May",
      "June", "July", "August",
      "September", "October",
      "November", "December"};

int
f1_fun1(int n)
{ . . . }

double
f1_fun2(double x)
{ . . . }

char
f1_fun3(char c1, char c2)
{   double months; . . . }
```

```
/* filetwo.c */

/* #define's and typedefs
   including  complex_t */

void
f2_fun1(int x)
{ . . . }

/* Compiler-notifying
   declarations -- no
   storage allocated */
extern const complex_t
        complex_zero;
extern const char
        *months[12];

void
f2_fun2(void)
{ . . . }

int
f2_fun3(int n)
{ . . . }
```

TABLE 12.1 Functions in Fig. 12.7 with Global Variable Access and Reasons

Function(s)	Can Access Variables of Class Extern	Reason
f1_fun1 and f1_fun2	complex_zero and months	Their definitions follow in the same source file the top-level defining declarations of complex_zero and months. The functions have no parameters or local variables by these names.
f1_fun3	complex_zero only	Its definition follows in the same source file the top-level defining declaration of complex_zero, and it has no parameter or local variable by this name.
f2_fun1	none	Its definition precedes the declarations that notify the compiler of the existence of complex_zero and months.
f2_fun2 and f2_fun3	complex_zero and months	Their definitions follow in the same source file the declarations containing keyword extern that notify the compiler of the existence of global names complex_zero and months. The functions have no parameters or local variables by these names.

Table 12.1 shows which functions are allowed to access globals complex_zero and months and why. We assume that any local variable declarations affecting access to the globals are shown.

Storage Classes static and register

static storage class of variables allocated only once, prior to program execution

C's remaining storage classes are static and register. Placing the **static** keyword at the beginning of a local variable declaration changes the way the variable is allocated. Let's compare variables once and many in the following function fragment:

```
int
fun_frag(int n)
{
      static int once = 0;
      int       many = 0;
      . . .
}
```

As a variable of storage class auto, many is allocated space on the stack each time fun_frag is called; for every call many is initialized to zero. Every time fun_frag returns, many is deallocated. In contrast, static variable once is allocated and initialized *one time*, prior to program execution. It remains allocated until the entire program terminates. If fun_frag changes the value of once, that value is retained between calls to fun_frag.

Using a `static` local variable to retain data from one call to a function to the next is usually a poor programming practice. If the function's behavior depends on these data, then the function is no longer performing a transformation based solely on its input arguments, and the complexity of its purpose from the program reader's perspective is vastly increased.

One situation in which the use of a `static` local variable does not degrade readability is in function `main`, since a return from this function terminates the program. On a system that allocates a relatively small run-time stack, one might wish to declare large arrays as `static` variables in function `main`. Then these arrays will not use up stack space.

register storage class of automatic variables that the programmer would like to have stored in registers

The final storage class, `register`, is closely related to storage class `auto` and may be applied only to local variables and parameters. In fact, C implementations are not required to treat `register` variables differently from `auto` variables. Designating that a variable is of storage class `register` simply alerts the compiler to the fact that this memory cell will be referenced more often than most. By choosing storage class `register`, the programmer indicates an expectation that the program would run faster if a *register*, a special high-speed memory location *inside* the central processor, could be used for the variable. Variables serving as subscripts for large arrays are good candidates for this storage class. Here are declarations of variables in storage classes `static` and `register`:

```
static double matrix[50][40];
register int row, col;
```

EXERCISES FOR SECTION 12.4

Self-Check

Reread the program in Fig. 10.12 that converts units of measure.

1. Identify the storage classes of the following names used in the program:

    `unit_max` (first parameter of `load_units`)
    `found` (in function `search`)
    `convert`
    `quantity` (in function `main`)

2. For which one of the variables in function `search` would it be a good idea to request storage class `register`?

12.5 Modifying Functions for Inclusion in a Library

When building a personal library based on functions originally developed for use in a specific context, usually some modifications are advisable. A library function should be as general as possible, so all constants used should be examined to see whether they could be replaced by input parameters. Any restrictions on the library function's parameters should be carefully defined.

In previous work, our functions have dealt with an error either by returning an error code or by displaying an error message and returning a value that should permit continued execution. In some situations, however, it is better not to permit continued processing. For example, manipulation of a large two-dimensional array can be very time-consuming, and it might be pointless to expend this time on a matrix that contains erroneous data. Similarly, if our `factorial` function is called with a negative number, there is no way it can return a valid answer. Therefore, we might want to print a message and then terminate execution of a program in which this error occurs.

C's `exit` function from the standard library stdlib can be used in these types of situations to terminate execution prematurely. Calling `exit` with the argument 1 indicates that some failure led to the exit. Using the value 0 in an `exit` call implies no such failure, just as a 0 returned from function `main` indicates successful function completion. The `exit` function may also use one of the predefined constants `EXIT_SUCCESS` or `EXIT_FAILURE` as its return value. These constants are an option for use in the `return` statement as well, provided that the standard library stdlib is included. Figure 12.8 shows a library form of function `factorial` that terminates program execution prematurely on a negative input.

The following syntax display describes the `exit` function.

FIGURE 12.8   Function factorial with Premature Exit on Negative Data

```
1.  /*
2.   * Computes n!
3.   * n is greater than or equal to zero -- premature exit on negative data
4.   */
5.  int
6.  factorial(int n)
7.  {
8.      int i,            /* local variables */
9.          product;
10.
11.     if (n < 0) {
12.         printf("\n***Function factorial reports ");
13.         printf("ERROR: %d! is undefined***\n", n);
14.         exit(1);
15.     } else {
16.         /* Compute the product n x (n-1) x (n-2) x . . . x 2 x 1 */
17.         product = 1;
18.         for  (i = n; i > 1; --i) {
19.             product = product * i;
20.         }
```

(continued)

FIGURE 12.8 (continued)

```
21.          /* Return function result */
22.          return (product);
23.     }
24. }
```

---

exit Function

SYNTAX: exit(*return_value*);

EXAMPLE:
```
/*
 * Gets next positive number from input
 * stream. Returns EOF if end of file
 * is encountered. Exits program with error
 * message if erroneous input is encountered.
 */
int
get_positive(void)
{
int n, status;
char ch;

for  (status = scanf("%d", &n);
          status == 1  &&  n <= 0;
          status = scanf("%d", &n)) {}

if (status == 0) {
      scanf("%c", &ch);
      printf("\n***Function get_positive ");
      printf("reports ERROR in data at ");
      printf(">>%c<<***\n", ch);
      exit(1);
} else if (status == EOF) {
      return (status);
} else {
      return (n);
}
   }
```

(continued)

INTERPRETATION: Execution of a call to `exit` causes program termination from any point in a program. The *return_value* is used to indicate whether termination was brought on by some type of failure. A *return_value* of 0 means normal exit. In general, the use of

```
exit(0);
```

should be avoided in functions other than `main` since placing "normal" termination of a program in one of its function subprograms tends to diminish the readability of function `main`. The use of

```
exit(1);
```

should be reserved for terminating execution in cases where error recovery is not possible or not useful.

EXERCISES FOR SECTION 12.5

Self-Check

1. Why should you `#include` the header file of a library in the library's own implementation file?

12.6 Conditional Compilation

C's preprocessor recognizes commands that allow the user to select parts of a program to be compiled and parts to be omitted. This ability can be helpful in a variety of situations. For example, one can build in debugging `printf` calls when writing a function and then include these statements in the compiled program only when they are needed. Inclusion of header files is another activity that may need to be done conditionally. For example, we might have two libraries, sp_one and sp_two, that both use a data type and operators of a third library, sp. The header files `sp_one.h` and `sp_two.h` would both have the directive `#include "sp.h"`. However, if we wanted a program to use the facilities of both sp_one and sp_two, including both of their header files would lead to inclusion of `sp.h` twice, resulting in duplicate declarations of the data type defined in `sp.h`. Because C prohibits such duplicate declarations, we must be able to prevent this situation. A third case in which conditional compilation is very helpful is the design of a system for use on a variety of computers. Conditional compilation allows one to compile only the code appropriate for the current computer.

Figure 12.9 shows a recursive function containing `printf` calls to create a trace of its execution. Compilation of these statements depends on the value of the condition

```
defined (TRACE)
```

FIGURE 12.9   Conditional Compilation of Tracing printf Calls

```
1.  /*
2.   *  Computes an integer quotient (m/n) using subtraction
3.   */
4.  int
5.  quotient(int m, int n)
6.  {
7.        int ans;
8.  #if defined (TRACE)
9.        printf("Entering quotient with m = %d, n = %d\n", m, n);
10. #endif
11.
12.       if (n > m)
13.             ans = 0;
14.       else
15.             ans = 1 + quotient(m - n, n);
16.
17. #if defined (TRACE)
18.       printf("Leaving quotient(%d, %d) with result = %d\n", m, n, ans);
19. #endif
20.
21.       return (ans);
22. }
```

The `defined` operator evaluates to 1 if the name that is its operand is defined in the preprocessor. Such definition is the result of using the name either in a `#define` directive or in a compiler option that simulates a `#define`. Otherwise, the `defined` operator evaluates to 0.

After creating functions like the one in Fig. 12.9, one need only include the directive

`#define TRACE`

somewhere in the source file prior to the function definition to "turn on" the compilation of the tracing `printf` calls. It is not necessary to explicitly associate a value with `TRACE`. Remember that, as for all preprocessor directives, the # of the conditional compilation directives *must* be the first nonblank character on the line. The `defined` operator exists exclusively for application in `#if` and `#elif` directives. The `#elif` means "else if" and is used when selecting among multiple alternatives, as in Fig. 12.10.

FIGURE 12.10   Conditional Compilation of Tracing printf Calls

```
1.  /*
2.   *  Computes an integer quotient (m/n) using subtraction
3.   */
4.  int
5.  quotient(int m, int n)
6.  {
7.        int ans;
8.
9.  #if defined (TRACE_VERBOSE)
10.       printf("Entering quotient with m = %d, n = %d\n", m, n);
11. #elif defined (TRACE_BRIEF)
12.       printf(" => quotient(%d, %d)\n", m, n);
13. #endif
14.
15.       if (n > m)
16.             ans = 0;
17.       else
18.             ans = 1 + quotient(m - n, n);
19.
20. #if defined (TRACE_VERBOSE)
21.       printf("Leaving quotient(%d, %d) with result = %d\n", m, n, ans);
22. #elif defined (TRACE_BRIEF)
23.       printf("quotient(%d, %d) => %d\n", m, n, ans);
24. #endif
25.
26.       return (ans);
27. }
```

One approach to the coordination of included files is illustrated in Fig. 12.11. Each header file is constructed so as to prevent duplicate compilation of its contents, regardless of the number of times the header file is included. The entire contents of a header file are enclosed in an #if that tests whether a name based on the header file name has been defined in a #define directive. Then the first time the header file is included, its entire contents are passed to the compiler. Since a #define of the critical name is in the file, additional #include directives for the same file will provide no code to the compiler.

C's #if and #elif directives are complemented by an #else directive to make possible a full range of selective compilation constructs. An #undef directive that cancels the preprocessor's definition of a particular name is also available.

FIGURE 12.11   Header File That Protects Itself from Effects of Duplicate Inclusion

```
1.   /*   Header file planet.h
2.    *
3.    *   abstract data type planet
4.    *
5.    *   Type planet_t has these components:
6.    *        name, diameter, moons, orbit_time, rotation_time
7.    *
8.    *   Operators:
9.    *        print_planet, planet_equal, scan_planet
10.   */
11.
12.  #if !defined (PLANET_H_INCL)
13.  #define PLANET_H_INCL
14.
15.  #define PLANET_STRSIZ 10
16.
17.  typedef struct { /* planet structure */
18.        char name[PLANET_STRSIZ];
19.        double diameter;       /* equatorial diameter in km            */
20.        int    moons;          /* number of moons                      */
21.        double orbit_time ,    /* years to orbit sun once              */
22.               rotation_time;  /* hours to complete one revolution on axis  */
23.  } planet_t;
24.
25.  /*
26.   *   Displays with labels all components of a planet_t structure
27.   */
28.  extern void
29.  print_planet(planet_t pl);  /* input - one planet structure         */
30.
31.  /*
32.   *   Determines whether or not the components of planet_1 and planet_2
33.   *   match
34.   */
35.  extern int
36.  planet_equal(planet_t planet_1,     /* input - planets to           */
37.               planet_t planet_2);    /*              compare         */
38.
39.  /*
40.   *   Fills a type planet_t structure with input data. Integer returned as
41.   *   function result is success/failure/EOF indicator.
42.   *        1 => successful input of planet
```

(continued)

FIGURE 12.11   (continued)

```
43.    *          0 => error encountered
44.    *          EOF => insufficient data before end of file
45.
46.    *   In case of error or EOF, value of type planet_t output argument is
47.    *   undefined.
48.
49.    */
50.    extern int
51.    scan_planet(planet_t *plnp); /* output - address of planet_t structure to
52.                                               fill                            */
53.
54.    #endif
```

EXERCISES FOR SECTION 12.6

Self-Check

1. Use conditional compilation to select an appropriate call to printf. Assume that on a UNIX-family operating system, the name UNIX will be defined in the C preprocessor; on a VMS-family operating system, the name VMS will be defined. The desired message on UNIX is

    ```
    Enter <ctrl-d> to quit.
    ```

    The desired message on VMS is

    ```
    Enter <ctrl-z> to quit.
    ```

2. Consider the header file shown in Fig. 12.11. Describe what happens (a) when the preprocessor first encounters a #include "planet.h" directive and (b) when the preprocessor encounters a second #include "planet.h" directive.

12.7   Arguments to Function main

Up to this point, we have always defined function main with a void parameter list. However, as another possibility, we could use the following prototype that indicates that main has two formal parameters: an integer and an array of pointers to strings:

```
int
main(int  argc,    /* input - argument count (including
                                program name)                    */
        char *argv[]) /* input - argument vector                 */
```

The way you cause your program to run varies from one operating system to another. However, most operating systems provide some way for you to specify values of options when you run a program. For example, on the ULTRIX operating system, one would specify options opt1, opt2, and opt3 when running a program named prog by typing the command line

```
prog opt1 opt2 opt3
```

command-line arguments options specified in the statement that activates a program

The formal parameters argc and argv provide a mechanism for a C main function to access these **command-line arguments**. If the program prog just mentioned were the machine code of a C program whose main function prototype had parameters argc and argv, then the command line

```
prog opt1 opt2 opt3
```

would result in these formal parameter values within main:

```
argc   4          argv[0]   "prog"
                     [1]    "opt1"
                     [2]    "opt2"
                     [3]    "opt3"
                     [4]    ""  (empty string)
```

Figure 12.12 shows a revised version of our program from Chapter 11 to make a backup copy of a text file. Rather than prompting the user for the names of the file to copy and the file to be the backup, the new version expects the user to enter this

FIGURE 12.12   File Backup Using Arguments to Function main

```
 1.  /*
 2.   *  Makes a backup of the file whose name is the first command-line argument.
 3.   *  The second command-line argument is the name of the new file.
 4.   */
 5.  #include <stdio.h>
 6.  #include <stdlib.h>
 7.
 8.  int
 9.  main(int    argc,     /* input - argument count (including program name) */
10.       char *argv[])    /* input - argument vector                        */
11.  {
12.       FILE *inp,       /* file pointers for input        */
13.            *outp;      /*      and backup files          */
14.       char  ch;        /* one character of input file    */
15.
16.       /* Verify argument count                                           */
17.       if (argc >= 3) {
```

(continued)

FIGURE 12.12   (continued)

```
18.
19.              /* Open input and backup files if possible                    */
20.              inp = fopen(argv[1], "r");
21.              if (inp == NULL) {
22.                      printf("\nCannot open file %s for input\n", argv[1]);
23.                      exit(1);
24.              }
25.
26.              outp = fopen(argv[2], "w");
27.              if (outp == NULL) {
28.                      printf("\nCannot open file %s for output\n", argv[2]);
29.                      exit(1);
30.              }
31.
32.              /* Make backup copy one character at a time                    */
33.              for (ch = getc(inp); ch != EOF; ch = getc(inp))
34.                  putc(ch, outp);
35.
36.              /* Close files and notify user of backup completion            */
37.              fclose(inp);
38.              fclose(outp);
39.              printf("\nCopied %s to %s\n", argv[1], argv[2]);
40.
41.          } else
42.              printf("Invalid argument list: Include two file names\n");
43.          return(0);
44. }
```

information on the command line. For example, if the program is named backup and the user activates it by typing

```
backup old.txt new.txt
```

the formal parameters of main will have these values:

```
argc  3           argv[0]  "backup"
                      [1]  "old.txt"
                      [2]  "new.txt"
                      [3]  ""
```

If the program encounters any difficulty in opening either of the files named by the user, it exits with an appropriate error message. Otherwise, it proceeds with the copy operation.

EXERCISES FOR SECTION 12.7

Self-Check

1. How many command-line arguments are expected by a program with this function heading for `main`?

   ```
   int main(int argc, char* argv[])
   ```

Programming

1. Write a program that takes a single command-line argument. The argument should be the name of a text file containing integers, and the program should sum the integers in the file. If any invalid data are encountered, the program should terminate with an error message that includes the file name and the invalid character.

12.8 Defining Macros with Parameters

We have consistently used the `#define` preprocessor directive we talked about in Chapter 2 for associating symbolic names with constant values. In Chapter 2, we discussed the fact that C's preprocessor actually revises the text of the source code, replacing each occurrence of a defined name by its meaning before turning the code over to the compiler. In this section, we study how to define **macros** that have formal parameters. The form of such a macro definition is

macro facility for naming a commonly used statement or operation

`#define` *macro_name(parameter list) macro body*

Like functions, macros allow us to give a name to a commonly used statement or operation. Because macros are handled through textual substitution, macro calls execute without the overhead of space allocation and deallocation on the stack that is associated with functions. Of course, since the macro's meaning appears in the program at every call, the object file produced by the compiler typically requires more memory than the same program would require if it used a function rather than a macro.

Figure 12.13 shows a brief program that uses a macro named `LABEL_PRINT_INT` to display the value of an integer variable or expression with a label (a string). Notice that in the directive that defines `LABEL_PRINT_INT`, there is no space between the macro name and the left parenthesis of the parameter list. This detail is critical, for if there were a space, the preprocessor would misinterpret the macro definition and would replace every occurrence of `LABEL_PRINT_INT` by

```
(label, num) printf("%s = %d", (label), (num))
```

The process of replacing a macro call such as

```
LABEL_PRINT_INT("rabbit", r)
```

FIGURE 12.13   Program Using a Macro with Formal Parameters

```
1.  /*  Shows the definition and use of a macro                          */
2.
3.  #include <stdio.h>
4.
5.  #define LABEL_PRINT_INT(label, num) printf("%s = %d", (label), (num))
6.
7.  int
8.  main(void)
9.  {
10.       int r = 5, t = 12;
11.
12.       LABEL_PRINT_INT("rabbit", r);
13.       printf("      ");
14.       LABEL_PRINT_INT("tiger", t + 2);
15.       printf("\n");
16.
17.       return(0);
18.  }
19.
20.  rabbit = 5      tiger = 14
```

by a copy of the macro body with appropriate parameter substitution,

```
printf("%s = %d", ("rabbit"), (r))
```

macro expansion
process of replacing
a macro call by its
meaning

is called **macro expansion**. When doing this replacement, the C preprocessor matches each macro parameter name with the corresponding actual argument. Then, in a copy of the macro body, every occurrence of a formal parameter name is replaced by the actual argument. This modified macro body takes the place of the macro call in the text of the program. Figure 12.14 illustrates the process of macro expansion of the last macro call in our sample program. Notice that only the macro name and its argument list are involved in the macro expansion process. The semicolon at the end of the macro call line is unaffected. It would be a mistake to include a semicolon at the end of the `printf` call in the macro body. If a semicolon were placed there, the statements resulting from macro expansion of our two macro calls would both end in *two* semicolons.

Use of Parentheses in Macro Body

You will notice that in the body of `LABEL_PRINT_INT`, each occurrence of a formal parameter of the macro is enclosed in parentheses. The use of adequate parentheses

FIGURE 12.14   Macro Expansion of Second Macro Call of Program in Fig. 12.13

```
LABEL_PRINT_INT("tiger", t + 2)
              ↓          ↙

LABEL_PRINT_INT(label, num)
```
parameter matching   →

```
                              "tiger"   t + 2
                                 ↓         ↓
              printf("%s = %d", (label), (num))
```
parameter replacement in body   →

```
                        printf("%s = %d", ("tiger"), (t + 2))
```
result of macro expansion

in a macro's body is essential for correct evaluation. In Fig. 12.15, we see a program fragment that uses a macro to compute n^2. We show two versions of the macro definition and the different program outputs that result.

Let's look at the different macro expansions that occur in Versions 1 and 2. Examination of Fig. 12.16 reveals that the incorrect results of Version 1 are a simple consequence of the operator precedence rules.

FIGURE 12.15   Macro Calls Showing Importance of Parentheses in Macro Body

Version 1   Version 2

```
#define SQUARE(n)  n * n                          #define SQUARE(n) ((n) * (n))
```

```
              . . .
              double x = 0.5, y = 2.0;
              int    n = 4, m = 12;

              printf("(%.2f + %.2f)squared = %.2f\n\n",
                     x, y, SQUARE(x + y));

              printf("%d squared divided by\n", m);
              printf("%d squared is %d\n", n,
                        SQUARE(m) / SQUARE(n));
```
```
(0.5 + 2.0)squared = 3.5                          (0.5 + 2.0)squared = 6.25

12 squared divided by                             12 squared divided by
4 squared is 144                                  4 squared is 9
```

FIGURE 12.16   Macro Expansions of Macro Calls from Fig. 12.15

Version 1	Version 2

`SQUARE(x + y)`
  becomes
`x + y * x + y`
Problem: Multiplication done
  before addition.
	`SQUARE(x + y)`
	  becomes
	`((x + y) * (x + y))`

`SQUARE(m) / SQUARE(n)`
  becomes
`m * m / n * n`
Problem: Multiplication and
  division are of equal precedence;
  they are performed left to right.
	`SQUARE(m) / SQUARE(n)`
	  becomes
	`((m) * (m)) / ((n) * (n))`

To avoid the problems illustrated in Figs. 12.15 and 12.16, use parentheses liberally in macro bodies. Specifically, parenthesize each occurrence of a parameter in the macro body, and enclose the entire body in parentheses if it produces a result value. For instance, here is a macro for finding one real root of a quadratic equation:

```
#define ROOT1(a,b,c)  ((-(b)+sqrt((b)*(b)-4*(a)*(c)))/(2*(a)))
```

The black parentheses are those normally required for proper evaluation of the expression. The parentheses in color are added in accordance with our guidelines for parenthesizing a macro definition.

One should avoid using operators with side effects in expressions passed as arguments in a macro call, since these expressions may be evaluated multiple times. For example, the statement

```
r = ROOT1(++n1, n2, n3);   /*  error: applying ++ in a macro
                               argument */
```

would be expanded as

```
r = ((-(n2)+sqrt((n2)*(n2)-4*(++n1)*(n3)))/(2*(++n1)));
```

resulting in a statement that violates the principle that the object of an operator with a side effect should not be reused in the expression.

We urge you to use parentheses routinely in macro bodies as described earlier, even if you cannot conceive of any circumstance when a given set of parentheses could matter. One needs only to work with macros a short time to realize how limited is this ability of a programmer to foresee *all* possible situations!

We also encourage you to use all capital letters in your macro names. Remembering that you are calling a macro rather than a function is critical in helping you avoid the use of operators with side effects in your actual arguments.

Extending a Macro over Two or More Lines

The preprocessor assumes that a macro definition fits on a single line unless the program indicates otherwise. To extend a macro over multiple lines, all but the last line of the definition must end with the backslash character \. For example, here is a macro that implements the header of a `for` statement to count from the value of `st` up to, but not including, the value of `end`:

```
#define INDEXED_FOR(ct, st, end)  \
     for  ((ct) = (st);  (ct) < (end);  ++(ct))
```

The following code fragment uses `INDEXED_FOR` to display the first `X_MAX` elements of array `x`:

```
INDEXED_FOR(i, 0, X_MAX)
     printf("x[%2d] = %6.2f\n", i, x[i]);
```

After macro expansion, the statement will be

```
for  ((i) = (0);  (i) < (X_MAX);  ++(i))
     printf("x[%2d] = %6.2f\n", i, x[i]);
```

EXERCISES FOR SECTION 12.8

Self-Check

1. Given these macro definitions, write the macro expansion of each statement that follows. If the expansion seems not to be what the macro definer intended (you may assume the macro names are meaningful), indicate how you would correct the macro definition.

    ```
    #define DOUBLE(x) (x) + (x)
    #define DISCRIMINANT (a,b,c)  ((b) * (b) - 4 * (a) * (c))
    #define PRINT_PRODUCT(x, y) \
         printf("%.2f X %.2f = %.2f\n", (x), (y), (x) * (y));
    ```

    a. `y = DOUBLE(a - b)*c;`
    b. `y = y - DOUBLE(p);`
    c. `if (DISCRIMINANT(a1, b1, c1) == 0)`
         `        r1 = -b1 / (2 * a1);`
    d. `PRINT_PRODUCT(a + b, a - b);`

Programming

1. Define a macro named `F_OF_X` that would evaluate the following polynomial for the x value passed as its argument. You may assume that the math library has been included.

$$x^5 - 3x^3 + 4$$

2. Define a macro to display its argument preceded by a dollar sign and with two decimal places.

12.9 Common Programming Errors

The most common problem in the development of large systems by teams of programmers is a lack of agreement regarding the details of a system's design. If you apply the software development method presented in earlier chapters, you can achieve a rational, stepwise division of a large problem into smaller subproblems that correspond to individual functions. Then, you can devise detailed descriptions of *what* each function is to do and *what type(s)* of data it is to manipulate. Only when representatives of all teams are in full agreement about this fundamental interface information is it wise to proceed with a system's implementation.

When developing personal libraries, it is easy to forget the long-range goal of having reusable functions in the rush of completing a current project. An unnecessarily restrictive assumption built into a library function can quickly negate the function's usefulness in another context.

Although macros provide a quick and often quite readable shorthand for the expressions they represent, they are also fertile ground for error growth. It is easy to slip and type a blank after the macro name in the definition of a macro with parameters, causing the preprocessor to misinterpret the definition. Operator precedence mistakes are sure to crop up unless the programmer is absolutely meticulous about parenthesizing every macro body that produces a result value as well as parenthesizing every occurrence of a macro parameter within the body. Following a consistent naming convention for macros can save hours of unnecessary debugging resulting from the programmer's erroneous assumption that a function, not a macro, is being called.

In the history of computing, the inappropriate use of global variables is notorious for corrupting a system's reliability. We cannot overemphasize the importance of maintaining visible interfaces among functions through their parameter lists. Only functions with visible interfaces are good candidates for reuse through inclusion in a library.

Chapter Review

1. C's facility for creating a personal library provides a means of encapsulating an abstract data type.
2. Dividing a library definition into a header file and an implementation file provides a natural separation of the description of *what* the library functions do from *how* they do it.
3. Defining a macro gives a name to a frequently used statement or operation.
4. The exit function allows premature termination of program execution.
5. Conditional compilation provides a means of customizing code for different implementations and of creating library header files that protect themselves from duplicate inclusion.
6. Designing function main with parameters argc and argv allows the use of command-line arguments.
7. Library functions must have meaningful names, have clearly defined interfaces, and be as independent as possible from globally defined constants.

NEW C CONSTRUCTS

C Construct	Meaning
Header File (with #if . . . #endif directives)	

```/* somelib.h */```
 ```#if !defined (SOMELIB_H_INCL)```
 ```#define SOMELIB_H_INCL```
 	
 ```#define SOMELIB_MAX 20```
 ```typedef struct {```
 ``` int comp;```
 ``` char s[SOMELIB_MAX];```
 ```} some_t;```
 	
 ```/* Purpose of function make_some```
 ``` */```
 ```extern some_t```
 ```make_some(int   n,```
 ```   const char str[]);```
 	
 ```/* other extern prototypes */```
 	
 ```#endif```
	somelib.h is a header file to be included (#include "somelib.h") in any program desiring to use its facilities. somelib.h uses conditional compilation (#if...#endif) to protect its contents from duplicate inclusion.

(continued)

NEW C CONSTRUCTS (continued)

C Construct	Meaning

Implementation File

```
/* somelib.c */
#include "somelib.h"
#include <string.h>


/*  Purpose of function make_some
 */
some_t
make_some(int          n,
          const char str[])
{
      some_t result;

      result.comp = n;
      strcpy(result.s, str);

      return (result);
}

/*  other function definitions */
```

somelib.c is the implementation file associated with somelib.h. Its object file must be linked to any other program that includes somelib.h.

Macro Definition and Call

```
#define AVG(x,y) (((x) + (y)) / 2.0)
. . .

ans = AVG(2*a, b);
```

Preprocessor will replace each call to AVG by its macro expansion. Statement shown becomes
```
      ans = (((2*a) + (b)) / 2.0);
```

exit Function

```
/*  Compute decimal equivalent of a
 *  common fraction
 */
double
dec_equiv(int num, int denom)
{
   if (denom == 0) {
      printf("Zero-divide: %d/%d\n",
             num, denom);
      exit(1);
   } else {
      return ((double)num /
              (double)denom);
   }
}
```

Function causes premature program termination if called with an invalid argument.

(continued)

NEW C CONSTRUCTS   (continued)

C Construct	Meaning

Arguments to Function main

```
int
main(int argc, char *argv[])
{
    if (argc == 3)
       process(argv[1], argv[2]);
    else
       printf
         ("Wrong number of options\n");
    return (0);
}
```

Function `main` is expecting two command-line arguments to pass to function `process`.

Quick-Check Exercises

1. A system designer who is breaking down a complex problem using _____ _____ will focus first on *what* a function is to do, leaving the details of *how* this is accomplished for later.

2. The process of protecting the implementation details of a lower-level module from direct access by a higher-level module is called _____.

3. The process of replacing a macro call by its meaning is known as _____.

4. In C, a(n) _____ file contains information about *what* a library's functions do. The _____ file contains the details of *how* these actions are accomplished.

5. Why do macro calls execute without the overhead of space allocation and deallocation on the stack?

6. When defining an implementation file `lib1.c`, why is it advantageous to `#include "lib1.h"`?

7. Given this definition of macro ABSDF,

   ```
   #define ABSDF(x, y)  (fabs((x) - (y)))
   ```

   show what this statement will be after macro expansion:

   ```
   if (ABSDF(a + b, c) > ABSDF(b + c, a))
        lgdiff = ABSDF(a + b, c);
   ```

8. Where are variables of storage class `auto` allocated and when? When are they deallocated?

9. When are variables of storage class `static` allocated? When are they deallocated?

10. Which of the following fragments would be followed immediately by the code of function `mangle`?

```
double                              extern double
mangle(double x, double y)          mangle(double x, double y);
```

11. When generalizing a function for inclusion in a library, named constants are often replaced by _____.

12. What directives could we add to header file `mylib.h` so that no matter how many `#include "mylib.h"` directives were processed, the contents of `mylib.h` would be compiled just once?

Answers to Quick-Check Exercises

1. procedural abstraction
2. information hiding
3. macro expansion
4. header, implementation
5. This is because macros are handled through textual substitution.
6. Any necessary macros and data types are defined in just one file, the header file, so modification of a macro or of a data type does not require changes in more than one place.
7. `if ((fabs((a + b) - (c))) > (fabs((b + c) - (a))))`
   `    lgdiff = (fabs((a + b) - (c)));`
8. The variables are allocated on the stack at the time when a function is entered. They are deallocated when the function to which they belong returns.
9. The variables are allocated before program execution. They are deallocated at program termination.
10. the fragment on the left
11. function parameters
12. `#if !defined (MYLIB_H_INCL)`
    `#define MYLIB_H_INCL`
    `    . . . rest of mylib.h . . .`
    `#endif`

Review Questions

1. Define *procedural abstraction* and *data abstraction*.
2. What feature of C encourages the encapsulation of data objects and their operators?
3. Compare the typical contents of a library header file to the contents of an implementation file. Which of these files defines the interface between a library and a program?

4. How does the C compiler know whether to look for an included file in the system directory or in the program's directory?

5. Compare the execution of the macro call

   `MAC(a, b)`

   to the execution of an analogous function call

   `mac(a, b)`

   Which of the following two calls is sure to be valid and why?

   `mac(++a, b)`   or   `MAC(++a, b)`

6. When you write the body of a macro definition, where should you use parentheses?

7. What are C's five storage classes? What are the default storage classes for variables declared in each of the following environments?

   declared at the top level
   declared as function parameters
   declared as local variables of a function

8. What is the purpose of storage class `register`?

9. Discuss this statement: If a program has five functions that manipulate an array of data values, it makes more sense to declare this array at the program's top level so that each function does not need to have an array parameter.

10. Why is the argument value 1 used much more often than the argument value 0 in calls to the `exit` function?

11. Describe the purpose of the `defined` operator.

12. If we wish to pass command line arguments using the main program, how many parameters have to be passed in the main function and which are they?

Programming Projects

1. Create a library that defines a structure type `high_precision_t` to represent a number with 20 decimal digits of precision. Include a 20-element integer array, a single integer to represent the position of the decimal point, and an integer or character to represent the sign. For example, the value –8.127 might be stored as

`.digits`	8	1	2	7	0	0	0	0	0	0	0	0	0	0	0	0	0	0	0	0

`.decpt`	1

`.sign`	–1

and 0.0094328 as

.digits	9	4	3	2	8	0	0	0	0	0	0	0	0	0	0	0	0	0	0	0

.decpt	-2

.sign	1

Your library should also define functions add_high, subtract_high, and multiply_high to perform simple arithmetic on high-precision structures. Include scan_high and print_high functions to facilitate I/O.

2. The bubble sort is another technique for sorting an array. A bubble sort compares adjacent array elements and exchanges their values if they are out of order. In this way, the smaller values "bubble" to the top of the array (towards element 0 of the array), while the larger values sink to the bottom of the array. After the first pass of a bubble sort, the last array element is in the correct position; after the second pass the last two elements are correct, and so on. Thus, after each pass, the unsorted portion of the array contains one less element. Create a user-defined library called "bsort.h" containing a function named bubbleSort for implementing the bubble sort algorithm. Write a C program that takes 100 random numbers with a maximum value of 100 and sorts them by using the bubbleSort function. The program must display the randomly selected numbers before displaying the numbers that are sorted by the bubbleSort algorithm.

3. Many operational engineering systems require complex scheduling of people, machines, and supplies to provide a service or produce a product. To schedule a system, one needs to know three things: The resources available to the system, the resources required to provide the desired service, and any constraints on the resources. Many sophisticated algorithms are available to minimize the cost or time required to provide a service. Here we will build a small library of functions useful for solving constrained scheduling problems.

You are head of maintenance scheduling for Brown Bag Airlines. You have three crews, with different qualifications as follows:

Crew Number	Skill Level	Cost of Crew Per Hour
0	1	$200
1	2	$300
2	3	$400

Crew 2 is certified to do all levels of maintenance work but costs more per hour than the other crews. Crew 1 can do maintenance work requiring skills

1 and 2 but not skill 3. Crew 0 can do maintenance work only at level 1. You need to schedule the following maintenance:

Aircraft ID	Level of Maintenance	Number of Hours
7899	1	8
3119	1	6
7668	1	4
2324	2	4
1123	2	8
7555	2	4
6789	3	2
7888	3	10

Write the following functions and create a scheduling library from them:

a. A function to scan and store crew data in an appropriate structure.
b. A function to scan and store in an appropriate structure the required maintenance data.
c. A function that checks maintenance level required against the crew abilities and returns the number of the lowest-cost crew that can perform the maintenance.
d. A function that checks the maintenance level required against the crew abilities and current schedule and returns the number of the qualified crew that will be free to perform the maintenance at the earliest time. If more than one crew satisfies the function's constraints, the number of the lowest-cost qualified crew is returned.
e. A function that accumulates hours required for each crew as each maintenance task is scheduled.

Write a main program that calls these functions and any others you feel are needed for scheduling crews to do the listed maintenance jobs. Assume that all three crews can work at the same time and that the crews are paid only when they work. Jobs must be done in their entirety by one crew. Develop one algorithm to find the quickest way to get the maintenance done and another to find the cheapest way to get the work done. How big is the difference between these two solutions in time required to complete the given list of maintenance jobs?

4. You are developing a personal library of functions to assist in solving monthly installment loan problems where simple interest is charged on the unpaid balance. You will include functions based on various forms of the formula

$$m = \frac{ip}{1 - (i + 1)^{-12y}}$$

where m is the monthly payment, i is the monthly interest rate (as a decimal fraction, not a percentage), p is the principal amount, and y is the number of years of the loan. Your library should have facilities for determining monthly payment (to the next whole dollar, i.e., `ceil(m)`) given p, i, and y, for determining the maximum principal that can be borrowed given a certain interest rate, monthly payment, and loan term, and also for determining the maximum annual interest rate at which a certain principal can be borrowed and repaid in y years with a monthly payment of m.

In addition, define a function that will print an amortization table for a loan by displaying in columns the payment number, the payment, the interest paid, the principal paid, and the remaining balance. The last payment must be calculated separately.

5. What are the changes required in the C program designed for Exercise 2 so as to sort the 100 random numbers in a descending order? The program must display the randomly selected numbers before displaying the numbers that are sorted by the `bubbleSortD` algorithm. (Hint: Create a new user-defined library called "bsort-descending.h" containing a function named `bubbleSortD` to implement the `bubbleSort` algorithm. This function must sort the given numbers in a descending order.)

6. Create a user-defined library called "ssort.h" containing a function named `selectionSort` for a selection sort algorithm (see Section 7.6 in Chapter 7 for details of the selection sort algorithm). Write a C program that takes 100 random numbers with a maximum value of 100 and sorts them by using the `selectionSort` function. The program must display the randomly selected numbers before displaying the numbers that are sorted by the `selectionSort` algorithm.

Pointers and Dynamic Data Structures

CHAPTER OBJECTIVES

- To understand dynamic allocation on the heap
- To learn how to use pointers to access structs
- To learn how to use pointers to build linked data structures
- To understand how to use and implement a linked list
- To understand how to use and implement a stack
- To learn how to use and implement a queue
- To understand basic concepts of binary trees
- To learn how to use and implement a binary tree

This chapter discusses **dynamic data structures**, structures that expand and contract as a program executes. C's facilities for creating these structures allow a program to defer until a later time its decision regarding how much space to use in processing a data set. A program that can procrastinate in this way is far more flexible than a comparable program that must make this decision on space earlier. In Chapter 7, we studied how to store a list of data in an array that we declared as a variable. Although we could handle lists of different lengths by only partially filling the array, the maximum list size had to be determined before the program was compiled.

In this chapter, we will study how the use of one dynamic memory allocation function allows us to delay the setting of the maximum list size until the program is already running. Using another function permits us to allocate space separately for each list member, so the program itself *never* actually sets an upper bound on the list size. Since the program can call these functions to request memory at any time, it can use information from the input data as the basis for determining how much space to request and what data types are to be stored in the blocks.

When allocating memory dynamically, a program can use the space to store any of the simple and structured data types and any of the data structures presented in earlier chapters. In addition, it can combine separately allocated structured blocks called **nodes** to form composite structures that expand and contract as the program executes. Such composite dynamic structures are extremely flexible. For example, it is relatively easy to add new information by creating a new node and inserting it between two existing nodes. It is also relatively easy to delete a node.

In this chapter, we will examine how to create and manipulate a composite data structure called a *linked list* and how to use this structure in forming lists, stacks, and queues of varying lengths.

13.1 Pointers

Because the creation and manipulation of dynamic data structures requires sophisticated use of pointers, we will begin by reviewing the nature of pointers and their uses discussed in earlier chapters. We saw in Chapter 6 that a pointer variable contains not a data value, but rather the address of another cell containing a data value. Figure 13.1 illustrates the difference between pointer variable num and integer variable num. The *direct* value of variable num is the integer 3, and the *direct* value

FIGURE 13.1

Comparison
of Pointer and
Nonpointer
Variables

Reference	Explanation	Value
num	Direct value of num	3
nump	Direct value of nump	Pointer to location containing 3
*nump	Indirect value of nump	3

of variable nump is the address of the memory cell where the 3 is stored. If we follow the pointer stored in nump, we can access the value 3, which means that 3 is the *indirect* value of nump. The reference nump means the direct value of nump. When we apply the indirection or "pointer-following" operator as in the reference *nump, we access the indirect value of nump.

Pointers as Function Parameters

In Chapter 6, we studied the use of pointers as output parameters of functions. By passing the address of a variable to a function, we give the function a means of storing one of its results in that variable. C defines the & address-of operator that gives the programmer access to the address of any simple variable or any array element. Figure 13.2 shows a long division function that has two input parameters, dividend and divisor, and two output parameters, quotientp and remainderp. Variables quotientp and remainderp are both pointers to integer variables, so a call to long_division must pass the addresses of two integer variables, as is done in the highlighted statement of function main:

```
long_division(40, 3, &quot, &rem);
```

Pointers Representing Functions

In Chapter 5, we learned that a function can be passed as a parameter to another function (see function evaluate in Fig. 5.16 on p. 298). In fact, C represents such a parameter as a pointer to the function's code, and there is an alternative parameter declaration that makes this pointer use more obvious. In Fig. 5.16, we declared the function parameter as

```
double f(double f_arg)
```

C also accepts the following function parameter declaration that makes explicit the fact that the implementation is using a pointer to represent f:

```
double (*f)(double f_arg)
```

FIGURE 13.2   Function with Pointers as Output Parameters

```
1.  #include <stdio.h>
2.
3.  void long_division(int dividend, int divisor, int *quotientp,
4.                      int *remainderp);
5.
6.  int
7.  main(void)
8.  {
9.     int quot, rem;
10.
11.    long_division(40, 3, &quot, &rem);
12.    printf("40 divided by 3 yields quotient %d ", quot);
13.    printf("and remainder %d\n", rem);
14.    return (0);
15. }
16.
17. /*
18.  *  Performs long division of two integers, storing quotient
19.  *  in variable pointed to by quotientp and remainder in
20.  *  variable pointed to by remainderp
21.  */
22. void long_division(int dividend, int divisor, int *quotientp,
23.                     int *remainderp)
24. {
25.    *quotientp = dividend / divisor;
26.    *remainderp = dividend % divisor;
27. }
```

Regardless of the way you declared f, its type would be "pointer to function taking a single type double argument and returning a type double result."

Pointers Representing Arrays and Strings

In Chapters 7 and 8, we studied how C uses pointers in its representation of array and string variables. Consider these variable declarations:

```
double nums_list[30];
char    surname[25];
```

When we wish to pass either of these arrays to a function, we use the array name with no subscript. C interprets the array name as meaning the address of the initial array element, so a whole array is always passed to a function as a pointer. For this

TABLE 13.1 Pointer Uses Already Studied

Use	Implementation
Function output parameters	1. Function formal parameter declared as a pointer type. 2. Actual parameter in a call is the address of a variable.
Arrays (strings)	1. Declaration of array variable shows array size. 2. Name of array with no subscript is a pointer: It means the address of initial array element.
File access	1. Variable declared of type `FILE *` is a pointer to a structure that is to contain access information for a file. 2. File I/O functions such as `fscanf`, `fprintf`, `fread`, and `fwrite` expect as arguments file pointers of type `FILE *`.
Function as a parameter of another function	1. Declaration may or may not include a *. 2. Name of a function alone (with no parameter list) is a pointer to the function's code.

reason, if we were passing the string `surname` to a function, the corresponding formal parameter might be declared as either

```
char n[]
```

or

```
char *n
```

Pointers to Structures

In Chapter 10, we saw that our own structure types were handled by C in exactly the same manner as built-in types. Specifically, we implemented structured output parameters as pointers to structures, and an array of structures was represented as a pointer to the first array element.

Summary of Pointer Uses

Table 13.1 summarizes the ways in which we have used pointers in earlier chapters. In addition to the uses noted above, it lists the fact that when we use program-controlled files, each file is represented as a pointer to a `FILE` structure.

EXERCISES FOR SECTION 13.1

Self-Check

1. The incomplete program below uses several pointer variables. Indicate which of the names listed are pointers, and for each pointer, note whether it is a file pointer, an output parameter, or an array.

a.	`num_list`	d.	`fracp`	g.	`denomp`
b.	`den_list`	e.	`inp`	h.	`slash`
c.	`i`	f.	`nump`	i.	`status`

```c
#include <stdio.h>
#define SIZE 15
int fscan_frac(FILE *inp, int *nump, int *denomp);

int
main(void)
{
    int num_list[SIZE], den_list[SIZE], i;
    FILE *fracp;

    fracp = fopen("fracfile.txt", "r");

    for (i = 0; i < SIZE; ++i)
        fscan_frac(fracp, &num_list[i], &den_list[i]);
    . . .
}

int
fscan_frac(FILE *inp, int *nump, int *denomp)
{
    char slash;
    int status;

    status = fscanf(inp, "%d %c%d", nump, &slash, denomp);
    if (status == 3 && slash == '/')
        status = 1;
    else if (status != EOF)
        status = 0;

    return (status);
}
```

2. In Fig. 5.19 on p. 302, the prototype of the iterative approximation function bisect was declared:

```c
double bisect(double x_left, double x_right, double epsilon,
              double f(double farg));
```

Write an alternative prototype that shows explicitly that parameter f is a function pointer.

13.2 Dynamic Memory Allocation

In this section, we meet another context in which C uses pointers—as a means of accessing a memory block allocated in response to an explicit program request. We have seen that declarations such as

```
int      *nump;
char     *letp;
planet_t *planetp;
```

allocate variables of types "pointer to `int`," "pointer to `char`," and "pointer to `planet_t`" where `planet_t` is a user-defined structure type like the one we defined in Chapter 10. If `nump`, `letp`, and `planetp` are local variables of a function, then they are allocated at the time the function block is entered, as shown in Fig. 13.3.

In order to allocate an integer variable, a character variable, and a structured `planet_t` variable dynamically, we call the C memory allocation function `malloc`, which resides in the stdlib library. This function requires a single argument, that is, a number indicating the amount of memory space needed. Applying the `sizeof` operator to the data type we plan to store in the dynamic block gives us precisely the needed number. Thus,

```
malloc(sizeof (int))
```

allocates exactly enough space to hold one type `int` value and returns a pointer to (the address of) the block allocated.

Of course, when we work with pointers in C, we always deal with a "pointer to some specific type," rather than simply a "pointer." Therefore, the data type (`void *`) of the value returned by `malloc` should always be cast to the specific type we need, such as

```
nump = (int *)malloc(sizeof (int));
letp = (char *)malloc(sizeof (char));
planetp = (planet_t *)malloc(sizeof (planet_t));
```

heap region of memory in which function `malloc` dynamically allocates blocks of storage

The result of these three assignment statements is shown in Fig. 13.4. Notice that the area in which the new memory blocks are allocated is called the **heap**. This

FIGURE 13.3

Data Area of a Function with Three Pointer-Type Local Variables

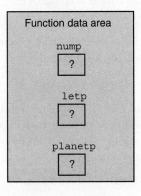

Function data area

nump

?

letp

?

planetp

?

FIGURE 13.4

Dynamic Allocation of Variables for an int, a char, and a Five-Component planet_t Structure

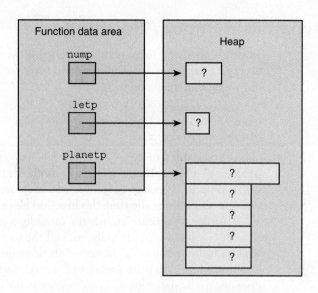

storage area is separate from the **stack**, the region of memory in which function data areas are allocated and reclaimed as functions are entered and exited.

Values may be stored in the newly allocated memory using the indirection operator (*), the same operator we used to follow pointers representing function output parameters. The statements

```
*nump = 307;
*letp = 'Q';
*planetp = blank_planet;
```

would lead to the memory snapshot in Fig. 13.5 if we assume the following declaration of `blank_planet`:

```
planet_t blank_planet = {"", 0, 0, 0, 0};
```

Accessing a Component of a Dynamically Allocated Structure

In Chapter 10, we saw that a component of a structure accessed through a pointer could be referenced using a combination of the indirection (*) and direct component selection (.) operators such as

```
(*planetp).name
```

We also met C's single operator that combines the function of these two operators. This *indirect component selection* operator is represented by the character sequence -> (a minus sign followed by a greater-than symbol). Thus, these two expressions are equivalent.

```
(*structp).component            structp->component
```

FIGURE 13.5

Assignment
of Values to
Dynamically
Allocated Variables

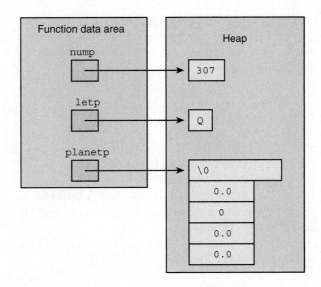

Either notation could be used to access a component of a dynamically allocated structure. We will use the more concise ->.

In Fig. 13.6 are statements that display our dynamically allocated planet (assuming the `planet_t` definition in Section 10.1).

Dynamic Array Allocation with calloc

We can use function `malloc` to allocate a single memory block of any built-in or user-defined type. To dynamically create an array of elements of any built-in or user-defined type, we use the contiguous allocation function from stdlib, `calloc`. Function `calloc` takes two arguments: The number of array elements needed and the size of one element. Function `calloc` initializes the array elements to zero. Figure 13.7 allocates and fills three arrays—an array of characters accessed through

FIGURE 13.6   Referencing Components of a Dynamically Allocated Structure

```
1.  printf("%s\n", planetp->name);
2.  printf("  Equatorial diameter:  %.0f km\n", planetp->diameter);
3.  printf("  Number of moons:  %d\n", planetp->moons);
4.  printf("  Time to complete one orbit of the sun:  %.2f years\n",
5.         planetp->orbit_time);
6.  printf("  Time to complete one rotation on axis:  %.4f hours\n",
7.         planetp->rotation_time);
```

FIGURE 13.7   Allocation of Arrays with calloc

```
1.   #include <stdlib.h>   /* gives access to calloc */
2.   int scan_planet(planet_t *plnp);
3.
4.   int
5.   main(void)
6.   {
7.        char      *string1;
8.        int       *array_of_nums;
9.        planet_t *array_of_planets;
10.       int        str_siz, num_nums, num_planets, i;
11.       printf("Enter string length and string> ");
12.       scanf("%d", &str_siz);
13.       string1 = (char *)calloc(str_siz, sizeof (char));
14.       scanf("%s", string1);
15.
16.       printf("\nHow many numbers?> ");
17.       scanf("%d", &num_nums);
18.       array_of_nums = (int *)calloc(num_nums, sizeof (int));
19.       array_of_nums[0] = 5;
20.       for (i = 1; i < num_nums; ++i)
21.            array_of_nums[i] = array_of_nums[i - 1] * i;
22.
23.       printf("\nEnter number of planets and planet data> ");
24.       scanf("%d", &num_planets);
25.       array_of_planets = (planet_t *)calloc(num_planets,
26.                                          sizeof (planet_t));
27.       for (i = 0; i < num_planets; ++i)
28.            scan_planet(&array_of_planets[i]);
29.       . . .
30.  }
```

```
Enter string length and string> 9 enormous

How many numbers?> 4

Enter number of planets and planet data> 2
Earth    12713.5 1  1.0 24.0
Jupiter 142800.0 4 11.9  9.925
```

FIGURE 13.8

Stack and Heap
After Program
Fragment in
Fig. 13.7

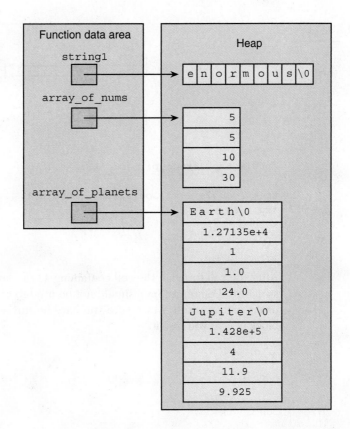

string1, an array of integers accessed through array_of_nums, and an array of planets accessed through array_of_planets. Figure 13.8 shows memory as we reach the end of the fragment in Fig. 13.7.

Returning Cells to the Heap

Execution of a call to the function free returns memory cells to the heap so they can be reused later in response to calls to calloc and malloc. For example,

```
free(letp);
```

returns to the heap the cell whose address is in letp, that is, the cell in which we stored a 'Q' (see Fig. 13.5);

```
free(planetp);
```

returns the entire structure pointed to by planetp.

Often, more than one pointer points to the same memory block. For example, the following statements result in the situation pictured in Fig. 13.9.

FIGURE 13.9

Multiple Pointers
to a Cell in the
Heap

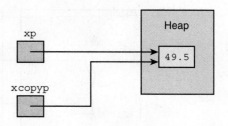

```
double *xp, *xcopyp;

xp = (double *)malloc(sizeof (double));
*xp = 49.5;
xcopyp = xp;
free(xp);
. . .
```

After the call to `free`, the cell containing `49.5` may be allocated as part of another structure. Pointer `xcopyp` should not be used to reference the cell after it is freed, or errors can result. Make sure you have no further need for a particular memory block before you free it.

 EXERCISES FOR SECTION 13.2

Self-Check

Consider Fig. 13.5. Write statements to accomplish the following:

1. Print the character accessed through `letp`.
2. Scan a new value into the location whose value is currently `307`.
3. Store the value `"Uranus"` in the name component of the structure.
4. Store in `nump` the address of a dynamically allocated array of 12 integers, and initialize all the array elements to zero.
5. Store in `letp` the address of a 30-character dynamically allocated string variable.

13.3 Linked Lists

linked list   a sequence of nodes in which each node but the last contains the address of the next node

A **linked list** is a sequence of nodes in which each node is linked, or connected, to the node following it. Linked lists are like chains of children's "pop beads," where each bead has a hole at one end and a plug at the other (see Fig. 13.10). We can connect the beads in the obvious way to form a chain and easily modify it. We can remove the color bead by disconnecting the two beads at both its

FIGURE 13.10 Children's Pop Beads in a Chain

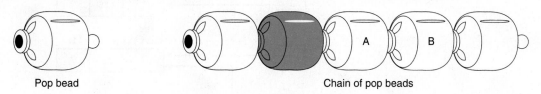

Pop bead   Chain of pop beads

ends and reattaching this pair of beads, add a new bead by connecting it to the bead at either end of the chain, or break the chain somewhere in the middle (between beads A and B) and insert a new bead by connecting one end to bead A and the other end to bead B. The following is a linked list of three nodes. In all nodes but the last, the linkp component contains the address of the next node in the list.

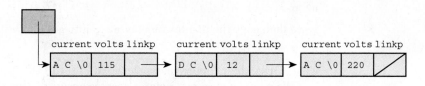

Structures with Pointer Components

To construct a dynamic linked list, we will need to use nodes that have pointer components. Because we may not know in advance how many elements will be in our lists, we can allocate storage for each node as needed and use its pointer component to connect it to the next node. A definition of a type appropriate for a node of the linked list pictured earlier is

```
typedef struct node_s {
      char            current[3];
      int             volts;
      struct node_s *linkp;
} node_t;
```

When defining a structure type in C, we have the option of including a *structure tag* such as node_s after the reserved word struct. Then the phrase struct node_s is an alternative name for type node_t. Here we use the type struct node_s * in the declaration of one component to indicate that the linkp component of our node points to another node of the same type. We use struct node_s * rather than node_t * because the compiler has not yet seen the name node_t.

FIGURE 13.11

Multiple Pointers
to the Same
Structure

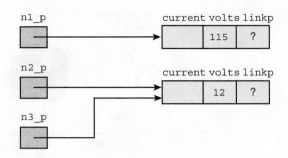

We can allocate and initialize the data components of two nodes as follows:

```
node_t *n1_p, *n2_p, *n3_p;
n1_p = (node_t *)malloc(sizeof (node_t));
strcpy(n1_p->current, "AC");
n1_p->volts = 115;
n2_p = (node_t *)malloc(sizeof (node_t));
strcpy(n2_p->current, "DC");
n2_p->volts = 12;
```

If we then copy the pointer value of `n2_p` into `n3_p`,

```
n3_p = n2_p;
```

we will have the memory values shown in Fig. 13.11.

We can compare two pointer expressions using the equality operators `==` and `!=`. The following conditions are all true for our `node_t *` variables `n1_p`, `n2_p`, and `n3_p`.

```
n1_p != n2_p    n1_p != n3_p    n2_p == n3_p
```

Connecting Nodes

One purpose of using dynamically allocated nodes is to enable us to grow data structures of varying size. We accomplish this by connecting individual nodes. If you look at the nodes allocated in the last section, you will see that their `linkp` components are undefined. Because the `linkp` components are of type `node_t *`, they can be used to store a memory cell address. The pointer assignment statement

```
n1_p->linkp = n2_p;
```

copies the address stored in `n2_p` into the `linkp` component of the node accessed through `n1_p`, thereby connecting the white and light-colored nodes as pictured in Fig. 13.12.

We now have *three* ways to access the `12` in the `volts` component of the second node: The two references that were also valid in Fig. 13.11,

```
n2_p->volts
```

and

```
n3_p->volts
```

FIGURE 13.12

Linking Two Nodes

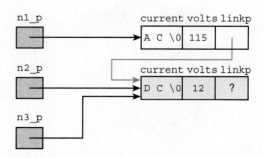

as well as one through the `linkp` pointer just assigned:

`n1_p->linkp->volts`

In Table 13.2, we analyze this third reference a section at a time.

The `linkp` component of our structure with three access paths is still undefined, so we will allocate a third node, storing its pointer in this link. Then we will initialize the new node's data components.

```
n2_p->linkp = (node_t *)malloc(sizeof (node_t));
strcpy(n2_p->linkp->current, "AC");
n2_p->linkp->volts = 220;
```

Now we have the three-node linked list shown in Fig. 13.13.

However, we still have an undefined `linkp` component at the end. Clearly, we cannot continue allocating nodes indefinitely. At some point our list must

TABLE 13.2 Analyzing the Reference n1_p->linkp->volts

Section of Reference	Meaning
n1_p->linkp	Follow the pointer in **n1_p** to a structure and select the `linkp` component.
linkp->volts	Follow the pointer in the `linkp` component to another structure and select the **volts** component.

FIGURE 13.13

Three-Node Linked List with Undefined Final Pointer

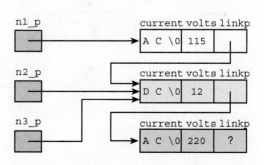

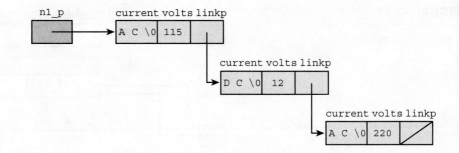

FIGURE 13.14

Three-Element
Linked List
Accessed Through
n1_p

empty list   a list of no
nodes; represented in
C by the pointer `NULL`,
whose value is `zero`

end, and we need a special value to mark the end showing that the linked list of nodes following the current node is empty. In C, the **empty list** is represented by the pointer `NULL`, which we will show in our memory diagrams as a diagonal line through a pointer variable or component. Executing the assignment

```
n2_p->linkp->linkp = NULL;
```

marks the end of the data structure pictured in Fig. 13.14, a complete linked list whose length is three. The pointer variable `n1_p` points to the first list element, or **list head**. Any function that knows this address in `n1_p` would have the ability to access every element of the list.

list head   the first
element in a linked list

Advantages of Linked Lists

A linked list is an important data structure because it can be modified easily. For example, a new node containing DC 9 can be inserted between the nodes DC 12 and AC 220 by changing only one pointer value (the one from DC 12) and setting the pointer from the new node to point to AC 220. This means of modifying a linked list works regardless of how many elements are in the list. The list shown in Fig. 13.15 is after the insertion; the new pointer values are shown in color.

Similarly, it is quite easy to delete a list element. Only one pointer value within the list must be changed, specifically, the pointer that currently points to the element

FIGURE 13.15

Linked List After
an Insertion

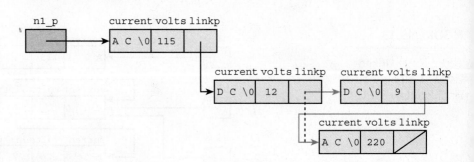

FIGURE 13.16   Linked List After a Deletion

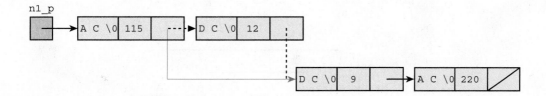

being deleted. The linked list is redrawn as is shown in Fig. 13.16 after the node containing DC 12 is deleted by changing the pointer from the node AC 115. The deleted node is effectively disconnected from the list and could be returned to the heap (if we had another pointer through which to access the node). The new list consists of AC 115, DC 9, and AC 220.

EXERCISES FOR SECTION 13.3

Self-Check

1. Here is the final linked list created in this section. What is displayed by the code fragment that follows it?

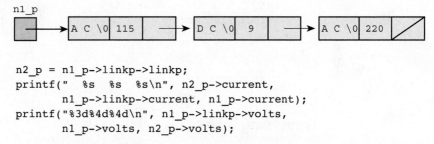

```
n2_p = n1_p->linkp->linkp;
printf("  %s  %s  %s\n", n2_p->current,
       n1_p->linkp->current, n1_p->current);
printf("%3d%4d%4d\n", n1_p->linkp->volts,
       n1_p->volts, n2_p->volts);
```

2. Complete the given code fragment so it will create a linked list containing the musical scale if the input is

```
do  re  mi  fa  sol  la  ti  do
```

```
typedef struct scale_node_s {
    char                note[4];
    struct scale_node_s *linkp;
} scale_node_t;
. . .
scale_node_t *scalep, *prevp, *newp;
int i;
```

```
scalep = (scale_node_t *)malloc(sizeof (scale_node_t));
scanf("%s", scalep->note);
prevp = scalep;
for (i = 0;  i < 7;  ++i) {

    newp = _____ ;

    scanf("%s", _____ note);

    prevp->linkp = _____ ;
    prevp = newp;
}


_____ = NULL;
```

13.4 Linked List Operators

This section and the ones that follow consider some common list-processing operations and show how to implement them using pointer variables. We assume that the structure of each list node corresponds to type `list_node_t`, declared as shown. Pointer variable `pi_fracp` points to the list head.

```
typedef struct list_node_s {
    int                 digit;
    struct list_node_s *restp;
} list_node_t;
. . .
{
    list_node_t *pi_fracp;
```

Traversing a List

In many list-processing operations, we must process each node in the list in sequence; this is called **traversing a list**. To traverse a list, we must start at the list head and follow the list pointers.

traversing a list
processing each node in a linked list in sequence, starting at the list head

One operation that we must perform on any data structure is displaying its contents. To display the contents of a list, we traverse the list and display only the values of the information components, not the pointer fields. Function `print_list` in Fig. 13.17 displays the digit component of each node in the existing list whose list head is passed as an input parameter (of type `list_node_t *`). If `pi_fracp` points to the list

pi_fracp

FIGURE 13.17   Function print_list

```
1.  /*
2.   * Displays the list pointed to by headp
3.   */
4.  void
5.  print_list(list_node_t *headp)
6.  {
7.      if (headp == NULL) {    /* simple case - an empty list          */
8.          printf("\n");
9.      } else {                /* recursive step - handles first element */
10.         printf("%d", headp->digit);  /*        leaves rest to       */
11.         print_list(headp->restp);    /*        recursion            */
12.     }
13. }
```

the function call statement

```
print_list(pi_fracp);
```

displays the output line

```
14159
```

We have chosen a linked list to store the decimal representation of the fractional part of π because this would permit us to save *many* more digits of this fraction than we could represent in an int or a double.

We observed in Chapter 9 that problems involving varying-length lists were well suited to recursive solutions, so we have written a recursive print_list. This function takes a typical recursive approach: "If there's anything in this list, I'll be happy to take care of the first element; but somebody else (i.e., another call to the function) will have to deal with the rest of the list."

Figure 13.18 compares recursive and iterative versions of print_list. The type of recursion we see in print_list is termed **tail recursion** because the recursive call is executed as the function's *last* step, if it is executed at all. Tail recursion is relatively easy to convert to iteration. Compilers for languages specifically developed for list processing even do such conversions automatically.

tail recursion any recursive call that is executed as a function's last step

Let's examine the header of the iterative version's for loop. This header makes traversing every element of a linked list as easy as a counting for loop makes processing every element of an array.

We want to begin by examining the linked list's first node, so we initialize our loop control pointer variable cur_nodep to the value of headp. We want to stay in the loop as long as there remain nodes to process, that is, as long as cur_nodep does not contain the NULL "end-of-list" pointer. Our loop control update effectively gets

FIGURE 13.18   Comparison of Recursive and Iterative List Printing

```
                        /* Displays the list pointed to by headp */
                        void
                        print_list(list_node_t *headp)
{                                      | { list_node_t *cur_nodep;
 if (headp == NULL) {/* simple case */ |
     printf("\n");                     |     for  (cur_nodep = headp; /* start at
 } else {          /* recursive step */|                            beginning */
     printf("%d", headp->digit);       |           cur_nodep != NULL; /* not at
     print_list(headp->restp);         |                         end yet    */
 }                                      |           cur_nodep = cur_nodep->restp)
}                                      |         printf("%d", cur_nodep->digit);
                                       |     printf("\n");
                                       | }
```

us to the next node of the list. Figure 13.19 shows how `cur_nodep` might appear before and after one such update.

Getting an Input List

Function `get_list` in Fig. 13.20 creates a linked list from a sequence of integers entered as input. Entry of the sentinel –1 marks the end of the data. The function's recursive algorithm recognizes the sentinel value as an empty data list and returns NULL, which is automatically converted to type `list_node_t *` upon assignment to `ansp`. Function `get_list` views a nonsentinel data item as the first value in the list it is creating, so it allocates a node and places the integer in the `digit` component. The problem is that the other component, `restp`, should point to the linked list constructed from the rest of the input. Like all good recursive algorithms, this one knows when it's time to call in an expert: It simply trusts that a function whose purpose is to form a linked list from some input data will do its job as advertised and calls `get_list` (i.e., itself) to find out the pointer value to store in `restp`.

FIGURE 13.19

Update of
List-Traversing
Loop Control
Variable

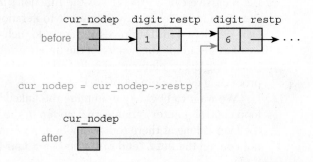

FIGURE 13.20   Recursive Function get_list

```
1.  #include <stdlib.h>  /*  gives access to malloc */
2.  #define SENT -1
3.  /*
4.   *  Forms a linked list of an input list of integers
5.   *  terminated by SENT
6.   */
7.  list_node_t *
8.  get_list(void)
9.  {
10.      int data;
11.      list_node_t *ansp;
12.
13.      scanf("%d", &data);
14.      if (data == SENT) {
15.            ansp = NULL;
16.      } else {
17.            ansp = (list_node_t *)malloc(sizeof (list_node_t));
18.            ansp->digit = data;
19.            ansp->restp = get_list();
20.      }
21.
22.      return (ansp);
23.  }
```

Figure 13.21 shows an iterative version of get_list.

Searching a List for a Target

Another common operation is searching for a target value in a list. A list search is similar to an array search in that we must examine the list elements in sequence until we find the value we are seeking or until we examine all list elements without success. The latter is indicated by advancing past the list node whose pointer field is NULL.

Function search in Fig. 13.22 returns a pointer to the first list node that contains the target value. If the target value is missing, search returns a value of NULL.

Avoid Following a NULL Pointer

Observe carefully that the order of the tests in the loop repetition condition of search is critical. If the order of the tests were reversed and if cur_nodep were NULL,

```
cur_nodep->digit != target  &&  cur_nodep != NULL
```

FIGURE 13.21   Iterative Function get_list

```
1.   /*
2.    *  Forms a linked list of an input list of integers terminated by SENT
3.    */
4.   list_node_t *
5.   get_list(void)
6.   {
7.        int data;
8.        list_node_t *ansp,
9.                    *to_fillp, /* pointer to last node in list whose
10.                                  restp component is unfilled         */
11.                   *newp;     /* pointer to newly allocated node      */
12.
13.       /* Builds first node, if there is one */
14.       scanf("%d", &data);
15.       if (data == SENT) {
16.            ansp = NULL;
17.       } else {
18.            ansp = (list_node_t *)malloc(sizeof (list_node_t));
19.            ansp->digit = data;
20.            to_fillp = ansp;
21.
22.            /* Continues building list by creating a node on each
23.               iteration and storing its pointer in the restp component of the
24.               node accessed through to_fillp */
25.            for  (scanf("%d", &data);
26.                  data != SENT;
27.                  scanf("%d", &data)) {
28.             newp = (list_node_t *)malloc(sizeof (list_node_t));
29.             newp->digit = data;
30.             to_fillp->restp = newp;
31.             to_fillp = newp;
32.            }
33.
34.            /* Stores NULL in final node's restp component */
35.            to_fillp->restp = NULL;
36.       }
37.       return (ansp);
38.  }
```

FIGURE 13.22 Function search

```
1.  /*
2.   *   Searches a list for a specified target value. Returns a pointer to
3.   *   the first node containing target if found. Otherwise returns NULL.
4.   */
5.  list_node_t *
6.  search(list_node_t *headp,    /* input - pointer to head of list */
7.            int          target)    /* input - value to search for     */
8.  {
9.      list_node_t *cur_nodep; /* pointer to node currently being checked */
10.
11.     for  (cur_nodep = headp;
12.           cur_nodep != NULL  &&  cur_nodep->digit != target;
13.           cur_nodep = cur_nodep->restp) {}
14.
15.     return (cur_nodep);
16. }
```

our program would attempt to follow the NULL pointer, an action that usually causes a run-time error. Because C always does short-circuit evaluation of logical expressions, we can be certain that in the original expression, there will be no attempt to follow cur_nodep if it is found to be NULL.

 EXERCISES FOR SECTION 13.4

Self-Check

1. Trace the execution of function search for a list that contains the three numbers 4, 1, and 5. Show the value of pointer cur_nodep after the update of each iteration of the for loop. Do this for the target values 5, 2, and 4.

Programming

1. Write a function that finds the length of a list of list_node_t nodes.
2. Write a recursive version of function search.

13.5 Representing a Stack with a Linked List

stack a list data structure in which elements are inserted in and removed from the same end, the *top* of the stack

In Chapter 7, we implemented the **stack** data structure as an array. We saw in Chapter 9 how a stack could be used to track multiple parameter and local variable values created by recursive function calls. Stacks are used extensively in computer system software such as compilers and operating systems.

FIGURE 13.23   Stack of three characters

Linked List
Representation of
Stacks

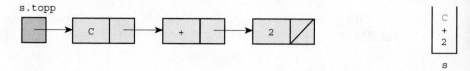

Stack after insertion (push) of   '/'

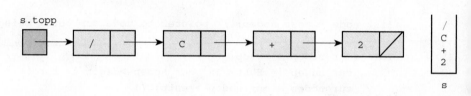

**last-in, first-out (LIFO)
structure**   a data
structure in which the
last element stored is
the first to be removed

We have seen that in a stack, elements are inserted (pushed) and removed (popped) at the same end of the list, the *top* of the stack. Since the element that is removed first is the one that has been waiting the shortest length of time, a stack is called a **last-in, first-out (LIFO)** list.

EXAMPLE 13.1

A stack can also be implemented as a linked list in which all insertions and deletions are performed at the list head. List representations of two stacks are shown on the left side of Fig. 13.23. The nodes that hold elements of the stack are typical linked list node structures with an information field plus a pointer field that points to the next node.

The stack s can be represented by a structure with a single pointer component, topp, that points to the top of the stack. The typedefs of Fig. 13.24 define such a stack type.

FIGURE 13.24   Structure Types for a Linked List Implementation of a Stack

```
1.  typedef char stack_element_t;
2.
3.  typedef struct stack_node_s {
4.       stack_element_t      element;
5.       struct stack_node_s *restp;
6.  } stack_node_t;
7.
8.  typedef struct {
9.       stack_node_t *topp;
10. } stack_t;
```

Figure 13.25 shows implementations of the functions push and pop and a driver program that first builds the stacks illustrated in Fig. 13.23 and then repeatedly pops and prints stack elements until the stack is empty.

FIGURE 13.25 Stack Manipulation with Functions push and pop

```
1.   /*
2.    *   Creates and manipulates a stack of characters
3.    */
4.
5.   #include <stdio.h>
6.   #include <stdlib.h>
7.
8.   /*  Include typedefs from Fig. 13.24 */
9.   void push(stack_t *sp, stack_element_t c);
10.  stack_element_t pop(stack_t *sp);
11.  int
12.  main(void)
13.  {
14.        stack_t s = {NULL}; /* stack of characters - initially empty */
15.
16.        /*  Builds first stack of Fig. 13.23        */
17.        push(&s, '2');
18.        push(&s, '+');
19.        push(&s, 'C');
20.
21.        /*  Completes second stack of Fig. 13.23    */
22.        push(&s, '/');
23.
24.        /* Empties stack element by element        */
25.        printf("\nEmptying stack: \n");
26.        while (s.topp != NULL) {
27.              printf("%c\n", pop(&s));
28.        }
29.
30.        return (0);
31.  }
32.
33.  /*
34.   *   The value in c is placed on top of the stack accessed through sp
35.   *   Pre:  the stack is defined
36.   */
```

(continued)

FIGURE 13.25   (continued)

```
37.  void
38.  push(stack_t        *sp, /* input/output - stack         */
39.       stack_element_t c)  /* input        - element to add */
40.  {
41.      stack_node_t *newp; /* pointer to new stack node */
42.
43.      /*  Creates and defines new node                */
44.      newp = (stack_node_t *)malloc(sizeof (stack_node_t));
45.      newp->element = c;
46.      newp->restp = sp->topp;
47.      /* Sets stack pointer to point to new node       */
48.      sp->topp = newp;
49.  }
50.
51.  /*
52.   *  Removes and frees top node of stack, returning character value
53.   *  stored there.
54.   *  Pre:  the stack is not empty
55.   */
56.  stack_element_t
57.  pop(stack_t *sp) /* input/output - stack */
58.  {
59.      stack_node_t     *to_freep;  /* pointer to node removed */
60.      stack_element_t ans;         /* value at top of stack   */
61.
62.      to_freep = sp->topp;             /* saves pointer to node being deleted  */
63.      ans = to_freep->element;         /* retrieves value to return            */
64.      sp->topp = to_freep->restp;      /* deletes top node                     */
65.      free(to_freep);                  /* deallocates space                    */
66.
67.      return (ans);
68.  }
69.
70.  Emptying stack:
71.  /
72.  C
73.  +
74.  2
```

Function push allocates a new stack node, storing the pointer to the current stack in the new node's restp component and setting the stack top to point to the new node.

EXERCISES FOR SECTION 13.5

Self-Check

1. Draw the stack resulting from execution of the following fragment. Assume you are working with a linked list implementation of a stack of individual characters, as illustrated in Fig. 13.23.

```
stack_t stk = {NULL};
push(&stk, 'a');
push(&stk, 'b');
pop(&stk);
push(&stk, 'c');
```

13.6 Representing a Queue with a Linked List

queue a list data structure in which elements are inserted at one end and removed from the other end

first-in, first-out (FIFO) structure a data structure in which the first element stored is the first to be removed

A **queue** is a data abstraction that can be used, for example, to model a line of customers waiting at a checkout counter or a stream of jobs waiting to be printed by a printer in a computer center. In a queue, new elements are inserted at one end (the rear of the queue), and existing elements are removed from the other end (the front of the queue). In this way, the element that has been waiting longest is removed first. A queue is called a **first-in, first-out (FIFO)** list.

We can implement a queue using a linked list that grows and shrinks as elements are inserted and deleted. We will need to keep track of both the first node of the linked list, which is the *front* of the queue, and the last node, which is the *rear*, since removing a node from the queue requires access to the front and adding a node requires access to the rear. In addition, we need to be able to find out the size of the queue, preferably without having to traverse the entire list-counting nodes. The `typedefs` in Fig. 13.26 define a queue type with the desired features.

FIGURE 13.26 Structure Types for a Linked List Implementation of a Queue

```
1.  /* Insert typedef for queue_element_t */
2.
3.  typedef struct queue_node_s {
4.       queue_element_t      element;
5.       struct queue_node_s *restp;
6.  } queue_node_t;
7.
8.  typedef struct {
9.       queue_node_t *frontp,
10.                   *rearp;
11.      int          size;
12.  } queue_t;
```

FIGURE 13.27

A Queue of
Passengers in a
Ticket Line

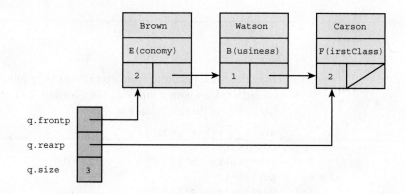

One queue we might wish to model is a line of passengers waiting to be served by a ticket agent. Figure 13.27 shows such a queue. The two primary operations required to maintain a queue are addition and removal of elements. The ability to display the queue is also helpful. Figure 13.28 shows a main function that creates and maintains a queue of passengers based on the user's input. The function's main control structure is a do-while loop to get user choices and an embedded switch statement to process each choice.

FIGURE 13.28   Creating and Maintaining a Queue

```
1.   /*
2.    *  Creates and manipulates a queue of passengers.
3.    */
4.
5.   int scan_passenger(queue_element_t *passp);
6.   void print_passenger(queue_element_t pass);
7.   void add_to_q(queue_t *qp, queue_element_t ele);
8.   queue_element_t remove_from_q(queue_t *qp);
9.   void display_q(queue_t q);
10.
11.  int
12.  main(void)
13.  {
14.       queue_t pass_q = {NULL, NULL, 0}; /* passenger queue - initialized to
15.                                            empty state */
16.       queue_element_t next_pass, fst_pass;
17.       char choice; /* user's request */
18.
19.       /* Processes requests */
20.       do {
```

(continued)

FIGURE 13.28   (continued)

```
21.          printf("Enter A(dd), R(emove), D(isplay), or Q(uit)> ");
22.          scanf(" %c", &choice);
23.          switch (toupper(choice)) {
24.          case 'A':
25.                  printf("Enter passenger data> ");
26.                  scan_passenger(&next_pass);
27.                  add_to_q(&pass_q, next_pass);
28.                  break;
29.
30.          case 'R':
31.                  if (pass_q.size > 0) {
32.                          fst_pass = remove_from_q(&pass_q);
33.                          printf("Passenger removed from queue: \n");
34.                          print_passenger(fst_pass);
35.                  } else {
36.                          printf("Queue empty - no one to delete\n");
37.                  }
38.                  break;
39.
40.          case 'D':
41.                  if (pass_q.size > 0)
42.                          display_q(pass_q);
43.                  else
44.                          printf("Queue is empty\n");
45.                  break;
46.
47.          case 'Q':
48.                  printf("Leaving passenger queue program with %d \n",
49.                          pass_q.size);
50.                  printf("passengers in the queue\n");
51.                  break;
52.
53.          default:
54.                  printf("Invalid choice -- try again\n");
55.          }
56.      } while (toupper(choice) != 'Q');
57.
58.      return (0);
59. }
```

Figure 13.29 shows functions `add_to_q` and `remove_from_q`. Because queue elements are always added at the end of the queue, `add_to_q` works primarily with the pointer `rearp`. The pointer `frontp` would be affected by an addition to the queue only if the queue were previously empty. On the other hand, elements are always removed from the front of a queue, so `remove_from_q` deals exclusively with the pointer `frontp` unless the element being removed is the only one remaining. Since queue nodes are dynamically allocated, we must explicitly free their memory when it is no longer needed. Function `remove_from_q` saves a copy of the `frontp` pointer in the variable `to_freep` before placing a new value in `frontp`. Then it uses `to_freep` to free the space allocated for the node being removed.

Figure 13.30 shows the addition of passenger Carson to a queue that already contains passengers Brown and Watson. The "After" diagram shows the changes in color. Figure 13.31 shows the removal of passenger Brown from the queue.

FIGURE 13.29 Functions add_to_q and remove_from_q

```
1.  /*
2.   *  Adds ele at the end of queue accessed through qp
3.   *  Pre:  queue is not empty
4.   */
5.  void
6.  add_to_q(queue_t          *qp,  /* input/output - queue   */
7.           queue_element_t  ele) /* input - element to add */
8.  {
9.      if (qp->size == 0) {                        /* adds to empty queue     */
10.         qp->rearp = (queue_node_t *)malloc(sizeof (queue_node_t));
11.         qp->frontp = qp->rearp;
12.     } else {                                    /* adds to nonempty queue  */
13.         qp->rearp->restp =
14.             (queue_node_t *)malloc(sizeof (queue_node_t));
15.         qp->rearp = qp->rearp->restp;
16.     }
17.     qp->rearp->element = ele;                    /* defines newly added node  */
18.     qp->rearp->restp = NULL;
19.     ++(qp->size);
20. }
21.
22. /*
23.  * Removes and frees first node of queue, returning value stored there.
24.  * Pre:  queue is not empty
25.  */
26. queue_element_t
27. remove_from_q(queue_t *qp) /* input/output - queue */
```

(continued)

FIGURE 13.29   (continued)

```
28.  {
30.      queue_node_t    *to_freep;      /* pointer to node removed          */
31.      queue_element_t  ans;           /* initial queue value which is to
32.                                          be returned                     */
33.      to_freep = qp->frontp;          /* saves pointer to node being deleted */
34.      ans = to_freep->element;        /* retrieves value to return        */
35.      qp->frontp = to_freep->restp;   /* deletes first node               */
36.      free(to_freep);                 /* deallocates space                */
37.      --(qp->size);
38.
39.      if (qp->size == 0)              /* queue's ONLY node was deleted    */
40.          qp->rearp = NULL;
41.
42.      return (ans);
43.  }
```

FIGURE 13.30

Addition of One
Passenger to a
Queue

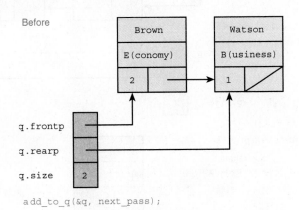

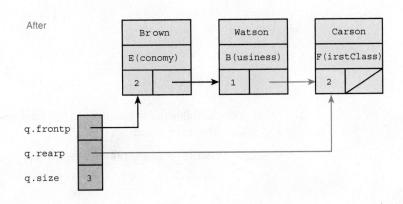

FIGURE 13.31

Removal of One
Passenger from a
Queue

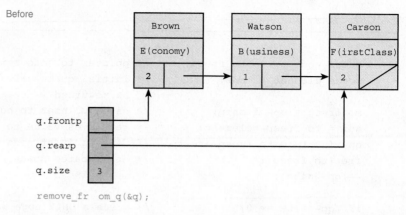

Before

remove_fr om_q(&q);

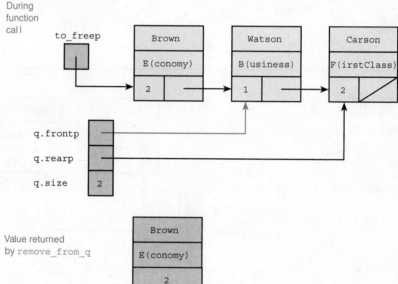

During
function
call

Value returned
by remove_from_q

 EXERCISES FOR SECTION 13.6

Self-Check

1. What does the following segment do to the final queue q, as shown in
    Fig. 13.31? Draw the result.

    ```
    queue_element_t one_pass = {"Johnson", 'E', 5};
    . . .
    ```

```
q.rearp->restp =
    (queue_node_t *)malloc(sizeof (queue_node_t));
q.rearp = q.rearp->restp;
q.rearp->element = one_pass;
q.rearp->restp = NULL;
++(q.size);
```

2. Draw the queue resulting from executing

    `one = remove_from_q(&pass_q);`

    if `pass_q` is

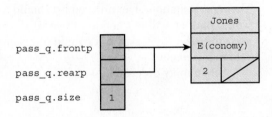

13.7 Ordered Lists

ordered list a data structure in which each element's position is determined by the value of its key component; the keys form an increasing or decreasing sequence

In queues and stacks, the time when a node was inserted in the list determines the position of the node in the list. The data in a node of an **ordered list** include a *key* component that identifies the structure (for example, an ID number). An ordered list is a list in which each node's position is determined by the value of its key component, so that the key values form an increasing or decreasing sequence as we move down the list.

Maintaining an ordered list is a problem in which linked lists are particularly helpful because of the ease with which one can insert and delete nodes without disturbing the overall list. As you might expect, we can use an ordered list to maintain a list of integers, real numbers, or airline passengers. We could modify the menu-driven program in Fig. 13.28 to maintain an ordered list of passengers instead of placing the passengers in a queue. By using the passenger's name as the key component, we would keep the list in alphabetical order. An advantage of using an ordered list is that we can delete *any* passenger from the list, whereas in a queue only the passenger at the front can be removed. Also, we can easily display the passengers in an ordered list in sequence by key field. Programming Project 1 at the end of this chapter asks you to modify the menu-driven program to use an ordered list of passenger data. We solve a simpler problem next.

CASE STUDY   Maintaining an Ordered List of Integers

PROBLEM

To illustrate some common operations on ordered lists, we will write a program that builds an ordered list of integer values by repeated insertions and then displays the size of the list and the values in the list. The next section of the program deletes values as requested, redisplaying the list after each deletion.

ANALYSIS

The representation of an ordered list should have a component to represent the list size so that we will not need to traverse all the nodes to count them whenever we need the size. Let's sketch a couple of ordered lists, and then we will specify our data requirements.

A nonempty ordered list would be

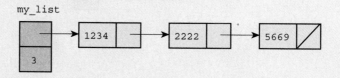

An empty ordered list would be

DATA REQUIREMENTS

Structure Types

ordered_list_t
  components:
    headp   /* pointer to first of a linked list
                              of nodes   */
    size   /* number of nodes currently in list   */

list_node_t
  components:
    key   /* integer used to determine node order   */
    restp   /* pointer to rest of linked list   */

Problem Constant

```
SENT    -999              /* sentinel value              */
```

Problem Input

```
int next_key             /* each record key             */
```

Problem Output

```
ordered_list_t my_list  /* the ordered list            */
```

DESIGN

ALGORITHM

1. Create an empty ordered list.
2. for each nonsentinel input key
      3. Insert the key in the ordered list.
4. Display the ordered list and its size.
5. for each nonsentinel input key
      6. Delete node marked by key.
      7. if deletion is successful
            8. Display the ordered list and its size.
      else
            9. Display error message.

IMPLEMENTATION

The type definitions and main function are shown in Fig. 13.32. Algorithm step 1 is accomplished through initialization of an ordered list variable at declaration. Steps 2 and 5 use typical sentinel-controlled `for` loops. Steps 6 and 7 are combined since we can design function `delete` to return as the function value a flag indicating the success or failure of its attempt to delete a node.

FUNCTIONS INSERT, DELETE, AND PRINT_LIST

Function `insert` is similar to our `add_to_queue` function in that both the size and pointer components of our ordered list structure will require modification. However, function `insert` differs from our queue functions in that we must first search our linked list of nodes for the proper place to insert. Finding the right place to insert is quite simple to conceptualize if we use a recursive approach. We use recursion in our design of helper function `insert_in_order`, the function that handles the linked list aspect of element insertion. Then function `insert` can simply increment the list size and update the value of the list head pointer with the value resulting from a call to `insert_in_order`.

FIGURE 13.32   Building an Ordered List Through Insertions and Deletions

```
1.   /*
2.    *  Program that builds an ordered list through insertions and then modifies
3.    *  it through deletions.
4.    */
5.
6.   typedef struct list_node_s {
7.         int                key;
8.         struct list_node_s *restp;
9.   } list_node_t;
10.
11.  typedef struct {
12.        list_node_t *headp;
13.        int          size;
14.  } ordered_list_t;
15.
16.  list_node_t *insert_in_order(list_node_t *old_listp, int new_key);
17.  void insert(ordered_list_t *listp, int key);
18.  int delete(ordered_list_t *listp, int target);
19.  void print_list(ordered_list_t list);
20.
21.  #define SENT -999
22.
23.  int
24.  main(void)
25.  {
26.        int             next_key;
27.        ordered_list_t my_list = {NULL, 0};
28.
29.        /* Creates list through in-order insertions */
30.        printf("Enter integer keys--end list with %d\n", SENT);
31.        for  (scanf("%d", &next_key);
32.              next_key != SENT;
33.              scanf("%d", &next_key)) {
34.           insert(&my_list, next_key);
35.        }
36.
37.        /* Displays complete list */
38.        printf("\nOrdered list before deletions:\n");
39.        print_list(my_list);
```

(continued)

FIGURE 13.32   (continued)

```
40.
41.         /* Deletes nodes as requested */
42.         printf("\nEnter a value to delete or %d to quit> ", SENT);
43.         for  (scanf("%d", &next_key);
44.               next_key != SENT;
45.               scanf("%d", &next_key)) {
46.            if (delete(&my_list, next_key)) {
47.                   printf("%d deleted. New list:\n", next_key);
48.                   print_list(my_list);
49.            } else {
50.                   printf("No deletion. %d not found\n", next_key);
51.            }
52.         }
53.
54.         return (0);
55. }
```

```
Enter integer keys--end list with -999
5  8  4  6  -999
Ordered list before deletions:
   size = 4
   list = 4
          5
          6
          8

Enter a value to delete or -999 to quit> 6
6 deleted.  New list:
   size = 3
   list = 4
          5
          8

Enter a value to delete or -999 to quit> 4
4 deleted.  New list:
   size = 2
   list = 5
          8

Enter a value to delete or -999 to quit> -999
```

Algorithm for insert_in_order

1. if the list is empty   /* simple case 1   */
    2. The new list is just a new node containing the new key and an empty
        `restp` component.
    else if the key to insert should precede   /* simple case 2   */
    the list's first node
    3. The new list is a new node containing the new key and with the old
        list as the `restp` component.
    else   /* recursive step   */
    4. The new list starts with the first value of the old list. The `restp` compo-
        nent is the rest of the old list with the new node correctly inserted.

Figure 13.33 illustrates the three possibilities, and Fig. 13.34 shows the
implementation.

FIGURE 13.33

Cases for
Recursive Function
insert_in_order

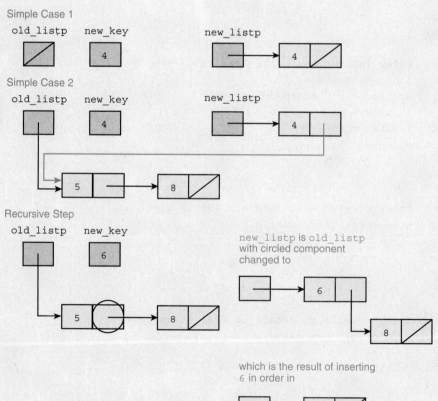

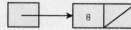

FIGURE 13.34   Function Insert and Recursive Function insert_in_order

```
1.  /*
2.   *  Inserts a new node containing new_key in order in old_list, returning as
3.   *  the function value a pointer to the first node of the new list
4.   */
5.  list_node_t *
6.  insert_in_order(list_node_t *old_listp,  /* input/output */
7.                  int          new_key)    /* input        */
8.  {
9.      list_node_t *new_listp;
10.
11.     if (old_listp == NULL) {
12.         new_listp = (list_node_t *)malloc(sizeof (list_node_t));
13.         new_listp->key = new_key;
14.         new_listp->restp = NULL;
15.     } else if (old_listp->key >= new_key) {
16.         new_listp = (list_node_t *)malloc(sizeof (list_node_t));
17.         new_listp->key = new_key;
18.         new_listp->restp = old_listp;
19.     } else {
20.         new_listp = old_listp;
21.         new_listp->restp = insert_in_order(old_listp->restp, new_key);
22.     }
23.
24.     return (new_listp);
25. }
26.
27. /*
28.  *  Inserts a node in an ordered list.
29.  */
30. void
31. insert(ordered_list_t *listp, /* input/output - ordered list */
32.        int             key)   /* input */
33. {
34.     ++(listp->size);
35.     listp->headp = insert_in_order(listp->headp, key);
36. }
```

For function `delete`, we need to traverse the list until we find the node to delete. Always on the lookout for an opportunity to reuse code previously developed and tested, we might expect that our function `search` from Fig. 13.22 would provide a good starting point. Let's consider the result of applying the algorithm of `search`'s `for` loop to our longest ordered list in search of the value 6 to delete.

```
for  (cur_nodep = headp;
       cur_nodep != NULL  &&  cur_nodep->digit != target;
       cur_nodep = cur_nodep->restp) {}
```

At loop exit, our memory status will be

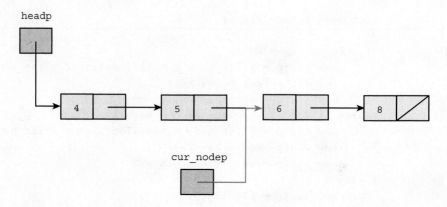

This memory status is a good news/bad news situation. The good news is that we did find the node to delete. The bad news is that we have no way of accessing the node whose `restp` component will need to be changed to carry out the deletion! Clearly, what we really need to search for is not the node we wish to delete, but rather the node that *precedes* the node we wish to delete. This immediately suggests that deleting the list's *first* node is a special case, leading us to the initial algorithm that follows.

Initial Algorithm for delete

1. if `target` is found in the list's first node
    2. Copy `headp` into `to_freep`.
    3. Change `headp` to point to rest of list.
    4. Free `to_freep`'s memory block.
    5. Decrement list size.
    6. Set `is_deleted` to 1.
    else
    7. Initialize `cur_nodep` to `frontp` and traverse list as long as the node `cur_nodep` accesses is not the last in the list, and the node after it does not contain the target.

8. if `target` is found
9. Copy the address of the node to delete into `to_freep`.
10. Move the `restp` pointer of the node being deleted into the `restp` component of the node accessed by `cur_nodep`.
11. Free `to_freep`'s memory block.
12. Decrement list size.
13. Set `is_deleted` to 1.

else

14. Set `is_deleted` to 0.

15. Return `is_deleted`.

If we trace this algorithm on a few lists, we find that this algorithm is actually a generic "delete from linked list" algorithm that does not take advantage of the fact that our list is ordered. Since the list is ordered, we actually do not always need to search all the way to the end of the list to know that our target is not present. As soon as we encounter a key greater than the target, we can give up. To do this, we need only to modify the last phrase of step 7 to read "and the node after it does not contain the target or a key greater than the target." In addition, we must add a test that allows us to handle a deletion request for an empty list. Figure 13.35 shows an implementation of this algorithm.

FIGURE 13.35 Iterative Function delete

```
1.  /*
2.   * Deletes first node containing the target key from an ordered list.
3.   * Returns 1 if target found and deleted, 0 otherwise.
4.   */
5.  int
6.  delete(ordered_list_t *listp,     /* input/output - ordered list   */
7.         int            target)     /* input - key of node to delete */
8.  {
9.      list_node_t *to_freep,        /* pointer to node to delete              */
10.                 *cur_nodep;       /* pointer used to traverse list until it
11.                                      points to node preceding node to delete */
12.      int         is_deleted;
13.
14.      /*  If list is empty, deletion is impossible              */
15.      if (listp->size == 0) {
16.          is_deleted = 0;
17.
```

(continued)

FIGURE 13.35   (continued)

```
18.      /*  If target is in first node, delete it                        */
19.      } else if (listp->headp->key == target) {
20.           to_freep = listp->headp;
21.           listp->headp = to_freep->restp;
22.           free(to_freep);
23.           --(listp->size);
24.           is_deleted = 1;
25.
26.      /* Otherwise, look for node before target node; delete target     */
27.      } else {
28.           for  (cur_nodep = listp->headp;
29.                   cur_nodep->restp != NULL && cur_nodep->restp->key < target;
30.                   cur_nodep = cur_nodep->restp) {}
31.           if (cur_nodep->restp != NULL  &&  cur_nodep->restp->key == target) {
32.                to_freep = cur_nodep->restp;
33.                cur_nodep->restp = to_freep->restp;
34.                free(to_freep);
35.                --(listp->size);
36.                is_deleted = 1;
37.           } else {
38.                is_deleted = 0;
39.           }
40.      }
41.
42.      return (is_deleted);
43.   }
```

By the time we handle all the special cases, our simple little search loop has become a fairly complex algorithm. Let's investigate to what extent writing a recursive delete_ordered_node helper function would simplify the process. Our insert_in_order helper function was quite straightforward, but then we did not have to deal with the possibility that the insertion might fail. We will pattern delete_ordered_node after insert_in_order with respect to its returning as its value a pointer to the first node of the revised list. We will also need an output parameter that is a flag indicating whether the deletion has occurred. Assuming the existence of our helper function makes delete's algorithm very simple, as shown in Fig. 13.36.

We can use the algorithm we developed for our iterative delete as a guide in identifying the cases to handle in function delete_ordered_node.

FIGURE 13.36 Function delete Using Recursive Helper Function

```
1.   /*
2.    *  Deletes first node containing the target key from an ordered list.
3.    *  Returns 1 if target found and deleted, 0 otherwise.
4.    */
5.   int
6.   delete(ordered_list_t  *listp,    /* input/output - ordered list   */
7.          int              target)   /* input - key of node to delete */
8.   {
9.        int is_deleted;
10.
11.       listp->headp = delete_ordered_node(listp->headp, target,
12.                                           &is_deleted);
13.       if (is_deleted)
14.            --(listp->size);
15.
16.       return (is_deleted);
17.  }
```

Algorithm for delete_ordered_node

1. if listp is NULL   /* simple case 1 */
   2. Set is_deleted output parameter to 0.
   3. Set ansp to NULL.
   else if first node contains target   /* simple case 2 */
   4. Set is_deleted output parameter to 1.
   5. Copy listp into to_freep.
   6. Set ansp to restp pointer of first node.
   7. Free memory block accessed by to_freep.
   else if key in first node > target key   /* simple case 3 */
   8. Set is_deleted output parameter to 0.
   9. Copy listp into ansp.
   else   /* recursive step */
   10. Copy listp into ansp.
   11. Use a recursive call to delete target from rest of list and store result in restp pointer of first node.
12. Return ansp.

Figure 13.37 shows an implementation of this algorithm. We will leave our print_list function as an exercise for you to do.

FIGURE 13.37   Recursive Helper Function delete_ordered_node

```
1.  /*
2.   *  If possible, deletes node containing target key from list whose first
3.   *  node is pointed to by listp, returning pointer to modified list and
4.   *  freeing deleted node. Sets output parameter flag to indicate whether or
5.   *  not deletion occurred.
6.   */
7.  list_node_t *
8.  delete_ordered_node(list_node_t *listp,        /* input/output - list to modify */
9.                      int         target,        /* input - key of node to delete */
10.                     int         *is_deletedp)  /* output - flag indicating
11.                                                    whether or not target node
12.                                                    found and deleted           */
13. {
14.      list_node_t *to_freep, *ansp;
15.
16.      /* if list is empty - can't find target node    - simple case 1       */
17.      if (listp == NULL) {
18.           *is_deletedp = 0;
19.           ansp = NULL;
20.
21.      /* if first node is the target, delete it       - simple case 2       */
22.      } else if (listp->key == target) {
23.           *is_deletedp = 1;
24.           to_freep = listp;
25.           ansp = listp->restp;
26.           free(to_freep);
27.
28.      /* if past the target value, give up            - simple case 3       */
29.      } else if (listp->key > target) {
30.           *is_deletedp = 0;
31.           ansp = listp;
32.
33.      /* in case target node is farther down the list,      - recursive step
34.         have recursive call modify rest of list and then return list       */
35.      } else {
36.           ansp = listp;
37.           ansp->restp = delete_ordered_node(listp->restp, target,
38.                                             is_deletedp);
39.      }
40.
41.      return (ansp);
42. }
```

EXERCISES FOR SECTION 13.7

Self-Check

1. Compare the original call to `delete_ordered_node` (from function `delete`)

```
listp->headp =
    delete_ordered_node(listp->headp, target, &is_deleted);
```

   and the recursive call to the same function

```
ansp->restp =
    delete_ordered_node(listp->restp, target, is_deletedp);
```

   Why does one call apply the address-of operator to the third argument and the other does not?
2. Modify helper function `insert_in_order` so that it will not insert a duplicate key. Use an output parameter to signal the success or failure of the insertion.

Programming

1. Write the `print_list` function called by the program in Fig. 13.32.
2. Write a function `retrieve_node` that returns a pointer to the node containing a specific key. The function should take a single `ordered_list_t` input parameter. If the desired node is not found, `retrieve_node` should return the `NULL` pointer.

13.8 Binary Trees

root node the first node in a binary tree

leaf node a binary tree node with no successors

left subtree the part of a tree pointed to by the left pointer of the root node

right subtree the part of a tree pointed to by the right pointer of the root node

We can extend the concept of linked data structures to structures containing nodes with more than one pointer field. One such structure is a *binary tree* (or *tree*) whose nodes contain two pointer fields. Because one or both pointers can have the value `NULL`, each node in a binary tree can have 0, 1, or 2 successor nodes.

Figure 13.38 shows two binary trees. For tree (a), each node stores a three-letter string. The nodes on the bottom of this tree have zero successors and are called **leaf nodes**; all other nodes have two successors. For tree (b), each node stores an integer. The nodes containing `40` and `45` have a single successor; all other nodes have no or two successors. A recursive definition of a binary tree is: A binary tree is either empty (no nodes) or it consists of a node, called the **root**, and two disjoint binary trees called its **left subtree** and **right subtree**, respectively.

In the definition for binary tree, the phrase *disjoint subtrees* means that a node cannot be in both a left and a right subtree of the same root node. For the trees shown in Fig. 13.38, the nodes containing `FOX` and `35` are the root nodes for each tree. The node containing `DOG` is the root of the left subtree of the tree whose root

FIGURE 13.38

Binary Trees

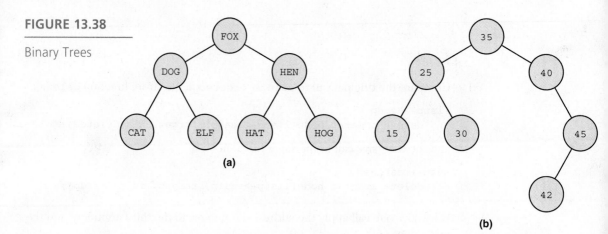

(a)

(b)

is FOX; the node containing CAT is the root of the left subtree of the tree whose root is DOG; the node containing CAT is a leaf node because both its subtrees are empty trees.

A binary tree resembles a family tree, and the relationships among its members are described using the same terminology as for a family tree. In Fig. 13.38 the node containing HEN is the *parent* of the nodes containing HAT and HOG. Similarly, the nodes containing HAT and HOG are *siblings,* because they are both *children* of the same parent node. The root of a tree is an *ancestor* of all other nodes in the tree, and they in turn are *descendants* of the root node.

For simplicity, we did not show the pointer fields in Fig. 13.38. Be aware that each node has two pointer fields and that the nodes in (b) containing integers 45 and 42 are stored as follows.

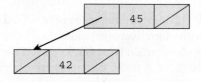

Binary Search Tree

In the rest of this section, we focus our attention on a particular kind of binary tree called a binary search tree—a tree structure that stores data in such a way that they can be retrieved very efficiently. Every item stored in a binary search tree has a unique key.

A *binary search tree* is either empty or has the property that the item in its root has a larger key than each item in its left subtree and a smaller key than each item in its right subtree. Also, its left and right subtrees must be binary search trees.

The trees in Fig. 13.38 are examples of binary search trees; each node has a single data field that is its key. For tree (a), the string stored in every node is alphabetically larger than all strings in its left subtree and alphabetically smaller than all strings in its right subtree. For tree (b), the number stored in every node is larger than all numbers in its left subtree and smaller than all numbers in its right subtree. Notice that this must be true for every node in a binary search tree, not just the root node. For example, the number 40 must be smaller than both numbers stored in its right subtree (45, 42).

Searching a Binary Search Tree

Next, we explain how to search for an item in a binary search tree. To find a particular item, say e1, we compare e1's key to the root item's key. If e1's key is smaller, we know that e1 can only be in the left subtree so we search it. If e1's key is larger, we search the root's right subtree. We now write this recursive algorithm in pseudocode; the first two cases are simple cases.

Algorithm for Searching a Binary Search Tree

1. if the tree is empty
    2. The target key is not in the tree.
   else if the target key is in the root item
    3. The target key is found in the root item.
   else if the target key is smaller than the root's key
    4. Search the left subtree.
   else
    5. Search the right subtree.

Figure 13.39 traces the search for 42 in a binary search tree containing integer keys. The pointer labeled Root indicates the root node whose key is being compared to 42 at each step. The colored arrows show the search path. The search proceeds from the top (node 35) down to the node containing 42.

Building a Binary Search Tree

Before we can retrieve an item from a binary search tree, we must, of course, build the tree. This process requires that we scan a collection of data items that is in no particular order and insert each one individually, making sure that the expanded tree is a binary search tree. A binary search tree builds from the root node down, so we must store the first data item in the root node. To store each subsequent data item, we must find the appropriate node to be its parent, attach a new node to the parent, and then store that data item in the new node.

When inserting an item, we must search the existing tree to find that item's key or to locate its parent node. If our search is successful, the item's key is already in

FIGURE 13.39   Binary Tree Search for 42

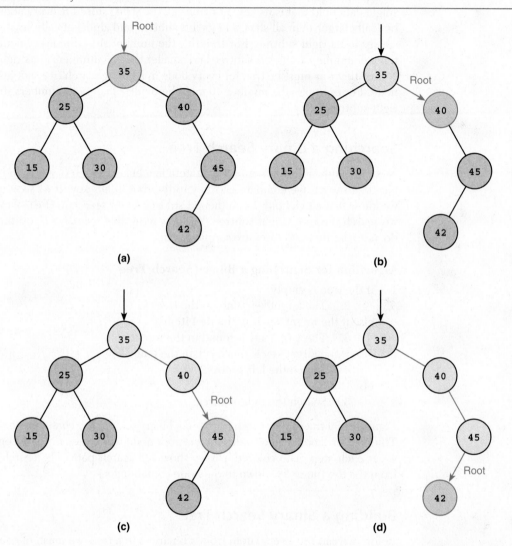

the tree, so we will not insert the item. (Duplicate keys are not allowed.) If unsuccessful, the search will terminate at the parent of the item. If the item's key is smaller than its parent's key, we attach a new node as the parent's left subtree and insert the item in this node. If the item's key is larger than its parent's key, we attach a new node as the parent's right subtree and insert the item in this node. The following recursive algorithm maintains the binary search tree property; the first two cases are simple cases.

Algorithm for Insertion in a Binary Search Tree

1. if the tree is empty
     2.   Insert the new item in the tree's root node.
    else if the root's key matches the new item's key
     3.   Skip insertion—duplicate key.
    else if the new item's key is smaller than the root's key
     4.   Insert the new item in the root's left subtree.
    else
     5.   Insert the new item in the root's right subtree.

Figure 13.40 builds a tree from the list of keys: 40, 20, 10, 50, 65, 45, 30. The search path followed when inserting each key is shown in color.

The last node inserted (bottom-right diagram) contains the key 30 and is inserted in the right subtree of node 20. Let's trace how this happens. Target key 30 is smaller than 40, so we insert 30 in the left subtree of node 40; this tree has 20 in its root. Target key 30 is greater than 20, so we insert 30 in the right subtree of node 20, an empty tree. Because node 20 has no right subtree, we allocate a new node and insert target 30 in it; the new node becomes the root of 20's right subtree.

Be aware that we would get a very different tree if we changed the order in which we inserted the keys. For example, if we inserted the keys in increasing order (10, 20, 30, . . .), each new key would be inserted in the right subtree of the previous key and all left pointers would be NULL. The resulting tree would resemble a linked list.

FIGURE 13.40   Building a Binary Search Tree

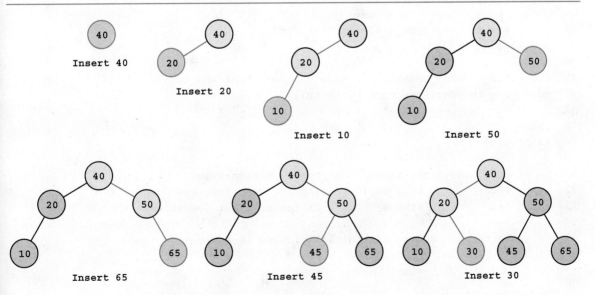

In Fig. 13.41, we show an implementation of our algorithm for insertion in a binary tree. The main function repeatedly scans integers and calls `tree_insert` to insert them in a binary search tree. In this implementation we define a macro that formalizes a standard pattern in dynamic allocation of nodes. If we are allocating a node of type `node_t`, we always cast the pointer to type `node_t *`. Using the macro

```
#define TYPED_ALLOC(type) (type *)malloc(sizeof (type))
```

we could give `nodep` the desired value simply by writing:

```
nodep = TYPED_ALLOC(node_t);
```

Function `main` displays the resulting ordered list after each insertion by calling function `tree_inorder`. Next, we study an algorithm that could be the basis of this display function.

FIGURE 13.41   Creating a Binary Search Tree

```
1.  /*
2.   *  Create and display a binary search tree of integer keys.
3.   */
4.
5.  #include <stdio.h>
6.  #include <stdlib.h>
7.
8.  #define TYPED_ALLOC(type) (type *)malloc(sizeof (type))
9.
10. typedef struct tree_node_s {
11.     int           key;
12.     struct tree_node_s *leftp, *rightp;
13. } tree_node_t;
14.
15. tree_node_t *tree_insert(tree_node_t *rootp, int new_key);
16. void tree_inorder(tree_node_t *rootp);
17.
18. int
19. main(void)
20. {
21.     tree_node_t *bs_treep;    /* binary search tree          */
22.     int          data_key;    /* input - keys for tree       */
23.     int          status;      /* status of input operation   */
24.
25.     bs_treep = NULL;   /* Initially, tree is empty */
26.
```

(continued)

FIGURE 13.41   (continued)

```
27.          /* As long as valid data remains, scan and insert keys,
28.             displaying tree after each insertion. */
29.          for  (status = scanf("%d", &data_key);
30.                status == 1;
31.                status = scanf("%d", &data_key)) {
32.             bs_treep = tree_insert(bs_treep, data_key);
33.             printf("Tree after insertion of %d:\n", data_key);
34.             tree_inorder(bs_treep);
35.          }
36.
37.          if (status == 0) {
38.                printf("Invalid data >>%c\n", getchar());
39.          } else {
40.                printf("Final binary search tree:\n");
41.                tree_inorder(bs_treep);
42.          }
43.
44.          return (0);
45. }
46.
47. /*
48.  *   Insert a new key in a binary search tree. If key is a duplicate,
49.  *   there is no insertion.
50.  *   Pre:  rootp points to the root node of a binary search tree
51.  *   Post: Tree returned includes new key and retains binary
52.  *         search tree properties.
53.  */
54. tree_node_t *
55. tree_insert(tree_node_t *rootp,    /* input/output - root node of
56.                                        binary search tree     */
57.             int          new_key) /* input - key to insert   */
58. {
59.      if (rootp == NULL) {                 /* Simple Case 1 - Empty tree  */
60.            rootp = TYPED_ALLOC(tree_node_t);
61.            rootp->key = new_key;
62.            rootp->leftp = NULL;
63.            rootp->rightp = NULL;
64.      } else if (new_key == rootp->key) {          /* Simple Case 2 */
65.            /* duplicate key - no insertion                        */
66.      } else if (new_key < rootp->key) {          /* Insert in     */
67.            rootp->leftp = tree_insert              /* left subtree  */ (continued)
```

FIGURE 13.41   (continued)

```
68.                                   (rootp->leftp, new_key);
69.        } else {                          /* Insert in right subtree */
70.            rootp->rightp = tree_insert(rootp->rightp,
71.                                      new_key);
72.        }
73.
74.        return (rootp);
75. }
```

Displaying a Binary Search Tree

To display the contents of a binary search tree so that its items are listed in order by key value, use the next recursive algorithm.

Algorithm for Displaying a Binary Search Tree

1. if the tree is not empty
    2.   Display left subtree.
    3.   Display root item.
    4.   Display right subtree.

For each node, the keys in its left subtree are displayed before the key in its root; the keys in its right subtree are displayed after the key in its root. Because the root key value lies between the key values in its left and right subtrees, the algorithm displays the items in order by key value as desired. Because the nodes' data components are displayed in order, this algorithm is also called an **inorder traversal**.

Table 13.3 traces the sequence of calls generated by the display algorithm for the last tree in Fig. 13.40. Completing the sequence of calls for the last step shown—"Display right subtree of node 40."—is left as an exercise at the end of this section. The trace so far displays the item keys in the sequence 10, 20, 30, 40.

inorder traversal
displaying the items in a binary search tree in order by key value

TABLE 13.3   Trace of Tree Display Algorithm

Display left subtree of node 40.
   Display left subtree of node 20.
      Display left subtree of node 10.
         Tree is empty—return from displaying left subtree of node 10.
      Display item with key 10.
      Display right subtree of node 10.
         Tree is empty—return from displaying right subtree of node 10.
      Return from displaying left subtree of node 20.

(continued)

TABLE 13.3   (continued)

Display item with key 2 0.

Display right subtree of node 2 0.

Display left subtree of node 3 0.

Tree is empty—return from displaying left subtree of node 3 0.

Display item with key 3 0.

Display right subtree of node 3 0.

Tree is empty—return from displaying right subtree of node 3 0.

Return from displaying right subtree of node 2 0.

Return from displaying left subtree of node 4 0.

Display item with key 4 0.

Display right subtree of node 4 0.

C IN FOCUS   VIVO 320

Videoconferencing from Your PC

Videoconferencing, which was long a feature of futuristic movies, today is one of the most rapidly growing sectors of the computer industry. The C language has played a major role in making videoconferencing an affordable and sought after technology.

In 1992 Dr. Staffan Ericsson realized that it was possible to perform all the video, audio, and communications processing necessary for videoconferencing in a high-end personal computer such as an Intel Pentium or Motorola PowerPC. This realization led him to found Vivo Software, Inc., a company that produces standards-based software that allows personal computers to serve as tools for visual communications.

It was when Ericsson, Dr. Bernd Girod, and Oliver Jones started to sort out the implementation issues that the videoconferencing project moved from the conceptual to the design phase. After buying a 486-based laptop computer and a copy of a highly efficient Watcom 32-bit C compiler, Ericsson and Girod programmed a prototype of the video compression and decompression software in about a month.

Drawing on their experience in signal processing, they used the C language as a high-level assembly language, getting the compiler to generate clever sequences of machine instructions to do the computations efficiently. Within a couple of months, the design team consisted of Mary Deshon, Ted Mina, Joseph Kluck, John Bruder, Gerry Hall, David Markun, Ericsson, and Jones.

The team anticipated difficulties in several areas. First, they knew the videoconferencing protocols required hard real-time performance and that ordinary PCs at that time would have a difficult time delivering this performance. Second, they knew that the video compression would consume as much computing power as they could dedicate to it; they were going to have to implement this part of the system extremely efficiently. Third, they knew this incredibly demanding software package would have to be Windows-friendly.

To handle the need for hard real-time processing, the team wanted to design a virtual device driver for the Windows environment. This virtual device driver needed to contain the software for handling the communications aspects of the videoconferencing system. With Markun's help, the team decided to implement the driver using the C language. Because it was

C IN FOCUS   VIVO 320 (continued)

implemented in C, the team could test and debug the 25,000 lines of code quite easily.

Throughout the development process, the C language demonstrated its strengths as a very good general-purpose language. It gave the team enough control over bits and bytes to allow them to implement international standard protocols exactly, yet had enough power and abstraction to allow large chunks of application code to be implemented rapidly. It also gave the programmers enough control over the generation of machine code to allow the development of computationally demanding algorithms. Finally, it allowed the creation of portable code. The development team not only achieved the goals of the original plan but also added many convenient user-interface features (programmed in Visual C++) to the Vivo 320 product once the basic communications and video components were working.

Today, videoconferencing is becoming an increasingly larger part of our lives. It has made possible video cellphone roaming, the online classroom, and has given smartphone users the capacity to broadcast real-time events from even the most remote locations of the world. Because of the success of the Vivo 320 design team and with recent developments in technology that have made videoconferencing more affordable, videoconferencing is no longer restricted to the world of science fiction and fantasy.

 EXERCISES FOR SECTION 13.8

Self-Check

1. Are the following trees binary search trees? Show the list of keys as they would be displayed by an inorder traversal of each tree. If these trees were binary search trees, what key values could be stored in the left subtree of the node containing key 50?

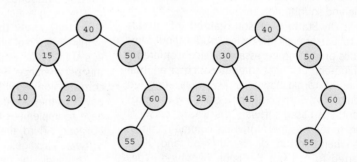

2. Complete the trace started in Table 13.3.
3. Show the binary search trees that would be created from the following lists of keys. What can you say about the binary search tree formed in parts (a) and (b)? Which of the four trees do you think would be most efficient to search? What can you say about the binary search tree formed in part (d)?

How do you think searching it would compare to searching a linked list with the same keys?

a.   25, 45, 15, 10, 60, 55, 12
b.   25, 15, 10, 45, 12, 60, 55
c.   25, 12, 10, 15, 55, 60, 45
d.   10, 12, 15, 25, 45, 55, 60

4.   What would be displayed by an inorder traversal of each tree in Question 3?

Programming

1.   Write function `tree_inorder` that is called in Fig. 13.41.

13.9   Common Programming Errors

Remember that the indirect selection operator `->` is correctly used to reference a component of a structure that is accessed through a pointer, so

`var->component`

is valid only if `var` is of a pointer-to-structure type.

There are a number of run-time errors that can occur when you are traversing linked data structures with pointers. The most common error is an attempt to follow a NULL pointer. This error can happen easily when traversing a list in a loop whose repetition condition does not explicitly check for the NULL. Any attempt to follow a pointer in an undefined variable will usually cause a run-time error as well.

Problems with heap management can also cause run-time errors. If your program gets stuck in an infinite loop while you are creating a dynamic data structure, it is possible for your program to consume all memory cells on the storage heap. This situation will lead to a `heap overflow` or `stack overflow` run-time error message.

Make sure your program does not attempt to reference a list node after the node is returned to the heap. Also, be careful to return a storage block to the heap before losing all pointers to it.

Because displaying the value of a pointer variable is not very informative, it can be difficult to debug programs that manipulate pointers. To trace the execution of such a program, you must display an information component that uniquely identifies a list element instead of displaying the pointer value itself.

When you are writing driver programs to test and debug list operators, it is often helpful to create a sample linked structure using the technique shown in Section 13.3. Use a sequence of calls to `malloc` and temporary pointer variables to allocate the individual nodes. Next, use assignment statements to define the data and pointer components of the structures.

Chapter Review

1. Function `malloc` from the stdlib library can be used to allocate single elements, or nodes, of a dynamic data structure.
2. Function `calloc` from stdlib dynamically allocates an array.
3. Function `free` from stdlib returns memory cells to the storage heap.
4. A linked list is constructed from nodes containing one or more information components and a pointer component providing access to the next list element. Linked lists can implement stacks, queues, and ordered lists.
5. A stack is a LIFO (last-in, first-out) structure in which all insertions (push operations) and deletions (pop operations) are done at the list head. Stacks have many varied uses in computer science including saving parameter lists for recursive modules and translating arithmetic expressions.
6. A queue is a FIFO (first-in, first-out) structure in which insertions are done at one end and deletions (removals) at the other. Queues are used to save lists of items waiting for the same resource (e.g., a printer).
7. A binary tree is a linked data structure in which each node has two pointer fields leading to the node's left and right subtrees. Each node in the tree belongs to either the left or right subtree of an ancestor node, but it cannot be in both subtrees of an ancestor node.
8. A binary search tree is a binary tree in which each node's key is greater than all keys in its left subtree and smaller than all keys in its right subtree.

NEW C CONSTRUCTS

Construct	Effect
Pointer Declaration	

`typedef struct node_s {`
`      int            info;`
`      struct node_s *restp;`
`} node_t;`
	The type name **node_t** is defined as a synonym of the type **struct node_s,** which is a structure containing an integer component and a component that is a pointer to another structure of the same type.

`node_t *nodep;` `int *nums;`	**nodep** is a pointer variable of type pointer to **node_t.** **nums** is a pointer variable of type pointer to **int.**
Dynamic Memory Allocation	

`nodep = (node_t *)`
`      malloc(sizeof (node_t));`
`nodep->info = 5;`
`nodep->restp = NULL;`
	A new structure of type **node_t** is allocated on the heap, and its address is stored in **nodep.** Values are stored in the new structure like this: 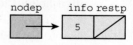

(continued)

NEW C CONSTRUCTS   (continued)

Construct	Effect
`nums = (int *)` `    calloc(10, sizeof (int));`	A new 10-element array of integers is allocated on the heap, and its starting address is stored in `nums`. The elements of the new array are all set to zero.

Memory Deallocation
`free(nodep);`
`free(nums);`
	The memory blocks accessed through the pointers `nodep` and `nums` are returned to the heap.

Pointer Assignment `nodep = nodep->restp;`	The pointer `nodep` is advanced to the next node in the dynamic data structure pointed to by `nodep`.

Quick-Check Exercises

1. Function _____ allocates storage space for a single data object that is referenced through a _____. Function _____ allocates storage space for an array of objects. Function _____ returns the storage space to the _____.

2. The area in which new memory blocks are allocated is known as the _____.

3. The C memory allocation function malloc, which resides in the stdlib library, is used to allocate a single block of memory. True or false?

4. If A and B are first inserted into a stack, then removed and inserted into a queue in the same order, what will be the order of removal from the queue?

5. Assume the following data type definition and declaration:

```
typedef struct node_s {
        int             num;
        struct node_s *restp;
} node_t;
...
node_t *headp, *cur_nodep;
```

Write a `for` loop header that causes `cur_nodep` to point in succession to each node of the linked list whose initial pointer is stored in `headp`. The loop should exit when `cur_nodep` reaches the end of the list.

6. The first element in a linked list is called the _____.

7. If a linked list contains three nodes with values "him", "her", and "its", and hp is a pointer to the list head, what is the effect of the following statements? Assume the data component of node type pro_node_t is pronoun, the link component is nextp, and np and mp are pointer variables.

```
np = hp->nextp;
strcpy(np->pronoun, "she");
```

8. Answer Exercise 7 for the following code fragment:

```
mp = hp->nextp;
np = mp->nextp;
mp->nextp = np->nextp;
free(np);
```

9. Answer Exercise 7 for the following code fragment:

```
np = hp;
hp = (pro_node_t *)malloc(sizeof (pro_node_t));
strcpy(hp->pronoun, "his");
hp->nextp = np;
```

10. Write a for loop that would place twos in the odd-numbered elements of the following dynamically allocated array:

```
nums_arr = (int *)calloc(35, sizeof (int))
```

11. If a binary search tree has an inorder traversal of 4, 5, 6, 7, 8, 9, and the root node contains 5 and has 7 as the root of its right subtree, what do we know about the order in which the numbers were inserted in this tree?

12. What is the relationship between the keys of the left child, the right child, and their parent in a binary search tree? Between the right child and the parent? Between a parent and all descendants in its left subtree?

Answers to Quick-Check Exercises

1. malloc, pointer; calloc; free, heap
2. heap
3. true
4. B, A
5. ```
   for  (cur_nodep = headp;
             cur_nodep != NULL;
             cur_nodep = cur_nodep->restp)
   ```
6. list head
7. replaces "her" with "she"
8. The third list element is deleted.
   ```

9. A new node with value "his" is inserted at the front of the list.
10.
```
for  (i = 1; i <= 35; i += 2)
     nums_arr[i] = 2;
```

11. 5 was inserted first, and 7 was inserted before 6, 8 and 9.
12. Left child < parent < right child; all descendants in left subtree < parent.

Review Questions

1. What are nodes?
2. Describe a simple linked list. Indicate how the pointers are utilized to establish a link between nodes. Also, indicate any other variables that would be needed to reference the linked list.
3. Give the missing type definitions and variable declarations and show the effect of each of the following statements. What does each do?

```
wp = (word_node_t *)malloc(sizeof (word_node_t));
strcpy(wp->word, "ABC");
wp->next = (word_node_t *)malloc(sizeof (word_node_t));
qp = wp->next;
strcpy(qp->word, "abc");
qp->next = NULL;
```

Assume the following type definitions and variable declarations for Questions 4–9.

```
typedef struct name_node_s {
    char                name[11];
    struct name_node_s *restp;
} name_node_t;

typedef struct {
    name_node_t *headp;
    int          size;
} name_list_t;
 . . .
{
    name_list_t list;
    name_node_t *np, *qp;
```

4. Write a code fragment that places the words Hello, C, and Language in successive elements of the linked list referenced by structure list. Define list.size accordingly.
5. Write a code fragment to insert the word Programming between C and Language.

6. Write a function called `delete_last` that removes the last element from any list referenced by structure `list`.

7. Write a function `place_first` that places its second parameter value as the first node of the linked list referenced by structure `list`, which is passed as the function's first argument.

8. Write a function called `copy_list` that creates a linked list (the function result) with new nodes that contain the same data as the linked list referenced by the single argument of `copy_list`.

9. Write a function that you could call to delete all nodes with name component `"Smith"` from a linked list referenced by structure `list`. The linked list and the name to delete are the function's two parameters.

10. What is meant by an ordered list? How can we overcome the problem of maintaining the ordered list?

11. Discuss the differences between a simple linked list and a binary tree. Compare, for example, the number of pointer fields per node, search techniques, and insertion algorithms.

12. Write a recursive algorithm to search for an element in a binary search tree.

Programming Projects

1. Rewrite the passenger list program whose main function is shown in Fig. 13.28 so that it uses an ordered list (alphabetized by passenger name) rather than a queue. Menu selection `'D'` (delete) should prompt for the name of the passenger to delete. In addition to the functions you write to manipulate the ordered list, you will need to write functions `scan_passenger` and `print_passenger`, which are mentioned in Fig. 13.28.

2. Rewrite the C program designed for Programming Project 1 to work with doubly linked lists. The C program must prompt the user to input two doubly linked lists and sort these lists in a descending order. Once sorted, merge the resulting two doubly linked lists into one doubly linked list.

3. Create header and implementation files (`"stack.h"` and `"stack.c"`) for a data type `stack_t` and operators for maintaining a stack of single characters. Use functions `push` and `pop`. Also, implement function `retrieve` whose header is given here:

```
/*
 * The value at the top of the stack is returned as the
 * function value. The stack is not changed.
 * Pre:  s is not empty
 */
int
retrieve(stack_t s)  /* input */
```

TABLE 13.4   Examples of Postfix Expressions

Example	Infix Expression	Value
5 6 *	5 * 6	30
5 6 1 + *	5 * (6 + 1)	35
5 6 * 9 −	(5 * 6) − 9	21
4 5 6 * 3 / +	4 + ((5 * 6) / 3)	14

4. A *postfix expression* is an expression in which each operator follows its operands. Table 13.4 shows several examples of postfix expressions.

    The grouping marks under each expression should help you visualize the operands for each operator. The more familiar *infix expression* corresponding to each postfix expression is also shown.

    The advantage of postfix form is that there is no need to group subexpressions in parentheses or to consider operator precedence. The grouping marks in Table 13.4 are only for our convenience and are not required. You may have used pocket calculators that require entry of expressions in postfix form.

    Use an adaptation of your stack library from Project 3 to write a program that simulates the operation of a calculator by scanning an integer expression in postfix form and displaying its result. Your program should push each integer operand onto the stack. When an operator is encountered, the top two operands are popped, the operation is performed on its operands, and the result is pushed back onto the stack. The final result should be the only value remaining on the stack when the end of the expression is reached.

5. Write and thoroughly test a program that creates a doubly linked list—a list in which each node contains two pointers, one to the node that follows the current node and one to the node that precedes the current one.

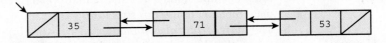

Develop functions to insert a node at the beginning of the list, at the end, and in front of a node with a designated key. Also, write a function to delete a node with a designated key and functions to display the list from any point to the end and from any point backward to the beginning.

6. Write a program to monitor the flow of an item into and out of a warehouse. The warehouse will have numerous deliveries and shipments for the item (a widget) during the time period covered. A shipment out is billed at a profit of 50% over the cost of a widget. Unfortunately, each shipment received may have a different cost associated with it. The accountants for the firm have instituted a first-in, first-out system for filling orders. This means that the oldest widgets are the first ones sent out to fill an order. This method of inventory can be represented using a queue. Each data record will consist of

S or O: Shipment received or an order to be sent
\#:   Quantity received or shipped out
Cost: Cost per widget (only for a shipment received)
Vendor: Character string that names company sent to or received from (up to 20 characters)

Write the necessary functions to store the shipments received and to process orders. The output for an order will consist of the quantity and the total cost for all the widgets in the order.

Hint: Each widget price is 50% higher than its cost. The widgets used to fill an order may come from multiple shipments with different costs.

7. Each student in the university may take a different number of courses, so the registrar has decided to use a linked list to store each student's class schedule and to use an array of structures to represent the whole student body. A portion of this data structure follows.

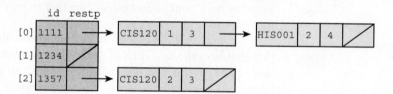

The records show that the first student (array element 0, id 1111) is taking Section 1 of CIS120 for 3 credits and Section 2 of HIS001 for 4 credits; the second student (array element 1, id 1234) is not enrolled, and so on. Define the necessary data types for creating this structure. Provide operators for creating the original array of student ID numbers, inserting a student's initial class schedule, adding a course, and dropping a course. Write a menu-driven main function to use this structure.

8. The *radix sorting algorithm* uses an array of 11 queues to simulate the operation of the old card-sorting machines. The algorithm requires that one pass be made for every digit of the numbers being sorted. For example, a list of three-digit numbers would require three passes through the list. During the first pass, the least significant digit (the ones digit) of each number is examined, and the number is added to the rear of the queue whose array subscript

matches the digit. After all numbers have been processed, the elements of each queue beginning with `queue[0]` are copied one at a time to the end of an 11th queue prior to beginning the next pass. Then, the process is repeated for the next-most significant digit (the tens digit) using the order of the numbers in the 11th queue. Finally, the process is repeated using the hundreds digit. After the final pass, the 11th queue will contain the numbers in ascending order. Write a program that implements the radix sort.

9. Write a program that takes certain given numbers as input and generates a binary search tree. Note that if a duplicate element is found, it must be neglected and must not be inserted into the tree. The output of the program must print the numbers per the inorder traversal on the constructed binary tree.

10. Write a C program that prompts the user to input two singly linked lists and sorts these lists in a descending order. Once sorted, merge the resulting two singly linked lists into one singly linked list.

11. Revise the Binary Search Tree program of Fig. 13.41 so the nodes of the tree contain both an integer key and a tree name (elm, oak, pine, etc.). After creating and displaying the tree with the associated keys and names, make a copy of the pointers to the tree nodes in an array of pointers in which each element is of type `tree_node_t *`. You will not need to do any dynamic allocation of space. Then call a function `sort_nodes` to sort the array of pointers in alphabetical order by tree name. Display the resulting list of ordered tree names and their associated keys. Follow this display with another call to `tree_inorder` to verify that your creation of the array of pointers did not alter your binary search tree.

Appendix A

MORE ABOUT POINTERS

Chapter 13 reviews the use of pointers as output and input/output parameters, function pointers, and as arrays and strings before presenting their use in dynamic memory allocation. In this appendix, we present two pointer topics not previously discussed—pointer arithmetic and a pointer to a pointer.

Pointer Arithmetic

C permits application of the addition and subtraction operators to pointer operands if the pointers reference elements of an array. If `p` is a pointer to an array element, the value of the expression

```
p + 1
```

depends entirely on the size of the memory block occupied by one array element. C guarantees that if `p` is the address of an array's nth element, then `p + 1` is the address of element n + 1.

FIGURE A.1 Pointer Arithmetic Example

```
typedef struct {
      char name[STRSIZ];
      double diameter;        /* equatorial diameter in km                    */
      int    moons;           /* number of moons                             */
      double orbit_time,      /* years to orbit sun once                     */
             rotation_time;   /* hours to complete one revolution on axis    */
} planet_t;

. . .

planet_t pl[2] = {{"Earth", 12713.5, 1, 1.0, 24.0},
                  {"Jupiter", 142800.0, 4, 11.9, 9.925}};
```

(continued)

FIGURE A.1 (continued)

```
int nm[5] = {4, 8, 10, 16, 22};
planet_t *p;
int *np;

p = pl + 1;
np = nm + 1;
printf("sizeof (planet_t) = %d        sizeof (int) = %d\n",
       sizeof (planet_t), sizeof (int));
printf("pl = %d            nm = %d\n", pl, nm);
printf(" p = %d (pl + %d)        ", p, (int)p - (int)pl);
printf("np = %d (nm + %d)\n", np, (int)np - (int)nm);
printf(" p - pl = %d\n", p - pl);
```

An example to illustrate the role of context in the evaluation of a pointer expression follows. In Fig. A.1, our example uses two arrays: pl, which is an array of planets, and nm, which is an array of integers. Figure A.2 shows the values of pointers p and np after they are assigned 1 more than pl and nm, respectively. In Fig. A.3, we see possible output produced when our example prints the contents of the four pointer variables as integers. We also see the effect of pointer subtraction on two pointers of the same type.

FIGURE A.2

Memory Snapshot at Completion of Pointer Arithmetic Example

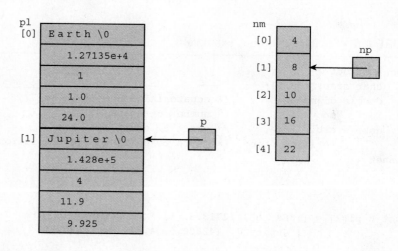

FIGURE A.3 Output from Pointer Arithmetic Example

```
sizeof (planet_t) = 48          sizeof (int) = 4
pl = 2145835092                 nm = 2145835316
 p = 2145835140 (pl + 48)       np = 2145835320 (nm + 4)
 p - pl = 1
```

Pointer to a Pointer

Since C uses pointers that are under programmer control both for output and input/output parameters and for access to dynamically allocated memory such as the nodes of a linked list, sometimes the occasion arises where a pointer variable that accesses dynamically allocated memory must be passed as an output or input/output argument to a function. Passing the address of a pointer variable creates a pointer to a pointer, a concept that requires very careful programming.

In Chapter 13, we implemented the stack data structure using a linked list. However, we hid this implementation detail from the client program by embedding the stack's top pointer in a `stack_t` structure type as illustrated below in Fig. A.4.

In Fig. A.5, we show an implementation of `push` and `pop` that uses the linked list without embedding it in a `stack_t` structure type. Since `push` and `pop` take the stack as an input/output parameter, these parameters are represented as pointers to pointers of type `stack_node_t **`. Figure A.6 illustrates the appearance of memory in the middle of the fourth call to `push` in function `main`, just prior to the last assignment statement in the code of function `push`.

FIGURE A.4 Structure Types for a Linked List Implementation of a Stack

```
typedef char stack_element_t;

typedef struct stack_node_s {
     stack_element_t       element;
     struct stack_node_s *restp;
} stack_node_t;

typedef struct {
     stack_node_t *topp;
} stack_t;
```

FIGURE A.5 Functions push and pop That Use a Linked List as a Stack

```c
/*
 *  Creates and manipulates a stack of characters implemented as
 *  a linked list of nodes
 */

#include <stdio.h>
#include <stdlib.h>

/* stack data structure and operations */
typedef char stack_element_t;

typedef struct stack_node_s {
      stack_element_t      element;
      struct stack_node_s *restp;
} stack_node_t;

void push(stack_node_t **top_stackpp, stack_element_t c);
stack_element_t pop(stack_node_t **top_stackpp);

int
main(void)
{
      stack_node_t *stackp = NULL;

      /* Builds stack of four characters */
      push(&stackp, '2');
      push(&stackp, '*');
      push(&stackp, 'C');
                              /* Figure A.6 shows memory */
      push(&stackp, '/');  /* during this call */


      /*  Empties stack element by element */
      printf("\nEmptying stack: \n");
      while (stackp != NULL) {
            printf("%c\n", pop(&stackp));
      }

      return (0);
}
```

FIGURE A.5 (continued)

```c
/*
 *  The value in c is placed on top of the stack implemented as
 *  a linked list of nodes accessed through top_stackpp
 */
void
push(stack_node_t **top_stackpp,  /* input/output - stack        */
     stack_element_t c)           /* input       - element to add */
{
      stack_node_t *newp;  /* pointer to new stack node */

      /* Creates and defines new node */
      newp = (stack_node_t *)malloc(sizeof (stack_node_t));
      newp->element = c;
      newp->restp = *top_stackpp;

      /* Sets stack top pointer to point to new node */
      *top_stackpp = newp;
}

/*
 *  Removes and frees top node of stack, returning character value
 *  stored there.
 *  Pre:  the stack is not empty
 */
stack_element_t
pop(stack_node_t **top_stackpp)    /* input/output - stack        */
{
      stack_node_t    *to_freep;  /* pointer to node removed     */
      stack_element_t ans;        /* value at top of stack       */
                                  /* saves pointer to node       */
      to_freep = *top_stackpp;            /*     being deleted     */
      ans = to_freep->element;    /* retrieves value to return   */
      *top_stackpp = to_freep->restp;  /* deletes top node        */
      free(to_freep);             /* deallocates space           */

      return (ans);
}
```

FIGURE A.6

Memory During
Use of Pointer to
Pointer

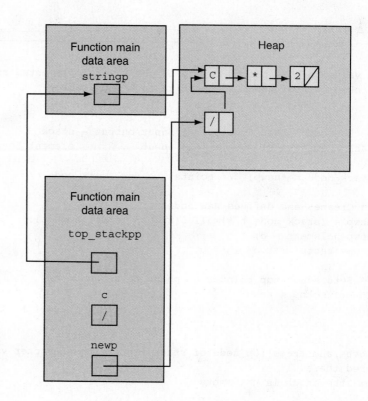

ANSI C STANDARD LIBRARIES†

LIBRARY FACILITIES ALPHABETIZED BY NAME

Syntax	Header File	Purpose
void abort(void);	stdlib.h	Abnormally terminates a program.
int abs(int x);	stdlib.h	Returns the absolute value of an integer.
double acos(double x);	math.h	Returns the arc cosine of the input value (argument must be in the range −1 to 1).
char *asctime (const struct tm *tblock);	time.h	Converts a time stored as a structure in *tblock to a 26-character string.
double asin(double x);	math.h	Returns the arc sine of the input value (argument must be in the range −1 to 1).
void assert(int test);	assert.h	If test evaluates to zero, assert prints a message on stderr and aborts the program.
double atan(double x);	math.h	Calculates the arc tangent of the input value.
double atan2(double y, double x);	math.h	Calculates the arc tangent of y/x.
int atexit(void (*func)(void));	stdlib.h	Registers a function to be called at normal program termination.
double atof(const char *s);	math.h	Converts a string pointed to by s to double.
int atoi(const char *s);	stdlib.h	Converts a string pointed to by s to int.
long int atol(const char *s);	stdlib.h	Converts a string pointed to by s to long int.

void *bsearch(const void *key,
  const void *base,
  size_t nelem, size_t[1] width,
  int (*fcmp)(const void *,
              const void *));
	stdlib.h	Binary search of the sorted array base: returns the address of the first entry in the array that matches the search key using the comparison routine *fcmp; if no match is found, returns 0.

---

†This table has been adapted from the Borland C++ Library Reference Manual with permission of Borland International, Inc.
[1]size_t is a type used for memory object sizes and repeat counts.

LIBRARY FACILITIES ALPHABETIZED BY NAME (continued)

Syntax	Header File	Purpose
`void *calloc(size_t nitems,` `          size_t size);`	`stdlib.h`	Allocates a memory block of size `nitems` × `size`, clears the block to zeros, and returns a pointer to the newly allocated block.
`double ceil(double x);`	`math.h`	Returns the smallest integer not less than `x`.
`void clearerr(FILE *stream);`	`stdio.h`	Resets `stream`'s error and end-of-file indicators to 0.
`clock_t`[2] `clock(void);`	`time.h`	Returns processor time elapsed since the beginning of program invocation.
`double cos(double x);`	`math.h`	Calculates the cosine of a value (angle in radians).
`double cosh(double x);`	`math.h`	Calculates the hyperbolic cosine of a value.
`char *ctime` `  (const time_t`[3] `*time);`	`time.h`	Converts date and time value pointed to by `time` (the value returned by function `time`) into a 26-character string representing local time.
`double difftime` `  (time_t time2, time_t time1);`	`time.h`	Calculates the difference between two times in seconds.
`div_t div(int numer,` `  int denom);`	`stdlib.h`	Divides two integers, returning quotient and remainder in a structure whose components are `quot` and `rem`.
`void exit(int status);`	`stdlib.h`	Terminates program. Before termination, all files are closed, buffered output (waiting to be output) is written, and any registered "exit functions" (posted with `atexit`) are called; status of 0 indicates normal exit; a nonzero status indicates some error.
`double exp(double x);`	`math.h`	Calculates the exponential function e^x.
`double fabs(double x);`	`math.h`	Calculates the absolute value of a floating-point number.
`int fclose(FILE *stream);`	`stdio.h`	Closes the named stream.
`int feof(FILE *stream);`	`stdio.h`	Predicate that detects end of file on a stream.
`int ferror(FILE *stream);`	`stdio.h`	Predicate that detects errors on a stream.
`int fflush(FILE *stream);`	`stdio.h`	Flushes a stream: If the stream has buffered output, `fflush` writes the output for `stream` to the associated file.
`int fgetc(FILE *stream);`	`stdio.h`	Gets a character from a stream.
`int fgetpos(FILE *stream,` `          fpos_t *pos);`	`stdio.h`	Gets the current file pointer and stores it in the location pointed to by `pos`.

[2]`clock_t` is used to represent processor time.
[3]`time_t` is used to represent calendar time.

LIBRARY FACILITIES ALPHABETIZED BY NAME (continued)

Syntax	Header File	Purpose
`char *fgets(char *s, int n,` `  FILE *stream);`	`stdio.h`	Copies characters from `stream` into the string `s` until it has read `n-1` characters or a newline character, whichever comes first. Marks the end of `s` with the null character.
`double floor(double x);`	`math.h`	Returns the largest whole number not greater than `x`.
`double fmod(double x,` `  double y);`	`math.h`	Calculates `x` modulo `y`, the remainder of `x` divided by `y`.

`FILE *fopen`
`  (const char *filename,`
`  const char *mode);`
	`stdio.h`	Opens file named by `filename` and associates a stream with it. Modes and meanings: `"r"` is read, `"w"` is write, `"a"` is append, `"r+"` is existing file update (reading and writing), `"w+"` is new file update (reading and writing), `"a+"` is update at the end of the file.

`int fprintf(FILE *stream,`
`  const char *format`
`  [, argument, ...]);`
	`stdio.h`	Writes formatted output to a stream.

`int fputc(int c, FILE *stream);`	`stdio.h`	Outputs a character to a stream.
`int fputs(const char *s,` `  FILE *stream);`	`stdio.h`	Outputs a string to a stream.

`size_t fread(void *ptr,`
`  size_t size, size_t n,`
`  FILE *stream);`
	`stdio.h`	Reads up to `n` items of data, each of length `size` bytes, from the given stream into a block pointed to by `ptr`; returns number of items read.

`void free(void *block);`	`stdlib.h`	Deallocates a memory block allocated by a previous call to `calloc`, `malloc`, or `realloc`.

`FILE *freopen`
`  (const char *filename,`
`  const char *mode,`
`  FILE *stream);`
	`stdio.h`	Associates a new file with an open stream; often used for redirecting standard streams.

`double frexp(double x,` `  int *exponent);`	`math.h`	Splits a `double` number into mantissa and exponent.

`int fscanf(FILE *stream,`
`  const char *format`
`  [, address, ...]);`
	`stdio.h`	Scans and formats input from a stream.

`int fseek(FILE *stream,` `  long int offset, int whence);`	`stdio.h`	Repositions the file pointer associated with `stream` to a new position that is `offset` bytes from the file location given by `whence`.
`int fsetpos(FILE *stream,` `  const fpos_t *pos);`	`stdio.h`	Positions the file pointer of a stream to a new position that is the value obtained by a previous call to `fgetpos` on that stream.

LIBRARY FACILITIES ALPHABETIZED BY NAME (continued)

Syntax	Header File	Purpose
`long int ftell(FILE *stream);`	`stdio.h`	Returns the current file pointer for `stream` as the number of bytes from the beginning of the file.

`size_t fwrite`
`  (const void *ptr,`
`  size_t size, size_t n,`
`  FILE *stream);`
	`stdio.h`	Writes n × `size` bytes to `stream` from the memory block pointed to by `ptr`.

`int getc(FILE *stream);`	`stdio.h`	Gets a character from `stream`.
`int getchar(void);`	`stdio.h`	Gets a character from `stdin`.
`char *getenv(const char *name);`	`stdlib.h`	Returns the value of a specified variable.
`char *gets(char *s);`	`stdio.h`	Gets a string (one line) from `stdin`; discards any newline character.
`struct tm *gmtime` `  (const time_t *timer);`	`time.h`	Converts date and time to Greenwich mean time (GMT).
`int isalnum(int c);`	`ctype.h`	Predicate returning nonzero if `c` is a letter or a decimal digit.
`int isalpha(int c);`	`ctype.h`	Predicate returning nonzero if `c` is a letter.
`int iscntrl(int c);`	`ctype.h`	Predicate returning nonzero if `c` is a delete character or an ordinary control character.
`int isdigit(int c);`	`ctype.h`	Predicate returning nonzero if `c` is a decimal digit.
`int isgraph(int c);`	`ctype.h`	Predicate returning nonzero if `c` is a printing character other than a space.
`int islower(int c);`	`ctype.h`	Predicate returning nonzero if `c` is a lowercase letter.
`int isprint(int c);`	`ctype.h`	Predicate returning nonzero if `c` is a printing character.
`int ispunct(int c);`	`ctype.h`	Predicate returning nonzero if `c` is a punctuation character.
`int isspace(int c);`	`ctype.h`	Predicate returning nonzero if `c` is a space, tab, carriage return, new line, vertical tab, or form feed.
`int isupper(int c);`	`ctype.h`	Predicate returning nonzero if `c` is an uppercase letter.
`int isxdigit(int c);`	`ctype.h`	Predicate returning nonzero if `c` is a hexadecimal digit (0 to 9, A to F, a to f).
`long int labs(long int x);`	`math.h`	Computes the absolute value of the parameter `x`.
`double ldexp(double x,` `  int exp);`	`math.h`	Calculates $x \times 2^{exp}$.

LIBRARY FACILITIES ALPHABETIZED BY NAME (continued)

Syntax	Header File	Purpose
`ldiv_t ldiv(long int numer, long int denom);`	`stdlib.h`	Divides two `long int`s, returning quotient and remainder in a structure whose components are `quot` and `rem`.
`struct lconv *localeconv(void);`	`locale.h`	Sets up country-specific monetary and other numeric formats.
`struct tm *localtime (const time_t *timer);`	`time.h`	Accepts the address of a value returned by `time` and returns a pointer to a structure of type `tm` in which the time is corrected for the time zone and possible daylight savings time.
`double log(double x);`	`math.h`	Calculates the natural logarithm of **x**.
`double log10(double x);`	`math.h`	Calculates $\log 10(x)$.
`void longjmp(jmp_buf jmpb, int retval);`	`setjmp.h`	Restores the task state captured by the last call to `setjmp` with the argument `jmpb`; then returns in such a way that `setjmp` appears to have returned with the value `retval`.
`void *malloc(size_t size);`	`stdlib.h`	Allocates a block of `size` bytes from the memory heap and returns a pointer to the newly allocated block.
`int mblen (const char *s, size_t n);`	`stdlib.h`	Returns the size in bytes of the multibyte character pointed to by **s** (**n** is the maximum size of the character).
`size_t mbstowcs(wchar_t *pwcs, const char *s, size_t n);`	`stdlib.h`	Converts up to **n** multibyte characters from string **s** to wide characters stored in array **pwcs**.
`int mbtowc(wchar_t *pwc, const char *s, size_t n);`	`stdlib.h`	Converts the multibyte character accessed by **s** to a wide character.
`void *memchr(const void *s, int c, size_t n);`	`string.h`	Searches the first **n** bytes of the block pointed to by **s** for first occurrence of character **c**.
`int memcmp(const void *s1, const void *s2, size_t n);`	`string.h`	Compares two blocks for a length of exactly **n** bytes; return value < 0 means **s1** less than **s2**, value = 0 means same as, and value > 0 means greater than.
`void *memcpy(void *dest, const void *src, size_t n);`	`string.h`	Copies a block of **n** bytes from **src** to **dest** (behavior undefined if **src** and **dest** overlap); returns **dest**.
`void *memmove(void *dest, const void *src, size_t n);`	`string.h`	Copies a block of **n** bytes from **src** to **dest** (copy is correct even if **src** and **dest** overlap); returns **dest**.
`void *memset(void *s, int c, size_t n);`	`string.h`	Sets the first **n** bytes of the array **s** to the character **c**.

LIBRARY FACILITIES ALPHABETIZED BY NAME (continued)

Syntax	Header File	Purpose
`time_t mktime(struct tm *t);`	`time.h`	Converts the time in the structure pointed to by `t` into a calendar time.
`double modf(double x, double *ipart);`	`math.h`	Splits a `double` into integer and fractional parts, both with the same sign as `x`.
`void perror(const char *s);`	`stdio.h`	Prints to the `stderr` stream the system error message for the last library routine that produced the error.
`double pow(double x, double y);`	`math.h`	Calculates x^y.
`int printf(const char *format [, argument, ...]);`	`stdio.h`	Writes formatted output to `stdout`.
`int putc(int c, FILE *stream);`	`stdio.h`	Outputs a character to `stream`.
`int putchar(int c);`	`stdio.h`	Outputs a character to `stdout`.
`int puts(const char *s);`	`stdio.h`	Outputs a string to `stdout`; terminates output by a newline character.
`void qsort(void *base, size_t nelem, size_t width, int (*fcmp)(const void *, const void *));`	`stdlib.h`	Sorts array `base` using the quicksort algorithm based on the comparison function pointed to by `fcmp`.
`int raise(int sig);`	`signal.h`	Sends a signal of type `sig` to the program. If the program has installed a signal handler for the signal type specified by `sig`, that handler will be executed.
`int rand(void);`	`stdlib.h`	Returns successive pseudorandom numbers in the range from 0 to `RAND_MAX` (constant defined in `stdlib.h`).
`void *realloc(void *block, size_t size);`	`stdlib.h`	Attempts to shrink or expand the previously allocated block to `size` bytes, copying the contents to a new location if necessary.
`int remove (const char *filename);`	`stdio.h`	Deletes the file specified by `filename`.
`int rename(const char *oldname, const char *newname);`	`stdio.h`	Changes the name of a file from `oldname` to `newname`.
`void rewind(FILE *stream);`	`stdio.h`	Repositions a file pointer to the beginning of a stream.
`int scanf(const char *format [, address, ...]);`	`stdio.h`	Scans and formats input from `stdin` stream.
`void setbuf(FILE *stream, char *buf);`	`stdio.h`	Causes the buffer `buf` to be used for I/O buffering instead of an automatically allocated buffer.
`int setjmp(jmp_buf jmpb);`	`setjmp.h`	Captures the complete task state in `jmpb` and returns 0.

LIBRARY FACILITIES ALPHABETIZED BY NAME (continued)

Syntax	Header File	Purpose
`char *setlocale(int category,` `   char *locale);`	`locale.h`	Selects a locale; if selection is successful, returns a string indicating the locale that was in effect prior to invoking the function.

`int setvbuf(FILE *stream,`
`   char *buf, int type,`
`   size_t size);`
	`stdio.h`	Causes the buffer **buf** to be used for I/O buffering instead of an automatically allocated buffer. The **type** parameter may be **_IOFBF** (fully buffered), **_IOLBF** (line buffered), or **_IONBF** (unbuffered).

`void (*signal(int sig,`
`   void (*func)(int sig)))`
`   (int);`
	`signal.h`	Specifies signal-handling actions.

`double sin(double x);`	`math.h`	Calculates the sine of the input value (angles in radians).
`double sinh(double x);`	`math.h`	Calculates hyperbolic sine.

`int sprintf(char *buffer,`
`   const char *format`
`[, argument, ...]);`
	`stdio.h`	Writes formatted output to a string.

`double sqrt(double x);`	`math.h`	Calculates the positive square root of a nonnegative input value.
`void srand(unsigned int seed);`	`stdlib.h`	Initializes random number generator.

`int sscanf(const char *buffer,`
`   const char *format`
`[, address, ...]);`
	`stdio.h`	Scans and formats input from a string.

`char *strcat(char *dest,` `   const char *src);`	`string.h`	Appends a copy of **src** to the end of **dest**; returns **dest**.
`char *strchr(const char *s,` `   int c);`	`string.h`	Returns a pointer to the first occurrence of the character **c** in the string **s** (or null).
`int strcmp(const char *s1,` `   const char *s2);`	`string.h`	Compares one string to another; return value < 0 means **s1** less than **s2**, value = 0 means same as, and value > 0 means greater than.
`int strcoll(const char *s1,` `   const char *s2);`	`string.h`	Compares two strings according to the collating sequence set by **setlocale**; return value < 0 means **s1** less than **s2**, value = 0 means same as, and value > 0 means greater than.
`char *strcpy(char *dest,` `   const char *src);`	`string.h`	Copies string **src** to **dest**, stopping after copying the terminating null character; returns **dest**.
`size_t strcspn(const char *s1,` `   const char *s2);`	`string.h`	Returns the length of the initial segment of string **s1** that consists entirely of characters *not* from string **s2**.
`char *strerror(int errnum);`	`string.h`	Returns a pointer to an error message string associated with **errnum**.

LIBRARY FACILITIES ALPHABETIZED BY NAME (continued)

Syntax	Header File	Purpose
`size_t strftime(char *s, size_t maxsize, const char *fmt, const struct tm *t);`	`time.h`	Formats time for output according to the `fmt` specifications; returns the number of characters placed into `s`.
`size_t strlen(const char *s);`	`string.h`	Returns the number of characters in `s`, not counting the null terminating character.
`char *strncat(char *dest, const char *src, size_t maxlen);`	`string.h`	Copies at most `maxlen` characters of `src` to the end of `dest` and appends a null character.
`int strncmp(const char *s1, const char *s2, size_t maxlen);`	`string.h`	Compares a portion (no more than `maxlen` characters) of one string to a portion of another; return value < 0 means portion of `s1` less than portion of `s2`, value = 0 means same as, and value > 0 means greater than.
`char *strncpy(char *dest, const char *src, size_t maxlen);`	`string.h`	Copies up to `maxlen` characters from `src` into `dest`, truncating or null-padding `dest` (which might not be null-terminated).
`char *strpbrk(const char *s1, const char *s2);`	`string.h`	Returns a pointer to the first occurrence in `s1` of any of the characters in `s2` (or returns null).
`char *strrchr(const char *s, int c);`	`string.h`	Returns a pointer to the last occurrence of the character `c` in string `s` (or returns null).
`size_t strspn(const char *s1, const char *s2);`	`string.h`	Returns the length of the initial segment of `s1` that consists entirely of characters from `s2`.
`char *strstr(const char *s1, const char *s2);`	`string.h`	Scans `s1` for the first occurrence of the substring `s2`.
`double strtod(const char *s, char **endptr);`	`stdlib.h`	Converts string `s` to a `double` value; if `endptr` is not null, it sets `*endptr` to point to the character that stopped the scan.
`char *strtok(char *s1, const char *s2);`	`string.h`	Searches `s1` for tokens, which are separated by delimiters defined in `s2`.
`long int strtol(const char *s, char **endptr, int radix);`	`stdlib.h`	Converts a string `s` to a `long int` value in the given radix; if `endptr` is not null, it sets `*endptr` to point to the character that stopped the scan.
`unsigned long int strtoul (const char *s, char **endptr, int radix);`	`stdlib.h`	Converts a string `s` to an `unsigned long int` value in the given radix; if `endptr` is not null, it sets `*endptr` to point to the character that stopped the scan.
`size_t strxfrm(char *s1, const char *s2, size_t n);`	`string.h`	Transforms strings so that `strcmp` of new strings has the same result as `strcoll` of original strings. Changes up to `n` characters of `s1`.

LIBRARY FACILITIES ALPHABETIZED BY NAME (continued)

Syntax	Header File	Purpose
`int system` `  (const char *command);`	`stdlib.h`	Executes an operating system command.
`double tan(double x);`	`math.h`	Calculates the tangent of an angle specified in radians.
`double tanh(double x);`	`math.h`	Calculates the hyperbolic tangent.
`time_t time(time_t *timer);`	`time.h`	Gives the current time, in seconds, elapsed since 00:00:00 GMT, January 1, 1970, and stores that value in the location pointed to by `timer`.
`FILE *tmpfile(void);`	`stdio.h`	Creates a temporary binary file and opens it for update.
`char *tmpnam(char *s);`	`stdio.h`	Creates a unique file name.
`int tolower(int ch);`	`ctype.h`	Converts an integer `ch` to its lowercase value. Non uppercase letter values are returned unchanged.
`int toupper(int ch);`	`ctype.h`	Converts an integer `ch` to its uppercase value. Non lowercase letter values are returned unchanged.
`int ungetc(int c,` `  FILE *stream);`	`stdio.h`	Pushes a character back into an open input stream.

`void va_start(va_list ap,`
`  lastfix);`
`type va_arg(va_list ap, type);`
`void va_end(va_list ap);`
	`stdarg.h`	Macros for implementing a variable argument list.

`int vfprintf(FILE *stream,`
`  const char *format,`
`  va_list arglist);`
	`stdio.h`	Writes formatted output to a stream: Writes the values of a series of arguments, applying the format specifiers from the format string.

`int vprintf(const char *format,` `  va_list arglist);`	`stdio.h`	Writes formatted output to `stdout`: Writes the values of a series of arguments, applying the format specifiers from the format string.

`int vsprintf(char *buffer,`
`  const char *format,`
`  va_list arglist);`
	`stdio.h`	Writes formatted output to a string: Writes the values of a series of arguments, applying the format specifiers from the format string.

`size_t wcstombs(char *s, const` `  wchar_t *pwcs, size_t n);`	`stdlib.h`	Converts a string of wide characters to a string of multibyte characters (changes no more than `n` bytes of `s`).
`int wctomb(char *s,` `  wchar_t wchar);`	`stdlib.h`	Stores in `s` the multibyte representation of wide character `wchar`.

LIBRARY FACILITIES BY HEADER FILE

assert.h
```
void assert(int test);
```

ctype.h
```
int isalnum(int c);
int isalpha(int c);
int iscntrl(int c);
int isdigit(int c);
int isgraph(int c);
int islower(int c);
int isprint(int c);
int ispunct(int c);
int isspace(int c);
int isupper(int c);
int isxdigit(int c);
int tolower(int ch);
int toupper(int ch);
```

locale.h
```
struct lconv *localeconv(void);
char *setlocale(int category, char *locale);
```

math.h
```
double acos(double x);
double asin(double x);
double atan(double x);
double atan2(double y, double x);
double atof(const char *s);
double ceil(double x);
double cos(double x);
double cosh(double x);
double exp(double x);
double fabs(double x);
double floor(double x);
double fmod(double x, double y);
double frexp(double x, int *exponent);
long int labs(long int x);
double ldexp(double x, int exp);
double log(double x);
double log10(double x);
double modf(double x, double *ipart);
double pow(double x, double y);
double sin(double x);
double sinh(double x);
double sqrt(double x);
double tan(double x);
double tanh(double x);
```

LIBRARY FACILITIES BY HEADER FILE (continued)

pthread.h
```
int pthread_create(pthread_t*, const pthread_attr_t*,
  void* (void *), void*);
int pthread_join(pthread_t, void**);
int pthread_mutex_init(pthread_mutex_t*,
  const pthread_mutexattr_t*);
int pthread_mutex_lock(pthread_mutex_t*);
int pthread_mutex_unlock(pthread_mutex_t*);
```

setjmp.h
```
void longjmp(jmp_buf jmpb, int retval);
int setjmp(jmp_buf jmpb);
```

signal.h
```
int raise(int sig);
void (*signal(int sig, void (*func)(int sig)))(int)
```

stdarg.h
```
void va_start(va_list ap, lastfix);
type va_arg(va_list ap, type);
void va_end(va_list ap);
```

stdio.h
```
void clearerr(FILE *stream);
int fclose(FILE *stream);
int feof(FILE *stream);
int ferror(FILE *stream);
int fflush(FILE *stream);
int fgetc(FILE *stream);
int fgetpos(FILE *stream, fpos_t *pos);
char *fgets(char *s, int n, FILE *stream);
FILE *fopen(const char *filename, const char *mode);
int fprintf(FILE *stream, const char *format[, argument, ...]);
int fputc(int c, FILE *stream);
int fputs(const char *s, FILE *stream);
size_t fread(void *ptr, size_t size, size_t n, FILE *stream);
FILE *freopen(const char *filename, const char *mode, FILE *stream);
int fscanf(FILE *stream, const char *format[, address, ...]);
int fseek(FILE *stream, long int offset, int whence);
int fsetpos(FILE *stream, const fpos_t *pos);
long int ftell(FILE *stream);
size_t fwrite(const void *ptr, size_t size, size_t n, FILE *stream);
int getc(FILE *stream);
int getchar(void);
char *gets(char *s);
void perror(const char *s);
int printf(const char *format[, argument, ...]);
```

LIBRARY FACILITIES BY HEADER FILE (continued)

stdio.h *(continued)*
```
int putc(int c, FILE *stream);
int putchar(int c);
stdio.h (continued)
int puts(const char *s);
int remove(const char *filename);
int rename(const char *oldname, const char *newname);
void rewind(FILE *stream);
int scanf(const char *format[, address, ...]);
void setbuf(FILE *stream, char *buf);
int setvbuf(FILE *stream, char *buf, int type, size_t size);
int sprintf(char *buffer, const char *format[, argument, ...]);
int sscanf(const char *buffer, const char *format[, address, ...]);
char *strncpy(char *dest, const char *src, size_t maxlen);
FILE *tmpfile(void);
char *tmpnam(char *s);
int ungetc(int c, FILE *stream);
int vfprintf(FILE *stream, const char *format, va_list arglist);
int vprintf(const char *format, va_list arglist);
int vsprintf(char *buffer, const char *format, va_list arglist);
```

stdlib.h
```
void abort(void);
int abs(int x);
int atexit(void (*func)(void));
int atoi(const char *s);
long int atol(const char *s);
void *bsearch(const void *key, const void *base, size_t nelem,
  size_t width, int (*fcmp)(const void *, const void *));
void *calloc(size_t nitems, size_t size);
div_t div(int numer, int denom);
void exit(int status);
void free(void *block);
char *getenv(const char *name);
ldiv_t ldiv(long int numer, long int denom);
void *malloc(size_t size);
int mblen (const char *s, size_t n);
int mbtowc(wchar_t *pwc, const char *s, size_t n);
size_t mbstowcs(wchar_t *pwcs, const char *s, size_t n);
void qsort(void *base, size_t nelem, size_t width,
  int (*fcmp)(const void *, const void *));
int rand(void);
void *realloc(void *block, size_t size);
void srand(unsigned int seed);
double strtod(const char *s, char **endptr);
```

LIBRARY FACILITIES BY HEADER FILE (continued)

stdlib.h *(continued)*

```
long int strtol(const char *s, char **endptr, int radix);
unsigned long int strtoul(const char *s, char **endptr, int radix);
int system(const char *command);
size_t wcstombs(char *s, const wchar_t *pwcs, size_t n);
int wctomb(char *s, wchar_t wchar);
```

string.h

```
void *memchr(const void *s, int c, size_t n);
int memcmp(const void *s1, const void *s2, size_t n);
void *memcpy(void *dest, const void *src, size_t n);
void *memmove(void *dest, const void *src, size_t n);
void *memset(void *s, int c, size_t n);
char *strcat(char *dest, const char *src);
char *strchr(const char *s, int c);
int strcmp(const char *s1, const char *s2);
int strcoll(const char *s1, const char *s2);
char *strcpy(char *dest, const char *src);
size_t strcspn(const char *s1, const char *s2);
char *strerror(int errnum);
size_t strlen(const char *s);
char *strncat(char *dest, const char *src, size_t maxlen);
int strncmp(const char *s1, const char *s2, size_t maxlen);
char *strpbrk(const char *s1, const char *s2);
char *strrchr(const char *s, int c);
size_t strspn(const char *s1, const char *s2);
char *strstr(const char *s1, const char *s2);
char *strtok(char *s1, const char *s2);
size_t strxfrm(char *s1, const char *s2, size_t n);
```

time.h

```
char *ctime(const time_t *time);
char *asctime(const struct tm *tblock);
clock_t clock(void);
double difftime(time_t time2, time_t time1);
struct tm *gmtime(const time_t *timer);
struct tm *localtime(const time_t *timer);
time_t mktime(struct tm *t);
size_t strftime(char *s, size_t maxsize, const char *fmt,
   const struct tm *t);
time_t time(time_t *timer);
```

unistd.h

```
int close(int);
int dup2(int, int);
int execl(const char *path, const char *file, . . ., NULL);
```

LIBRARY FACILITIES BY HEADER FILE (continued)

unistd.h *(continued)*
```
pid_t fork(void);
pid_t getpid(void);
int pipe(int[]);
size_t read(int, void*, size_t);
ssize_t write(int, void*, size_t);
```

wait.h
```
pid_t wait(int*);
```

MACRO CONSTANTS, VARIABLES, AND TYPES BY HEADER FILE

Construct by Header File	Meaning
errno.h	
EDOM	Error code for math domain error
ERANGE	Error code for result out of range
errno	Variable whose value is set to indicate type of error when an error in a system call occurs
stddef.h	
NULL	Null pointer value
ptrdiff_t	Pointer difference data type
size_t	Type used for memory object sizes and repeat counts
wchar_t	Wide-character constant type
assert.h	
NDEBUG	If defined, **assert** is a true function; otherwise, **assert** is a macro.
locale.h	
	The first argument passed to **setlocale** specifies which aspect of the locale is changed:
LC_ALL	all behavior
LC_COLLATE	behavior of **strcoll** and **strxfrm** facilities
LC_CTYPE	character-handling functions
LC_MONETARY	monetary information returned by **localeconv**
LC_NUMERIC	decimal point and nonmonetary information returned by **localeconv**
LC_TIME	behavior of **strftime** facility
NULL	When passed as second argument to **setlocale**, the function returns a pointer to a string that is the name of the current locale for the indicated category.
struct lconv	Type used to store strings that represent the settings for the current locale
math.h	
HUGE_VAL	Overflow value for **math** functions
setjmp.h	
jmp_buf	Type of buffer used to save and restore the program task state

MACRO CONSTANTS, VARIABLES, AND TYPES BY HEADER FILE (continued)

Construct by Header File	Meaning
signal.h	
sig_atomic_t	Atomic entity type
SIG_DFL	Means that a signal should receive its "default" handling, which may cause the program to terminate
SIG_IGN	Means that a signal should be ignored, no action
SIG_ERR	Means that an error code should be returned
	Each macro below stands for a standard signal:
SIGABRT	abnormal termination
SIGFPE	erroneous arithmetic operation
SIGILL	illegal computer instruction
SIGINT	interrupt or attention signal
SIGSEGV	invalid memory access
SIGTERM	a termination signal from a user or another program
stdio.h	
	Each macro below expands to values that can be used for parameter **type** in a call to **setvbuf** indicating:
_IOFBF	fully buffered file
_IOLBF	line buffered file
_IONBF	unbuffered file
BUFSIZE	Default buffer size used by **setbuf**
EOF	Indicates that the end of a file has been reached
FILE	Type used to represent file control information
FILENAME_MAX	Maximum length for a file name
FOPEN_MAX	Number of streams that may be open simultaneously (at least 8)
fpos_t	A file position type
L_tmpnam	Size of an array large enough to hold a temporary file name string
	In a call to **fseek**, the constants below indicate from which point the offset should be measured:
SEEK_CUR	from the current position
SEEK_END	from the end of the file
SEEK_SET	from the beginning of the file
size_t	Type used for memory object sizes and repeat counts
stderr	Standard error output device
stdin	Standard input device
stdout	Standard output device
TMP_MAX	Maximum number of unique file names
stdlib.h	
	Constants defining exit conditions for call to **exit** function:
EXIT_FAILURE	abnormal program termination
EXIT_SUCCESS	normal program termination
MB_CURR_MAX	Maximum number of bytes used to represent a multibyte character in the current locale
RAND_MAX	Maximum value returned by **rand** function
div_t	Integer division return type
ldiv_t	Long integer division return type

MACRO CONSTANTS, VARIABLES, AND TYPES BY HEADER FILE (continued)

Construct by Header File	Meaning
`time.h`	
`CLOCKS_PER_SEC`	The number of time units ("clock ticks") per second
`clock_t`	Type used to represent the processor time
`time_t`	Type used to represent the calendar time
`struct tm`	Structure type defining the broken-down calendar time

TABLE OF IMPLEMENTATION LIMITS

Constant	Minimum Magnitude
`limits.h`	
`CHAR_BIT`	8
`CHAR_MAX`	`UCHAR_MAX` or `SCHAR_MAX`
`CHAR_MIN`	0 or `SCHAR_MIN`
`INT_MAX`	+32767
`INT_MIN`	−32767
`LONG_MAX`	+2147483647
`LONG_MIN`	−2147483647
`MB_LEN_MAX`	1
`SCHAR_MAX`	+127
`SCHAR_MIN`	−127
`SHRT_MAX`	+32767
`SHRT_MIN`	−32767
`UCHAR_MAX`	255
`UINT_MAX`	65535
`ULONG_MAX`	4294967295
`USHRT_MAX`	65535
`float.h`	
`DBL_DIG`	10
`DBL_MANT_DIG`	
`DBL_MAX_10_EXP`	+37
`DBL_MAX_EXP`	
`DBL_MIN_10_EXP`	−37
`DBL_MIN_EXP`	
`FLT_DIG`	6
`FLT_MANT_DIG`	
`FLT_MAX_10_EXP`	+37
`FLT_MAX_EXP`	
`FLT_MIN_10_EXP`	−37
`FLT_MIN_EXP`	
`FLT_RADIX`	2
`LDBL_DIG`	10
`LDBL_MANT_DIG`	
`LDBL_MAX_10_EXP`	+37

TABLE OF IMPLEMENTATION LIMITS (continued)

Constant	Minimum Magnitude
float.h *(continued)*	
LDBL_MAX_EXP	
LDBL_MIN_10_EXP	-37
LDBL_MIN_EXP	
DBL_MAX	1E+37
FLT_MAX	1E+37
LDBL_MAX	1E+37

Constant	Maximum Value
float.h	
DBL_EPSILON	1E-9
DBL_MIN	1E-37
FLT_EPSILON	1E-5
FLT_MIN	1E-37
LDBL_EPSILON	1E-9
LDBL_MIN	1E-37

C OPERATORS

Table C.1 shows the precedence and associativity of the full range of C operators. In this table, an ellipsis (. . .) at the beginning of a group of operators indicates that these operators have equal precedence with those on the previous line. The precedence table is followed by a table listing each operator along with its name, the number of operands required, and the section of the text that explains the operator. New operators are marked by lowercase Roman numerals keyed to the descriptions following Table C.2.

TABLE C.1   Precedence and Associativity of Operations

Precedence	Operation	Associativity
highest	`a[..]   f(..)   .   ->`	left
(evaluated first)	postfix `++` postfix `--`	left
prefix `++` prefix `--` `sizeof` `~` `!`		right
`...` unary `+` unary `-` unary `&` unary `*`		
	casts	right
	`*   /   %`	left
	binary `+` binary `-`	left
	`<<   >>`	left
	`<   >   <=   >=`	left
	`==   !=`	left
	binary `&`	left
	binary `^`	left
	binary `|`	left
	`&&`	left
	`||`	left
	`?  :`	right
	`=    +=    -=    *=   /=   %=`	right
	`...  <<=   >>=   &=   ^=   |=`	
lowest	`,`	left
(evaluated last)		

TABLE C.2   Where to Find Operators in Text

Operator	Name	Number of Operands	Where Found
a[..]	subscript	2	7.1
f(..)	function call	varies	3.2
.	direct selection	2	10.1
–>	indirect selection	2	10.2
++	increment	1	5.4
––	decrement	1	5.4
sizeof	size of memory block	1	11.2
~	bitwise negation	1	App C
!	logical negation	1	4.2
&	address-of	1	6.1
*	indirection	1	6.1
	or multiplication	2	2.5
(type name)	cast	1	2.5
/	division	2	2.5
%	remainder	2	2.5
+	unary plus	1	2.5
	or addition	2	2.5
–	unary minus	1	2.5
	or subtraction	2	2.5
<<	left shift	2	App C
>>	right shift	2	App C
<	less than	2	4.2
<=	less than or equal	2	4.2
>	greater than	2	4.2
>=	greater than or equal	2	4.2
==	equality	2	4.2
!=	inequality	2	4.2
&	bitwise and	2	App C
^	bitwise xor	2	App C
|	bitwise or	2	App C
&&	logical and	2	4.2
||	logical or	2	4.2
? :	conditional	3	App C
=	assignment	2	2.3
+= –= *=	compound assignment		
/= %=	(arithmetic)	2	5.3
<<= >>=	(shifts)	2	App C
&= ^= |=	(bitwise)	2	App C
,	sequential evaluation	2	App C

Bitwise Operators

In Chapter 2, we noted that positive integers are represented in the computer by standard binary numbers. For example, on a machine where a type int value occupies 16 bits, the statement

n = 13;

would result in the following actual memory configuration:

n   0 0 0 0 0 0 0 0 0 0 0 0 1 1 0 1

Ten of the operators given in Table C.1 take operands of any integer type but treat an operand as a collection of bits rather than as a single number. These operations are described below.

(i) Bitwise negation   Application of the ~ operator to an integer produces a value in which each bit of the operand has been replaced by its negation, that is, each 0 is replaced by a 1, and each 1 is replaced by a 0. Using our n value just shown, we compute ~n as follows:

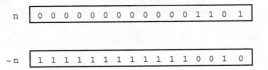

n   0 0 0 0 0 0 0 0 0 0 0 0 1 1 0 1

~n   1 1 1 1 1 1 1 1 1 1 1 1 0 0 1 0

(ii) Shift operators   The shift operators << (left) and >> (right) take two integer operands. The value of the left operand is the number to be shifted and is viewed as a collection of bits that can be moved. To avoid problems with implementation variations, it is best to use left operands that are nonnegative when right shifting. The right operand is a nonnegative number telling how far to move the bits. The << operator shifts bits left, and the >> operator shifts them right. The bits that "fall off the end" are lost, and the "emptied" positions are filled with zeros. Here are some examples:

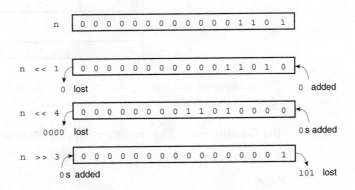

The compound assignment operators <<= and >>= cause the value resulting from the shift to be stored in the variable supplied as the left operand.

(iii) Bitwise and, xor, and or   The bitwise operators & (and), ^ (xor), and | (or) all take two integer operands that are viewed as strings of bits. The operators determine each bit of their result by considering corresponding bits of each operand. For example, if we denote the ith bit of operand n by n_i and the ith bit of operand m by m_i, then the ith bit of result r (r_i) is defined for each operator as shown in Table C.3.

TABLE C.3   Value of Each Bit of Result r for &, ^, and | with Operands n and m

Operator	Value of r_i	Explanation
&	n_i & m_i	r_i is 1 only if both corresponding operand bits are 1
^	n_i + m_i == 1	r_i is 1 only if the corresponding operand bits *do not* match
|	n_i | m_i	r_i is 1 if at least 1 of the corresponding operand bits is **1**

The following is an example of applying each operator:

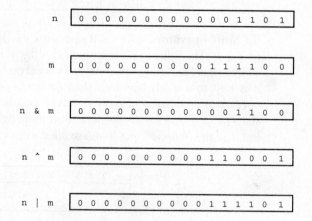

The compound assignment operators &=, ^=, and |= cause the result value to be stored in the variable supplied as the left operand.

(iv) Conditional   The conditional operator ? : takes three operands:

c ? *r1* : *r2*

The value of an expression using the conditional is the value of either its second or third operand, depending on the value of the first operand. This evaluation could be expressed in pseudocode as

if *c*
   result value is *r1*
else
   result value is *r2*

The conditional might be used in defining a macro to find the minimum of two values,

```
#define MIN(x,y) (((x) <= (y)) ? (x) : (y))
```

(v) Sequential evaluation   The comma operator , evaluates its two operands in sequence, yielding the value of the second operand as the value of the expression. The value of the first operand is discarded. Following are two examples of the comma's use. In the first example, the value of the result of the comma's application is actually used: It is assigned to x. In the second example, the comma is merely a device to allow execution of two assignments in a context where only one expression is permitted.

EXAMPLE C.1   The effect of the assignment statement

```
x = (i += 2, a[i]);
```

is the same as the effect of these two statements:

```
i += 2;
x = a[i];
```

Notice that the parentheses around the comma expression in the first version are essential since the precedence of the assignment operator is higher than the precedence of the comma. Here are "before" and "after" snapshots of memory:

Before		After	
a[0]	4.2	a[0]	4.2
[1]	12.1	[1]	12.1
[2]	6.8	[2]	6.8
[3]	10.5	[3]	10.5
i	1	i	3
x	?	x	10.5

EXAMPLE C.2   In the code fragment that follows, the two loop control variables are initialized to 0. One of these variables is incremented by 2 at the end of each loop iteration while the second variable is incremented by the new value of the first.

```
for  (i = 0, j = 0;
      i < I_MAX && j < J_MAX;
      i += 2, j += i)
    printf("i - %d, j = %d\n", i, j);
```

The comma operator should be used sparingly, since frequent use greatly increases the code's complexity from the reader's point of view.

Quick-Check Exercise

Assume that you have 16-bit int variables instruction, opcode_mask, operand1_mask, and operand2_mask whose binary values are as shown below. Trace the statements that follow, recording the resulting values of int variables opcode, operand1, and operand2.

instruction	0 1 0 1 0 0 1 1 1 0 0 1 1 1 0 1
opcode_mask	1 1 1 1 0 0 0 0 0 0 0 0 0 0 0 0
operand1_mask	0 0 0 0 1 1 1 1 1 1 0 0 0 0 0 0
operand2_mask	0 0 0 0 0 0 0 0 0 0 1 1 1 1 1 1
opcode	
operand1	
operand2	

```
opcode = instruction & opcode_mask;
opcode >>= 12;
operand1 = instruction & operand1_mask;
operand1 >>= 6;
operand2 = instruction & operand2_mask;
```

Answer to Quick-Check Exercise

opcode	0 0 0 0 0 0 0 0 0 0 0 0 0 1 0 1
operand1	0 0 0 0 0 0 0 0 0 0 0 0 1 1 1 0
operand2	0 0 0 0 0 0 0 0 0 0 0 1 1 1 0 1

CHARACTER SETS

The charts in this appendix show the following character sets: ASCII (American Standard Code for Information Interchange), EBCDIC (Extended Binary Coded Decimal Interchange Code), and CDC[†] Scientific. Only printable characters are shown. The integer code for each character is shown in decimal. For example, in ASCII, the code for "A" is 65, and the code for "z" is 122. The blank character is denoted by □.

Left Digit(s) \ Right Digit	0	1	2	3	4	5	6	7	8	9
3			□	!	"	#	$	%	&	'
4	(	)	*	+	,	−	.	/	0	1
5	2	3	4	5	6	7	8	9	:	;
6	<	=	>	?	@	A	B	C	D	E
7	F	G	H	I	J	K	L	M	N	O
8	P	Q	R	S	T	U	V	W	X	Y
9	Z	[	/	]	^	−	`	a	b	c
10	d	e	f	g	h	i	j	k	l	m
11	n	o	p	q	r	s	t	u	v	w
12	x	y	z	{			}				

ASCII (table heading)

Codes 00–31 and 127 are nonprintable control characters.

[†]CDC is a trademark of Control Data Corporation.

EBCDIC

Left Digit(s)	0	1	2	3	4	5	6	7	8	9
6					□					
7					¢	.	<	(	+	|
8	&									
9	!	$	*	)	;	¬	_	/		
10							^	,	%	—
11	>	?								
12			:	#	@	'	=	"		a
13	b	c	d	e	f	g	h	i		
14						j	k	l	m	n
15	o	p	q	r						
16			s	t	u	v	w	x	y	z
17								\	{	}
18	[	]								
19				A	B	C	D	E	F	G
20	H	I								J
21	K	L	M	N	O	P	Q	R		
22							S	T	U	V
23	W	X	Y	Z						
24	0	1	2	3	4	5	6	7	8	9

Codes 00–63 and 250–255 are nonprintable control characters.

CDC

Left Digit	0	1	2	3	4	5	6	7	8	9
0	:	A	B	C	D	E	F	G	H	I
1	J	K	L	M	N	O	P	Q	R	S
2	T	U	V	W	X	Y	Z	0	1	2
3	3	4	5	6	7	8	9	+	−	*
4	/	(	)	$	=	□	,	.	?	[
5	]	%	≠	⌐	∨	∧	↑	↓	<	>
6	≤	≥	¬	;						

ANSI C RESERVED WORDS

auto	double	int	struct
break	else	long	switch
case	enum	register	typedef
char	extern	return	union
const	float	short	unsigned
continue	for	signed	void
default	goto	sizeof	volatile
do	if	static	while

GLOSSARY

Abstract data type (ADT) A data type combined with a set of basic operations.

Abstraction The process of modeling a problem by extracting the essential variables and their relationships.

Acceptance test A system test that demonstrates that a program meets its functional requirements in a real environment.

Accumulator A variable used to store a value being computed in increments during the execution of a loop.

Activation frame Representation of one call to a function.

Actual argument An expression used inside the parentheses of a function call; its value is passed into the function and associated with the function's corresponding formal parameter.

Address of a memory cell The relative position of a memory cell in the computer's main memory.

Algorithm A list of steps for solving a problem.

Application Software used for a specific task such as word processing, accounting, or database management.

Arithmetic overflow An error that is an attempt to represent a computational result that is too large.

Arithmetic underflow An error in which a very small computational result is represented as zero.

Array A collection of data items of the same type.

Array element A data item that is part of an array.

Array subscript A value or expression enclosed in square brackets [] after the array name, specifying which array element to access.

Assembly language Mnemonic codes that correspond to machine language instructions.

Assignment statement An instruction that stores a value or a computational result in a variable.

auto Default storage class of function parameters and local variables; storage is automatically allocated on the stack at the time of a function call and deallocated when the function returns.

Background color The default color for all of the pixels in a display window.

Batch mode A mode of program execution in which the program scans its data from a previously prepared data file.

Binary file A file containing binary numbers that are the computer's internal representation of each file component.

Binary number A number made up of a sequence of the digits 0 and 1; a base-2 number.

Binary operator An operator with two operands.

Bit A binary digit—0 or 1.

Blu-ray disk High-density optical disk read with a blue-violet laser.

Booting a computer Loading the operating system from disk into memory.

Bottom-up testing The process of separately testing individual functions of a program system.

Buffer An area of memory where data to be displayed or printed is temporarily stored.

Byte The amount of storage required to store a single character.

Cancellation error An error resulting from applying an arithmetic operation to operands of vastly different magnitudes: effect of smaller operand is lost.

Cast (see type cast) Converting an expression to a different type by writing the desired type in parentheses in front of the expression.

Central processing unit (CPU) The "brain" of a computer; consists of arithmetic logic unit and control unit.

Cohesive function A function that performs a single operation.

Collating sequence A sequence of characters arranged by character numeric code number.

Command-line arguments Options specified in the statement that activates a program.

Comment Text beginning with /* and ending with */ that provides supplementary information that is ignored by the preprocessor and compiler.

Compiler Software that translates a high-level language program into machine language.

Compound statement A group of statements bracketed by { and } that are executed sequentially.

Computer A machine that can receive, store, transform, and output data of all kinds.

Computer chip (microprocessor chip) A silicon chip containing the circuitry for a computer processor.

Computer theft (computer fraud) Illegally obtaining money by falsifying information in a computer database.

Concatenation Joining of two strings.

Concurrent programming Writing sets of program instructions that can execute at the same time independently of one another.

Condition An expression that is either false (represented by 0) or true (usually represented by 1).

Constant macro   A name that is replaced by a particular constant value before the program is sent to the compiler.

Contents of memory cell   The information stored in a memory cell, either a program instruction or data.

Control structure   A combination of individual instructions into a single logical unit with one entry point and one exit point; controls which instructions are executed and in what order.

Counter-controlled loop (counting loop)   A loop whose required number of iterations can be determined before loop execution begins.

Cursor   A moving place marker that indicates the next position on the screen where information will be displayed.

Data abstraction   Separation of the logical view of a data object (*what* is stored) from the physical view (*how* the information is stored).

Data retrieval   Copying the contents of a particular memory cell to another storage area.

Data storage   Setting the individual bits of a memory cell to 0 or 1, destroying the cell's previous contents.

Data structure   A composite of related data items stored under the same name.

Data type   A set of values and of operations that can be performed on those values.

Database   A vast electronic file of information that can be quickly searched using subject headings or keywords.

Debugging   Removing errors from a program.

Decision step   An algorithm step that selects one of several actions.

Declarations   The part of a program that tells the compiler the names of memory cells used.

Digital video disk (DVD)   Silvery plastic platter with data bits packed in a tight spiral.

Direct component selection operator   A period placed between a structure type variable and a component name to create a reference to the component.

Directory   A list of the names of files stored on a disk.

Disk   A circular sheet of metal or plastic coated with a magnetic material used for secondary data storage in a computer.

Disk drive   A device used to store and retrieve information on a disk.

Double buffering   A technique used in graphics programming to reduce display flicker by allocating two buffers: The second buffer is filled while the contents of the first buffer are displayed and then the roles of each buffer are reversed.

Driver   A short function written to test another function by defining its arguments, calling it, and displaying its result.

Dynamic data structure   A structure that can expand and contract as a program executes.

Empty list   A list of no nodes; represented in C by the pointer NULL, whose value is 0.

Empty string   A string of length zero: the first character of the string is the null character.

Encapsulate   Packaging a data object and its operators together as a unit.

Enumerated type   A data type whose list of values is specified by the programmer in a type declaration.

Enumeration constant   An identifier that is one of the values of an enumerated type.

Executable statements   Program lines that are converted to machine language instructions and executed by the computer.

extern   Storage class of names known to the linker.

Extraction operator (>>)   An operator that takes values from an input stream for storage in variables.

Fetching an instruction   Retrieving an instruction from main memory.

Field width   The number of columns used to display a value.

FIFO (first-in, first-out) structure   A data structure in which the first element stored is the first to be removed.

File   A collection of related information stored on a disk.

File server   The computer in a network that controls access to a secondary device such as a hard disk.

Flag   A type `int` variable used to represent whether or not a certain event has occurred.

Flash drive   Device that plugs into USB port and stores data bits as trapped electrons.

Flowchart   A diagram that shows the step-by-step execution of a control structure.

Foreground color   The new color of pixels that are part of a graphics object in a display window.

Formal parameter   An identifier that represents a corresponding actual argument in a function definition.

Format string   In a call to `printf`, a string of characters enclosed in quotes (`""`), which specifies the form of the output line.

Function argument   Expression enclosed in parentheses following the function name in a function call; provides information needed by the function.

Function call   Code that activates a function.

Function keys   Special keyboard keys used to select a particular operation; the operation selected depends on the program being used.

Global variable   A variable that may be accessed by many functions in a program.

Graphics mode   A display mode in which a program draws graphics patterns and shapes in an output window.

Graphical user interface   Pictures and menus displayed to allow user to select commands and data.

Hand trace (desk check)   Step-by-step simulation of an algorithm's execution.

Hard disk   A disk drive that is built into the computer and normally cannot be removed.

Hardware   The computer's physical devices.

Header file Text file containing the interface information about a library needed by a compiler to translate a program system that uses the library or by a person to understand and use the library.

Heap Region of memory in which function `malloc` dynamically allocates blocks of storage.

Hierarchical structure A structure containing components that are structures.

High-level language Machine-independent programming language that combines algebraic expressions and English symbols.

Icon A picture representing a computer operation.

Implementation file File containing the C source code of a library's functions and any other information needed for compilation of these functions.

Indirect component selection operator The character sequence -> placed between a pointer variable and a component name that creates a reference that follows the pointer to a structure and selects the component.

Indirect reference Accessing the contents of a memory cell through a pointer variable that stores its address.

Infinite loop A loop that executes forever.

Information hiding Protecting the implementation details of a lower-level module from direct access by a higher-level module.

Inorder traversal Displaying the items in a binary search tree in order by key value.

Input data The data values that are scanned by a program.

Input operation An instruction that copies data from an input device into memory.

Input (output) stream Continuous stream of character codes representing textual input (or output) data.

Input/output function A C function that performs an input or output operation.

Install Make an application available on a computer by copying it from CD to the computer's hard drive.

Integrated circuit (IC) or Chip A sliver of silicon containing a large number of miniature circuits.

Integrated development environment (IDE) Software package combining a word processor, compiler, linker, loader, and tools for finding errors.

Integration test A test of the interactions among functions,.

Interactive mode A mode of program execution in which the user responds to prompts by entering (typing in) data.

Leaf node A binary tree node with no successors.

Left subtree The part of a tree pointed to by the left pointer of the root node.

Library A collection of useful functions and symbols that may be accessed by a program.

LIFO (last-in, first-out) structure A data structure in which the last element stored is the first to be removed.

Linker Software that combines object files and resolves cross-references to create an executable machine language program.

List head The first element in a linked list.

Local area network (LAN) Computers, printers, scanners, and storage devices connected by cables for inter-communication.

Logic error An error caused by following an incorrect algorithm.

Logical complement (negation) The complement of a condition has the value 1 (true) when the condition's value is 0 (false); the complement of a condition has the value 0 (false) when the condition's value is nonzero (true).

Logical expression An expression whose value is (false) or nonzero (true); may include one or more of the logical operators && (and), || (or), ! (not).

Loop A control structure that repeats a group of steps in a program.

Loop body The statements that are repeated in a loop.

Loop boundaries Initial and final values of the loop control variable.

Loop control variable The variable whose value controls loop repetition.

Loop repetition condition The condition that controls loop repetition.

Machine language Binary number codes understood by a specific CPU.

Macro Facility for naming a commonly used statement or operation.

Memory cell An individual storage location in memory.

Modem A device that converts binary data into audio signals that can be transmitted between computers over telephone lines.

Mouse An input device that moves its cursor on the computer screen to select an operation.

Multidimensional array An array with two or more dimensions.

Nested if statement An if statement with another if statement as its true task or its false task.

Newline escape sequence The character sequence \n, which is used in a format string to terminate an output line.

Nodes Dynamically allocated structures that are linked together to form a composite structure.

Null character Character "\0" that marks the end of a string in C.

Null pointer Pointer whose value is NULL.

Processor An entire CPU on a single chip.

Object file File of machine language instructions that is the output of a compiler.

Operating system (OS) Software that controls interaction of user and computer hardware and that manages allocation of computer resources.

Optical drive   Device that uses a laser to access or store data on a compact disk.

Ordered list   A data structure in which each element's position is determined by the value of its key component; the keys form an increasing or decreasing sequence.

Output operation   An instruction that displays information stored in memory.

Parallel arrays   Two or more arrays with the same number of elements used for storing related information about a collection of data objects.

Pixel   A picture element on a computer screen.

Placeholder   A symbol beginning with % in a format string that indicates where to display the output value.

Pointer   A memory cell whose content is the address of another memory cell.

Pointer variable   A memory cell that stores the address of a data item.

Pop   Remove the top element of a stack.

Postcondition   A condition assumed to be true after a function executes.

Precondition   A condition assumed to be true before a function call.

Preprocessor   A system program that modifies a C program prior to its compilation.

Preprocessor directive   A C program line beginning with # that provides an instruction to the preprocessor.

Print list   In a call to `printf`, the variables or expressions whose values are displayed.

Printer   An output device that produces a hard copy of information sent to it.

Procedural abstraction   A programming technique in which a main function consists of a sequence of function calls and each function is implemented separately.

Processor   An entire CPU on a single chip.

Program   A list of instructions that enables a computer to perform a specific task.

Program documentation   Information (comments) that enhances the readability of a program.

Program output   The lines displayed by a program.

Prompt (prompting message)   A message displayed to indicate what data to enter and in what form.

Pseudocode   A combination of English phrases and C constructs to describe algorithm steps.

Push   Insert a new element at the top of the stack.

Queue   A list data structure in which elements are inserted at one end and removed from the other end.

Random access memory (RAM)   The part of main memory that temporarily stores programs, data, and results.

Read-only memory (ROM)   The part of main memory that permanently stores programs or data.

Record   A collection of information about one data object.

Recursive function   Function that calls itself or that is part of a cycle in the sequence of function calls.

Reference parameter   A parameter into which the address of the corresponding actual argument is stored, so the function/operator can refer to the original copy of the argument.

Register   High-speed memory location inside the CPU.

`register`   Storage class of automatic variables that the programmer would like to have stored in registers.

Representational error   An error due to coding a real number as a finite number of binary digits.

Reserved word   A word that has special meaning in C.

Right subtree   The part of a tree pointed to by the right pointer of the root node.

Root (zero of a function)   A function argument value that causes the function result to be zero.

Root node   The first node in a binary tree.

Run-time error   An attempt to perform an invalid operation, detected during program execution.

Scope of a name   The region in a program where a particular meaning of a name is visible.

Secondary storage   Units such as disks or tapes that retain data even when the power to the disk drive or tape drive is off.

SeedSeed for a random number generator is an initial value used in the computation of the first random number.

Selection control structure   A control structure that chooses among alternative program statements.

Sentinel value   An end marker that follows the last item in a list of data.

Short-circuit evaluation Stopping evaluation of a logical expression as soon as its value can be determined.

Side effect   A change in the value of a variable as a result of carrying out an operation.

Simple case   Problem case for which a straightforward solution is known.

Single buffering   The default case for graphics mode in which only one buffer is allocated.

`sizeof`   Operator that finds the number of bytes used for storage of a data type.

Software   The set of programs associated with a computer.

Software piracy   Violating copyright agreements by illegally copying software for use in another computer.

Source file   File containing a program written in a high-level language; the input for a compiler.

Stack   A data structure in which the last data item added is the first data item processed.

Standard identifier   A word having special meaning but one that a programmer may redefine (but redefinition is not recommended!).

`static`   Storage class of variables allocated only once, prior to program execution.

`stdin`   System file pointer for keyboard's input stream.

`stdout`, `stderr`   System file pointers for screen's output stream.

Stepwise refinement   Development of a detailed list of steps to solve a particular step in the original algorithm.

Stored program concept   Computer's ability to store program instructions in main memory for execution.

String length   In a character array, the number of characters before the first null character.

Structure chart   A documentation tool that shows the relationships among the subproblems of a problem.

Structure type   A data type for a record composed of multiple components.

Stub   A skeleton function that consists of a header and statements that display trace messages and assign values to output parameters; enables testing of the flow of control among functions before this function is completed.

Subdirectory   A list of the names of files that relate to a particular topic.

Subscripted variable   A variable followed by a subscript in brackets, designating an array element.

Substring   A fragment of a longer string.

Syntax   Grammar rules of a programming language.

Syntax error   A violation of the programming language's grammar rules, detected during program translation (compilation).

System stack   Area of memory where parameters and local variables are allocated when a function is called and deallocated when the function returns.

System test   A test of a whole program in the software/hardware context in which it will be used.

Tail recursion   Any recursive call that is executed as a function's last step.

Terminating condition   A condition that is true when a recursive algorithm is processing a simple case.

Text file   A named collection of characters saved in secondary storage.

Text mode   A display mode in which a program displays only characters.

Top-down design   A problem-solving method in which you first break a problem into its major subproblems and then solve the subproblems to derive the solution to the original problem.

Traversing a list   Processing each node in a linked list in sequence, starting at the list head.

Unary operator   An operator with one operand.

union   A data structure that overlays components in memory, allowing one chunk of memory to be interpreted in multiple ways.

Unit testing   A test of an individual function.

Value parameter   A parameter into which the value of the corresponding actual argument is stored, so the function/operator has its own copy of the argument value.

Variable   A name associated with a memory cell whose value can change.

Variable declarations   Statements that communicate to the compiler the names of variables in the program and the kind of information stored in each variable.

Virus   Code attached to another program that spreads through a computer's disk memory, disrupting the computer or erasing information.

void function   A function that does not return a value.

Volatile memory   Memory whose contents disappear when the computer is switched off.

Wide area network (WAN)   A network such as the Internet that connects computers and LANs over a large geographic area.

World Wide Web (WWW)   A part of the Internet whose graphical user interfaces make associated network resources easily navigable.

Worm   A virus that can disrupt a network by replicating itself on other network computers.

INDEX

REFERENCE GUIDE TO ANSI C CONSTRUCTS

Construct	Page	Example of Use
library header inclusion	67	`#include <stdio.h>`
constant macro definition	67	`#define LIMIT 100`
macro with parameters	712	`#define AVG(x,y) (((x) + (y)) / 2.0)`

structure type definition	593	`typedef struct {`
		`        char name[20];`
		`        int quantity;`
		`        double price;`
		`} part_t;`

linked list node type definition	737	`typedef struct node_s {`
		`    int data;`
		`    struct node_s *restp;`
		`} node_t;`

function prototype	146	`double next_approx(double previous);`
comment	68	`/* C construct examples */`
main function heading	69	`int` `main(void)`
with parameters	708	`int` `main(int argc, char *argv[])`

variable declaration
simple
	73	`int q, r;`
		`double x, y;`
		`char ch;`

array	398	`int ages[LIMIT];`
structure	593	`part_t one_part;`
pointer	338	`double *fracp;` `node_t *listp;`
array of pointers	500	`char *words[20];`
file pointer	340	`FILE *infilep, *outfilep;`

with initialization	284
	400
	
	505
		`int sum = 0;`
		`char hex[16] = {'0','1','2','3','4','5','6',`
		`        '7','8','9','A','B','C','D','E','F'};`
		`char *greetings[2] = {"Hi", "Bye"};`